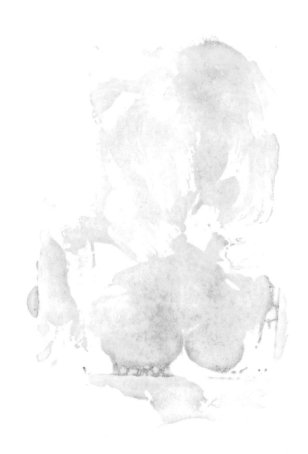

JAN 2 8 1991

POLITICAL SCANDALS AND CAUSES CELEBRES SINCE 1945:
AN INTERNATIONAL REFERENCE COMPENDIUM

Other titles from St James Press include the following:

Political Parties of the World, 0-912289-94-5, $85.00

Trade Unions of the World, 1-55862-014-1, $85.00

Elections Since 1945, 1-55862-017-6, $150.00

Religion in Politics, 1-55862-051-6, $75.00

Political and Economic Encyclopaedia of the Pacific, 1-55862-033-8, $85.00

Political and Economic Encyclopaedia of the Soviet Union and Eastern Europe, 1-55862-070-2, $85.00

Political and Economic Encyclopaedia of Western Europe, 1-55862-072-9, $85.00

Communist and Marxist Parties of the World, 2nd edition, 1-55862-073-7, $85.00

POLITICAL SCANDALS AND CAUSES CELEBRES SINCE 1945:
AN INTERNATIONAL REFERENCE COMPENDIUM

Contributors

**Louis Allen (LA), Kate Devereux (KD), Rupert Dickens (RSD),
Alan Doig (RAD), Ian Gorvin (IPG), F. J. Harper (FJH),
Martin Harrison (MH), Lawrence Joffe (LJ), Hans Lohneis (HL),
Patricia McCullagh (PLM), Maria Moore (MM), Lorimer Poultney (LP),
William Stallard (WS), Melanie Sully (MS), David Weatherup (DW)**

StJ

ST. JAMES PRESS
CHICAGO AND LONDON

POLITICAL SCANDALS AND CAUSES CÉLÈBRES SINCE 1945:
AN INTERNATIONAL REFERENCE COMPENDIUM

Published by Longman Group UK Limited, Westgate House,
The High, Harlow, Essex, CM20 1YR, United Kingdom.
Telephone (0279) 442601
Telex 81491 Padlog
Facsimile (0279) 444501

Published in the USA and Canada by St James Press,
233 East Ontario Street, Chicago 60611, Illinois, USA

ISBN 0-582-03065-X (Longman)
ISBN 1-55862-009-5 (St James)

© Longman Group UK Limited

British Library Cataloguing in Publication Data
Political Scandals and Causes Célèbres since 1945: An International Reference Compendium
1. Politics. Scandals
I. Title
320
ISBN 0-582-03065-X

CONTENTS

ALBANIA

Shehu Affair (1981–83) 1

AUSTRALIA

Petrov Affair (1954) 3
Holt Affair (1967) 6
Gorton Affair (1971) 8
Whitlam Dismissal Affair (1975) 11
Royal Commissions on Crime and Corruption (1980–86) 14

AUSTRIA

Habsburg Affair (1961–66) 17
Olah Affair (1964–69) 18
Lutgendorf Affair (1976) 20
Androsch Affair (1978–88) 21
Reder Affair (1985–86) 23
Waldheim Affair (1986–90) 24
Lucona Affair (1987–90) 26
Noricum Affair (1987–88) 27

BAHAMAS

Pindling Affair (1983–88) 29

BELGIUM

Ibramco Affair (1973–74) 31
Vanden Boeynants Affair (1982–89) 33

BULGARIA

Markov Affair (1978) 35

BURMA (MYANMAR)

Aung San Affair (1947) 37

CANADA

Gouzenko Affair (1945–46) 43
Rivard Affair (1964–65) 46
Munsinger Affair (1966) 48
Trudeau Affair (1970) 50
Mulroney/"Sleaze Factor" (1985–   ) 51

CZECHOSLOVAKIA

Masaryk Affair (1948) 54
Slansky Affair (1952) 57

FRANCE

Wine Scandal Affair (1946–53) 64
Generals' Affair (1949–51) 66

Leakages Affair (1954–56) 69
Mitterrand Affair (1959–65) 71
Ben Barka Affair (1965–67) 73
Markovic Affair (1969–70) 76
Canard Enchaîné Affair (1973–80) 78
De Broglie Affair (1976–1982) 80
Boulin Affair (1979–83) 84
Bokassa Diamonds Affair (1979–81) 86
L'Auriol Massacre Affair (1981–85) 88
Sniffer Aircraft Affair (1976–84) 90
Rainbow Warrior Affair (1985–90) 92
Crossroads of Development Affair (1983–90) 94
Luchaire Affair (1984–87) 95
Pechiney Affair (1988–   ) 97

WEST GERMANY

Spiegel Affair (1962–65) 98
Flick Affair (1982–   ) 102
Guillaume Affair (1974) 104

GREECE

Lambrakis Affair (1963–1966) 107
ASPIDA Affair (1964–1966) 109
Papandreou Affair (1987–1990) 112
Koskotas Affair (1988–90) 115

HUNGARY

Imre Nagy Affair (1956–58) 118

INDIA

Maruti Affair (1977–81) 122
Bofors Affair (1987–89) 124

IRELAND

Arms Smuggling Affair (1970) 127

ISRAEL

Lavon Affair (1954–64) 129
Rabin Affair (1977–80) 132
Flatto-Sharon Affair (1977–83) 133
Kahan Commission Affair (or Sabra and Chatila
Massacre Affair) (1982–83) 135
Shin Bet Affair (1984–1988) 137
Vanunu Affair (1986–88) 140
Bank Leumi Affair (1984–90) 141

ITALY

Lockheed Affair (1976–79) 144
Banco Ambrosiano Affair (1981–85) 145
P-2 Affair (1981–89) 149

JAPAN

Kakuei Tanaka/Lockheed Affair (1976–86) 153
Recruit Scandal Affair (1984–   ) 161

NETHERLANDS

Prince Bernhard/Lockheed Affair (1976) 168

NIGERIA

Dikko Affair (1983–84) 169

NORWAY

Treholt Affair (1984–85) 172

PANAMA

Noriega Affair (1983–90) 174

PHILIPPINES

Marcos Affair 177

POLAND

Katyn Massacre (1940–90) 180
Popieluszko Affair (1984) 183

SOUTH AFRICA

Muldergate Affair (1978–79) 188
Terre'Blanche Affair (1988–89) 194

SOVIET UNION

Rust Affair (1987) 195
Yury Churbanov and the Uzbekistan Cotton Scandal (1976–90) 198

SPAIN

Matesa Affair (1969–1975) 201
Rumasa Affair (1983–89) 202

SWEDEN

Raoul Wallenberg Affair (1945–90) 205
Palme Assassination Affair (1986–89) 207

UNITED KINGDOM

Groundnuts Affair (1946–51) 211
Sherman Pools Affair (1948–49) 213
Klaus Fuchs Affair (1949–50) 215
Crichel Down Affair (1950–54) 217
Burgess and Maclean Affair (1951) 219
Commander Crabb Affair (1956) 221
Suez Collusion Affair (1956) 223
Bank Rate Leak Affair (1957–58) 226
George Blake Affair (1961–90) 228
Vassall Affair (1962) 230
Profumo Affair (1963) 233
Commander Courtney Affair (1965–66) 236
"D" Notice Affair (1967) 238
Cecil King Affair (1968) 239
Enoch Powell Affair (1968) 240
Maudling Affair (1972–76) 241

Lord Lambton Affair (1973) 245
Lord Jellicoe Affair (1973) 247
Slag Heap Affair (1974) 249
Crown Agents Affair (1974) 252
Stonehouse Affair (1976) 255
Wilson Resignation Honours Affair (1976) 258
Thorpe/Scott Affair (1976) 262
Philby Affair (1963) 265
Blunt Affair (1979–80) 267
Kincora Boys' Home Affair (1980–1990) 269
Geoffrey Prime Affair (1981–82) 271
Commander Trestrail Affair (1982) 272
General Belgrano Affair (1982–86) 273
Parkinson Affair (1983) 275
Bettaney Affair (1983–84) 278
Sarah Tisdall Affair (1983–84) 280
Oman Cementation Affair (1984) 281
Clive Ponting Affair (1984–85) 284
Stalker Affair (1984–88) 286
Westland Helicopters Affair (1985–86) 288
Zircon Affair (1987) 291
Spycatcher Affair (1987–89) 292
Gibraltar Shootings Affair (1988) 294
Cathy Massiter Affair (1985) 296
Maurice Oldfield Affair (1987) 297

UNITED STATES OF AMERICA

"Hollywood Ten" Affair (1947) 302
Harry Dexter White Affair (1947–53) 303
William Remington Affair (1948–53) 309
Hiss/Chambers Affair (1948–50) 310
Communist Party "Top Eleven" Affair (1948–56) 319
Gerhard Eisler Affair (1949) 322
James Forrestal Affair (1949) 323
Atom Spies Affair (1950–53) 325
Joseph McCarthy Affair (1950–54) 331
Gen. MacArthur Affair (1951) 339
Oppenheimer Affair (1954) 343
Sherman Adams Affair (1958) 346
Martin/Mitchell Espionage Affair (1960) 347
Bay of Pigs Affair (1961) 348
Soblen Affair (1962) 350
John F. Kennedy Assassination Affair (1963–79) 351
Gulf of Tonkin Affair (1964–71) 363
Adam Clayton Powell Affair (1967) 365
Martin Luther King Assassination Affair (1968–79) 366
Abe Fortas Affair (1968–69) 369
Chicago Seven Affair (1968–70) 370
Chappaquiddick Affair (1969) 373
My Lai Massacre Affair (1969–71) 376
Kent State Massacre Affair (1970) 378
Pentagon Papers Affair (1971–74) 380
Thomas Eagleton Affair (1972) 384
Watergate Affair (1972–74) 385
Spiro Agnew Affair (1973) 410
Mitchell/Stans/Vesco Affair (1973–74) 413
John Connally Affair (1973–75) 414
CIA "Family Jewels" Affair (1974–76) 415
Bert Lance Affair (1977) 420

Tongsun Park Affair (1977–79) 422
Agent Orange Affair (1978–88) 423
Hamilton Jordan Affair (1979) 423
Billy Carter Affair (1980) 424
Abscam Affair (1980–82) 426
Westmoreland Libel Affair (1982–85) 427
Sleaze Factor Affair (1984) 428
Geraldine Ferraro Affair (1984) 430
Raymond Donoval Affair (1984–87) 431
Edwin Meese Affair (1984–88) 432
Samuel Morison Affair (1985) 435
Walker Family Espionage Affair (1985) 436
Jonathan Pollard Affair (1985–87) 438
Michael Deaver Affair (1986–87) 439
Iran-Contra Affair (1986–90) 441
Gary Hart Affair (1987) 453
Joseph Biden Affair (1987) 454
Bork/Ginsburg Affair (1987) 455
Wedtech Affair (1987–90) 457
Dan Quayle Affair (1988) 459
Jim Wright Affair (1989) 461

ZIMBABWE

Willowgate Affair (1988–89) 463

Index 465

FOREWORD

Any compilation of political scandals and *causes célèbres* must of necessity involve subjective judgement as to the claims for inclusion of individual "affairs", and indeed the weighting to be given to different nations.

Within that limitation two broad considerations have governed the selection of entries for the present volume. The first is that each "affair" should be genuinely political in content or implications. In most cases, the principal figures have been politicians, although this has not excluded various affairs (especially involving espionage) where the principals may have come from other walks of life but the controversy has had consequences for domestic politics or international relations.

Secondly, each affair has had to have identifiable contours as a self-contained episode. This consideration has had particular significance in the selection of entries by country. In many parts of the world, for much of the period since 1945, individual instances of corruption, extra-legal governmental activity, and repression simply do not stand out from the general background. In the case of Eastern Europe, for example, the entries selected come largely from (on the one hand) the beginnings of the consolidation of Communist rule after World War II, and (on the other) the disintegration of that rule in recent years. Some of the cases (such as the Nagy Affair in Hungary, or Katyn in Poland) effectively span the period in a particularly poignant way.

This is, inescapably, a book which is largely concerned with the politics of democracies. The concept of the *cause célèbre* is almost the definition one which belongs to the open society: it assumes the existence of loci of power outside the executive—in independent legislatures, or an autonomous judiciary, or a free and campaigning press. It likewise assumes the vulnerability of those who rule to overturning by means other than revolution or assassination; the existence of public opinion as an articulate factor in the political equation; and the durability of institutions which can survive the fall or discrediting of the individuals who temporarily lead. It is those major Western countries with the longest democratic traditions—the United States of America, Britain, and France—which contribute the largest number of scandals to this volume. A theme in what follows is the emergence—or at times collapse—of democratic institutions, and the adjustment of the powers of such institutions. In that sense the significance of political scandals and *causes célèbres* goes beyond their narrow historical contexts—they represent the turning points at which societies define their essential values or start out in new directions.

FJH

ALBANIA

Shehu Affair (1981–83)

Kadri Hazbiu, Defence Minister (1980–82), brother-in-law of Mehmet Shehu.

Enver Hoxha, leader of the Party of Labour of Albania (1941–85).

Feçor Shehu, Interior Minister (1980–82), nephew of Mehmet Shehu.

Mehmet Shehu, Prime Minister (1954–81).

Outside an élite circle of officials in that most closed and secretive of countries, little can be known with any certainty about the circumstances in which the Albanian Prime Minister, Mehmet Shehu, met his death on Dec. 17, 1981, aged 68. The official version has always been that he committed suicide, and a year after Shehu's death Albania's Stalinist leader, Enver Hoxha, proffered the scenario that Shehu had killed himself after being unmasked as a long-time agent of Albania's enemies, both East and West. Many foreign observers, however, have speculated that Shehu was either executed or murdered, or at least compelled to take his own life, as the consequence of a power struggle with Hoxha. In the wake of Shehu's death, and especially after his public denunciation, the regime apparently engaged in a purge of its supposed opponents which extended to senior members of the Communist party, state and military leadership.

Mehmet Shehu commanded the Communist-led Albanian resistance movement during World War II. He became Chief of Army General Staff when the communists established a provisional government in 1944, and following the declaration of a People's Republic in 1946 he was named Interior Minister. A close ally of Enver Hoxha, leader of the ruling Party of Labour (PLA), Shehu was appointed Prime Minister in July 1954, thus becoming the second most senior figure in the regime.

An official announcement on Dec. 18, 1981, said that Shehu had committed suicide on the previous evening in "a moment of nervous distress". No further details were given at that time, and consequently considerable speculation was immediately aroused abroad, especially as Shehu was not given a state funeral, nor did he receive the normal eulogy nor any posthumous honours. Rumours about Shehu's death spread rapidly particularly in neighbouring Yugoslavia, where the weekly magazine *Nin* alleged that Shehu had clashed with Hoxha (then aged 72) at a PLA central committee meeting on Dec. 17 and that an exchange of gunfire had occurred in which Shehu had been mortally wounded and Hoxha had also been injured (Hoxha was not seen again in public until nearly a full month later). While Western observers reacted cautiously to the gun-battle scenario, they were unanimous in retrospectively detecting signs of a power struggle possibly centring on differences over foreign policy, especially the questions of how to respond to Soviet overtures for improved relations, and whether Albania should seek an accommodation with the West.

The power struggle theory was initially vigorously denied by Albanian officials, and for nearly a year there was official silence on the subject of Shehu. However, in an address on Nov. 10, 1982, Hoxha accused Shehu of having been "one of the most dangerous traitors and enemies" of his country. He claimed that Shehu had worked since before the war for the US, Yugoslav and Soviet intelligence services in turn, and had been plotting to kill Hoxha and other Albanian leaders. Hoxha elaborated on these accusations in a book published in the following month entitled *The Titoists*. He claimed that the Yugoslav secret service and the US Central Intelligence Agency (CIA) had ordered Shehu to kill him, supplying poison for that purpose, and that on Dec. 16, 1981, Feçor Shehu (then the Interior Minister, and Mehmet Shehu's nephew) had gone to his uncle's home to deliver an order from the Yugoslavs for the immediate elimination of Hoxha "at all costs". The plot had been discovered, however, and Mehmet Shehu had committed suicide, having first flushed the poison down the toilet. In June 1983 Hekuran Isai, Feçor Shehu's successor as Interior Minister, alleged that Mehmet Shehu had been plotting to overthrow the PLA regime and establish a "bourgeois political system" in Albania with the aid of Kadri Hazbiu, his brother-in-law and then the Minister of People's Defence.

The official suicide claim began to look particularly suspect in the light of a statement in the PLA newspaper *Zëri i Popullit* on Feb. 27, 1985, that Mehmet Shehu had been "liquidated" after "meeting with the unbreakable unity of the party with the people". Foreign observers interpreted the mention of "liquidation" as an admission that Shehu had in fact been executed, but an Albanian embassy official in Vienna a few days later rejected that interpretation, stating that "liquidation" was meant only in a political sense.

Shehu's successor as Prime Minister, Adil Çarçani, immediately dropped Feçor Shehu from his government, and several other ministers considered to be close associates of Mehmet Shehu were removed in the course of 1982, including Foreign Minister Nesti Nase, Health Minister Llambi Ziçishti, and Hizbiu. In February 1983 Fadilj Hodza, an ethnic-Albanian member of Yugoslavia's collective presidency, suggested that since Shehu's death Albania had been undergoing the most extensive purge of state and party officials since the establishment of Communist rule, which he claimed was evidence of "grave differences" within the leadership over internal and foreign policy. Feçor Shehu, Ziçishti and Hazbiu were unofficially reported to have been executed in September 1983, together with up to 30 other senior officials (including military officers thought to be loyal to Hazbiu), after being convicted of spying for the USA, the Soviet Union and Yugoslavia. Several others, including Nase and Mehmet Shehu's widow and two sons, were reportedly sentenced to long terms of imprisonment. Albanian officials would confirm only that a treason trial had taken place.

IPG

AUSTRALIA

Petrov Affair (1954)

Dr Herbert Evatt, Leader of the Australian Labour Party (1951–60).
Robert Menzies, Prime Minister (1939–41; 1949–66).
Evokiya Petrov, Wife of Vladimir Petrov and cipher clerk at the Soviet Embassy, Canberra, (1951–54).
Vladimir M. Petrov, Third Secretary and Consul, Soviet Embassy, Canberra (1951–54).

The first major dispute involving Australia with a Great Power occurred in April 1954, when she refused to hand back to the Soviet Union their Third Secretary and Consul in Canberra, Vladimir Petrov, who had been granted political asylum in Australia. His defection not only caused a break in diplomatic relations between the two countries until March 1959, but also left its mark on the Australian domestic political scene. The repercussions from it were felt by the opposition Labour Party rather than the governing Liberal-Country Party coalition, led by Prime Minister Robert Menzies. The Petrov affair also contained real-life drama that might have come straight out of a fictional spy story.

On April 10 in a statement regarded by many MPs as the most sensational to occur in the House of Representatives since Australia went to war with Japan in 1941, Menzies announced that Petrov, who worked under diplomatic cover for the MVD (a forerunner of the KGB), had been granted political asylum. He had actually defected a week earlier, having handed over a large number of documents to the Australian Security and Intelligence Organization and asked for Australian citizenship. "I no longer believe in Communism", he said, "since I have seen the Australian way of life". For his actions Petrov received £5,000 from the Australian government.

As a result of this case the government appointed a Royal Commission on April 14 to investigate evidence of systematic espionage and attempted subversion in Australia. At a press conference at the Soviet Embassy the same day, Ambassador Generalov dismissed Menzies' statements about the defection as "nonsense", while Evokiya Petrov, who was also present, said she believed her husband had been kidnapped by Australian security officers and had not sought asylum. Mrs Petrov, however, captured the headlines far more dramatically five days later. On April 19, a crowd of around a thousand people, including many Russian, Ukrainian and Czech immigrants, gathered at Mascot aerodrome in Sydney to try and prevent her from boarding a BOAC airliner under the escort of three Soviet officials.

For eight minutes there were scuffles among the crowd, the police and Soviet officials as they fought for possession of Mrs Petrov, who was heard to cry out in Russian, "I don't want to go — save me", before her escorts dragged her into the plane for the first part of the journey home to Russia.

Before the plane's departure for Darwin the Australian authorities briefed the BOAC captain to use his crew to try and find out what Mrs Petrov's real wishes were. During the flight an air hostess was instructed to follow Mrs Petrov to the ladies' cloakroom and question her at an appropriate opportunity. When she did so, Mrs Petrov confided to the air hostess that she had no desire to return to Russia, but was too terrified to say so publicly for fear of her escorts. This information was immediately passed on to the authorities, which meant that when the plane arrived in Darwin at dawn seven hours later the waiting Australian officials knew what she was thinking. During the ensuing conversation between the Acting Administrator of the Northern Territory and Mrs Petrov, her escorts became aggressive and tried to push the police and officials aside. When one of the escorts thrust his hands into his pocket, the police quickly intervened and found that both men were carrying loaded revolvers. They were disarmed, but then allowed to continue their journey. Once Mrs Petrov, who herself worked for the MVD, had spoken to her husband on the telephone to confirm he was still alive, she asked for and was granted political asylum.

The consequences of the Petrovs' defection adversely affected the Labour Party under Herbert Evatt, a brilliant lawyer who had been leader since 1951. The party was moving away from a rigid adherence to socialist doctrine in order to broaden its popular appeal, though Evatt's views on the right of the Australian Communist Party to exist and the need for Australia to be less dependent on Great Britain had caused some controversy. Nevertheless, the political tide was turning in Labour's favour in the run-up to the federal elections on May 29 as tough economic measures to combat inflation were making the government unpopular. Evatt, therefore, was sanguine about his chances of the premiership. However, he alluded in parliament to the establishment of the Royal Commission and the timing of the election as a political manoeuvre by the government to gain electoral advantage. But Menzies never made the Petrov affair an open issue during the election campaign, though it was widely discussed in the press.

The coalition was returned to power, but with a reduced majority. This was a bitter disappointment for Evatt, who felt that he had been the victim of a political conspiracy; but it is impossible to determine whether the Petrov case really influenced the election result. Any effect it may have had could only have benefited the government, who tended to play upon the sensitivities of the Australian public over Communism. The Cold War remained a live issue and Sir Arthur Fadden, the Country Party Leader, had remarked on what he considered to be Evatt's indulgence towards Communists in the past.

Evatt, however, allowed the Petrov affair to damage him irreparably. His frustrations could be detected in his behaviour and statements before the Royal Commission, where he defended two of his staff, who had been named in the Petrov documents as possible contributors of information to the Soviet Embassy. Evatt drew comparisons between the Commission and McCarthyism and accused Petrov of conspiring to forge papers and produce charges detrimental to the Labour Party's election chances. In its interim report on Oct. 21 the Commission dismissed all this, describing Evatt's charges of conspiracy, fraud and blackmail as "fantastic and wholly unsupported by any credible evidence". Meanwhile, internal dissensions were splitting the Labour Party. The right-wing and Roman Catholic elements, who were hostile towards the Communists in the Trade Union movement, had been antagonized by the Party's defence of its members implicated in the Petrov affair. Evatt accused the right-wingers of disloyalty and subversion, but this only served to widen the breach and in 1955 some of them broke away to form the Democratic Labour Party.

The Commission published its final report in October 1955, concluding that all the Petrov documents were authentic and that for many years the Soviet Union had used its Embassy as a cloak under which to control and operate espionage organizations in Australia. It found that the only Australians who knowingly assisted in this were Communists and their sympathizers. Petrov's task had been to promote MVD activities and establish an "Illegal Apparatus" (an espionage organization or fifth column, which could operate in Australia if war caused the withdrawal of the Soviet Embassy, the "Legal Apparatus"). As far as the Commission could learn, the MVD had not succeeded in gaining any information directly involving the security and defence of Australia, but it had some success in indirectly affecting the security of the country by building up a spy network. The Soviet Embassy looked to recruit people to sabotage vital installations in an emergency; to persuade Communist university students to join the Foreign Affairs Department; and to terrorize, if need be, Australian migrants with relatives behind the Iron Curtain.

One consequence of the Commission's enquiries was that many Australians had their loyalty and conduct called into question, which adversely affected their reputations and prospects of employment since fellow travellers or "Pinkies" were unlikely to be welcomed into the Public Service. During the debate on the Commission's report in the House of Representatives on Oct. 19, 1955, Evatt spoke of the fact that no spies had been discovered and nobody was to be prosecuted. He accused Menzies of having had no security grounds for the enquiry and of saving up the Petrov Affair for the 1954 election as a "red bogey" scare. He then revealed he had sent a letter to Soviet Foreign Minister Molotov, asking whether the Petrov documents were genuine. This was a politically naive move on the part of Evatt because the Soviet government was never going to admit their authenticity. In their reply to him, the Soviets described the documents as "falsifications fabricated by people interested in the deterioration of USSR–Australian relations and in discrediting their political opponents".

Menzies called a general election for Dec. 10, 1955, on the grounds that it made sense to combine an election to the Senate (constitutionally required by that date) with one to the House of Representatives as well. But Menzies was also too shrewd a politician not to strengthen his position by exploiting the erosion in Evatt's credibility resulting from the Molotov letter and the disarray in the Labour Party. At the general election the coalition increased its majority and so weakened the Labour Party that it remained out of power for the next 17 years.

DW

Holt Affair (1967)

Anthony Grey, British journalist and former Reuter's correspondent in Beijing.
Harold Holt, Prime Minister (1966–67).

The presumed death from drowning of Harold Holt on Dec. 17, 1967, brought an untimely end to a political career that had achieved the highest office through quiet determination, administrative ability, and a likeable personality. The first photograph of Holt as Prime Minister, taken at his seaside home at Portsea just before he went spear fishing, reflected a style and informality that contrasted sharply with his patriarchal predecessor in office, Sir Robert Menzies. Nobody expected him to dominate as Sir Robert had done, so when Holt was questioned on the art of leadership, he said he wanted to be the captain of a team, not its master. His career had been worthy and uncontroversial, but 16 years after his death the British journalist Anthony Grey claimed in his book *The Prime Minister was a Spy* that Holt had not drowned, but had actually defected to Communist China, for whom he had been spying for over 30 years.

Harold Edward Holt was born in Sydney on Aug. 5, 1908, the son of a teacher who later became the London representative for an Australian theatre group. He went to school at Wesley College in Melbourne and then went on to graduate in law from the university there in 1930. After working as a barrister and solicitor, he entered the federal House of Representatives in 1935 following his by-election victory at Fawkner and achieved office four years later as a minister without portfolio in the government of Robert Menzies, the leader of the United Australia Party. In March 1940 he volunteered for overseas service as a private in the Australian Imperial Force, but following the death of three ministers in an air crash that October, he was recalled to the War Cabinet as Minister of Labour and National Service. The Menzies government fell in September 1941, but Holt remained an MP and helped in the resurrection of the United Australia Party as the Liberal Party in the mid-1940s. In 1946 he married Zara Fell, a fashion designer in Melbourne.

After the victory of the Liberals (in coalition with the Country Party) in the general election in December 1949, he held a succession of ministerial posts in the Menzies administrations and also became deputy leader of the party and leader of the House of Representatives. On Sir Robert's retirement in January 1966, Holt was elected unopposed as Liberal Party leader, which automatically gave him the premiership. He was less sentimental than his predecessor towards Britain, and his period of office was noteworthy for its strong stress on the American alliance and the importance of Asia in Australian affairs. He travelled widely in 1966, touring several Asian countries, Britain and the United States. One of his first major decisions was to treble the number of Australian troops in Vietnam, and on his visit to Washington in June to meet American President Lyndon B. Johnson, he said he would go "all the way with L.B.J." The President returned this compliment by visiting Australia that November, where the anti-war demonstrators were vastly outnumbered by the huge crowds welcoming him.

Holt's loyalty to the American cause and the opposition Labour Party's policy of an immediate Australian withdrawal from Vietnam were contributory factors in his landslide victory in the general election of November 1966. However, the following year witnessed a steady decline in the fortunes of the government, whose internal problems were being exploited by Gough Whitlam, Labour's vigorous new leader. Reports of the extravagant use of VIP flights by politicians and officials embarrassed the government, while a threatened backbench revolt forced Holt to appoint a royal commission to investigate the loss of a naval destroyer. The coalition was also under strain because the Country Party was uneasy about Holt's decision not to devalue the Australian currency in the wake of the sterling devaluation in November 1967.

But this was the last crisis he was to handle. During a weekend trip to Portsea shortly before Christmas, he decided to go for a swim with friends on the Sunday. He was an experienced swimmer and his companions, who were much nearer the shore, last saw him about 60 yards out, swimming in the surf amid 15-foot waves. When Holt was reported missing, police, servicemen and volunteers launched a search of the beaches and sea that lasted six days, but to no avail. His body was never recovered and he was presumed drowned, either from being sucked under or swept out to sea. His memorial service was on a scale usually reserved for Heads of State and no other event in Australian history had attracted such a distinguished gathering. Holt was Prime Minister for less than two years, so perhaps it was the manner of his death that added a greater than usual significance to the occasion. Among the leaders and senior representatives of 26 nations who attended were President Johnson, Prince Charles (who was representing his mother, Queen Elizabeth II) and British Prime Minister Harold Wilson.

Holt's disappearance prompted some public speculation that it was more than just accidental drowning. The idea of suicide was mooted and various rumours claimed he was either alive and living in another country, or had been assassinated. None, however, received official credence and public interest soon died down. But it revived in 1983 following the publication of Grey's book, which was based on information from Ronald Titcombe, a former Australian naval officer, who claimed it came from official Chinese sources and contacts in the Australian security service. According to the book, Holt became interested in China as a young man and was recruited as an informant by the Kuomintang government in the 1930s. After the 1949 revolution in China, the Communist regime took him over and paid him large sums of money not only to try and influence Australian foreign policy in a pro-Chinese direction, but also to support his glamorous life style. Believing himself under suspicion by the Australian Security and Intelligence Organization (ASIO), Holt decided to defect and did so by swimming out that fateful December day to rendezvous with Chinese frogmen waiting to take him to a submarine bound for the People's Republic of China.

This story was received with scepticism, not to say ridicule, in Australia and Britain. The Chinese government refused to comment on it, while the Australian Attorney-General, Senator Gareth Evans, denied that ASIO had ever investigated Holt and expressed the opinion that "the whole tale seems to be out of fruitcake land". One British newspaper, *The Observer*, poured such scorn on the story that Titcombe sued it for libel. Though initially prepared to defend its comments, the newspaper eventually made an out-of-court settlement (reported by *Private Eye* to be £40,000) with Titcombe in October 1988, having first apologized in open court for describing the story as a hoax.

DW

Gorton Affair (1971)

Malcolm Fraser, Minister of Defence (1969–71).
John Gorton, Minister of Defence (1971) and Prime Minister (1968–71).
John McEwen, Leader of the Country Party and Deputy Prime Minister (1958–71); Prime Minister (December 1967–January 1968).
William McMahon, Deputy Leader of the Liberal Party (1966–71); Prime Minister (1971–72).

The ministerial career of John Gorton was marked in its later stages by infighting and personality clashes that were exceptional even in Australian politics, with its reputation for contention and invective. His sacking as Minister of Defence on Aug. 12, 1971, was as controversial and unexpected as his election to the premiership three years earlier. The decision by Prime Minister William McMahon to dismiss him arose from an article in the *Sunday Australian* four days previously, in which Gorton had defended his own premiership (1968 to 1971) against criticisms of it contained in *The Gorton Experiment*, a book by Alan Reid, the political correspondent of the *Sydney Daily Telegraph*. Gorton was attacked for his arrogance, obstinate simple-mindedness and for the influence he allowed his private secretary, Ainsley Gotto, to have over him. But what McMahon took exception to was not that Gorton had defended himself, but that he had accused some of his ministerial colleagues of divulging Cabinet information to their wives and the news media. Gorton's resignation was asked for because his article had "breached Cabinet solidarity and unity and reflected on the integrity of Ministers".

John Grey Gorton achieved far more in his political career than was generally expected. Born on Sept. 9, 1911, in Melbourne, the son of a prosperous fruit grower and his mistress, he was educated at Geelong Grammar School and Brasenose College, Oxford, where he read Philosophy, Economics and History. In 1935 he married an American, Bettina Brown, and the following year took over the management of the family orange orchards in Victoria. During World War II he served as a fighter pilot with the Royal Australian Air Force in South-East Asia and the Pacific; after being shot down and seriously wounded, he underwent plastic surgery and was invalided out in December 1944. His political career began in 1949 with his election as Senator for Victoria, a post he held until 1968, when he became the Liberal Member of the House of Representatives for Higgins.

From 1958 onwards Gorton held a succession of junior ministerial posts in the governing coalitions of Prime Minister Robert Menzies, gaining a reputation for hard work and effectiveness; but he did not achieve Cabinet rank until his appointment in 1966 as Minister of Education and Science in Prime Minister Harold Holt's government. The untimely death from drowning of Holt in December 1967 (see *Holt Affair, 1967*) unexpectedly thrust Gorton into the centre of the political stage, at a time when he was leader of the government in the Senate and not generally regarded as a major contender for the leadership. But Liberal–Country Party politics were rent with divisions in the fight for the succession: John McEwen, Deputy Prime Minister and leader of the minority Country Party in the coalition, refused to serve under McMahon, then deputy leader of the Liberals. Gorton, therefore, became a compromise candidate, supported by many Liberal backbenchers in marginal constituencies, who regarded him as a gritty campaigner with a good TV image. They also thought his reputation as a dissenter from the Liberal Establishment had electoral appeal. On Jan. 9, 1968, Gorton became party leader and Prime Minister by defeating Paul Hasluck, the able but reserved Minister of External Affairs, in the second ballot for the leadership.

Gorton assumed office under a number of disadvantages. He had to transfer from the Senate to the House of Representatives, which was a far livelier chamber, and to deal in Cabinet with colleagues of wider experience than himself. Accordingly, these disadvantages made it difficult for him to provide convincing leadership during a period when Labour Party fortunes were improving and the questions of Australian involvement in Vietnam and defence issues in South-East Asia required a steady hand. Public disenchantment with Gorton's performance was reflected in the general election results of October 1969, when the coalition's majority fell from 38 seats to seven.

This prompted McMahon to make a close, but unsuccessful, challenge for the leadership. The Byzantine manoeuvring over this did nothing for the Liberal Party's image; neither did Gorton's Cabinet purge afterwards, when he appointed a front bench of henchmen rather than a ministry of all the talents. Three ministers were sacked, including Dudley Erwin, who had helped Gorton in his bid for the leadership. Erwin responded by attacking the Prime Minister in unprecedented terms, accusing Gorton of tossing him out on account of "a shapely political manoeuvre that wiggles", a reference to Miss Gotto, whom he described as ruthless and authoritarian and who had denied him access to the Prime Minister. Gorton denied Erwin's allegations about his involvement in attempts to oust Holt from the premiership before his death. However, he found it more difficult to refute claims about his membership of "the mushroom club", a faction in the Liberal Party, whose members were all in the 1969 ministry and whose motto regarding backbenchers was said to be "keep 'em in the dark and feed 'em bullshit".

Gorton continued to be beset by problems. His virtual ignoring of the American Ambassador on one particular occasion, whilst a guest at his Embassy in Canberra, was widely viewed as discourteous and undiplomatic. In domestic affairs, the Labour Party was organizing a campaign of civil disobedience against the Vietnam war; there was a financial scandal involving mining shares; and disputes between the Federal and State governments over off-shore mineral rights forced the Prime Minister to postpone legislation to avoid a possible revolt from his own backbenchers. In foreign affairs, there were divisions in the government about security issues in South-East Asia, the scale of the Australian withdrawal from Vietnam, and the handling of the situation in Papua New Guinea, where the independence movement was organizing fierce demonstrations.

Against this background it was only a matter of time before Gorton's opponents in his own Party seized their chance to remove him. This came on Feb. 1, 1971, with the retirement of McEwen, whose refusal to serve under McMahon had kept Gorton in power. Malcolm Fraser, who resigned as Minister of Defence on the grounds that Gorton had deceived him, accused the Prime Minister in Parliament on March 9 of seriously damaging the Liberal Party and of showing a dangerous reluctance to consult his Cabinet colleagues. Gorton was further criticized for his obstinate determination to get his own way and his tendency to ridicule the advice of the Public Service unless it supported his own view. He was, according to Fraser, unfit to hold the office of Prime Minister. On March 10, in the face of such criticism and an opposition motion of no confidence, Gorton called a meeting of the Parliamentary Liberal Party to discuss his position. After a three-hour session the result of the vote was 33–33, so he used his casting vote against himself and vacated the premiership and party leadership, which McMahon won in a subsequent ballot. Gorton was elected Deputy Leader and took over the post of Defence Minister. He described his reaction to events as one of disappointment and surprise rather than bitterness, while leading figures in the Labour Party said of him that he had made the Establishment feel uncomfortable and been destroyed by Sir Frank Packer and the press barons. Within five months Gorton's ministerial career had ended and he returned to the backbenches until his retirement from politics in 1975.

DW

Whitlam Dismissal Affair (1975)

Malcolm Fraser, Leader of the Liberal Party (1975) and Prime Minister
   (1975–83)
Sir John Kerr, Governor-General (1974–77)
Gough Whitlam, Prime Minister (1972–75)

The 18th-century British statesman and political thinker, Edmund Burke, stated that of all the trusts vested in the Crown, the most critical and delicate was the use of its prerogative to dissolve Parliament. And so it proved with Sir John Kerr, the Governor-General and Queen Elizabeth II's representative in Australia, who had the right to exercise this prerogative. His dismissal of Gough Whitlam, leader of the governing Labour Party, on Nov. 11, 1975, was the greatest constitutional crisis in Australian history and the first instance in 200 years of the Crown removing an elected Prime Minister from office. The Governor-General took this action to resolve a political deadlock that had begun the previous month, when the Liberal–Country Party opposition decided to use its majority in the Senate to reject two Supply (i.e. Finance) Bills.

The son of a high-ranking public servant, Edward Gough Whitlam was born on July 11, 1916, and educated at schools in Melbourne and Canberra before graduating from Sydney University in 1938 with a Bachelor of Arts degree. His marriage to Margaret Dovey, a social worker and daughter of a judge, took place in 1942 during World War II, when he saw active service in the Pacific as a navigator with the Royal Australian Air Force. After the war he qualified as a barrister and was elected to the House of Representatives in 1952 as Labour MP for Werriwa. A charismatic figure with a commanding presence and a gift for oratory, he became party leader in 1967, though his determination to discard doctrinaire socialist policies and alter Labour's stance over Australian commitments in Vietnam brought him into conflict with party traditionalists. But Whitlam's success in altering the Party's image could be measured by its increased representation in the Senate after the 1967 elections. However, his sometimes impetuous and determined approach was not always popular among his colleagues and in April 1968 he had to fight off a leadership challenge from Dr James Cairns.

Public disenchantment with the performance of the Liberal–Country Party coalition governments of John Gorton (1968–71) and William McMahon (1971–72) finally brought Labour to power in the general election in Dec. 1972, after a period of 23 years out of office. Whitlam's administration was marked by a heavy programme of legislation, including increased expenditure on social welfare and the abolition of conscription. However, many Bills were blocked by the Senate (the Upper House), which could impede legislation to the point where the leader of the House of Representatives (the Lower House) could request the Governor-General for a double dissolution, an election where both Houses faced the electorate. If the Senate still failed to pass a Bill after the dissolution, the Australian Constitution allowed for a joint sitting of both Houses, at which the larger membership of the Lower was expected to prevail, thereby breaking the deadlock.

However, Whitlam held back from adopting this course and calling a general election in case he lost control of the Lower House. When he did go to the country in May 1974 in the hope of winning a majority in the Senate, the election issues centred on the high levels of taxation and unemployment at the time. The result was that Labour's majority in the House of Representatives fell to only five seats, while in the Senate it had parity with the opposition, with two independents holding the balance of power. But Labour was soon in a minority in the Upper House when one of the independent senators rejoined the Liberal Party and two previously Labour-held seats went to independents.

Further changes on the political scene occurred in March 1975, when Malcolm Fraser became leader of the opposition. In answer to press questions about whether he would use his majority in the Senate to force a general election, Fraser replied he would do so "only in the most exceptional circumstances", but refused to elaborate on what these might be. Whitlam's political problems were increasing: the economy was in difficulties; his government was virtually bankrupt through overspending; and a financial scandal (see *Overseas Loans Affair, 1974–77*) forced him to dismiss Cairns, the Deputy Prime Minister, and to ask on Oct. 14 for the resignation of Reginald Connor, the Minister for Minerals and Energy.

The following day the Opposition exploited the government's position by using its majority in the Senate to defer consideration of two Supply Bills until Whitlam agreed to elections for both Houses of Parliament. At a press conference Fraser censured the Prime Minister for his government's maladministration and incompetence, while later that day in a television broadcast Whitlam stated his intention of carrying on in the face of "blackmail" and pressure from vested interests, such as newspaper proprietors. On Oct. 16 he warned of the "utter financial chaos" that would result from blocking the Supply Bills, but the Senate showed its disregard by delaying their passage three times during the next three weeks.

In early November attempts were made to break the deadlock and Fraser offered a compromise solution after meeting the Governor-General. He announced on Nov. 3 that the opposition would allow the immediate passage of the Supply Bills on condition that an election for the House of Representatives would be held at the same time as that for one-half of the Senate seats, which had to take place before June 30, 1976. Fraser had, in effect, challenged Whitlam either to defy the constitution or allow the Australian people to vote, but the Prime Minister refused either to advise a dissolution or accept the compromise. He stated he would not call a general election for at least a year, claiming that his government had enough financial resources and that the current political problems had to be settled in Parliament and not "by some back-door deal".

The crisis reached its climax the following week. After an unsuccessful meeting with Fraser on Nov. 11, the Prime Minister, with the unanimous support of his party, proposed to ask the Governor-General to call an election in December for half the Senate. But on his arrival at Government House early that afternoon to seek approval, Whitlam was immediately informed that the Governor-General had withdrawn his commission as Prime Minister. Within an hour Fraser had been sworn in as Prime Minister of a caretaker government, with a view to dissolving both Houses and holding new elections. Shortly after the swearing in, the Senate passed the necessary Bills, after which the Governor-General granted the double dissolution. Meanwhile, the House of Representatives passed a vote of no confidence in the Fraser administration before despatching the Speaker to ask the Governor-General to reverse his decision. But it was too late. The dissolution proclamation had already been read outside Parliament House. It concluded with the words "God save the Queen", after which Whitlam was reported to have said: "Well may we say God save the Queen, because nothing will save the Governor-General. The proclamation which you have just heard read by the Governor-General's official secretary was countersigned by Malcolm Fraser, who will undoubtedly go down in Australian history from Remembrance Day 1975 as Kerr's cur."

The next day the Labour Party condemned the Governor-General for "deception" of an elected government and for "a squalid intrigue" with the Establishment. For some days afterwards there were widespread and, in some cases, violent demonstrations in many parts of Australia in protest against the Prime Minister's dismissal. Shortly before Sir John's visit to London in December to report to the Queen, Whitlam sent her a letter, giving his own views on the dismissal. He accused the Governor-General of favouring the coalition parties and endangering the monarchy in Australia by arousing strong republican sentiments on account of his action. Furthermore, he was critical of Sir John for failing to indicate his intentions to him; for rejecting his advice not to see the Chief Justice, Sir Garfield Barwick; and for relying on the advice of the Opposition legal spokesman, Robert Ellicott. Whitlam voiced his suspicions about a conspiracy theory in a dramatic debate in the House of Representatives on March 4, 1976, when he accused Ellicott (the then Attorney-General) of plotting with his cousin, the Chief Justice, to overthrow the elected government. Ellicott immediately responded by challenging Whitlam to take the matter to court, but the allegations were withdrawn after the intervention of the Speaker.

All the protagonists in the Whitlam dismissal are open to criticism for their roles in the affair. Though the Governor-General acted constitution-ally, whether he did so with political skill is questionable. The government had enough money until the end of November, so he should have delayed his intervention for as long as possible in order to avoid accusations of precipitate action or partisanship in his search for a solution. Sir John did not indicate his intentions to Whitlam so that he could judge the Prime Minister's reactions for himself, nor did he issue an ultimatum. The Senate can be criticized for playing politics and using its constitutional powers to further party interests; the opposition parties for engineering a deadlock to provoke a premature general election; and Whitlam for refusing to accept a compromise or advise a double dissolution. Ironically, when opposition leader in 1970, he declared that a government should resign when a major taxation Bill was defeated in the Senate and political deadlock ensued. There was also the double irony that his dismissal was at the hands of a Governor-General he himself had appointed and who had also been a personal friend up till then.

The whole affair produced unprecedented controversy throughout Australia, with emotions running high and talk in some quarters of a general strike and blood in the gutters. But in the campaign for the general election on Dec. 13, the only incident was when a beer can was thrown at Fraser. The opposition's victory by a record majority could be interpreted as an endorsement of the Governor-General's actions by the electorate. After relinquishing the Labour leadership in 1977, Whitlam resigned as an MP the following year and retired from politics.

DW

Royal Commissions on Crime and Corruption (1980–86)

Francis Costigan, QC, Barrister and Solicitor; President of the Australian Bar Association (1979).

Mr Justice Lionel Murphy, a Justice of the High Court of Australia (1975–86).

Mr Justice Donald Stewart, a Justice of the New South Wales Supreme Court (1981–84).

Sir Laurence Street, Chief Justice of the New South Wales Supreme Court (1974 to the present).

Neville Wran, Premier of New South Wales (1976–87); National President of the Australian Labour Party (1980–86).

Public concern about corruption and malpractice in Australian political, professional and business life led to the establishment of several Royal

Commissions during the early 1980s to look into its extent. One of these, headed by Francis Costigan, QC, a leading barrister and solicitor, was appointed in September 1980 to investigate allegations of widespread criminal activities within the Federated Ship Painters' and Dockers' Union. In an interim report to Parliament on Feb. 25, 1982, the Commission found that certain members of the union were guilty of tax evasion, amounting to more than A$2,000,000, while a further report six months later revealed that other members had been involved in 15 murders and 23 serious assaults on the waterfront in the 1970s. In addition to the revelations about the union, the Commission also disclosed that thousands of companies had avoided paying tax; that the government taxation office had failed to take action after detecting tax evasion schemes; and that a senior government official in Perth had been involved in organized prostitution.

Following disclosures in the Senate on Sept. 7, 1982, that a hitherto secret section of this report had indicated the existence of a large criminal organization based in Sydney, the Costigan Commission's brief was extended to investigate criminal and corrupt practices in other areas. These included the daily fixing of horse races, organized prostitution, extortion, crooked gambling games, concerted shoplifting raids, and the production of pornographic material, much of which featured drugged children. In May 1983 a member of the Commission, Douglas Meagher, QC, issued a summary of its current findings and expressed the view that controlling organized crime in Australia was one of the main challenges of the 1980s. The government set up a National Crime Authority after the submission of the Commission's final report in November 1984, though only five of its 11 volumes were made public.

In March 1986 Costigan accused the state government of New South Wales of having hindered the fight against organized crime and criticized the close relationship between people of political, commercial and criminal influence within the state. Allegations about the activities of the state Premier, Neville Wran, resulted in the establishment in May 1983 of a Royal Commission under Sir Laurence Street, Chief Justice of the New South Wales Supreme Court. Wran was alleged to have influenced the outcome of court proceedings in 1977 by asking the then chief stipendary magistrate of New South Wales, Murray Farquhar, to use his influence to secure the acquittal of Kevin Humphreys, the executive director of the New South Wales Rugby League, who had been accused of misappropriating funds. The Commission heard of a close relationship between Farquhar and Wran, but cleared the latter of any role in the decision to acquit Humphreys. However, Farquhar was sentenced to four years' imprisonment on March 15, 1985, for his illegal involvement in the case.

Wran also featured in the investigations of the Royal Commission set up in June 1981 under Mr Justice Donald Stewart, a Justice of the New South Wales Supreme Court, in order to investigate the drugs traffic in Australia. Its interim report in May 1983 uncovered sufficient evidence of widespread corruption within the law enforcement agencies to conclude that it was dealing not merely with "a few rotten apples", but "the tip of an iceberg of institutionalized corruption". Police corruption, it stated, had enabled criminal elements to build up a large-scale network in Australia for the distribution of heroin and other illegal substances originating in South-East

Asia. The Commission's brief was then extended to look into the affairs of the Nugan Hand merchant banking group, which was suspected of being involved in drug trafficking, under-cover international arms deals, and tax avoidance within Australia. In April 1985 the Attorney General asked the Commission to examine 524 pages of transcripted telephone conservations, which had been illegally recorded by police investigating organized crime. Extracts from these had been published in the Melbourne newspaper *The Age* in 1984, but Wran and other senior Labour politicians dismissed them as fabrications.

However, the Commission's authentication of the tapes, together with a High Court ruling allowing the use of such evidence in criminal proceedings, opened the way for the prosecution of Mr Justice Lionel Murphy in December 1984. In the first ever indictment of an Australian High Court judge, Mr Justice Murphy was arraigned for attempting to pervert the course of justice by seeking to influence the court case against Sydney Ryan, a lawyer. He was accused of conspiracy involving an immigration racket and his conversations with Mr Justice Murphy had been taped. In September 1985 Mr Justice Murphy was found guilty and sentenced to 18 months' imprisonment, but released on bail pending an appeal on several points of law. This was successful and the conviction was quashed on the grounds that his trial had involved several miscarriages of justice.

Despite his acquittal, allegations of misconduct continued against Mr Justice Murphy, so a parliamentary commission of enquiry was set up in May 1986 to advise on whether he should resume his seat on the bench. However, two months later it was disclosed Mr Justice Murphy was suffering from terminal cancer, so the commission disbanded without reporting and he resumed his judicial duties on Aug. 1. After his death that October Mr Justice Murphy was described by Bob Hawke, the Australian Prime Minister, as "a great Australian and one of our finest jurists". In March 1987 Wran, who had been a close personal friend of the judge, was fined A$25,000 for contempt of court following his suggestion (made while the Murphy case was still under judicial review) that the judge had been innocent of the charges against him.

DW

AUSTRIA

Habsburg Affair (1961–66)

Otto Habsburg, eldest son of the last Emperor of Austria.
Bruno Kreisky, Foreign Minister (1959–66).

The word scandal in this affair was invoked by the Socialist Party in Austria
and relates to the judgment of the Administrative High Court published in
May 1963. Otto Habsburg, the eldest son of the last emperor Karl, had to
make a declaration of loyalty as a prerequisite for an Austrian passport.
The government procrastinated and the High Court passed judgment
that the declaration was sufficient for a return by Otto Habsburg to
Austria.

The "Habsburg Act" of 1919 exiles all members of the House of Habsburg
unless they declare their loyalty to the republic and renounce claims to the
throne. This declaration has to be checked by the government and the
Main Committee in parliament. In June 1961 Otto Habsburg offered his
declaration of loyalty but the government was divided on the issue. A
"grand coalition" had been in existence since the end of World War II
consisting of the People's Party (ÖVP) and the Socialist SPÖ. The ÖVP
had always provided the Chancellor and the SPÖ the Vice-Chancellor in a
neat balance which was designed to overcome the pre-war polarization in
political life which had proved so catastrophic. In the 1960s, tension in the
arrangement began to develop and critics urged a reform of the coalition
mechanism which would allow for more flexibility. The coalition survived
but increasingly came under attack for failing to produce clear decisions
and for encouraging two-party political horse-trading.

The Habsburg issue was a delicate case and revived old fears of the
monarchy leading to a heated debate between the main protagonists.
The ÖVP considered the loyalty declaration to be adequate but this was
vehemently rejected by the Socialists. In the government, unanimity was
necessary and deadlock ensued. The Main Committee in parliament could
not promulgate on this question because of the paralysis in the government.
Consequently Otto Habsburg appealed to the Constitutional Court and then
to the Administrative High Court, after the former declared the matter
to be outside its jurisdiction. The latter took the view that the 1919 Act
requiring the approval of the Main Committee had been made invalid by
subsequent law.

A tumultuous session of parliament ensued in June 1963: the SPÖ
demanded a retrospective law to overrule the Administrative High Court

but the ÖVP accepted the judgment. In the constitutional committee in parliament, the SPÖ and the small right-wing "Freedom Party" (FPÖ), then in opposition, accepted a proposal that the return of Otto Habsburg to Austria would be "unwelcome". The SPÖ Foreign Minister, Bruno Kreisky, and the socialist Minister of the Interior, Franz Olah, decided that they would not, on the basis of this, issue a passport to Otto Habsburg. Besides the question of the monarchy, Franz Olah was interested in liaising with the FPÖ to undermine the "grand coalition" and pave the way for a small coalition with the FPÖ under the leadership of the Socialists. Otto Habsburg finally received a passport from the single-party government which was formed by the ÖVP in 1966. He entered Austria in 1967 and even met Bruno Kreisky several times in the 1970s and '80s.

MS

Olah Affair (1964–69)

Christian Broda, Minister of Justice (1960–66).
Franz Olah, President of the Austrian Trade Union Federation (1959–63); Minister of the Interior (1963–64)
Bruno Piterrmann, head of the SPÖ and Vice-Chancellor (1957–66).

Franz Olah was born in Vienna in 1910 and in the 1930s was imprisoned for political activities as a Revolutionary Socialist. In 1938 he was captured and spent the war years in a concentration camp. After the war he became Central Secretary of the Construction and Woodworkers' Union and in 1955 became Vice-President of the Trade Union Federation (ÖGB). He also became deputy president in the National Assembly and leader of the parliamentary party for the Socialists. In 1959 he took over as President of the ÖGB. There was no doubting Olah's energy, talent and ambition. He was regarded as a forceful politician with a strong will-power and sense of destiny. His charismatic personality exercised a strong hold on his union members and he assumed an influential position on the right wing of the Socialist Party. During the four-power occupation (1945–55), Olah was active on behalf of the Americans preparing secret broadcasts to the eastern part of Austria under Soviet control. It was Olah too who led the workers in 1950 in their successful efforts to squash the Communist uprising of that year.

Olah was a member of the dominant socialist group in the ÖGB and was responsible for the administration of its accounts. He was later

accused of misuse of trade union funds and for helping to finance one
of the FPÖ's election campaigns. With union savings books he granted
security for secret credit which was used to finance a popular tabloid
newspaper (*Kronen Zeitung*). He used this paper as a platform to build
up his position in the party, with the apparent aim of striving for the
leadership of the SPÖ and possibly one day of becoming Chancellor of
the republic.

His main adversaries in the party were Christian Broda, the left-wing
Minister of Justice, and the then chairman of the party, Bruno Pittermann.
He was distrusted by the left in the party who disliked his pro-American
sympathies and were suspicious of his greed for personal power. Olah was
a practising catholic and a convinced anti-marxist. His brash, unorthodox
style made many enemies in the party.

In 1963 he became Minister of the Interior and announced in public
that a slander campaign was being waged against him in the SPÖ. He
gave up his post as trade union boss but continued to enjoy the loyalty
of members in his union. In a televised appearance he claimed to have
discovered personal files kept by the state police and called for a thorough
reform in the security system. He even went so far as to discredit members
of his own party for abuse of power in office. The party presidium warned
him against this behaviour and he was obliged to surrender the office
of Minister of the Interior. Soon after, strikes in sympathy with Olah's
position broke out amongst the workers supporting their hero. Although
the demonstrations on the streets in favour of him continued, he was
subsequently expelled from the party. During these strikes the electricity
was periodically cut off and the trams in Vienna ground to a halt. Such
action was in express defiance of the orders of the ÖGB and the workers
demanded the resignation of the party leadership and the reinstatement of
Olah. The discovery that Olah had misappropriated union funds lost him
sympathy and weakened his cause.

In July, 1965, Olah founded his own party, the Democratic Progressive
Party (DFP), and used this as a power base to launch further attacks
on the SPÖ leadership through the medium of the tabloids like the
Kronen Zeitung. Suddenly in February 1966 two editions of the paper
were confiscated and its offices occupied by the ministry of Justice. The
official reason was a claim of the ÖGB's that it was the legitimate owner
of the paper. For the SPÖ the Olah case proved to be a disaster and in
the federal election in March 1966 the conservative ÖVP won an absolute
majority. The SPÖ was divided and confused and its traditional discipline
and unity was severely tested.

The Olah crisis came at a time when the party was at low ebb and
lacking clear policies and leadership. The DFP won 3.3 per cent of the
votes, but because of the electoral system did not qualify for parliamentary representation. To add to the disarray the Communists, who were
historically unpopular in Austria, asked their supporters to turn out for
the SPÖ thus alienating many "liberal" voters. In 1966 therefore the ÖVP
was able to form the first single party government ending 20 years of the
"grand coalition".

In 1967 the ÖGB's claim to be the rightful owner of the *Kronen Zeitung*
was dismissed in the courts but the Federation persisted by tabling a charge

of breach of trust against Olah. He was forced to stand trial for fraud and a verdict was passed in 1969 which led to Olah's imprisonment for one year, but he was cleared of acting for his personal enrichment.

Shortly after this the DFP won seats in the municipal elections in Vienna. The large socialist majority there decided not to allow Olah into the chamber because of the decision reached after his trial. Olah's claim to fame subsequently subsided particularly after Bruno Kreisky, who had supported Olah, took over as leader and started to open up the party, scoring election victories and building bridges with the FPÖ. Olah became a *persona non grata* in the party's history and memories of the damage he inflicted are still vivid and bitter.

MS

Lütgendorf Affair (1976)

Karl Lütgendorf, Minister of Defence (1971–77).

In December 1976, the export of 400,000 cartridges of snipers' ammunition, destined for Syria from Austrian army stocks, was intercepted at Vienna International Airport. The weekly magazine, *Wochenpresse*, publicised this in January 1977 and a special session of parliament was called. Austria's status as a neutral country, adopted in 1955, prohibits the export of weapons to countries in a state of war.

The exporter was Alois Weichselbaum, a former brothel keeper and close friend of the Minister of Defence, Karl Lütgendorf. Parliament set up a special committee of inquiry and closed sessions took place in March and April. The socialist speaker in the national assembly, Anton Benya, excluded journalists from parliament. The investigation lasted until May and a report was drawn up. This concluded that the Minister of Defence had not informed the chancellor, Bruno Kreisky, either in full or accurately. Lütgendorf subsequently offered his resignation which was accepted. A more rigid scrutiny of the export of arms followed.

The background to this scandal in the socialist government is especially abstruse. Lütgendorf was on friendly terms with Mustafa Tlass, the Syrian Minister of Defence. Tlass, Lütgendorf and Weichselbaum were in fact hunting friends. At one such hunt in the autumn of 1975, the deal was reported to have been struck. Lütgendorf offered to supply Syria with Austrian army ammunition and in January 1976 the contract was signed.

In May 1976, Lütgendorf visited Syria on an official visit and claimed bank credit.

When the ammunition was stopped by customs officers at the airport in December 1976, Lütgendorf ordered a change in the declared name of the exporter from "Weichselbaum" to the "Austrian army". As this too proved to be useless the consignment was routed by train to a Yugoslavian port. When the scandal was made public, Lütgendorf and Weichselbaum agreed to declare unanimously that the ammunition would be shipped to Tunisia, a country not in a state of war at this time.

Lütgendorf, a former brigadier, had been a member of the socialist government since 1971 although he was not a party member. His appointment was part of a tactic by Kreisky to bring non-party ministers into his cabinet in an effort to woo the votes of the liberal thinking. Lütgendorf was one of the few high-ranking officers who accepted a major army reform involving the reduction of military service from nine to six months, a central slogan of the SPÖ election campaign in 1971. Later on Lütgendorf was additionally involved in the Lucona affair (see below) in which, as Minister of Defence, he gave substantial support to Udo Proksch.

Lütgendorf was reported as having committed suicide in October 1981 but there have been frequent rumours since that he was murdered.

MS

Androsch Affair (1978–88)

Hannes Androsch, Minister of Finance (1970–81); Vice-chancellor (1976–81).

The Androsch affair is linked with the infamous general hospital or AKH building project in Vienna. The hospital, including university clinics, was originally erected by Joseph II at the end of the 18th century and was newly constructed in the 1960s. At the end of the 1970s, wild discrepancies in estimated costs, chaotic planning and impossible target dates came to light. The inflated costs were the result in part of underhand transaction deals involving high-ranking politicians.

In a special parliamentary committee of inquiry in 1980, the questions of the conservative opposition concerned for the most part the planning firm Ökodata, of which it was said that the then Minister of Finance, Hannes Androsch, was a partner, a claim which was officially contested by Androsch. In 1975, Androsch bought a luxury villa in a smart residential quarter of Vienna. Although the purchase was an extremely good opportunity (the seller was a socialist-dominated insurance company), he had to spend money belonging to him and his family from "black" accounts. In all there were about 10 special accounts which had existed since 1966–67 to which Androsch had access during the entire time he was Minister of Finance (1970–81). In 1978 the weekly magazine, *Profil*, latched on to the story and published the irregularities. Lengthy and involved investigations followed during which a friend of Androsch claimed the accounts to be his, although he had declared his "lack of means" shortly before. It was clear Androsch was part of a complex "clan" sometimes referred to in the press as the "AKH-Mafia". In 1981, Androsch, who in the meantime had become Vice-Chancellor, was dismissed by Kreisky from his cabinet. Androsch had been a prodigy of Kreisky and treated almost like a favoured son. His ostentatious behaviour hurt Kreisky deeply as inappropriate for a socialist politician. In spite of this, Androsch's dismissal from the cabinet was hardly a personal tragedy. With help from the FPÖ, he went on to become chairman of the *Creditanstalt*, Austria's largest bank, and a recipient of a generous salary, the envy of many humble cabinet ministers. During the scandal, Androsch was backed by the powerful union boss and socialist, Anton Benya.

In 1983, *Profil* returned to the case again and published details of evidence provided by Androsch's successor as Finance Minister, Herbert Salcher. The case dragged on into 1986 during which time Androsch renewed his contact with the Bank. The Minister of Justice at this time was Harald Ofner of the FPÖ, then in coalition with the Socialists. In 1987 the Austrian equivalent of the Inland Revenue found Androsch guilty of tax evasion (more than 6,000,000 Schillings) and in 1988 he was found guilty of giving false evidence before a parliamentary committee of inquiry. He was obliged under these circumstances to retire from his banking position — but of course with a lucrative full pension. The criminal case for his tax evasion continued late into 1990.

The political importance of the Androsch case lies not only in the near comic figure of a tax-evading Minister of Finance but calls into question the effective workings of a democracy and political accountability. It also illustrated, in the sphere of political morals, the failure of a highly talented social democrat, espousing one theory but living a somewhat contradictory life-style in practice. The Androsch affair became a symbol in Austria for a new type of politician, the *Macher*; the efficient, competent and unashamed rich multi-functionary. Franz Vranitzky, now socialist Chancellor and ex-banker, was a former secretary of Androsch, a twist of history which provoked a bitter response from the former Chancellor Bruno Kreisky.

MS

Reder Affair (1985–86)

Leopold Gratz, Minister of Foreign Affairs, Socialist deputy in parliament
   and mayor of Vienna.
Walter Reder, former SS major.

Walter Reder, "SS-Sturmbahnführer" (major), was a prisoner of war
condemned to "life" imprisonment because of his involvement in brutal
actions against anti-fascist guerrillas and civilians in Italy. For these actions
he became known as the notorious "butcher of Marzabotto". When the
Italian authorities decided in December 1984 to pardon Reder and to allow
him to return to Austria they requested that the return should not be made
public. As Reder arrived by plane in January 1985, the then Minister of
Defence Friedhelm Frischenschlager, a member of the liberal-pan-German
nationalist FPÖ, met him personally at the airport and even shook his hand
on welcoming him home, suggesting Reder was returning as a "prisoner of
war". This caused a furore in domestic politics and the conservative ÖVP
attacked both Frischenschlager for this insensitivity and the FPÖ's coalition
partner, the SPÖ.

   The socialist Foreign Minister, Leopold Gratz, also shared responsibility
for the arrangements concerning Reder's return and was severely censured
by some members in his own party and even cabinet colleagues. Gratz in
his youth had been a pupil of the Nazi NAPOLA and his role in the affair
was particularly unfortunate. This was not the last time that Gratz was to
make the headlines for suspect activities and his name occurs frequently in
the annals of Austrian scandals (see also *Lucona Affair, 1987–90; Noricum
Affair, 1987–88*, below).

   Eventually the SPÖ-FPÖ coalition, after a strained session, agreed that
Frischenschlager should not resign because of his action. Many Socialists
were however unhappy with this decision and it was another episode in
the luckless experiment of a small "social-liberal" coalition. The incident
did little to help Austria's image abroad and the general reaction of
the international press was negative and hostile. The Frischenschlager
"handshake" occurred at a time when Austrian politics was entering an
uncertain period of turbulence, especially noticeable after the illusory calm
of the Kreisky era (1970–83). In addition to the Reder affair, there was also
the occasion of the Austrian wine scandal when it was discovered that high
quality wines from Burgenland contained a constituent of anti-freeze. The
cosy *gemütlich* image of the Mozart-loving friendly Austrians was further
blown apart by revelations of the darker side of Austria's past which
somehow many Austrians had managed to avoid facing. The Reder case
was symptomatic of such a failure but was soon dwarfed by the international
reprobation provoked by the Waldheim affair.

                                                              MS

Waldheim Affair (1986–90)

Kurt Waldheim, President (1986–); Foreign Minister (1968–70). Elected
  secretary-general of the United Nations (1971 and 1976).

In June 1986, Kurt Waldheim, formerly UN Secretary-General, was elected
Federal President of Austria on a second ballot with 53.9 per cent of the
vote. He was the first non-socialist to hold that office since the war. In April
1987 the US government placed Waldheim on the "watch list" under the
Holtzmann amendment of 1978, effectively debarring him from entering
the United States. With few exceptions, Waldheim has been internationally
isolated during his term of office and confined to purely routine duties
within Austria.

The reason for this extraordinary treatment of the Austrian head of state
concerns Waldheim's wartime past and, more particularly, his version of it,
which often seemed at odds with historical investigation. In March 1986, the
magazine *Profil* released information which suggested that Waldheim had
omitted crucial aspects of his past, including his membership of National
Socialist organizations and his full involvement in the Balkan occupation
led by the German Wehrmacht. His autobiography is curiously incomplete
on these points; a fact which only came to light during the subsequent
debate in the election campaign and after. Waldheim's response was often
inconsistent and confused and when he did concede ground it was only
as a result of pressure. This gave the impression that he had something
more serious to hide and contributed to a loss of credibility abroad. He
demonstrated throughout a surprising lack of sensitivity, given the fact that
he had served in a particularly brutal theatre of the war.

The campaign was one of the hardest and most emotive in Austria's
post-war history. Until then it seemed almost an unwritten law that
presidential campaigns were to be fairly tedious, low-key affairs. Before
the story broke the press anticipated the worst, since Waldheim and his
socialist opponent, Kurt Steyrer, were lacking anything newsworthy. The
campaign, however, was to prove anything but dull as both sides launched
into a diatribe of invective, polarising society and even families in the
process.

The ÖVP, which backed Waldheim, insisted that its candidate was
the victim of a co-ordinated campaign to blacken Waldheim, the first
non-socialist who, it seemed, might make it to the Hofburg. Regrettably
the debate took the form of allegations against Jews, Socialists and
others who might be involved in the plot to "stop Waldheim". Latent
anti-semitism was used by some in the ÖVP to discredit the accusations
made by the World Jewish Congress based in New York. By the time of
the election it was almost impossible to conduct an objective discussion on
the issue. The matter was made even more complex by the involvement
in this domestic storm of the international press who were quick to sketch
out the alleged Austrian role in past atrocities and the Holocaust. There
was much speculation as to how Waldheim's wartime past had escaped
attention, especially given his former position as Secretary-General of the

UN. Far more was at stake than the wartime past of an hitherto mediocre politician, and Waldheim became caught up in the transition taking place in the political culture of Austria. Much of these changed attitudes can be traced to the scandals in the nationalized industries which coincided with the Waldheim affair and revealed the bankruptcy of mismanagement which had been commonplace in the public sector for so long. The bills of the Kreisky era were beginning to flow in and, with the nationalized steel industries in trouble, jobs were abruptly lost. Many Austrians had been accustomed to heavy protection in the large nationalized industries; they were not used to lay-offs and disillusionment was inevitable. The situation contributed to the emergence of a new climate in Austria. It was also linked to the growing dissatisfaction with the socialist management of the economy. The SPÖ had been in power since 1970 and in coalition with the FPÖ since 1983. The "small coalition" was not popular even with its members and the Waldheim election provided an outlet to voice this dissatisfaction. The scrutiny of the outside world, to make matters worse, looked like foreign meddling and a defensive reaction developed in which Austrians defiantly stated they would vote for the candidate they wanted.

The immediate consequence of Waldheim's victory was the resignation of Chancellor Sinowatz who was succeeded by the urbane technocrat, Franz Vranitzky. The SPÖ therefore managed to reap some harvest from the debacle since it had found an attractive and popular personality who saved them from greater defeat in the November elections of the same year. The Waldheim affair dragged on to plague the great coalition, formed by Vranitzky in 1987 with the ÖVP. Despite unease in the socialist ranks, Vranitzky gave muted support to Waldheim as the elected President of the Republic.

A minor breakthrough for Waldheim came in the summer of 1990 when a joint visit was paid by the German and Czechoslovak presidents to Salzburg, where they met Waldheim.

Waldheim was not, according to an international historians' commission, a war criminal. The picture emerges of a careerist with an especially selective memory who made undeserved news through his own insensitive reaction to the accusations. The Waldheim case surfaced once more during the commemoration of the 50th anniversary of the German occupation of Austria in 1938. After a renewed discussion during this epilogue to the story, Austrian voters seemed bored with the affair and most international observers begrudgingly accepted Waldheim's continuation in office at least until the next election. In 1990 Waldheim made the headlines again by intervening in the Gulf crisis to rescue Austrian hostages held by Saddam Hussein, the Iraqi President. He built on his good relations with the Arab World stemming from his time as UN Secretary-General, but was criticized outside Austria for breaking international solidarity against Saddam.

MS

Lucona Affair (1987–90)

Udo Proksch, owner of Demels *Konditorie/Kaffeehaus*, Vienna.

One of the more bizarre scandals to break in Austria in the 1980s was the Lucona case. In January 1977, the ship *Lucona* sank in the Indian Ocean and six of the crew were drowned. In the autumn of 1987 Udo Proksch, owner of the Demel Coffee House in Vienna's fashionable inner city, claimed 212,000,000 schillings from the Bundesländer insurance company. Proksch claimed that on board the *Lucona* was equipment for processing uranium which had been en route for a deal in the Far East. The insurance company suspected foul play and refused to pay, hiring a private investigator to unravel the case. Information was given to the Salzburg police in July 1983 but the Minister of the Interior, the socialist Karl Blecha, ordered a halt to the police investigations. The Minister of Justice, Harald Ofner (FPÖ), further slowed down proceedings in January 1985 although suspicion was growing that the "uranium-processing equipment", supposedly the ship's cargo, was in fact worthless scrap. The police authorities in Lower Austria were required for further inquiry but Blecha once again blocked the case. Nevertheless a judge ordered the arrest of Proksch (and his partner Daimler) in February 1985. Foreign Minister Leopold Gratz immediately asked the Austrian Embassy to furnish plans of the uranium plant from Romania by diplomatic mail in an effort to clear his friend Proksch. These documents later turned out to be forged. In October 1986 Proksch and Daimler were once more arrested but were soon released.

In January 1987, with the formation of a "grand coalition", a new Minister of Justice, Egmont Foregger (non-party) came to office. An indictment was worked out later that year and Proksch and Daimler left Austria to go into hiding in the Philippines. He was arrested in October 1989, after an obscure tip-off when travelling with a forged passport via the UK, and placed on a plane for Vienna.

Udo Proksch was more than the proprietor of a smart coffee and cakes establishment. His premises were used as a contact centre by the socialist equivalent of its high society. "Club 45", as it was known, was the rendezvous above Demels, frequented by prominent socialists, many mesmerized by Proksch's personality and keen to further their own careers. In October 1988 a committee of inquiry had been set up by parliament. One of the main points which emerged in the murky story was that access to the explosives of the Austrian army was offered to Proksch in 1976 by the former Minister of Defence, Karl Lütgendorf (see also *Lütgendorf Affair, 1976*, above).

Blecha and Gratz resigned in January 1989 and Blecha retired from parliament and all party functions in April 1989. The parliamentary inquiry learnt that Blecha had influenced the testimony of the director of the Salzburg police before he was to give evidence. The trial of Proksch started in 1990 at which he was accused of attempted fraud and multiple murder. He pleaded not guilty. If convicted hc faces the maximum penalty of life imprisonment.

MS

Noricum Affair (1987–88)

Karl Blecha, general secretary of the Socialist Party, MP and Minister of the Interior.
Fred Sinowatz, Chancellor for the SPÖ (1983–86).

In 1977, a law regulating the export of weapons was passed, one of the results of the Lütgendorf affair (see above). In 1979 VÖEST, a state-owned industrial conglomerate, decided to produce guns in its special subsidiary company, Noricum. Chancellor Bruno Kreisky, under whose sphere of influence the state industries came, concurred. As the State treaty of 1955 prohibits guns in Austria with a range longer than 30 km, the conclusion was that the howitzers were for export.

In 1980–81, Iraq bought 200 guns which were delivered to Jordan. In 1984, Iran too ordered 200 guns which officially were marked destined for Libya. The deal was organized by a weapon trader, Hadji Dai, who in July 1985 complained to Amry, the Austrian ambassador in Athens, that he was not getting his share. Iran had set up a camouflage firm, Fasami, to avoid payments. Amry informed the Foreign Ministry, but died mysteriously shortly afterwards.

The Foreign Minister, Leopold Gratz, instructed the relevant officials not to check the Libyan end-user certificates. In August 1985 the magazine *Basta* investigated the death of Amry since it was rumoured that he had been murdered by poison. In an urgent meeting, Chancellor Fred Sinowatz and Minister of the Interior, Blecha, agreed that the Minister for the nationalized industries, the socialist Ferdinand Lacina, should "examine" the case. Nothing however came of this.

In November 1985 a subsidiary company of VÖEST, Intertrading, collapsed after oil-speculating ventures which necessitated huge subsidies from the Austrian taxpayer. The fired boss of Intertrading threatened to publicize the details on the exports of the guns but decided against this after receiving a large sum of hush money from Noricum.

In January 1986, US officials demanded a halt to the sale of guns to Libya because of the tensions with Gaddafi, the Libyan leader. In February, Sinowatz, Blecha and Gratz declared formally in the committee on foreign affairs that no exports to Iran had taken place. In March 1986, Austrian police were informed by the Japanese Embassy that Fasami was an Iranian camouflage firm.

In June 1986, Chancellor Sinowatz and Foreign Minister Gratz resigned as a result of the Waldheim election (see *Waldheim Affair, 1986–90*, above). The new Chancellor, Franz Vranitzky, was informed of the Iran exports by his personal secretary. In 1987 and 1988 Karl Blecha, who was Minister of the Interior in the SPÖ/ÖVP coalition, had a hand in faking and destroying important documents relating to the gun exports and, in particular, to the last telex of Herbert Amry.

In September 1989 a parliamentary committee of inquiry, under pressure from the ÖVP and FPÖ, was set up and the scandal was fully documented under the public eye. The aim was to ascertain who knew of the arms shipment and who gave the go-ahead. It was concerned to probe the extent of the knowledge of politicians and to decide how much they were misinformed by the managers. The trial against the Noricum management for violating Austria's neutrality was still in process in late 1990 and legal proceedings against the politicians involved were being prepared.

MS

BAHAMAS

Pindling Affair (1983–88)

Everette Bannister, Businessman.
Sir Lynden Pindling, Prime Minister (from 1973).
Sir James Smith, former Chief Justice of the Bahamas.

The Pindling Affair helped demonstrate the extent to which corruption connected with drug trafficking could spread through the fabric of the society of a small nation.

The geographical position of the Bahamas, to the south-east of Florida and on a direct route to the USA from the drug-producing areas of South America, combined with the existence of numerous small sparsely inhabited islands, made it a natural stopping place for the light aircraft and fast boats shipping illegal drugs into the USA. Its banking and company confidentiality laws also made it an ideal place for "laundering" drug profits.

Lynden Pindling, a British-trained barrister, became the Bahamas' first Prime Minister on the country's independence from Britain in 1973. His party, the Progressive Liberal Party, had first formed a government in 1967. Pindling's position as the champion of the black population earned him continued electoral support in subsequent general elections, although many criticized his lavish lifestyle and that of his flamboyant wife.

Local politicians and officials were bribed by drug smugglers to turn a blind eye to illegal activities, but by November 1983 allegations involving senior politicians and Pindling himself had reached such a pitch that Pindling announced the creation of a Royal Commission to investigate all aspects of drug-related corruption in the Bahamas. The Commission was chaired by Sir James Smith, a former Chief Justice, with Bishop Drexel Gomez of Barbados and Edwin Willes, a former Canadian police officer.

The hearings, which continued until August 1984, revealed the extent to which drug-related money had permeated through Bahamian society. In Pindling's own case the hearings revealed numerous gifts and loans made to him by businessmen and individuals and personal expenditure far in excess of his official salary. Two government ministers, Kendal Nottage and George Smith, resigned on Oct. 8 after being implicated in the hearings. Arthur Hanna, the Deputy Prime Minister, also resigned and two of his colleagues were dismissed on the same day after an unsuccessful attempt to force Pindling to resign.

The Commission's report, published on December 17, said that corruption had reached senior levels of government and had caused "serious social and economic ills". The report singled out Howard Smith, assistant commissioner of police, George Weech, a government MP and Everette

Bannister, a businessman and friend of Pindling, for particular criticism. A minority report by Bishop Gomez went further in its criticism of Pindling and although the Commission could not find enough evidence to link Pindling with drug-related money it stated that his acceptance of large financial gifts had been unwise. Pindling regarded the Commission's report as clearing his name and vigorously refused opposition demands for his resignation or fresh elections.

In the aftermath of the scandal Bahamian banking and company laws were strengthened and more anti-drug measures taken, in co-operation with the USA. The suspicions surrounding Pindling did not disappear however, and as late as 1988 attempts were being made in the USA to organize an indictment against him for accepting bribes while an appeal in London cleared him of allegations of failing to reveal a number of personal cash gifts.

LP

BELGIUM

Ibramco Affair (1973–74)

Willy Claes, Socialist Minister for Economic Affairs.
Edmond Leburton, Prime Minister.

The three-party coalition government in Belgium which lasted from January 1973 until March 1974 was beset by the sort of ideological rifts which are common in any such collection of diverse political parties struggling to live together. Nothing illustrated these rifts more dramatically than the Ibramco Affair which was to lead to the government's downfall. A joint venture between Belgium and Iran to build an oil refinery near Liège had been entered into by the previous Belgian government and it was pursued by the coalition government with great vigour by the Socialist ministers and with great suspicion by their partners from the Christian Social and Liberal parties. This divergence of view led to the government exceeding the deadline set by the Iranians for a final decision on the project, with the consequence that the Iranians pulled out. The Belgian Socialists then resigned from the Cabinet leading to a collapse of the government and a general election.

The Ibramco Affair began with a convention, signed in December 1972, between Belgium and the National Iranian Oil Company (NIOC), providing for the establishment of a joint enterprise, to be known as the Iranian-Belgian Refining and Marketing Company (Ibramco). The convention was signed on behalf of Belgium by a caretaker government which had assumed responsibility when the previous administration had resigned the month before. On Jan. 24, 1973 the Socialist Budget Minister, André Cools, appointed four Belgian members of the Ibramco board, all of them members of his own party.

When the coalition government of Socialists, Christian Socials and Liberals under the Prime Minister, Edmond Leburton, took over the next day it became apparent that there were different views about the project among the coalition partners. Criticism was expressed about the way Socialist ministers had handled the affair during the interim government, with accusations that they had exceeded their authority. It was pointed out that the decision of a ministerial committee in early December 1972 to go ahead with the project had specified that initially it would be a joint feasibility study, but in the course of 1973 it seemed likely that the company was proceeding with work on the construction of the refinery near Liège.

In a heated debate in the Belgian parliament in May, spokesmen for the Liberals and the Christian Socials expressed their disquiet at the way the project was being handled. The Liberals said they could not support the gradual nationalization of economic life. In reply, the Socialist Minister for Economic Affairs, Willy Claes, stated that Ibramco was still only a research company and that a final decision on the construction of the refinery would depend on its potential profitability. On the strength of this, a motion of censure on the government over the affair was defeated.

In a further statement to parliament in June, Claes confirmed that the Belgium share in Ibramco would be completely state-owned and also announced the setting up of a committee for oil policy, to include government representatives and other interested parties to which all proposals for future action on Ibramco would be referred.

It was agreed in the autumn of 1973 that Belgium would make a final decision on whether to proceed with the project by Dec. 2, although Leburton later secured an extension of the deadline until Jan. 15, 1974. Discussions within the government continued and it was not until after a Cabinet meeting held on the night of Jan. 15–16 that the government issued a statement expressing approval of the project subject to certain conditions.

The statement specified that as long as Ibramco existed the NIOC should undertake to supply the refinery with all the crude oil it required at the market place, and maintained that in view of recent changes in the oil market further clarifications were necessary: to this end the government would send a delegation to Iran as soon as possible.

The Belgian Government received a telegram on Jan. 16 from the assistant director general of the NIOC, stating that, in view of the expiry of the deadline of Jan. 15, the 1972 convention must be considered as no longer valid. The Belgian Ministry of Foreign Affairs announced that the telegram had been sent before the Iranian authorities had learnt of the decision of the Belgian Cabinet. However, Claes then received another telegram from the chairman of NIOC, stating that, as it appeared that the decision of the Belgian government was dependant on various conditions and further negotiations at government level, the NIOC had decided to abandon the project immediately and to terminate all discussions relating to the proposed refinery.

The collapse of the Ibramco project was swiftly followed by that of the government. The resignation of the Socialist members of the Cabinet was announced on Jan. 18, and following unsuccessful attempts to form another coalition, a general election was called.

RSD

Vanden Boeynants Affair (1982–89)

Paul Vanden Boeynants, Prime Minister (1966–68; 1978–79).

There was widespread sympathy among the Belgian public when the former Prime Minister, Paul Vanden Boeynants, was kidnapped in Brussels in January 1989. There was genuine relief too when he was released unharmed a month later apparently after the payment of a large ransom by his family. The flamboyant self-made millionaire had always held a fond place in the mind of his fellow Belgians and it was perhaps not surprising that they should identify themselves with the plight of a man of nearly 70 years of age suffering from a heart condition falling into the hands of a ruthless kidnap gang.

What might appear surprising is that this sympathy was in no way diminished by the knowledge that Vanden Boeynants had been convicted three years earlier of systematic tax fraud and branded a compulsive cheat by the court which handed him a suspended prison sentence. Some observers went so far as to say that Vanden Boeynants' popularity had been enhanced by his indulgence in tax fraud, once described by a public prosecutor as Belgium's national sport.

Paul Vanden Boeynants was born in 1919 and began his working life as a butcher's assistant. He became the owner of a meat-processing chain and eventually made a fortune through land deals in and around his native Brussels. Entering politics at the end of the war, he was elected to parliament as a Christian Social deputy for Brussels at the age of 29, and was also active in municipal politics in the capital. He was Minister for the Middle Classes from 1958 to 1961, and after the 1961 elections he became President of the Christian Social Party. He became Prime Minister in 1966 and stepped down two years later over the issue which has come to haunt Belgian politics — the split between the French and Dutch-speaking parts of the country. In 1978–79 he again served as Prime Minister, heading a caretaker coalition after the fall of the government of Leo Tindemans.

One of an increasingly rare breed of Belgian anti-federalist politicians, Vanden Boeynants opposed the devolution of government to French and Dutch-speaking regions. He himself spoke both languages (equally badly, according to one unkind commentator). A Brussels newspaper, *Le Soir*, described him thus: "Whether you love him or hate him — or do both at the same time — Paul Vanden Boeynants incarnates down to his fingertips a certain type of Belgianism".

Whether this type of Belgianism included attracting the attention of the tax authorities is uncertain. But in 1982 a file with detailed allegations of tax fraud was passed to the Belgian parliament for examination and the deputies duly obliged by lifting Vanden Boeynants' immunity from prosecution. His trial on 137 charges of tax fraud and forgery took place in June 1986. The prosecution alleged that he had evaded taxes through various operations of buying and selling stock in several companies — some of them "ghost companies" — in Belgium, Switzerland and Liechtenstein. One of the major charges was the forgery of a document about the sale of shares to the former Lebanese ambassador to Belgium, Antoine Francis. All the experts agreed that the signature of the late Francis was forged but the defence argued that Vanden Boeynants would have had nothing to gain from such a crude action.

In general, the former Prime Minister's defence was that he had been much too busy and had left his financial affairs to advisers, who were therefore to blame for any irregularities. The court found him guilty of most of the charges and sentenced him to three years imprisonment, suspended, and a fine of BFr 620,000. One of the judges said he was "a compulsive cheat" who had imposed laws on others but failed to respect them himself. The authorities continued to scrutinize Vanden Boeynants' affairs by examining allegations that he had taken bribes while Defence Minister in the 1970s.

The second chapter of the Vanden Boeynants Affair opened with the news in January 1989 that the former Prime Minister had been kidnapped outside his flat in Brussels. A previously unknown group calling itself the Socialist Revolutionary Brigade demanded a ransom, two-thirds of which was to be sent to the Third World. A month after the kidnapping, Vanden Boeynants arrived home after midnight in a taxi after being dumped by his abductors in the town of Tournai, 80 km away on the French-Belgian border. He told police that he had been generally well treated. The kidnappers had administered medicine for his heart condition, and had even given him a pipe to replace one left behind in his flat. His hearing aid had also been left and negotiations had been conducted through writing.

It transpired that the family had paid a large ransom for his release (possibly BFr 63,000,000) and that the police had co-operated during the negotiations. The authorities no longer took seriously the claims of left-wing involvement in the kidnapping. They were conducting a straightforward criminal investigation and made a number of arrests during 1989.

RSD

BULGARIA

Markov Affair (1978)

Gen. Ilya Kashev, chief of security for President Todor Zhivkov.
Georgi Markov, exiled writer and broadcaster.
Grigor Shopov, department head in security service.
Mircho Spassov, head of Bulgarian Communist Party security department.
Lt.-Gen. Dimitur Stoyanov, Interior Minister.
Todor Zhivkov, first secretary of Bulgarian Communist Party (1954–89), President of the State Council (1971–89).

It is as the "case of the poisoned umbrella" that most people remember the killing of Georgi Markov in London in 1978. That Markov, an outspoken émigré critic of the regime in his homeland, fell victim to an assassin sponsored by that regime is widely believed, but has yet to be proved.

Georgi Markov, a celebrated writer of fiction, drama and essays, fled Bulgaria in 1969 after his play "I was him", being staged at the Theatre of Satire in Sofia, was banned after its dress rehearsal. He defected in Italy, but lived in the United Kingdom from 1971. He worked for the Bulgarian section of the BBC World Service, but it was his freelance broadcasts for Radio Free Europe (based in Munich, West Germany, and financed by the United States) and the West German radio service *Deutsche Welle* which were believed to have made him a target for the Bulgarian security service. Markov used his intimate knowledge of the lifestyle of Bulgaria's hardline leader Todor Zhivkov and his associates, acquired during Markov's years in Bulgaria as a favoured writer, to denounce the political system in talks broadcast to the country by these stations.

On Sept. 7, 1978, Markov was standing at a bus stop on London's Waterloo Bridge when a man jabbed him in the leg with what appeared to be an umbrella. Four days later Markov died in hospital, at the age of 49. A post mortem examination revealed a tiny metal pellet in his right thigh, apparently fired from the umbrella, which forensic scientists determined had contained a fatal dose of the poison ricin. An inquest concluded on Jan. 2, 1979, that Markov had been unlawfully killed by an unknown person.

A similar attack had been made on another Bulgarian émigré, Vladimir Kostov, in Paris in late August 1978, but the pellet had lodged in his back, where the poison had been able to work less effectively than in Markov's case, and Kostov had survived. Kostov was a former head of the Paris bureau of Bulgarian state radio and television, and had defected to the West in June 1977.

Allegations were made in various quarters that the Bulgarian security service had carried out the attacks on Markov and Kostov as part of a campaign to eliminate émigré opponents of the regime. Some commentators went so far as to note that Sept. 7 was Zhivkov's birthday, and to suggest that Markov's assassination was meant as a present to him. The Bulgarian authorities denied all involvement, and the identity of the assailant in each case remained unknown.

Zhivkov's hardline regime was overthrown in November 1989 by reformist members of the Communist leadership, and a free multiparty democratic system was introduced early in 1990. Encouraged by these developments, Markov's British-born widow Annabel travelled to Bulgaria in January 1990, and in a meeting with the new Communist Party leader Aleksandur Lilov she secured his support for an official investigation to establish whether her husband's death had been ordered by Bulgaria's rulers. However, in February an Interior Ministry spokesman insisted that the idea that Markov had been assassinated by the Bulgarian security service was a fiction put about by the British press, and he accused the *Sunday Times* of having invented the umbrella scenario after British agents had planted the poisoned pellet on Markov's body. On March 1 a vigil was held in Sofia by several hundred people holding open umbrellas to protest at the failure of the authorities to fulfil Lilov's pledge to Annabel Markov. *The Guardian* of March 2 claimed that the authorities' change of heart was because four of the five men suspected of complicity in the killing were still alive, namely Zhivkov; former Interior Minister Dimitur Stoyanov; Grigor Shopov, who had been responsible for security operations involving Bulgarians living abroad; and Mircho Spassov, a former head of the Communist Party's security department. The fifth man was Gen. Ilya Kashev, former head of Zhivkov's presidential guard, who had died in suspicious circumstances (unofficial reports spoke either of suicide or murder) in 1986.

Markov was posthumously rehabilitated to the Bulgarian Writers' Union in January 1990. His works are once again being published in Bulgaria.

IPG

BURMA (MYANMAR)

Aung San Affair (1947)

Aung San, President Anti-Fascist People's Freedom League, 1945; member of Executive Council.
Maj. Gen. Sir Hubert Rance, last British Governor of Burma, (1946–48).
Thakin Nu (U Nu), Aung San's successor, 1947.
U Saw, former Premier (1941) leader of Myochit (Patriotic) Party, executed 1948.

By the time the Japanese surrendered at the end of World War II, the British were once again masters of most of the territory of Burma which they had lost to the invading Japanese in 1942. The exception was the coastal strip of Tenasserim. Yet within two-and-a-half years they had been compelled to leave Burma forever. It became an independent republic, the first country to leave the British Commonwealth. The young man chiefly responsible for this spectacular turn of events was Aung San. A Rangoon student in the 1930s, he had collaborated with the Japanese in 1942 and was given command of a force they raised, the Burma National Army, under the government of Dr Ba Maw. Discontent with the inadequate independence conceded by the Japanese in 1943 led Aung San to negotiate secretly with the British, and on March 27, 1945, he led the Burma National Army over to them.

As the chief figure of what became Burma's main post-war political party, the Anti-Fascist People's Freedom League (AFPFL), Aung San led the political struggle to ensure that Britain's military victory in Burma did not allow the post-war regime, under the returned Governor Sir Reginald Dorman-Smith, to re-establish itself. He was successful, and the new British Labour Government's expectations that three years of direct rule would be needed before elections could be held were soon swept aside. The AFPFL did not want to wait half a decade for the transfer of power. Immediate complete self-government was the aim. There were still British officials in Burma, and also on the staff of the Supreme Commander, South-East Asia, Lord Louis Mountbatten, who did not want to work with Aung San, and considered he should be tried for treason and murder, for crimes committed in 1942. But as even Dorman-Smith had to recognize, Aung San was the most important figure in Burma at that time, and it was with him the British would have to negotiate. Dr Ba Maw had fled with the retreating Japanese armies and was still in hiding in Japan. When he finally returned to Burma he took little part in politics. The only real rival to Aung San was the crafty politician U Saw, then 43, who had been leader of the pre-war Myochit (Patriot) Party and Premier in 1941. In that year he was (correctly) suspected of treasonable negotiations with the Japanese and was interned by the British in Uganda for the rest of the war. Back in Rangoon once the war was over, he bore the British no malice and was ready to enter the political fray once more, confident he would soon sweep away the naive youths of the AFPFL, who lacked his administrative experience, and his wide bonhomous acquaintance among the British officials. In spite of his betrayal (no worse than Aung San's), he was a welcome guest at official parties, and on good terms with Dorman-Smith. The Burmese represented by the AFPFL, on the other hand, mistrusted the British and were sure they would not grant independence, at least not so fully and quickly as the Burmese wanted it. In fact, the number of British troops in Burma (weakened by repatriation and military intervention elsewhere in South-East Asia) could hardly support a military solution, if the Burmese chose to rebel. The majority of government forces were Indian troops — nearly 80,000 — and the Government of India was wary of allowing them to be used in any action which could be interpreted as suppressing Asian nationalism. The same problem occurred in the Netherlands East Indies (later Indonesia) and French Indo-China (later Vietnam).

Eventually, the London government, under its Prime Minister Clement Attlee, grew tired of Dorman-Smith's inability to deal with the situation in Burma and a new Governor, Sir Hubert Rance (Aug. 31, 1946) was instructed to create an executive council to map out Burma's future form of government, avoiding the use of the terms "Dominion Status" and "Independence". A Rangoon police strike soon convinced Rance that his executive council was outmoded, and he decided to negotiate where the power lay, i.e. with Aung San and the AFPFL. Aung San was named Deputy Chairman of the new council. U Saw was member for education and planning, a minor post he did not want. There was dissension in the AFPFL. Communists split off from non-Communists. After some hesitation, the British Government reluctantly announced at the end of 1946 that it would bring forward the time when Burma's independence would be achieved, "either within or without the Commonwealth".

A Burmese delegation, led by Aung San, and including U Saw, nego-tiated with the Labour Government in London in January 1947. A final agreement was reached on Jan. 26, from which U Saw and another pre-war politician, Ba Sein, dissented. Contrary to what the British had intended, Burma was now further along the path to independence than India whose future — unity or partition? — had not yet been decided. And whereas in India the Viceroy presided over the interim government meetings, in Burma the Governor only attended those which directly concerned his special powers. Otherwise Aung San presided. He was by this time, the *de facto* ruler of Burma. Strikes and rioting had already occurred, but these ceased when Aung San returned to Rangoon with the guarantee of independence. Next, the hill peoples' future was settled: at Panglong a conference was held which concluded that a Shan Counsellor should have a seat on the Executive Council, with two deputies, a Chin and a Kachin. The largest minority group, the Karens, did not accept this. They were not entirely a hill people, since two-thirds of them lived in the Delta, so although they wanted a separate state, there were obvious geographical difficulties. They had two seats on the Executive Council.

In the general elections (April 9–10, 1947), Aung San's AFPFL won a landslide victory. The pre-war parties had negligible support, the Karens refused to take part, the Communists won only three of 91 constituencies, so Aung San controlled 204 of the 210 seats in the Constituent Assembly, which was presided over by Thakin Nu, one of Aung San's wartime "Thirty Comrades" of the Japanese days. The British Government was told independence must be announced early in 1948 and that Burma would be a republic. This last provision effectively removed Burma from the British Commonwealth, since there was in 1947 no machinery for retaining in it any state which did not accept the British Crown as head. The Executive Council became, to all intents and purposes, a provisional government.

On July 19, 1947, while the Executive Council was meeting in the Secretariat Building, four gunmen — Maung Soe, Thet Hnin, Maung Sein and Yan Gyi Aung — entered the building and made for the Council Room. They burst in and sprayed it with automatic gunfire. Aung San was killed, together with the Finance Minister, Thakin Mya, the Karen leader Mahn Ba Khaing, the President of the Burma Muslim League, Abdul Razak, Ba Win, Aung San's eldest brother, and a Deputy Secretary, Maung Ohn. Two other ministers later died of wounds in hospital. The Council was debating the arrest of U Saw, who was suspected of preparing to use force against the Executive Council.

The assassins had arrived in a jeep bearing British Army markings, and were wearing British uniforms. A guard outside the door, who was shot, stated that the men were from the 4th Burma Rifles. The situation was fraught with dangerous possibilities: one group of Communists was said to have prior knowledge; there were vague rumours of a general insurrection; and British complicity was almost universally assumed. The Governor, Sir Hubert Rance, acted promptly to defuse the situation by asking Aung San's colleague, Thakin Nu, to take Aung San's place and form a new Executive Council, which he did. The police had had U Saw's house under observation for some time (he himself had been wounded when driving his jeep through Rangoon), and a jeep with five men wearing singlets was seen to arrive there soon after 11.00 am on July 19 (the assassination had taken place at 10.30 am). In the afternoon, the police raided U Saw's house, and took him and 10 others into what was termed "protective custody". They also seized a large quantity of weapons and ammunition, all packed in air-tight tins and sunk in the lake behind U Saw's house, about 10 yards from the bank. A further cache was retrieved from a house in Rangoon belonging to U Saw's party organization.

Weapons and ammunition — both British and Japanese — were not particularly hard to come by in Burma, in the immediate aftermath of the Japanese surrender. But the use of British markings on jeep and uniforms was obviously meant to divert attention to the British, and the government soon revealed that a British Army officer seconded to the police had easy access to Ordnance Depots and had sold quantities of arms to U Saw. This made it easy for Burmese speakers at rallies to accuse the British Government of contriving the elimination of Aung San and replacing him and his Executive Council by a group favourable to Burma remaining inside the British Commonwealth. As it happens, the same case was made in the House of Commons by a Labour MP, Tom Driberg, who accused "comfortable Conservative gentlemen here [who] have incited U Saw to treachery and sabotage". Anthony Eden repudiated the charge on July 24. Thakin Nu, on the other hand, though deeply suspicious of British involvement, appealed to the Burmese press not to inflame public feeling. British Army officers and civilians had, it was well known, visited U Saw socially, and on at least one occasion, when drunk, he was reported to have boasted of an arms cache in the nearby lake. British XII Army headquarters knew this, but apparently it was not passed on immediately to the CID.

The British were prepared for violence to break out at any moment, and attacks on Europeans were feared. There were seven battalions (British, Indian, Gurkha) in Burma at the time, five in the Rangoon area; a battalion was standing by in Malaya, and a cruiser in Ceylon. But Thakin Nu issued a statement from the first meeting of the new Executive Council declaring they regarded rumours of British collusion in the assassinations as utterly unfounded. In a speech at Jubilee Hall (July 27, 1947) he even proclaimed that both he and the late Aung San were "convinced that in spite of her economic setback after World War II Britain [was] the one nation with the stature to lead the world intellectually and morally."

Complications arose when letters from U Saw in Insein Jail, addressed to John S. Bingley of the British Council, were shown to the authorities. They asked for help, and referred to a third person called "VV". This was taken to refer to a Captain David Vivian, who had been seconded from the Army to the Police Supply Department. Bingley was about to leave for home on a BOAC plane, but the Governor had him stopped and questioned. There was no alternative, Rance pointed out, since Thakin Nu was convinced the British Council was a cloak for an intelligence organization. After questioning by the Burmese police, Bingley was allowed to fly home on Sept. 4, 1947, "a victim of circumstances" in the Governor's view. Vivian was not so lucky, and not so innocent. He was arrested along with another officer, and enquiries were set in train about the activities of two more.

The Army authorities had without doubt been negligent. A Major Moore, Indian Army Ordnance Corps, Commandant of the Base Ammunition Depot, had become very friendly with U Saw, and visited his house on a number of occasions. He made a statement to Burma Command on June, 1947, that U Saw had spoken to him of arms supplies he had received. It so happened that Moore himself was a suspect, as a result of investigations into large-scale arms and ammunition thefts from British Army depots, and was believed to have been implicated in an arms case in war-time India when he was a Warrant-Officer. Further, as a pre-war NCO in Burma he had, it was believed, been on the Civil Police Suspect list. His statement was made orally to an investigating officer on June 26 and repeated in writing to the Deputy Provost Marshal of Burma Command on July 5. General Briggs, GOC Burma Command, told the Governor he thought Moore had made the statement to deflect suspicion from himself, since he knew investigations into arms thefts had started. On June 24, the Base Ordnance Depot had issued 200 Bren guns to men falsely claiming to be police, and using forged documents. This was discovered on July 14. On July 12, ammunition was missed from the Base Ammunition Depot north of

Mingaladon: 25,000 rounds of sten ammunition and 100,000 rounds of small arms ammunition. Again, a bogus police lieutenant using forged papers was responsible.

Moore's statement was passed on to the Brigadier, General Staff, Burma Command, Brigadier Duke. Duke should, naturally, have made it available to the CID, but by an oversight failed to do so. Even when the ammunition thefts were reported to him, he did nothing about Moore's statement. It was only after the assassinations that Duke recalled the document, which he had first seen on July 8. However innocent Duke's forgetfulness may have been, it can only have fuelled anti-British feeling in the AFPFL whose members' characteristic reaction — mediated to the Governor by the Home Member, Thakin Kyaw Nyein — was that U Saw must have been subsidized and that European business firms had probably helped him.

The wish to defuse this anti-British anger had a slight effect on U Saw's trial. He was tried under the Special Crimes (Tribunal) Act 1947 (Burma Act No. LIII of 1947) by a special bench of three judges including a High Court judge, Mr. Justice Kyaw Myint, who presided. It was originally intended to involve the well-known Left-wing lawyer, D. N. Pritt, KC, MP in the defence, but Lord Listowel, Secretary of State for Burma, begged Pritt not to act, since the fact of an eminent English KC who was also a Member of Parliament taking on the defence would make relations with the Labour Government in London difficult. Pritt re-assured him, but said that English counsel should be sent out to ensure a fair trial. The firm of Henry Polak (Danes Inn House, Strand) instructed Captain Benjamin Raphael Vertanes, a former High Grade pleader of Rangoon, to go to Burma, but insisted that because of his political views he should be granted special protection, and a promise of immunity against action against himself by the Burmese Government.

The case was opened on Sept. 25, 1947, at Insein Central Gaol, where most of the accused were being held. But it was not held *in camera*. The trial was public. The Burmese Advocate-General, U Tun Byu, named four of the defendants as the actual assassins: Maung Soe, Thet Hnin, Maung Sein and Yan Gyi Aung, but emphasized that U Saw had conceived, planned and directed the murders. He also claimed that it had been planned to kill Thakin Nu as well. One of the original accused, Ba Nyun, had turned King's Evidence, and said that he had been ordered by U Saw to shoot down Thakin Nu, but had not been able to find him in the Constituent Assembly Building.

U Saw's reactions in court have been very variously reported. Reuter's described him on October 15, 1947, as sitting in the dock, "listening silently, and looking glum". E. V. Foucar says that "throughout the long proceedings U Saw remaind cheerful and irrepressible, always smiling". In December, 1947, Derek Curtis-Bennett KC, arrived from England to take over from Vertanes as senior counsel; the trial was adjourned from October to December to enable him to reach Rangoon. In the upshot, his arrival had no effect. U Saw and the other eight accused were found guilty and sentenced to death by hanging. U Saw sat impassive and unmoved as he heard the verdict, and when asked by the President of the tribunal if he understood the sentence, replied in a low but firm voice, "Yes, I do".

While the trial was proceeding, the Governor, Sir Hubert Rance, was preparing to leave Burma for good. On the basis of a treaty signed between Thakin Nu and Clement Attlee, the British Prime Minister, on Oct. 17, 1947, Burma declared its intention of being independent, outside the Commonwealth, on Jan. 4, 1948.

Saw continued to proclaim his innocence. Had he admitted the crime, Thakin Nu later said, he would not have been given the death sentence. He went to the scaffold in debonair fashion, saying "Good Morning" to his jailers and laughing as he climbed up to the gallows.

Vivian was jailed, and in 1949, when Karen rebels against the government captured Insein and reached the outer suburbs of Rangoon, he was freed by them. Several months later, in a clash in the hills between government forces and Karens, a European was killed, and the body was declared to be Vivian's. The Consul-General, a canny and sceptical official, refused to register the death for lack of proof; quite correctly, because Vivian turned up on the Burma-Thai border years later and contacted the British Embassy in Bangkok asking to be repatriated. No extradition treaty existed between Thailand and Burma, and Vivian was flown home, to end his days in obscurity.

The influence of the murdered Aung San, now Burma's national hero, remains strong. Burma's former military dictator, Ne Win, still the power behind the scenes, and another of Aung San's war-time "Thirty Comrades", later displaced Thakin Nu (U Nu) and instituted a spartan and inefficient one-party socialist dictatorship. The chief elements in the repressed opposition to Ne Win is Aung San's daughter, Daw Aung San Suu Kyi, who was brought up by Sir Paul Gore-Booth, once British ambassador to Burma. She married an Oxford don and was still in August 1990 under house arrest in Rangoon, though her party triumphed in the recent Burmese elections. Her father remains the most significant symbol in Burmese politics, not in spite of his assassination, but perhaps because of it.

LA

CANADA

Gouzenko Affair (1945–46)

Igor Gouzenko, cipher clerk in the Soviet Embassy in Ottawa (1943–45).

A classic spy scandal, the Gouzenko affair involved a junior cipher clerk working in the Soviet Embassy in Ottawa, who betrayed his country by passing secret documents to the Canadian government divulging information about a Soviet spy ring operating in Canada. The intent of the Soviet operation was to uncover atomic bomb secrets and any technological information that would be useful to the Russians in their efforts to "build the bomb".

Igor Gouzenko was born in Rogachov, USSR on Jan. 13, 1919, received a superior education, and trained as an architect. With the advent of World War II, Gouzenko entered into military service, and was recruited to military intelligence, where he received instruction in ciphering as a junior officer in 1942. This training was in preparation for the young Gouzenko to go abroad, and with the opening of the Soviet Embassy in Canada in the Spring of 1943, he was recruited as a cipher clerk to the military attaché and arrived in Ottawa in June 1943.

Gouzenko was not prepared for the life that awaited him in Canada. The relative freedom and wealth contrasted sharply with the deprivation he had experienced in the Soviet Union. In Ottawa, although low in the diplomatic hierarchy, Gouzenko led a comparatively affluent life by Soviet standards with his wife Anna and son Andrei. In 1945 Gouzenko learned that he and his family were to be sent home, and he decided to defect.

Igor Gouzenko left the Soviet Embassy on Sept. 5, 1945, with an armful of documents, heading straight for the newsroom of the Ottawa *Journal*, one of two English-language newspapers in Ottawa. Although one might expect that an admission of this kind would receive immediate attention by the press, the city editor of the newspaper indicated that he was too busy, and because it was late most of the senior staff had gone home for the night. Gouzenko was told to come back in the morning, or to go directly to the Royal Canadian Mounted Police (RCMP).

Growing increasingly desperate, he then went to the office of the Minister of Justice, where by that time it was nearly midnight and the minister and his staff were long gone. Gouzenko was told to come back the next morning. The morning of Sept. 6 proved to be equally fruitless. With his wife at his side, Gouzenko tried once again to get through to the Minister of Justice, Louis St Laurent. Turned away from the Minister's offices, the Gouzenkos again tried the Ottawa *Journal*, but were told to go away.

Upon returning home, the Gouzenkos noticed that their apartment was being watched by two men sitting in a park opposite, and took refuge with their son in the apartment of a neighbour. The men, as it happened, were not agents of the Soviet embassy, but those of the Prime Minister of Canada, William Lyon Mackenzie King, who had by this time been informed that there was something suspicious about Gouzenko.

When representatives of the Soviet embassy did come to call on Gouzenko on the eve of Sept. 6, they broke down the door of his apartment, thereby attracting the attention of the Ottawa city police. The RCMP were contacted, who subsequently got in touch with the Under-Secretary of State for External Affairs, Norman Robertson. After speaking with William Stephenson of British intelligence, Robertson ordered that Gouzenko be brought in the next morning.

It was then, some 36 hours after Gouzenko left the Soviet embassy, that he finally presented the evidence he carried with him to the RCMP. The Canadian authorities were convinced that they faced a domestic espionage ring that had ramifications for the United States and Great Britain. The mass of information that Gouzenko had brought was thus sorted and translated, while he and his family were sent out of Ottawa to a tourist camp.

The Canadian Prime Minister soon informed the British High Commissioner, Malcolm MacDonald, and the American ambassador, Ray Atherton, of the Gouzenko case. This affair had specific implications for the British as one of the spy ring, Kay Willsher, was found to be operating inside MacDonald's own office. The British secret service therefore sent two agents to Ottawa to help with the investigation (one agent was Roger Hollis of MI-5), and the Americans sent several FBI agents.

Prime Minister King was slow and cautious in dealing with the Gouzenko case. He went personally to speak with the American President Truman in Washington indicating that Gouzenko had revealed that there was an assistant secretary working in the Secretary of State's Department who was implicated in the case. King's discussion with the American President proved relatively inconsequential, and Truman later asserted that he was not as concerned as MacKenzie King was about the atomic secrets.

In October, King met with British Prime Minister Clement Attlee in London. Both agreed with Truman's view to delay opening the case to the public until they had secured as much information as they could in the UK and the USA. The Canadian Prime Minister was persistent, however, in his attempts to persuade the British to arrest the nuclear physicist Dr Alan Nunn May, code named *Primrose* in Gouzenko's documents.

During November and December little progress was made between the three leaders, although they agreed to continue with atomic co-operation. The police investigation into the Gouzenko case continued secretly in Canada, but no news was made public until as late as Feb. 4, 1946 when an American journalist told his radio audience that President Truman had been advised by Prime Minister King of a Soviet spy ring in Canada, information that had obviously been leaked.

MacKenzie King appointed two Supreme Court of Canada justices, Robert Taschereau and R. L. Kellock as commissioners, and a Royal Commission began its operations on Feb. 6. The Commission functioned behind closed doors until Feb. 14, when the commissioners advised the government that there was enough evidence to arrest and detain 12 men and women named in the documents and testimony. The arrests took place at 7.00 am on Feb. 15, following which King's first statement on the Gouzenko case was released to the public.

Although the Soviet Union was tactfully not mentioned, the official Russian response came five days later as an admission of guilt. The Royal Commission released an interim report on March 2, 1946, naming the principal members of the Soviet military attaché, Col. Zabotin's staff who had conducted espionage in Canada. Most of the information sought by those named was about the atomic bomb, the production of explosives and chemicals, ways to recruit agents and allied troop movements. A further report released on March 14 named some of the Canadian suspects, as did a third interim report which gave more evidence of Canadian involvement.

The final *Report of the Royal Commission* was released to the public on July 15 and revealed that a member of Parliament, Fred Rose, had been active in the spy ring as a recruiter and transmitter of information. He had been arrested on March 14, 1946, under a police warrant alleging conspiracy to persuade others to commit breaches of the Official Secrets Act. Along with Sam Carr, who fled Canada to evade arrest, Rose allegedly found recruits, gave them instructions, and passed on their information to Zabotin or his officers.

In spite of the public revelations surrounding the Gouzenko case, evidence of the Royal Commission was not made public for 35 years, late in 1981. Of the 18 people brought to trial, eight were convicted and received prison sentences, one was fined and nine were acquitted. Sam Carr was arrested in the United States in 1949, and he and Fred Rose were sentenced to six years' imprisonment and were incarcerated for almost their entire terms. Alan Nunn May was tried in Britain, was found guilty and sentenced.

Gouzenko's testimony suggested that a British mole codenamed *Elli* worked in MI-5. According to Chapman Pincher in his *Their Trade is Treachery* (London, 1981), Elli was Sir Roger Hollis, the man who eventually rose to head MI-5 and who, ironically, had been sent to Canada to assist the RCMP and the government in handling the Gouzenko case.

The Gouzenko case then, reads like a true spy novel. The identity of *Elli* is still unresolved and even Igor Gouzenko's death in 1982 is shrouded in mystery. Gouzenko, who since September 1945 lived under complete police protection and never appeared in public unless masked, died suddenly at his home near Toronto. The date of his death is unclear, and Gouzenko was buried before any announcement was made. Photographs of Gouzenko (unmasked) and his wife were printed in the Canadian newspapers allegedly taken earlier but never published until his death.

PLM

Rivard Affair (1964–65)

Raymond Denis, executive assistant to Immigration Minister.
Guy Favreau, Minister of Justice (until 1965).
Pierre Lamontagne, prosecuting lawyer.
Guy Masson, Montreal Liberal organizer.
Lester Pearson, Prime Minister (until 1967).
Lucien Rivard, Montreal thug, ringleader in Mafia.
Guy Rouleau, Parliamentary Secretary to Pearson.

The Rivard affair, which plagued the Liberal government of Lester Pearson for nearly eight months between 1964 and 1965, was a complex web of bribery and neglect, by which a drug syndicate with Mafia connections successfully penetrated the offices of the Prime Minister of Canada and some of his top Ministers.

At the centre of the affair was Lucien Rivard, a criminal and ringleader in the North American drug trade who was arrested in Montreal on June 19 and taken to the Bordeaux Jail on charges of narcotics smuggling. His arrest followed the confession of another Montreal thug, Michel Caron, who admitted that he was a courier in a network run by Rivard after being caught by US customs officials with 76 pounds of pure heroin. The United States government applied for Rivard's extradition, and the Canadian Justice Department appointed Pierre Lamontagne, a young Montreal lawyer, to prosecute the case.

The Montreal underworld, anxious to keep Rivard away from the US authorities, wasted no time trying to arrange for his bail. With the aid of two shady characters, Robert Gignac and Eddy Lechasseur, Rivard's wife managed to pull together $60,000, while Gignac began the circle of bribery, which soon reached Ottawa. The first culprit was Guy Masson, a Liberal organizer in Quebec, who was offered $1,000 by Gignac to help arrange Rivard's bail. Masson's link in Ottawa was Raymond Denis, the executive assistant to the Immigration Minister, with whom Masson had several meetings. Denis then proceeded to offer his old friend Pierre Lamontagne $20,000 if he withdrew his opposition to Rivard's release on bail, on the grounds that Rivard was a Liberal Party supporter.

Lamontagne began receiving threats from Gignac and Rivard's lawyer, Raymond Daoust, claiming that he had taken the bribe and questioning his inaction. Growing increasingly worried, Lamontagne warned Denis that he would call in the RCMP if the threats did not stop. They did not stop, and Lamontagne was receiving more pressure for intervention from other Liberals including Guy Lord and André Letendre, assistants to the Justice Minister, and Guy Rouleau, parliamentary secretary to the Prime Minister. The frightened Lamontagne revealed the whole story to an RCMP Inspector on Aug. 11, who in turn passed the details on to Guy Favreau, the Minister of Justice.

Favreau initiated an RCMP investigation of Denis, Lord, Letendre and Rouleau, but neglected to inform any other senior Ministers of the case. Denis was forced to tell his boss, the Immigration Minister René Tremblay, of the allegations against him, and submitted his resignation. The Prime Minister, who had no previous knowledge of the case, was made aware of the bribery allegations and the RCMP investigation by Favreau on a short government flight. He was, however, spared the details of the narcotics issue, and assured that he would receive a full report when the investigations were complete. Upon receiving the RCMP report two weeks after his conversation with Pearson, Favreau reviewed the contents, and without any further evaluation, dismissed the case, never mentioning it again to the Prime Minister, least of all to inform him that his own parliamentary secretary was seriously implicated.

The Rivard affair erupted in the House of Commons on Nov. 23, 1964, when Erik Nielsen, a Conservative MP notorious for digging up dirt on the Liberals, unearthed the whole case. In spite of rumours that had been circulating around the corridors of power for a month, and the warnings Favreau had received about the information Nielsen had gathered, this was to be the first time that the Prime Minister was made aware of the seriousness of the Rivard affair. With no strategy formulated, Pearson announced that he would set up a commission of inquiry into the affair. When he finally saw the RCMP report that evening, he demanded Rouleau's immediate resignation. The Prime Minister was questioned in the House the next day as to when he had first been made aware of the Rivard case, and his response caused him much grief. Pearson said that his Justice Minister had only informed him of the affair the previous day, and promptly left on a political tour of Western Canada.

While the Prime Minister was away, Favreau divulged their airplane conversation of Sept. 2 to his Cabinet colleagues. Pearson was contacted in Manitoba by the acting Prime Minister, Paul Martin, concerned that the government would appear to have misled Parliament. The Prime Minister chose to continue his tour. The badly shaken Liberals were forced to accept a wider set of terms for the Rivard inquiry to include an investigation into the Justice Minister's conduct.

The hearings began on Dec. 15, 1964, led by Chief Justice Frédéric Dorion who was to question the 12 men involved. When the Dorion Commission wound up the Ottawa hearings on March 2, 1965, it was to the news that Lucien Rivard had escaped from Bordeaux Jail. Favreau, who had by this point suffered irreversible strain, came under renewed attack by the Conservatives who laid the blame for Rivard's escape on him. The Liberal government showed signs of weakening, but were relatively dismissive of the scandal, describing it as press sensationalism.

The final verdict became clear with the tabling of the Dorion Commission's report by the government on June 29, 1965. Denis, Gignac and Lechasseur were all sentenced to prison terms, while Favreau received the harshest indictment when his judgment was put in question. Favreau immediately submitted his letter of resignation to the Prime Minister, but was convinced by Pearson and Cabinet colleagues to remain in the Department of Justice. The Rivard scandal thus ended without bringing down the Liberal government.

PLM

Munsinger Affair (1966)

Lucien Cardin, Minister of Justice (1965–68).
John Diefenbaker, Prime Minister (1957–63).
Davie Fulton, Minister of Justice under Diefenbaker.
Gerda Munsinger, prostitute and alleged Russian spy from East Germany.
Lester Pearson, Prime Minister (1963–68).
Pierre Sévigny, Associate Minister of Defence (1960–61).

This scandal revolved around a Montreal prostitute and alleged Russian spy, Gerda Munsinger, and two Conservative Ministers, Pierre Sévigny and George Hees, with whom she was said to have been involved in 1960. The Munsinger affair, which broke six years after the fact, brought into question a breech of national security in Canada, although allegations against the former Conservative Prime Minister, John Diefenbaker, proved relatively inconclusive.

Born in East Germany, Gerda Heseler married an American soldier, Michael Munsinger, and was arrested by German border police in 1949, charged with espionage activities for the Russians. Munsinger thereby became known to Western Intelligence sources and when she tried to follow her husband to the United States, she was denied entry because of her criminal record. Gerda was divorced from Munsinger in 1954, and was admitted to Canada in 1955, becoming a prostitute in Montreal. She was classed as a security risk by the CIA in Washington, and although this information was passed on to the RCMP, there was no evidence that she did anything to breach security while in Canada.

The Munsinger case first came to the attention of the Prime Minister in December 1964 when he received a summary of the Sévigny–Munsinger dossier from the RCMP Commissioner, George McClellan. The Justice Minister, Guy Favreau, who had one week earlier been implicated in the Rivard affair (see above), also received a copy of the file.

Pearson approached John Diefenbaker on the matter by way of a personal letter, but the Opposition Leader did not respond. Instead, he visited the Prime Minister in person, and there was reportedly a heated exchange. The Munsinger case was seen to be good ammunition by some Ministers (particularly Favreau) to use against the Conservatives who had been digging up improprieties in the Liberal Party. However, this was vehemently opposed by other Cabinet Ministers who threatened to resign if the confidential Munsinger file was opened.

It was not until February 1966 that the Munsinger affair came to light. Guy Favreau, then President of the Privy Council, threatened the former Conservative Justice Minister, Davie Fulton, with disclosure of the scandal if the Conservatives did not let up on their demands for an inquiry into the arrest of George Victor Spencer. Spencer, a public servant accused of spying for the Russians, had been convicted without a trial, angering many Members of Parliament from all parties. Pearson finally succumbed to demands from Opposition MPs and some of his own Ministers for an inquiry into the Spencer case. The Justice Minister Lucien Cardin, incensed by the Prime Minister's sudden reversal, blurted out a reference to Munsinger in the House of Commons while in a fiery debate with the Leader of the Opposition.

The press began digging and Cardin, still furious about Pearson's actions, offered his resignation, which he later withdrew after several Liberal caucus members pleaded with him to stay. Cardin held a press conference on March 10, describing the Munsinger affair, and leaving journalists in a flurry to track down the woman in question. Gerda Munsinger, whom Cardin claimed had died in East Germany, was found in Munich by a keen reporter anxious to get a scoop.

The allegations against Sévigny were simple; by having an illicit sexual relationship with Gerda Munsinger, the beautiful German spy, he too became a security risk. But there were further implications for the former Prime Minister of Canada, John Diefenbaker. Having failed to place the Munsinger file before the Department of Justice in 1960, he had compromised national security. Pearson, who by this time had become distraught by the whole Munsinger affair, realized the implications of investigating a former Prime Minister's judgment. Perhaps he was reminded of his own actions in the Rivard affair two years earlier (see above).

On March 14, 1966, Pearson announced the terms of reference of the Munsinger inquiry and appointed Mr. Justice W. F. Spence of the Supreme Court of Canada to lead it. By mid April the hearings had begun. Sévigny denied that Munsinger had been his mistress, despite her claim that he paid for her apartment. Davie Fulton, it was revealed, had been made aware of this liaison by the RCMP on Dec. 7, 1960 and was presented with a full report five days later, which he passed on to Diefenbaker. Sévigny was then confronted by the Prime Minister, who, satisfied that there was no breach of security, simply told him to end his affair with Munsinger.

The Spence report, published on Sept. 23, 1966, concluded, however, that Sévigny had become a security risk through his affair with Munsinger, and that John Diefenbaker was at fault for not dismissing his Minister or consulting his Cabinet before ignoring the case. George Hees, who had made a statement in the House of Commons on the day the inquiry was announced admitting that he had lunch with Munsinger on two occasions, was mildly reprimanded for his lack of discretion.

Apart from providing the Canadian public with intrigue over a glamorous blonde German spy who had reportedly plagued the Diefenbaker years, the Munsinger affair was inconsequential. It was unsuccessful in toppling a government, as the government in question had been out of power for three years. In spite of Justice Minister Cardin's claim that "the Munsinger affair was worse than the Profumo case" (see United Kingdom: *Profumo Affair, 1963*), it had the distinct appearance of a retaliatory measure by the Liberals following the exposure of the Rivard affair. Neither scandal helped the credibility of either party.

PLM

Trudeau Affair (1970)

James Cross, British Trade Commissioner.
Pierre Laporte, Quebec Minister of Labour.
Pierre Elliot Trudeau, Prime Minister (1968–84).

Throughout Pierre Elliot Trudeau's 14 years as Prime Minister of Canada, nothing distinguished him as significantly as his response to the events of October 1970. A *cause célèbre* in Canadian politics, the October Crisis implicated the FLQ in kidnappings and murder, and shocked the country. The Quebec Liberation Front (Front de Libération du Québec or FLQ), intent upon the separation of Quebec from the rest of Canada, had been carrying out a spate of terrorist activities since 1963. There was no limit to the extremes undertaken by the FLQ during the events of the October Crisis.

The British trade Commissioner, James Cross, was abducted from his Montreal home on Monday, October 5, 1970 at 9.10 am. His kidnappers, the FLQ, demanded $500,000 in gold bullion and the release of 23 FLQ members who were in jail on bomb charges, and threatened to kill Cross if these demands were not met. The federal and Quebec governments rejected the kidnappers' demands, and it wasn't until five days later, when the FLQ took their second victim, that something was done.

The Quebec Minister of Labour, Pierre Laporte, was kidnapped on Oct. 10 while playing football in front of his house in Montreal. The crisis suddenly heightened, and the Quebec Premier, Robert Bourassa, agreed with Trudeau and his advisers that the appropriate response was to invoke the War Measures Act. On Friday Oct. 16 at 4.00 am the Act was put into force for the first time in peacetime Canada, following unanimous approval by the Federal Cabinet.

The War Measures Act made FLQ membership a criminal offence, banned political rallies and gave the police the right to arrest, interrogate, and detain suspects for up to 90 days, thereby suspending *habeas corpus*. The FLQ wasted no time in retaliating. On Oct. 17 Laporte's body was found by Montreal police in the trunk of a car after a tip-off from the FLQ. Trudeau was distraught, and declared on national television a day later "the FLQ has sown the seeds of its own destruction". The FLQ bombings that had killed or maimed people in Montreal since 1963 could not touch this atrocity; the Canadian public was outraged.

The October Crisis was effectively over after the discovery of Laporte's body. Cross, however, was to remain in captivity for 60 days, hand-cuffed and hooded and in terrible discomfort, leaving his sight partially impaired. He was released on Dec. 3 after negotiations took place between the kidnappers and Montreal police, who agreed to give the FLQ members safe passage to Cuba the same day. The last two members of the group of kidnappers were arrested on Dec. 28, and Paul Rose and Francis Simard were sentenced to life imprisonment for the murder of Laporte.

Trudeau, whose international reputation was enhanced by his actions during the October Crisis, also came under scrutiny by some Canadians when it was over. Nearly 500 suspects were arrested, but only 62 were charged. The Prime Minister was criticized for this abuse of civil liberties. Paradoxically, the vast majority of Canadians supported the War Measures Act. A Gallup Poll taken at the time of the Crisis measured 85 per cent support for the War Measures Act; another poll, in April 1971, showed that by a margin of more than two to one, Canadians wanted the Act continued even after a lapse of several months.

Whatever the dictates of public opinion, it is undisputable that the October Crisis was a *cause célèbre* in Canadian history and a personal accolade for Pierre Trudeau. There were to be no further bombings or acts of violence by the FLQ. Trudeau did, however, receive criticism for his handling of the affair, by those who saw his actions as being cold and self-serving. During a television interview at the height of the October Crisis Trudeau was asked how far he would go to crush the FLQ. Trudeau retorted with his now famous line "Just watch me".

PLM

Mulroney/"Sleaze Factor" (1985–)

Suzanne Blais-Grenier, Minister of the Environment.
Robert Coates, Minister of Defence (1984–85).
John Fraser, Minister of Fisheries and Oceans.
Marcel Masse, Minister of Communications.
Sinclair Stevens, Minister of Industry.
Michael Wilson, Finance Minister.

The government of Brian Mulroney has been plagued by a steady stream of scandals and questionable ethical behaviour on the part of some of his Cabinet Ministers since he was swept into office in September 1984. This spate of scandal has come to be known as the "sleaze factor" in the Conservative Party. Within three years of assuming power, the man who won the largest majority in Canadian history also achieved the lowest standing in the polls. Mulroney's reputation had been scarred, and yet the folly that has plagued the Conservatives continues in 1990.

The first affair seriously to damage Mulroney's reputation involved his Defence Minister, Robert Coates. When Coates and two of his aides set off on a Canadian Armed Forces jet for a 12-day NATO tour, Mulroney could not have predicted what lay in store for him. The three men visited a sleazy strip bar not far from the Canadian base at Lahr, West Germany, late on Nov. 29, 1984. "Tiffany's" featured strippers and pornographic films and was said to be a haven for prostitutes. Coates, who was chatted up at the bar by a stripper, did not take the decision to leave.

The impropriety first surfaced in an article published in the Ottawa *Citizen* on Feb. 12, 1985. Coates tendered his resignation immediately and Mulroney, when questioned on the matter, claimed he had first heard of Coates' escapades on Jan. 22. After receiving reports on the incident, Mulroney was satisfied that there was no security breach and let the issue drop. When the story broke two weeks later, the Prime Minister reluctantly accepted his Defence Minister's resignation.

Following revelations in the spring of 1985 that two of Mulroney's key ministers had been giving lucrative government contracts to family members, the next scandal hit. "Tunagate", as its name implies, forced the resignation of the Minister of Fisheries and Oceans, John Fraser. Fraser personally overruled his own officials when he released close to a million cans of tuna onto the marketplace that was deemed "unfit for human consumption". He had been made aware of the problem in February 1985, and warned several times thereafter about the danger of putting the tuna on the supermarket shelves. In an attempt to protect the jobs of 400 employees at the *Star-Kist* plant in New Brunswick, Fraser ignored all advice and decided to release the tuna in March of that year.

The scandal did not erupt until it was aired on a television programme on Sept. 17. In a press conference given by the Prime Minister two days later, he admitted that he had known about the rancid tuna for a few weeks. To make matters worse, Fraser and Mulroney both claimed in separate news conferences that it had been their own decision to remove the tuna from supermarkets. John Fraser was forced to resign as Fisheries Minister on Sept. 23, in part due to his own neglect, and in part for his contradiction of the Prime Minister's statements.

Three days after Fraser resigned, Mulroney lost his Minister of Communications, Marcel Masse. When Masse became aware that he was being investigated by the RCMP (Royal Canadian Mounted Police) for alleged spending irregularities during the 1984 federal elections, he did the honourable thing and submitted his resignation. Mulroney, who had only heard of this matter an hour before his Minister resigned was taken completely by surprise. The Conservative party director, Jerry Lampert, swore that he had advised senior staff in the Prime Minister's office of the investigation, but Mulroney insisted he had heard nothing of it. The incident ended in Lampert resigning, Mulroney coming out clean, and Masse returning to Cabinet in December, 1985.

The extravagant public spending habits of some of Mulroney's ministers also caused him some grief. Suzanne Blais-Grenier, the Environment Minister, reportedly spent $64,000 of taxpayers' money on two European trips in the spring of 1985. On one trip, which came to be known as "April in Paris", Blais-Grenier spent vast amounts of money on chauffeur-driven cars and luxurious hotels for herself, her husband and two aides. In June and July, she took several of her staff members on a 15-day tour of Europe, reportedly costing around $47,000. Blais-Grenier was demoted to Junior

Transport Minister, and on New Year's Eve, 1985, she resigned from the Cabinet.

The Sinclair Stevens affair erupted on April 29, 1986 when it was learned that his wife Noreen negotiated a $2.6 million loan for his own firm, Cardiff Investments Ltd., from a company with massive government dealings, Magna International Inc. The loan negotiated by Noreen Stevens, vice-president of her husband's company, carried one year's free interest, worth $300,000.

The allegations of conflict-of-interest against Stevens mounted when his wife was accused of approaching three major Toronto investment dealers about putting $5 million into her husband's money-strapped company. These firms were later employed by Stevens to help the government sell off several Crown corporations. After denying any wrongdoings, Stevens resigned on May 12, 1986 and a special inquiry was launched into the affair.

Stevens' resignation made a total of five of Mulroney's ministers to leave in just over a year. Two days later a backbench Conservative MP, Robert Toupin, decided to leave the caucus and sit as an Independent, and another Conservative MP was charged with over 50 counts of bribery and influence peddling the following day.

The ensuing scandals and incidence of wrongdoings in the Mulroney government between 1986 and 1990 are too numerous to mention. Suffice to say that the "sleaze factor" in the Conservative Party was only getting worse. Cabinet ministers continued to award huge government contracts to friends and family, and Mulroney himself decided to infuse money into his own riding by investing millions of dollars in airport renovations and a new prison in his constituency. Another Cabinet Minister was sacked on January 1987 over allegations of impropriety in land transactions for a Low Level Air Defence Contract, and yet another resigned a month later due to allegations of influence peddling over government contracts.

In spite of the rot within the Conservative party and the Prime Minister's decreasing popularity (he dropped to 22 per cent in the polls, the lowest showing by a government since Gallup began its political polling during the last war), Mulroney went on to win the 1988 general election. The "sleaze factor" may have caused Mulroney great stress, but it did not topple his government, nor did it cause the Conservatives to lose power in Canada.

The scandals in the Conservative party have not died yet. There were plenty of conflict-of-interest cases involving government contracts in 1989. Even Mulroney's Finance Minister, who was notorious for steering out of trouble when other Cabinet ministers erred, came under attack when his entire 1990 budget was leaked. This was considered a *cause célèbre* in Canadian budget history as Michael Wilson was forced to deliver the budget on national television. Although his resignation was called for, the Finance Minister did not leave.

Only time will tell whether the scandals and improprieties that have plagued the Mulroney years will have a long-term effect on his leadership. At the very least, the "sleaze factor" has kept many writers and journalists busy, and has possibly amazed a few readers in its wake.

PLM

CZECHOSLOVAKIA

Masaryk Affair (1948)

Dr Edvard Beneš, President of the Republic (1935–38; 1945–48).
Lavrenti Beria, head of Soviet People's Commissariat for Internal Affairs—NKVD (1938–53).
Klement Gottwald, leader of Communist Party of Czechoslovakia (1929–48; 1951–53); Prime Minister (1946–48).
Dr Jan Masaryk, Foreign Minister (1945–48).
Maj. Augustin Schramm, officer in Czechoslovak security service.

Did he jump, or was he pushed? Did he fall at all? Such is the essence of the enduring mystery surrounding the death of Jan Masaryk, Czechoslovakia's Foreign Minister and the son of Tomas Masaryk, his country's chief founder and first President. On the night of March 9–10, 1948, less than two weeks after the communists had seized power in Czechoslovakia, Jan Masaryk's body was found in the courtyard of the Foreign Ministry in Prague. The official verdict on his death was that he had committed suicide by jumping from his bathroom window, although there was widespread suspicion that he had been murdered.

Born in 1886 in Prague, Jan Masaryk in 1919 joined the diplomatic service of the new Czechoslovak Republic founded in the previous year. His father had been named as first President of the Republic, holding that post until 1935. Jan Masaryk served first in his country's missions in Washington DC and London, returned to Prague in 1921 as secretary to Foreign Minister Edvard Beneš (who succeeded Tomas Masaryk as President in 1935), and from 1925 to 1938 was ambassador to Great Britain. After Czechoslovakia's dismemberment by Nazi Germany and its allies in 1938–39 Jan Masaryk served as Foreign Minister in the Czechoslovak government-in-exile in London, whence he made a series of wartime radio broadcasts to his occupied homeland (published in English in 1944 under the title "Speaking to my country") which earned him great respect and popularity among Czechoslovaks.

Following Czechoslovakia's liberation in 1945 Masaryk took the portfolio of Foreign Minister in the National Front coalition government (comprising parties from across the political spectrum), and Beneš returned as President. The National Front coalition was continued after elections in 1946, with the Communist Party leader Klement Gottwald as Prime Minister (the Communists were the largest single party in the Constituent Assembly, and with their allies the Social Democrats they had a narrow majority in the Assembly over the other coalition parties). Disagreements between the

Communists and the right-wing parties in the National Front, principally over the Communist-sponsored nationalization programme, Communist control of the police, and the appointment of Communists to government posts led to a Cabinet crisis in February 1948. Ministers from three right-wing parties resigned, and a Communist-dominated government was able to take power on Feb. 25 by a combination of constitutional methods and extra-parliamentary pressure. Masaryk, who was not affiliated to a political party, remained as Foreign Minister, apparently at the urging of President Beneš.

On March 10 the government announced that Jan Masaryk had committed suicide by throwing himself from a window of his apartment into the courtyard of the Czernin Palace (the Foreign Ministry) in the early hours of the morning. The official announcement suggested that as a result of overwork and insomnia Masaryk had decided to take his own life "in a moment of nervous breakdown". However, it continued: "The day before his tragic end, and also during the evening, Minister Masaryk did not show any evidence of mental depression, but, on the contrary, was full of active life and of his usual optimism."

Masaryk's supposed suicide made a profound impression both in Czechoslovakia and the West. It was widely thought in the West that, in view of Masaryk's devotion to democratic principles and his known aversion to totalitarianism, his suicide had been motivated by political developments in Czechoslovakia. On the other hand the Czechoslovak government and the Communist-controlled press attempted to place responsibility for Masaryk's death on the attitude of Western countries towards those developments: Interior Minister Václav Nosek claimed that telegrams had been found in Masaryk's rooms from individuals and organizations in Great Britain and the United States criticizing Masaryk for participating in the new government, and that these "recriminations from the West" must have depressed him enough to disturb his frame of mind.

Rumours immediately began to circulate underground in Czechoslovakia about whether Masaryk might not have been murdered. In the most significant development, Maj. Augustin Schramm, a Moscow-trained officer in the Czechoslovak security service, in June 1948 was murdered by a Czech student underground movement, apparently in revenge for the death of Masaryk. The student accused of killing Schramm was subsequently executed.

It was not until the short-lived period of political liberalization in 1968, known as the "Prague Spring", that demands for an investigation into whether Masaryk had been murdered were publicly voiced inside Czechoslovakia. An open letter to the Czechoslovak Attorney-General was published by Ivan Svitak, a philosopher, on April 2, 1968, in *Student*, organ of the Czechoslovak National Students' Organization, in which Svitak specifically demanded an answer to the question: "Was Jan Masaryk murdered 20 years ago as the first victim on the road to a totalitarian dictatorship?" As possible evidence that Masaryk's death might not have been a case of suicide but of foul play Svitak listed a series of strange and, he alleged, hitherto unexplained occurrences surrounding the events at the Czernin Palace on the night of March 9–10, 1948. He cited various reports of witnesses indicating that other persons were in Masaryk's bedroom on his last night; that a struggle might have taken place; that Masaryk's physician had not been allowed to see the body; and that the doctor who signed the official autopsy report had also not been closer to the body than 10 feet. On the day after the publication of Svitak's open letter the Czechoslovak State Prosecutor's Office announced that an investigation would be held into Masaryk's death, and a five-member commission was established for that purpose.

Two Czechoslovak newspapers, *Smena* of Bratislava and *Svobodne Slovo* of Prague, published on April 7, 1968, first-person accounts by eye-witnesses purporting to shed light on the events at the Czernin Palace of the night of March 9–10, 1948.

Smena published an interview with a former employee of the Foreign Ministry, Pavel Straka, who said that on the night of Masaryk's death he had been on duty at the Czernin Palace. Between 8.30 and 9.00 pm that night Masaryk had gone to his apartment to work, but at about 11.00 pm he (Straka) had noticed an unusual amount of noise in the usually quiet building and the sound of cars in the courtyard outside. He had discovered that his telephone had gone dead, and that his door had been locked from the outside. After a quarter of an hour the noise had stopped, but at about 2.00 am he had heard more cars entering the courtyard, the telephone had come alive again, and the door had been unlocked. He had rushed out of the door and encountered the porter who, frightened, at first had refused to talk, but who had finally told him to look in the courtyard. Here, said Straka, he had found the body of Masaryk lying under the window of his apartment, but, looking up, he had seen that the window was closed. Expressing his conviction that Masaryk had not committed suicide, Straka said that he had kept silent for the past 20 years for fear of reprisals. (Straka had been dismissed from the Foreign Ministry in 1949, tried for treason at the time of the Stalinist purges in 1951–52, and given a 12-year prison sentence; he had been released in 1960, and in 1968 was working in a brewery in Slovakia.)

The second witness, a former taxi-driver employed in 1948 by the state security service, was identified only by the initials "B.J." He told *Svobodne Slovo* that on the night in question in 1948 he had been told at about 4.00 am to drive to the Czernin Palace, and on entering the courtyard had been shown by the porter Masaryk's body covered with a blanket and wearing pyjamas. While a physician examined the body, "B.J." noted that the soles of the feet were injured, but when he helped to put the body on a stretcher he had seen no other injuries, nor was there any sign of blood. He had also noticed that the body was not lying directly beneath the window, but at least three yards from the side of the wall and slightly to the side of the window. Like Straka, "B.J." (who had been arrested in 1949 and imprisoned for two years without explanation before being released) said that he had kept silent for 20 years but was now willing to talk to the authorities.

The Czechoslovak Communist Party newspaper *Rude Pravo* suggested on April 16 that Lavrenti Beria, the notorious former chief of the Soviet secret police, and Maj. Schramm might have had a hand in Masaryk's death, and called upon the Soviet authorities to render assistance to the State Prosecutor's investigation. However, on May 7 the Soviet news agency Tass issued a statement emphatically denying that any Soviet person had been involved in

Masaryk's death. It described reports to that effect as "lies from beginning to end", inspired by "hostile propagandists" inside Czechoslovakia and in the West who sought to "sow distrust" between Czechoslovakia and the Soviet Union and to "stir up anti-socialist sentiments among politically unstable people".

Investigation of Masaryk's death during the Prague Spring was halted by the Warsaw Pact invasion of Czechoslovakia in August 1968 which ended the reforms. The suicide verdict regained undisputed official currency. However, in the wake of the overthrow of the Communist regime in November 1989 and the installation of a democratically elected government, it seems likely that the Masaryk case will be reopened once again.

IPG

Slánský Affair (1952)

Klement Gottwald, leader of Communist Party of Czechoslovakia (1929–48; 1951–53); Prime Minister (1946–48); President (1948–53).
Anastas Mikoyan, member of Soviet Communist Party politburo (1929–66).
Rudolf Slánský, general secretary of the Communist Party of Czechoslovakia (1948–51).
Marshal Joseph Stalin, Soviet Communist Party leader (1922–53).
Konni Zilliacus, former British Labour Party MP.

In the years 1949–54 the Communist Party of Czechoslovakia (CPCz), which had seized power in February 1948, indulged in a Stalinist reign of terror involving a wholesale purge of its own ranks and persecution of non-Communist opponents, both real and imagined. The most notorious of the many political trials of that period was that of Rudolf Slánský, the second most senior member of the CPCz leadership, whose conviction and execution at the end of 1952 on obviously false charges of treason and espionage cast a lasting shadow over Czechoslovak Communism

A Czech of Jewish extraction, Slánský joined the nascent Communist Party in 1921, at the age of 20. After two years' service as a regional party leader he was elected to the party central committee in 1929. He was prominent in the party leadership formed in Moscow following the banning of the CPCz in Czechoslovakia in 1938, being considered one of the closest associates of general secretary Klement Gottwald and also one of the Czechoslovaks closest to Stalin. During World War II Slánský saw military service with the Red Army on the Ukrainian front and with partisan forces during the Slovak uprising of 1944. He played a major role in the 1948 Communist takeover in Czechoslovakia, and after Klement Gottwald assumed the post of President of the Republic in June 1948 Slánský succeeded him as CPCz general secretary.

From 1949 Slánský was himself one of the prime movers in the purge of Communist ranks (allegedly at the urging of the notorious Soviet state security chief Lavrenti Beria), having been during the previous year a main author and an enthusiastic advocate of the purging of non-Communists. On Sept. 7, 1951, however, Slánský was removed from the post of CPCz general secretary as part of what purported to be a reorganization of senior party posts, his duties being once again assumed by Gottwald. Two days later he was appointed as a Deputy Prime Minister, but on Nov. 27 it was announced that he had been stripped of that post and arrested on charges of "conspiracy against the state".

Slánský went on trial on Nov. 20–27, 1952, along with 13 other former high-ranking Communist officials. Accused collectively with Slánský were Dr Vladimir Clementis, who became Foreign Minister following the apparent suicide of Jan Masaryk in 1948 (q.v.) but resigned in 1950 after being denounced at a Slovak Communist Party congress; Bedrich Geminder, formerly head of the CPCz foreign affairs committee; Otto Sling, former CPCz leader in Brno; Gen. Bedrich Reicin, former Deputy Minister of Defence and Chief of Intelligence; Karel Svab, former Deputy State Security Minister and chief of the secret police; Ludvik Frejka, former economic adviser to the government; Jozef Frank, former deputy general secretary of the CPCz; Artur London and Vavro Hajdu, both former Deputy Foreign Ministers; Dr Evzen Löbl and Rudolf Margolius, both former Deputy Ministers of Foreign Trade; Otto Fischl, a former Deputy Minister of Finance and ambassador to East Germany; and André Simone, a former editor of the CPCz newspaper *Rude Pravo*.

The indictment described the accused as "Trotskyist-Titoist-Zionist-bourgeois-nationalist traitors and enemies of the Czechoslovak people", and alleged among other things that they had plotted to overthrow the Communist regime; that they were "tools of Western imperialism" and "agents of the British, American and French intelligence services"; and that they had attempted to sabotage the Czechoslovak economy. A notable feature of the charges was the emphasis laid on the fact that 11 of the 14 accused were of Jewish origin, and that the charge of "Zionism" had been added to the by now all too customary charges of "Titoism" and "Trotskyism" for the first time in any mass trial in post-war Communist-dominated Eastern Europe. Among Western "agents" and "imperialists" with whom the accused persons were alleged to have been in contact were Herbert Morrison (deputy leader of the British Labour Party); John Foster Dulles (then Secretary of State-elect in the Cabinet of US President Dwight D. Eisenhower); former British, French and US ambassadors in Prague; and Konni Zilliacus (a former British Labour MP).

All 14 defendants were officially declared already to have made full confessions of the charges brought against them, and during the trial itself all pleaded guilty to the charges of high treason, espionage for the Western powers, "Titoism", "Trotskyism" and "Zionism" (it is widely assumed that these confessions were secured under physical and psychological torture). Slánský, who told the court that he had "never been a real Communist", said that he had become a "Trotskyite" in 1927 and an "agent of the bourgeoisie" in 1935. He described himself as the leader of a "Jewish bourgeois nationalist group" pledged to overthrow the Communist regime, and admitted responsibility for the appointment of the 13 other accused to high party and government posts. Up to 1949, he said, his main contact with the Western powers had been through Gen. Pika, until the latter had been tried for espionage and hanged. In addition, he had collaborated closely with Zilliacus, whom he had seen three times in Prague between 1946 and 1948 and to whom he had expressed anti-Soviet feelings; with "Titoist agents"; and with the Zionist Movement, with which he had collaborated mainly through economic help to Israel "to the disadvantage of Czechoslovakia". In the course of his evidence Slánský said that he had been in touch with the British authorities since 1946 through Zilliacus (whom he described as having "posed as a left-wing socialist to camouflage his true aims"); that the purpose of his contacts with Zilliacus had been "to plan the restoration of capitalism in Czechoslovakia as had happened in Yugoslavia"; that he had introduced Zilliacus to Clementis and other defendants; and that he had received secret instructions and material from Zilliacus through the intermediary of a former attaché at the Czechoslovak Embassy in London. In addition, Slánský pleaded guilty to charges of having passed on information to former US ambassador Laurence Steinhardt; of having ordered members of his "conspiratorial group" to transmit regular military intelligence reports to the British and US military attachés in Prague; and to having caused the death in 1944 of Jan Sverma, a wartime resistance leader, by failing to give him medical treatment during the abortive uprising against the Nazis in Slovakia. Slánský attributed his crimes against the state to his "bourgeois origin".

The summing up by public prosecutor Dr Jiri Urvalek on Nov. 26 was characterized by its vitriolic attacks directed particularly at Zionism. He demanded the death penalty for all the 14 accused. On Nov. 27 the court passed sentence of death on Slánský and 10 others, the remaining three (London, Hajdu and Löbl) being sentenced to life imprisonment. The condemned men were hanged on Dec. 3.

In 1956, in a general climate in Eastern Europe of repudiating Stalinism following Nikita Khrushchev's exposure of Stalin's crimes at the 20th congress of the Soviet Communist Party, most charges against Slánský and his co-accused were withdrawn, and London, Hajdu and Löbl were released from prison and rehabilitated. Nevertheless, at that time allegations surfaced for the first time of Slánský's collaboration with Beria and of his responsibility for political purges in 1948–51. All the charges of the original indictment against Slánský and eight of the 10 defendants executed with him were finally quashed by the Appeal Court in August 1963. The two not fully rehabilitated were Svab and Fischl, who despite being absolved of criminal offences against the state remained guilty of "unlawful exercise of authority". Membership of the CPCz was posthumously restored to Slánský in 1968.

In April 1968, at the height of the short-lived period of liberal Communist rule known as the "Prague Spring", Karol Bacilek, who at the time of Slánský's arrest and trial had held the post of Minister of National Security (and thus was in charge of the Czechoslovak secret police), alleged in an interview with the Czechoslovak newspaper *Smena* that Stalin had personally ordered the trial of Slánský and other "Titoists". Bacilek claimed that this order had been conveyed during a visit to Prague in 1951 by Soviet politburo member Anastas Mikoyan, who had complained to Gottwald that while trials of "Titoists" had been held in Poland and Hungary, none had taken place in Czechoslovakia. According to Bacilek, Gottwald had at first resisted this pressure, whereupon Mikoyan had telephoned Stalin from the Soviet embassy in Prague and had then told the Czechoslovak leaders that Stalin insisted that the trials must proceed. It was, said Bacilek, only with reluctance that Gottwald eventually agreed to hold the trials.

Shortly before Bacilek made these disclosures, *Rude Pravo* published an interview with Urvalek in which he disclosed that Soviet experts had helped to draw up the charges against Slánský and the other accused. Urvalek justified his own role in the Slánský trial by saying that legal officials had been required to carry out orders from the party leadership, and that he and other members of the prosecution had been convinced at the time of the guilt of the accused. He also said that microphones had been installed in the judges' room during the trial and that "a judge or prosecutor who expressed doubt would have become a victim himself".

More than 37 years after his execution, Slánský's story was furnished with an unexpected footnote in the wake of the overthrow of Czechoslovakia's Communist regime by the popular uprising of November 1989. In a gesture laden with political symbolism, Czechoslovakia's new president, Václav Havel, in February 1990 appointed Slánský's son, also named Rudolf and like Havel a long-standing former dissident, to serve as Czechoslovakia's ambassador to the Soviet Union.

IPG

FRANCE

France is the classic land of the political scandal. Nowhere else has the *affaire* been so much of the warp and woof of political history. Nowhere else have the characteristics of scandal developed into so instantly recognizable a pattern of behaviours and attitudes. This is not because the French are exceptionally liable to misbehave but rather that the troubled course of their history over more than two centuries has repeatedly made affairs the terrain of political warfare. The historical importance of any scandal depends less on the gravity of the behaviour giving rise to it than on the political exploitation that ensues. Thus the leakages affair of the mid-1950s is inseparable from the efforts of the Fourth Republic's enemies to discredit and overthrow it, and the Markovic affair of 1969 was significant less for light it shed on the links between politicians and the demi-monde than for its use as a weapon in the struggle to succeed President de Gaulle.

In one respect the Markovic affair was untypical. French scandals rarely turn on the private lives of public men; a Profumo or Gary Hart affair is barely imaginable there. The only other scandal of sexual mores to approach major proportions in recent years was the *ballets roses* affair of 1958. Even there paedophile orgies in high places did not rouse the commotion they would have done in Britain or the United States. Ministers may have a string of mistresses, a president may bump a milk lorry on his way home at dawn; they may attract private ribaldry or censure but run little risk of public exposure — not even in the hypocritical form of concern for "security". They are at risk only if their behaviour may genuinely have compromised their public role.

But by no means all disgraceful public behaviour constitutes a "scandal". Some of the murkiest episodes of recent years do not feature here, such as the widespread torture of suspects during the Algerian war and the illegal seizures of the few newspapers prepared to denounce it, the police riot that left dozens of Algerian bodies in the Seine, the death of peaceful demonstrators at police hands at the Charonne metro station in Paris — just two of a legion of occasions when police "overstepping the mark" have gone unpunished. Scandalous though they were, they did not fall within the French understanding of an affair. Nor do the plots in which French history is also rich — whether the "Whitsun Plot" of 1949, when Gaullists with complicities in the armed forces were said to have conspired against the Fourth Republic, the so-called "thirteen plots of the 13th May" which preceded the regime's downfall or the diehard conspiracies against the Fifth Republic once de Gaulle moved towards Algerian independence.

Nevertheless, seditious plots and scandals were often closely related. The frequency of both reflected the fact that from the Revolution of 1789 until a very recent past, every French regime was under challenge. (None of the dozen or so systems has yet survived more than 70 years.) For much of this period a disaffected extreme Right, by turns royalist or fascistic, unable to prevail over the Republic through the ballot box, repeatedly fell back on conspiracy and the exploitation of scandal against the hated enemy. (In later years the Communists, with a common interest in discrediting the Republic, at times leaped on the scandal bandwagon once it was rolling, though they rarely took the initiative.) Some scandals were genuine enough: the president whose brother-in-law sold official decorations and the deputies who took bribes to pass a Bill saving the insolvent Panama Company. And of course the greatest affair of all, the Dreyfus case, in which Military Intelligence resorted to forgery and perjury and protected a traitor in discrediting the innocent Captain Dreyfus. Others were far less substantial or even flagrant inventions, such as the attempt by members of the far Right to present the suicide of the mentally unstable son of one of its leaders as a police murder involving senior ministers. But however substantial or flimsy the event at its core, since, in France, no scandal has an incontrovertible outcome, each in turn drew sustenance from its predecessors and eased the path of its successors.

The affair would never have become so prominent a feature of politics had it not drawn on wider features of French society, particularly during the Third Republic (1875–1940), when the genre developed its characteristic form and dynamics. Many people were not reconciled to the Republic; many more were suspicious of politicians as self-serving and venal and were contemptuous of the spectacle offered by the weak, fleeting cabinets of those years, and the intrigues and croneyism surrounding their rise and fall. This was a climate in which it was easy for unscrupulous financiers and favour-mongers to reach the corridors of power. The combination of kaleidoscopic governments and a fragmented bureaucracy produced a chronic blurring of responsibility. Moreover, when malpractice was exposed, power-holders expected the police and the judiciary to bend to their will — not without success. Regimes facing a constant threat of subversion sought safety in multiplying police forces, with which unhealthily close relationships could develop. There were always policemen who pursued personal advancement through accommodating the powers that be (or might be), just as there were always members of an underpaid judiciary of highly uneven calibre who were tempted to take the easy path to promotion despite their nominal independence.

Yet if the legal system at times smothered scandal, on other occasions the laxity of court procedures and ineffectual libel laws turned the courts into a vehicle for unscrupulous, hate-filled politicians and lawyers to launch calumnies, confident that they would reach the widest possible audience through an exceptionally vicious press. A brief extract from an anthology of material from the anti-republican *L'Action Française* shows leading politicians being assailed as "blackguards, filth, guttersnipes, traitors who ought to have a stick of dynamite stuck up their backsides, criminals whose dirty carcasses will be ripped up, nauseous creatures, spawn of the brothel, cowards, cads, stinkers, sons of Prussians, sons of murderers, sons of thieves, Peeping Toms, keyhole sniffers . . .".[1]

What was even worse than this wilful debasing of political vocabulary was the systematic creation of a climate in which almost any allegation could be believed and, however tenuously based, once launched, feed the endemic distrust and cynicism about politicians. As Georgette Elgey puts it:

"The mechanism is always the same: in the beginning a genuine fact; the opposition seize upon it, embroider it, create a whole theory, incriminate members of parliament and ministers. The judicial authorities become involved; the enquiry lasts for months and months and most of the prominent figures are found innocent. But the public, 'brainwashed' by the campaign of slander and insinuation launched when the affair blew up, will not be fooled by that. Its long-established and engrained tendency to anti-parliamentarianism leads it to revel in the certainty of the dishonesty, contemptible or criminal behaviour of the powers that be. It is determined to cling to its conviction of their guilt. And if the courts or parliamentary committees reach the conclusion they are innocent, it sees in this a fresh source of scandal. 'Slander away! Slander away! Something always sticks!' "[2]

In reflecting on the 1946 wine scandal, the first major affair of the post-war years, she was also underlining a more general point about how scandals emerge and are played out. Determined though the new generation of politicians that emerged after the Liberation were to break with the discredited politics of the past, when scandals did break out they instinctively turned to the only model they had — the attitudes, understandings and behaviour they inherited from the Third Republic. And the inheritance factor has been sustained. Each of the scandals discussed here was played out within a context shaped by its predecessors, to which it was recognizably kin, and with which it frequently shared principal actors.

This is not to suggest that the French scandal is unchanging. The emergence during the 1960s of a substantial consensus about the terms on which France is to be governed means that the political exploitation of scandal is now directed more at discrediting individuals or parties than at undermining the Republic or democracy itself. The terms on which affairs are conducted are milder and politicians are more uneasily aware that the short-term advantages from even the most legitimate exposure of scandal may rebound on them or tarnish the image of politicians still further.

Other features of the classic scandal remain. Major affairs invariably drag on for years, thereby overlapping with others. One reason for this, apart from the protracted nature of French legal processes, is that major scandals are invariably extraordinarily complex. Most have a large cast of characters, some of them familiar from earlier affairs; they tend to involve complex machinations by rival police forces, a fog of bureaucratic obstruction, a mix of tensions and pressures surrounding the operations of the judiciary, and a perplexing mass of dead ends, red herrings, wild speculations and picturesque conspiracy theories. Though the necessarily simplified accounts that follow have had this luxuriant undergrowth pruned, enough remains to convey that flavour. Above all, there remain unresolved questions; today, as in the past, the one certainty about French scandals is an absence of certainty.

A review of French scandals, then, not only produces some bizarre political episodes; it also throws revealing light on how individuals and institutions operate under stress, on the rules of how politics functions in practice rather than in theory. On the one hand we gain some insights into the attitudes of the political class as to how power is to be used. On the other light is shed on episodes which have played a not unimportant role in shaping the attitudes of ordinary men and women towards the members of that political class.

MH

1.   L. Ducloux, *From Blackmail to Treason*, Andre Deutsch, 1958, p. 52.

2.   G. Elgey, *La République des Illusions*, Fayard, 1965, p. 189.

Wine Scandal Affair (1946–53)

Yves Farges, Minister of Food (1946). Officially non-party, later fellow-travelling politician and journalist.
Félix Gouin, Socialist deputy for Marseilles (1924; 1945–58), Prime Minister (1946).
Pierre Malafosse, Director of Alcohol Division, Ministry of Food (1945–46).

Even stereotypes are sometimes true: wine has so important a place on the tables of most French families that a shortage is an affair of state. And in the summer of 1946 it was cruelly lacking. The wine harvest had been the smallest since 1879, 40 per cent below requirements. In many areas the official ration could not be honoured. The government decided to authorise imports from Algeria. Those lucky enough to receive licences to import or transport this wine could expect rich rewards.

The Ministry of Food's Alcohol Division was a by-word for incompetence and malpractice. At the Liberation its entire staff had been replaced by former prisoners of war, most of them lacking administrative experience and knowledge of the wine trade. Under one director almost all import licences were assigned to a dealer who was engaged to his daughter. He was sacked — and the engagement collapsed. His successor, who came from a wine-trading family, devised an allocation scheme of unworkable complexity which had to be withdrawn. At this point Yves Farges was appointed minister. A flamboyant figure with a chequered background pre-war but an outstanding Resistance record, Farges declared war on corruption and black-marketeering. He did not trust Malafosse, who learned from his morning paper four weeks later that he had been sacked. Farges refused to explain but commissioned a report into the division which revealed widespread confusion and fraud, and claimed he had stopped a major source of supplies to the black market.

With elections approaching the matter rapidly became politicized. Jean Fraissinet, a far-Right deputy from Marseilles alleged that Malafosse (who was also Socialist mayor of Béziers) had colluded with Gaston Defferre, the Socialist mayor of Marseilles, and that Defferre had bought a ship, pulled strings to get it derequisitioned, and was cashing in on the wine trade. Further, "ghost ships" were illegally ferrying wine from Algeria to the mainland, shipments of wine to Belgium were being monopolized by a dealer with an entrée to Félix Gouin, the Socialist Vice-Premier (at the time the second ranking office in the State, and Defferre's patron in Marseilles), and the father of a member of Gouin's staff had organized a swap deal between Swiss textiles and Algerian wine, using a company based on Marseilles — with much of the wine being diverted to the black market. Later, Gouin himself was said to be involved in wine deals. Certainly he had interceded with Farges to grant Malafosse a hearing.

"Was Gouin really involved?" a Socialist deputy asked Farges. "Undoubt-edly", was the reply — later denied, but too late to prevent a row that immediately leaked to the press. Vainly the government protested that neither parties nor individuals had been compromised, the affair was launched, overshadowing debate on the new constitution. It dragged on for years, through a parliamentary committee of enquiry whose proceedings ran to 1,779 pages and a host of trials and journalistic investigations, zealously fanned by the Communist Party as a means of discrediting the Socialists and particularly their arch enemy, Jules Moch, the minister of the interior, whose impeachment they sought for complicity in suppressing a supposedly key document.

Yet, even after these years of charges and counter-charges it was unclear whether there had been a scandal on anything approaching the scale Farges alleged, not least because official statistics were hopelessly unreliable. The swap deal had occurred months before Gouin took office and apparently none of the wine had reached the black market. The Belgian contract had also been agreed months before Gouin became premier, and charges that his office had intervened to obtain barrels for the company involved were found baseless. Payment for the deal, which was only partially fulfilled, was authorised by Farges himself. There was not a scintilla of evidence against Defferre; his enemies had played on the similarity between his name and that of the ship's previous owner (Daher). The allegation against Gouin was found to rest on a telephone tap leaked to Farges by a "public-spirited" policeman, which scrutiny showed had had Gouin's name added subsequently to a tap on someone else. Such is the stuff of scandal-mongering.

What did emerge was a picture of Gouin as a man with no ministerial experience, coming to office amid almost indescribable confusion, with a staff he scarcely knew but which had been selected for its war record rather than its competence. Before he became Prime Minister, the head of his personal secretariat, a lawyer who confessed to knowing nothing about administration, overwhelmed with work, gave a prominent Socialist activist from Marseilles, who was seeking backing for his employer, a local ship owner, a sheet of Gouin's headed paper, and let him draft a letter himself and sign it on Gouin's behalf. Indiscretions by the head of Gouin's personal staff seemed to have led to a company gaining advance knowledge of a lucrative contract. And a longstanding acquaintance with ready access to his office was clearly involved in shady deals.

A court noted that Malafosse's "brilliant qualities were no substitute for the experience gathered over time by civil servants reaching senior positions after a lengthy intellectual and moral preparation". Of Gouin the Court of Appeal would eventually say in 1953, "Farges has not demonstrated that Gouin fell short of the standards of honour, probity or propriety in the high offices he filled", though he had been "ill advised in the choice of his entourage", which had included some "doubtful elements". Neither Gouin nor Farges ever held office again.

MH

Generals' Affair (1949–51)

Paul Coste-Floret, Christian Democrat Minister for Indo-China (1948–49).
Col. Fourcaud, Deputy director of the secret service until 1958.
Captain Girardot, secret service officer.
Gen. Mast.
Jules Moch, Socialist Minister of the Interior (1947–50).
Roger Peyré, wheeler-dealer influence pedlar; later residing in La Paz.
Henri Queuille, Radical Prime Minister (1948–49).
Paul Ramadier, Socialist Minister of Defence (1948–49).
Gen. Revers, Chief of the General Staff.

It began as a scuffle between a soldier and two Indo-Chinese students and developed into an affair that carried the seeds of destruction of the Fourth Republic. For, when searched at the police station, one of the students was found to be carrying a copy of a top secret report by the chief of the general staff, Gen. Revers, which was highly critical of the policy being pursued in Indo-China (where France had been fighting the Viet-Minh since 1947) and advocating the appointment of a soldier as High Commissioner. A second document was a eulogistic account of General Mast, a friend of Revers and head of the *Institut des hautes études de défense nationale*.

A series of police searches rounded up over 70 copies of the report, of which only 50 had officially been printed. Enquiries also led to Roger Peyré, manager of a small import-export business who, after being interrogated by the counter-espionage service for 32 hours, admitted receiving the report from Mast, with Revers's consent, and passing it to two Indo-Chinese whom he believed to be pro-French. One of these had given him 2.5 million francs which he had distributed to the generals and a former Socialist minister. Appalled at the prospect of a scandal involving the chief of the general staff while delicate negotiations were due to start with the Americans, Ramadier, Moch and Queuille hurriedly decided to hush the affair up. The generals, whose links with Peyré were undeniable, but who denied taking money, agreed to retire quietly on the understanding that there would be no prosecution.

But Paul Coste-Floret, whose policy Revers had attacked, and who was not involved in the decision not to prosecute, smelled a plot. He believed that not only had Revers leaked his report to help Mast, to the eventual profit of Peyré and his friends, but that financial and trading concessions granted by Mast would bring profits to Socialist funds. News of the leak soon reached the press, identifying Revers and alleging he had been paid. Revers promptly refused to retire — but did not sue.

The deputy head of the secret service (SDECE), Colonel Fourcaud, intervened. A friend of Revers, he concluded that Moch and Ramadier were covering up spying for their own sordid purposes and should be shot. Peyré had at one time been a "correspondent" of SDECE and Fourcaud instructed his former contact officer, Captain Girardot, to warn Peyré his life was in danger. However, if Peyré made a new statement clearing Revers and incriminating Socialist politicians he would be helped to leave the country. Peyré spun a coin to decide which story to tell. South America won. The day after he left France his new version appeared in a Gaullist paper, which alleged that the troops in Indo-China were being betrayed by politicians at home and blamed Ramadier for the leaks. ("A cheque for a million for the fat cats . . . a bullet in the back for our soldiers.") Opposition papers alleged that knowledge of the Revers report had helped the enemy militarily. Revers was sacked.

Meanwhile DST, the counter-espionage service, had hauled Girardot in for questioning. Fearing he was to be the scapegoat he decided to tell a parliamentary enquiry all he knew — an event almost unique in such matters. The enquiry spent much of its time in wild goose chases and settling political scores. It took only a reference to a mysterious "Paul" in a telegram for the spotlight to play in turn on the son of the President of the Republic and two generals bearing that name, though there was not a shred of evidence of any of them being even remotely involved. Though the proceedings were nominally secret the Communist member assiduously leaked them to the party daily, L'Humanité. Another member resigned after the disclosure that he was in correspondence with Peyré. Three more resigned after it was discovered that they had separately interviewed a member of SDECE who had failed to attend the full committee.

The government behaved little better. It promised full co-operation but the documentation it supplied was woefully incomplete, especially on the notorious traffic in Indo-China piastres through which prominent pockets (and, it was alleged, party coffers) were being amply lined. Many procedural irregularities came to light, and key documents were destroyed. Attempts to obtain Peyré's extradition were suspiciously feeble.

Counter-attacking, Revers blamed the leak on the negligence of the Ministry for Overseas France, which had got the DST to stage the Gare de Lyon incident to throw responsibility elsewhere. The DST had gone along with this plan because it was packed with Gaullists who had not forgiven him for remaining in France during the war; indeed it had recently attempted to poison him. (Revers was not alone in wondering whether the incident had not happened a shade too neatly.) What damned him, however, was his association with Peyré, a pre-war fascist with a criminal record, whose conviction for wartime collaboration had been quashed partly through Revers' testimony as to his Resistance activities, about which he now told the enquiry he knew nothing! Peyré was clearly a go-between in all manner of unsavoury activities, though how much influence he really enjoyed never became clear. Revers had used him to try to block promotion of a rival and to gain his own fifth star.

The committee reached the view that the report had passed from Revers to Mast and then Peyré, with Revers's knowledge, and on to a Vietnamese who was a secret Communist sympathizer and thence to the Viet-Minh. It exonerated Ramadier for halting the prosecution on the ground that although that would normally have been a criminal misuse of his powers he had acted in the national interest. It criticized the irregularities of the DST, and called for reorganization of the secret services and an enquiry into the traffic in piastres. It was unable to discover for whom Peyré was working, whether he was a patriotic Frenchman or a spy and, if the latter, on behalf of whom, or was he simply an opportunist adventurer? It is unlikely we will ever know.

In the debate on the report in November 1950 the Communists seized the opportunity to assail their hated enemy Moch; their impeachment motion received 235 votes to 207 because some 40 Christian Democrats joined with the Communists for their own purposes — but this was 50 less than the absolute majority required. A week later, after almost 18 months' delay and under the pressure of military disaster, the policy of the Revers report was adopted with the appointment of Gen. de Lattre de Tassigny as High Commissioner in Indo-China.

The affair provided the Communists and Gaullists with unparalleled opportunities to expose, respectively, the "dirty war" in Indo-China and the shortcomings of Fourth Republic politicians. It also drove a wedge of suspicion into the alliance of Socialists and Christian Democrats which was crucial to the arithmetic of the regime's survival. It deepened the cynicism of the public and the military, who were to believe increasingly that the politicians would profit from the war as long as possible only to sell out when it suited their purposes. Above all, the failure of ministers to deal firmly with military misbehaviour was the first of a series of losses of nerve leading to the regime's final collapse in 1958.

MH

Leakages Affair (1954–56)

André Baranès, journalist and informer.

Jean Dides, Chief Inspector in charge of anti-communist section of the police in Paris.

Pierre Mendès-France, Radical Prime Minister (1954–55).

François Mitterrand, Minister for the Colonies (1953–55).

Jean Mons, Secretary of the National Defence Committee.

Jean-Louis Tixier-Vignancour, defence counsel to Baranès, extreme-right deputy, presidential candidate 1965.

In substance one of the gravest scandals since the war, the leakages affair was rendered even more serious by the cut-throat manner in which it was fought and its contribution to discrediting the Fourth Republic.

In the summer of 1954 Pierre Mendès-France became premier. A long-standing critic of policy in Indo-China, where a colonial war was increasingly unpopular and unsuccessful, Mendès formed a government excluding many prominent politicians and embarked on negotiations that were to lead to the Geneva agreements. His lucidity and political courage earned the respect of history, but at the time he was more detested and vilified than any politician of his generation. All means were good that might bring him down.

In July 1954 Chief Inspector Jean Dides, head of a unit at the Prefecture of Police specializing in Communist activities, approached the minister for Tunisian and Moroccan affairs with a report of a meeting of the Politburo of the Communist Party in which a senior party leader had "vouched for" Mendès-France to the Russians and then read a detailed account of the last meeting of the National Defence Committee, whose proceedings are secret. The person responsible for this leak, Dides implied, was his hierarchical superior, the Minister of the Interior, François Mitterrand.

The minister informed Mendès, who discovered this was only the latest in a series of leaks from the Committee — a matter on which the outgoing government had not seen fit to brief him. He ordered an investigation, but failed to tell Mitterrand — an omission which permanently clouded relations between the two men.

Dides also sent his report to the President of the Republic via a right-wing deputy who leaked it to journalists and opposition politicians, who enthusiastically spread word about Communist backing for Mendès and Mitterrand's "treason". But the report had in fact been doctored, mingling an accurate account of Committee proceedings and complete invention regarding remarks to the Politburo. Even had he been so minded, Mitterrand could not have been the source of the leaks because he did not attend all the meetings concerned.

The DST identified Dides' source as André Baranès, a journalist with a fellow-travelling newspaper who was also a paid police informer. Dides, who persistently kept his superiors in the dark about his activities, was arrested in September with carbon copies of reports on further meetings of the Committee; his subordinates promptly destroyed his records. Baranès disappeared. Dides claimed the Communists had murdered him, also alleging that the head of the DST was a secret Communist. But Baranès had simply gone to ground in a monastery and was soon arrested. He first presented himself as a dedicated Communist who had been disinforming Dides on the CP's behalf, then claimed to be a patriotic Frenchman who had been risking his life as a double agent. His story later changed again.

Political exploitation of the affair was now in full swing. Right-wing politicians insinuated that Mitterrand had been forced to resign from the previous government because his treachery had been unmasked. Mitterrand demonstrated that he had resigned over Indo-China policy; his enemies were relying either on forgeries or on "evidence" like the supposedly damning presence of a car which in fact had a registration one digit different from his. Such were the lengths to which hatred and a total lack of scruple led opponents in their determination to bring their targets down.

Meanwhile, investigations led to Jean Mons, the Defence Committee's secretary, and two members of his staff — both opponents of the war. With their arrest the leaks ceased. The trial in 1956 became as much a trial of the political class of the Fourth Republic as of the accused. The judge allowed singular latitude to Baranès' counsel, Jean-Louis Tixier-Vignancour, a brilliant but utterly unscrupulous advocate who detested the Republic and seized every opportunity to smear his opponents. Quite apart from his activities the trial revealed a murky world of disloyal civil servants, rival police forces playing politics and misleading the authorities, and governments repeatedly trying to influence the course of justice.

Baranès was acquitted, on the ground that although he had improperly obtained state secrets he had acted on Dides' orders. Dides, astonishingly, was not put on trial, though he was dismissed. Mons was acquitted of negligence, but his assistants were sentenced to four and six years respectively. The trial had done nothing to illuminate Baranès' true loyalties; was he simply a police informer or was he playing some more complex game? If so, on whose behalf? We may never know.

What is clear is that the affair was crucial to the process by which the French Right re-emerged from the justified ignomony of its wartime record to proclaim itself the guardian of patriotism. The democratic Left was thrown on the defensive, tainted by lack of national feeling or outright treason. The paralysing effects on any who might have been tempted to "sell out" Algeria as Indo-China had been were painfully evident in the years ahead. Above all, the affair tarnished the image of democratic politics in ways which could only serve democracy's enemies on the Right and Left.

MH

Mitterrand Affair (1959–65)

François Mitterrand, at the time opposition senator, later leader of the
  Socialist Party and President of France (1981–).
Robert Pesquet, one-time Gaullist, then Poujadist deputy, diehard defender
  of French Algeria, with close contacts with the terrorists.

Of all affairs of the post-war period none remains more perplexing or more
intriguing since its central figure was to become president. The original
version went like this. On Oct. 16, 1959, François Mitterrand left the
restaurant in the Latin Quarter where he had been dining. Sensing that
another car was following him he made a sudden left turn, braked sharply,
jumped over a fence and hid in a bed of geraniums. A volley of shots rang
out, seven bullets striking his vehicle, one of which embedded itself in the
driver's seat. Mitterrand escaped unscathed.

A sensational event, but entirely in keeping with the climate of that
time. Following de Gaulle's offer of self-determination in Algeria Paris
was buzzing with political intrigues and rumours of military pressure and
terrorist plots. Tracts were circulating threatening public figures who
favoured a negotiated solution with assassination. A few hours earlier
a Gaullist deputy had warned that "commandos of killers have crossed
the Spanish frontier with lists of public figures marked for extermination".
As a longstanding object of right-wing enmity Mitterrand knew he was a
strong candidate for any such list.

But all was not as it had seemed. A few days later Robert Pesquet, an
ex-deputy who had links with the "patriotic terrorists", published a detailed
account alleging that Mitterrand had sought his help in staging a fake
attack; the shots were fired by Pesquet's gardener after Mitterrand himself
had given the signal. Mitterrand's motive, he alleged, was to force the
government to crack down on right-wing groups. To substantiate his story
he had posted two registered letters to poste restante before the attack,
outlining his discussions with Mitterrand and the resulting scenario.

Mitterrand acknowledged having met Pesquet on three occasions, when
Pesquet had warned him his life was in danger. This was not as improbable
as it might seem. Former prime minister Mendès-France confirmed that a
member of the extreme Right had warned him in similar terms two years
earlier and an attack followed in which his police bodyguard had been
severely wounded. Another ex-minister testified he had been warned by
Pesquet of an attempt on his life, which he had passed to the Sûreté
Nationale without identifying Pesquet. But Mitterrand had not told the
police about the warning either before or after the attack, nor had he
conveyed it to other politicians Pesquet had named. Indeed he had
told the police he could shed no light on the matter. The prosecutor's office, acting it was said on instructions from the prime minister,
Michel Debré, laid a charge against him roughly equivalent to contempt
of court.

Mitterrand's response was that his three meetings with Pesquet had been
too brief to work out the suggested scenario, that Pesquet's letters were

less circumstantial than had been claimed, and could have been written after the event, and that he had not divulged Pesquet's warning to the police because he had given his word not to and Pesquet's own life might have been in danger. Was it really credible that someone with his political experience and background would embark on such a crazy venture with someone of Pesquet's ilk? He implied that the affair had been concocted by the unofficial police forces he had opposed when Minister of Justice, then manipulated against him by repeated and improper government intervention in the conduct of the case. He also implied a connection with the bazooka plot of 1957, when he was Minister of Justice and a gang had attempted to assassinate the Commander in Chief in Algeria, who was suspected of being insufficiently dedicated to keeping Algeria French. Rumour had repeatedly linked Michel Debré with that attack.

Mitterrand never came to trial. In 1963 Pesquet, who had fled to Spain, was sentenced *in absentia* to 20 years for leading a terrorist group in Normandy. In 1965 he alleged that the government had offered to allow him to return to France in exchange for his silence. He now claimed that the attack had been organized by his defence counsel, Tixier-Vignancour, with the assistance of another extreme rightist, Jean-Marie Le Pen. Denying the charge, Le Pen alleged that Pesquet had operated on behalf of a "parallel" police force; more surprisingly he exonerated Mitterrand. In 1975 Pesquet changed the story again, accusing Debré and another leading Gaullist of organizing the affair.

What really happened? While Pesquet's word was worthless there was the evidence of the letters — or could they have somehow been written after the event? Probably not. Had Mitterrand indeed staged the whole melodramatic incident? Again, probably not; so harebrained a scheme seems uncharacteristic of so subtle a politician — though in his younger years Mitterrand took some rash chances. And if the attack was genuine was its intention to assassinate Mitterrand physically or politically — and who, in that case, were its true authors?

The likeliest explanation is Mitterrand's own, that he fell into a trap to discredit him. But if so, his enemies had to be very sure of their man, for success depended on Mitterrand's telling nobody either before or after the attack, and so being incapable of providing corroboration of his story. Very much a political loner, Mitterrand is a man who might well have chosen to play his hand that way. If so, he played into his enemies' hands and paid a heavy price. Even some of his closest political friends found his explanation hard to credit, and many were highly critical of his behaviour, as a former Minister of Justice, in withholding information from the police. Subsequently his career of course recovered triumphantly, but for years after the episode the politics of the French Left were not entirely comprehensible without an appreciation of the resulting legacy of distrust.

MH

Ben Barka Affair (1965–67)

Mehdi Ben Barka, exiled Moroccan opposition leader.
Georges Figon, gangster.
Antoine Lopez, traffic officer Orly airport, SDECE agent.
General Mohamed Oufkir, Moroccan Minister of the Interior.
Louis Souchon, head of narcotics squad, Prefecture of Police.

On Oct. 29, 1965, Mehdi Ben Barka arrived at Orly airport from his home in exile in Geneva. He took a taxi to a fashionable brasserie at St Germain des Prés, where he was to discuss a film about decolonization with a film director, Georges Franju, Philippe Bernier, a left-wing journalist and Georges Figon, an ex-convict with intellectual pretensions. He was intercepted by two plain clothes policemen, Louis Souchon and Roger Voitot and driven off in an official car, which also contained Antoine Lopez, an SDECE (secret service) informer and friend of Gen. Oufkir, the Moroccan minister of the interior, and Julien Le Ny, a "retired" gangster. He was driven to the suburban home of Georges Boucheseiche, a friend of Lopez, former Gestapo agent, police informer and disposer of bodies.

Lopez and Boucheseiche telephoned Oufkir to say, "Your guest has arrived". Oufkir and his right-hand man, Ahmed Dlimi, flew separately to Paris. They were taken to Boucheseiche's villa by Lopez, where Oufkir tortured Ben Barka, who was taken to Lopez' home (in Lopez' absence) and never seen again. Oufkir flew to Geneva, where Ben Barka kept his papers, and Dlimi returned to Casablanca.

When Ben Barka's disappearance became known Oufkir came under suspicion. Having returned to France in connection with an official visit by King Hassan he and Dlimi hastily flew home. For months the Moroccans had been seeking to persuade Ben Barka to return; negotiations having failed they had decided to "recover" him by "unorthodox" means. Oufkir had approached Boucheseiche, who needed his goodwill to establish a chain of brothels. Figon and Bernier were enlisted and Ben Barka was enticed to Paris with the offer to finance a film to be shown at the forthcoming Tricontinental Revolutionary Congress.

Thus far this was a Moroccan plot, albeit executed by Frenchmen. The French dimension centred on SDECE. It knew of previous attempts on Ben Barka's life, and Lopez had warned his superiors of the Moroccans' readiness to employ unorthodox means. Had that information been passed to ministers or the police there would have been no Ben Barka affair. For whatever reason it was not. Lopez compromised SDECE further by presenting himself as operating on its behalf in persuading Inspector Souchon, a highly experienced officer with an excellent record, and his assistant Roger Voitot, to help him, ostensibly in setting up a meeting between Ben Barka and the King of Morocco, adding that "Foccart is in the know" (Jacques Foccart was officially de Gaulle's adviser for African affairs and unofficially co-ordinator of secret service matters for the President.) The reluctant Souchon was finally convinced by telephone confirmation of his assignment from someone claiming to be the head of the Minister of the Interior's personal staff.

At the subsequent trial Le Roy-Finville, Lopez' case officer, was acquitted of failing to report a crime. However, the impression of SDECE that emerged was one of complacent inertia followed by panicky attempts at a cover-up involving selective amnesia, concealment of information and lying and inconsistent testimony. In demonstrating it was not culpable SDECE conveyed a powerful impression of being incapable. The Director-General was sacked, responsibility for supervising the service was moved from the Prime Minister to the Minister of Defence, several agents were dismissed or "blown" and one who was despatched to Morocco to investigate was murdered. Morale and operational efficiency were affected for years afterwards.

Meanwhile, Commissaire Jean Caille, head of political intelligence at the Paris Prefecture of Police, was involving himself in the case. A highly energetic officer, his actions against the extreme-Right Secret Armed Organization combating Algerian independence had earned him bitter enemies. They had also brought him into contact with Maître Pierre Lemarchand, a Gaullist deputy who had recruited "barbouzes" — the unavowed counter-terrorists, often with a criminal background, who were enlisted to fight the OAS — and who also happened to be Figon's lawyer. He, too, was a target for right-wing enemies of the regime, as well as the gangsters, who sought to demonstrate his involvement either to get their revenge and damage the government or to persuade the authorities they would be wiser to hush the whole matter up. Their attempts to tie him into the plot were unsuccessful, though Lemarchand inspired less than complete confidence as a witness, so muddying the waters still further.

Through an informer Caille learned that Figon was boasting in bars about his part in a kidnapping and of Lopez' involvement. At Caille's request Lemarchand telephoned Figon, who called on Lemarchand and told his story. According to Figon Caille was also present. Caille and Lemarchand denied this, and Lemarchand denied even meeting Figon then. Accused before the Bar Council of unprofessional conduct he admitted the meeting, saying he was arranging a deal by which Figon would talk in exchange for immunity. He subsequently retracted this story in court; asked why he had told it he replied, "Why, to get acquitted". However, Figon's subsequent behaviour was consistent with the belief that he would not be prosecuted.

The regular police were also involved. Bernier had reported the Moroccans' approach and Figon's role and warned that Ben Barka was unlikely to survive in Moroccan hands. The detective who interviewed him omitted this warning from his report as "exactly the sort of thing one doesn't want to put on record from a witness". It was 19 days before Figon's house was searched. By then Boucheseiche and his confederates had fled the country.

Similarly when the Assistant Director of the Police Judiciaire asked Souchon to contact Lopez, Souchon's ensuing confession was concealed from the detective in charge of the case and the examining magistrate. Lopez' statement reached the Ministry of the Interior's desk as Oufkir and his assistant were flying back to Morocco after an official visit. No attempt had been made to question them. The minister explained that the evidence was too flimsy — and that to arrest Oufkir might have had disastrous consequences for the French community in Morocco. Behind-the-scenes efforts to persuade King Hassan to dismiss Oufkir were fruitless. These negotiations were later semi-officially advanced as the reason for withholding Souchon's confession and concealing its date. Asked subsequently in court whether he realised that this was illegal the director of the Police Judiciaire replied, "only too well". Some commentators speculated that the delay reflected concern that disgust at police implication might affect de Gaulle's decision to stand in the forthcoming presidential election. Only after two months in prison did Souchon reveal to the examining magistrate that he had confessed on Nov. 3 and again on the 13th, obediently concealing the earlier confession.

The impression that the investigation was not being pursued with due diligence was enhanced by Figon's antics. He stayed in Paris cocking snooks at the police — he was photographed for *Paris-Match* outside the office of the detective handling the case — strengthening suspicions that he enjoyed police protection. But in January, following a sensational account in *L'Express* of Ben Barka's treatment after the kidnapping, which was attributed to Figon (but denied), he lost his self-confidence, possibly fearing reprisals. A week later, acting on a tip-off, the police raided the flat where he was hiding. They found him — with a bullet in his head. The authorities announced he had committed suicide and the enquiry into his death was wound up in three weeks rather than the more customary months or year. The inevitable rumours that he had been murdered by the police were fed by the fact that the examining magistrate was not allowed to see the results of the enquiry, by serious deficiencies in police procedure and by conflicting statements about the forensic evidence and Figon's state of mind. Conspiracy theorists had a field day. Whatever the truth of the matter, the last available witness to Ben Barka's fate would not now tell his story.

Public suspicion deepened that the government was trying to hush the affair up. When *Le Monde's* legal commentator, a judge, said as much the Minister of Justice took disciplinary action. "Punishment at last!", the paper ironically commented. His peers imposed a reprimand — the lightest possible sentence.

For those who maintain that the inquisitorial system of justice, unlike the adversarial approach, is committed to rooting out what really happened, the ensuing trials offer salutary food for reflection. The first, in 1966, was strewn with hints that more was known in high places than was being revealed and that certain accused and witnesses were protecting their superiors. As the defence was making its closing speeches, Dlimi arrived "to defend my personal honour". At a fresh trial in 1967 Bernier, Dlimi, Le Roy, Voitot and another Moroccan were all acquitted. Lopez and Souchon were convicted of making an illegal arrest and sentenced to eight and six years respectively. Oufkir, another Moroccan and the gangsters were sentenced *in absentia* to life. (Oufkir would have had a happier fate had he submitted; he was subsequently executed for plotting against King Hassan; his family was still detained in 1990.)

The aims of the plot and the exact circumstances of Ben Barka's death have never been authoritatively elucidated. Simple assassination would surely have been executed more straightforwardly. It seems more likely that the intention was to return Ben Barka to Morocco by force or to extract details about names and funds from him and then kill him. At some point the plan seems to have gone wrong. Almost certainly he died shortly after being abducted.

Privately incensed, de Gaulle publicly dismissed French responsibilities as "vulgar and secondary"; good citizens could be reassured. But even if the SDECE had not been hand in glove with the Moroccans, as some believed, or if the CIA was indeed involved as some Gaullists darkly hinted, there could be no reassurance when a senior policeman would act with flagrant illegality at the behest of an unknown official or a Lopez, or when official police forces and the secret service were locked in bitter rivalry, ostensibly respectable politicians, officials and lawyers had friendly links with common criminals and people in senior positions connived at delaying or misleading the police without suffering disciplinary action. The resignation of the responsible minister — Roger Frey at the Interior — was neither sought nor seriously expected. Several highly-placed people had, literally, got away with murder — and the well-springs of distrust on which suspicion of politicians draws had again been amply replenished.

MH

Markovic Affair (1969–70)

Georges Pompidou, Prime Minister (1962–68), President (1969–74).

This was an exception to two general rules; that French scandals are not about sex and that there is no smoke without fire. This was the least substantially based of all post-war scandals, and its alleged substance the least relevant to the conduct of public affairs.

In October 1968 the body of a young Yugoslav, Stefan Markovic, was found on a rubbish tip near Paris. He had been murdered. The case seized the imagination of the popular press because he was a former bodyguard and friend of the film actor Alain Delon. The headlines grew still larger when it transpired that he had left a letter accusing Delon and another Yugoslav, also a former bodyguard of Delon, should he meet a suspicious end.

The police found themselves in a seamy world of drugs, orgies, compromising photographs and blackmail. Among the prominenti mentioned was "a former minister's wife", later identified in society gossip, then in the press, as Claude Pompidou, wife of the Gaullist former prime minister. As far as can be gauged the rumours were baseless, though the Pompidous' circle of acquaintance was such that they could not be dismissed out of hand, and the context within which they circulated gave them a highly charged political significance. De Gaulle's long reign was clearly approaching its close; manoeuvring for the succession was under way. Pompidou, whom de Gaulle had recently put out to grass, but who nevertheless looked best placed, had opponents within the Gaullist party who were prepared to use the Markovic affair to destroy his chances. Here lay the real scandal.

On being informed that Pompidou's name had come up during the investigation de Gaulle conferred with his prime minister, Maurice Couve de Murville, and the ministers of the interior and justice. It was decided that justice should take its course, if only because any attempt to stifle the investigation would surely leak. Couve was to brief Pompidou. But Couve, whose relations with Pompidou were distant, failed to do this. For a fortnight Pompidou remained in ignorance while all around him tongues wagged. Finally a former member of his staff broke the silence.

Pompidou was incensed at the accusations and what he saw as an attack on his aspirations by way of his wife. He was furious that the investigation had been allowed to proceed and at the delay in informing him. He was particularly indignant that the examining magistrate heard testimony from a prisoner who said he had attended a wild party at which he was told the prime minister's wife was present. How was it, he demanded, that a letter in excellent French from a semi-literate crook, who was in gaol at the time of the crime, was being received so respectfully? Why had so vast an investigation been launched into something quite unconnected with the murder? Why were senior policemen feeding such heavy hints to the media? Why were so many senior Gaullists so assiduously peddling the latest gossip?

Pompidou protested to de Gaulle at the failure to stamp on the rumours; the General, he said, "did not seem very pleased with himself". De Gaulle had in fact expressed his displeasure to the Minister of Justice, but Pompidou felt de Gaulle had failed him. Though the latter invited the Pompidous to dine at the Elysée, in implicit testimony to their innocence, the relationship was never the same again. A few weeks' later de Gaulle's constitutional reform was rejected in a referendum and he resigned, retiring from public life. Georges Pompidou became the second president of the Fifth Republic. And there was no place in the governments formed under that presidency for those who had failed him in the Markovic affair. "They will never be forgiven", he had vowed. And they never were.

MH

Canard Enchaîné **Affair (1973–80)**

Founded during World War I to combat official propaganda and censorship, *Le Canard Enchaîné* has been a thorn in the side of governments of every hue, specializing in leaks of material the powerful would prefer to conceal and in exposing abuses of power. But on this occasion it was the focus of scandal rather its impertinent chronicler.

One evening the paper's chief cartoonist, André Escaro, took a walk past the paper's new, as yet unoccupied, offices. Finding policemen with walky-talkies outside the building and a light in what was to be the editor's room he investigated. He found five men claiming to be working on the central heating, holes in the walls and floor, coils of wire, boxes and two transmitters. They were unable to tell him which company they represented or what connection there was between their equipment and the heating system which was already working satisfactorily. They had told the caretaker they were putting up the curtains. On leaving to telephone his editor Escaro heard, through one of the walky-talkies, "Follow that man who's coming out. We're dropping everything. Get out of here". By the time he returned with his colleagues the men had gone, having hastily patched the walls and floor but leaving some of their bugging equipment behind.

Characteristically, the journalists remade the next day's issue with the banner headline addressed to the Minister of the Interior, "Oh Marcellin, What a Watergaffe!", adding, "Read the *Canard Enchaîné*, the most listened-to newspaper". More prosaically it lodged a complaint for violation of domicile and an attempt to record conversations in a private place.

That someone would wish to bug the *Canard* was no surprise. Its journalists had long assumed they might be followed or have their phones tapped to unmask their sources, so little was gleaned through these means. The new offices, however, were too good an opportunity for someone to miss. But who? The regular police denied all involvement, insisting none of their men had been in the area. Pride was at stake here; their "plumbers" would never have done such a botched job! Government supporters tried to blame the CIA or a left-wing plot, while the prime minister, Pierre Messmer, suggested the *Canard* had staged the affair itself to boost circulation.

Such explanations were exploded when the examining magistrate found more devices in the chimney and the adjoining building, and the next issue of the paper carried a detailed report, based on a major leak, alleging that the bugging had been ordered by Marcellin and naming the DST (counter-espionage) agents involved. Few believed Marcellin's protestation that he was the victim of a plot. The director of the DST claimed that vehicles identified as being in the vicinity at the appropriate time were engaged in an independent anti-terrorist operation; he refused to let his men be questioned for security reasons and declared that the *Canard* was "a nest of spies". Meanwhile, week by week the paper revealed more details, including the fact that the police's "Intelligence" branch had originally been considered for the operation but had been considered too leaky!

By now everyone "knew" what had happened, but almost nobody can have expected that anyone would be brought to book; the only remaining question was how they would escape. The issue of whether the DST agents could be required to appear before the examining magistrate was aired in a succession of courts until mid-1975 before the final ruling that they could. The promotion of the examining magistrate engendered further delays. A year later the director-general of the national police was again refusing to let his men testify.

The dénouement was a classic of its kind. On Dec. 29, 1976 the second examining magistrate issued a ruling tantamount to acquittal. Its arrival on New Year's Eve was calculated to make it as difficult as possible for the paper to appeal within the three-day limit prescribed. Its reasoning was also remarkable: the paper was not in full occupation of the premises, therefore there was no violation of domicile. Further, there had been no invasion of privacy "because in a workplace journalists could only hold conversations of a political, general or professional nature, by definition excluding any reference to private life". However, since the *Canard* had complained "in good faith" it would not have to contribute to the costs of the case. Seven months later the court of appeal confirmed this ruling. It did not comment on the refusal of witnesses to attend, but held the *Canard*'s refusal to reveal its sources to be "unacceptable" and the manner in which it had accused the police "regrettable".

In June 1978 the highest court of appeal, the Cour de Cassation, overturned this judgment. In French law, an allegation of misconduct by an *officier de police judiciaire* must be referred to the Cour de Cassation. The officer who allegedly led the operation had this status, yet the experienced examining magistrate had failed to do this. Consequently he and his successor were incompetent to handle the matter and everything they had done was null and void.

In October 1978 another court ruled that the acts complained of did not constitute a "crime"; violation of domicile by an official was not "an arbitrary act or one injurious to personal freedom or the civil rights of one or more citizens". The DST's actions were mere misdemeanours, and since over three years had elapsed without valid proceedings being initiated the matter was now time-expired. Though it was the responsibility of the examining magistrate or the prosecutor to refer to the Cour de Cassation, since the *Canard* had not itself raised the matter it had "allowed the action to fall out of time". Finally, over six years after the "plumbers'" expedition, the Cour de Cassation upheld this ruling. As *Le Quotidien de Paris* put it, "the *Canard Enchaîné*, which conducted the enquiry in place of the police is in effect being punished for not having also conducted the legal action on behalf of the prosecutor". The *Canard* headlined its commentary, "Everything saved — except honour". Technically the reasoning was doubtless impeccable, but if one wanted one example why French opinion is sceptical about its judiciary in political cases one need look no further.

MH

De Broglie Affair (1976–1982)

Jean de Broglie, right-wing politician, unsuccessful financier.
Gerard Frèche, murderer.
Michel Poniatowski, Minister of the Interior.
Patrick de Ribemont, unsuccessful businessman.
Guy Simone, police inspector.
Pierre de Varga, fraudster.

On Christmas Eve 1976 Jean de Broglie, a right-wing deputy from Normandy, was shot dead in a Paris street by a young man who made his escape. Aged 55, he had served in several governments during the 1960s, had been one of the chief negotiators of the Evian agreements which enshrined Algeria's independence in 1962, and a co-founder with President Giscard d'Estaing of the Independent Republican party (later a constituent element in the Giscardian *Union pour la Démocratie Française*).

Two days later the police made a series of arrests, and two days after that the Minister of the Interior, Michel Poniatowski, held a press conference to announce that the case was "sewn up" — a flagrant disregard of due process that earned a merited rebuke from the Ministry of Justice. Despite this precipitate assurance that all was known, the affair was just beginning. As always the situation was not entirely as it seemed — or as Poniatowski wished it to seem. The official explanation was that de Broglie had acted as guarantor of a loan of some £400,000 to Patrick de Ribemont and Pierre de Varga, owners of a restaurant suffering cash-flow problems. De Broglie's commission would be £60,000; as the loan was repaid his shares passed to his partners, but if he died before repayment they all passed to them. Herein lay the motive.

Who killed de Broglie was never in doubt. Gerard Frèche, a small-time crook confessed almost immediately, incriminating de Ribemont and de Varga. Frèche had been recruited by one Serge Tessèdre, acting as a go-between for a crooked police inspector, Guy Simone, who was already under suspicion for involvement in a hold-up, the murder of his mistress and other shady incidents — despite which he had recently been put on the promotion list. Simone, who owed de Broglie money, also confessed, naming de Ribemont and de Varga as the instigators. De Ribemont had a background of business failure; de Varga had a criminal record and was to appear on a fraud charge the week after the murder. He was also an informer for the police intelligence branch. Both men were desperately short of money.

Such were the associates of this respectable public figure. But how respectable was he? The customary message of condolence was not forthcoming from President Giscard d'Estaing; senior politicians shunned the funeral, pleading "bad weather". De Broglie was a political outcast. Apparently his dubious business activities had been known in political circles for years. Giscard had barred his election as chairman of the Assembly's finance committee because several of his companies were under investigation by the tax authorities. His party had edged him away from posts of responsibility; he was on the verge of leaving it to join the Gaullists.

A picture emerged of a man involved in unsuccessful and at times dubious business deals — including a project for issuing fake treasury bonds that never got off the ground — sinking deeper into financial difficulties and lending his name to schemes from which he drew little profit but in which he became ever more compromised. Though ostensibly worth £2.5 million he left debts of £1.3 million.

What led the affair to drag on so long and so poisonously were doubts about the motive and the behaviour of the police. Shortly after the murder de Broglie's chateau in Normandy was burgled and papers stolen, then the restaurant manager was attacked and his car dismantled, again in an apparent search for papers, while a relative of de Varga had a handbag with relevant documents stolen. It emerged that the anti-gang squad had been tapping Simone's telephone and monitoring his movements for six months, raising questions about how much the police had known, and when, and to whom they had communicated their knowledge. And how had the "rotten apple", Simone, survived so long unless he had protection? Poniatowski accused critics of hypocritically exploiting the murder for political purposes; his denials were received with seasoned scepticism.

In a bizarre detour an extreme-Right weekly alleged that de Varga's lawyer had tried to obtain false testimony from de Broglie's cardiologist, Dr Nelly Azerad, who had earlier been suspected of helping secure the release of a number of prisoners, including de Varga, on bogus medical grounds. (The senior medical officer in the prison service was killed by a parcel bomb about this time.) The cardiologist, whose appointment diary covering the relevant period had disappeared, was charged with destroying evidence. The lawyer was suspended.

Still the affair dragged on. In May 1978 Poniatowski, who had left the government, declined to appear before the examining magistrate, saying he could shed no light on the matter. A change of examining magistrate caused further delays. Simone's lawyers contended the police enquiry was "carefully setting aside everything relating to the political and public relationships of de Broglie and his entourage", alleging that the government was trying to hide the true nature of the affair.

Scarcely had the examining magistrate completed her enquiries when, in April 1980, the *Canard Enchaîné* published two leaked police reports confirming that they had known that de Broglie's life might be in danger. One report, three months before the murder, stated that "as a result of his dishonesty in an earlier affair [de Broglie] would shortly be killed by criminals". Shortly afterwards the police began following Simone — a coincidence, they said; they suspected him of preparing an armed robbery. How much did the government know? Why had de Broglie not been informed? Jean Ducret, director of the police judiciaire, insisted he had withheld nothing from the examining magistrate. The information held by the police had not been substantial enough to refer to higher authority. De Broglie had been neither warned nor protected. He refused to say who had known of the threats at the time though Poniatowski strenuously denied prior knowledge.

With elections approaching the affair became thoroughly politicized.

Poniatowski, one of Giscard's chief lieutenants, accused critics of dirty electoral politics; the Left demanded his impeachment for concealing evidence and failing to assist a person in mortal danger. (Ironically, de Broglie himself had presided over the only impeachment trial in the Fifth Republic.)

The parliamentary committee set up to consider whether impeachment should be initiated heard evidence that Poniatowski had no prior knowledge of the threat to de Broglie but had greater difficulty in elucidating police behaviour. They had withheld their reports from the examining magistrate, who learned of them through an informer. He obtained copies through "unofficial channels" and felt unable to communicate them to the defence. Why had Ducret earlier insisted he had no advance knowledge, only to tell the committee that one of his inspectors had reported the threats to him? The police explanation that they had been protecting their informer was not entirely persuasive, especially as Ducret's account did not square with that given by the first examining magistrate. To the opposition, Ducret was so unreliable a witness as to cast doubt on his assurance the Poniatowski had known nothing of the threats before the murder. On a straight party vote the committee declined to hear Inspector Roux who made the reports. Socialist members interviewing him separately learned that word of a "contract" against de Broglie had been circulating in the underworld for some time before the murder. There had been three previous, unsuccessful attempts to kill him. Roux's informant had even shown him the getaway car several days beforehand, making it hard to understand why the information was not treated more seriously. Ducret now acknowledged that the telephone of one of those approached to undertake the killing had been tapped, but insisted that, like the tailing of others involved, this had no connection with the murder. The head of the anti-gang brigade insisted it had no wind of the affair although Roux was emphatic that he had kept them informed. A former member of the brigade was emphatic they had known. Transcripts of relevant phone taps were not available because, despite their possible relevance, they had been destroyed when the enquiry was two years' old.

The de Broglie affair was rapidly becoming the Poniatowski affair. Just as in the Ben Barka case (see *Ben Barka Affair, 1965–67*), the criminals had been arrested within days, yet years afterwards the behaviour of the police and their responsible minister remained shrouded in murky mystery. Poniatowski protested his manifest innocence, alleging that the Socialists' widening of the scope of the enquiry was infringing the separation of powers in a near-criminal manner. In the hope of bringing the affair to a speedy end he agreed to meet the committee. But tension between the coalition partners meant that, with a presidential election approaching, the Gaullists were now in no hurry. Poniatowski acknowledged for the first time that he had been informed about the reports four days after the crime, but insisted he had no responsibility for their reaching the examining magistrate. Why had he not mentioned them to the examining magistrate? "I said I was available to answer questions; he did not ask me." This was less than might have been expected of a senior minister, and a *prime facie* violation of the penal code — of which several policemen were equally culpable. None was charged and no disciplinary action ensued. Indeed, the Minister of Justice, Christian

Bonnet, defended Ducret: "Let him who has never made a mistake cast the first stone."

In January 1981 the parliamentary committee approved, on a straight party vote, a report concluding that two of the three allegations against Poniatowski were misdemeanours which were now time-expired under the statute of limitations, while the third could not be invoked against ministers. Since prosecution was legally impossible it was inappropriate for it to reach any conclusions whatsoever. This satisfied the UDF's need to prevent impeachment while suiting the Gaullists by falling short of a whitewash. "Do we laugh or cry?" asked *Le Monde*.

Meanwhile, following publication of the police reports, de Varga had initiated proceedings against the police. As a judge involved at an earlier stage had observed, the accusation that the police had, in effect, allowed the crime to happen, was "extremely grave" and "necessarily implies the agreement of the highest authorities in the State". Yet there was apparently no attempt to follow the enquiry through. In a further bizarre twist Dr Azerad and one Serge Gehrling were accused of trying to murder de Varga by shooting him from a window overlooking the Santé prison while he exercised in the prison yard. Why Azerad, who was awaiting trial on charges of destroying evidence to protect Varga might wish now to kill him was unclear. She claimed to have been approached by Gehrling, a former mercenary, and to have pretended to go along with his proposal in order to study his psychopathic behaviour.

The trial of Frèche, Tessèdre, Simone and de Varga opened in November 1981. (De Ribemont, whose guilt Poniatowski had so publicly proclaimed, had long been dismissed from the case.) It was as much a trial of the witnesses as of the accused. It was marked by controversy over the advocate-general's criticism of the examining magistrate for concealing the police reports from his successor, and over the presiding judge's outburst against Poniatowski (before he testified) for lying by omission and against senior policemen for withholding evidence. Justice, he said, had been "held of little account". *Le Monde* commented on the "lamentable confusion, mutual contempt and suspicion among all who should have co-operated loyally to discover the truth". Senior officials had lied and passed the buck, the silences of the politicians had been eloquent, and justice had been impotent in the face of the contempt of the powerful. In the end, de Varga, Simone and Frèche were sentenced to 10 years' imprisonment, Tessèdre to five. But the real mysteries of the de Broglie affair were as obscure at the close of the trial on Dec. 23, 1981 as when three revolver shots ended de Broglie's life five years less one day before. And that probably surprised nobody.

MH

Boulin Affair (1979–83)

Robert Boulin, Gaullist Minister of Labour.
Alain Peyrefitte, Gaullist Minister of Justice.
Henri Tournet, building promoter.

On the morning of Oct. 30, 1979, the body of Robert Boulin, Minister of Labour in the government of Raymond Barre, was found in a muddy pond in the forest of Rambouillet. Both the circumstances of his death and the manner in which it was greeted contrasted sharply with the de Broglie affair (see above). He had apparently swallowed a tube of sleeping tablets, then drowned himself in two feet of water, leaving a suicide note at the Ministry. Colleagues rushed to defend his memory against "slanderers" and "rumour mongers"; President Giscard d'Estaing, in writing to his widow, referred to "circumstances which provoke our indignation" as a factor in his death.

An able and respected minister tipped to be the next prime minister, he had apparently been driven to suicide by accusations of involvement in a real estate scandal, first aired by the far-Right weekly *Minute*, then followed up by the *Canard Enchaîné*.

The allegations were that, in 1973, Boulin had bought five acres of choice woodland near the Riviera from a promoter, old friend and longstanding Gaullist, Henri Tournet, for £40,000. Within four months he had obtained a building permit, though no other permits had been given to build in the woodland before or since. This multiplied the value of the site many times. Boulin had intervened with the local authorities area to get Tournet planning permission for 26 houses (without success) and in 1979 recommended him for a decoration. Shortly afterwards Tournet was accused of selling the land twice; he was awaiting trial. It was clear that Boulin had not been entirely sure that the deal with Tournet was above board because he had twice caused enquiries to be made which assured him that all was well. Boulin insisted that his behaviour had been entirely honourable, that at worst he had been hoodwinked by a swindler.

The affair came at a bad moment for the government. It had lost popularity as it wrestled with the post-1973 slump and relations between the main coalition partners, Gaullists and Giscardians, were increasingly difficult. The de Broglie affair (see above) was unresolved; the affair of Bokassa's diamonds (see below) was causing further embarrassment and prime minister Barre himself had been accused of buying a prime site on the Riviera at a remarkably low price and then obtaining permission to build there no less remarkably rapidly. Boulin's death was seized on as an opportunity to expose the tragic consequences of muck-raking journalism. Parallels were drawn with the suicide of Roger Salengro, the Socialist Minister of the Interior who killed himself in 1937 after the extreme Right press falsely accused him of desertion in World War I.

But the following day Agence France-Presse received a letter from Boulin in which he denounced the collusion between a mythomaniac crook, the *Canard*, a vindictive and publicity-seeking examining magistrate and "certain political circles, from which, alas, my own friends are not excluded". He was particularly bitter at breaches of the secrecy of the judicial investigation which "left cold a Minister of Justice (Alain Peyrefitte, a fellow Gaullist) who is more preoccupied with his own career than the proper functioning of the judicial system". "I prefer death to suspicion."

Peyrefitte replied that he had simply let the enquiry take its course, and had ordered an enquiry into leaks before Boulin's death. (This concluded that there had been no violation of judicial secrecy.) Boulin of course knew as well as anyone that such strict propriety was by no means the rule where public figures were involved. "There is no Boulin affair", Raymond Barre told the Assembly, in unconscious echo of a distant predecessor assuring the Senate some 80 years earlier, "There is no Dreyfus affair". Yet, inevitably, the affair had a political angle; it was suggested (though indignantly denied) that the leaks against Boulin were attributable to the Gaullist party, which could not forgive him for so ably serving President Giscard d'Estaing, now the arch-rival of their leader, Jacques Chirac. The opposition was divided. The Socialists were prepared to draw political capital from the affair; the Communists' high-minded refusal to deal in personalities fanned Socialist suspicions that, with the left-wing alliance wearing increasingly thin, they were behaving as "objective allies" of Giscard.

Shortly before his trial in November 1980 Tournet fled to the Balearic islands. He was found convicted *in absentia* of forgery and sentenced to 15 years. However, the court also reached the view that he had in effect given Boulin the land in recompense for Boulin's efforts on his behalf; the "sale" was fraudulent and the money Boulin had ostensibly paid found its way back to him through covert channels.

Boulin's family was outraged at the fact and manner of this posthumous "conviction" and sought to overturn it. At the hearing in May 1983, Mme Boulin claimed her husband had been murdered, but that she had been prevailed upon to go along with the idea of suicide in the interests of her children. However, no evidence emerged to sustain this belated claim. The overwhelming balance of probability remained suicide. Boulin may have been duped by a crook as he had claimed, but at the least the transactions warranted scrutiny.

MH

Bokassa Diamonds Affair (1979–81)

Jean Bedel Bokassa, military ruler and president of the Central African
   Republic (1966–76), Emperor of the Central African Empire (1976–79).
Roger Delpey, writer and adventurer.
Valéry Giscard d'Estaing, Finance minister (1969–74), President
   (1974–1981).

Better handled, this might have been the affair that never was. As it
was, it dogged Valéry Giscard d'Estaing during the dying months of his
presidency and almost certainly contributed to his defeat in 1981. It began
in October 1979 when the *Canard Enchaîné* published a photocopy of an
order for diamonds, placed by President Bokassa in 1973, for presentation
to Giscard, who at that time was Finance Minister.

   That important visitors to Bangui frequently came away with gifts of ivory
or diamonds had long been rumoured. The *Canard*'s revelations followed
swiftly on the overthrow of Bokassa, in which French paras had played a
major role and French agents had removed his private papers to the French
Embassy. Although the Minister for Co-operation denied knowledge of
that operation — unsurprisingly since it had been run from the presidential
palace by Giscard's adviser on African affairs — it had been witnessed by
several journalists. But, as the *Canard*'s story showed, not everything had
been safely retrieved.

   With the de Broglie affair (see above) unresolved, the opposition calling
for an enquiry and *Le Monde* concluding that the only acceptable explanation would be that the gift had been returned, Giscard's political nose
should have told him he must dispose of the matter rapidly. Instead he
adopted a lofty disdain that was to serve him badly. His spokesman said it
was not "in keeping with the office of president to have to justify oneself or
reply to stories that can be classed as defamation or a concerted campaign
rather than genuine news". Agence France-Presse was informed that "the
exchanges of gifts, which are customary when members of the government
visit foreign states, in no event have the character or value mentioned by
certain publications". To some this sounded more like a semi-confirmation
than a denial.

   On Giscard's behalf it must be said that the rules governing such gifts were
far from clear. Customarily French presidents give up valuable gifts on leaving
office and de Gaulle had meticulously refused them. But Giscard was not yet
president in 1973. As speculation continued the Elysée maintained its lofty
tone: the president would dispose of the matter at an appropriate moment.
"The president", explained Poniatowski, "cannot defend himself because he
cannot engage in debate with a satirical weekly".

   Over six weeks elapsed before Giscard broke his silence in a TV interview. After a lengthy preamble on his treatment of gifts since becoming
president came a single, opaque sentence on the diamonds: "Finally, on the
question you put to me about the value of what I am said to have received
when Minister of Finance, I respond with a categorical and contemptuous
denial."

In December the Canard published further documents; official sources dismissed them as forgeries (they were not). In January 1980 it published a register of gifts to French officials and politicians kept by Bokassa. This was met by official silence. Nor was there any response to further documents published by the *Canard* in March on the extent of those gifts. In September 1980 Bokassa himself telephoned the *Canard* from exile in Abidjan to confirm that he had presented diamonds to Giscard on four occasions, and that he had handed documents dealing with his relations with Giscard to one Roger Delpey for transmission to his lawyers. His telephone was cut off the next day.

Testimony from such a discredited and embittered source must obviously be treated with the utmost caution. Delpey was a writer-adventurer hired by Bokassa, who gave him a large quantity of documents. In May 1980 he was arrested as he left the Libyan embassy and charged with illegal "intelligence with agents of a foreign power" detrimental to France's external interests. His case was referred to the Court of State Security, a special court created by de Gaulle to deal with the diehard terrorist defenders of French Algeria. It operated in camera. Delpey was held for six months before being released to face trial. By his account he had visited the Libyan embassy as Bokassa's message boy on seven occasions, all very brief. Though interrogation by the DST (counter-espionage service) had focused mainly on his links with Bokassa, all documents relating to the diamonds affair had been removed from the dossier. The prosecutor alleged that he had been seeking Libyan backing for a scheme detrimental to French interests, but Delpey claimed he was "the president's prisoner", held on trumped-up charges to stop him making further embarrassing revelations. In November 1981 he would be acquitted on all charges.

Meanwhile, in November 1980, the Minister of Justice, Roger Peyrefitte, launched a prosecution of *Le Monde* for five articles over a three-year period allegedly "seeking to cast discredit on acts and decisions of the courts in conditions such as to impair the authority and independence of the judicial system." This was widely seen as a reprisal for its coverage of the diamonds affair and the doubts it had expressed about the independence of the Court of State Security. The government brought the charges in such a way that the paper could not defend itself by demonstrating its accuracy. (The case was dropped after the Socialist victory the following year.)

The presidential election, in which Giscard was seeking a second term, was now imminent. Official leaks revealed that the diamonds had been valued professionally at only £10,000 in current money (£4,000 at the time of gift). In February 1981 Giscard sent a cheque for the latter sum to the Central African president and another for the capital gain to three Central African charities.

The diamonds affair was one of many strands, some considerably more substantial, contributing to Giscard's defeat. Exploited by his opponents, it formed part of the malaise that clouded the last stages of his presidency. While he apparently did nothing that other public figures had not done, his failure to defuse the issue promptly served him badly, keeping it alive for many months. He was less than candid, and his restitution was grudging and belated. Especially so since the country concerned was among the poorest in the world. And here was far greater ground for scandal — the policy under which, under successive presidents, France sustained one of the bloodthirsty and corrupt regimes of the time and financed the nauseating extravagance of Bokassa's megalomaniac coronation. Finally, when a massacre of children made him too embarrassing, he was disposed of. But the underlying policy remained; Africa and the French political process were the poorer.

MH

L'Auriol Massacre Affair (1981–85)

Paul Debizet, national leader of SAC.
Jean-Bruno Finochietti, member Marseilles SAC.
Jean-Joseph Marie, acting leader Marseilles SAC.
Jacques Massie, leader Marseilles SAC.

One July evening in 1981 five men burst into l'Auriol, the home of Pierre Massie, a trainee police inspector in Marseilles. They killed five members of his family with exceptional savagery, then Massie himself when he returned home. Though they set fire to the villa to eradicate traces they left clues which led to their rapid arrest and eventual conviction. In 1985 three were sentenced to life imprisonment, two to 20 years and one to 15 years.

Though such a brutal attack was unusual even by the standards of Marseilles, which is no stranger to multiple murders, what distinguished this particular crime was that Massie and all those convicted were members of the same political organization — the Service d'Action Civique (SAC), and that it precipitated the organization's downfall.

The Service d'Action Civique was formed in 1958 as a praetorian guard of Gaullist activists. In its heyday its help was gratefully saluted by the Gaullist leadership; Georges Pompidou was honorary president, senior Gaullists attended its annual congress and SAC leaders were treated deferentially by state officials. When the OAS was seeking to assassinate de Gaulle SAC members were among those who fought terrorist fire with counter-terrorist fire, though the organization as a whole was not involved. Nonetheless the priorities and personal contacts formed in a period when murder and patriotism merged brought the SAC dubious recruits, attracted by the protection its tricolour-flashed membership card conferred.

Even after the return to normality following the end of the Algerian war the SAC retained its criminal fringe. One study linked it with no fewer than 12 major political and financial scandals and 164 other crimes in a decade. In

1971, President Pompidou ordered a purge of the organization; 7,000 of its 12,000 members were excluded. But the criminal element was by no means eliminated, notably around Marseilles, where the links between Gaullism, the SAC and the underworld were particularly close, even allowing for political hyperbole in the allegation by Gaston Defferre, Socialist mayor of Marseilles and Minister of the Interior in the 1981 Socialist government, that the SAC was involved in three-quarters of the city's organized crime.

The massacre appears to have stemmed from rivalry between Jacques Massie, leader of the SAC in the Marseilles region, and Jean-Joseph Marie, who stepped into his shoes while he was on a training course and had ambitions to supplant him permanently. Maria suspected Massie's expensive life-style was sustained by milking SAC funds. Massie (who was also suspected of involvement in gun running) refused to resign, warning his critics that he possessed documents implicating them in political and racialist bomb attacks. The Auriol raid was intended to deal with Massie and recover these documents.

The Auriol slaughter broke the whole deterioration of the SAC into the open. Although the secretary-general of the Gaullist party expressed his indignation at the way it was being linked to the SAC the association was too well-established for this to be convincing. While the criminal investigation continued, a parliamentary committee of enquiry investigated the SAC. Its right-wing minority members soon withdrew, leaving the left-wing majority to write a report chronicling the organization's degeneration and its unhealthy mix of policemen, politicians and criminals. Its traditionally close links with the Gaullist party had loosened but remained numerous. Soon afterwards the government declared that the SAC was "based on violence and on practices akin to banditism" and ordered its dissolution.

While the decision was clearly politically motivated it was also appropriate. Although the original purposes of the SAC were proper enough successive right-wing governments, finding its "muscle" useful, had been prepared to turn a blind eye to unhealthy relationships and the behaviour of an unsavoury fringe, so long as they were not too blatant, to the point where the apparent invulnerability of this riff-raff became notorious. And so the SAC met an ignominious end. But the problem did not end with it. A few years later the head of the Gaullist party's "stewards" was a man who had allegedly belonged to one of the Delta commando groups formed to assassinate de Gaulle.

MH

Sniffer Aircraft Affair (1976–84)

Aldo Bonassoli, "inventor".
Albin Chalandon, President of ELF-Acquitaine after 1977.
Valéry Giscard d'Estaing, President of France (1974–81).
Pierre Guillaumat, President of ELF-Acquitaine oil to 1977.
Alain de Villegas, "businessman".

Grave though it was, the "sniffer" aircraft affair was unusual in arousing more hilarity than revulsion — a hilarity provoked by the embarrassment of the powerful at being so thoroughly hoodwinked.

In 1976 the partly public oil company ELF-ERAP was approached by a Belgian, Alain de Villegas de Saint-Pierre-Jette, an Italian technician, Aldo Bonassoli and a French lawyer, Maître Jean Violet. They had backing from an international consortium including the president of the *Union des banques suisses* and Antoine Pinay, a former prime minister whose name was a byword for financial rectitude. They offered a revolutionary technique for petroleum prospecting, involving the installation of sophisticated electronics in the nose of aircraft. It promised quicker and cheaper surveys and consequent economies in the purchase of terrestrial prospecting permits, since the success rate in drilling wells would be much higher.

ELF signed a contract with Fisalma, a Swiss-Panamanian company, to develop and exploit the technique. ELF was headed by Pierre Guillaumat, a longstanding oil man and graduate of the Ecole Polytechnique, France's top technological university; he was also a former senior Gaullist minister. (He was succeeded in 1977 by Albin Chalandon, another former Gaullist minister.) Following the 1973 oil crisis France was desperate for sure supplies of relatively cheap oil, for economic reasons and because of the link in Gaullist minds between energy autonomy and national independence.

The operation was approved by President Giscard d'Estaing in June 1976 using procedures which kept the project hidden from ELF shareholders. "Project X" was classified as a military secret.

Over the ensuing two years some £100 million plus expenses was made available to the "inventors". However, doubts grew. Two public demonstrations, one attended by Giscard d'Estaing, underlining the importance attached to the project at the highest level, were unsuccessful. André Giraud, the Minister for Industry, commissioned an independent report which concluded that the project had been a fraud from start to finish. A further simple test confirmed the point. Chalandon managed to recover half the money, but about £50 million was irretrievably lost. De Villegas and Bonassoli disappeared abroad.

Asked to investigate, the Court of Accounts, which scrutinizes public expenditure, reported to the President and Prime Minister in December 1980. With a presidential election imminent it was, not surprisingly, not published and no action was taken against the crooks. After the ensuing Socialist victory Giscard and Raymond Barre took their copies with them on leaving office; the first President of the Court, Bernard Beck, apparently deeming it his patriotic duty to see that such embarrassing material did not see the light of day, improperly destroyed all the Court's copies on his retirement in October 1982. Thus no copy remained in the State archives.

The affair began unravelling when tax inspectors queried unexplained outgoings in ELF's accounts but were unable to penetrate the curtain of military secrecy. The *Canard Enchaîné* broke the story in June 1983. Socialist ministers ordered further enquiries, and in December the *Canard* revealed the disappearance of the Court of Accounts report and the fact that Barre had called on the Court to maintain total secrecy even after the fraud was known.

The junior minister for the budget, confirming the story to parliament, called it a "gigantic swindle". Opposition leaders complained of a campaign of calumny and accused the government of putting party politics before their patriotic duty. Certainly the Socialists were happy to distract attention from their own difficulties with so juicy an affair, which compromised the image of competence central to both Giscard's and Barre's political stock in trade. But the opposition's implication that the government should have perpetuated the cover-up offered a no less revealing insight into its view of politics.

Giscard appeared on television brandishing his copy of the report and offering an account of the affair that was peppered with inaccuracies. In January 1984 the Prime Minister, Pierre Mauroy, took the unusual step of publishing the report in full, attacking his predecessors for their poor judgment, interference with judicial processes and bending of regulations. Barre, who feared that he was becoming the prime political target in the affair, complained bitterly at this "irresponsible" behaviour, while Giscard declared that Mitterrand was no longer qualified to represent France because he had allowed ELF, Beck and himself to be criticized.

In time the political polemics subsided, substantial sums were recovered from the "inventors", who thus avoided prosecution. It emerged that the same team had operated in several countries since 1965, sometimes in respect of oil and sometimes water. Journalists had a field day tracing the links between actors in the affair and bodies as varied as the SDECE (secret service), the Franco regime, the CIA, the Vatican, the Banco Ambrosiano, Otto de Habsburg's Pan-European Union, so producing that tangled web characteristic of a classic "affair".

But how had a company of ELF's stature come to be so successfully hoodwinked? Partly because of the impressive range of public figures the conspirators had persuaded to let their names be associated with the project, partly because official secrecy limited the circle of knowledge of discussion, and partly because, among those in the know, junior staff with doubts hesitated to challenge the judgment of their seniors and fellow Polytechnique graduates. But chiefly, as so often with confidence tricks, people were deceived because they so desperately wanted to solve the problems of cheap oil supplies and "energy independence". Once the fraud was realised the conduct of the affair proceeded on the principle that the highest law of politics is the eleventh commandment — thou shalt not be found out. Thanks, yet again, to the *Canard* the attempt failed.

MH

Rainbow Warrior Affair (1985–90)

Charles Hernu, Socialist defence minister (1981–85).
Alain Mafart, alias Alain Turenge, DGSE agent.
François Mitterrand, President (1981–   ).
Dominique Prieur, alias Sophie Turenge, DGSE agent.

On the evening of July 10, 1985 a bomb exploded on the Greenpeace vessel *Rainbow Warrior*, which was preparing to sail from Auckland harbour to monitor, publicize and harass nuclear weapon tests at Mururoa atoll in French Polynesia. A member of the crew died in the explosion and the ship sank. On July 12, New Zealand police arrested two "Swiss tourists", "Alain" and "Sophie Turenge", who had been "acting suspiciously", and (thanks to the unwitting help of the French authorities in identifying the telephone numbers they carried) rapidly identified them as agents of the DGSE (formerly SDECE, the French Secret Service).

A day or so later, François Mitterrand was warned by his Minister of the Interior that France might be compromised in the affair. He apparently took no action until Aug. 8 when, aware that fresh revelations were imminent, he instructed Prime Minister Laurent Fabius to commission a "rigorous" enquiry into this "absurd and criminal affair", and seek out the guilty "however high their status". On Aug. 25 Bernard Tricot, the senior official charged with conducting the enquiry, reported that he had no reason to believe that any of the five agents sent to New Zealand had exceeded instructions to gather information about Greenpeace's intentions. "Everything I have heard and seen makes me certain that, at governmental level, no decision was taken to damage the *Rainbow Warrior*".

Doubts whether Tricot had got to the bottom of the matter widened into certainty on Sept. 17 when *Le Monde* showed that he had been told a pack of lies. The Minister of Defence, Charles Hernu, who had ordered surveillance of the *Rainbow Warrior*, had either approved the attack or failed to prevent it. The chief of staff, the head of the DGSE and Mitterrand's personal military adviser were all in some way implicated. And there had been a third team of agents, unknown to Tricot, who had planted the bomb and escaped undetected.

Hernu repeatedly denied that any attack had been ordered by his department. Subsequently he claimed that the truth had been concealed from him. Too late; on the 20th he was dismissed for repeatedly lying to the Prime Minister and the President, and the director-general of DGSE was sacked for refusing to answer questions. On the 23rd the Prime Minister acknowledged that the agents had acted on orders and promised that France would pay compensation to New Zealand and the family of the dead photographer.

The sequels dragged on for years. The government refused to let agents who escaped face trial in New Zealand. The two who were captured were sentenced to 10 years for manslaughter. Using the threat of barring access for New Zealand butter to the European Community, France forced a deal by which she apologized and paid compensation, and the agents were to be transferred to an isolated atoll in French Polynesia for three years.

In 1987 the Chirac government repatriated one agent without New Zealand's consent, and on the eve of the 1988 election it brought the second agent back, again without following the agreed procedure. New Zealand protests resulted in the matter being taken to international arbitration. In 1990 the panel found for New Zealand in one instance and France in the other, but decided it was now too late to return the agent affected. France was not ordered to pay compensation but was called on to establish a fund to improve understanding between the two countries.

Meanwhile, in 1987 Hernu had admitted responsibility for conducting "an action of the State" in respect of the *Rainbow Warrior*. However, to his death in 1989 he insisted bitterly that he had been betrayed by colleagues and made the scapegoat of the affair. Certainly no evidence had come to light that he had ordered the sinking in as many words; he had, however, underlined the word "forestall" in a memorandum by a senior admiral on the effect of Greenpeace's activities on the test programme. This seems to have been taken as a green light along the lines of "will nobody rid me of this turbulent priest?"

The outstanding remaining question was about Mitterrand's role. Publicly he presented himself as outraged by the unauthorised conduct of wayward subordinates. But some continued to believe that such an operation would only be sanctioned at the highest level; others could not believe he would compromise himself in such a way. Investigation produced no smoking gun in the presidential office, though the financial arrangements for the operation were approved by the head of Mitterrand's military staff. The most that could be safely said was that Mitterrand did not emerge from the affair with his status enhanced; at the very least his inertia in the period before French involvement became public suggested a readiness to see the affair hushed up. What thwarted this tactic was the unusual determination with which the French press sought to demonstrate, in the wake of Watergate, a hitherto unsuspected talent for investigative journalism (see United States: *Watergate Affair, 1972–74*).

MH

Crossroads of Development Affair (1983–90)

Yves Chalier, head of Nucci's private office.
Christian Nucci, Minister for Co-operation.
Charles Pasqua, Minister of the Interior (1986–88).

In 1983 the Socialist government set up an agency named Crossroads of Development to foster support for aid to the Third World. After it was wound up in January 1986 it was discovered that between £2 million and £5 million was missing. In April the new right-wing Minister for Development discovered the scandal, and with a mixture of sorrow and satisfaction pronounced it the gravest he had known in 35 years of public life.

The hunt for the missing money soon focused on Yves Chalier, the former chef de cabinet of the previous Minister for Development, Christian Nucci. Chalier, however, had disappeared after writing a letter of exculpation to the current minister. The investigation brought to light the purchase of an apartment in Paris and the acquisition of a chateau which was subsequently resold to Chalier and a former assistant to the Socialist minister for women's rights. Also, ghost companies had overbilled the French government for arranging a conference in Burundi. What turned the matter from an administrative scandal to a political one was that some of the cheques bore Nucci's name. Nucci claimed his signature had been forged. However, some of the missing funds had gone to pay for his election posters. Chalier later alleged from Paraguay that one of Mitterrand's advisers, Guy Penne, was involved.

Red-faced, the Socialist Party reimbursed Nucci's printer the sums improperly paid from the Crossroads account. However, embarrassment was now spread when Chalier revealed that he had been advised to leave France as the scandal was breaking by an official of the Ministry of the Interior. It emerged that he had been supplied with a "genuine-false" passport prepared by the DST on the request of the minister, Charles Pasqua. The examining magistrate's attempts to investigate were blocked by a declaration that the matter was covered by "military secrecy". Even though Chalier had once had links with the SDECE (secret service) this reflected a bizarre notion of the needs of national security. It was assumed that Chalier's flight had been eased so that he would be produced when his reappearance would cause maximum damage to the Socialists.

In January 1987 the examining magistrate found a *prima facie* case that Nucci had committed offences while a minister. It now rested with parliament to decide whether to initiate impeachment proceedings. He also ordered the arrest of the official who had given Chalier his passport. The official's anger at the melodramatic arrest at dawn gave way to the fury of the judiciary when he was released a few hours later after Pasqua had leaned on the prosecutor's office. The prosecutor's office also ruled, and was upheld on appeal, that "military secrecy" had been invoked properly, the court appearing to take the minister's judgment as being beyond question.

In May 1987 the prosecutor agreed that Nucci would have to be judged by parliament, describing him as "one of the principal beneficiaries of a fraudulent system", who had gained improper access to about £700,000. In September 1987 parliament voted to initiate impeachment proceedings — only the third time the procedure had been used against a minister since 1815. A Socialist attempt to impeach Pasqua was rejected, and an attempt by Nucci himself to have Pasqua prosecuted for harbouring a malefactor was also unsuccessful. In 1990 a Socialist minister of justice again declined to move for Pasqua's impeachment. In April 1990 the panel of senior judges considering the case concluded that there was sufficient evidence for impeachment in respect of some £200,000. However, while discussing a Bill to put the financing of parties and elections on a more regular basis some weeks earlier the Assembly had approved an amnesty for earlier offenders in terms that were tailor-made for Nucci (who meanwhile had been found employment on the staff of Fabius, now president of the National Assembly). Accordingly, the judges concluded that Nucci could not be brought to trial. Unprecedentedly they added comments criticizing the amnesty law that led to this outcome. Chalier, who had returned to France and been released from custody after a hunger strike in 1987, still awaited trial for forgery, misappropriation and breach of trust, along with 13 others. (Three more were charged in relation to the false passport — but not, of course, Pasqua.) "One law for the politicians, one law for the rest", he commented bitterly. A judgment shared by many of his countrymen.

MH

Luchaire Affair (1984–87)

Charles Hernu, Socialist defence minister (1981–85).
Jean-François Barba, senior defence official.

On the eve of the 1986 elections a local newspaper reported illegal sales of munitions by the Luchaire company to Iran. The Minister of Defence, Paul Quilès, initiated an enquiry. Following the Socialists' defeat his successor, André Giraud, commissioned a report from Jean-François Barba, a controller-general of the armed forces. This confirmed the illegal export of 450,000 shells, alleging the operation had been covered by the staff of the then Minister of Defence, Charles Hernu. Moreover, commissions had been paid into Socialist Party funds.

The gist of Barba's report appeared in the newsweekly *L'Express* in January 1987, attracting little attention during a wave of public service strikes. It was not until November that a fresh leak, coinciding with other affairs, made it a major issue. Barba also asserted that the head of DGSE (secret service) had alerted Mitterrand in 1984, and that Mitterrand had told them to brief Hernu. But the illegal traffic persisted. Hernu denied this but the *Rainbow Warrior* incident (see *Rainbow Warrior Affair, 1985–90*) had shown what his word might be worth. Meanwhile a legal investigation was marking time because the examining magistrate was not authorised to see the report, which was classed as a military secret. A leak of the full text to *Le Figaro*, neatly timed in relation to the presidential election, led to its being declassified.

The Right made much of Mitterrand's involvement as commander-in-chief and the DGSE briefing — though the Socialists claimed this had been very imprecise. Humiliatingly for Mitterrand, though he had ordered a ban on deliveries to Iran, they had continued — not least because of the electoral damage if the company collapsed. The Ministry of Defence knew what was happening; notes to Hernu's office were left unanswered. In effect officials were being tacitly covered. The enquiry found no evidence of commissions being paid into Socialist coffers and Barba said he had been "subjected to political pressures linked to the change in government in March 1986". Politically, what remained was the question of how the law and the President's will had been flouted for four years.

The outcome was a classic of its kind. In June 1989 the case was dropped with acquittals all round. The prosecutor's report demonstrated that, although the original complaint had been laid by a Minister of Defence, successive ministers, both Left and Right, had blocked the investigation by refusing to communicate evidence required for a successful prosecution to the examining magistrate — with the aim of protecting their own officials. A customs enquiry reported no evidence of customs regulations being breached — a ludicrous conclusion in the light of clear proof that Luchaire had sent shells to Iran. The prosecutor therefore took the view that the refusal of the complainant to supply evidence undermined the rights of the defence; accordingly he declined to proceed against the managing director of Luchaire alone — the only other "exposed" figure, having died in 1988.

There was anger in the judiciary that, yet again, the political class had escaped. The one positive aspect of the affair was that it produced the first steps towards a new law on the financing of political parties, which was so long overdue.

MH

Pechiney Affair (1988–   )

Alain Boublil, head of finance minister's private office.
Roger-Patrice Pelat, businessman.
Max Théret, businessman.

In November 1988 the big nationally owned company Pechiney made a bid for the American canning and packaging group, Triangle. Soon after, the US Securities and Exchange Commission notified the stock exchange watchdog body, the *Commission des Opérations de Bourse*, that in the three days before the announcement, during which the shares rose sharply, one third of the deals originated inside France. Among those making deals were Max Théret, a businessman who had contributed generously to Socialist Party funds, and Roger-Patrice Pelat, a close friend of President Mitterrand since their prisoner of war days. This was not the only such incident; a little earlier there had been similar allegations over a highly profitable dawn raid on another major company, *Société Générale*. But the Pechiney allegations came very close to the President, conflicting with his publicly-expressed distaste for mammon and with the Socialists' self-image of political and financial rectitude.

Alain Boublil, the abrasive *chef de cabinet* to the Finance Minister, to whom rumour pointed as the source of the leak, resigned to defend his reputation. Some opposition politicians found the temptations too great: "France", declared the general secretary of the Gaullist party, "has the most corrupt Left in the world". This sparked an uncharacteristically sharp riposte from the Prime Minister, Michel Rocard, reminding the Right of the Ben Barka affair, the bugging of the *Canard Enchaîné*, the murder of de Broglie and the death of Boulin (see above for all four "Affairs"). Pierre Joxe, the Minister of the Interior, ridiculed the notion that the finance minister, Pierre Bérégovoy, might be involved; "Look at his suits, his shoes, his socks . . .". Beregovoy's thoughts on this line of defence are not recorded.

The COB reported there was evidence of criminal behaviour, naming six people, including Pelat and Théret. These two were charged with insider dealing, but Pelat died of a heart attack a few days later — killed, Théret declared, by the stress of the affair. Now that "the president's friend" was dead the political heat went out of the affair. With the case still to come to trial it seemed that, though there was indeed a scandal of insider dealing, on the political level little of substance had come to light.

MH

WEST GERMANY

Spiegel Affair (1962–65)

Konrad Adenauer, Federal Chancellor.
Conrad Ahlers, Journalist.
Franz Josef Strauss, Defence Minister.

In 1962, the year of the Spiegel Affair, West Germany was a "fair-weather democracy", a country with democratic structures but with a weak democratic political culture. This was the conclusion arrived at by a cross-national study published by Almond and Verba (*The Civic Culture*). The reasons had as much to do with her Nazi past as with the threatened position of West Germany. The state had been founded in the teeth of Soviet opposition, had joined NATO in 1955 because its defence was only possible within a larger alliance, while the building of the Wall through Berlin in 1961 did nothing to make the country feel more secure. Internally, the ideology which all the parliamentary parties subscribed was anti-communism, a result of the existence of the GDR. Since 1956 the Communist party had been banned in West Germany and public prosecutors and judges were busy applying the political penal code against Communists. All this contributed to keeping the authoritarian state tradition, the "*Obrigkeits-staat*, very much alive and the methods employed by the state authorities during the Spiegel affair reflected that.

On Oct. 10, 1962 the political weekly *Der Spiegel* published an article (by Conrad Ahlers) on the NATO exercise "Fallex 62" with the title "Of limited value for defence" (*Bedingt abwehrbereit*). In the article the scenario of a Russian attack on Western Europe was considered and it was stated that the German *Bundeswehr* (Army) was deficient in manpower, weapons and equipment, unable to prevent a Soviet attack with conventional forces. The article ended: "'Fallex 62', however, has proved that neither for forward defence, nor as a deterrent can nuclear missiles or grenade throwers replace conventional brigades". This article constituted a severe attack on the defence policies of the Federal Government and in particular on the Defence Minister and the leader of the Bavarian CSU, Franz Josef Strauss. He had been Minister of Defence since 1956 and had shown great vigour in establishing the new West German army. He was an outspoken, clever politician and perhaps the most brilliant orator of the Federal Parliament. But he was also a dyed-in-the-wool Bavarian conservative, he talked about massive nuclear retaliation against a Soviet attack, even about a pre-emptive strike, long after the Kennedy administration had adopted a "flexible response" strategy. He also insisted on nuclear carrier weapons for the *Bundeswehr*. All this sounds peculiar as the Federal Republic had (and has) no nuclear weapons of its own. But it made Strauss the *bête noire* of left-wingers and of all those who opposed such federal defence policies. Strauss was a colourful personality, a man of "business affairs", surrounded by a whiff of corruption. To quote but one example: His name was linked to the building of barracks for American soldiers (FIBAG). His feud with *Der Spiegel* was long-standing. *Der Spiegel* had extensively reported on the various "affaires" not merely because it sold more copies as a result but also because Rudolf Augstein, the publisher, had come to the conclusion that Strauss was not a democrat and must be stopped from becoming chancellor if at all possible.

But the Spiegel Affair also involved the chancellor Konrad Adenauer and the authority of his government. In 1962 he was 86 years old and calls for his retirement had increased over the years. In 1959 he had toyed with the idea of becoming federal president with the proviso that he would decide on and guide his successor — a ploy, as it turned out, to exclude the CDU's favourite Ludwig Erhard. When the CDU leadership refused to accept his *diktat* he declared himself indispensable and continued as chancellor. In the federal elections of 1961 the CDU/CSU lost its absolute majority and had to find a coalition partner. But their obvious choice, the conservative Liberals, had just achieved their highest vote ever with the campaign slogan "Governing with the CDU but without Adenauer". Adenauer, as astute as ever, outsmarted them by negotiating with the SPD which forced the FDP — under pressure from their supporters in industry — to bite the bullet and accept Adenauer as chancellor. By way of thanks the Liberals were dubbed the "break-promise party". It comes as no great surprise that the new coalition government was one of unease and mutual distrust.

Following a charge of treason and bribery by a professor of constitutional law (and reserve officer), the Federal Prosecutor's Office approached the Ministry of Defence for an expert opinion on *Der Spiegel* article. Ministry officials judged that treasonable statements had been made. The permanent undersecretary, Volkmar Hopf, visited the prosecutor's office and put pressure on its staff to proceed with the full force of the law. He also offered technical assistance. Long before the police action started the Ministry of Defence was informed and involved. On the night of Friday, Oct. 26 the editorial offices of *Der Spiegel* in Hamburg and Bonn were searched and sealed. The publisher, Rudolf Augstein, was arrested as well as the two managing editors. Conrad Ahlers, on holiday in Spain at the time, was detained by the Spanish police and despatched to Germany "of his own free will" (accompanied by Spanish CID officials). Other people arrested were the journalist Hans Schmelz, the acting editor Becker, and Colonel Wicht of the counter intelligence service who had read the article in advance of publication. A strong police force plus officials occupied the offices of *Der Spiegel* for about a month. One prosecutor even scrutinized the forthcoming issue of *Der Spiegel* (Oct. 29) for possible treasonable contents and then allowed its publication, an action clearly contrary to Art. 5 Basic Law which stated "there shall be no censorship". All this might have led to financial ruin and the end of *Der Spiegel* altogether, had it not been for many offers of help from other publishers, including even the conservative Springer Press. Virtually the entire spectrum of newspapers as well as radio and TV condemned the night-time police raid. Even though the prisoners on remand were gradually released Augstein himself was held for more than 100 days. The legal aftermath of the Spiegel Affair dragged on for years through the courts but none of the Spiegel journalists were ever convicted of treason. The counter-charges of Spiegel journalists against members of the government also came to nothing.

Public prosecutors are subordinate to ministries of justice. This fact alone made government involvement likely. Surprisingly, it turned out that the federal Minister of Justice, Wolfgang Stammberger (FDP), the minister in question, had not been informed about the impending proceedings. In a tortuous statement by Adenauer and Strauss much later it was said that Adenauer wanted prior knowledge of the police action confined to a small circle but did not give instructions to keep Stammberger in ignorance. Strauss always maintained that Adenauer had given such instructions. This makes it clear that Adenauer was informed in advance and that Strauss was deeply involved in the preparation of the prosecution.

Leaving Stammberger uninformed was an obvious sign of distrust (and interference in the internal workings of a government department). There-fore, on Oct. 31, Stammberger tended his resignation. But this would have meant a coalition crisis which Adenauer was not prepared to risk. Instead he worked out a compromise which led to the dismissal or suspension of the permanent undersecretaries of defence and justice as those held allegedly responsible.

From the beginning it was widely assumed that Franz Josef Strauss was involved and that he would use this godsent opportunity to get even with *Der Spiegel*. To start with, however, he said repeatedly that he had nothing whatever to do with the matter. But persistent questioning of the government in the *Bundestag* by SPD and FDP MPs elicited the fact that Strauss had phoned the German military attaché in Spain twice (thus interfering with Foreign Office business), instructing him to see that Conrad Ahlers was arrested.

Adenauer's attitude was highly ambiguous. It seems that he tried to use the treason charge to eliminate a political opponent. In answering parliamentary questions he maintained that the matter was *sub judice* and the government could not possibly interfere with legal processes, but on the other hand he did his utmost to smear the *Der Spiegel* publisher personally by saying that he was a man who earned money by committing treason. In a radio broadcast before the Bavarian state elections (Nov. 23) he maintained that the treason charge would be proved without a doubt. Parliamentary questioning went on for weeks and the truth only came out gradually.

This explains why the FDP's executive demanded a cabinet reshuffle on Nov. 19 without clearly insisting on the dismissal of Franz Josef Strauss. On Nov. 22 — to lend teeth to this demand — the five FDP ministers resigned. This was three days before the Bavarian state elections in which the CSU emerged with an increased majority. But even this could not save Strauss, as Adenauer's future as chancellor was increasingly questioned. So Strauss had to resign on Nov. 30, holding the FDP responsible for this decision. Adenauer weathered this crisis by an extensive government reshuffle even if it was not clear at first whether the FDP would again enter a coalition under his leadership. As in 1961, negotiations with the SPD did the trick but the weakening of Adenauer's authority was only too apparent: for the first time it was publicly announced that he would resign the chancellorship in September/October 1963 and the aims of the coalition government of CDU/CSU/FDP were enshrined in a written contract.

The long-term effects of the Spiegel Affair are far-reaching. In retrospect it was the making of *Der Spiegel*. It became the major political weekly of West Germany; an institution, developing its own distinctive style, with excellent contacts with government officials, ideally placed to report extensively on all subsequent political scandals.

Franz Josef Strauss was down but not out. In 1966 he became Minister of Finance in the CDU/SPD government. But his record was not forgotten. When, in 1980, he stood as chancellor candidate of the CDU/CSU, one of the factors that led to his severe electoral defeat was the memory of the Spiegel Affair. In party politics the affair reinforced one of the major conflicts within the conservative spectrum, the conflict between the CSU and the FDP, a permanent feature of the West German party system.

The Federal Constitutional Court ruled that even in treason cases the defence had to be given access to all the material of the prosecution in order to allow a fair trial. The inadequacies and flaws in the existing treason laws were recognized, and after the SPD had entered government these laws were modified. The most important long-term effect, however, was on the political culture of the Federal Republic. In abstract terms it was a conflict between the extent of press freedom and the security of the State. Contrary to what had happened in more authoritarian times the "State" did not win this time. It was established that press freedoms and state security were of equal importance and it was no longer possible to muzzle the press. This view was endorsed by widespread public support; students demonstrated, professors (usually pillars of the state) protested and intellectuals sent petitions. Clearly the Spiegel Affair did not lead to such widespread protests as the student revolt some years later, but it was the first sign that democratic values had taken root and that individuals stood up and defended them. In this sense this affair sounded the death knell of the authoritarian state.

HL

Flick Affair (1982—   )

Friedrich Flick, German industrial magnate.

The Flick Affair — named after the large Flick concern — lasted with all its repercussions nearly 15 years.

Traditionally the founder of the Flick empire, Friedrich Flick had attempted to establish good relations with politicians. In the Third Reich he belonged to the circle of friends around Heinrich Himmler, the SS leader, and it is estimated that his donations to the SS and the Nazi party totalled DM 8,000,000, a considerable sum in those days. In return he acquired valuable property rights in the East, concessions and contracts. After 1945 he was also sentenced as a war criminal, largely for his employment of slave labour. (In the middle of the Flick Affair, in the 1980s, his heir suddenly announced a general compensation payment to the victims of DM 5,000,000, a sum that had been demanded since 1968.) Thus the habit of seeking close relations with politicians simply followed family tradition.

Almost from the establishment of the Federal Republic the Flick concern paid considerable sums to individual politicians, mainly to influential members of the CDU/CSU and the FDP. Some money also went to the SPD after 1969. On the whole these payments were passed on to the respective party coffers, even if they were used — for example — to finance the election campaigns of individuals. The discovery of these payments led to charges of bribery and corruption against the general manager Eberhard von Brauchitsch in 1982, but the prosecution was unable to prove that they had been made in return for specific favours. Rather, corruption of a more subtle kind was revealed; that of close links between leading politicians and industry. The "political bureau" of Flick in Bonn certainly followed political events closely and was not slow to exert influence and single out certain politicians for special favours. There were also regular meetings — both formal and informal — with leading CDU/CSU and FDP members were employees of the Flick empire discussed their general concern and interest in political matters. The concern must have felt that these contacts were profitable for its business interests.

The Flick concern first entered the limelight in the mid '70s when it sold a large quantity of Daimler-Benz shares to the Deutsche Bank. About one billion DM were owed in Sales Tax on this transaction and not unnaturally Flick sought to minimize his tax liabilities. However, the Economic Minister (working in conjunction with the Finance Minister) is entitled to waive the tax payment if the proceeds of such a sale are reinvested in the national interest. The economics ministers in question were Hans Friderichs and his successor Graf Lambsdorff, both at some time treasurers of the FDP. Payments were made to them and they maintained close personal relations with Brauchitsch, but again it could not be proved that these payments were for specific favours rather than for party funds. In the end — not least because Flick had acquired shares in Grace Brothers (USA) — a large part of the sales tax had to be paid.

The Flick Affair has also been called the "donations to political parties" affair and this is really the aspect that took longest to solve. All the parliamentary parties in the Federal Republic, though far more generously supported from public funds than other West European parties, feel that they are short of money and as a result are very eager to collect as many donations as possible. But political parties (till the new Party Law of 1984) had no charity status and therefore tax has to be paid on such donations. The party law of 1967 also laid down that the donors of sums in excess of DM 20,000 had to be named. But the donors disliked the publicity and the tax liability and the parties obliged by setting up a number of dummy charitable organizations whose sole (or major purpose) was to transfer such funds to the parties in question. This procedure also avoided unwanted publicity. In other words, parties assisted in large tax evasion schemes, in turn involving Inland Revenue Offices which initially had to confer charitable status and were then supposed to supervise charities. Apparently politicians used their influence to obtain charitable status and ensure a lax supervision. When, in the 1980s, large numbers of industrialists (at one stage there were over 900 cases pending) were summoned to answer charges of tax evasion, their defence was that parties themselves had advised them to pay donations to certain — apparently charitable — organizations and arranged receipts for tax purposes.

However, the great variety of supposedly charitable organizations was not the only tax avoidance dodge. For example, Rainer Barzel, the president of the West German parliament, had a contract as a legal consultant with Flick and received very large payments for minor legal services. When this was revealed he had to resign. Another notable tax evasion scheme was set up with the help of Flick's general manager von Brauchitsch. The "Society of the Divine Word", a Catholic missionary society, of St Augustin near Bonn, received over the years DM 12,300,000 and issued tax-deductible receipts for it. The Society then returned 80 per cent of the sum in cash to von Brauchitsch for his political slush fund, 10 per cent to the party treasurer of the CDU while 10 per cent went to the missionary society. All this was a conspiracy to defraud the Inland Revenue and it was this and other tax evasion cases that finally resulted in the jailing of the Flick manager in 1987.

In the early 1980s many industrial managers saw themselves arraigned for tax evasion because of previous donations to political parties. The leaders of the CDU, CSU and FDP, fearing that their source of funds might dry up if these cases were allowed to proceed, proposed an amnesty in the *Bundestag*. It was largely the fury of the rank-and-file of the FDP that scotched this plan. The failure of the amnesty meant that court cases dragged on for years, although by 1990 most of them were settled by a fine. The direct result of the Flick Affair was the new Party Law of 1984 which safeguarded the income of political parties in two ways: (i) Parties were effectively accorded charity status by making donations of up to DM 100,000 per annum tax deductible. (This violates the basic democratic principle of equality but was accepted in a ruling of the Federal Constitutional Court); (ii) the size of public funds for political parties was significantly increased. Donations were only recognized as tax-deductible if the name and address of the donor was publicized in the party accounts.

The Flick concern sold some of its holdings and has taken a very low political profile. Graf Lambsdorff, who was fined for tax evasion, had to resign but some years later was elected leader of the FDP and then became the leader of the FDP in a united Germany, a clear sign that party members regard tax evasion on behalf of a political party as a minor offence.

The parliamentary investigation committee of 1983 charged with looking at the links between the Flick concern and leading politicians, and whether undue influence had been exerted, interviewed virtually all the leading politicians of Federal Germany but with indeterminate results: no case of individual bribery could be established, the same conclusion that had been reached by the court cases.

HL

Guillaume Affair (1974)

Willy Brandt, Federal Chancellor.
Günter Guillaume, Personal assistant to Brandt.

Günter Guillaume, a refugee from East Germany, had worked for years as an SPD official in the West before he started work in the Chancellor's office in 1970 and became one of Willy Brandt's personal assistants. In April 1974 he was arrested together with his wife, Christel, and four others, and charged with espionage for East Germany. According to a statement by the Attorney General, Herr Guillaume had confessed to being an officer in the "National People's Army" and to having worked for the East German Ministry for State Security.

The discovery of an East German spy in a government department was rare; in the Chancellor's Office, the hub of government, it was unheard of, but for it to lead to the resignation of Willy Brandt, the Chancellor himself, was quite astounding. After all, this leader of the SPD had won the most glorious election victory for the party in 1972. For the first time since 1949 the SPD had become the strongest party in the *Bundestag* and at the same time Brandt's *Ostpolitik* had received a rousing endorsement by the electorate. But Brandt proved unable to form a coalition government in a determined way and showed deficiencies both as a party leader and as head of government. As SPD leader he was unable to control the increasingly bitter debate between left — and right — wingers on economic and social issues; as Chancellor his government's response to the oil crisis was considered weak and ineffectual. Senior figures of the SPD began to criticize the Chancellor openly. Herbert Wehner said, for example, that the Chancellor "likes it lukewarm". The SPD also lost a number of regional elections in 1973/74. So it was not merely mid-term blues that had already weakened the Chancellor's position well before the Guillaume Affair.

The main issue of the Guillaume affair centred on the security implications. Guillaume had been vetted both by the organization reponsible for internal security (*Bundesamt für Verfassungsschutz*) and by the Federal Intelligence Office (BND) responsible for external security. The former had found no grounds for withholding security clearance from Guillaume in 1970, while the head of the BND had advised the then head of the Chancellor's office to confront Guillaume with the allegations made against him — surely a somewhat naïve procedure. As a result Guillaume had signed a declaration stating that he had never worked for East German intelligence. Because of these suspicions the BND further advised that he should not be employed in the Chancellor's Office and that further investigations should be made. This advice had been disregarded, not least because the SPD defence minister at the time had written a letter to the head of the Chancellor's office guaranteeing Guillaume's personal and political reliability. Brandt, who used Guillaume principally as liaison officer with the SPD, regarded him as a tried SPD official, as "one of the family" and as a personal friend.

At first it was stated categorically that Guillaume had had no access to secret papers and therefore his importance as a spy was not very great. Later, however, it turned out that this was not true. In his letter of resignation Brandt gave three reasons: while on holiday in Norway in 1973 he was accompanied by Guillaume and at that time secret papers had inadvertently been allowed to pass through his assistant's hands. He also felt constrained by his policy towards the East knowing there was a spy in his office. (Later the point was made that Guillaume's reports on the motives and background of *Ostpolitik* showed to the policy-makers in the East that Brandt's motives were those openly stated and that these reports promoted rather than hindered his policy.) Thirdly, Brandt felt that his "private life would have been dragged into speculations concerning the espionage case. It is and remains grotesque that a German Chancellor could be open to blackmail". These rather oblique references refer to Brandt's having a number of girl friends (something he had never made any secret about) and that somehow it might be possible to blackmail him on this account. Willy Brandt had always been a sensitive man and preferred to withdraw when matters became too personal, especially as the CDU/CSU had no qualms exploiting this point and argued that a man who — in Christian terms — led an immoral personal life might also pursue public policies that were immoral. But he also felt that he had to resign out of "respect for the unwritten rules of democracy" as he stated in his letter to the Federal President.

The Guillaume affair highlighted, even if it did not solve, the security issue. The main reason why the West German government machinery contained so few spies had to do with the civil service status of its employees. Two state examinations and an "open career" including repeated security vetting, excluded virtually all potential spies. On the other hand, all government ministers brought with them advisers and assistants who were then given temporary civil servant status. The civil servants' organizations suggested in earnest after the Guillaume Affair — because Guillaume had been an outsider — that ministers should only employ professional civil servants in future to minimize the security risk. This was not acceptable to the politicians.

Helmut Schmidt, Brandt's successor as Chancellor, steered a far more right-wing economic course and as far as possible muzzled the left-wingers in the SPD. Brandt's loss of the chancellorship was also a blow for left-wing socialist policies and for the left wing in the SPD.

HL

GREECE

Lambrakis Affair (1963–66)

Konstantinos Karamanlis, Prime Minister, resigned in 1963.
Spyros Kotzamanis, and Emmanuelidis, Emmanuel, members of para-state
    right-wing groups, who killed Lambrakis in 1963.
Grigoris Lambrakis, medical doctor, independent MP for Pireus
    (1961–1963).

The death of Grigoris Lambrakis in Thessaloniki, Greece, in 1963 was an
event that split Greek society and political life, exposing the existence of
secret para-military gangs which had set themselves the task of "purging"
Greek society of progressive and leftist groups and individuals.

Lambrakis was a distinguished medical doctor who lived and practised in
Pireus. Later, while a Professor of Medicine at the University of Athens,
he continued his practice, offering his services free of charge to needy
people. He was also a Balkan Games long jump champion and an Olympic
athlete. He was associated with EDA (Greek Democratic Left), although
he was not a member of this or any other party. In the 1961 elections
Lambrakis won a seat as an independent Deputy for Pireus. It was
Lambrakis who established the Peace Movement in Greece, becoming
its leader and thus a very popular and well known personality throughout
the country.

In March 1963 Lambrakis was invited to represent the Greek Peace
Movement at a peace march organized by Bertrand Russell. While in
London Lambrakis became involved with a group of Greeks who had
relatives who had been imprisoned or exiled following the Greek Civil War
(1944–1949). They were led by the English wife of Tonis Ambatiellou, who
had already served 16 years of a life sentence. These people were seeking
official help in re-opening the old trials and securing the release of their
relatives. The Greek Queen, Frederiki, was in London at that time on
a private visit, and because of the known political power she wielded
in Greece they mounted demonstrations seeking her help. Lambrakis
himself wanted to see the Queen on their behalf, but she refused to
receive him.

On his return from England, Lambrakis organized the First Marathon
Peace March from Marathon to Athens. The march was banned. Nevertheless many people tried to complete it, and about 2,000 individuals
were arrested. Lambrakis completed the march alone since as an MP
he had immunity. Even so, at the end of the march he was arrested.
This prompted the newspapers to expresss the enormous public outrage

felt against the police and especially against those para-state groups whose complicity with the police was beginning to be revealed. Lambrakis's life now appeared to be under threat from these secret groups.

On May 22, 1963, he was invited to speak at a Nuclear Disarmament rally in Thessaloniki. He appeared at a meeting held in the headquarters of the Peace and Nuclear Disarmament Movement. As he left the meeting to be greeted by the people who had gathered outside, he was run down and knocked unconscious by a motorcycle. He was immediately taken to hospital but died four days later, on May 27, without regaining consciousness.

Lambrakis's body was taken to Athens by train. On May 28, 1963, half-a-million people attended his funeral carrying signs reading "Lambrakis lives" or "Every young person is Lambrakis". Lambrakis's death shocked the nation and for Greek youth in particular he became a hero. A movement called "Grigoris Lambrakis Democratic Youth" was formed only two weeks after his death. Mikis Theodorakis, the composer, was its first leader.

On Oct. 4 Lambrakis's assassins were brought to a trial which was to last two years. This trial brought into the open the existence of conspiratorial underworld forces which had been created when, in 1952, the Constitution provided for the right of free association. Spyros Kotzamanis and Emmanuel Emmanuelidis, who were the drivers of the motorcycle which had run down Lambrakis, had been members of the "League of Fighters and Victims of the National Resistance in Northern Greece", an extreme right wing para-state organization. Now that its purposes had been exposed by the trial, the Ministry of the Interior banned it as a criminal organization. The leader of the League, Xenophon Yosmas, was proved to have been the instigator of the assassination and was arrested. It was he who had recruited Kotzamanis and Emmanuelidis and provided them with identity cards issued by the Thessaloniki police. In 1946, although found guilty of collaboration with the Germans, he had never been punished. In 1957 he had worked in Athens with Fascist gangs.

A report published on June 22, 1963 found that the police outside the building next to where Lambrakis had been assassinated had made no move to protect or assist him, despite the fact that a demonstration against him was taking place outside the Peace meeting. During the trial Emmanuel Kapelonis, a gendarmerie officer, was exposed as the "moral instigator" of the incident. He was immediately arrested and when he decided to speak out he revealed that the demonstration against Lambrakis had been planned by Yosmas and the State Security Police of Thessaloniki. He also claimed that a high ranking officer who had visited him in prison had asked him to keep silent. This confession came as a bombshell and the trial was eagerly re-assumed.

Gen. Mitsiou, the Chief of State Police in Northern Greece, was proved to have known all about the plan to kill Lambrakis; he was arrested, together with 18 other officers, and charged with criminal negligence and abuse of authority. But in September 1968 Gen. Mitsiou and three other officers were released by the military Junta and re-appointed to their original positions in the Army. As for Kotzamanis, he was sentenced to 11½ years' imprisonment, but in November 1969 he was released by the Junta after serving only three-and-a-half years.

Political parties had begun to accuse Karamanlis of responsibility for the death of Lambrakis immediately after the event. Yiorgos Papandreou issued a statement in which he accused the Karamanlis Government of "moral responsibility" for the death of Lambrakis through its recognition of so many para-state groups. Karamanlis, nervous of these accusations, ordered an immediate inquiry, forcing the resignation of the Thessaloniki Chief of Police. The local police were accused of co-operating with Lambrakis's attackers. Demonstrations against Karamanlis flared up in the streets of Athens. Lambrakis's death was seen as a deliberate government action and for the Communists in particular he became a martyr. On June 1, 1963, Karamanlis resigned, ostensibly because of a disagreement with the King over the dates of the latter's official visit to London. Karamanlis tried to convince the King not to go to London during this period of domestic upheaval and when the Greeks of London had demonstrated such strong opposition to the monarchy.

MM

ASPIDA Affair (1964–66)

Constantine of the Hellenes, King (1964–1967).
Andreas Papandreou, son of the Prime Minister, Minister in the Prime Minister's Office.
Yiorgos (George) Papandreou, Prime Minister (1963–1965).

ASPIDA ("Shield") is the acronym of the (Greek) phrase "Officers Save Fatherland, Ideas, Democracy and Meritocracy". Under this name a conspiracy originating within the Greek Army was made public, involving politicians in its network and forcing Yiorgos Papandreou, the then Prime Minister, to quarrel with King Constantine and then to resign. The affair shook Greek society, which all of a sudden felt itself threatened by the Army's attempts to reform itself through association with left-wing ideas and to become a more independent body free of monarchist sympathizers. Right-wing and left-wing newspapers each made accusations against their respective political opponents, and a variety of conflicting views were expressed as to which army personnel were responsible for supporting the movement and its ideology. There began a trial, *in camera*, which ended in 1967 with the indictment of 28 army officers.

Yiorgos Papandreou came to power by a narrow majority in the November 1963 elections. To strengthen his position he called for fresh elections, which were held in March of the following year and which he won by an overwhelming majority. Immediately he began to implement economic and educational reforms which for a conservative country seemed daringly progressive, alarming conservative politicians and voters.

The King was the constitutional Commander-in-Chief of the Greek Armed Forces, many of whose most senior officers were closely associated with him, keeping up the long tradition of the Army's monarchist and right-wing outlook. Its loyalty to the king and its right-wing ideals seemed to Yiorgos Papandreou too limited and too conservative for it to be able to accept his more advanced domestic and foreign political reforms.

In January 1965 Gen. Grivas, former leader of EOKA (the militant wing of the Greek nationalist movement in Cyprus), reported to the King and to the Minister of Defence, Konstantinos Garouphalias, a secret leftist conspiracy among Greek Army Officers in Cyprus and the alleged implication therein of Andreas Papandreou. These reports were kept secret in Greece until newspapers started to disclose them, at the same time accusing Andreas Papandreou of being a principal figure among the Army conspirators. Yiorgos Papandreou was forced to start an official inquiry. Thus the so-called ASPIDA affair started to be uncovered in May 1965.

Papandreou, in his efforts to reform Greek politics, had attempted gradually to purge the Army of right-wing sympathizers. He set himself the task of replacing some of the older high-ranking right-wing officers with younger ones more sympathetic to his own political views. Konstantinos Garouphalias, as a conservative close to the King, used his position to ensure that Papandreou's liberal policies would not interfere with the King's position and the nation's security. So when Papandreou asked him to accept a list of Army transfers and retirements, and especially the replacement of the Chief of Defence Staff, Gen. Gennimatas, Garouphalias refused to do so, obviously suspicious of Papandreou's attempts to win the Army over to his side in order to pursue his policies free of its opposition. Papandreou dismissed Garouphalias, informing the King that he wanted to take over the Defence Ministry himself. The King accepted Garouphalias's dismissal but refused to accept Papandreou as Minister of Defence on the grounds that his son Andreas was under investigation for his alleged involvement in the ASPIDA affair.

Meanwhile the ASPIDA investigation continued, with Andreas Papandreou's name inextricably associated with it. Papandreou and the King exchanged letters defending their respective positions. Papandreou insisted that the King had exceeded his constitutional rights and was interfering in politics, while the King declared himself to be protecting the Army from political involvement. Papandreou told the King that he would resign, but in fact never presented a formal note of resignation. Even so the King requested the formation of a new government. This in effect forced Papandreou's hand and on July 15, 1965 he resigned. The King, after several attempts, managed in September of that year to form a new government under the leadership of Stephanos Stephanopoulos, Papandreou's Deputy Prime Minister. He had the support of the conservative ERE (National Radical Union), though by a majority of only two seats. Demonstrations in the middle of Athens followed Papandreou's resignation and right-wing politicians accused Papandreou's supporters of creating a common front with the Communists. Papandreou's party seemed to fall apart; many senior members resigned, Greek politicians were split between, on the one hand, the new Government and the Palace advisers who tried to maintain control and, on the other hand, Andreas Papandreou who had moved closer to EDA, denounced NATO and spoken out against the King and the USA. People in the streets were divided on the issue, which created heavy tension in the country.

The ASPIDA trial now continued under the new right-wing government, with many politicians eager to see Andreas Papandreou clearly implicated in the conspiracy. Andreas Papandreou was a deputy at that time and had immunity against any accusations. Lt.-Gen. Simou initiated investigations in Athens and Cyprus between May 1 and 25. After examining numerous witnesses, on June 1, 1965, he published his report. In it he stated that in Cyprus a movement called ASPIDA had been organized by a group of army captains for the purpose of mutual assistance within the army. Andreas Papandreou went to Cyprus in 1965 and in a report written by Gen. Grivas to Garouphalias, in May 1965, he was stated to have broken up the agreement the officers had built up amongst themselves and to have made accusations against officers belonging to ERE, the right-wing party. Simou also stated that it was not clear who was the leader and what were the purposes of its members. On June 8, 1965 he requested the punishment of those chiefly responsible for initiating officers into the ASPIDA organization. Garouphalias, the Minister of Defence, who was a prosecution witness, decided with Papandreou's agreement to send 10 officers before the investigating committee. Court martial proceedings were started against this group and it was found that there had been a plan to infiltrate the military forces with republican and socialist ideas. On Oct. 10, 1966, the results of the investigation into ASPIDA were issued in a 500-page special report based on the testimony of 645 witnesses. The entire investigation lasted 16 months.

In October 1966, 28 officers faced two charges: firstly, that of association for the purpose of rebellion; and secondly, that of conspiracy to execute an act of high treason. They were sentenced to terms of imprisonment ranging from two to 18 years. Thirteen were acquitted. Cols. A. Papaterpos, D. Chondrokoukis and P. Anagnostopoulos were found responsible for founding and supporting of the organization, the rest were considered agitators. The trial had begun on April 14, 1966 and lasted until March 16, 1967.

The Public Prosecutor, Konstantinos Kollias, wanted to lift the parliamentary immunity of deputies and make an open accusation against Andreas Papandreou, although no direct evidence could be found against him. It was obvious that with the dissolution of Parliament before the election campaign Andreas Papandreou would be under arrest. The Centre Union worked hard to pass a law extending parliamentary immunity during the election campaign. This shocked the caretaker government of Paraskevopoulos, who, refusing to accept such a plan, resigned. The King asked Konstantinos Kanellopoulos, the leader of ERE, to form an interim government until the next elections on May 28. But in the early morning of April 21 a group of Army officers led by Yiorgos Papadopoulos seized power, catching the King, the government and all politicians off guard and forcing many left-wing individuals into exile. The dictatorship of "the Colonels" was to last until November 1973.

MM

Papandreou Affair (1987–90)

Agamemnon Koutsogiorgas, Minister of Justice and Minister in the Prime Minister's Office in 1988 (resigned 1989).

Dimitra Liani, former air hostess, married to Andreas Papandreou in 1989.

Andreas Papandreou, Prime Minister (1981–1989).

Andreas Papandreou was born on Feb. 5, 1919. His father was the politician and former Prime Minister Yiorgos (George) Papandreou. He was educated at an American school in Athens and subsequently at Athens University, where he read Law. In 1939 he left Greece for the USA, where he lived for the next 20 years. In 1943 he received a doctorate in Economics from Harvard University, where he also taught. He became an American citizen and served in the navy in World War II. In 1951 he divorced his first wife and married Margaret Chad, a 25-year-old language student at the University of Minnesota. They had four children, Yiorgos, Sophia, Nikos and Andreas. In 1955 he became a Professor of Economics at the University of Berkeley, California. He returned to Greece in 1959 to establish the Centre of Economic Research. With Karamanlis's support he became adviser to the National Bank of Greece.

After his father had become Prime Minister following the February 1964 elections, and he himself an MP for the Achaia district, he became an adviser to his father and held various ministerial posts. In the 1977 elections Andreas Papandreou's PASOK Party (Pan-Hellenic Socialist Party) won 93 seats and became the official opposition to the New Democracy Party of Karamanlis. PASOK proclaimed radical socialist policies, including the idea of de-centralization and worker self-management. It also opposed Greek membership of the EC and was hostile towards NATO and to the presence of US military bases in Greece.

On Oct. 18, 1981 Andreas was elected Prime Minister. He tried to create a modern welfare state, but the country lacked the necessary resources. In 1984 he was re-elected, though by this time his socialist policies had been severely compromised. In 1987 Papandreou announced a series of new measures to halt the country's economic decline. Six of the largest Greek corporations were deeply in debt. Forty-three private companies in financial difficulties had been taken over by the State in 1983 and by 1987 they were closing down, with great job losses in consequence. For the first time in Greece VAT was introduced. Although public work programmes were announced, there was continual industrial unrest and high national unemployment. On Jan. 15, 1987, workers went on strike protesting against the meagre wage rises that Papandreou had promised.

In March of the same year a new crisis erupted when the Turks sent their ship *Sismic* to survey the Aegean for oil outside Turkish territorial waters, near the Greek islands of Lesbos, Lemnos and Samothrace. Papandreou put the Army on alert and also made the Americans believe that he would close the American bases if hostilities started. The situation created great fear in Greece but was eventually defused following a meeting of NATO ambassadors in Brussels.

1988 was the year that Papandreou's personal life severely damaged his party's image and that corruption scandals involving his ministers and close associates helped to erode his socialist policies. In September he travelled to Harefield Hospital in London with a serious heart condition. It took him two months to recover from a heart-valve replacement operation. With him in London was his lover, Dimitra Liani, a former air hostess whom he had met in 1986 and who had been his constant companion over the past months, accompanying him to summit meetings and other official functions instead of his wife Margaret. Photographs of Liani's private life and details of their liaison had been headline news in daily newspapers for months and had contributed to the fall of the PASOK Party.

On his return to Greece a month later Papandreou announced his intention of divorcing his wife Margaret, after 37 years of marriage, in order to marry Dimitra Liani, herself recently divorced from her second husband. Andreas Papandreou was 70 years old and Dimitra Liani 35. Thirty days after Papandreou obtained his divorce from Margaret, and three weeks after his electoral defeat, they were married at an Orthodox church in the Athens suburb of Ekali. None of Papandreou's children attended the wedding and no wedding reception was given afterwards. Papandreou's affair with Liani had been the focus both of serious criticism and of much salacious and satirical writing. As soon as they were married, however, the hostility and criticism evaporated. But the affair had already done much to damage Papandreou's image and that of the PASOK party to which his own fortunes had always been so closely tied.

It was while Papandreou was in hospital in London that the Koskotas scandal had broken out, revealing the economic corruption of Papandreou's ministers (see also *Koskotas Affair, 1988–90*, below). This scandal, which had so drastically influenced the political climate of Greece, was again discussed in Parliament. Papandreou now faced three charges. The first charge was that he had taken money from Koskotas via Louvaris while he was still in London for his operation, in order to conceal Koskotas's illegal activities. Much was made in the press of the testimony of one of Papandreou's former bodyguards that he had seen money slipped into a ministerial car in a nappy disposal bag — money said to have been paid by Koskotas. The second charge against Papandreou was that he had given an order to the head of DECO to deposit money in the Bank of Crete in 1988 when the bank was without funds and under investigation. The third charge was that he had given an order to his Minister of Economics, Dimitris Tsovolas, to settle the debts of Sokratis Kalkani (owner of the King George Hotel in Athens) and to guarantee for Papandreou the purchase of a plot of land in Rhodes by the Ionian Bank in co-operation with the Bank of Crete. Papandreou was also allegedly responsible for having instructed various State enterprises to deposit public funds amounting to some £50,000,000 in the Bank of Crete, all the while knowing the state of the Bank's affairs.

The Papandreou government was also accused, by Defence Minister Evstathios Yiotas, of other corrupt activities. These included the illegal re-sale to South Africa of firearms purchased from Italy ostensibly for sale to Paraguay, and the purchase of aircraft for the Greek Air Force at inflated prices, the proportionately higher commission allegedly paid to a consultancy firm (which upon inquiry turned out to be non-existent) presumably finding its way into various private accounts.

A further scandal in which Papandreou was indirectly implicated was the Yugoslavian corn scandal. In 1986, 20,000 tonnes of corn bought from Yugoslavia, and shipped from a Greek port, was sold to the European Community as Greek produce. The state trading company ITCO set up the fraud in order to avoid paying £600,000 in duties to the EC. It is alleged that Andreas Papandreou covered up the facts of this transaction, though he himself denies any part in the affair. The EC fined Greece $2,500,000 dollars for this fraud. In Greece the former Deputy Finance Minister, Nikos Athanassopoulos, along with Sotiris Apostolopoulos, the president of ITCO, its sales manager and four other finance ministers and customs officials were put on trial. In August 1990 Athanassopoulos was sentenced to three-and-a-half years' imprisonment. More convictions would follow.

The parliamentary investigating committee set up to investigate the Koskotas scandal also uncovered further corruption — extensive illegal telephone tapping allegedly instigated by Andreas Papandreou. Two state agencies, the National Information Service (EYR) and the Greek Telecommunications Organization (OTE) — both directed by Papandreou's confidants Kostas Tsimas and Theophanis Tombras — had carried out the telephone tapping of politicians, newspaper editors and journalists, and even members of Papandreou's own security guard. Papandreou's responsibility was traced to a former head of EYR who admitted that such activities would have been unthinkable without the Prime Minister's approval.

The various scandals severely weakened Papandreou's control over his government and party. There was great confusion in the country and demands for an election from the opposition parties and the Communists. Papandreou's eight years of power in Greece ended in the inconclusive elections of June 1989. After a fortnight of negotiations an interim government was established under Tzannis Tzannetakis, a conservative New Democracy back-bencher, with the support of a Communist coalition of the Left. The new government was committed to "katharsis" — a cleaning up of the scandals left behind by PASOK. New elections were set for November. Although Papandreou accepted political responsibility for the scandals, he denied any personal involvement, denouncing his accusers as irresponsible fanatics intent on the demolition of his party.

Judicial investigation of the corruption scandals associated with the Papandreou government continued throughout 1990, but with no clear evidence emerging against Papandreou himself.

MM

Koskotas Affair (1988–90)

Yiorgos Koskotas, a Greek American financier, owner of the Bank of Crete.

Agamemnon Koutsogiorgas, Minister of Justice and deputy Prime Minister (1988).

Andreas Papandreou, Prime Minister (1981–1989).

The Koskotas affair was a major economic scandal during the government of Andreas Papandreou, allegedly involving high-ranking politicians, including Papandreou himself, and throwing the entire economy of Greece into confusion (see also *Papandreou Affair, 1987–1990*, above).

Yiorgos Koskotas was a Greek American who came to Greece in 1983, and who within five years achieved immense economic power and political influence. Although only in his early 30s, he quickly impressed Greek society with his numerous activities and immense wealth. He bought the two right-wing newspapers *Kathimerini* and *Vrathini* with the aim of eventually turning them into organs of PASOK (Pan-Hellenic Socialist Party). He also controlled a radio station and was involved in "Olympiakos", one of the top football teams in Greece. He created "Grammi", a technologically advanced publishing company valued at 10 billion drachmas. Eventually, in 1984, he bought and became president of the Bank of Crete, the second largest bank in the country. His bank borrowed money from other Greek banks, paying out higher interest than the other banks, and his bank was always able to dispense large sums of money. He also bought properties in many Greek cities, with the idea of turning them into part of the MacDonald's business.

In 1986 Koskotas was introduced to Andreas Papandreou by Papandreou's son Yiorgos, who was then Minister of Education. Papandreou met him only three times, but Koskotas gave money to Yiorgos Louvaris, a personal friend of Papandreou who bought property for Papandreou in Athens.

In the summer of 1988 rival newspapers in Greece started publishing allegations concerning various irregularities in the Bank of Crete's affairs. Koskotas did not respond, relying upon the law which protected the confidentiality of deposit accounts. The idea was that the central Bank of Greece knew of these transactions but avoided any further investigtions on the grounds of not wanting to jeopardize the Bank of Crete's standing with depositors. A later investigation into Koskotas's affairs implicated Andreas Papandreou in the receipt of money to ensure that the Bank would be left untouched following the rumours of irregularities appearing in the newspapers. But the government, though under pressure to investigate the allegations against the Bank, changed the law so that these allegations would not go any further. This prevented the Bank of Greece from investigating Koskotas's illegal import of money from America. During the investigation, however, it was made clear by the Central Bank of Greece that two statements of accounts showing investments with major international investment banks were forgeries. This led to Koskotas being charged, on Nov. 3, 1988, with forgery and the embezzlement of $200,000,000. On Oct. 31 Koskotas had been forbidden to leave Greece while the investigation was in process. The Government had already accused him of trying to obstruct the legal process by preventing the release of documents detailing payments to leading members of the administration, including the Prime Minister's son.

On Nov. 5, 1988, despite strict surveillance by the security forces, Koskotas disappeared. It was never discovered who had organized his escape from Greece. He was traced to Brazil, but because there was no extradition agreement with Greece he was able to go to the USA, claiming that his life was in danger. But on arrival there he was arrested accused of financial corruption in the United States. Following this incident the Minister of Public Order in Greece resigned. On Nov. 11, the Minister of Justice, Athanasios Koutsogiorgas, also resigned, accused of illegal financial transactions with Koskotas. On Nov. 16 charges were brought against the Government, accusing some of its members of involvement in the Koskotas scandal. In the same year, in a confession broadcast from a private radio station in Athens, one Dimitris Stergiou accused a number of politicians of financial transactions with Koskotas. Evangelos Averoff and Konstantinos Mitsotakis, although they admitted they had met Koskotas in private from time to time, denied that they had ever accepted money from him.

In an interview given in prison in March of the following year and published in *Life* magazine, Koskotas claimed that between 1986 and 1988 the Bank of Crete had regularly paid quantities of the Bank's funds to PASOK officials. Also he directly implicated the Prime Minister. To this Papandreou made no response and even promoted Koutsogiorgas to the office of Minister in Charge of the Prime Minister's office. Papandreou dismissed the Minister of Education and Religious Affairs, Stephanos Tzoumakas, for criticizing his government. By December 1988 there was a series of resignations and five outgoing ministers accused Papandreou's government of inertia in the face of corruption charges.

In June 1989 Papandreou was defeated after eight years in power. In the summer of 1989 Tzannis Tzannetakis, the Prime Minister of the coalition government, called for the prosecution of Papandreou and three members of his cabinet — Agamemnon Koutsogiorgas, Yiorgos Petsos and Dimitris Tsovolas — for their part in the Koskotas affair. Parliament voted in a secret ballot to set up a commission of inquiry; if sufficient evidence existed legal action would be taken against them. Agamemnon Koutsogiorgas, Deputy Prime Minister, was accused, under the law concerning ministerial responsibility, of accepting bribes and assisting a criminal. The accusation was that £200,000,000 had been paid into a Swiss bank account in Koutsogiorgas's name after he had changed the law in order to protect Koskotas from investigation by the Bank of Greece. Koutsogiorgas replied that he did not know how the money had found its way into his account.

Yiorgos Petsos, Minister of Transport, was also accused of contravening the law of ministerial responsibility concerning bribery. He was another who had received money from Koskotas. He gave orders to the general director of the Post Office (ELTA), to the manager of the Greek Telecommunications Organization (OTE) and to the director of Olympic Airways to deposit large sums of money in the Bank of Crete at the time the Bank was without funds. He also illegally granted a licence to Koskotas to build an extension to the publishing company Grammi's building in Pallinini in Attica.

Dimitris Tsovolas, Minister of Economics, was also accused of settling debts owed by Sokratis Kalkanis, owner of the King George Hotel in Athens, which was deeply in debt to the State. Koskotas wanted to buy the hotel free of debts. Tsovolas worked through illegal means to secure a guarantee from the Bank of Crete which enabled Kalkanis to clear his debts to the State and Koskotas to buy the hotel.

Eleni Vlachou, the well-known newspaper owner, was another of those implicated in the Koskotas scandal. When she sold the newspaper *Kathimerini* to Koskotas, she received only half the money in Greece, the rest being deposited by the Bank of Crete in her name in an English bank, contrary to Greek law. She too said she had no idea how the money had got into her account.

The trial of those implicated in the Koskotas scandal, including Koskotas himself, is set for January 1991.

MM

HUNGARY

Imre Nagy Affair (1956–58)

Yury Andropov, Soviet ambassador to Hungary (1954–57); general secre-
tary of Communist Party of the Soviet Union, President of the USSR
Supreme Soviet Presidium (1982–84).
János Kádár, leader of Hungarian Socialist Workers' Party (1956–88);
Prime Minister (1956–57, 1961–65).
Gen. Pal Maleter, Defence Minister (November 1958).
Imre Nagy, Prime Minister (1953–55, October–November 1958).

On June 16, 1989, a painful chapter in Hungary's history was brought to a
close when, at a state funeral in Heroes' Square in Budapest, the Hungarian
nation laid properly to rest Imre Nagy, the man who had led it in its failed
uprising against Communist totalitarianism and Soviet domination in 1956.
There had been a rush towards Nagy's rehabilitation in the space of only
a few months, coinciding with the beginnings of Hungary's rejection in
1989 of one-party Communist rule and its transformation into a multiparty
democracy.

Imre Nagy was born into a peasant family at Kaposvar in 1896. Drafted
into the Austro-Hungarian army in World War I, he was captured by the
Russians, and after the 1917 Bolshevik revolution he joined the Bolshevik
party and fought in the Red Army, returning to Hungary only in 1922.
He was summoned to Moscow in 1930 to explain unorthodox views on
agricultural reform expressed by him at the second Hungarian Communist
Party congress in Vienna (the party was banned inside Hungary, then
under the right-wing Horthy regime), and remained there working as
an agricultural scientist until being mobilized in World War II. During
this period he rose within the hierarchy of the Hungarian Communist
Party, and in December 1944 he was named Agriculture Minister in the
provisional coalition government established at Debrecen in the wake of
the Soviet invasion of Hungary, serving also in coalition governments (in
which the Communists increasingly held sway) formed after elections in
1945 and 1947. Elections in 1949 ushered in one-party Communist rule,
but in August of that year Nagy was excluded from the government and
from the politburo of the Hungarian Workers' Party (HWP, formed in
1948 by the merger of the Communist Party with the Social Democratic
Party) for opposing the immediate collectivization of agriculture.

He was readmitted to the topmost ranks of the party and government
after 1951, and in June 1953 became Prime Minister upon the resignation of
Mátyás Rákosi (who remained general secretary of the HWP). During the

next two years Nagy instigated a number of important measures to mitigate
the repressions which had characterized Rákosi's premiership, including
abandoning the policy of compulsory agricultural collectivization, closing
internment camps, releasing political detainees, and permitting a partial
return to private enterprise. In April 1955, however, Nagy was deposed
from the premiership and deprived of party membership after his "new
course" economic policy had been violently denounced as "right-wing
deviationist" and "anti-Marxist". Following Nikita Khrushchev's denunciation of Stalin in February 1956, Rákosi was replaced as HWP leader by
Ernö Gerö, and Nagy (who had taken up a teaching post) was readmitted
to party membership.

Mass demonstrations broke out in Budapest and other cities on Oct.
22–23, 1956, in support of a return to democracy, the withdrawal of
Soviet forces from Hungary, and Nagy's reinstatement as Prime Minister.
An attempt by Soviet troops to suppress the demonstrations provoked a
popular uprising which spread throughout the country. As a concession,
Nagy was reappointed Prime Minister on Oct. 24, while János Kádár succeeded Gerö as HWP first secretary on the following day. Nagy announced
on Oct. 31 that Hungary would leave the Warsaw Pact and pursue a
policy of absolute neutrality, and on Nov. 3 he formed a government in
which all the political parties existing in 1945 were represented, together
with the Hungarian Socialist Workers' Party (HSWP), newly formed by
Kádár on the basis of the HWP. On Nov. 4 the Soviet army launched a
massive offensive, and immediately afterwards Kádár defected from Nagy's
government and was named as head of a puppet HSWP government set up
with Soviet backing (the then Soviet ambassador to Hungary and thus a
protagonist in the suppression of the revolt was Yury Andropov, who was
much later to become Communist Party leader and President of the Soviet
Union). By Nov. 10 the revolt was crushed, and a brutal "normalization"
programme was instituted.

Nagy sought refuge in the Yugoslav embassy on Nov. 4 with a number
of his political associates and their families, but on Nov. 22, after Kádár
had given written and verbal assurances to the Yugoslav government that
Nagy and his associates would be allowed to return to their homes without
molestation and that no action would be taken against them, they left
this sanctuary voluntarily. Despite Kádár's promise, however, Nagy and
his associates were abducted by Soviet troops shortly after leaving the
Embassy in a bus made available by the Hungarian authorities. On the
following day they were deported to Romania. The Yugoslav government
issued strongly-worded protests to the Hungarian and Soviet governments,
but was reportedly told in reply that the Hungarian government considered
that Nagy had left for Romania voluntarily, and insisted that the matter was
solely within Hungarian jurisdiction.

In a broadcast on Nov. 26 Kádár, while attacking Nagy for having
countenanced a "murderous counter-revolution" and for having "deserted
his post" by taking refuge in the Yugoslav embassy, explained: "Imre
Nagy, who legally left the territory of his country by stepping into the
Yugoslav embassy, later asked to leave the country entirely . . . . After
the Romanian government said that it was prepared to give him sanctuary,
he and his party left for Romania on Nov. 23. Despite his grave deeds, we

plan no criminal proceedings against him, and we will keep that promise. We do not consider him permanently exiled. But we think it better that he remain outside the country for the time being, because some of the many counter-revolutionaries who are still in hiding might assassinate him and try to place the blame on the government."

Nothing more was heard of Nagy and his associates until the announcement in Budapest on June 17, 1958, that Nagy had been sentenced to death and executed after trial by a "people's court". The announcement also stated that Gen. Pal Maleter (the Defence Minister in Nagy's Cabinet, who had been arrested on Nov. 4, 1956, while conducting negotiations at the invitation of the Soviets for their withdrawal from Hungary) and the journalists Jozsef Szilagyi and Miklós Gimes similarly had been sentenced and executed, and that five others had been given prison sentences ranging from five years to life.

The announcement stated that the accused had been charged with unleashing a "counter-revolutionary armed revolt" with the aim of overthrowing the legal order of the Hungarian People's Republic. In addition Nagy, who was accused of having plotted the revolt since December 1955, had been charged with treason and Maleter and Sandor Kopacsi with mutiny. According to the announcement, Nagy, Maleter and Szilagyi had protested their innocence to the end, but the other defendants had pleaded guilty.

Kádár was sidelined to a purely ceremonial post in the HSWP leadership in May 1988, and reformers began increasingly to hold sway in the party. At the end of January 1989 Imre Pózsgay, the most outspoken reformist in the HSWP politburo, threw the party into a state of crisis when he disclosed that a HSWP central committee historical commission, of which he was chairman, had produced a report reappraising the 1956 revolt not as a "counter-revolution" but as a "popular uprising . . . against an oligarchic system of power which had humiliated the nation".

It was announced on Jan. 26, 1989, that Hungary's parliament had authorised the exhumation of the remains of Imre Nagy and of other people executed following the 1956 uprising, so that their families might conduct proper burial services. The remains of Nagy were disinterred on March 29 from an unmarked plot in a Budapest cemetery, and shortly afterwards the remains were also disinterred of Maleter, Szilagyi, Gimes, and Geza Losonczy, a close associate of Nagy who had died in prison while awaiting trial.

The state funeral on June 16, 1989 (the 31st anniversary of Nagy's execution), was attended by some 300,000 people. The remains of Nagy, Maleter, Szilagyi, Gimes and Losonczy were reinterred, and an empty coffin was buried with them to symbolize the 245 other persons who had been executed in the aftermath of the uprising. Wreaths were laid by Hungary's Prime Minister Miklós Nemeth, by Pózsgay and by the parliamentary speaker Mátyás Szürös. All Warsaw Pact member states except Romania sent delegations to the funeral (although the Soviet delegation was of only junior rank), and it was widely reported in the official media in those countries. In particular the Soviet media reported, in the words of Moscow home service, that Nagy and the others had been "executed under the sentence of an unjust court" and that their "humane" reburial would "serve the purpose of national reconciliation".

On July 6, 1989, Nagy's rehabilitation was completed when the Supreme Court declared null and void the verdicts handed down at the trial in 1958. The court accepted a petition by the chief public prosecutor that no crimes had been committed by Nagy and his co-defendants, since their activity aimed at changing the existing social system had not violated the Constitution. Ironically, Kádár died on the same day as the Supreme Court passed its judgment.

IPG

INDIA

Maruti Affair (1977–81)

Indira Gandhi, Prime Minister.
Sanjay Gandhi, head of the Maruti company.

The Maruti affair revolved around the business activities, political ambitions and lifestyle of Sanjay Gandhi, youngest and favourite son of Indira Gandhi, India's Prime Minister 1966–77 and 1980–84, and was presented as evidence of the misuse of power by the Gandhi family.

The Maruti company had been surrounded by controversy since its inception. The company had been formed in 1969 to build a locally designed and produced compact car for the domestic market. Sanjay Gandhi, then aged 23, had been given the licence to produce the Maruti in the face of 17 other competitors, many of them major national companies. Sanjay's only engineering experience came from an incomplete apprenticeship with Rolls-Royce, and his financial backing was limited. Questions were also raised about the acquisition of the land for the factory, seen by many as a political gesture by the then Chief Minister of Haryana to gain favour. Design and production of the car soon ran into difficulties and only a handful were actually produced. Instead the factory concentrated on building bus bodies to fulfil contracts placed by state governments. The rumours surrounding the Maruti car company and the other companies formed by Sanjay with the Maruti name intensified as Sanjay's political career and influence grew.

Sanjay Gandhi's aggressive and populist image earned him both many supporters and many enemies. He soon became a close confidant of his mother and attained substantial political influence without holding any formal position. As leader of the Youth Congress he was heavily involved in the unpopular mass sterilization campaign during the state of emergency (1975–77).

After Mrs Gandhi's defeat in the 1977 general election the Janata Party government announced on May 29 the creation of an inquiry, headed by D. S. Mathur, a former Chief Justice of the Allahabad High Court, into the affairs of Maruti. The inquiry was to investigate how the licence had been obtained, how the land for the factory had been obtained, the company's foreign exchange transactions and evidence of any bribes or "kickbacks". Sanjay's passport was confiscated and loans to the company frozen in an attempt to retrieve some of the money. Sanjay had already been convicted on charges of criminal conspiracy surrounding the destruction of an anti-Indira Gandhi film, although he was to be released later after a successful appeal. Mathur resigned in July and was replaced by Justice Alak Chandra Gupta. The company was ordered to be wound up by the state government on March 6, 1978. Liabilities totalled Rs 60 million, and as there was no product the company was judged to have few business prospects.

The commission reported on May 31, 1979. It revealed numerous improprieties committed by the company during its history. Among its conclusions the report stated that Sanjay Gandhi had ignored the conditions of the licence prohibiting foreign goods or collaboration in the production of the car as the prototype had been fitted with an imported engine for its official road test. The car had subsequently been approved by the Heavy Industry Ministry in spite of proving unroadworthy. It also criticized the way in which Maruti had obtained the land for its factory at a low price from the state government of Haryana after local farmers had been dispossessed. Objections from the Defence Ministry about the siting of the plant near to military installations had also been disregarded. Maruti's financing activities had also circumvented the standard procedures for raising share capital and there had been no public issues of shares. The report concluded by saying that the way in which Maruti had achieved its ends and the way in which it had received favourable treatment from politicians and government officials displayed evidence of the close interest of Mrs Gandhi in the company. It said that "one is left in no doubt as to the origin of the power that made such a state of affairs possible. Mr Sanjay Gandhi exercised only a derivative power; its source was the authority of the Prime Minister".

The Maruti Affair, although damaging to the reputation of the Gandhis, was, in the light of the collapsing Janata coalition in 1979, quickly super-seded by events surrounding Mrs Gandhi's dramatic return to power. Sanjay's influence with his mother grew strongly as he played an impor-tant role in securing her return to government and his own position as "heir-apparent", supported by a clique of like-minded followers. He also secured his own election to Parliament for the first time. But on June 23, 1980, he was killed in an aircraft accident when the plane in which he was performing aerobatics crashed over New Delhi. On Oct. 14 the government nationalized Maruti in order to prevent the completion of the bankruptcy proceedings and on July 28, 1981, the Cabinet formally rejected the findings of the commission's report.

LP

Bofors Affair (1987–89)

Martin Ardbo, managing director of AB Bofors.
Win Chaddha, manager of Anatronic General Corporation.
Rajiv Gandhi, Prime Minister (from 1984).

The Bofors Affair effectively ruined Rajiv Gandhi's reputation for being "Mr Clean", and played a major part in the opposition campaigns against him leading to the election victory of the National Front in November 1989, in spite of the lack of direct evidence of his personal involvement. ·

Rajiv Gandhi was born on Aug. 20, 1944, the eldest son of Mrs Indira Gandhi, Prime Minister of India 1966–77 and 1980–84. Unlike his younger brother Sanjay, Rajiv kept out of politics and pursued a career as an airline pilot. The sudden death of his brother in a flying accident in mid-1980 led to his rapid advancement as "heir-apparent" in the Nehru family dynasty. In 1981 he won his brother's parliamentary seat of Amethi in a by-election and became General Secretary of the Congress (I) Party in 1983. Following his mother's assassination by Sikh extremists in October 1984 Rajiv Gandhi was immediately put forward as Prime Minister. In the subsequent general election he secured a massive majority, capitalizing on the sympathy vote for the Gandhi family. Rajiv was also seen by many as representing a new generation of younger politicians and technocrats, untainted by association with the past and with corruption.

By early 1987 this reputation for incorruptibility was growing tarnished after a series of allegations, in particular those surrounding illegal payments connected with defence contracts. A ruling made in 1980 by Mrs Gandhi had forbidden Indian middlemen or the payment of commission in negotiations for defence contracts. In April the Defence Minister, V. P. Singh, resigned after criticism of his investigations into illegal commissions paid in defence contracts and in particular a deal involving the purchase of West German submarines. He had earlier been moved to the Defence portfolio from Finance, where he had also aroused controversy by hiring a US detective agency to investigate corruption. Many loyalists in the Congress Party saw this latest inquiry as a criticism of Rajiv Gandhi who had previously held the Defence portfolio himself.

It was in this political climate that a Swedish radio station on April 16 broadcast allegations relating to a contract signed in 1986 with the Swedish company, AB Bofors, for 400 155 mm howitzers. The station alleged that Bofors had made payments totalling US$4.6 million into Swiss bank accounts as bribes to senior Indian officials and defence personnel to secure the contract. The Indian government denied the allegations but asked Sweden to investigate. Sweden agreed to Indian requests for the Swedish national audit bureau to carry out an investigation.

The report of the bureau, apart from some sections classified as secret, was passed to the Indian government and thence to the press on June 4. It suggested that commissions had been paid to Indian nationals, although Bofors had stated that they had been in connection with "winding-up" payments for deals made before the reiteration by Rajiv Gandhi to the

Swedish government in late 1985 of the rule that no middlemen or agents should be involved in contract negotiations. The amounts totalled about 2 to 3 per cent of the total order (about US$32 million). The report did not, however, mention any names, apart from that of the Anatronic General Corporation, which had acted as agent for Bofors in India and which had been engaged to assist with what were termed "administrative services".

The Bofors Affair was seized upon by opposition politicians who attempted to force a debate on the issue when parliament reconvened at the end of July. Rajiv Gandhi vigorously denied allegations that he had personally received "kickbacks" in the deal. On Aug. 6 a parliamentary committee was established to investigate the issue. Most opposition groupings boycotted the committee complaining about its lack of powers. The repercussions of the affair also affected the Congress (I) Party. In mid-July V. P. Singh and three other Congress MPs were expelled from the party, freeing Singh to pursue an anti-corruption campaign through the states.

The president of Bofors, Per Ove Morberg, and other senior officials of the company, appeared before the parliamentary committee in September. He said that Bofors had provided the Indian government with the names of three non-Indian companies that had been recipients of "winding-up" payments, but refused to give details of the arrangements. Win Chaddha of the Anatronic Corporation also appeared before the committee and denied receiving any "winding-up" payments or any connection with the three recipients. An investigation by the Swedish public prosecutor, started in August 1987, was dropped in January 1988 citing a lack of evidence. The parliamentary committee reported on April 26, 1988 and stated that there was no evidence of middlemen or of any payments, apart from the "winding-up" costs. Opposition members staged a walk-out in protest.

The affair refused to go away, however, and in July the *Hindu* newspaper published a series of documents which it alleged identified the companies through which money had been paid. It also claimed that one of them had a close working arrangement with the Anatronic Corporation. A report by the Comptroller and Auditor General on July 18 criticized the government's handling of the affair, but exonerated Rajiv Gandhi from personal responsibility. The opposition demanded another parliamentary inquiry into the issue. When Gandhi refused their calls to resign, 71 opposition MPs resigned en masse.

In October the *Hindu* published what it claimed were parts of the Swedish national audit bureau report that had been kept secret. These allegedly showed evidence of payments to Chaddha in May 1986 of "commission" totalling US$26 million. Further extracts, said to be from the diary of Martin Ardbo, then managing director of Bofors, provided links between payments and a "Gandhi Trust Fund".

These revelations helped build up the affair into a major issue during the election campaign and were a factor in the defeat of Gandhi's Congress (I) Party in the election held on Nov. 22–26, 1989. In December V. P. Singh, as the new Prime Minister, promised to uncover the full facts about the affair. On Jan. 22, 1990 the Central Bureau of Investigation filed preliminary charges, including those of criminal conspiracy and corruption, against Chaddha, Ardbo and G. P. Hinduja, a London-based businessman.

LP

IRELAND

Arms Smuggling Affair (1970)

Charles Haughey, government minister from 1961, later Prime Minister.

The election of Charles Haughey as Prime Minister of the Irish Republic in December 1979 marked one of the most extraordinary political comebacks of modern times. Less than a decade earlier he had stood in the dock of a Dublin court, charged with conspiring to smuggle arms into the country. The prosecution alleged that the weapons were to have been passed to Nationalists in Northern Ireland to defend themselves against possible attacks by Loyalists. It was assumed by many that this meant the arms could have ended up in the hands of the most notorious of the Republican terrorist groups — the IRA. Although Haughey and his three co-defendants were acquitted, few observers doubted that his once promising political career was at an end. But they were reckoning without the tenacity and determination which made Charles Haughey such a survivor.

Charles Haughey was born on Sept. 16, 1925 in Castlebar, County Mayo, where his parents had taken refuge after Protestant raiders burned the family farm in the northern county of Derry. After studying accounting and law in Dublin, he worked as an accountant and dabbled in real estate, ultimately amassing a fortune from land transactions. Elected to the *Dáil* as a representative of the *Fianna Fáil* party, Charles Haughey became Minister of Justice in 1961. He was later appointed Minister for Agriculture and Fisheries and by 1970 he had become Minister of Finance.

If Haughey's rise was rapid, his fall was even quicker. In late April 1970, the *Fianna Fáil* Prime Minister, Jack Lynch, was informed by the police of a plot to smuggle arms into Dublin from the Continent. Since there was evidence implicating Haughey and the Minister for Agriculture and Fisheries, Neil Blaney, Lynch interviewed both ministers and subsequently asked for their resignation, stating that it was essential that no suspicion should attach to any member of the Government on a matter of this kind. Both ministers denied the allegations and refused to resign, whereupon they were dismissed. The Minister for Local Government, Kevin Boland, resigned in protest at their treatment.

Little more than three weeks later, on May 28, the sacked ministers were arrested and brought before Dublin District Court, charged with conspiring to import unlawfully arms and ammunition. Blaney was discharged through lack of evidence, but Haughey and three others were committed for trial.

The appearance of so senior a figure in a trial of this nature was eagerly awaited by the international media, but the event was to be an anti-climax at first. The trial was less than a week old when the judge discharged the jury and ordered a new trial on the grounds that one of the defence counsel had questioned his impartiality. The new trial began on Oct. 9 and this time the waiting journalists were not disappointed. The allegations outlined by the prosecution went to the heart of the troubled politics of Ireland — specifically, to the debate about how best to help the embattled Nationalist population in Northern Ireland who were perceived to be facing persecution from the Loyalists, backed up by the British authorities.

The prosecution case began with Haughey's co-defendants. James Kelly, an intelligence officer with the Irish Army, was said to have visited Northern Ireland in the course of his duties and to have met John Kelly, the chairman of the Belfast Citizens' Defence Committee, a group protecting the interests of the Catholic community. The two had conceived a plan to get arms to the Committee by arranging for consignments to be brought through Dublin without being examined by customs. The prosecution alleged that Haughey had been approached with this idea and had issued orders that two cargoes of weapons should be exempt from customs scrutiny. The fourth defendant, Albert Luykx, was the director of a firm to which the consignments were to have been taken.

According to the prosecution, the first consignment was to have arrived in Dublin on board a merchant vessel, the City of Dublin, on March 25, 1970. Guns and ammunition were to have appeared on customs documents as "mild steel plate" but the cargo was never loaded due to difficulties with the customs in Belgium. The second attempt was to have involved arms flown into Dublin Airport on board an Aer Lingus plane on April 17 or shortly thereafter. The prosecution maintained that Haughey had ordered the abandonment of this attempt after the Justice Department had raised objections to the proposal to exempt the cargo from customs inquiries.

The prosecution case was backed up by witnesses from various government departments and agencies who testified to conversations involving the four defendants. The defence claimed that most of these conversations were ambiguous and contradictory and failed to prove that the four had been involved in a joint enterprise. During his time in the witness box, Haughey said he had indeed given blanket permission for certain arms imports to be exempt from customs examination — but only because he believed that James Kelly's request for him to do so had the official backing of the Irish Army. He denied granting specific permission for the two projects outlined by the prosecution. On Oct. 23 the jury found all four defendants not guilty and they were carried shoulder-high from the court room by well-wishers.

There followed three years in the political wilderness for Charles Haughey before he re-entered the *Dáil* in 1973. *Fianna Fáil* lost that election, but four years later they were returned to Government and he was made Minister for Health and Social Welfare. In 1979, faced with runaway inflation, a large balance of payments deficit and a series of crippling strikes, Prime Minister Lynch resigned. Two days later Charles Haughey became *Fianna Fáil* leader and he was formally elected Prime Minister a week after that. He served until election defeat in 1982 and was returned to office in 1987.

RSD

ISRAEL

Two features characterize political scandals in Israel — most if not all are connected to the great strategic issues and conflicts that plague the young state; and many also bear the hallmark of long-standing feuds between a small elite of ambitious politicians, often within the same party.

Founded as the world's only Jewish nation on May 14, 1948, Israel has since been at a state of war with all its Arab neighbours, apart from Egypt after 1979. After independence, the new state was invaded from all sides but survived. Some 750,000 Arabs from old Palestine fled or were expelled, leaving a Jewish majority within Israel but also a refugee problem that still exists. The dual threat from Arab state armies and Palestinian guerrillas and terrorists makes national security a priority. It was a perceived breach in this security that spawned the first major scandal in Israel — the Lavon Affair.

Lavon Affair (1954–64)

David Ben-Gurion, Prime Minister (1955–63).
Chaim Cohen, Supreme Court Judge, head of 1960 inquiry.
Moshe Dayan, Chief of Staff.
Ya'akov Dori, former Chief of Staff, joint head of 1955 inquiry.
Benjamin Jibli, Chief of Military Intelligence.
Pinchas Lavon, Defence Minister till 1955, Director-General of the *Histadrut* till 1961.
Yitzchak Olshan, Supreme Court Judge, joint head of 1955 inquiry.
Shimon Peres, Director-General of the Defence Ministry.
Moshe Sharett, Prime Minister (1953–55).

Although the Lavon Affair reached its climax in 1960–61, its origins lay in an event that happened in 1954; and its repercussions led to the resignation of Prime Minister David Ben-Gurion in 1963. The affair set a model for future security scandals and exacerbated political divisions.

When Gamal Abdel Nasser took power in Egypt in 1954 he verbally attacked Israel and demanded that Britain vacate the Suez Canal Zone. Some Israeli Defence Force (IDF) personnel thought Britain should be stung into action against Israel's chief enemy. To this end the IDF Intelligence Branch sent secret agents into Egypt and launched a clandestine firebombing campaign on July 14. But a week later things backfired — almost literally — when a bomb that one agent carried in his pocket ignited prematurely at a Cairo theatre. He was arrested and Egypt Radio announced the discovery of an Israeli spy-ring.

While officially Israel called the whole affair a "base libel" perpetrated by Egypt, Prime Minister Moshe Sharett and Chief of Staff Moshe Dayan soon found out it was true. They subsequently denied any hand in planning the operation, but their initial response to the news was to keep quiet.

The trial of six Israelis and two Egyptian Jewish allies opened in Cairo on Dec 11. Max Bennett, Israel's highest ranking spy who covered as a German businessman, was arrested in Egypt, and committed suicide on 21 Dec., the day before he was to stand trial. On Jan. 27, 1955 two of the other Israelis were sentenced to death and four to long terms of imprisonment. Meanwhile in the Israel Supreme Court Justice Yitzhak Olshan and ex-Chief-of-Staff Ya'akov Dori opened a secret commission of inquiry. Defence Minister Pinchas Lavon was rumoured to be behind the campaign. Some said he hid details of the operation from colleagues, notably Dayan and the Director-General of the Defence Ministry, Shimon Peres, even going to the length of forging official documents. When such rumours appeared in the Israeli press, Lavon accused Dayan and Peres of prompting the leaks.

On Jan. 13, 1955 the two-man commission concluded: "We. . .have not been convinced beyond a reasonable doubt that the Chief of Intelligence [Benjamin Jibli] did not receive orders from the Defence Minister [Lavon]. However, neither are we sure that the Defence Minister actually issued the orders ascribed to him." Lavon offered to resign, but threatened to publicly reveal his motives. Fearing this would open a new can of worms within the ruling *Mapai* (Labour) Party, Sharett urged Lavon to retract his resignation, but he would only do so if Jibli and Peres were dismissed. When Sharett refused to accede to this demand, Lavon formally resigned on Feb. 2.

The details of the Egyptian operation were kept from the public, who were told that Lavon had resigned because of misgivings over the structure of the Defence Ministry and the IDF. Jibli resigned too, and Lavon became Secretary-General of the influential *Histadrut* labour federation. But divisions within *Mapai* refused to go away. The moderate Sharett was criticized for poor leadership, and Ben-Gurion, who had retired as Prime Minister in December 1953, was recalled to the Defence Ministry on Feb. 17, 1955. *Mapai* lost ground in the mid-July elections and Ben-Gurion resumed his premiership on Nov. 2, 1955.

The storm seemed to have abated, but then in mid-1960 Lavon took what he called "new evidence" to Ben-Gurion. It was information given to him by former IDF Intelligence Branch officer Col. Yosef Harel which suggested that Jibli had forged documents to exonerate himself from the "unfortunate business", and instead shift the blame onto Lavon. After two months' investigation, Ben-Gurion's Military Secretary accepted that forgery had taken place, and ordered a new board of inquiry, to be headed by Supreme Court Judge Chaim Cohen.

Lavon demanded that his name be cleared immediately, and this time he had the popular press on his side. Ben-Gurion rejected his demand, but as pressure grew he allowed Lavon to testify before the *Knesset* (Parliamentary) Foreign Affairs and Defence Committee. There Lavon accused the whole defence establishment of "economic imperialism" and inefficiency. He blamed Jibli for planning the Egyptian sabotages, and Dayan and Peres for betraying him before the 1954 Dori-Olshan Commission. Peres returned from abroad to defend himself, saying he had testified in secret in 1954 on orders from the commission chairman. Lavon retorted that it had been "beneath his dignity to consult Dayan and Peres" at the time. Ben-Gurion staunchly defended Peres, and soon found himself attacking Lavon directly.

The Cohen Commission concluded that there had indeed been forgeries and pressures leading to perjury; but Ben-Gurion, now convinced that Lavon was at least as much to blame as Jibli, demanded a legal investigation. Compromise proposals were brushed aside, and on Oct. 30, 1960, Justice Minister Pinhas Rosen set up a committee of seven ministers. But it exceeded its brief by asking who gave the original order for the sabotage campaign. Peres and Dayan grew worried, and approached Ben-Gurion to resolve the issue once and for all. On Dec. 21 the committee found that "Lavon did not give the order and [the affair] was not executed with his knowledge". A furious Ben-Gurion damned the committee as "biased" and called its conclusions "devoid of truth and justice". Flying in the face of *Mapai's* near-universal acceptance of its findings, Ben-Gurion insisted on a full legal inquiry. When that was not granted he submitted his own resignation on Jan. 31, 1961. New rumours even suggested that Israeli spies were double agents.

Fearful of losing Ben-Gurion, still the national hero albeit now tarnished by his stubborn attitude, the *Mapai* Central Committee met secretly on Feb. 4 and agreed to dismiss Lavon as head of the *Histadrut*. Ben-Gurion was appeased and stayed on as Prime Minister, but the seeds of mistrust and recrimination were sown. On June 16, 1963, the weary Old Man resigned as Prime Minister and was replaced by Levi Eshkol. Soon afterwards Ben-Gurion came across new evidence incriminating Lavon, but on May 2, 1964 Eshkol revoked the 1961 decision to dismiss Lavon. When the Attorney-General backed Ben-Gurion's call for a legal investigation, Eshkol threatened to resign. Soon afterwards Ben-Gurion came across new evidence incriminating Lavon, but on May 2, 1964 Eshkol revoked the 1961 decision to dismiss Lavon. When the Attorney-General backed Ben-Gurion's call for a legal investigation, Eshkol threatened to resign. In an ironical replay of Ben-Gurion's own proffered resignation in January 1961, the cabinet backed Eshkol. Ben-Gurion resigned to form the new "Rafi" party in 1965, but his political force was spent and in time the party was re-absorbed into the Labour Alignment.

LJ

Rabin Affair (1977–80)

Aharon Barak, Attorney-General, head of initial inquiry.
Shimon Peres, second-in-command of Labour Party.
Leah Rabin, wife of Yitzchak Rabin.
Yitzchak Rabin, Prime Minister and leader of Labour Party.
Yehoshua Rabinovich, Finance Minister.

Levi Eshkol led Israel to its crushing victory in the 1967 Six Day War, when
it occupied vast territories previously in the hands of Egypt, Jordan and
Syria. Golda Meir became Prime Minister after Eshkol's death in 1969.
Following Israel's near-defeat in the 1973 Yom Kippur War, she and
Defence Minister Moshe Dayan resigned after an inquiry criticized the
nation's lack of war preparedness. Yitzchak Rabin ensured that Labour's
rule continued as it had done since independence, but he was dogged
by his "Mapai" party rival Shimon Peres whom he had beaten in the
leadership battle.

Rabin tried to patch up bruised national morale and restore an economy
suffering from wartime losses, an Arab oil boycott and inflation. Menachem
Begin's *Likud* opposition expected to pick up disgruntled Labour voters in
the election set for May 17, 1977. His popularity grew among the poorer
Sephardic Jews, Oriental immigrants who felt excluded from the Ashkenazi
establishment and suffered inflation the worst. As terrorist attacks on
Israel and Israelis overseas increased, *Likud's* tough advocacy of Jewish
settlements in the territories appealed to those seeking strong leadership,
while Rabin seemed unable to control even his own Cabinet.

Finance Minister Rabinovich introduced a new tax system in late 1976
designed to net the many self-employed businessmen thriving in Israel's
"black economy". Just then a rash of scandals implicated top officials in
misappropriation of public funds. A fortune went missing from the Britain-
Israeli Bank. Asher Yadlin, Labour's new appointee as Governor of the
Bank of Israel, received five years' imprisonment for accepting bribes and
filing a false income tax declaration. And on Jan. 2, 1977 Avraham Ofer,
the Housing Minister, committed suicide after a barrage of unsubstantiated
reports in the popular press alleged that he had tampered with the finances
of the *Histadrut* Housing Company when he was its director-general.

But worst of all, on the eve of the 1977 election and less than a month
after Rabin had again narrowly defeated Peres in party leadership elections,
he and his wife Leah were themselves accused of breaking an Israeli law by
keeping a bank account in New York. It was an event which sealed the fate
of three decades of Labour rule.

A Treasury regulation forbade citizens to keep foreign currency accounts
abroad, ostensibly to stop "black market" gains being spirited away. When
reports emerged in the *Ha'aretz* newspaper on March 15, 1977 that such
an account existed in the name of Mrs Rabin, the Treasury ordered an
inquiry. Yitzchak Rabin had been Israel's ambassador to Washington from
1968 to 1973, and the account was, he said, the balance of their savings from
that period. Rabin's lawyer contacted the Finance Ministry and submitted

details about the account. The law did not specify what actions the ministry could take if guilt were established, so Rabinovich appointed a committee to look into this matter. Normally for amounts under $5,000 the courts did not level criminal charges and only imposed a fine, so Attorney-General Aharon Barak assured Rabin there was little to worry about.

But when he discovered there were two bank accounts totalling $23,000, Barak told Rabin he had no choice but to place Leah on trial and demand a full Foreign Currency Division committee investigation, with representatives of the Ministries of Finance, Police and Justice present. On April 5 this latter committee ordered the Rabins to pay a fine. Before Leah's trial Barak tried to dissuade Rabin from sharing responsibility with his wife, but Rabin rejected this; and on April 7 he withdrew his nomination as candidate for Prime Minister. (Israeli law disallows caretaker Prime Ministers from resigning, and as cabinet chairman Peres became effective party leader.) Leah was tried by district court and on April 17 was fined 250,000 Israeli pounds. A month later *Likud* beat Labour in the general election. Rabin won more popular support in adversity than he did in power, but smarted from a perceived smear campaign by Peres. On Nov. 22, 1980 he accused the French magazine *L'Express* of libel for alleging that a shady Tel Aviv businessman, Bezalel Mizrachi, lent him money to pay Leah's fine. Rabin implicated Peres in the affair and had him sign an affidavit to prosecute the publication jointly. The paper retracted its story, but only after an Israeli inquiry revealed Rabin had another foreign bank account totalling $73,000. Peres resoundingly beat Rabin in party elections that year, and went on to become Prime Minister in later years, though Rabin re-emerged as a strong Defence Minister under Shamir in the 1980s. In 1990 opinion polls showed Rabin to be the most popular politician in the country, but at the time of going to print Peres had still prevented him from unseating him as party leader.

LJ

Flatto-Sharon Affair (1977–83)

Menachem Begin, Prime Minister (1977–83).
Samuel Flatto-Sharon, Member of *Knesset* (1977–81).
Ya'akov Halfon, his campaign manager.

The case of Flatto-Sharon was a quirky affair centred on an eccentric criminal, but it raised profound questions about the efficacy of Israel's political and legal system. Born in Poland in 1930, Samuel Flatto came to France after surviving the Nazi holocaust. He grew into a wealthy financier, but when charged with fraud involving hundreds of millions of francs, he fled to Israel in 1972. Under the Israeli Law of Return, all Jews throughout the world can claim instant Israeli citizenship. But the law is meant to serve genuine immigrants or refugees fleeing persecution, not criminals. To avoid possible extradition back to France, Flatto-Sharon (as he was now called), decided in 1977 to stand as a one-man party list for the *Knesset* (Parliament). If elected he knew he would have immunity.

Standing as the "Peace and Development Party" under the slogan "the lonely man to the *Knesset*", Flatto-Sharon, who could hardly muster a word of Hebrew, won enough votes to justify two seats in the 160-seat *Knesset*, and joined the new *Likud*-led government. He won public sympathy as an alleged victim of French anti-Semitism, but his success was also due to the wealth and expertise of his campaign manager, Ya'akov Halfon. The latter had held high rank in the *Mapai* (Labour) party and especially fund-raising bureaucracy. Before the election and during the Yadlin trial (see Rabin Affair, 1977–80) Halfon claimed that political parties had received the equivalent of US$40 million "under the table" to finance campaigns. Meanwhile Flatto-Sharon was raising funds for a task force to track down Ugandan President Idi Amin.

Soon there were allegations that Halfon had "bought votes" for his candidate, but it was not until May 1979 that the Attorney General levelled five charges of contravening the election law and one of conspiracy against Halfon, Flatto-Sharon and another colleague. Apparently the candidate has promised flat accommodation for young couples (during a mounting housing crisis), and had actually paid up to US$30 per vote. Others claimed he bought votes via leaders of ethnic groups.

But as long as Flatto-Sharon was an MK (Member of the *Knesset*), he could not be prosecuted. In August 1979 the Knesset voted by 61 to 31 to remove his immunity. This did not mean that he would be extradited, only brought to face the Attorney General's charges. The *Jerusalem Post* newspaper suggested that 30 MKs voted for him for fear of what his trial would reveal about their own electoral malpractices, and Halfon threatened to prove how he had "vote-contracted" in the same way for the main parties in previous elections. The Israeli State Comptroller (ombudsman) duly demanded a full review of existing election laws, especially those regarding finance.

In September French authorities convicted Flatto-Sharon *in absentia* for fraud, forgery and tax evasion, but Israel still refused to allow his extradition. Relations between the two countries deteriorated in October 1980 after the bombing of the Rue Copernic synagogue in Paris. Israeli Premier Begin held the "anti-Zionist" policy of the French government responsible, and Flatto-Sharon called for an Israeli vigilante force to defend European Jewish communities from further attack.

Flatto-Sharon re-entered the headlines that year, accused of smuggling expensive stolen cars from Israel to Egypt, and burying them under the Sinai desert until "the heat was off". This time the MK was more co-operative with the authorities — after all, one of the buried cars, a US$80,000 Mercedes complete with television and bar, was his own. On May 11, 1981,

Flatto-Sharon became the first MK to be convicted of electoral bribery, and was sentenced to three years' imprisonment with 27 months suspended. The *Knesset* house committee voted to suspend his parliamentary membership, but the High Court of Justice overruled this. Flatto-Sharon nonetheless failed to be re-elected in 1981 and again in 1984. On Jan. 11, 1983 he lost his appeal to overturn his bribery conviction; though on June 27 the Supreme Court reduced his sentence to 18 months in prison with all but three months suspended, which he served as a "day prisoner" from October. As a bizarre tailpiece to the affair, French security forces arrested him in Italy on Oct. 28, 1985, but the ever-enterprising Flatto-Sharon escaped in disguise to Israel the next April. He continues to appear in the news, most recently in 1990 as a salesman for a perfume called "Eau de Flatto". In the same year new allegations of vote-buying and misappropriation of political party funds have been levelled at Rabbi Aryeh Der'i, leader of the religious Sephardic "Shas" party and a key member of Shamir's government.

LJ

Kahan Commission Affair (or Sabra and Chatila Massacre Affair) (1982–83)

Menachem Begin, Prime Minister, (1977–83).
Raphael Eitan, Chief of Staff.
Bashir Gemayel, President of Lebanon and leader of the Christian *Phalange*, assassinated before the massacre in 1982.
Yitzchak Kahan, Supreme Court Judge.
David Levi, Deputy Prime Minister.
Yitzchak Navon, President of the State of Israel.
Yehoshua Saguy, head of Israeli Military Intelligence.
Yitzchak Shamir, Foreign Minister.
Ariel Sharon, Minister of Defence (later Minister Without Portfolio and Minister of Trade and Industry).

On June 6, 1982, a week after signing the final peace accords with Egypt, Israel invaded Lebanon in an operation called "Peace for Galilee". The pretext was the attempted assassination of Israel's Ambassador to Britain, but in fact Israel had long wanted to wipe out the Palestine Liberation Organization (PLO) military presence in southern Lebanon. For years its *fedayeen* had raided Israel from an area nicknamed "Fatahland" after the

PLO faction. Israel had retaliated before, but never had they gone so far. Instead of stopping at the Litani River, the Israeli Defence Forces (IDF) drove on to the capital, Beirut, base of PLO Chairman Yasser Arafat.

Documents revealed later show how divided the Israeli Cabinet was about the extent of the invasion, but the hawkish Defence Minister Ariel Sharon prevailed. After fierce battles and heavy civilian casualties the PLO was forced to vacate Lebanon. Most PLO troops had left by September, but hundreds of thousands of other Palestinians remained in crowded refugee camps.

Among the biggest was Sabra and Chatila, on the outskirts of Beirut and near the headquarters of their implacable enemies in the seven-year old civil war, the Christian Lebanese *Phalange*. Nominally the region was under IDF control, so it was assumed that whatever happened there was Israel's responsibility. On Sept. 16, the day after the newly elected Christian President of Lebanon Bashir Gemayel died in a bomb blast, *Phalange* troops entered the camp and began a three-day massacre, killing an estimated 700 or 800 people. As soon as news reached Israel, some 350,000 furious citizens rose up in the largest protest seen in the country. Many were related to troops embroiled in what was rapidly becoming an unpopular war, but until then no one major incident had focused their anger. They demanded to be told if the IDF knew of the *Phalange's* plans, or even directed the massacre?

Prime Minister Menachem Begin denied that there was any Israeli involvement, as international leaders had alleged. "*Goyim* [non-Jews] kill *goyim* and they come to hang the Jews", he said. But Jewish protest grew in Israel — President Navon demanded an investigation and 100 IDF officers called on Sharon to resign; the Liberal Minister Yitzchak Berman resigned in protest, as did Menachem Milson, the West Bank Civil Administrator, and Gen. Amram Mitzna. Begin rejected Labour opposition calls for an inquiry, but after the National Religious Party threatened to leave the coalition government, Begin on Sept. 28 agreed to a full commission of inquiry under Supreme Court Justice Yitzchak Kahan, assisted by former Attorney-General Aharon Barak and Brigadier-General Yonah Ephraim.

The commission called 48 witnesses in all before publishing its 122-page report on Feb 8, 1983. It concluded that Israel did not order the massacre, but senior officials should and could have prevented it. During the hearings Prime Minister Begin had admitted overseeing a Cabinet decision to allow the *Phalange* in, though later evidence showed they were already there and the Cabinet effectively rubber-stamped this. Now both he and Foreign Minister Shamir were castigated for delegation of responsibility, and not having heeded Deputy Prime Minister David Levi and others' warnings of a possible massacre. Defence Minister Sharon "disregarded acts of revenge", erred in allowing the *Phalange* into the camp and so did not act as a responsible minister should have done. Kahan recommended that he resign. Chief of Staff Raphael Eitan was held to be guilty of a breach of duty, IDF Intelligence Head Yehoshua Saguy was dismissed for his "indifference, and closing of his eyes and ears"; two senior IDF officers were sacked for gross negligence. Kahan criticized the decision-making process of the army and government which prevented Begin being informed of the excesses (he learnt about it from BBC Radio).

Sharon was the only minister to vote against accepting the report. One anti-Sharon demonstrator became the first Jew in Israel to die in a protest when a bomb exploded at a rally on Feb. 10. Sharon resigned his defence post on Feb. 13, but stayed on the periphery of the Cabinet as minister without portfolio (a precedent repeated in 1990 when Ezer Weizmann was sacked for talking to the PLO). As a tailpiece to the saga, Sharon, by now rehabilitated as Trade and Industry Minister, sued the US *Time* magazine for slander after it said he knew more, and began a prolonged case against it in New York. *Time's* defence lawyers referred to an unpublished annex of the Kahan Commission, though when this annex was read it did not bear out their allegations. Sharon won the case, but had to pay huge costs — a Pyrrhic victory at best. In subsequent years he has risen in the *Likud* establishment to challenge Shamir for leadership from the right, and was largely responsible for rejecting the Baker Peace Plan and so scuttling the *Likud*–Labour coalition government of 1989–90.

Israeli reaction ranged from shame at the massacre to resentment that there should be an inquiry at all. In between were those who believed that the very fact of the inquiry somewhat vindicated Israel's constitutional status as unique in the Middle East. The Sabra-Chatila incident spawned a number of new peace groups, and internal pressure was a major factor in forcing the IDF to withdraw most units from Lebanon by 1985.

LJ

Shin Bet Affair (1984–88)

Moshe Arens, Defence Minister.
Moshe Bar-Kochba, Maj.-Gen. in charge of the bus-storming party.
Yosef Harish, successor to Zamir.
Yehudit Karp, Assistant Attorney-General.
Moshe Landau, Supreme Court Judge, head of 1987 inquiry.
Moshe Levy, Chief-of-Staff.
Avraham Shalom, head of *Shin Bet* (Israel's internal intelligence service).
Yitzchak Zamir, Attorney-General till 1986.
Meir Zorea, former Maj.-Gen. and officer in charge of the initial 1984 defence department inquiry into the bus raid.

The mid-1980s were a time of violent terrorist attacks on Israel and her citizens abroad. Palestinians were frustrated at the lack of progress towards peace talks and Israel's continued occupation of the territories. Israel in turn was frustrated by the PLO's ability to regroup in south Lebanon and launch cross-border raids — it was precisely to prevent this that she had invaded

Lebanon in the first instance. While Israeli security vigilance is legendary, Israeli law has a broad remit to prosecute excessive action by her forces. In 1984 one incident threw into relief the division between legalists and the military, and within Israeli society.

On April 12 four guerrillas attacked a bus carrying 35 passengers en route from Tel Aviv to Ashkelon. They released a pregnant woman who raised the alarm. Israeli Defence Forces (IDF) marksmen chased the bus and shot out its tyres near Rafah in the Gaza Strip. The attackers demanded safe passage to Egypt and the release of 500 PLO members from Israeli prisons, but negotiations broke down after 10 hours and soldiers stormed the bus. Two guerrillas and one passenger were killed, and seven passengers were wounded. Within hours an Israeli newspaper alleged that the hijackers had been captured alive and subsequently killed, a view supported by the deceased parties' relatives and eyewitnesses.

On April 27 Defence Minister Moshe Arens ordered a secret departmental committee of inquiry headed by retired Maj.-Gen. Meir Zorea. A month later it concluded that the allegations were by and large true — both of the hijackers had died from blows sustained *after* the gun battle. Arens condemned the behaviour of the security forces, which he said was "in clear contravention of the rules and norms incumbent on all".

There things may have been left, but on June 1, 1985, Chief-of-Staff Moshe Levy formally reprimanded Maj.-Gen. Moshe Bar-Kochba about the incident. Two days later police launched their own inquiry under Yonah Blattman to determine who the guilty soldiers were. Brig.-Gen. Yitzchak Mordechai was identified and Attorney General Yitzchak Zamir ruled that he should be prosecuted. But on Aug. 18, 1985, a military disciplinary board acquitted him of "violent behaviour", finding him not "unreasonable" in pistol-butting the hijackers as he feared they may have left a bomb on board the bus. In June, Zamir had upset the right wing by insisting that Jewish underground terrorists be prosecuted for murder; now he angered the right again with his liberal views. Determined to get to the bottom of the bus incident, Zamir felt sure the *Shin Bet*, the internal security and counter-intelligence service, was suppressing evidence.

After an internal *Shin Bet* disciplinary hearing, three of the highest-ranking officers, Reuven Hazak, Peleg Radai and Rafi Malka, testified that their boss had forced them to lie, and tried to get Mordechai to shoulder responsibility for the bus incident. They insisted that he resign and take the blame, which Zamir told Peres, Rabin and Shamir. Due to retire, Zamir chose to stay on despite protests from politicians.

Traditionally the head of the *Shin Bet* is a secret appointment, but the American television ABC News revealed the name of the chief, Avraham Shalom (whose surname translates as "peace" in Hebrew). Zamir forced the Cabinet to order a police inquiry into Shalom's role on May 25, 1986; but after insisting Shalom be prosecuted, Zamir was replaced as Attorney General by Yosef Harish on June 1. Prime Minister Peres and Foreign Minister Shamir both opposed a prosecution. Peres conceded that a secret inquiry may be useful, but Shamir, premier at the time of the original incident and who some said actually authorised the killings, called for the investigation to end, saying "the security service needs secrecy like humans need oxygen". To him the killings were at worst an accident.

In February 1984 a Cabinet commission of inquiry under Assistant Attorney-General Yehudit Karp issued a report on human rights violations in the occupied territories, which the *Likud* government had only released in December 1985. Now Karp alleged that Shalom had lied to the Zorea and Blattman investigations. On June 25, 1986, Shalom resigned after President Herzog granted him and his three colleagues immunity from prosecution (Yosef Hermalig, former chief from 1964 to 1974, was recalled to replace him). Immediately the Labour wing of the coalition government protested that the President had no right to pardon them before guilt had been admitted. Karp showed that Shalom had posted Yossi Ginossar as a fifth column on the Zorea Commission. In his defence Shalom said he was merely acting according to an understanding reached with the then Premier Shamir in 1983. On July 2, 1986, the Supreme Court asked the government why there had been no investigation, and six days later Shalom admitted before the court that he had indeed "worked to conceal the roles of the *Shin Bet* men in the killings of the terrorists." On July 14 the cabinet agreed a compromise — a police investigation into *Shin Bet* rather than a full state inquiry — though a former Treasury minister left the Cabinet in protest at Peres's insistence on an inquiry.

The Karp report unleashed a welter of accusations from people mis-treated by *Shin Bet*, notably an informer, Nafsu Izat, who was falsely held for seven years as a suspected PLO double agent; and an IDF private, Daniel Shoshan, forced to confess to a crime he did not commit. New Attorney-General Yosef Harish pursued these and other cases. A commission of inquiry on May 31, 1987, headed by Justice Moshe Landau, produced the toughest ever findings levelled at Israeli intelligence. While acknowledging *Shin Bet's* "devotion", Landau said that for 16 years it had deliberately misled Israeli courts on a "norm based on false testimony" and threatened to "destroy Israel's reputation as a law-abiding state". Only when its officials lied to their own internal inquiry was the full extent of the corruption revealed, said Landau.

The upshot of the affair was a tarnished reputation for *Shin Bet*, and persistence of bus hijackings; on March 7, 1988, PLO forces overran a bus en route to the sensitive Dimona area (see *Vanunu Affair, 1986–88*) and in July 1989 a Palestinian killed 16 when he forced a bus over a ravine. On Nov. 12, 1987, Harish ordered an investigation into the death in *Shin Bet* custody of Awad Hamdan in July, and on Feb. 18, 1988, he called for the agent responsible to stand trial. The Palestinian *intifada* in the occupied territories began in December 1987, and remains active. *Shin Bet* was blamed for not anticipating it, despite their network of Palestinian collaborators, hundreds of whom have since died in the violence. On March 27, 1988, Hermalig was suddenly replaced as head of the *Shin Bet*. Amnesty International has reported deaths by summary execution, reminiscent of the original bus incident. In March 1989 *Shin Bet's* newly pragmatic top brass joined other intelligence leaders to call for cabinet negotiations with the PLO — but its agents continued to spread disinformation in the territories in an only partly successful bid to stifle the *intifada*.

LJ

Vanunu Affair (1986–88)

Shimon Peres, Prime Minister (1984–86).
Margaret Thatcher, UK Prime Minister.
Mordechai Vanunu, former technician at the Dimona nuclear plant.

In none of the Arab-Israeli wars have any of the parties threatened the use of nuclear weapons, for the simple reason that, despite rumours to the contrary, none of them admit to having any. For her part Israel has never signed the Nuclear Non-Proliferation Treaty. Hence her profound embarrassment when the British *Sunday Times* of Oct. 5, 1986, quoted an Israeli nuclear physicist who claimed to have evidence of an arsenal of up to 200 thermonuclear bombs built up over 20 years.

A Moroccan-born Jew, Mordechai Vanunu, had worked since 1976 at Israel's sole atomic energy generation plant in Dimona, deep in the Negev desert in southern Israel. In 1982 the previously apolitical Vanunu suddenly joined left-wing and pro-Palestinian causes and felt guilty over his involvement in the nuclear programme. In November 1985 he was dismissed from Dimona, and left for Australia where he converted to Christianity. There he met a Columbian journalist, Oscar Guerrero, who persuaded him to sell his story and photographs to the *Sunday Times*. It now appears that when he left Australia for Britain, Australian security forces tipped off their Israeli counterparts, *Mossad*.

While Israel denied the newspaper report, British nuclear experts confirmed that Vanunu's account seemed technically accurate. Prime Minister Peres met leading Israeli journalists and won their promise to keep a lid on the affair, but the meeting was leaked. What happened next has all the hallmarks of a James Bond film. On Oct. 20, 1986, the US *Newsweek* magazine said that Vanunu had been captured by *Mossad* agents after a blonde woman called Cindy lured him onto a yacht in the Mediterranean. Other reports said he had been packed in a crate and taken to Israel as diplomatic baggage, reminiscent of Nigeria's Dikko incident (see Nigeria: *Dikko Affair, 1983–84*).

Whatever the case, on Nov. 9 the Israeli government confirmed that Vanunu was "lawfully detained" in Haifa and had attended a court hearing. By now rumours abounded in Britain that UK Prime Minister Margaret Thatcher knew well in advance of Israel's intention to catch Vanunu, and had sanctioned her own security forces to co-operate with *Mossad*. Under pressure from MPs the British government asked Jerusalem how Vanunu had arrived back in Israel. On Nov. 14 it was told that he had left voluntarily and that no UK laws or regulations had been broken. Yet while being driven to a Jerusalem court Vanunu was photographed showing his hand on which he had written "I was hijacked in Rome".

After a secret trial, on March 27, 1988, Vanunu was sentenced to 18 years' imprisonment for treason and disseminating information with intent to damage the security of the state. The magistrates were not convinced that he had acted out of ideological motives, and hence did not impose the death penalty (the ultimate sentence for treason, though never to date used). Vanunu appealed to the Supreme Court, but ultimately lost his case on May 28, 1990. The 89-page report explaining the decision remains secret. In September 1988 a leading Italian magistrate, Dominico Sica, claimed that Vanunu was himself a *Mossad* agent, and that the whole affair had been deliberately staged to scare Israel's Arab foes over her nuclear strength.

Most regard this as too far-fetched. Indeed, *Shin Bet* (Israel's internal security service) was known to be embarrassed about giving Vanunu security clearance in the first place; *Mossad*, by contrast, was proud of their role in abducting him. (In September 1990, however, *Mossad* was embarrassed by the publication of a book by the Canadian Ostrovsky, a former agent, who alleged that the organization used extreme subterfuge and murder to achieve their ends.) The affair suggested close links between British and Israeli intelligence; although in later years Britain was to expel *Mossad* agents after serious incidents, and angered Israel by criticizing her over the Palestinian issue. The longer-term repercussions were to confirm that Israel probably does have a highly sophisticated nuclear arsenal which may deter aggressors like Iraq from attack. In the late 1980s Israel showed off her long-range rockets and even launched satellites into space. As for Vanunu, his case has been adopted by Amnesty International and Israeli civil rights activists, though most of his compatriots still see him as a traitor.

LJ

Bank Leumi Affair (1984–90)

Dr Moshe Beijsky, Supreme Court Judge and head of the initial inquiry.
Eli Hurwitz, successor to Japhet.
Ernest Japhet, Managing Director of Bank Leumi, dismissed in 1986.
Moshe Mandelbaum, Governor of the Bank of Israel.
Yitzchak Moda'i, Finance Minister since 1988.
Shimon Peres, Prime Minister (1984–86).
Yitzchak Shamir, Prime Minister (1983–84); (1986–present).
Yitzchak Tunik, State Comptroller.

Likud had benefited from the financial shenanigans which brought down Labour in 1977, but in power were far from immune to such scandal themselves. In 1981 the Religious Affairs Minister, Abu-Hatzeira, was indicted for accepting bribes while distributing funds to religious institutions. He was convicted and resigned in April 1982. Elected on a free enterprise ticket, *Likud* presided over massive inflation. In October 1983 the Tel Aviv stock exchange itself collapsed after a sudden rush to withdraw shares. Banks who had encouraged unprecedented private speculation could not honour their shares. Prime Minister Shamir immediately devalued the shekel and halved government subsidies, began nationalizing the banks and appointed a public commission under Supreme Court Justice Dr Moshe Beijsky, which reported in April 1986.

Bank Leumi, Israel's largest bank with assets of $22.2 billion at the end of 1985, seemed to be the worst offender. In August 1984 the government charged it and the three other major banks of forming a cartel to illegally depress interest rates on bank deposits held by the public in 1983. By January 1985 dozens of customers started suing Bank Leumi for misleading them into buying shares just before they collapsed. The State Comptroller, Yitzchak Tunik, blamed the government for turning a blind eye when banks bought their own share issues and lent money to potential investors. Between 1977 and 1983 banks boosted their stock by $116 billion by expanding overseas operations.

By now a *Likud*–Labour coalition was in power struggling to contain inflation which had topped 450 per cent in 1984, and Israel desperately sought $5 billion-worth of aid from the USA. A rash of fraud cases was reported involving Bank Leumi overseas — in October 1983 a dividend manager was charged with stealing $5 million from his New York investment company and depositing it in accounts at Bank Leumi, Fifth Avenue; in March 1984 a telex operator and businessman at *Crédit Suisse* in London were jailed for sending a false computer message to deposit $7 million in Bank Leumi, Geneva; in June 1986 four were indicted for fraud of $11 million by depositing invoices from bogus companies in Bank Leumi, New York; and in August 1987 two senior officials of the same branch were sentenced for embezzlement and acceptance of bribes.

On April 20, 1986, the Beijsky report called for the resignation of the governor of the Bank of Israel (the central bank), Dr Moshe Mandelbaum, and criticized former finance ministers, Yoram Aridor and Yigael Hurwitz, for not curbing banks engaged in dubious share regulation practices. It also called for the removal of the heads of four banks, including Ernest Japhet of Bank Leumi. The report welcomed restrictions on capital movements out of the country, and urged that commercial banks be barred from managing provident funds.

Three weeks later Japhet resigned and was replaced by Eli Hurwitz, but in May he argued that hyper-inflation compelled banks to "regulate their own share-prices". The scandal was far from over — on Aug. 13 police started investigating reports that Leumi and others had set up front companies in Switzerland and the Dutch Antilles to finance illegal purchase of their own shares between 1977 and 1983. And on Jan. 9, 1987 Bank Leumi's new board of directors temporarily suspended Japhet's excessive severance pay of $4.5 million and pension of $30,000 per month. After 10,000 bank employees went on strike in protest at the payments the board voted to resign en masse. Prime Minister Shamir tried but failed to postpone this action. Political opponents saw this as an attempt to shield his coalition partner, Liberal Party leader Ari Dulczin, who was implicated.

On April 10 Bank Leumi's new board began court action against Japhet, demanding the return of payments he had received. On June 30 a court froze $2.5 million in assets belonging to Japhet, now resident in New York. Meanwhile Bank Leumi reported that its earnings had fallen by 95 per cent in 1986.

American creditors now demanded the return of money they had lost by loaning to Israeli banks, and in February 1989 the Israeli Government struck a deal with wealthy *kibbutzim* (collective farms) to raise $400 million owed to them. Between 1985 and 1989 the government spent $7 billion buying back shares from the public. On March 2, 1990 Yitzchak Moda'i, Finance Minister in the new post-coalition right-wing government, announced a change — the four major banks would be sold back to the public over the next two years. To maximize proceeds they would be broken up and lose all non-banking operations. Government spokesmen admitted they were unlikely to recoup more than $2.5 billion of the taxpayer's money used to buy back shares, but clearly it felt it had to disengage from the banking minefield. Between them the four banks control three-quarters of Israel's non-governmental business, so a successful resolution is vital for the future.

LJ

ITALY

Lockheed Affair (1976–79)

Gen. Duilio Fanali, former Chief of Air Staff.
Luigi Gui, Christian Democratic politician and former minister.
Giovanni Leone, President of the Republic.
Mario Tanassi, Social Democratic politician and former minister.

The effects of the revelations by the Lockheed Aircraft Corporation that it had paid bribes to politicians were felt in many countries (see also Japan: *Kakuei Tanaka/Lockheed Affair, 1976–86*; Netherlands: *Prince Bernhard/Lockheed Affair, 1976*). In Italy the scandal led to the first conviction of a Cabinet minister on a charge of corruption. It also led indirectly to the resignation of the President, Giovanni Leone, and left the Italian body politic tainted with scandal.

In February 1976 evidence was brought before the subcommittee on multinational corporations of the US Senate's Foreign Relations Committee that the Lockheed Aircraft Corporation, one of America's major aerospace companies, had given payments to politicians in a number of foreign countries in connection with deals for the purchase of its aircraft.

In reference to Italy the evidence presented on Feb. 4 concerned two former ministers of defence, Luigi Gui and Mario Tanassi, who were alleged to have received over US$700,000 in payments related to the purchase of 14 Hercules C-130 transport planes by the Italian Air Force in 1969.

On April 2 an Italian parliamentary committee opened an inquiry into the allegations against the two men. In the meantime, as a result of the allegations against them, Gui had asked not to be included in the new government being formed by Aldo Moro, while Tanassi had been defeated as party leader at the annual congress of the small Social Democratic Party (PSDI). A number of other figures in the scandal, not protected by parliamentary immunity, were arrested. These included Gen. Duilio Fanali, Chief of the Air Staff at the time of the purchase and Camillo Crociani, president of the state-owned company Finmeccanica.

Allegations were also made in the press that one of the Christian Democratic Prime Ministers in the period between 1965 and 1969 (Aldo Moro, Giovanni Leone and Mariano Rumor) had accepted payments as well. It was in this atmosphere of rumour that Aldo Moro's minority government collapsed on April 30.

On Dec. 1, the commission laid charges against Gui and Tanassi of "serious corruption", together with former Prime Minister Mariano Rumor. The charges against Rumor were later dropped, but the parliamentary immunity of Gui and Tanassi was lifted to allow them to be prosecuted. Charges against Leone by the small Radical Party of involvement in the Lockheed Affair were rejected by the commission.

The trial of the two ex-ministers, plus nine others (and two *in absentia*), opened on April 10, 1978. It concluded on March 1, 1979 with Tanassi receiving a sentence of 28 months' imprisonment and the loss of his parliamentary seat. Gui, by contrast, was aquitted. Of the other defendants, five were sentenced to terms of imprisonment ranging from 18 to 28 months, including Gen. Fanali.

In June 1978 Giovanni Leone, who was coming to the end of his term as President of the Republic, resigned before the expiry of his term after a sustained press campaign linking him to the Lockheed affair and other financial scandals. The left-wing newspaper *L'Expresso* led the campaign, publishing allegations about Leone and his family. He was closely linked with the Lefebvre brothers who had acted as lawyers in the deal and who were then facing trial. Leone denied the allegations, but his resignation was seen by some as a tacit admission of guilt.

LP

Banco Ambrosiano Affair (1981–85)

Roberto Calvi, banker and president of Banco Ambrosiano.
Flavio Carboni, Sardinian businessman.
Licio Gelli, grand master of the P-2 masonic lodge.
Archbishop Paul Marcinkus, president of the Vatican Bank.

The collapse of Italy's largest privately owned bank, Banco Ambrosiano, in the summer of 1982 was the biggest banking failure in Europe in the post-war period. The financial scandal was compounded by the mysterious death of the bank's president, Roberto Calvi, and the revelations about his activities, spanning at least a decade and involving, among others, the Vatican's own bank. The fate of Calvi and Banco Ambrosiano was also linked with that of the secret masonic lodge P-2, which was discovered in 1981. The scandal raised numerous questions about Italian financial and business methods and also raised questions about the judgment of the Vatican authorities, including, ultimately, that of the Pope himself.

Roberto Calvi was born in 1920 and, after World War II, pursued a career as a banker, joining the Milan-based Banco Ambrosiano. He rose steadily to become its managing director and then president in the 1970s. Calvi had a secretive and dour personality, but proved a clever and efficient financier. He was the mastermind behind the bank's expansion into merchant banking by using front companies (often based abroad) to circumvent the banking laws preventing banks from buying directly into non-banking companies. In this way Banco Ambrosiano was transformed into Italy's largest bank in private hands, and one of the country's major financial institutions. In 1971 Calvi acquired control of La Centrale which was to become the vehicle for the expansion of Banco Ambrosiano's domestic ambitions. These included the Credito Varesino, the Banco Cattolica del Veneto and the Toro insurance group. The complex dealings and share transfers involved in Calvi's numerous deals did not go unnoticed, however, and were investigated by the central Bank of Italy during 1978 and 1979. Further investigations were derailed by scandal at the Bank of Italy itself during 1979. Calvi had also been involved in the deals made by Michele Sindona, a Sicilian-born financier, who had been made bankrupt in 1974 and who had fled the country to avoid arrest on charges of fraud and false accounting. Sindona continued to operate from New York, but in 1979 he was finally arrested and tried in the USA and sentenced to 25 years' imprisonment.

Sindona had introduced Calvi to the Vatican Bank, known as the Institute for Religious Works (Instituto per le Opere di Religione — IOR), and its president, Archbishop Paul Marcinkus, and managing director, Luigi Mennini. The IOR, with its special status and obsessive secrecy, provided an ideal route for Calvi's operations in transferring money abroad and then back to Italy. For the IOR, Banco Ambrosiano was a respected bank with good Catholic credentials (it had been founded by a Catholic priest), and the bank's expansion under Calvi brought enhanced revenues to the Church, which needed money to meet its rising expenditure. The IOR's keenness to diversify its holdings outside Italy meant that Marcinkus was willing to allow the IOR's money to become involved in Calvi's convoluted dealings, as long as it benefited the Holy See.

In the mid-1970s Calvi also became a member of the secret masonic lodge Propaganda Due (P-2), and a close friend of its grand master, Licio Gelli. Calvi used his position as a banker to help P-2 members, for example by providing support for the Rizzoli publishing group (whose senior executives were also P-2 members) and its influential daily newspaper, *Corriere della Sera*. In April 1981 La Centrale acquired 40 per cent of Rizzoli (which by then was in serious financial trouble) for a total cost of 176 billion lire. This proved a strain for the bank and prompted questions about Ambrosiano's other activities.

After the discovery by the authorities of the existence of P-2 and the seizure of documents from Gelli, including those which implicated Calvi, investigations into Calvi's affairs gathered pace. On May 20, 1981, he was arrested in connection with La Centrale's share dealings over Toro and Credito Varesino. Other executives of the companies involved were also arrested. Calvi was brought to trial and on July 20 sentenced to a fine of 16 billion lire and four years' imprisonment for the illegal export of currency. He was released on bail pending an appeal.

The full implications of the state of Banco Ambrosiano's finances were not revealed for another year. Calvi returned as the bank's head, despite being a convicted criminal, but was increasingly pressurized by creditors and by investigators from the Bank of Italy. On June 10, 1982 he disappeared from his flat in Rome. Initial fears that he had been kidnapped were soon discounted. In his absence he was replaced as bank president by the Governor of the Bank of Italy, who had also helped organize a group of banks to step in and rescue Banco Ambrosiano. Calvi's disappearance had removed the bank's remaining credibility and there was a rush by investors and creditors to retrieve their money. Banco Ambrosiano's subsidiaries abroad were revealed to have lent large sums which could no longer be guaranteed. In addition, the bank had spent money illegally supporting its share price on the Milan stock exchange. Support of the troubled subsidiaries proved impossible and on July 12 it was revealed that Banco Ambrosiano Luxembourg had defaulted on its loan repayments to the UK Midland Bank and a number of other British and European banks. The overseas network was forced into liquidation and on Aug. 6 Banco Ambrosiano itself was liquidated after the consortium of banks stated that it could no longer support it. The bank proved unable not only to satisfy its creditors abroad, but also its depositors at home as withdrawals worsened the bank's deficit. The bank had lent US$774,000,000 to its subsidiaries that could no longer be recovered, while $1,300 million had virtually disappeared after being lent to Panamanian-registered front companies. On Aug. 9 the remaining assets of the bank were transferred to a new institution founded by the consortium of banks, to be called Nuevo Banco Ambrosiano.

Meanwhile, Calvi himself had fled to London, accompanied by Flavio Carboni, a Sicilian building contractor with underworld connections, and Silvano Vittor, a small-time smuggler who acted as Calvi's bodyguard. He entered Britain on a false passport and maintained a low profile, undetected by the authorities. On the night of June 17 he went out alone and was discovered the next morning, dead, hanging from a rope attached to scaffolding underneath Blackfriars Bridge. There were stones in his pockets and over £7,000 in foreign currency. Calvi's body was soon identified, but speculation as to the strange manner of his death remains unresolved. There were no signs of violence on Calvi's body, but the unusual method of suicide and a number of unanswered questions led some to suggest that he had been murdered. Elaborate theories of masonic ritual killings were also proposed. The initial inquest into his death, strongly influenced by the medical advice from the post-mortem, recorded a verdict of suicide. This was subsequently overturned by the High Court after protests by the Calvi family. The new inquest, which concluded on June 27, 1983, reached an open verdict. During the inquest the Calvi family said that Calvi was preparing to reveal the details and names involved in his deals when he appeared in court for his appeal against conviction for illegal currency export. The first hearing had been due 11 days before he disappeared from Rome. They also said that Calvi had been attempting to reach an agreement with the IOR for the repayment of debts to Banco Ambrosiano to cover the money lent by the foreign subsidiaries.

The collapse of Italy's largest privately owned bank proved a blow to the financial world, and a further serious scandal to add to the long list of scandals that had plagued Italian politics and business. It also exposed some of the practices that the IOR had been willing to condone, even though the Vatican continued to deny involvement in Banco Ambrosiano's demise. Marcinkus had been a member of the board of several of Banco Ambrosiano's overseas companies and the Panamanian-registered front companies that had received the US$1,300 million in loans from Banco Ambrosiano subsidiaries were discovered to be owned directly or indirectly by the IOR. The money had been used in part to buy undisclosed holdings in Ambrosiano companies, but the destination of the bulk of it remains a mystery. In July 1983 the Vatican set up its own commission of three lay Catholic bankers to investigate the links between the IOR and Banco Ambrosiano. The involvement of the IOR in the bank's collapse led to a deterioration in relations between the Italian government and the Holy See. The Treasury Minister, Beniamino Andreatta, in a speech to parliament, accused the Vatican of being directly responsible for Banco Ambrosiano's collapse. The senior officials of the IOR were forced to remain inside the Vatican for fear of arrest if they stepped into Italian territory. On Dec. 24, however, Pope John Paul II stated that the Vatican would co-operate fully to discover the truth, and a six-member joint commission was set up. The healing of the breach in relations was sealed in February 1984 with the signing of a new Concordat between the Italian state and the Holy See. In May the IOR agreed to pay 109 creditor banks up to US$250,000,000 in "recognition of moral involvement" of its part in the affair, but refused to accept responsibility. In return the banks agreed to drop their claims for the outstanding debts, even though the sum agreed was far short of the total amount of debt outstanding.

The Italian government responded to the scandal by stating that it would impose new controls on the foreign-based subsidiaries of Italian companies. Luxembourg gave Italian companies an ultimatum to give guarantees to cover any debts incurred by their subsidiaries in Luxembourg. Banco Ambrosiano Luxembourg Holdings had lost US$1,000 million. On June 29, 1984 eight former directors of Banco Ambrosiano and a number of others involved with the bank were committed to trial on charges involving illicit share deals and contravention of foreign exchange controls. On March 13, 1985, 10 of them were convicted, including Roberto Rosone, former vice-chairman, who received a suspended six-year sentence, although the sentences were later reduced at appeal. As for the Rizzoli group, both Angelo Rizzoli and Bruno Tassan Din, the managing director, were arrested and charged with fraud and concealment of debts. Their interests in the firm were later seized by the authorities.

LP

P-2 Affair (1981–89)

Licio Gelli, grand master of the P-2 lodge.

The P-2 Affair was the most significant scandal in Italian politics since World War II. The discovery of a parallel state within the state, encompassing a wide cross-section of the establishment, and its subsequent outlawing and disbanding, proved a challenge to Italian democracy. Born during the difficult period of the 1970s when Italy had faced attack from left-wing terrorism, P-2 posed a threat from the right, described by Giovanni Spadolini (Prime Minister from 1981 to 82) as a "creeping coup". Its true influence and the threat it posed remains uncertain, however. Many saw P-2 simply as a useful way of using contacts to circumvent red tape, and many of the grander ideas may have been just wishful thinking by the lodge's mastermind, Licio Gelli.

Freemasonry had long been part of Italian politics before the growth of P-2. Its secrecy, anti-clerical and nationalist associations made it an ideal vehicle for republicanism and liberalism, and secret societies played an important role in the forging of a unified Italian state in the mid 19th century. The masonic lodge known as Propaganda Due (or P-2 for short) had existed for many years, but it was not until Licio Gelli became its grand master during the 1970s that its influence grew. Although nominally affiliated to the orthodox Grand Orient rite of Italian freemasonry, P-2 soon developed an independence and peculiar style of its own. Gelli had been expelled from the Grand Orient rite in 1976 and when the scandal broke the official freemasons denied any links with P-2, although their records were seized by the authorities. The lodge's obsession with secrecy meant that few people, other than Gelli and his deputy, Umberto Ortalini, had any idea of the organization's true extent. When the membership list was published many were surprised to see colleagues listed alongside their own names. Gelli's initiation ceremonies were simple and held behind the anonymity of hotel rooms with few people present.

Licio Gelli was born in 1919. He had built up a substantial personal fortune in the textile business, both in Italy and abroad. A large part of his life had been spent in South America, and he had been a personal friend of the Argentinian president Juan Perón. Gelli also held dual Italian-Argentinian citizenship. He was assiduous in cultivating acquaintances and contacts — something he pursued on a larger scale as head of P-2. The use of favours and bribes, augmented when necessary by blackmail and extortion, were the basis of P-2's web of influence, and provided Gelli with great power as the organizing genius behind the lodge. P-2 quickly attracted members who broadly shared the same right-wing political stance, even if they belonged to political parties ranging from the Socialists (PSI) to the neo-fascist MSI-DN. In the complicated world of Italian business and politics P-2 provided an easy way to use contacts to get things done quickly and avoid bureaucracy and delay.

In March 1981 the secret of the lodge's existence was accidentally exposed when investigating magistrates from Milan, working on the case of bankrupt financier Michele Sindona, were given a lead to Gelli by a suspect they were questioning. Gelli's villa and office in Arezzo were raided by the customs police (Guardia di Finanza). In Gelli's office they found a briefcase containing a list of 962 members of P-2 and files revealing the lodge's activities. Gelli was away from home at the time of the raid, and subsequently went into hiding, possibly in South America.

After numerous rumours and speculation in the press, the list was finally published on May 21, 1981. It comprised the names of numerous senior figures within the establishment, including politicians, businessmen, members of the armed forces and police, the media and the bureaucracy. They included two current serving Cabinet ministers, other politicians who had previously held high office, senior military officers such as the chief of general staff, Adm. Giovanni Torrisi; the head of military intelligence, Gen. Guiseppe Santovito; the past and present heads of the customs police, the former head of the civil service, members of the judiciary, the directors of radio and television news, and many businessmen.

The publication of the list caused an outcry against those named and a rash of investigations into the lodge and its members. The report of the investigating magistrates claimed that P-2 amounted to a state within the state, using blackmail and bribery to achieve its ends. P-2 was discovered to be linked to events and scandals in the recent past, including the activities of Michele Sindona (a P-2 member), whose financial empire had collapsed in 1974 and who was currently in prison in the USA for fraud and for staging his own kidnapping; the Bank of Italy scandal in 1979; and the bombing of Bologna railway station in 1980 by an extremist neo-fascist group.

The Prime Minister, Arnaldo Forlani, from the Christian Democratic Party, set up a three-member commission to investigate the lodge. They concluded that P-2 was a "secret society" and therefore in breach of the constitution which outlawed such societies. One of the first casualties of the affair was the Forlani government itself. The governing coalition collapsed on May 26 after the refusal of the Socialists to join the other three parties in the coalition to discuss the affair. The implication of two Christian Democrat ministers on the P-2 list had already undermined the government's credibility. A new five-party coalition was eventually formed in June 28 with Giovanni Spadolini, leader of the small Republican Party (PRI) as Prime Minister — the first time since 1945 that the premiership had not been held by a Christian Democrat.

Spadolini promised firm action to deal with P-2. The organization was outlawed and government ministries were ordered to take internal action against civil servants who were lodge members. Numerous public officials, such as chiefs of police, military officers and secret service agents were dismissed or sent on immediate leave. The heads of the armed forces were reshuffled in July in an unprecedented reorganization. The directors of radio and television news, Franco Colombo and Gustavo Selva, were suspended from their posts, and the editor of the influential Milan-based daily newspaper, *Corriere della Sera*, Franco di Bella, resigned. (The senior executives of the *Corriere's* parent group, the Rizzoli group, Angelo Rizzoli and Bruno Tassan Din, were also on the P-2 list and were later arrested and charged with fraud — see *Banco Ambrosiano Affair, 1981–85*, above.) On the day before the list's publication another of P-2's members, the banker

Roberto Calvi, had been arrested in connection with illegal share dealings and the case against him was to be bolstered by the documents found in Gelli's office.

Although by now a fugitive, Gelli continued to contact Calvi and others from hiding, partly to blackmail money from Calvi's Ambrosiano. On Sept. 13, 1982 Gelli was arrested in Geneva, Switzerland, after attempting to withdraw US$55,000,000 from an account with money allegedly transferred from Banco Ambrosiano's foreign subsidiaries. Bank staff who were suspicious of Gelli alerted the police. Gelli was discovered to be in disguise and travelling on a false passport. He was imprisoned by the Swiss authorities and the Italian government immediately requested his extradition to stand trial on charges of political conspiracy, criminal association, extortion and fraud. On Aug. 10, 1983, shortly before the final hearing in his extradition case, Gelli escaped from his maximum security prison, apparently with the aid of his warder who drove him across the French border to a waiting private jet.

Meanwhile, many of the cases against those accused of being members of P-2 were gradually dropped for lack of sufficient evidence. Many of the civil servants who had been suspended were reinstated in their jobs. In March 1983 the investigating magistrates on the case agreed with Achille Gallucci, the Rome public prosecutor, to drop most of the remaining cases. However, some were successfully brought to trial and convicted. In May 1983 Gen. Raffaele Giudice and Gen. Donato Lo Prieto, formerly the head and chief of staff of the customs police, were fined 50,000 million lire for their part in an oil tax evasion scandal in 1980 and Giudice received a term of seven years' imprisonment.

In May 1984 the official report of the parliamentary commission into P-2, chaired by a former Christian Democratic labour minister, Tina Anselmi, was published, which upheld the validity of the list and most of the names mentioned on it. The report stated that many of the senior military officers named on the list had "played a central role in particularly significant episodes in the recent history of our country, including events of a subversive nature". These were taken to be references to small-scale right-wing coup plots during the 1970s. The report was critical of how many of those implicated in the P-2 affair had escaped relatively lightly, although the report itself was circumspect about the politicians of all parties involved in P-2. None of the politicians was named in the report, but, as a result of the publicity surrounding the publication, Pietro Longo, the leader of the small Social Democratic Party (PSDI) and Minister of the Budget, was forced to resign. Longo's name had appeared on the original P-2 list although he denied any connection with the lodge.

After making statements that he would like to return to Italy if he could be granted immunity, Licio Gelli eventually came out of hiding and surrendered to the Swiss authorities on Sept. 21, 1987. He was taken to hospital suffering from a heart condition. The Italian government again sought his extradition, this time adding new charges of subversion in connection with the Bologna railway station bombing. Gelli first had to serve a two-month sentence imposed by the Swiss authorities for possession of a false passport and for his escape from prison in 1983. Gelli was extradited to Italy on Feb. 17, 1988, but under the terms of the extradition treaty he could only serve a term of imprisonment for conviction under the original charges against him and not the charges of subversion. In trial of those suspected of involvement in the Bologna bombing Gelli received a sentence of eight years' imprisonment for financing right-wing terrorism, but was found not guilty of subversive association, along with Gen. Musameci, former deputy head of intelligence and a P-2 member. Gelli, by this time a sick man, was released temporarily on grounds of ill-health, but was committed to trial on the charges of political conspiracy, criminal association, extortion and fraud on April 7, 1989.

Of other figures in the lodge, Umberto Ortalini fled to Brazil, where he is still wanted by the Italian police. Sindona was extradited to Italy in 1984 to stand trial for fraudulent bankruptcy and was sentenced to 15 years' imprisonment, plus a life sentence for the murder of the liquidator of his banking assets in 1979. On March 22, 1986 he died, after being given cyanide in prison in mysterious circumstances.

LP

JAPAN

Kakuei Tanaka/Lockheed Affair (1976–86)

J. W. Clutter, head of Lockheed's Tokyo office.
Hiro Hiyama, Chairman, Marubeni Corpn. 1972.
Yoshio Kodama, fixer and go-between.
A. C. Kotchian, Vice-chairman, Lockheed, 1973.
Yasuhiro Nakasone, Prime Minister (1982–1987).
Kakuei Tanaka, Prime Minister (1972–1974).

On Oct. 14, 1989, the former Japanese Prime Minister, Kakuei Tanaka, announced that he would retire from politics at the end of his current term as a member of the House of Representatives. The announcement was not made in Tokyo, but in Tanaka's regional base Nagaoka (Niigata Prefecture) in North-West Japan, by his son-in-law, Naoki Tanaka, also a member of the Diet. So came to an end a career of unmatched political influence and skullduggery in Japan's major political party, the right-wing Liberal Democrats.

When Kakuei Tanaka became Japan's youngest (54) Prime Minister in July 1972, he had been a Diet member since 1947, and had held a number of ministerial posts: posts and telecommunications, finance, international trade and industry. More important, he had been secretary-general of the ruling party. Not only by his comparative youth was he different from the senior men who had been Prime Minister in the post-war period. He was socially different: from relatively obscure origins, with only an elementary school education, he lacked the social graces of the older generation. He was the complete successful outsider. Journalists called him "the computerised bulldozer". He was cocky, self-confident, fast-talking and histrionic at the microphone. He was also greedy for money, and that was to be his downfall.

In Niigata, where he was born in 1918 into a farming family, his father had been a failure, moving from job to job. Tanaka himself spent much of his childhood at home, after an early attack of diphtheria. After working as a building labourer, he left for Tokyo and a succession of odd jobs, clerk, reporter, novelist, and at the age of 19 started his own construction business. He was inducted into the army and took part in the fighting against Soviet forces at Nomonhan in Manchuria in 1939, where he caught pleurisy and pneumonia. Back in Japan in 1940, his construction company contracted to build factories in Manchuria and China. He never served in the army again, but he was a success as a builder: by the time the war was over, his construction company was one of the largest in Japan.

Entering politics in 1947, he was Vice-Minister for Justice in Shigeru Yoshida's Cabinet (1948) and, in a pattern he was tragically to repeat, was arrested and jailed for taking bribes, a charge of which he was cleared on appeal. As Minister for Posts and Telecommunications, he introduced commercial television. He appeared often on television, becoming known as a "developer" minister, explaining how fast Japan's gross national product was growing, with new hydroelectric resources and new industrial sites.

When Prime Minister Eisaku Sato did not stand for re-election, Tanaka, by then head of a powerful faction in the Liberal Democrats, secured the succession as party president, a role which ensures being Prime Minister. He won on a second ballot (282 votes to his competitor Fukuda's 190).

As Prime Minister, Tanaka achieved spectacular results. The "oil shock" of 1973, which caused hyper-inflation in Japan, the world's most susceptible oil importer, was an inauspicious beginning, but he rode out the crisis. He cut ties with Taiwan and normalized diplomatic relations with mainland China, visiting Beijing in September 1972. He put forward an ambitious development programme entitled "Remodelling the Japanese Archipelago". Published in book form, the plan indicated likely development areas, particularly for new industrial cities, which naturally led to huge increases in land prices in the areas named. The town of Tsuyama was thus designated, and Mitsubishi Estates Company promptly bought up land near it. In southern Kyushu, land close to designated Shibushi Bay increased 10-fold in price. This blatant courting of property giants caused Tanaka's popularity to drop; the powerful University of Tokyo-educated bureaucracy mistrusted him as a parvenu, and the right-wing intellectual monthly, *Bungei Shunju* (October 1974) tore his reputation apart in a 60-page article entitled "An Anatomy of Kakuei Tanaka, His Money and His Men". He had bought land that year for six or seven times the amount of his declared income; and he was accused of using political funds for private purposes. *Bungei Shunju* also revealed his connection with a former bar hostess who acted on his behalf in handing out vast sums to keep members of his faction happy. His popularity in the opinion polls shrank to 16 per cent, and in November 1974 he resigned from office, after publicly acknowledging responsibility for the damage done to his party by his reputation for shady deals.

Stepping down did not end his career as power broker. Far from it. As head of the party's largest faction, he was, inevitably, a king-maker, with the final decision on the choice of Prime Minister and cabinet members. Then, in February 1976, the blow fell which was to bring him to a jail sentence and effectively end his career. It came, first, from the outside. A United States Congressional investigation revealed that the Lockheed aircraft company had achieved sales of its Tristar jet airliner and its P-3C Orion anti-submarine patrol aircraft to All Nippon Airways (ANA) and Japan's Maritime Self-Defence Force by bribing Tanaka, who had been Prime Minister at the time, to the tune of ¥500 million. Tanaka was arrested by the Tokyo District Public Prosecutor's office on July 27, 1976. To cushion the blow against his party, Tanaka left it, but continued to sit in the House of Representatives as an independent; and, of course, to wield patronage, since his faction in the LDP continued to obey his orders.

After the pre-trial hearings, the Tokyo District Court began four separate trials in the Lockheed case, reflecting the various "routes" by which the bribe reached Tanaka: (i) Marubeni Corporation; (ii) All Nippon Airways; (iii) Kenji Osano; (iv) Yoshio Kodama. We should look at these separately.

Marubeni Corporation acted as Lockheed Aircraft Corporation's agents in Japan. On Aug. 23, 1972, Marubeni's chairman, Hiro Hiyama, met Tanaka at the latter's residence in Mejirodai and asked him to use his influence to ensure that All Nippon Airways (ANA) purchased Tristar aircraft, either by persuading ANA personally, or by having the Transport Minister convey an order to ANA; in return, a sweetener of ¥500 million was proposed. "Yossha, yossha" (OK, OK), Tanaka is said to have replied.

Hiyama was accompanied by Marubeni's head of aircraft sales, Toshiharu Okubo, descendant of a famous 19th-century statesman, Toshimichi Okubo. At the crucial moment, Okubo was told to make himself scarce, but in the car returning from Mejirodai he asked Hiyama how much had been promised. Hiyama spread out the fingers of his left hand, at which Okubo asked "Do you mean ¥50 million or ¥500 million?" "¥500 million of course", Hiyama testily replied. (It was not an unusual sum. The Nissho Iwai Company paid Raizo Matsuno, a former defence minister, the same amount for ensuring the Japanese Government bought F-4E fighter planes made by McDonnell Douglas.)

After ANA agreed to buy the Tristars, on Oct. 30, 1972, Tanaka pressed for payment (June 1973). Okubo requested A. C. Kotchian, vice-chairman of Lockheed, to supply the cash, and he agreed to do so, but in four instalments. These were duly handed over to Marubeni by Lockheed's Tokyo office and then conveyed to Hiroshi Itoh, a Marubeni managing director, to Toshio Enomoto, Tanaka's secretary, from the boot of a car at four different locations in Tokyo.

When the prosecution asserted this, Enomoto produced alibis which were promptly torn apart. Enomoto had confided in his ex-wife, and asked her what he should do. "You pretend it never happened", she told him, as she freely admitted in court. Clearly, Enomoto, like the Marubeni people, perjured himself. In fact perjury was a conspicuous feature of the Lockheed case from the start. The pre-trial enquiry had called on a number of witnesses, under oath, who all denied any knowledge of what was alleged to have happened. During the court proceedings, all were shown to have lied.

Hiyama's and Enomoto's evidence was vital, since two points had to be established through them: that an "entreaty" had been made by Marubeni to Tanaka on Lockheed's behalf, and that funds had actually changed hands. The word "entreaty" seems odd, but it is the word used in the official English translation of the Japanese penal code. The defence naturally claimed that the money was a "political contribution", in which case no charge of bribery could stand. But it was pointed out that Marubeni was known to make political contributions, and invariably did so by cheque, not cash. And if the money had not been *abunai kane* ("dangerous money", a euphemism for a bribe) there would have been no need for the clandestine rendezvous.

Tanaka claimed that Hiyama's account of their Oct. 23, 1972 meeting could not be accurate, since he would not have used the phrase "yossha, yossha", which was Kansai dialect, whereas he was from North-West Japan. Hiyama modifed the phrase to "yosha, yosha" but the Tokyo District Court accepted the substance of his testimony. On Oct. 12, 1983, after a trial lasting six years and eight months, the three Marubeni go-betweens were found guilty by a panel of three judges, of bribery, of violating the Foreign Exchange Control Law, and of perjury. Hiyama was sentenced to two-and-a-half years imprisonment, and Itoh to two years. Both gave notice of appeal and were released on bail of ¥60 million and ¥45 million respectively. Okubo was given two years, suspended for four years, and did not appeal. Enomoto was sentenced to one year, suspended for three years, for violating the Foreign Exchange Control Law.

The prosecution asked for the maximum sentence for Tanaka, and a forfeiture of ¥500 million. Judge Mitsunori Okada reduced this to four years, the longest sentence ever awarded in a bribery case, adducing in Tanaka's favour that the ANA purchase had not damaged Japan's aircraft industry, that he had not solicited the bribe, and that he had given many years' service to Japan. Tanaka was granted bail of ¥300 million, continued to maintain his innocence, and refused to give up his Diet seat.

The prosecution had had to establish a chain of proofs involving four points:

1.   Whether or not the actual "entreaty" was made to Tanaka (and if he agreed to comply). In pre-trial testimony, Hiyama affirmed this, but withdrew it in court, saying he merely confirmed an offer of ¥500 million from Lockheed to Tanaka as a donation. This was very thin. Why on earth should Lockheed make such a donation unless to bring Tanaka's influence to bear? In this way, Hiyama hoped to represent Marubeni as no more than Lockheed's emissary. Okubo's testimony on the conversation in Hiyama's car was vital in countering this.
2.   Whether or not the payments reached Tanaka. The prosecution alleged four sites were used for the payment from the boot of Enomoto's car: a street behind the British Embassy, a spot behind the Kudan High School, the car park of the Hotel Okura, and Itoh's house. Itoh maintained he delivered the money on four occasions.
3.   Whether or not Enomoto's alibis were acceptable. Enomoto, in his pre-trial testimony, admitted Itoh had delivered four boxes of cash, but reversed his story in court. However, alibis to prove Enomoto was elsewhere at the four times failed to convince the court. His chauffeur's log had been doctored and in any case other chauffeurs might have been used. It was also claimed that, once the case surfaced, Tanaka had offered to return the bribe. He could hardly have done this if he had not received it.
4.   Whether or not, as Prime Minister, Tanaka had authority to influence a private airline's decision to buy aircraft. This was an important point, since Tanaka could not be convicted of bribery if it could not be shown that he had the authority to do what was asked of him. If he had not, he would merely be guilty of violating the Foreign Exchange Control Law. The prosecution asserted that (a) Tanaka could use his personal

influence on ANA, but also, as Prime Minister, had authority to order his Transport Minister to compel ANA to buy Tristar. Under the Civil Aviation Law, a choice of new aircraft constitutes a change of business plan and needs the Transport Minister's approval; and Tanaka could ensure that.

When considering the other "routes", two facts should be noted. The Japanese Cabinet had already decided, on Nov. 20, 1970, to authorize wide-bodied jetliners on domestic air routes. And at the US–Japan summit in Hawaii on Sept. 1, 1972, President Richard Nixon had suggested to Tanaka that the imbalance of US–Japan trade should be rectified, and buying Tristars was one way of doing this. Tanaka is said to have borne this in mind when acceding to Marubeni's representations.

The case against Tanaka and Marubeni lasted longest. The shortest was the case against the ANA board chairman, Tokuji Wakasa, and five other ANA defendants, which ended in October 1980. Wakasa and the other five were accused of receiving ¥160 million in return for buying Tristars. The money had not been entered in ANA's books, and was said to be for winning favour from politicians. Two politicians implicated in the case were the Transport Minister, Tomisaburo Hashimoto (sick for much of the trial) and his Vice-Minister, Takayaki Sato.

On Jan. 26, 1982, all ANA defendants were convicted and given suspended prison terms, ranging from three years to six months. Their trial had lasted five years four months, from Jan. 31, 1977. On June 8, 1982, Hashimoto and Sato were found guilty of "accepting bribes upon entreaties" from ANA executives, and were sentenced to two-and-a-half years and two years respectively, as well as to forfeits of ¥2.5 million and ¥2 million. These verdicts were seen at the time as hardening the case against Tanaka and his Marubeni co-defendants.

The ANA case was not so much concerned with aircraft purchase as with delaying a decision to bring jumbo jets into domestic service. JAL were ready to do so, and ANA were not, so they wanted the Ministry to delay a decision until they were, i.e. after 1974. The repercussions on the Tanaka trial were made clear by Judge Kazunobu Aragu, who decided that the ANA bribes were part of a ¥30 million sweetener from Lockheed, via Marubeni, to persuade ANA to buy Tristars instead of McDonnell Douglas DC 10s. Part of the bribe, the judge accepted, had gone to Tanaka and four high-ranking "grey officials" — "grey" because they were not named. He proceeded to name them: Susumu Nikaido, secretary-general of the Liberal Democratic Party and a close ally of Tanaka; Hideyo Sasaki, former Transport Minister; Kazunori Kikunaga, former chairman of the LDP aviation committee and Mutsuki Kato, former Vice-Minister of Transport (they were not indicted either because of the statute of limitations or because they were said to have no control over national aviation policy).

Hashimoto, who had been secretary-general of the LDP, was a creature of Tanaka's who had failed to be re-elected to the Diet in 1980. Sato was an independent Diet Representative from Hokkaido, and opposition parties called on him to resign. The judge offered a very odd reason for the suspended sentences: the defendants had not expected rewards for performing their duties, and Marubeni had provided payoffs whether the defendants had willed it or no. Hiroshi Itoh, who had made the "entreaty" to Tanaka, was involved here too: he had given Hashimoto ¥5 million in cash 22 months after Wakasa's entreaty to him as Transport Minister.

The case of Kenji Osano has similar links with Tanaka. Osano, a wealthy property developer with extensive interests in Hawaii, was approached in August 1972 by Yoshio Kodama, a nationally known "fixer" and former war crimes suspect, to help promote Lockheed's aircraft sales in Japan. In July 1973, A. C. Kotchian, vice-chairman of Lockheed, asked Kodama and Osano to help with sales of the P-3C anti-submarine patrol plane to the Maritime Self-Defence Force. In thanks, Osano received a cheque for $200,000 at Los Angeles airport. Osano was asked to appear before the Budgetary Committee of the House of Representatives on Feb. 16, 1976 in connection with the Tanaka affair. He made a blanket denial of any links, and was indicted for perjury on Jan. 21, 1977. Six months later, the hearing of the case began, and on March 26, 1981, the prosecution asked for a sentence of two years' hard labour. He was given one year with hard labour, and promptly appealed.

Kotchian had met Osano at the latter's office, in the presence of Yoshio Kodama, and agreed to approach ANA to buy Lockheed airbuses. He made an approach through Naoji Watanabe, vice-president of ANA. The $200,000 he received at Los Angeles airport from Lockheed's Tokyo representative, John W. Clutter, in November 1973, was part of a consultancy fee and commission payment to Kodama from Lockheed. Like Enomoto, Osano had heart trouble during the hearings; so did Kodama, so effectively in fact that scores of hearings were held at his bedside. Osano, a close friend of Tanaka for many years, said that he had asked ANA to buy Tristars, at Tanaka's request. The court's acceptance of this statement in November 1981 was a powerful factor in closing the ring of evidence against Tanaka two years later.

Although Kodama was too ill to appear at the court ruling on his case, his aide Tachikawa was not, and was sentenced before the ruling on Osano. He was given four months (with a two-year stay of execution) for conspiring to purchase a Hong Kong Company, Brown Lee Ltd., to make it appear that Lockheed payments to Kodama were made to that firm. John W. Clutter, then head of Lockheed's Tokyo office, carried out the purchasing procedures for the Hong Kong firm, but Kodama provided 3,000 shares at a cost of ¥300,000 which meant *he* was the real purchaser. At a Tokyo hotel, Tachikawa received ¥80 million from Clutter, as payment for Brown Lee Ltd., and delivered it to Kodama, as consultancy fee and commission in the sale of Tristars to ANA.

Kodama's own role as agent of Lockheed was secret, as opposed to Marubeni's public role as sales promotion agent. From pre-war days, Kodama had an unsavoury reputation as an ultra-right–wing bully-boy and "fixer", who had made money in Shanghai as a supplier to the Imperial Japanese Navy. He had been held as a war crimes suspect, but was never tried, and used his wealth to help found the LDP. He admitted to receiving, from 1969 on, an annual sum of ¥50 million as consultant to Lockheed, but no more; and this was for his opinions, not as sales agent. The prosecution, on the other hand, estimated his consultancy fees as in the region of ¥1 billion, and charged him also with evading nearly ¥2 billion in income tax, on a total of ¥2.5 billion earned from Lockheed in his role as "fixer".

Kodama first appeared before the Tokyo District Court on June 2, 1977, after 16 months of prevarication. The prosecution could not link him with bribes of officials, but concentrated on the tax evasion and violation of the Foreign Exchange Control Law (for having accepted large fees from a US company without authorisation from the Bank of Japan). It was asserted that Kodama had been a secret consultant for Lockheed since 1958, without a contract, and always insisted on being paid in cash.

One result of his activities was a reversal of the Japanese government's decision to buy Grumman fighters, in favour of the Lockheed F104. Kodama received large sums before and after this reversal. It was at Kotchian's urging that Kodama approached Osano in the summer of 1972. Kodama explained that a figure of ¥500 million would be needed for a billionaire businessmen like Osano. At roughly the same time, Kodama is said to have introduced Kotchian to Ryoichi Sasakawa, president of the private Japan Shipbuilding Industry Foundation, to obtain Sasakawa's help in appeasing local residents near Osaka airport who opposed the landing of airbuses.

The hearing of the US Senate Subcommittee on Multinational Corporations identified Kodama as a Lockheed secret agent. The Japanese court accepted the Senate Subcommittee's findings, just as they accepted the statements of the Lockheed executives, Kotchian and Clutter, which were made in the USA on promise of immunity from proceedings in Japan. The prosecution asked the court for three-and-a-half years' imprisonment for Kodama and a ¥700 million fine. They were able to prove his tax evasion. On the other hand, they could not say how he had channelled funds from Lockheed to politicians or officials. Either the bedside interrogations were too brief, said one newspaper, or Kodama's parsimony meant that he did not in fact put the money to use for his client, but simply pocketed it.

It would be natural to suppose that a political and financial scandal of such dimensions would have as its first effect the loss of Tanaka's national popularity. Indeed, the *Bungei Shunju* investigations of 1974 had compelled him to resign the premiership. But the Lockheed scandal had almost the opposite effect. Certainly, on the day he was sentenced, there were nation-wide demonstrations organized by the opposition parties at 230 places all over Japan, involving 350,000 people, demanding that he resign his seat in the Diet. In Tokyo, demonstrators at a rally in Meiji Park marched through the streets shouting "Tanaka! Go to jail quickly!"

But his own faction in the LDP stood behind him. So did the unshakeable block in his constituency in Niigata, showing the immense power of the Japanese *oyabun/kobun* (boss/beneficiary) tradition. In 1974, Tanaka's faction in the LDP numbered 74 Diet members. By 1982 this had risen to 110, roughly one quarter of the LDP members in the Diet, and it played a decisive role in establishing the Nakasone Cabinet. Tanaka's 1974 *Bungei Shunju* critic, Takashi Tachibana, emphasized the extraordinary circumstances of a man who had left his party, because of a financial scandal, continuing to rule the major faction within that party and so being able, while in court defending himself against criminal charges, to replace the Prime Minister at his discretion.

The attention Tanaka had paid to his followers over the years had paid off. The worse his position became, the less likely were his faction members to abandon him: it would be a grave sin of disloyalty to do so. A faction spokesman, Kozo Watanabe, was quite blunt:

> Although it may seem to laymen that the Lockheed case is a serious blow, politicians do not think that way. Most politicians sympathize with him . . . . Whether or not a politician is "clean" about money is judged according to how he spends it.

It had been assumed, continued Watanabe, that the new Justice Minister in the Nakasone cabinet, one of Tanaka's protégés, would quietly hint to the prosecutor general to drop the case. But the mass media had given it such coverage that the minister could not exercise his authority secretly in that way, "however much we may wish the minister to do so". An interesting afterthought. No other Prime Minister has his charisma, claimed Watanabe: "Is there anyone else but Mr. Tanaka who is so reliable and attractive in the political world?"

The Lockheed scandal had electoral repercussions: in the December 1983 election for the House of Representatives, the Liberal Democratic party under Nakasone, who had come to power under Tanaka's aegis, lost over 30 seats and failed to win a simple majority in the House (it won 250 seats out of 511, six short of a majority). On the other hand, politicians connected with the Lockheed scandal, and others, were returned to the Diet. Earlier in the election year, a political writer, Naoki Komuro, educated at Kyoto and Harvard, voiced a widely held opinion:

> I like, love and admire Mr. Kakuei Tanaka. He is the sole Japanese politician who deserves the title of statesman.

Komuro described Tanaka as a man of quick decision and quick action, whose acceptance of Lockheed bribes was no more significant than shop-lifting tissues from a supermarket, by the standards of today's corrupt political world. It was relatively corruption-free politicians who dominated pre-war Japan, he claims, and led the country into a disastrous war. Corruption is the cost the Japanese have to pay for democracy.

These egregious sentiments were echoed in Tanaka's base in North-West Japan. Tanaka always used his influence in public construction projects to further the interests of his constituency. Niigata was "snow country", with a reputation for strong *sake* and good rice; but quite outside Japan's major industrial areas. It now has an international airport, a new university, and the bullet trains (*Shinkansen*) stop there. In 1983 it ranked first of Japan's 47 prefectures in *per capita* public works investment. One example is the Shiodani Tunnel. Shiodani is a small village which was regularly cut off in winter by 12 feet of snow. A tunnel through the mountains was built, which linked it with the rest of the wintry world, at a cost of around ¥1 billion, i.e. ¥17 million per household. Little wonder that in 1983, by the time the scandal was seven years old, Niigata people still rated Tanaka as their favourite son, greater by far than Admiral Isoroku Yamamoto, the victor of the attack on Pearl Harbor. Two months after Tanaka's 1983 conviction, Niigata returned him to the Diet in an election in which he was opposed by the novelist Akiyuki Nosaka, who had resigned a seat in the Upper House deliberately to fight the seat on an anti-corruption platform. Nosaka gained 28,045 votes: Tanaka 220,761.

Neither the demands of the opposition parties that he should resign his seat, nor his own conscience, troubled him. In the end, nature took a hand. Tanaka suffered a mild stroke on Feb. 27, 1985, with the result that the right side of his body was paralyzed and he had a slight speech defect. On March 4, his doctors announced his condition to be worse than they had expected, though his life was not in danger. His faction now numbered 123, but the power had shifted gradually from Tanaka himself to Noboru Takeshita, Finance Minister in the Nakasone Cabinet, who had formed his own 40-strong "study group" inside the faction and was aiming at the premiership. Tanaka closed his political office on June 6, 1985 and was taken by his daughter to the resort at Karuizawa to recuperate.

LA

Recruit Scandal Affair (1984–   )

Hiromasa Ezoe, Chairman, Recruit Co.
Takeo Fujinami, Chief Cabinet Secretary, 1989.
Toshiki Kaifu, Prime Minister from August 1989.
Yasuhiro Nakasone, former Prime Minister.
Noboru Takeshita, Prime Minister 1986.

In the summer of 1988, a number of highly placed Japanese — politicians, government officials, businessmen — admitted having bought unlisted shares in a property company called Recruit Cosmos Ltd. The company was a subsidiary of Recruit Co., originally a company dealing in employment magazines, which had become a vast conglomerate involved in the renting of computers, the sale of telephone circuits, and property, with 72 branches throughout Japan, 5,600 employees, 27 subsidiaries and eight publications. In 1984, 76 eminent and influential people had been offered pre-flotation stock at ¥1,200 per share, on the surface to raise funds for the parent company, in fact to extend its tentacles of influence throughout the Japanese Government. Two years later the stock was publicly traded, and the share price rose to more than ¥5,000. Recipients of the pre-flotation shares made huge killings. Some were secretaries of highly-placed politicians, including Ikei Aoki, secretary to the then Prime Minister, Noboru Takeshita. On July 7, 1988, Takeshita told the press that he had no idea how many shares Aoki had bought nor what he did with his profits (¥4 million). Aoki himself claimed to have forgotten the details, but apologized for "causing trouble". Other politicians similarly named included Shintaro Abe, Secretary-General of the ruling Liberal Democratic Party, and Kiichi Miyazawa, Finance Minister; as well as two aides of the previous Prime Minister, Yasuhiro Nakasone.

It was a bad moment for Takeshita, who was intending to introduce major tax reforms and needed the co-operation of the opposition parties to see them safely through the Diet. Now, the Japan Socialist Party was sure to use the revelations to demand heavier taxes on capital gains. Repercussions spread to the media. Ko Morita, president of Japan's most prestigious economic journal, *Nihon Keizai Shimbun*, admitted buying 20,000 shares, and making a profit of around ¥80 million. Recruit's board chairman, Hiromasa Ezoe, also resigned.

The Japan Socialist Party named 19 people who should be asked to give evidence to the House of Representatives Budgetary Committee, including both Takeshita and Nakasone. At first, the Finance Minister, Miyazawa, told the Budgetary Committee that the Securities and Exchange Law or the Code of Criminal Procedure could not be invoked in the case. On the other hand, the Director-General of the Securities Bureau, Masahiko Kadotani, told the Committee (Aug. 22, 1988) that the sale of Recruit Cosmos shares *might* have violated Article 4 of the Act, which requires the sale of shares to more than 50 unspecified buyers to be reported to the Finance Minister. The Minister said he had no authority to supply the list of 76 names requested by a Japan Socialist Party Diet member, who demanded that Recruit's chairman, Ezoe, be brought to testify before the House. Miyazawa himself was hardly neutral. He claimed neither he nor his secretary, Tsuneo Hattori, had bought shares, but two years later withdrew the claim, admitting that in the summer of 1986 Hattori had discussed an offer of 10,000 shares.

The issue affected not simply the probity of Japan's financial world, but also the entire basis of the "money-power politics (*kinken seiji*)" on which the Liberal Democratic Party had been run for decades, and which was almost implicit in the electoral structure. A Diet member might receive from the state around ¥20 million annually, but he could be expected to spend around ¥100 million. The extra cash would be found by officially sanctioned fund-raising organizations and parties, tickets for which would be bought at astronomical prices by business firms. As an indirect way of funding individual politicians, the system was wide open to bribery; but it must be remembered that Japan is traditionally a "gift-giving" society, where a gift is a social gesture, not necessarily a currying of influence. "No clear line has been established", said Hiroshi Itakura, professor of criminal law at Nippon University, "between bribes and gifts in Japan".

The law does provide for disclosure of gifts above a certain value. Politicians are required to report donations and how they intend to use them. If they do this, the donations are tax-free. There is also another method of avoiding tax. Capital gains from stock sales are virtually tax free, and politicians can use them as they wish. So companies or individuals, desirous of influencing a politician, could structure stock transactions to permit the politician to draw an easy profit. Under the Securities and Exchange Law, this would only be illegal if it could be shown that the share prices had been manipulated, a proviso which does not seem to have been enforced. So Recruit sold pre-flotation shares to politicians and officials (or members of their entourage) who would then profit from the almost certain rise in stock values once they were listed. Since, in theory, the stock values could fall as well as rise, the recipients could claim they were not in receipt of a bribe.

The kind of influence sought by Recruit can be illustrated by the employment journals it published, a very lucrative trade in Japan. Jobs in these journals often turned out to be vastly different from the terms advertised, and the Ministry of Labour's Employment Security Bureau began to investigate the problem and propose legislative tightening-up of the system. Pressure from Recruit, it was claimed, put a stop to the investigations. The Labour Vice-Minister, Takashi Kato, who bought 3,000 Recruit shares, was head of the Employment Security Bureau; and a bureau chief at the Labour Ministry was charged with receiving "entertainment" worth ¥1.35 million on 39 occasions from Recruit.

So the tentacles spread, tarnishing the world of politics, business and the civil service. Takashi Hasegawa, appointed Justice Minister on Dec. 27, 1988, resigned three days later when it was learned that his fund-raising organization had received ¥6 million from Recruit. Piquantly, he was also president of the newly formed inter-party league in the Diet to promote political ethics. Other resignations followed. Ken Harada, Director-General of the Economic Planning Agency, resigned on Jan. 24; one of his support organizations had been funded by Recruit for 10 years. Three Cabinet ministers had gone in two months.

At the eye of the storm, Recruit's chairman, Hiromasa Ezoe, was arrested with three executives on Feb. 13 and indicted on March 4 on charges of offering bribes to officials of NTT (Nippon Telegraph and Telephone). Other Recruit executives were roped in, and the former chairman of NTT, with his aide, was arrested on March 6, 1989.

The public prosecutor's decision to proceed in this way implied that the offer and transfer of shares which were certain to rise was going to be considered as bribery. And the politicians' use of their secretaries as lightning-conductors was frustrated by the Public Prosecutor's ruling that they were responsible for their secretaries' purchases of shares, if it could be proved that the politicians in question were, by virtue of their office, in a position to influence decisions on Recruit. Such politicians were not named in the investigation but were described as "grey" politicians because of the lack of clarity in their association with Recruit. They included the former Prime Minister, Yasuhiro Nakasone, and the current premier, Noboru Takeshita, who finally admitted (April 11, 1989) before a Diet committee that he had been the beneficiary of a total sum of ¥151 million from Recruit between 1985 and 1987, but claimed the funds had been handled legally in accordance with the Political Fund Control Law of 1976. He did in fact detail the various Recruit affiliates and the sums donated; on the other hand, none of these appeared in the Home Affairs Ministry documents listing donations to parties and politicians (a large donation did not need to be reported if it was divided into small amounts and given to a variety of political support groups). The reaction on the committee was sharp: "Your hands are dirty", asserted Kanji Kawasaki, a Japan Socialist Party member at the committee session. He told Takeshita that the revival of democracy in Japan depended on his resignation, a summons Takeshita rejected, saying lamely that he must retain responsibility for political reform. An odd comment, since three of his Cabinet ministers had already resigned for accepting far smaller sums from Recruit.

Finally, on April 25, 1989, Takeshita yielded to pressure and announced he would resign after his budget was passed. The announcement was long overdue. His popularity in opinion polls had sunk to an unprecedented 3.9 per cent.

Even the most blasé of political commentators were amazed by the sheer number of politicians and officials involved in the Recruit scandal. The press described it as a watershed in national politics, since — it was asserted — all politicians henceforth would be more aware of ethical improprieties, and the public would be far less tolerant of the evils of "money-power politics". In the loss of public esteem, the Liberal Democrat ruling party of course suffered most, but some opposition parties were also sullied by association. A *Komeito* ("Clean Government") Party Diet member, Katsuya Ikeda, received ¥14 million from a Recruit subsidiary and was indicted on May 22, 1989, on the same day as the Chief Cabinet Secretary, Takeo Fujinami. And the Democratic Social Party chairman, Saburo Tsukamoto, was also involved. On May 29, 1989, the Tokyo District Public Prosecutor's Office ended the investigation (it had lasted 260 days) with 16 indictments. A total of 43 people — politicians, civil servants, journalists, businessmen — had been forced to resign. Most of these, it was noted, were in the private sector, and the Japan Socialist Party promptly asserted that the "political route" into the bribery scandal had been inadequately probed.

The comparison with the Lockheed scandal was, of course, in everyone's minds, but there were structural differences (see *Kakuei Tanaka/Lockheed Affair, 1976–86*). Lockheed was seen as a "vertical" process, focused on one main actor, whoever else was involved. Recruit spread "horizontally", the tentacles of the share offers being spread widely among figures in government, bureaucracy and the commercial world. And it seemed harder to fix guilt; it was far from clear, for instance, that block purchases of tickets for a political fund-raising party could constitute a criminal offence.

The difficulty was further emphasized when the new Justice Minister, Kazuo Tanikawa, presented his final report on Recruit to the Diet on June 12, 1989. It failed to indicate who were the "grey" politicians, though they had been widely referred to in the press. The Director-General of the Ministry's Criminal Affairs Bureau, Yasuchika Negoro, maintained that it was legally impossible to determine whether the politicians had the *official* power to grant favours to Recruit in return for cash and shares. A clear connection between gifts and favours had to be proved before legal action could be taken. The former Prime Minister, Nakasone, was not mentioned in the report, though sections of the press had clamoured for his resignation.

The Japanese people then began to give their verdict through the ballot box; but it was not entirely an unambiguous one. The first by-election to the Upper House under the regime of Takeshita's successor, Sosuke Uno, took place on June 25, 1989 in Niigata Prefecture — Kakuei Tanaka's old power base and a conservative stronghold. The Liberal Democrat candidate was beaten by a Japan Socialist Party candidate — a woman — by 464,096 votes to 45,889. The fact that the victor was a woman was no coincidence. Uno added his own personal scandal to the Recruit mix: his extra-marital affair with a *geisha* had been widely publicized, which had an undoubted effect on the women's vote.

Next, in the July 3, 1989 election to the Tokyo Metropolitan Assembly, the Liberal Democrats lost 20 of their 63 seats to the Socialists. In a final gesture of disgust with money-power politics, the election to the House of Councillors on July 23, 1989 resulted in the Liberal Democrats losing their hold over the House for the first time, while the Socialists upped their strength from 42 to 66 seats (of a possible total of 252). The ruling party still held 109 seats but this was less than a simple majority of 127. Uno accepted responsibility for the defeat, and indicated he would resign the premiership. Not only did his extra-marital affairs play a role: the farmers' hostility to the (slight) opening of the Japanese market to foreign food produce, and hatred for the almost universally unpopular 3 per cent consumption tax, added to the resentment born of the Recruit scandal. The result was a harsh verdict for what one newspaper called the ruling party's "arrogant insensitivity to the public wish for clean, faithful and consistent politics" (*Japan Times*, Aug. 12, 1989). Toshiki Kaifu, former Education Minister, reputed to be free of the Recruit taint, was named as new president of the party on Aug. 8, 1989, thus becoming the new Prime Minister.

The trial of Hiromasa Ezoe, Recruit's chairman, resulted in his being arraigned for tax evasion on a colossal scale. He was to pay a penalty tax of ¥2 billion, having failed to report an income of ¥3.3 billion. On the other hand, though he was undoubtedly the spider at the centre of the web, it seemed strange that none of the 77 people involved in making profits from their Recruit shares were to be taxed. The reason, according to the National Tax Administration Agency, was that their stock transactions were inside the tax-exemption limit (50 transactions a year of less than 200,000 shares).

Then came the Lower House elections in February 1990. The Liberal Democrats were left with 275 seats, the Socialists with 136, and the Clean Government Party with 45. The Liberal Democrats had failed to retain the control of the Lower House they had won in 1986. But here again the verdict was not unambiguous. Candidates tainted by the Recruit scandal were re-elected, with the sole exception of the Vice-Minister for Education. Even Nakasone, who had felt compelled to resign from the Liberal Democrats and stand as an independent, was re-elected, though on a much reduced vote (115,000 down to 86,000). Nakasone, in fact, through his secretaries, was perhaps the largest buyer of Recruit shares (29,000); three of his aides had made ¥64 million on them. He took his re-election as the voters' absolution: "The election has purified me", he proclaimed.

When Kaifu had formed his first Cabinet, in August 1989, eight of its members had Recruit funds, ¥37.31 million in all. For his second Cabinet, after the February elections, he stressed that he wanted scandal-free ministers. He then proceeded to inform the Lower House that he and six of his new ministers had received a total of over ¥48 million, in political donations or sales of tickets for fund-raising events, from Recruit. All of this, his Chief Cabinet Secretary hastened to add to a news conference, "within the limits of the Political Fund Control Law".

The ramifications of the Recruit affair are multiple, and still need to be fully explored. Had the opposition parties, or some of them, not been tarred with the same brush, they might have succeeded in replacing the Liberal Democrats. They still have a long way to go.

LA

NETHERLANDS

Prince Bernhard/Lockheed Affair (1976)

Prince Bernhard, consort to Queen Juliana of the Netherlands, Inspector General to the Dutch Armed Forces.

When a congressional committee in the United States heard allegations in 1976 that the Lockheed Aircraft Corporation had paid bribes to "a high Dutch official" it seemed at first to be just another example of corruption in international commerce. But when the official turned out to be Prince Bernhard of the Netherlands, the husband of the sovereign, and a major figure in his own right through his war record and business activities, the scandal was elevated onto a higher plane. The Prince was eventually forced to resign from most of his public functions after a Dutch Government inquiry strongly criticized his conduct.

Prince Bernhard of Lippe-Biesterfeld was born in Germany in 1911, becoming a naturalized Dutch citizen shortly before his marriage in 1937 to the heir to the Netherlands throne, Princess Juliana. When the Nazis invaded the Low Countries in 1940, Prince Bernhard escorted the royal family to safety in England before returning to serve with what remained of the Netherlands Army. After the German occupation he became Chief Liaison Officer between the Dutch forces in exile and the British forces. In the closing phase of the war the Prince took command of the Dutch resistance forces and as the Allied advance swept across the Netherlands he was among the early arrivals in a long series of liberated towns.

Princess Juliana succeeded to the throne in 1948 and Prince Bernhard took his part in the public life of the kingdom, accompanying the Queen on state occasions and royal visits abroad. Among a wide variety of interests he held honorary directorships of the Dutch national airline, KLM, the VFW Fokker aircraft company and the Hoogovens steel company. In recognition of his services during the war, the Prince was appointed to the specially-created post of Inspector General to the Dutch Armed Forces, which involved extensive contacts with suppliers of military equipment. It was his activities in this field which were to lead to his downfall.

In February 1976 a sub-committee of the US Senate committee on multinational corporations began uncovering evidence that the Lockheed Aircraft Corporation had made monetary payments to government officials and leading politicians in various foreign countries including Japan, Italy and the Netherlands (see also Japan: *Kakuei Tanaka/Lockheed Affair, 1976–86*; Italy: *Lockheed Affair, 1976–79*). In his testimony to the sub-committee on Feb. 6, Carl Kotchian, a vice-chairman of Lockheed, stated that the company had paid $1,100,000 to a "high Dutch official" in 1961–62 to aid the sale of F-104 G Starfighter aircraft to the Netherlands Air Force. The official was immediately identified by a source in Washington as Prince Bernhard.

The Prince denied that he had received any money from Lockheed and the Dutch Government set up an inquiry headed by Dr Andreas Donner, a member of the Court of Justice of the European Communities. The Commission's report — published in August 1976 — found no unequivocal evidence that money from Lockheed had found its way to Prince Bernhard, although a sum of money from the company had been drawn from a Swiss bank account by an associate of the Prince's mother. The report found that in 1974, the Prince had written two letters to Lockheed asking for commission of $1,000,000 to be paid to him in the event of the Netherlands Navy ordering Lockheed Orion aircraft for anti-submarine duties. The money was never paid because the order did not go through. The Commission concluded that Prince Bernhard had "entered much too lightly into transactions which were bound to create the impression that he was susceptible to favours". The report also said that he had "showed himself open to dishonourable requests and offers" and had been tempted "to take initiatives which were completely unacceptable".

In a statement to parliament, the Dutch Prime Minister said that the Government accepted the Commission's findings and had concluded that the Prince's actions had damaged the national interest. However, the Government had decided not to open a criminal investigation because it was unlikely to result in court proceedings. In a letter to parliament, Prince Bernhard accepted the report's conclusions and admitted that he had made mistakes and failed to exercise proper caution in his dealings with Lockheed. He would resign from all his functions connected with the armed forces and discontinue all his business activities.

The scrutiny of the Prince's activities was not yet over, however. He had told the Commission that the sum of $1,000,000 from Lockheed was destined for the World Wildlife Fund, of which he was president. The Fund subsequently denied having received the money and in September 1976, the Prince wrote to them declaring that he would step down as president when his term ran out in December.

RSD

NIGERIA

Dikko Affair (1983–84)

Alexander Barak, Israeli businessman and secret service agent.
Umaru Dikko, Nigerian Minister of Transport (1979–83).
Maj.-Gen. Haldu Hananiya, Nigerian High Commissioner in London.

The bizarre discovery of a former Nigerian cabinet minister in a crate marked "diplomatic baggage" about to be loaded onto a plane bound for Lagos might at first sight seem farcical, but it nevertheless soured the normally cordial relations between Nigeria and its former colonial ruler and raised important questions about the abuse of diplomatic privilege.

Alhaji Dr Umaru Dikko was born on Dec. 31, 1936. He worked in London for the BBC's Hausa service during the 1950s and 1960s before returning to Nigeria to become involved in politics. He was charged with corruption in the aftermath of the overthrow of Gen. Gowon's government in 1975, but in October 1979 was appointed Minister of Transport in the newly elected civilian government of President Shehu Shagari (a relation by marriage). When the Shagari government was overthrown on Dec. 31, 1983 in the military coup led by Maj.-Gen. Mohammed Buhari, Dikko succeeded in fleeing to Britain via Benin. Once in Britain he became actively involved in opposition to the military government.

The new Nigerian government was keen to secure his return to stand trial on charges of corruption arising from his position as head of a task force supervising the import and sale of rice and also for his management of Shagari's election campaign in 1983. In both cases he was alleged to have built up a substantial private fortune. He was also alleged to have received many bribes from companies involved in contracts for transport projects and equipment and used his position close to the president to amass money. However, no formal request was made to the British government for his extradition.

On July 5, 1984, at about 12.30 pm, Dikko was seized by three men from outside his luxury flat in Portchester Terrace in Bayswater, London, and bundled into a van. Police discovered Dikko later that evening at Stansted airport in Essex, together with a man with a syringe, in a crate marked "diplomatic baggage" due to be loaded onto a Nigeria Airways freight flight. Two other men were found in a second crate. Dikko had been drugged and was immediately taken to hospital. The crates, addressed to the Ministry of Foreign Affairs in Lagos, had arrived with two cars with diplomatic licence plates accompanied by Okon Edet, an attaché at the Nigerian High Commission. A customs officer had noticed irregularities in the labelling and documentation of the crates and the crates were subsequently opened in the presence of Edet.

The British government reacted strongly to this apparent abuse of diplomatic privilege. The Foreign Secretary, Sir Geoffrey Howe, stated that diplomats should respect the laws and regulations of host countries. The Nigerian High Commissioner in London, Maj.-Gen. Haldu Hananiya, was summoned to the Foreign and Commonwealth Office to explain the incident. He denied any involvement by the Nigerian government, but did say, however, that the kidnappers could have been "patriotic friends of Nigeria". Relations between the two countries deteriorated further when the Nigerians reacted to the detention of their aircraft and crew at Stansted by recalling a British Caledonian passenger flight from Lagos and seizing the aircraft, crew and passengers. It was not until after a meeting between the British High Commissioner and the Minister of External Affairs that the passengers were released on July 6, with the aircraft leaving Lagos the following day after the Nigerian plane had been allowed to leave Stansted.

Several people were questioned by police over the incident, including Edet, but all were later released apart from four who were charged with abducting Dikko and administering drugs in order to kidnap him. The accused were identified as Mohammed Yusufu, a Nigerian diplomat (but not on the Diplomatic List and therefore not covered by diplomatic immunity), and three Israelis found in the crates at Stansted: Alexander Barak, a businessman; Lev-Arie Shapiro, a consultant anaesthetist; and Felix Messoud Abitbol. The Israeli government issued a statement denying any involvement in the affair. Later press reports in Israel linked the affair to businessmen owed large sums of money in Nigeria.

The Nigerian government refused British requests for members of the High Commission to be interviewed by the police and, on July 12, two members of the Nigerian High Commission were expelled from Britain. Maj.-Gen. Hananiya, who had been recalled to Lagos as a protest, was also strongly urged not to return. The Nigerian government retaliated by expelling two British diplomats and seeking the recall of the British High Commissioner.

The four kidnappers were committed to trial and on Feb. 12, 1985 sentenced to terms of imprisonment of between 10 and 14 years, after pleading guilty to the charges. According to the evidence presented in court, Alexander Barak (who was revealed as an agent in Mossad, the Israeli secret service) had organized and led the kidnapping. Abitbol had acted as look-out, while Shapiro had administered the drugs. Yusufu, a Nigerian security officer, had been introduced to the Israelis by Maj.-Gen. Hananiya and acted as liaison officer with the High Commission.

Relations between the two countries continued to be overshadowed by the Dikko affair for some time, despite the wishes of many on both sides to resume cordial relations. The overthrow of Buhari by Maj.-Gen. Ibrahim Babangida in August 1985 was soon followed by a visit by the British Foreign Secretary, Sir Geoffrey Howe, in September and a gradual restoration of links between the two countries. As for Dikko, he was released from hospital on July 9 and given police protection. On Jan. 25, 1985, Nigeria formally asked for Dikko's extradition to face corruption charges and on June 6 the Home Office refused Dikko's request for political asylum. Dikko appealed, however, and in June 1987 was granted asylum by an immigration tribunal, but in May 1989 this decision was overturned when he was told that his residence permit would not be renewed.

LP

NORWAY

Treholt Affair (1984–85)

Arne Treholt, Norwegian diplomat and politician.

Standing as they did at the forefront of the Cold War between East and West, the Scandinavian countries have had their fair share of spy scandals. But of the 50 or so espionage cases in Norway since World War II, none has had such a wide ranging impact as that of Arne Treholt, a career diplomat and politician who was arrested in 1984, and found to have been passing top level secrets to the Soviet Union and Iraq for up to 15 years.

Arne Treholt was born in 1942, the son of Thorstein Treholt, a politician who rose to become Agriculture Minister between 1971 and 1976. Treholt junior became an idealistic young activist in the Labour Party. According to information at his trial, much of which he contested, his first innocent meetings with Soviet diplomats began in 1971. Gradually invitations to restaurants began to take a more sinister form. What started as small favours to the Russians, such as buying books from a local shop, developed into a conspiracy in which Treholt furnished the KGB with hundreds of secret documents.

Treholt rose through a series of government posts during the 1970s, holding such positions as personal secretary to the Minister of Trade in 1973. The following year he became personal secretary at the Ministry of the Law of the Seas and took part in negotiations with the Soviet Union. Between 1976 and 1978 he held the rank of deputy minister which gave him access to cabinet documents. In 1979 he joined the Norwegian delegation to the United Nations in New York, where he stayed until 1982, when he was admitted to the Defence College in Oslo. From 1983 until the time of his arrest the following year, Treholt was the head of the press section of the Norwegian Foreign Ministry.

The CIA, the FBI and the security service of his own country had been on to Treholt for some years. At the time of the last Norwegian spy scandal in 1977, a former clerk to the Norwegian Embassy in Moscow, Gunvor Galtung Haavik, had told the CIA after her arrest on suspicion of espionage that there was a "mole" at a high level in the Norwegian establishment. Treholt had been under investigation at the time of his application to join the defence college — an institution which would allow him access to classified NATO documents. Yet his application was approved for fear that refusal would arouse his suspicion and jeopardize the investigation. He was eventually arrested at Oslo Airport, on Jan. 20, 1984, while on his way to Vienna to hand over documents to the KGB concerning the recent visit to Norway of the American Secretary of State, George Shultz.

The subsequent interrogation of Arne Treholt, and the fruits of the previous investigation, were to reveal the extent of his treachery. His trial on more than 50 charges of espionage began on Feb. 23, 1985, and lasted for 50 days. The prosecutors revealed that he had been photographed in a Vienna street on Aug. 20, 1983 with Gennady Titov, a high ranking KGB officer, who they claimed had been his contact since the mid-1970s. Treholt was said to have passed on a large variety of sensitive information relating to the defence interests of Norway, Sweden, Denmark, the United States and NATO as a whole. Treholt affirmed his innocence, and has done so ever since in a series of unsuccessful appeals culminating in the Supreme Court in August 1988. He claimed that he had acted merely as an unconventional diplomat striving to enhance contacts between East and West in an unusual manner. The Court, however, did not believe him. He was convicted on all but one of the charges, sentenced to the maximum term of imprisonment of 20 years and ordered to pay court costs and fines totalling more than £100,000.

Arne Treholt's activities certainly had their effect on East–West relations. A special meeting of the Norwegian Cabinet concluded after his arrest that Norway's interests abroad and possibly her defence had been harmed. The Chairman of Norway's Joint Chiefs of Staff from 1977 to 1982, General Sverre Hamre, said later that Treholt's espionage would necessitate a redrawing of NATO's merchant shipping plans for times of crisis. The Treholt affair also led to the expulsion of Soviet diplomats from Norway and the inevitable Soviet retaliation.

Treholt's motives for his treachery remain unclear. The prosecution at the trial maintained that he had received substantial payment from the Soviet Union and Iraq. There was also a report that he had an 18-year-old daughter born to a mistress in Czechoslovakia which might have allowed the KGB to put pressure on him. Certainly, his friends always denied that he was a Communist.

The story of Arne Treholt has a bizarre postscript. In June 1986 the authorities at the prison where he was held made a routine search of a fellow inmate who was leaving for weekend parole. They discovered documents relating an elaborate plot hatched by Treholt for his escape. He was to have got away during a Saturday evening while the Brazil–France football match in the World Cup was being shown on television. From there, Treholt would have been kept in safe house in Oslo before being spirited away to Senegal in West Africa. The fellow prisoner and an accomplice were charged while Treholt was moved to a maximum security prison to continue paying his debt to society.

RSD

PANAMA

Noriega Affair (1983–90)

Gen. Manuel Antonio Noriega, Head of Panama's armed forces and *de facto* leader of Panama (1983–89)

The American invasion of Panama in December 1989 stands out in recent history for one reason — it was conceived entirely as an attempt to remove from power one man, Gen. Manuel Antonio Noriega. That the world's most powerful nation should resort to unleashing 23,000 troops on one of the smallest and poorest countries is a measure of the frustration endured by Washington in its crusade to get rid of its errant former protégé. For Noriega had once been very much favoured by the Americans, working for the CIA and carrying out delicate diplomatic missions on behalf of the Pentagon. When allegations surfaced that he had simultaneously provided information to Cuba and the Soviet Union, and had collaborated with drug barons smuggling cocaine into Florida, Washington's favour was abruptly withdrawn and a two-year campaign to oust him culminated in the 1989 invasion. Noriega took refuge in the papal mission in Panama City, before giving himslef up to face criminal charges in the American courts.

Manuel Antonio Noriega was born in a poor *barrio* in Panama City in February 1938. At that time his country was effectively controlled by the United States, having been created some 35 years earlier in order that a government friendly to Washington should take charge of the area of the planned Panama Canal. Noriega has claimed that he wanted to become a doctor but was frustrated by lack of funds. Instead he pursued a military career by attending a military academy in Peru before entering the Panamanian National Guard.

In 1969 Noriega used his already powerful intelligence network to foil a coup attempt against the then dictator, Brig.-Gen. Omar Torrijos. He was subsequently promoted to head of military intelligence and his prospects were advanced still further when Torrijos was killed in an air crash in July 1981. In August 1983 Noriega was appointed as commander of the Panamanian Defence Forces, becoming *de facto* leader of the country. During the next four years he tightened his grip on the country — according to his political opponents his tactics included a ruthless use of the secret police to suppress opposition, electoral fraud, blackmail and intimidation.

Things began to go wrong for the General in 1987 when his second-in-command, Roberto Diaz Herrera, accused him of subverting the 1984 presidential elections; of taking part in the murder of Torrijos in 1981; and of conspiring to murder an opposition leader, Hugo Spadafora, who died in 1985. Herrera was swiftly replaced. Media reports in the United States had already carried claims that Gen. Noriega had been involved in drug smuggling and in June 1987 the US Senate passed a resolution urging him to step down while the allegations were investigated. In September, the Senate approved a bill to fund an investigation by the CIA into the claims and that resulted, in February 1988, in federal grand juries in Miami and Tampa (Florida) issuing two indictments against the General. They charged him with turning Panama into a "vast criminal enterprise" and with obtaining $4,600,000 from helping a Colombian drug cartel move more than 4,000 lbs of cocaine into the USA, and of conspiring to import marijuana worth over $1,000,000 into the USA.

Opposition to Noriega's rule continued to grow in Panama itself, with a series of strikes and demonstrations, culminating in an attempt to remove him from his post as head of the armed forces. President Eric Delvalle, originally a Noriega appointee, announced in February 1988 that his mentor had been dismissed, but the Legislative Assembly promptly voted to replace Delvalle with a more amenable candidate. The pressure grew with the announcement in March of US economic sanctions against Panama, including the suspension of all US payments and preferential trade agreements.

Against this background, presidential elections were held on May 7, 1989. Counting was suspended eight hours after the polls closed with both the opposition and the pro-Noriega candidates claiming victory. The election was annulled three days later on the grounds of fraud — a move widely interpreted as a ploy to deny victory to the opposition. A less conventional, but equally unsuccessful, attempt to remove Noriega came in October in the shape of a coup mounted by disgruntled military officers. The rebel troops took over the military headquarters of the Panamanian Defence Forces and held Noriega captive for four hours. In a broadcast they described it as "an internal coup" to put a stop to military corruption, but they had no intention of handing over the General to face the American drugs charges. Troops loyal to Noriega surrounded the barracks and after several hours of fighting the rebels surrendered. The ringleaders were killed (some sources said they were executed personally by Noriega). A ruthless purge of the armed forces followed.

The US administration denied at first that it had been involved in the coup attempt but later admitted that it had communicated with the leaders before the event and had used American troops to block certain roads leading to the barracks. The administration faced criticism in Congress and the media for not offering more support.

The strained patience of the Americans finally snapped after a declaration on Dec. 15 by the Panamanian National Assembly, making Noriega the formal head of government, and Noriega's subsequent announcement that Panama was in a state of war with the USA. The next day an off-duty US marine was killed by a member of the Panamanian Defence Forces and there was violence against another US soldier and threats against his wife, providing Washington with a further pretext for action.

The invasion began on Dec. 20, using 13,000 troops who were already in the country and 9,500 flown in from the USA. The troops, supported by aircraft, tanks and artillery, took control of key installations. The Panama

Canal was closed for the first time in its history. The US forces destroyed the headquarters of the Panamanian Defence Forces, captured several other bases and secured the airport. The US Defence Department announced the next day that organized resistance had been crushed and 1,500 Panamanian soldiers had been captured. Preliminary US casualty figures issued later in the month referred to 320 military dead, including 23 US personnel, and 230 civilian dead. The main opposition leader, Guillermo Endara, who was widely held to have won the aborted presidential elections of May, was sworn in as the new president.

Although street fighting continued for many days, the US invasion had clearly been a military success, but for one crucial factor: they failed to capture Noriega. For several days his whereabouts were unclear until it was discovered that he had taken refuge in the papal nunciature in Panama City on Dec. 24. There followed a diplomatic stand-off with Noriega claiming sanctuary, the papal authorities declining to hand him over to the Americans and the Americans insisting that they did. US troops surrounded the building and played loud rock music incessantly in an attempt to discomfort their quarry. The General evidently became convinced that he could not escape for he walked out of the nunciature of his own accord on Jan. 3, 1990, and surrendered to the US forces. He was immediately flown to Florida, appearing in court in Miami the next day to face the drug-smuggling charges.

It soon became apparent that the case would be far from a foregone conclusion. The defence lawyers gave notice that they would challenge the seizure of Noriega as illegal under international law and claimed that the publicity surrounding the case would make it impossible to get a fair hearing. They also indicated that they would seek to obtain documents relating to Noriega's involvement with the CIA which could prove embarrassing to the US Government, the more so because President George Bush had been the director of the CIA during 1976–77. Delays were caused by the US decision to freeze some $20,000,000 in Noriega's bank accounts around the world. The courts later released part of the money to help Noriega pay his legal bills. With the trial postponed until 1991, the possibility remains that Noriega might once again outwit his American foes.

RSD

PHILIPPINES

Marcos Affair (1981–90)

Adnan Khashoggi, international arms dealer.
Ferdinand Marcos, President of the Philippines (1965–86).
Imelda Marcos, first lady of the Philippines (1965–86).

The overthrow in 1986 of the 20-year regime of Ferdinand Marcos in the Philippines was one of the most remarkable political events of recent years. The turning point came when hundreds of thousands of people took to the streets of the capital, Manila, to stand in the path of troops and tanks moving to attack a barracks taken over by rebel soldiers. That incident embodied the spirit of a revolution which was to become known as "people power".

But the aftermath of the revolution was, perhaps, even more extraordinary, as the extent of the Marcoses' web of corruption was gradually revealed by investigators of the new Philippines Government. An international legal battle followed as the government sought to trace and recover billions of dollars plundered from the national treasury. The search was to go on after the death of Ferdinand Marcos in Hawaii in 1990, and the acquittal by a New York court of his widow, Imelda, on charges connected with the transfer of some of the Philippines money into the United States.

Ferdinand Edralin Marcos was born in Ilocos Norte, Luzon, in September 1917. He studied law at the University of the Philippines, and during the Pacific War apparently distinguished himself in combat against the Japanese, being decorated for valour. Later evidence suggested, however, that Marcos was, in fact, a collaborator.

In 1946 Marcos was made special assistant to the then President and in 1949 was elected to the House of Representatives. In 1959 he entered the Senate, becoming President of that body. A Liberal until 1964, he successfully stood as the Nationalist Party candidate in the 1965 presidential elections and was re-elected President in 1969.

In 1972, before completing a maximum of two four-year terms in office, Marcos imposed martial law to deal with subversive activity and to introduce drastic reforms. His term of office was extended by referendum in 1973 and again in 1977. By experimenting with various forms of government and by the skilful use of patronage, Marcos maintained his grip on power and was able to neutralize political dissent. Although he lifted martial law in January 1981, he retained wide-ranging powers and won another six years in office in June of that year in elections boycotted by the opposition.

Corruption and economic adversity, however, began to cost him popular support, and, following the assassination of the opposition leader, Benigno Aquino, in which he was implicated, his position as president became increasingly untenable.

Snap elections were called by Marcos in November 1985 and held on Feb. 7, 1986. Discredited by the blatant vote-rigging which he used to try to claim election victory, Marcos was on Feb. 25 forced to flee the Philippines for the United States when opposition forces and key military figures staged the so-called "people power" revolution.

The opponents of Marcos had long railed against his extravagant lifestyle, maintained while many of his people were in poverty. But when thousands of people stormed the Malacanang Palace in Manila hours after the dictator had fled they found concrete proof of their suspicions. Marcos's wife Imelda was found to have left a wardrobe full of expensive dresses and handbags, and a collection of more than 3,000 pairs of shoes. More important still, documents about the Marcoses' financial affairs were found which were to be the basis for an international legal battle.

The new government of Corazon Aquino alleged that the Marcoses had systematically plundered up to US$10,000 million from the Philippines treasury, spending it on high living, depositing large sums in foreign banks and buying property abroad. Government lawyers set out to track down and retrieve the Marcos fortune, soon finding themselves bogged down with what seemed interminable court battles in the courts of Switzerland. By December 1989 the Swiss authorities had returned only about $2 million.

There was more success for the Aquino government in the United States where they achieved co-operation from the judicial authorities and a court judgment freezing the Marcoses' assets. The Americans began to build their own case against Marcos and his associates, alleging that they had broken US law in transferring and concealing some of the Philippines money. The Marcoses were indicted by a Grand Jury in October 1988 under the Racketeer-Influenced and Corrupt Organizations Act, after failing to respond to subpoenas issued in August.

But Ferdinand Marcos was never to face trial. His health had steadily deteriorated since his arrival in Hawaii after fleeing the Philippines and he was excused the trip to New York in late October for his arraignment. Imelda Marcos went alone, entered a plea of not guilty and was released on $8.5 million bail, provided by a friend. Ferdinand Marcos spent two spells in hospital with heart and kidney problems and died in September 1989. President Aquino, beset by economic problems and the ever-present threat of a coup, refused permission for Marcos's body to be allowed home for burial. She said her decision was "in the interest of the safety of those who will take the death of Marcos in widely and passionately conflicting ways". Aquino was reported to have alerted Philippino and US authorities to guard against attempts to smuggle the body back.

In March 1990 Imelda Marcos faced trial by a New York court on charges of helping her late husband steal more than $200 million from the Philippines and illegally investing much of it in the United States. She was also accused of fraudulently obtaining loans from US banks and of obstructing justice. With her in the dock was Adnan Khashoggi, a Saudi Arabian arms dealer, a long-time friend of the Marcoses, reputed to be one of the richest men in the world. He was charged with fraud and obstructing justice by helping the Marcoses conceal some of the stolen money.

The prosecution alleged that the former first lady had "built a spider's web in a dark corner of a room that reached from Manila to New York", while systematically looting her country. The case included the allegation that the Marcoses had bought four skyscrapers in Manhattan between 1981 and 1983, initially as an insurance policy against the possibility of a Communist takeover in the Philippines. Khashoggi was said to have pretended to own the buildings after the US Government froze the Marcoses assets. The prosecution said he had drawn up documents of sale in 1987 and backdated them to 1985 — before the assets were frozen.

Among the 95 witnesses called by the prosecution was Oscar Carino, the former manager of the New York branch of the Philippine National Bank, who testified that Imelda Marcos had treated his branch as her "personal piggy bank" whenever she visited the city. He had regularly delivered cash sums of up to $100,000 to her hotel to finance shopping sprees. State investigators had discovered that unreimbursed withdrawals on the bank's books had amounted to $22 million.

The defence chose not to call any witnesses but to rely instead on the eloquence of the flamboyant lawyer for Imelda Marcos, Gerry Spence, who addressed the jury in his usual attire of stetson and cowboy boots. He explained his client's collection of 3,000 shoes by saying that footwear manufacturers in the Philippines would routinely deliver dozens of pairs of shoes as a courtesy, most of which did not fit. He suggested that Imelda Marcos had not known where her accumulated wealth had come from. "She may have been a world-class shopper", said her lawyer, "but she is also a world-class decent human being who was guilty only of loving her husband".

The jury delivered its verdict in early July: both defendants were acquitted of all charges. Imelda Marcos described the decision as a perfect present on her 61st birthday. The reaction from Manila was less sanguine. A government spokesman said civil proceedings would continue in the United States, Switzerland and the Philippines itself to recover the stolen money. Imelda Marcos would not be allowed back to her homeland for fear that she would try to destabilize the country. If she did return she would be put on trial.

RSD

POLAND

Katyn Massacre (1940–90)

Lavrenti Beria, head of Soviet People's Commissariat for Internal Affairs—NKVD (1938–53).

Nazi Germany and the Soviet Union on Aug. 23, 1939, signed a non-aggression pact. Attached to it were secret protocols dividing Eastern Europe into German and Soviet spheres of influence. The protocols partitioned Poland between them, and the Nazi German invasion on Sept. 1 was followed on Sept. 17 by Soviet occupation and annexation of the eastern half of the country.

Immediately after the Soviet occupation, around 200,000 Polish service-men, including some 10,000 officers (mostly reservists mobilized during the German invasion and drawn from the intelligentsia and the professions), were rounded up by the NKVD (the Soviet security service) and deported to the Soviet Union for internment. Many of them were later released to fight in the Soviet Red Army or were transferred to Polish units in Great Britain and the Middle East. However, a contingent of around 15,000 men, including almost all of the imprisoned officers, was to suffer a fate which was to overshadow Polish-Soviet relations for the next 50 years, and is widely regarded in Poland as having wiped out the best men of a generation.

The Polish government-in-exile in London was able to establish quite soon after the event that most of the 10,000 officers taken prisoner by the Soviets had been interned in NKVD camps at Kozelsk (east of Smolensk in western Russia), Starobelsk (near Kharkov, in the east Ukraine) and Ostashkov (near Kalinin in western Russia), the numbers of inmates of those camps being, at Kozelsk, nearly 5,000 (including 4,500 officers), at Starobelsk, 3,920 (all officers, except for some 100 civilians), and at Ostashkov, 6,570 (380 officers). The internees initially were allowed to remain in contact with their families in eastern Poland by letter, but in April–May 1940 all such communication from the camps ceased. The Polish government-in-exile learned that in April 1940 the Soviet authorities had started to empty the camps, groups of 60–300 men being removed every few days until the middle of May.

The Nazi-Soviet non-aggression pact was abrogated in June 1941 when the Germans invaded the Soviet Union. One consequence of this was the conclusion of a Polish-Soviet Treaty and a Military Agreement in July and August 1941, whereupon the Polish government proceeded to form a Polish Army on Russian soil. It had been expected that the officers from the Kozelsk, Ostashkov and Starobelsk camps would take commands in that

Army, but fewer than 400 former inmates of the three camps arrived at Polish Army HQ, representing a contingent of prisoners deported from the three camps in question to a camp at Gryazovets near Vologda in northern Russia. Missing were about 8,300 officers, together with some 7,000 others (NCOs and civilians). In the course of the next year the Polish government made repeated requests for information from the Soviets about the fate of the missing prisoners, but was told that all Polish officers had been released under an amnesty following the 1941 Polish-Soviet treaties.

The German armies thrust deep into the Soviet Union in the two years before their advance was stopped and they were thrown back. On April 12, 1943, the German News Agency claimed that German occupation forces had discovered in the Katyn forest, outside Smolensk, mass graves containing the remains of Polish officers (the first reports said 10,000, but subsequent investigations put the figure at somewhat more than 4,000) who, it was alleged, had been murdered by the NKVD. Each one had been executed by means of a single bullet through the back of the neck. The Germans claimed that owing to the nature of the soil the bodies had not decomposed but become mummified and that, as documents were still in their pockets, they were identifiable. They were the missing former inmates of the Kozelsk camp.

The German allegations were immediately denounced by the Soviet authorities as "vile fabrications", but the Polish government-in-exile on April 16 called on the International Red Cross to investigate, albeit declaring that it denied to the Germans "the right to draw from a crime which they ascribe to others arguments in their own defence". On April 19 the Soviet Communist Party newspaper *Pravda* declared that the Polish government's appeal to the International Red Cross constituted direct assistance to the enemy, and on April 25 the Soviet government severed relations with the Polish government, accusing it of undertaking, under the influence of pro-Nazi elements within its ranks, a hostile campaign against the Soviet Union in direct collusion with the Germans. News of this development was hailed in Berlin as the "first rift in the Allied front". The Soviets thereafter sponsored the formation of a rival Polish government-in-exile inside the Soviet Union.

The International Red Cross received from the German Red Cross organization as well as from the Polish government a request for an inquiry by its International Committee into the discovery of the Katyn graves, but at the end of April 1943 it refused to undertake the inquiry unless a request was also received from the Soviet government (none was forthcoming). Nevertheless, the Germans arranged for an international medical commission to be sent to Katyn, comprising specialists in forensic medicine from 12 countries, and also allowed Polish Red Cross representatives to examine the bodies. Both groups corroborated the German version of events, putting the time of the massacre during the spring of 1940.

Moscow radio, in a statement broadcast on April 18, 1943, called the German allegations a "hideous frame-up" by the Gestapo, and claimed that the bodies found at Katyn were those of a number of former Polish prisoners who, following the Soviet retreat from the Smolensk area in 1941, had fallen into German hands, along with those of Soviet citizens killed by the Germans, on which falsified Polish documents had been planted.

This version of events was substantially reiterated in the findings, published on Jan. 26, 1944, of an official Soviet commission which investigated the Katyn graves after the Smolensk area had been recaptured by the Red Army. The report stated that the graves, situated 10 miles from Smolensk along the highway to Vitebsk, in an area of Katyn Forest called Kozie Gory 220 yards from the highway, had been reopened in the presence of the Special Commission members and coroners, and discovered to contain corpses clothed in Polish military uniforms. Reportedly, witnesses from among the local population had also been interviewed. The Commission concluded that the graves contained the remains of Polish prisoners of war left behind in the Soviet retreat from the Smolensk area and executed by the Germans in the autumn of 1941, and of other Poles executed by the Germans at other locations and placed in the Katyn graves in the spring of 1943.

In the interests of their wartime alliance with the Soviet Union, the British and US governments publicly supported the Soviet version of events at Katyn, albeit believing privately the version established by the Germans. The latter version was also believed by most Poles, who saw in the massacre of Polish officers a deliberate Soviet policy to undermine the Polish nation by depriving it of its élite, in order more easily to "sovietize" annexed eastern Poland. After the war the US administration changed its public position on the Katyn massacre, a US congressional committee finding in 1951 that it had been committed "beyond any reasonable doubt" by the Soviet NKVD. This finding was accepted by most other Western governments, with the exception of the UK government, which as late as 1988 continued to insist that responsibility for the massacre remained unclear.

Under Soviet direction a Communist regime was installed in post-war Poland, which publicly in its official pronouncements and its history books, and on monuments to the Katyn victims, continued to accept the Soviet version of the massacre. Whatever doubts Poles felt about the veracity of this version remained unarticulated until the latter part of the 1980s, when the reformist Soviet leader Mikhail Gorbachev, appointed in March 1985, introduced the policy of *glasnost* ("openness") to the Soviet media and the interpretation of Soviet history.

At a meeting in Moscow on April 21, 1987, Gorbachev signed with Gen. Wojciech Jaruzelski, Poland's head of state and leader of the Communist Polish United Workers Party (PUWP), a declaration on co-operation between the PUWP and the Soviet Communist Party in the fields of ideology, science and culture. This included a commitment to resolve the "blank spots" in the history of Polish-Soviet relations, and as a result it was announced that Polish and Soviet historians were to form a joint commission to investigate controversial matters in Polish-Soviet history, including the Katyn massacre. On the strength of findings by this commission, on March 7, 1989, the Polish authorities for the first time contradicted the official Soviet verdict and openly accused the Soviet Union of responsibility, the government spokesman declaring that "everything indicates that the crime was committed by the Stalinist NKVD".

The Soviet authorities on April 13, 1990, finally admitted Soviet responsibility for the Katyn massacre, as well as for the deaths of the inmates of

Starobelsk and Ostashkov. The admission, on the eve of a visit to Katyn by Jaruzelski, came in a statement by the Tass news agency. This said that Soviet historians recently had discovered documents revealing that in April–May 1940 all but 394 inmates of the camps at Kozelsk, Starobelsk and Ostashkov had been turned over to NKVD administrations in Smolensk, Voroshilovgrad and Kalinin, and had been "never again mentioned in NKVD statistical accounts". Avoiding mention of exactly what befell the victims, the statement added that the archive material led to the conclusion that "direct responsibility for the crime committed in Katyn forest" fell to NKVD chief Lavrenti Beria and his subordinates. It concluded: "The Soviet side, expressing profound regret over the Katyn tragedy, declares that this is one of the gravest crimes of Stalinism". At a meeting in Moscow on April 13 Jaruzelski received from Gorbachev copies of the NKVD lists of the names of Polish internees in the three camps.

A statement by the Polish government said that the question of responsibility for the Katyn massacre had "weighed particularly painfully" on Polish-Soviet relations, and that the "long-awaited" Soviet admission made possible a relationship based on "partnership and true friendship". It continued: "Reconciliation can only be built on truth."

Following this admission of Soviet responsibility, it was announced that the Soviet authorities would begin a search for the graves of the internees of the Starobelsk and Ostashkov camps. Not long afterwards, during June 1990, it was disclosed that these had been found in a forest outside Kharkov and at Mednoye near Kalinin.

IPG

Popieluszko Affair (1984)

Lt. Waldemar Chmielewski, officer in state security service.
Lt. Leszek Pekala, officer in state security service.
Col. Adam Pietruszka, deputy director of Interior Ministry department for monitoring church affairs.
Capt. Grzegorz Piotrowski, officer in state security service.
Maj.-Gen. Zenon Platek, director of Interior Ministry department for monitoring church affairs.
Fr Jerzy Popieluszko, Warsaw Roman Catholic priest.

Poland's Roman Catholic Church claims some 90 per cent of the country's 38 million people as its adherents. For Poles the Church has great cultural and historical significance as the only institution which unified the Polish nation and preserved its identity through centuries of invasion and subjugation, and their identification with the Church is strong and highly emotional. Throughout the more than 40 years of Communist rule in Poland relations between the Roman Catholic Church and the state were contentious and frequently highly ambiguous: although from the late 1950s a pragmatic agreement existed not to interfere in each other's spheres, the Church had no legal status, and frequently disputed with the authorities.

Following the emergence of the free Solidarity trade union movement in 1980 the Roman Catholic Church officially remained neutral and attempted to act as a mediator with the state authorities. Nevertheless, many members of lay Catholic groups joined Solidarity and rose to prominence, and radical members of the clergy openly preached support for the Solidarity movement even after it was banned. In 1984 there was national outrage and the Solidarity cause gained its most prominent martyr when one such priest, Fr Jerzy Popieluszko, was murdered by officers of Poland's security services.

Fr Jerzy Popieluszko was born in 1947, and at the time of his death was priest of the parish of St Stanislaw Kostka in Warsaw. A prominent supporter of Solidarity while the movement was operating underground in the wake of the December 1981 imposition of martial law in Poland, he had been placed under judicial investigation in October 1983 and formally charged in mid-July 1984 with abuse of religious freedom and concealing arms and ammunition, but the charges against him had been suspended a few days later under the terms of an amnesty.

On Oct. 19, 1984, Fr Popieluszko was being driven from Warsaw to the town of Torun when his car was stopped by three men, one of whom was posing as a police officer. Both Fr Popieluszko and his driver, Waldemar Chrostowski, were beaten up, and Fr Popieluszko was forced into the boot of an unmarked police car, but Chrostowski was able to escape, and raised the alarm.

An extensive police investigation into Fr Popieluszko's disappearance began immediately, and on Oct. 24 three members of the security forces were placed under provisional arrest on suspicion of complicity in the kidnapping. Three days later Interior Minister Gen. Czeslaw Kiszczak (who had personally taken charge of the investigation) announced on television that one of the suspects, Capt. Grzegorz Piotrowski, had confessed to killing Fr Popieluszko; however, the other two, Lt. Waldemar Chmielewski and Lt Leszek Pekala, claimed that Fr Popieluszko was still alive.

Fr Popieluszko's body was found weighted down in a reservoir on the Vistula river near Wloclawek, west of Warsaw, on Oct. 30. A post mortem examination revealed that he had been bound and badly beaten, and had probably choked to death on his own blood. Popieluszko's funeral, at the church of St Stanislaw Kostka on Nov. 3, was turned into a huge demonstration of support for Solidarity, attended by up to 250,000 mourners.

What was now a murder investigation led on Nov. 2 to the suspension from duty of Maj.-Gen. Zenon Platek, the director of the department at the Ministry of the Interior for monitoring church affairs, "for failing to exercise sufficient supervision" of his subordinates, and to the detention of Col. Adam Pietruszka, Platek's deputy. Pietruszka was charged on

Nov. 5 with involvement in the plot against Fr Popieluszko. The three officers arrested on Oct. 24 were formally charged with murder on Nov. 6.

The indictment against Piotrowski, Pekala and Chmielewski charged them not only with the murder of Fr Popieluszko, but with the attempted murder of Chrostowski and also with an attempt on Fr Popieluszko's life on Oct. 13, 1984, when they had allegedly tried to cause his car to crash. Pietruszka was indicted on charges of inciting his three co-defendants to kidnap and kill Fr Popieluszko. The trial began in Torun on Dec. 27, 1984, and ended on Feb. 7, 1985, with the four defendants being found guilty as charged. Piotrowski and Pietruszka were each sentenced to prison terms of 25 years, Pekala to 15 years and Chmielewski to 14 years (these sentences were confirmed by the Supreme Court on April 12).

Gen. Wojciech Jaruzelski, then Poland's Prime Minister and first secretary of the ruling Polish United Worker's Party (PUWP), on Oct. 26, 1984, condemned the kidnapping of Fr Popieluszko as "an act of political banditry". Although the kidnapping and the discovery of Fr Popieluszko's body led to widespread unrest including emotional pro-Solidarity demonstrations at Fr Popieluszko's church in Warsaw and elsewhere, it was generally accepted that the government was not responsible, and the Church and Solidarity appealed for calm. Opposition activists linked the kidnapping with earlier attacks on Solidarity supporters, which were believed to have been carried out by vigilante groups of police officers or members of the security forces who were connected with hardline elements in the PUWP leadership and who reportedly called themselves the Anti-Solidarity Organization.

Under cross examination at their trial Popieluszko's killers claimed to have believed that they had high-level protection, and would be rewarded for their action. However, the state prosecutor declared in his summing up that there was no evidence of a broader plot, nor of a conspiracy to discredit the government, as had been claimed in some quarters. These assertions were repeated in official comment on the trial in *Trybuna Ludu*, the PUWP newspaper, and in other party organs in Eastern Europe, among them the Czechoslovak Communist Party newspaper *Rude Pravo*, which called the murder "an individual act with which the authorities have nothing in common". Speaking on Feb. 12, Jaruzelski expressed his confidence that all those responsible for the killing of Fr Popieluszko had been brought to justice.

Western observers on the other hand speculated that the heavy sentence passed on Pietruszka was designed to place on him the brunt of the blame and limit the danger of the indictment going any higher. Nevertheless, after the trial Platek, a trial witness and the subject of allegations in Pietruszka's testimony, was dismissed from his Interior Ministry post. Furthermore, in mid-May 1985 Lt.-Gen. Miroslaw Milewski was removed from the PUWP politburo, secretariat and central committee, having been responsible for special supervisory control of party members in the Ministry of the Interior until that responsibility had been transferred to Jaruzelski on Nov. 6, 1984. Although Milewski's "resignation" was ascribed officially to "purely personal reasons", it was described in *The Times* as the "final political reckoning for the murder of Fr Popieluszko".

Earlier, suspicions of a wider political plot to discredit the government had been strengthened by the arrest, reported on Nov. 18, 1984, of Kazimierz Mijal, a former émigré who was charged with re-entering the country with forged papers and with distributing illegal documents. Mijal, an associate in the 1950s of Poland's Stalinist leader Boleslaw Bierut and a member of the "Natolin" (pro-Soviet) faction in the PUWP, had been a party central committee member and government minister until being removed because of his Stalinist views in 1957. He had defected to Albania in 1966, where he had set himself up as general secretary of an organization calling itself the Communist Party of Poland, and had made regular broadcasts on the Polish service of Radio Tirana.

Recommendations for major organizational changes in the security service and other law enforcement agencies, a response to the murder of Fr Popieluszko, were announced by Jaruzelski in late December 1984. These included introduction of a form of positive vetting to test political allegiances, closer PUWP supervision of the Interior Ministry, and measures to end nepotism in the Interior Ministry and improve the educational standards of the police.

In mid-1986 the Polish government approved a review of the cases of perpetrators of a range of crimes including politically motivated offences. As a result almost all of Poland's political prisoners were freed, but the review also led in October to a cut in prison sentences for Pietruszka (to 15 years), Pekala (to 10 years) and Chmielewski (to eight years). In December 1987 the Supreme Court ordered reductions in the sentences of all four defendants in the Popieluszko case, Piotrowski's sentence being cut to 15 years, Pietruszka's to 10 years, Pekala's to six years, and Chmielewski's to four-and-a-half years (consequently, Chmielewski was released from prison in April 1989). The second set of sentence reductions was justified by officials on humanitarian grounds following pleas from the murderers' families concerning the welfare of their children, and the health of Pietruszka and Chmielewski.

Comparisons with the murder of Fr Popieluszko suggested themselves very easily following the deaths in suspicious circumstances of three Roman Catholic priests linked to the political opposition during 1989. According to Church representatives and lawyers, 74-year-old Fr Stefan Niedzielak died at his home in Warsaw on Jan. 21 from blows to the neck, although the Interior Ministry denied that he had been murdered. On Jan. 30 Fr Stanislaw Suchowolec, 31, was found asphyxiated in his Bialystok flat, the official inquest report published in June finding that his death was due to inhaling fumes from a faulty electric heater. The third priest was Fr Sylwester Zych, a controversial figure who had been imprisoned between 1982 and 1986 for alleged complicity in the killing of a Warsaw policeman. He was found dead at a bus stop in the coastal resort of Krynica Morska, more than 250 km from his parish at Skierniewice. The regional prosecutor in Elblag ruled on Aug. 24 that Zych had died of alcohol poisoning, that bruises and bone fractures had probably been caused during efforts to revive him, and that there was insufficient evidence to suggest foul play.

As the result of a power-sharing agreement between the PUWP and Solidarity, elections in June 1989 saw Solidarity deputies enter Poland's parliament, and led eventually to the formation of a Solidarity-led government. On Aug. 3 the *Sejm*, the lower house of parliament, approved a motion by Solidarity deputies to set up a special parliamentary commission to investigate accusations that the police and security services had committed up to 100 "political murders" since the imposition of martial law in December 1981.

IPG

SOUTH AFRICA

Muldergate Affair (1978–79)

Balthazar Johannes Vorster, Prime Minister (1966–78); State President (1978–79).
Dr Cornelius Petrus "Connie" Mulder, Minister of Information and Interior; Minister of Plural Affairs and Information; provincial leader Transvaal National Party.
General Hendrik van den Bergh, Head of Bureau of State Security (BOSS).
Dr Eschel Rhoodie, Secretary of Information in Department of Information.
Pieter Willem (P. W.) Botha, Minister of Defence, National Party provincial leader (1966–78); Prime Minister (1978–84).

In 1972 the South African government had decided to establish a secret fund to promote South Africa abroad by influencing western opinion via the media, and by cultivating allies among influential foreigners. The source of the fund was to remain secret, with neither the Cabinet nor parliament knowing how the fund was being used. Only three Cabinet members knew about the fund's activities: Prime Minister B. J. Vorster, his Finance Minister Owen Horwood, and Dr Cornelius P. "Connie" Mulder, then Minister of Information and the Interior, and later of Plural (i.e. Black) Affairs and Information. Two non-Cabinet figures were closely involved: Gen. Hendrik van den Bergh, the head of the Bureau of State Security (BOSS, the secret police) and Dr Eschel Rhoodie, a journalist and publicist. Van den Bergh was a close friend of Vorster—both men had been detained together during World War II for being pro-Nazi. The secret fund was concealed in the Defence budget, but was administered by Rhoodie as Secretary for Information, reporting to Mulder.

In June 1978 Vorster ordered the reorganization and renaming of the Department of Information following criticism expressed by the Auditor-General of unauthorised expenditure of public money by the Department's officials, and after a parliamentary committee had also expressed concern at the activities of the Department.

Rhoodie, (whose suspension as Secretary for Information was announced in June), had revealed on May 6 that he had been operating a secret fund for which he said he was accountable only to a three-member Cabinet committee and which had never been approved by Parliament. Vorster made known in Parliament two days later that he had personally authorised the Department of Information to use secret funds without parliamentary approval for purposes which were "in the highest national interest", and in order to combat what he described as "the psychological and propaganda onslaught" against South Africa abroad. Nonetheless he said there would be an investigation into the alleged irregularities.

On Sept. 27 Vorster announced that a parliamentary commission of inquiry had found no irregularities in the accounts of the Department. However, a wider inquiry was still in progress to examine the purposes for which the money had been spent and to establish whether the officials had received any financial gain for their actions. The next day the caucus of the ruling National Party (NP) held an election to choose Vorster's successor as party leader, and thereby Prime Minister. (Vorster had suddenly announced on Sept. 20 that he was to resign as Prime Minister for reasons of health, but would be available for election as State President to replace Dr Nicolaas J. Diederichs, who had died in August.) Mulder, the NP leader in the Transvaal, had up till then been considered likely to succeed Vorster, but he was defeated by 98 votes to 74 in the second ballot by the Cape Province party leader, P. W. Botha. The continuing allegations of corruption in Mulder's Department of Information undoubtedly ruined his chances of becoming party leader. Vorster was sworn in as State President on Oct. 10, 1978.

Press investigations played a major role in the exposure of the scandal. In late October 1978 a report in the Johannesburg weekly *Sunday Express*, later backed up by the Erasmus Commission (see below), claimed that the equivalent of almost $14 million of the discredited department's funds had been used to launch an English-language newspaper, the *Citizen*, in 1976. This newspaper was intended to counter the anti-government reporting of most of the existing English-language press. The *Citizen* was 25 per cent foreign-owned, but the paper had refused to disclose the identity of its South African ownership, leading to speculation that government officials were involved.

The influential *Rand Daily Mail* followed these disclosures with a report that a further $15 million of the Department's money had "disappeared".

Judge Anton Mostert was appointed as a one-man commission to investigate the activities of the Department's officials. On Nov. 2, despite a request by the Prime Minister not to do so, Mostert published some of the evidence given to him by witnesses who included Vorster, Mulder, Gen. van den Bergh, and Louis Luyt, a South African fertilizer magnate. Mostert's evidence implicated Mulder in the scandal; protesting his innocence, he resigned from the Cabinet on Nov. 7.

According to Mostert's evidence, there had been massive misuse of public money through the secret fund, involving unsuccessful attempts to purchase influential media groups, namely (i) South African Associated Newspapers (SAAN), whose publications included English-language opposition papers the *Rand Daily Mail*, the *Sunday Times* and the *Sunday Express* (both of Johannesburg), and the *Cape Times*; and (ii) a US newspaper, the *Washington Star*.

The evidence indicated that the Department had loaned six million rand (approximately $7 million) to Luyt to finance the purchase of SAAN; this bid having failed, Luyt was then loaned at favourable terms money to start and maintain the *Citizen*, the editorial content of which was under the control of Rhoodie. According to Mostert's investigation, Luyt sold the *Citizen*, which had a wide readership among conservative whites, but was making losses, in February 1978, and invested the Department of Information's capital in his fertilizer business.

Both these attempts to buy media influence apparently involved a right-wing US publisher, John McGoff, who nonetheless denied the allegations. Mostert maintained that both McGoff and the German tabloid newspaper tycoon Axel Springer had offered to help finance Pretoria's bid to purchase SAAN.

In the face of evidence which revealed that Mulder knew about public money being used to set up the pro-National Party *Citizen*, Mulder maintained that he had acted in the best interests of his country, but declared on Nov. 3 that he had been guided by the principle that no rules applied when the continued existence of the country was at stake. Following his resignation from the Cabinet, he said that he "had no pangs of conscience about the entire matter" and had resigned only to "assist the Prime Minister". On Nov. 11 he was forced to resign as leader of the Transvaal NP.

Botha terminated Mostert's commission of inquiry on Nov. 7, partly on the grounds that the judge had made public "unverified evidence . . . in an unevaluated way". Four days earlier Botha announced the appointment of a judicial commission consisting of three lawyers chaired by Justice Rudolph P. B. Erasmus. The Commission's brief was to inquire into the questions of "any irregularities or unlawful gaining of advantage by individuals or bodies, or the misappropriation of public funds by the former Department of Information and/or any person connected with that". Botha's action in respect of Judge Mostert was criticized by, among others, the chairman the General Bar Council, who argued that it could be interpreted as interference with the independence of the judiciary.

In the course of November 1978 it emerged that (i) the Foreign Affairs Association, described as "an independent multiracial organization committed to promoting South Africa's contact with the outside world" had been funded by the Department of Information, but was now to be disbanded; and (ii) the Southern Africa Freedom Foundation had been largely funded by the Department to the tune of R 1,000,000 (approximately $1,150,000 at current rates of exchange), and that the Foundation had close links with the "Club of Ten" which had placed advertisements in UK and US newspapers defending South African government policies.

The Erasmus Commission published an interim report on Dec. 5, 1978. This revealed the extent of the defunct department's secret projects, said to number between 160 and 180. Funds for these activities had first been allocated via BOSS as being for "security services", although they were in fact "intended for sensitive projects" of the Department of Information. The report explained that the department of the Prime Minister, under which BOSS fell, did not want to carry the secret fund and shifted it onto the Department of Defence because it did not know to what extent it was exempt from audit. P. W. Botha, as the then Minister of Defence, did not want this secret fund either, but was forced to accept it against his will; he however insisted on an internal accountant and proper auditing. The report noted however that "apart from the approval of some projects by the Minister [of information] the utilization and control of the fund were exclusively in the discretion of [Rhoodie]".

Rhoodie, as Secretary for Information, had insisted that everything connected with the secret fund was secret; that it was therefore "not possible to keep conventional books and to let other officers into secrets" and that he had not discussed all projects with Mulder. An internal auditor had reported that he had been unable to obtain adequate information on how the fund was spent, and testified that Rhoodie had, without authority, raised loans abroad to the value of about R 16,000,000. Rhoodie also claimed that in 1976 he had destroyed documents on the orders of the then Prime Minister Vorster and Gen. van den Bergh when it emerged that the Auditor-General was asking questions about the Department's expenditure.

Vorster maintained that he did not know about the source of the *Citizen*'s funding until April 1977. In his testimony Vorster said that he had been informed by an official of BOSS named Loot Reynders in November 1977 about the likelihood of corrupt practices in the allocation of funds, and that more than R 20,000,000 of government money had by November 1977 been spent on the *Citizen*. Vorster said that, on learning this, he informed Mulder that to use public funds for running a newspaper was not "morally or ethically justifiable". Both Rhoodie and Mulder asserted however that Vorster had approved of the idea when it was first hatched in 1975.

The Commission noted that the *Citizen* had cost the government nearly R 32,000,000 in total. In June 1978 Luyt had agreed to repay nearly R 14,000,000 in instalments over seven years.

The Commission's interim report totally exonerated Vorster, Botha, and Finance Minister Horwood from implication in the irregular allocation of funds from the secret account. In respect of Mulder, however, it stated that he "wrongly interpreted his function as head of his department and . . . fulfilled it incompetently".

The report said that when Mulder discovered in the budget for the 1977–78 financial year that no provision had been made for the secret fund due to the fact that Botha as Minister of Defence had refused to make funds available, he was informed by Rhoodie that foreign loans had been raised to tide the department over, but Mulder never personally satisfied himself whether and how the financing had been provided for. Thus, through Mulder's negligence, Rhoodie was placed in total control of between R 14 million and R 17 million; the report concluded that "in this sense the responsibility for the misappropriations by Rhoodie out of the secret fund must be placed squarely on Mulder's shoulders".

It also emerged that Mulder had pressurized Reynders to produce a false initial report to Vorster to clear the department of irregularities, and that Reynders had indeed done so, at a time when it was obvious that Vorster was about to resign as Prime Minister, and when Mulder was clearly a strong candidate for the succession.

The Commission castigated Rhoodie for destroying records which would reveal incidents of fraud and theft, and for numerous claims by him for subsistence, travelling etc. which could not be substantiated.

Gen. van den Bergh, who had resigned as head of BOSS in September, also came out badly from the investigation. It concluded that he "saw himself as the power behind the throne", and that in attempting to influence events, particularly regarding Vorster's successor as Prime Minister, in which he strongly supported Mulder, he "sometimes withheld facts from Vorster and sometimes gave him only selected facts". He was "in charge of a formidable network of agents whose qualities he described in sinister terms", and the commission found that "there was a real danger at all times of material irregularities being covered up through van den Bergh's action and interference".

Gen. van den Bergh denounced the Commission's report as "the biggest character assassination in the history of South Africa". Justice Erasmus promptly called for him to be charged with contempt of commission, but on Jan. 24, 1979 it was announced that he would not be prosecuted as this would involve the disclosure of evidence detrimental to state security.

Mulder resigned his parliamentary seat at Botha's request on Jan. 24 because of his involvement in the scandal. Earlier in the month, the official opposition had threatened to introduce a motion of censure against him on the ground that he had made untrue statements to the House of Assembly. On April 6 he was expelled from the NP for refusing to accept the Erasmus Commission's findings and for publicly accusing Vorster of having lied about the extent of his involvement.

Meanwhile Rhoodie fled abroad in November 1978 after testifying before the Erasmus Commission. In March 1979 he surfaced in France, where he threatened to publish tape recordings detailing 180 secret projects, and information which would he said, reveal Vorster's tacit consent to the use by the Department of any means to improve South Africa's image abroad—including the setting aside of sums with which to bribe foreign politicians, business people and journalists.

Among other things, the projects included funding to help secure the defeat of anti-apartheid politicians in the USA, support for a right-wing party in Norway, bribes for trade unionists in the USA and Japan not to participate in boycotts of South African products, etc.

Gen. van den Bergh secretly met Rhoodie in Paris on March 10, promising him employment abroad and a large sum of money in return for his silence on the events. Soon afterwards, however, Gen. van den Bergh's own passport was confiscated by the state.

A further interim report was published by the Erasmus Commission on April 2, 1979, again exonerating Vorster, P. W. Botha and all members of his Cabinet from having any prior knowledge of irregularities occurring in the Department. Among other things, it found that (i) Rhoodie's assertion of the existence of a cabinet committee was "a figment of the imagination"; (ii) Horwood had no knowledge of the *Citizen* project during the period concerned; (iii) P. W. Botha did not know for what purpose the Department of Information had in 1974 transferred to the Union Bank of Switzerland an amount of $10,000,000 channelled through the Department of Defence, of which Botha, then Minister of Defence, had been aware; and (iv) Horwood had no knowledge, before September 1978, of the details of secret projects of the Department of Information, for which provision was made in successive budgets.

Rhoodie alleged that the sum of $10,000,000 had been used by the pro-South African McGoff to buy the Californian paper, the *Sacramento*

Union after he had failed in his earlier attempt to buy the *Washington Star*.

In its final report, however, published on June 4, the Erasmus Commission amended its interim report of April 2 and stated that President Vorster had to bear joint responsibility for corruption in the Department of Information when he was Prime Minister.

Vorster was accused of failing to take steps to end a wrongful state of affairs, and in particular had (i) wrongly sanctioned the Reynders report which he knew falsely cleared Mulder and others of irregularities; and (ii) failed for more than a year to stop state spending on the *Citizen*, of which he had been aware since August 1977.

Among other things the final report stated (i) that it was "incredible" that some $6,350,000 could not be accounted for out of a total of $11,000,000 sent to McGoff for his attempt to buy the *Washington Star*; and (ii) that legislation should be passed to enable prosecution of a person (such as Rhoodie or van den Bergh) without the state being blackmailed with the threat to disclose official secrets. It also recommended prosecution of Rhoodie's brother, Professor Nic Rhoodie (whom Rhoodie had appointed as his own secretary in the Department of Information), and another businessman who had "lined his pockets" with money entrusted to him by the Department.

Vorster's resignation as State President was announced by Prime Minister Botha on June 4, 1979. Botha and Horwood were ultimately cleared of complicity, the report stating that they had "inherited" the scandal from Vorster's time as Prime Minister.

Rhoodie was apprehended by the French authorities in July 1979 and the following month was extradicted to South Africa. He stood trial in September, and received a six-year prison sentence for fraud, which was later overturned.

On Aug. 30 Mulder was cleared of a charge of contempt for refusing to testify before the Erasmus Commission, the Supreme Court finding that the Commission had overstepped its brief in seeking to gather further information regarding the government's attempts to buy the *Washington Star*.

The scandal rocked the Afrikaner community to its foundations. Vorster, who became Prime Minister in 1966, had for many South Africans personified supposed Afrikaner values of determination and moral rectitude. His disgrace, and the revealed extent of government involvement in the scandal, was a severe blow to the community's self confidence. The affair nonetheless did much to strengthen the *verkrampte* (inward-looking, non-reformist) wing of the NP; its exponent Andries Treurnicht replaced Mulder as party leader in the Transvaal, and was appointed to the Cabinet. As with "Watergate" in the USA, (see United States: *Watergate Affair, 1972–74*), the exposure of "Muldergate" was very much the work of investigative press reporters, and depended on the integrity of judges; similarly it outraged long-standing supporters of the establishment as well as liberals.

KD

Terre'Blanche Affair (1988–89)

Eugene Terre'Blanche, leader Afrikaner Resistance Movement.

The leader of the extreme right-wing Afrikaner Resistance Movement (AWB), Eugene Terre'Blanche, was arrested on Dec. 27 1988, and accused of causing "malicious damage" to the entrance gates of the Boer War memorial at Paardekraal near Johannesburg during a nocturnal visit there by him in the company of a female journalist. In Krugersdorp on April 30, 1989, charges against him were dropped, the magistrate finding that the police had brought no adequate evidence to support their allegations.

Terre'Blanche denied any improper liaison with Jani Allen, who had written several feature articles about him for the English-language mass circulation *Sunday Times* of Johannesburg. He claimed that at the time of the alleged incident, he was waiting with her at the memorial for a Portuguese television crew to arrive. Critics of Terre'Blanche within the AWB alleged that despite the movement's strict moral code, he abused his position by drinking and womanizing.

Supporters of Terre'Blanche rallied round him, unanimously endorsing him as leader at a special meeting in January, but reports of his dubious activities caused a split in the movement. A splinter group was formed, calling itself the Boer Freedom Movement, and including among its members Jan Groenwald, whom Terre'Blanche had suspended as AWB deputy leader on Jan. 3, 1989.

KD

SOVIET UNION

Rust Affair (1987)

Mikhail Gorbachev, general secretary of the Communist Party of the Soviet
   Union (1985–).
Marshal Aleksandr Koldunov, Deputy Minister of Defence and Com-
   mander-in-Chief of air defence forces.
Mathias Rust, West German amateur pilot.
Marshal Sergei Sokolov, Minister of Defence.

Every year, May 28 is celebrated in the Soviet Union as Border Guards'
Day. How great the embarrassment, therefore, that on May 28, 1987,
a young West German amateur pilot, Mathias Rust, should achieve
an astonishing breach of Soviet air defences by flying a light aircraft,
unauthorised and unimpeded, from Helsinki in Finland and across more
than 750 km of Soviet airspace to the centre of Moscow, where he landed
beside the walls of the Kremlin (the seat of the Soviet government), close
to Red Square. Ironically, this humiliation of the defenders of the Soviet
Union played straight into the hands of Soviet leader Mikhail Gorbachev by
providing a much-looked-for opportunity to strengthen control by the ruling
Communist Party (CPSU) over the military establishment, considered one
of the main bastions of resistance to Gorbachev's reformist policies.
   Herr Rust, aged 19, had chartered a single-engined Cessna 172 aeroplane
from his Hamburg flying club for a tour of Scandinavia. He had flown
single-handed first to Reykjavik in Iceland and then via the Faroe Islands
and Norway to Finland, where he told air traffic controllers upon leaving
Helsinki's international airport at Malmi that he was bound for Stockholm,
Sweden. Instead, he headed south-east towards the Estonian coast, and his
failure to show up on radar screens along his declared course prompted
Finnish coastguards to mount a search in the belief that he might have
ditched into the sea.
   In order to enter Soviet airspace, Rust was at first assumed to have
successfully evaded the Soviet Union's extensive air defence network by
flying low enough to avoid radar detection. However, in an official
statement issued following a meeting of the CPSU central committee
politburo on May 30 (called specifically to discuss Rust's breach of Soviet
air defences) it was revealed that the plane had been detected by Soviet air
defence forces as it had approached Soviet airspace off the north coast of
Estonia near the town of Kohtla-Järva, and that Soviet fighter aircraft had
twice circled the plane, but that confusion over its origins had prevented
its being intercepted. (Rust confirmed at his trial that he had switched off

his radio to avoid being challenged when approached by Soviet aircraft.) Observers speculated that responsible officials had either assumed the plane to be domestic, or that they had been reluctant to act for fear of repercussions similar to those which had followed the shooting down in 1983 of a South Korean airliner which had intruded into Soviet airspace over the Pacific island of Sakhalin.

Shortly after landing on a slip road leading into Red Square, the Soviet state's most hallowed ground, Herr Rust was arrested. Initially, comments by officials and the Soviet media gave the impression that the authorities would be unlikely to deal harshly with Rust, but subsequently the media began to allege that although Rust "had no malicious intent" he had not been acting alone: the CPSU newspaper *Pravda* on June 5 suggested that he had been sent on a "suicide mission" to precipitate a crisis in Soviet–West German relations. Meanwhile, the West German government issued a statement on June 1 calling Rust's flight a "foolhardy act" which might have had "extremely unfortunate consequences for himself and for political developments".

Herr Rust went on trial on Sept. 2 before the Soviet Supreme Court on charges of unlawful entry into the Soviet Union, violation of international flight rules, and malicious hooliganism. He faced a maximum sentence of 10 years' imprisonment relating to the second charge. He initially pleaded guilty to all three charges, but subsequently withdrew his guilty plea in respect of the charge of hooliganism, declaring that he had been careful not to endanger lives. In an 80-minute statement to the court Rust declared that he had been on a peace mission prompted by his disappointment at the failure of the October 1986 Reykjavik summit meeting between Gorbachev and US President Ronald Reagan to produce an agreement on disarmament, and that he had flown to Moscow in the hope of meeting Gorbachev "to tell him my thoughts". Rust acknowledged that he had not properly considered the consequences of his actions, and asserted that he had acted entirely alone. The trial lasted three days, at the end of which Rust was sentenced to four years in a labour camp for "malicious hooliganism"; his claim that he had been engaged in a peace mission was rejected and his aim was declared to have been that of "seeking publicity" (according to a witness testifying at the trial, on emerging from the plane in Moscow Rust had told onlookers that he had flown to Red Square "for fun"). Rust was also given concurrent sentences of three years for violating international flight rules and two years for illegal entry into the Soviet Union. Sentences handed down by the Supreme Court were not open to appeal. However, Rust was released on Aug. 3, 1988 (having completed only 11 months of his sentences). He was immediately deported to West Germany.

A communiqué issued following the CPSU politburo meeting of May 30 observed that the air defence forces had displayed "impermissible lack of concern and resolve in attempting to intercept the intruding aircraft without resorting to combat means", and that "this points to serious shortcomings in the organization of the performance of combat duty in guarding the country's airspace, and to a lack of due vigilance and discipline and to major omissions in the leadership of the troops on the part of the USSR Ministry of Defence". Marshal Aleksandr Koldunov was relieved of his duties as Commander-in-Chief of the air defence forces and as a Deputy Minister of Defence, and the official announcement of the politburo session was immediately followed by the announcement that Marshal Sergei Sokolov had retired as Minister of Defence and had been replaced by Gen. Dmitry Yazov. Shortly afterwards Yazov also replaced Sokolov as a candidate (non-voting) member of the politburo.

Even before the Rust affair provided the opportunity for this shakeup in the topmost military ranks, the armed forces had become the subject of increasing criticism in the official media for tardiness in introducing reforms and for widespread indiscipline and low morale. Some Western observers had interpreted this as part of a CPSU-initiated campaign to diminish the military's prestige in order to weaken its role in security and foreign policy formulation, the military establishment being considered hostile to international arms control initiatives and plans to cut spending on armaments manufacture. The criticism intensified immediately after Rust's flight to Moscow, with the armed forces newspaper *Krasnaya Zvezda* on June 4 attacking "sluggishness and conservatism" in the work of the military. A fortnight later the same newspaper reported a meeting of CPSU activists from the Moscow air defence district at which a number of officers, including two Air Force generals, an Army general and a colonel were expelled from the party. In an address to the meeting Boris Yeltsin, then the first secretary of the CPSU committee in Moscow, accused the district's military leadership of demoralizing troops by bullying, idleness and corruption and revealed that Marshal Anatoly Konstantinov had been replaced as commander of the Moscow air defence district even before the Rust affair for failing to "translate party congress political directives into specific action".

IPG

Yury Churbanov and the Uzbekistan Cotton Scandal
(1976–90)

Col-Gen. Yury Churbanov, USSR First Deputy Interior Minister (1980–84).
Telman Gdlyan, chief corruption investigator at the USSR State Procurator's Office.
Nikolai Ivanov, chief corruption investigator at the USSR State Procurator's Office.
Sharaf Rashidov, first secretary of Uzbek Communist Party (1960–84).
Gen. Nikolai Shcholokov, USSR Interior Minister (1969–82).

The latter years of the rule of President Leonid Brezhnev, who died in 1982, are now denigrated in official Soviet pronouncements as the "period of stagnation", when corruption was rife, and a deep-seated malaise afflicted public morale and morality. Nowhere were the crimes of fraud, embezzlement and bribery more prevalent than in the Soviet Central Asian republic of Uzbekistan. Here, local government and Communist Party bosses ran their departments or regions like fiefdoms, and amassed vast personal fortunes principally by creaming off profits from the cotton harvest, the mainstay of the Uzbek economy.

Brezhnev's successor, Yury Andropov, began a clampdown against corruption, and this was stepped up by Andropov's former protégé Mikhail Gorbachev after he assumed the leadership of the Communist Party (CPSU) in 1985. Numerous officials were dismissed, arrested and tried. One of the highest ranking figures to be convicted as a party to the corruption of the Uzbek bosses was Col.-Gen. Yury Churbanov, a one-time First Deputy Minister of the Interior, and the son-in-law of none other than Brezhnev himself.

Born in 1936, Yury Churbanov was a lowly functionary in the Interior Ministry until in 1971 he married Galina Brezhneva, daughter of Leonid Brezhnev. Thereafter he made a spectacular rise through Interior Ministry ranks until in 1980 he was appointed First Deputy Minister, and in addition he was named a candidate (non-voting) member of the CPSU central committee and a deputy to the Supreme Soviet (parliament) in the Russian republic. However, following the death of his father-in-law in November 1982 Churbanov's fall was just as precipitate: he was demoted to a minor post in the Interior Ministry in November 1984, and lost his candidate membership of the CPSU central committee in March 1986 at the 27th party congress.

Before Yury Churbanov's involvement in the Uzbekistan cotton affair became known the Churbanovs had already been touched by public scandal. On Jan. 20, 1982, Gen. Semyon Tsvigun, the deputy head of the State Security Committee (KGB), died suddenly in mysterious circumstances, widespread rumour speaking of suicide after a heated argument with Mikhail Suslov (the CPSU's chief ideologist and a close associate of Brezhnev). The KGB had apparently resolved to arrest Boris Buryatia (a.k.a. "Boris the Gypsy"), a performer with the Moscow State Circus and a close friend of Galina Churbanova, on charges of illicit dealings in large quantities of diamonds and other jewels, and was thereby thought to have threatened serious embarrassment for President Brezhnev. However, Suslov himself died on Jan. 25, and Buryatia was arrested by the KGB on Jan. 29, the day of Suslov's funeral.

Furthermore, Churbanov's former boss, Gen. Nikolai Shcholokov, committed suicide in 1983 together with his wife while under criminal investigation for corruption, having been dismissed by Andropov as Interior Minister in 1982. An exposé of Shcholokov in the newspaper *Literaturnaya Gazeta* in May 1988 revealed that during his 16 years in office he had embezzled some 700,000 roubles (more than US$1,000,000) of state funds.

What became known as the "Uzbekistan cotton scandal" came to light in 1983 when a new Soviet military satellite revealed that much of the land in Uzbekistan which officials claimed was producing cotton was in fact barren. Investigators sent into the republic gradually discovered (in the face of concerted efforts by local officials to thwart them) that between 1976 and 1983 Uzbek government and Communist Party officials had embezzled some 3,000 million roubles from the state by inflating cotton production statistics and pocketing the money paid by the state for cotton which was never grown. They paid large bribes to Interior Ministry officials to keep the matter secret. Following discovery of the scandal numerous officials began to be arrested and tried, and there were a number of executions. However, the investigation came too late to net the man regarded as the "godfather" of the scandal, Uzbek Communist Party first secretary Sharaf Rashidov, who died in 1983.

Churbanov's arrest on suspicion of corruption and bribe-taking was confirmed on Feb. 3, 1987. He went on trial in Moscow on Oct. 5, 1988, with eight other defendants, all police officials from Uzbekistan, accused of accepting bribes from Uzbek officials to provide protection from corruption investigations. The trial received considerable Soviet media coverage, scathing newspaper articles invariably depicting Churbanov as a weak, impressionable and vain man who had been promoted beyond his capabilities following his marriage to Galina Brezhneva. On Dec. 30 Churbanov was convicted of accepting bribes worth 90,000 roubles and of abuse of power, and was sentenced on Dec. 30, 1988, to 12 years in a harsh regime corrective labour camp. Six other defendants were also imprisoned for terms of between 10 and 12 years.

Meanwhile Galina Churbanova had suffered a further indignity when in July 1988 it had been announced that Brezhnev's relatives were to be stripped of their "undeserved" pensions and privileges.

The Uzbekistan cotton scandal took an entirely new turn in April–May 1989 when Telman Gdlyan and Nikolai Ivanov, chief corruption investigators at the USSR State Procurator's Office who had helped uncover the scandal, were accused in the official press of "grave violations" of their office. The CPSU newspaper *Pravda* on April 30 published a letter from a lawyer accusing Gdlyan of intimidating corruption suspects, and shortly afterwards the official press reported Gdlyan's "inhuman conduct" in securing the wrongful imprisonment of a prominent Estonian nationalist. Gdlyan and Ivanov in turn alleged that they were victims of a smear campaign backed by senior officials who had been implicated in corruption, and claimed that among them was Yegor Ligachev, the CPSU central committee politburo and secretariat member who was widely regarded as the leader of the party's conservatives. A special commission was set up to look into the complaints against Gdlyan and Ivanov.

In September Ligachev was officially exonerated of the corruption allegations made against him by Gldyan and Ivanov. USSR Deputy Procurator General V.I. Kravets told the official Tass news agency that claims that Ligachev had received bribes from Inamszhan Usmankhodzhayev, first secretary of the Uzbek Communist Party between 1984 and January 1988, had been concocted by Usmankhodzhayev himself during interrogations following his arrest on corruption charges in October 1988, but that Usmankhodzhayev had since claimed that they had been extorted from him by Gdlyan using threats to arrest members of Usmankhodzhayev's family (Usmankhodzhayev was sentenced at the end of December to 12 years in prison for receiving bribes worth some 50,000 roubles).

The controversy surrounding the work of Gdlyan and Ivanov came to a head on April 18, 1990, when the USSR Supreme Soviet voted to refuse a request by the USSR State Procurator's Office that it rescind the mandates of the two men to sit in the Congress of People's Deputies, so that they might face criminal charges relating to coercion of suspects and witnesses. However, it agreed to a demand that Gdlyan and Ivanov be dismissed from working in the Procuracy, and in a resolution it warned them that their parliamentary immunity from prosecution could yet be withdrawn if they persisted in making "groundless" statements attacking the country's leaders. They had already been expelled in February from the CPSU by the Procuracy's party branch committee for "slander, violating the law, political extremism and gross abuses of party rules". The Supreme Soviet decisions were based on findings by the commission set up in May 1989. Chaired by former dissident Roy Medvedev, the commission confirmed that the investigators had committed "gross violations of the law", but shifted the ultimate blame onto the Procuracy for failing to exercise proper supervision.

Their pursuit of high-level official corruption, and the perception that they were being victimized for it, had earned Gdlyan and Ivanov significant public support. While their case was being debated in the USSR Supreme Soviet on April 17, around 10,000 of their supporters had demonstrated outside the Kremlin, part of a series of rallies in Moscow and Leningrad which since February had attracted crowds of up to 30,000 people.

IPG

SPAIN

Matesa Affair (1969–1975)

Juan Vila Reyes, businessman.

The interrelationship between business and politics in the Spain of Gen. Franco was never illustrated so potently as in the Matesa affair which started as a routine case of corruption and ended in a major political scandal. The central figure, Juan Vila Reyes, had experienced several brushes with the Spanish courts and was finally sentenced to more than 200 years in prison for fraud in connection with his textile company. His close ties with members of the government led to a full-scale purge of the Cabinet but he was released from prison after little more than six months under a general amnesty granted after Franco's death.

As early as 1967 Juan Vila Reyes was ordered by a special court for monetary offences to pay a fine of 21 million pesetas for having secretly exported to Switzerland banknotes to the value of 104 million pesetas. In May 1970 he was sentenced to three years' imprisonment and ordered to pay 1,658 million pesetas on charges that he and 47 other defendants had exported without authorization during 1965–69 some 5,631 million pesetas. The sentence was quashed under an amnesty declared by Gen. Franco in September 1971.

Vila Reyes was already under investigation for other matters connected with his textile firm, Maquinaria Textil del Norte de España, SA, known as Matesa. The inquiry had been ordered by the director general of customs in March 1968 and Vila Reyes and his brother, Fernando, had been removed from their posts in the company in mid-1969. Criminal proceedings against them were initiated in August, followed three days later by the announcement of a special commission to investigate the affair. This concluded that 10,000 million pesetas-worth of credits granted by the Industrial Credit Bank for the export of looms had largely ended up in private hands; Vila Reyes subsequently faced more than 400 charges of falsification, bribery and fraud.

Those charged over the Matesa affair claimed they were innocent because senior politicians, bankers and finance officials had known all about their dealings and had done nothing to stop them. Reports of this defence led to a widespread reshuffle of the Cabinet in October 1969. The amnesty of September 1971, from which Vila Reyes benefited through the quashing of his previous sentence, also granted immunity from prosecution over the Matesa Affair to 10 politicians and five former banking and finance officials, some of whom were to feature in the Matesa trial.

After having been twice postponed during 1974, the main Matesa trial against Juan Vila Reyes and seven others opened in April 1975. The defence was conducted by José Maria Gil Robles, a prominent politician from the Christian Democrat party. Pursuing the claims that his client's dealings had been known by senior members of the administration at the time, Gil Robles called as witnesses the former minister of commerce, two former finance ministers and several other politicians. A request to call Gen. Franco himself was rejected by the court. A month after the trial began all the defendants were found guilty. Vila Reyes was sentenced to a total of 223 years' imprisonment and ordered to pay fines and compensation of more than 10,000 million pesetas. Three other defendants, including Fernando Vila Reyes, were each given jail sentences of 108 years, while the remaining four, all bankers, were banned from holding public posts for one year.

In practice, the prison sentences served for the Matesa convictions would be much less severe than they appeared. The Spanish penal code laid down that the maximum sentence served could not exceed three times the sentence imposed for the most serious offence. (In the case of Juan Vila Reyes this meant 21 years, which would be reduced still further in view of the amount of time he had already served in jail.) The death of Gen. Franco in November 1975 meant there was a further shortening of Vila Reyes' sentence. King Juan Carlos issued a decree pardoning certain prisoners to mark the beginning of his reign. Vila Reyes was included and he walked free on Dec. 2.

RSD

Rumasa Affair (1983–89)

José Maria Ruiz Mateos, businessman.

In some ways the Rumasa Affair can be seen as a dramatization of the changes undergone by Spain as she struggled to throw off the yoke of dictatorship under Franco and to embrace democracy and the coming to power of a Socialist government. José Maria Ruiz Mateos, born into a modest family business, built up one of the most impressive business empires in the world, the Rumasa holding company, which accounted at one time for nearly 4 per cent of Spain's gross national product. He owed his success to his driving self-belief, and close ties with the establishment of Gen. Franco. But after Franco's death and the election of the Socialist Party, Rumasa was expropriated by the government on the grounds that it was insolvent, and its founder began six years of flight from the law, facing extradition from West Germany, escaping from custody and eventually conducting a successful election campaign for the European Parliament while a fugitive from justice.

José Maria Ruiz Mateos was born in 1930 into a family running a medium-sized sherry business in the town of Jerez in southern Spain. He soon proved himself to be an entrepreneur of stature by winning a major contract in 1958 to supply sherry to the British importers, Harveys of Bristol. In 1961 he established the Rumasa holding company (the name came from Ruiz Mateos, SA) to extend his burgeoning business empire from the drinks trade to banking, hotels and insurance. The 1960s was a time of growth in the Spanish economy fuelled by the lack of state controls. Ruiz Mateos made use of his cordial relations with the government of Gen. Franco and close ties with members of the Opus Dei organization — a secretive Roman Catholic lay body with an influential membership in business and commerce. By 1980 Rumasa owned more than 400 companies, including 20 banks, employed more than 60,000 people and accounted for 3.8 per cent of Spain's gross national output. Official tax returns showed that Ruiz Mateos was the richest man in the country.

The death of Gen. Franco in 1975 and the election of a Socialist government was to bring about a dramatic change of fortune for Rumasa and its flamboyant founder. Government investigators came to believe that Rumasa was using the proceeds of its banks to finance further company acquisitions. They also formed the opinion that Rumasa was insolvent, owing more money than it was worth, but found this hard to substantiate since Rumasa, as a private company, had never published any accounts. The government did not want to risk the damage to the economy which might have resulted from the collapse of such a large concern, so they acted quickly in February 1983 to expropriate Rumasa with the aim of selling its constituent companies back to the private sector. The decision provoked a political storm with the opposition challenging the legality of the government's action. It was upheld, however, by two decisions of the Constitutional Court in 1983 and 1984. A parliamentary commission reported in 1985 that the Rumasa Affair could be put down to "the passivity and, on occasions, the complicity and even the explicit support of governments prior to 1977". The uncontrolled expansion of Rumasa was said to have begun in 1969 when the company acquired two banks with the support of the Bank of Spain. From then until 1977, said the report, "the attitude of those responsible for Spanish economic policy was one of actively favouring the expansion of a group which was absolutely unknown as regards its objectives and solvency".

Ruiz Mateos was outraged by the seizure of his company, which he blamed on personal and political spite. Facing criminal charges including fraud and falsification, he and his wife and 13 children fled to Britain, with whom Spain had no extradition treaty. He then added to the wrath of the Spanish authorities by accusing King Juan Carlos of accepting a bribe to engineer the dismissal of certain banking officials. It seemed he had not forgiven the King for signing the official expropriation decree, but his outburst resulted in another criminal charge, of insulting the King, which carried a heavy prison sentence.

When his British permit ran out a year later, Ruiz Mateos moved from country to country, but was arrested at Frankfurt Airport after flying in from the United States. After a legal battle he was extradited to Spain in November 1985 and held in prison for two months before being released into house arrest. He faced trial on two charges, of fraud and falsifying commercial documents, since these were the only charges on which he was extradited.

As the investigation into his case dragged on, Ruiz Mateos became exasperated. He refused to answer to bail on six occasions and was eventually consigned to a maximum security prison. On a visit to the High Court in Madrid in October 1988, he staged a bizarre escape by donning a false moustache and dark glasses and climbing through a window. After his recapture, Ruiz Mateos's long delayed trial began in March 1989. It was to be a short-lived affair. The former tycoon declared that the trial was a farce and dismissed his defence lawyer, causing the hearing to be suspended.

Released on bail once more, Ruiz Mateos pursued a campaign against a former government minister, Miguel Boyer, who was responsible for taking over Rumasa in 1983. First he hired a private plane to "buzz" Boyer's holiday home on the Costa del Sol. Then he issued a libel writ, obliging the ex-minister to turn up at court, and physically assaulted him in a corridor of the courthouse before the television cameras. Ruiz Mateos went into hiding again while a warrant for assault was issued, carrying a possible 20-year prison sentence.

There followed the most extravagant of all Ruiz Mateos's stunts: he stood for the European Parliament in the elections of June 1989 while still a fugitive from Spanish justice. He secretly posted campaign literature and turned up at a meeting of the finance minister in a disguise sufficiently convincing to enable him to secure the minister's autograph, signed "to José Maria with affection". When the result was declared it transpired that Ruiz Mateos had comfortably won two seats, one of which he gave to his son-in-law. One of Spain's European Commissioners, Manuel Marin declared that "no normal country would have voted in a fugitive from justice". Two days later a Madrid court quashed the arrest warrant leaving José Maria Ruiz Mateos, MEP, able to pursue his quest for vindication without fear of seizure by the Spanish police.

RSD

SWEDEN

Raoul Wallenberg Affair (1945–90)

Raoul Wallenberg, Swedish diplomat.

Of all the political *causes célèbres* in the post-war period none has been so enduring as that of Raoul Wallenberg, the Swedish diplomat who saved tens of thousands of Hungarian Jews from the Nazi Holocaust. Did Wallenberg die of a heart attack in a Soviet prison in 1947, after his arrest by the Russians two years earlier? Or did he live on in Soviet prison camps, as suggested by a welter of reported sightings? And then there is the most intriguing question of all: is he alive today, still imprisoned by a Soviet Union unable to retract its past lies about him?

Raoul Wallenberg was born into a privileged and well-known Swedish family in 1912. His father, an officer in the Swedish navy, died three months before Raoul was born. His mother married again and had two further children. But Raoul was always considered to be a Wallenberg and he was watched over by senior members of his family, many of whom were bankers and diplomats. Raoul studied architecture in the United States and worked briefly in South Africa and Israel before returning to Sweden and joining the import-export business of a German-Jewish refugee, Koloman Lauer, selling foodstuffs all over central Europe. When the war broke out in 1939 it became difficult for Jews to travel on business and Raoul fulfilled this role for the company, making use of his skill in languages.

By the Spring of 1944 it was no longer possible to ignore the evidence of the mass extermination of Europe's Jews being carried out by the Nazis. Attention was focused on the 750,000 Jews in Hungary which was formally an ally of Germany and was partially occupied by the Nazis in March. The War Refugee Board, set up by the United States to save Jews from persecution, asked neutral countries to send more diplomats to Hungary on the grounds that it would be more difficult for the Nazis to carry out atrocities with international observers present. Sweden was the first neutral country to respond. Raoul Wallenberg was chosen for the task, because of the connections of his family and the position of his business partner, Koloman Lauer, in the exiled Jewish community.

Raoul Wallenberg's original brief for his mission to Budapest was relatively modest: to save some 400–500 Jews with family or business links to Sweden. He was appointed first Secretary to the Swedish Legation in Budapest arriving there by train in July 1944.

It was already clear that Germany was losing the War, a fact that Wallenberg was able to exploit in his dealings with Hungarian and German officials. He was able to hint that those who co-operated with his efforts to help the Jews would get better treatment when Russian troops occupied Hungary. If that did not work, Wallenberg used other resources, including threats and bribery, using the vast resources of his American backers.

At least 20,000 Jews at risk were given Swedish passports; perhaps as many as 100,000 others escaped through being hidden in a network of "safe houses" established in the city under the protection of the Swedish flag. Wallenberg's intervention was occasionally direct and dramatic. He would embrace groups and individuals bound for the extermination camps of Auschwitz and Riga and place them under his personal protection. More than once he came up against the most feared of the Nazi persecutors, Adolf Eichmann, a senior SS officer who seemed to have made it his personal mission to make sure that Hungary's Jews would not escape Hitler's "Final Solution". Wallenberg's efforts to frustrate his purpose led Eichmann to issue a number of dire threats and some sources maintain that he made at least one attempt on Wallenberg's life. Eichmann himself escaped to South America after the war before being captured, tried and executed in Israel in one of the most celebrated War Crimes trials.

Wallenberg's reputation among the Jewish community had reached legendary proportions, but that did not help him when Russian troops finally entered Budapest in January 1945. Stalin's Soviet Union was deeply suspicious of Sweden's role in the war, believing that the Swedes had hidden behind their neutrality while continuing to trade with the Nazis. Wallenberg's American connections also aroused suspicion and there is evidence that the Russians regarded him as a spy for Washington. Whatever the reason, Wallenberg was arrested by the NKVD, the predecessors of the state security organization, the KGB. He and his Hungarian driver Vilmos Langfelder were taken to Moscow and put in separate cells in the Lubyanka Prison.

There followed many years of confusion about Wallenberg's fate. Some reports said he had been killed by Hungarian bandits during the Russian advance. Attempts by the Swedish government to discover his whereabouts were met with stonewalling replies by the Russians. The Swedish Ambassador to Moscow, Staffan Soderblom, raised the matter with Stalin himself in June 1946 and received a half-hearted promise to look into the case. Yet Soderblom's reluctance to press the matter firmly during these early months has been blamed by some historians of the Wallenberg Affair for giving the impression to the Russians that the Swedes did not attach a high priority to their diplomat. The Swedes continued to approach the matter in a low-key manner, apparently fearing that it would be counter-productive to put too much pressure on the Russians. In August 1947 the Soviet deputy foreign minister, Andrei Vyshinsky, contradicted the previous Moscow line by denying that Wallenberg had ever fallen into Russian hands. He told the Swedes: "Wallenberg is not in the Soviet Union and is unknown to us."

This did not satisfy Wallenberg's relatives and supporters who continued to believe that he was being held in the Soviet Union. Their contention was supported by prisoners returning from the Soviet Union who spoke of communicating with Wallenberg through tapping on the walls of various prisons. In February 1957 the Soviet government dramatically reversed its previous position by admitting that Wallenberg had been a prisoner. The then deputy foreign minister, Andrei Gromyko, replied to persistent Swedish inquiries that Wallenberg had died of a heart attack in July 1947.

The Soviet Union has stuck to its story ever since but Wallenberg's friends and relatives have refused to believe it. Former inmates of prison camps in many parts of the Soviet Union have spoken of seeing Wallenberg throughout the 1960s and '70s. The most recent reported sightings are in 1981 and 1986. In the spirit of *glasnost*, the Russians invited a group of Wallenberg supporters to visit Moscow and discuss the case in October 1989. They met officials of the KGB and the foreign ministry and were given some of Wallenberg's personal possessions including his diplomatic passport and some notebooks. The officials also presented a death certificate signed by the Lubyanka prison doctor apparently confirming the cause of death as a heart attack. The group went away unconvinced. In May 1990 an international commission of inquiry headed by Professor Irwin Cotler of McGill University in Montreal concluded that the Soviet explanation was untrue and that, without contrary evidence, it was reasonable to assume that Wallenberg must be still alive. The inquiry based its findings on the reported sightings and on discussions with the late Soviet physicist and human rights activist, Dr Andrei Sakharov, who had taken a personal interest in the case.

Forty-five years after his capture by the Russians, Wallenberg's fate remains a mystery. There is an understandable scepticism about the explanation that an apparently fit man could have died conveniently of a heart attack at the age of 35. Some writers have pointed out that it was common in the period of the Stalinist purges for prisoners to be summarily executed and then a death certificate falsified to show death by natural causes. Others say it has also been known for prisoners to become "lost" in the vast Soviet prison system for many years. Many cling to the belief that Wallenberg survives to this day in a Soviet prison.

RSD

Palme Assassination Affair (1986–89)

Olof Palme, Prime Minister (1969–76 and 1982–86).
Christer Pettersson, murder suspect.

The assassination of Olof Palme, Sweden's Prime Minister and best known international statesman, was a large enough blow to the national psyche.

But the chaotic police investigation which followed, ending with the acquittal on appeal of the man initially convicted of the murder, was held by many to herald the end of the "age of innocence" for Swedish society and the realization that Sweden had fallen prey, like the rest of the West, to violence on the streets and corruption in the corridors of power.

Olof Palme had served as Prime Minister for a total of 10 years when he met his death. He was born in 1927 to wealthy parents, attended exclusive schools and finished his education in the United States. He joined the Social Democratic Party in 1952 and a year later was appointed to the staff of the then Prime Minister, Tage Erlander. He became a minister in 1963 and succeeded Erlander as Prime Minister in 1969. The Social Democrats were defeated in 1976 but they returned to government in 1982. Palme had built a formidable reputation as a campaigner for progressive causes — opposing nuclear weapons, colonialism and Third World poverty.

Late at night on Feb. 28, 1986 Olof Palme and his wife, Lisbet, left the Grand Cinema in Stockholm after watching a première of a Swedish film. They started to walk home through the snow-covered streets. Palme had been assigned two bodyguards, but he used them only for official functions; he was fond of boasting that he could pass safely among his fellow citizens in a way which would have been impossible in any other capital city. What followed was to shatter that conviction for ever. A single gunman approached from behind and fired two armour-piercing bullets from a Smith and Wesson .357 revolver into the Prime Minister's back. One of the bullets then grazed Lisbet Palme. Palme died minutes later in his wife's arms.

From the beginning the murder investigation was beset with problems. The police failed to seal off the area and there was a delay in mounting a watch at ports and airports. Rumours quickly began to circulate in the Swedish media, fed by apparently competing elements in the security services. A man connected with an extreme right-wing group in West Germany was arrested three weeks later and charged with complicity in the murder, but he was soon released for lack of evidence. The police turned their attention to a group of left-wing Kurdish refugees, the Kurdish Workers' Party. They were believed to have held a grudge against Palme because two of their number had been jailed in Sweden for the murder of a defector from the group. There was a series of raids on Party members and up to 30 were held for questioning, but embarrassment followed when the Chief Prosecutor for Stockholm publicly disagreed with the police over the strength of evidence against the Kurds. They were all released. But the suspicion against Kurdish groups remained, fuelled by a report from the secret services that a diplomat from the Soviet Union had formed contacts with these groups and gained prior knowledge that an attempt was to be made on Palme's life.

During 1988 there was a bizarre intervention by a publisher, Ebbe Carlsson, who became convinced of the Soviet connection and began his own private investigation, assisted by some police officers and apparently sanctioned by the Justice Minister, Anna-Greta Leijon. She and the national police chief, Nels-Erik Ahmansson, were forced to resign when this became public knowledge. Carlsson, two secret service agents and five current and former police officers were later charged with attempting to smuggle illegal bugging devices into Sweden to help with their investigation.

It was almost three years after the murder that the name of Christer Pettersson, a 42-year-old alcoholic and drug abuser with a list of convictions for violence, first came under close inspection from the police. A case was gradually constructed which supposed that Pettersson had seen the Palmes in the street, impulsively decided to murder them, quickly obtained a gun, carried out the shooting, and escaped on foot. He was identified from a police video by Palme's widow. At his trial which began on June 5, 1989, Lisbet Palme and other witnesses testified that they had seen him at the scene of the crime, although none could remember seeing him with a gun. Pettersson himself strongly denied the charge. The evidence against him appeared largely circumstantial; there was no motive, no murder weapon was ever found and there was no forensic evidence. The suspicion was aired in some sections of the Press that he was a convenient scapegoat. Nevertheless, on July 27 Pettersson was convicted and sentenced to life imprisonment.

His appeal, which began on Sept. 12, led to the discrediting of the prosecution case and his acquittal and release on Oct. 12. Pettersson had spent nine months and 29 days in custody. The Swedish government announced on April 19, 1990 that he was to receive at least £10,000 in compensation. The murder of Olof Palme remained as much a mystery as it had appeared on that cold night in February, 1986.

RSD

UNITED KINGDOM

Unlike the United States, where most of the major "affairs" of the post-war period have involved conflict between the different branches of government, the typical British scandal has focused on the downfall of a single individual. And, to an extent matched in few countries, the cause of such downfalls has often lain in sexual indiscretion, or the allegation of it. Those whose careers were terminated or badly damaged by allegations of sexual impropriety have included a Secretary of War (John Profumo), two government ministers in separate cases in one month in 1973 (Lords Lambton and Jellicoe), a party leader (Jeremy Thorpe) and a chairman of the Conservative Party (Cecil Parkinson). A sexual dimension has also been present in many other cases, including many of the leading espionage cases from Burgess and Maclean to Blunt.

Not all British "affairs" have concerned individuals rather than institutions. Bureaucratic incompetence, red-tape and corruption have been themes through the years in cases such as the Groundnuts Scheme (incompetence), Crichel Down (red-tape) and the Crown Agents Affair (corruption). In a country where discretion and secrecy are the prevailing ethos in public life, some cases (and increasingly so in recent years) have involved the right of the public to know what its political masters are doing. Such cases have included Suez (where the government misled Parliament), the "D" Notice affair (where light was cast on semi-formal censorship of the press), the continuing controversy over the Kincora Boys Home, and a whole sequence of 1980s cases (Tisdall, Ponting, Stalker, Massiter, Oldfield, Zircon and Spycatcher) in which current or former public servants leaked confidential information or made allegations about malpractice. Such recent cases have prompted some to demand a written Constitution and a Freedom of Information Act on the American model. Such demands have made little headway, however, in the face of the stability — or inertia — of British political institutions and often unspoken assumptions about the inherent superiority of a system in which decision-making can proceed (unlike in the USA) untrammelled by publicity or threat that the decision-makers may abruptly find themselves being prosecuted as criminals. The fact that the government is formed by the majority party in Parliament has also meant that cases which might in other circumstances develop into great struggles between the executive and the legislature, often simply fade away. Conversely, however, a government minister under the British system who once loses the confidence of his parliamentary colleagues faces a more certain exit than (for example) a

US cabinet officer who serves essentially at the pleasure of the President.

The British libel laws have served as a significant deterrent to full reporting and investigation of some cases. A vigorous litigant can use the law to curtail comment in ways which are arguably unhealthy in a democracy, and punitive libel awards in some recent cases have stirred doubts about the integrity of freedom of speech in some quarters. Serious investigative journalism — in contrast to the merely scurrilous muckraking of the tabloid press — has arguably declined in recent years. It would be wrong to overstate these trends, however, and they have been offset to some degree by a movement towards greater openness in Whitehall and the establishment of all-party parliamentary investigation committees which have weakened the grip of the executive.

FJH

Groundnuts Affair (1946–51)

Leslie Plummer, Chairman of Overseas Food Corporation.
John Strachey, Minister of Food.
J. A. Wakefield, colonial agriculture expert.

The Groundnuts Scheme was a worthy idea which developed into a disaster through haste, inefficiency, bad management and political interference. The original scheme to grow and harvest groundnuts from large mechanized plantations in Africa was born out of the severe food and foreign exchange shortages experienced by Britain immediately after World War II. The newly elected Labour government hoped that by expanding production in the colonies food and raw materials could be supplied to Britain for post-war reconstruction, while at the same time boosting the economies and infrastructure of colonies progressing towards self-government and eventual independence. State central planning, marketing and distribution would also help define a new relationship between Britain and her colonies, one divorced from the traditional colonial structure. Groundnuts provided a good and cheap source of vegetable fats, and it was hoped that modern mechanized farming would produce large yields.

A mission led by J. A. Wakefield, a former Director of Agriculture for Tanganyika, to investigate groundnut cultivation visited East Africa in mid-1946. The Wakefield Mission Report proposed three sites in Tanganyika — Kongwa and Urambo on the central railway and Nachingwea in the Southern province — as the first developments in what was planned as a series of sites throughout British Africa. In the three sites 3,210,000 acres of otherwise uninhabited and barren bush were to be cleared by 1953 to provide an anticipated crop yield of 600,000 tons. Extensive mechanization was to be used to achieve such a large task on schedule. Unlike other colonial projects, the groundnuts scheme was to be administered directly by the Ministry of Food, with the United Africa Co. (part of Unilever) acting as agent. The funds were also to come from central government rather than the colonial budget.

For a while the Groundnuts Scheme seized the public imagination. Thousands of men, recently demobilized, applied for jobs on the project. Work began on clearing land at Kongwa, against the advice of the Tanganyika government. The scheme soon ran into problems. The Wakefield Mission had only spent nine weeks in East Africa and had not collected sufficient data on soils, rainfall and local conditions. Rainfall in Kongwa proved very different from areas only 10 or 12 miles away where the climate statistics had been gathered. The fact that the areas were sparsely inhabited, which had first attracted the Wakefield mission, meant lack of labour for essential tasks and maintenance. The lack of transport infrastructure made the supply of spares, stores and the possibilities for export difficult. Much of the machinery destined for the project also proved unsuitable for the soils of Kongwa. Heavy tractors were required to deal with the hard soil. By November 1949 three-quarters of the 200 tractors which had arrived in August (originally due to have arrived in February) had broken down. Many of them were ex-US army bulldozers from the Philippines which had not been serviced prior to being transported to Kongwa. Sherman tanks were hastily converted to provide tougher machinery, but the difficult soils continued to provide problems. The harvesting equipment arrived late, and even then left many nuts in the ground which had to be gleaned by hand.

In April 1948 the Overseas Food Corporation (OFC) was set up under the chairmanship of Leslie Plummer and assumed responsibility for the project. By this time details of the actual progress in the field were attracting attention and the scheme was severely criticized in the House of Commons. John Strachey, the Minister of Food, admitted in Parliament on May 14 that the scheme would cost twice as much as originally estimated, but claimed that higher commodity prices would make up the deficit. The first plan for 3,250,000 acres to be cleared was to be scaled down to 2,000,000 acres producing the same yield through intensive farming and with the rotation of sunflower crops.

On Nov. 21 the first annual report of the Overseas Food Corporation revealed losses of £23,000,000. Only 46,620 acres had been cleared and sown, producing only 1,566 tons of oil-bearing crops in the 1947–48 harvest. In the 1948–49 harvest, drought had wilted plants, the soil had baked rock-hard, disease had affected the crop at Urambo, and the failure of the machinery meant that much of the crop would be harvested by hand.

Strachey came under severe criticism for the Ministry's handling of the project in a debate on the OFC's annual report in the House of Commons. However, he maintained his post and attempts to force a public inquiry failed. Wakefield and John Roas, the chief financial officer, were, however, dismissed from the Board of the OFC, partly to allay continued press criticism.

The report of the Public Accounts Committee on the OFC's annual report was published on June 12, 1950. It highlighted many of the problems that had surrounded the project and stated that while the managers were to some extent responsible for the problems in the field, the Ministry of Food should take the blame for the over-hasty implementation of the plan.

The Groundnuts Scheme continued on a reduced scale until its land and assets were acquired by Unilever in 1953. Mechanized production was abandoned and the yields never reached the optimistic targets once predicted. The Scheme distorted Tanganyika's development, creating a "ghost town" at Kongwa and railway links to a port at Mtwara that had little use, while writing off the sum of £36,000,000, equivalent to the total expenditure of the Tanganyika government between 1946 and 1950.

LP

Sherman Pools Affair (1948–49)

Clement Attlee, Labour Prime Minister (1945–51).
John Belcher, former railway clerk and trade unionist; Labour MP (1945–49); Parliamentary Secretary to the Board of Trade (1946–48).
Sidney Stanley, con-man and wheeler-dealer.

The downfall of Labour politician John Belcher had its origins in the restrictions and frustrations of an economically-exhausted and war-weary country. Elected in 1945 against a general expectation that a grateful country would return the victorious Conservative Prime Minister Winston Churchill, the Labour Government was finding peace and prosperity more intractable than the defeat of the Third Reich. Its ambitious strategy to nationalize large areas of industry, shift the industrial war machine to peacetime production and create a comprehensive welfare state came at a time of demobilization and associated manpower problems, food and clothing rationing, and housing and fuel shortages. These latter difficulties led to intrusive state control, petty bureaucracy and endless quotas and permits. Equally inevitable was the growth of the barter or cash economy, corner-cutting, favours, backhanders and informal networks which attempted to satisfy market demand and circumvent the official restrictions that hampered normal economic activities. Many such restrictions could only be overcome with the appropriate form signed by the appropriate civil servant. Knowing whom to approach, how and for what therefore became a pivotal feature of this shadowy world. At the bottom end were the "spivs", who could provide the extra petrol, the rare turkey, and at the top were the "contact-men", the intermediaries who knew their way around town halls and Whitehall.

In 1945 John Belcher was elected Labour MP for Sowerby, Yorkshire: he was 40 years old. His was the classic career of a clever working-class boy who had risen through the trade union movement. A scholarship boy at the local grammar school, he had begun work as an office boy at 17, jointed the Great Western Railway as a clerk and become immersed in trade union and then Labour Party politics. Within a year he was asked to become parliamentary secretary to the Board of Trade, the first step on the government promotions ladder, where first Sir Stafford Cripps and then Harold Wilson was president. Notwithstanding his ministerial salary, the family had had to work hard to make ends meet. Louise Belcher, his wife, was to describe her life in 1948: two sets of tenants shared their Enfield home, she opened her first bank account in 1947, shopped at the Co-op, had worked for the first 13 years of marriage and "could have wrung anybody's neck who said . . . that I had had hundreds of pounds of gifts, because I do not rely on gifts, I rely on my own saving up".

Her outburst, sincere and tearful, came during the hearing of a Tribunal established to ascertain whether government ministers, including her husband, had been the recipients of favours, gifts and bribes from businessmen and intermediaries, primarily from Sidney Stanley. A man of uncertain background but with several aliases, Stanley was the quintessential wheeler-dealer; smooth, well-dressed, self-assured, with a flat in Park Lane; a habitué of dog racing, boxing and fashionable clubs, with a bank account that in 1948 had a turnover of £60,000. He kept up fortuitous meetings with public figures, whom he courted with promises to help them fight communism, and claims of widespread commercial influence both in Britain and the United States. As his circle of political acquaintances grew, so his ever-expanding largesse paid for birthday parties, trips to sporting events and the occasional prize and holidays; Belcher and other politicians steadily accepted Stanley as an influential friend.

Stanley was also parading these contracts before businessmen, trying to trade his supposed influence with them for commission payments. In 1947 Stanley offered three businessmen his influence to circumvent Board of Trade regulations, persuading them to part with large sums of money; £12,000 came from Sherman Pools to avoid prosecution for paper quota infringements, £10,000 from Berger and Sons Ltd., paintmakers, for licences to redevelop premises and £10,000 from Stagg and Russell Ltd., to import amusement arcade machinery. One of the businesses involved in the last deal suspected a con-trick and reported Stanley's activities to the police. The pools promoter, Harry Sherman, likewise complained bitterly to a civil servant over the worthless security Stanley gave him in return for his payment which, he alleged, Stanley had asked for to buy political influence. The civil servant reported this allegation to the President of the Board of Trade, Harold Wilson, who called in the police. In each case the name of Stanley's contact was Wilson's junior minister, John Belcher, and in each case the payments were allegedly intended to bribe him.

Rumours began circulating of a political scandal. Labour Prime Minister Clement Attlee moved swiftly to counteract them, choosing to set up a public inquiry through a quasi-judicial tribunal before which three Cabinet Ministers appeared; Charles Key, Hugh Dalton and John Belcher together with George Gibson, former General Secretary of the Trade Union, the Confederation of Health Service Employees and a government-appointed Director of the Bank of England. Key had only reached the early stages of cultivation by Stanley and Dalton maintained that he had turned down Stanley's blandishments.

The real focus of the Tribunal, however, was on Gibson and Belcher. Gibson was viewed by the Tribunal as under Stanley's influence while Belcher's evidence suggested that he knew that Stanley was expecting some return on the steady drip of entertainment, holidays and gifts he was receiving. The Tribunal concluded that Belcher had done several favours, once in relation to a matter that was the responsibility of another department and once against earlier departmental statements, for Stanley's friends and other businessmen.

Belcher resigned from the Government during the Tribunal proceedings and from Parliament after it reported. He returned to his former job as a railway clerk until 1963: he died the following year.

RAD

Klaus Fuchs Affair (1949–50)

Klaus Fuchs, British scientist and Soviet spy.

During World War II and the immediate post-war period the Soviet Union was anxious to obtain details of Allied atomic research that was denied to them. As the Cold War intensified after 1945 this need became more urgent as the Soviet Union sought to match the USA's nuclear capability. The Fuchs Affair provided one of the first examples of how successful they had been in obtaining atomic secrets and how security was breached.

Emil Julius Klaus Fuchs was born in 1911 near Frankfurt, Germany, the son of a Lutheran pastor, and educated at Leipzig and Kiel Universities. In 1932 he joined the German Communist Party in order to combat Nazism. In 1933, after Hitler's rise to power, he was forced to flee Germany, and went first to France and then Britain. Once in Britain he attended Bristol and Edinburgh Universities, firstly to gain his doctorate and then as a research assistant. Interned as an alien in 1940 he was deported to Canada, but in 1942 was released and returned to Britain to help Prof. Peierls at Birmingham University with projects into atomic research. In July 1942 he applied for naturalization as a British citizen. This was granted, in the view that he was engaged in important research work for national security.

It was also in mid-1942 that he first made contact with the Soviet Union through the secretary to the military attaché's office at the Soviet embassy in London. Fuchs did not disguise his Communist sympathies, although he was not a party member, and regarded his actions as simply informing what was then an allied power of the progress in his research. In December 1943 Fuchs was part of the British team sent to the USA to help in the atomic bomb project. There the Russians provided another agent, Harry Gold, to receive Fuchs' information. This included full details of the first test explosion of the atomic bomb at Alamagordo, New Mexico, and full details of the components, size, construction methods and scientific data for the plutonium bomb then under development.

Fuchs returned to Britain in 1946 and became head of theoretical physics at the Atomic Energy Establishment at Harwell. Contact with the Russians was not resumed until 1947. In January 1947 Prime Minister Attlee and a small group of colleagues secretly decided to authorize the development of Britain's own atomic bomb. Fuchs was assigned to do the technical work for a plutonium bomb. Meanwhile investigations in late 1949 by the American CIA revealed leaks of atomic secrets that could not have come from the spies so far discovered. In the autumn of 1949 American cryptographers successfully started deciphering old messages sent by the Soviet Union during World War II. The correlation between the information and the time spent by Fuchs in America narrowed the hunt down to a member of the British team and eventually to Fuchs himself.

Although Fuchs was under suspicion, the security authorities were reluctant to expose his activities by confronting him directly. Ironically it was Fuchs' own reservations about the security implications of the appointment of his father to a post at Leipzig University in East Germany that prompted a series of interviews with members of the security services. In particular he confided in Wing-Cdr. Henry Arnold, the head of security at Harwell, who passed him to MI-5's best interrogator, William Skardon. It was during these interviews that Fuchs confessed to passing technical data to the Soviet Union.

He was arrested on Feb. 3, 1950, and charged on four counts under the Official Secrets Act. He pleaded guilty and on March 1 he was convicted and sentenced by Lord Chief Justice Goddard to 14 years' imprisonment. The case against him rested on his own written confession and the oral interviews. In his defence it was stated that Fuchs had a sort of split personality where he could both work conscientiously yet, at the same time, find nothing wrong in betraying secrets. In his confession Fuchs said that after the war he had become increasingly disillusioned with communism as practised in the Soviet Union. Once in prison Fuchs was interviewed by the Americans about his US links. He identified photographs of Gold and supplied information that was to lead to the arrest of Gold and the other "atom spies" in the USA (see USA: *Atom Spies Affair, 1950–53*).

Fuchs only served nine years of his sentence and was released in 1959. He resettled in East Germany where he became deputy director of the Nuclear Research Institute near Dresden. He became director in 1964, retiring in 1977. He died in 1988.

The press and public response to the Fuchs trial was muted at the time, concentrating on Fuchs' "disloyalty", but not attaching any of the blame to ministers or officials. Attlee, in a statement to the House of Commons, summed up the Fuchs Affair as "a most deplorable and unfortunate incident", but said that no-one was to blame. The case did, however, have repercussions in Britain's relations with the USA. British laxity over security cast serious doubts over future Anglo-US co-operation in nuclear development, while the knowledge that the USSR had obtained the atomic secrets prompted Truman's decision to proceed with development of the hydrogen bomb. His former superior in East Germany, who defected to the West in 1964, later claimed at a US Congressional hearing that Fuchs had saved the USSR about two years' work in the development of their atomic bomb.

LP

Crichel Down Affair (1950–54)

Sir Thomas Dugdale, Minister of Agriculture.
Christopher Eastwood, Permanent Commissioner of Crown Lands.
Lt-Cdr. George Marten, landowner and farmer.
Claude Wilcox, Under-Secretary at the Ministry of Agriculture.

The Crichel Down Affair is always cited as an example for students of British politics of a minister accepting responsibility for a failure in his department, rather than for a personal failing of his own.

Crichel Down consisted of 725 acres of land in Dorset compulsorily purchased by the Air Ministry in 1940. In 1950, when the land was no longer needed for military purposes, the land was transferred to the Agricultural Land Commission, a body set up to administer land held by the Ministry of Agriculture. The land was then sold for £15,000 to the Commissioners of Crown Lands and rented out to a tenant farmer.

The actions of civil servants that had led to this decision and the exposure of the methods by which they had ignored the claims of others only came to light after persistent complaints, led by Lt.-Cdr. George Marten, whose wife had inherited title to part of the land. He led a petition to the Minister of Agriculture, Sir Thomas Dugdale, on Sept. 28, 1953, and after further correspondence persuaded him to change his mind and set up a public inquiry into the case. This was duly established under Sir Andrew Clark on Nov. 12.

According to the evidence presented at the inquiry, the Agricultural Land Commission had decided to equip Crichel Down and rent it out as a single farm. The subdivision of the land, or letting neighbouring farmers rent parts of it was deemed to be unsuitable at a time when food shortages meant that all productive land should be put to good use. As the Commission's plans for the future of the land percolated out, a number of prospective tenants expressed an interest and made attractive offers which would have spared the Commission the expense of equipping the farm. One of these was from a local farmer, Christopher Tozer.

Shortly afterwards the Crichel Estate (owning that part of the land on Crichel Down inherited by Lt.-Cdr. Marten's wife) applied to buy back that part of land. The Land Commission failed to consider this offer properly as they did not realize that they had the authority to sell the land. Marten wrote to his local MP to present the minister with his objections to Crichel Down being maintained as a single unit when the land had been compulsorily purchased from a number of landowners. The Joint Parliamentary Secretary in the Ministry of Agriculture, Ian Nugent, responded by requesting a report from the Land Commission as to whether the land should be sold to Marten. He received in return a report which contained numerous inaccuracies and without a covering letter casting serious doubts on the cost of equipping Crichel Down as a single unit to rent.

In November 1952 Lord Carrington, the other Joint Parliamentary Secretary, visited Crichel Down at Dugdale's request. He concluded that the land should be kept and farmed as a whole, based on the disadvantages of selling the portion claimed by the Crichel Estate and retaining the remainder. He did not, however, visit any of the adjoining landowners and based his findings on the past reports.

In January 1953 Wilcox suggested to Eastwood that Crichel Down could be bought by Crown Lands, but by the time the file containing previous tenancy applications had been discovered the Crown Lands were already committed to giving Tozer the tenancy. When Lt.-Cdr. Marten wrote to Ian Nugent to suggest that he should become the tenant for Crichel Down, the Crown Lands commitment was not mentioned. Meanwhile Crown Lands had had the land valued and proceeded to buy it after funds were forthcoming from the Treasury. Yet in correspondence with Marten, in spite of stating that the land was unlikely to come up for resale, Crown Lands failed to reply to Marten's proposition to rent the land, proceeding with the tenancy agreement with Tozer which was signed in September.

Sir Andrew Clark's report was published on July 20, 1954. Whereas it revealed no corruption or misconduct by officials, it strongly criticized the way in which government departments had handled the case. In particular it singled out Wilcox for "grave error of judgment" and Eastwood for suggesting that applicants could be misled. It criticized their attitude of hostility towards Marten who was merely attempting to pursue what he thought were his rights. The civil servants were accused of being irritated that anyone should question their judgments.

Sir Thomas Dugdale announced his resignation on the same day at the end of his opening speech in the debate on the affair in the House of Commons. He stressed that it was not his position to endorse what his officials had done or shield them from the consequences of their actions, but to accept the constitutional precept of ministerial responsibility. "I, as Minister, must accept full responsibility to Parliament for any mistakes and inefficiency of officials in my department." A committee chaired by Sir John Woods was created to consider whether the civil servants involved should be transferred and its report accepted by the government. It recommended the transfer of Eastwood and Wilcox (who had already been moved to the post of Principal Financial Officer at the Ministry of Agriculture). It concluded by stating that the public should have confidence in civil servants and that civil servants, in return, should respect the rights and feelings of the individual. Eastwood was eventually transferred to the Colonial Office.

Lord Carrington and Ian Nugent both offered their resignations to the Prime Minister, Sir Winston Churchill, on July 21, after criticism in Parliament of their part in the affair, and both resignations were refused. In February 1955 Crichel Down was offered to Marten for sale at £15,000 — a proposal he eventually accepted "under protest".

LP

Burgess and Maclean Affair (1951)

Guy Burgess, Donald Maclean, Harold "Kim" Philby, Foreign Office
    diplomats and Soviet agents.

The names of Burgess and Maclean have become synonymous with treachery and have become inseparably linked, even though they were not close friends. Their sudden flight from England in May 1951 exposed the infiltration of British intelligence circles by the Soviet Union in the war and post-war years and started the hunt for further spies.

Guy Burgess was born in Devonport in 1911. Originally destined for a naval career, he eventually went to Trinity College, Cambridge, in 1930. Donald Maclean was two years his junior, the son of Sir Donald Maclean, a former Liberal politician. Both soon became involved in left-wing circles in Cambridge and were recruited as Soviet agents. Burgess moved from

The Times to the BBC in 1936 where his work brought him many valuable contacts with politicians and people of influence. His homosexuality, fondness for drink, and flamboyant behaviour also brought him to people's notice. This, together with a wide circle of acquaintances, helped disguise his Communist sympathies. At the outbreak of war in 1939 he joined the special intelligence division of MI-6. He joined the Foreign Office News Department in 1944 and later became personal spokesman for Hector McNeil, Minister of State at the Foreign Office. After being moved around several departments he was sent in November 1950 as second secretary to the embassy in Washington, DC, with a special brief to look after Far Eastern affairs.

Maclean had studied foreign languages at Cambridge and entered the Foreign Office in 1934 after abandoning an idea to teach in Russia. Although a model career diplomat, he was also prone to bouts of heavy drinking and aggressive behaviour . Burgess also led him into homosexuality. Maclean's positions as First Secretary and then Head of Chancery at the British Embassy in Washington, DC, gave him wide access to a range of British and US secrets. He served as secretary and British representative on the Combined Policy Committee on Atomic Development and was a frequent visitor to the headquarters of the US Atomic Energy Commission. As such he was able to supply the Soviets with important information, such as the supply, price and delivery of uranium, thereby revealing how many bombs the USA was making.

In 1949 the CIA started to have doubts about Maclean after monitoring the amount of coded information being relayed at regular intervals from the Soviet consulate in New York. It was soon established that the flow of ciphered information coincided with Maclean's twice-weekly visits to the consulate to pass on his information. Other lapses in the ciphering allowed the CIA to identify the British Embassy as the source, and Maclean in particular. The British authorities did not act directly, though, transferring Maclean to Cairo after the strain began to affect his work. His drinking increased, however, and he eventually suffered a nervous breakdown and was placed under psychiatric treatment. On a partial recovery he was appointed Head of the American Department at the Foreign Office in London. As such he was privy to a wide range of secret information, particularly disturbing at a time when he was under suspicion of passing information to the Soviet Union. He was also in a position to supply the Russians with information about US attitudes towards the Korean War, then in progress.

Burgess had meanwhile been living at the house in Washington, DC, of Harold "Kim" Philby, a friend and another of the "Cambridge spies" (see *Philby Affair, 1963*, below). Philby had access to information that revealed that Maclean was under suspicion. Burgess's recall from the USA in May 1951 for bad behaviour gave Philby the opportunity to warn Maclean. MI-5 delayed the date of their interrogation of Maclean for several weeks and Anthony Blunt, a former tutor at Trinity College and also a Soviet agent who had contacts within MI-5 (see *Blunt Affair, 1979–80*, below), was able to warn Burgess and Maclean of the exact date of the interrogation.

On May 25, 1951, two days before the expected date, Burgess hired a car and drove to Maclean's house at Tatsfield in Surrey. Both men then drove to Southampton and boarded a boat bound for St Malo in Brittany. Burgess had two tickets for the boat, originally intending to take an American friend he had met on the boat returning from the USA. From France they made their way to the Soviet Union. The Government officially admitted their disappearance on June 7, making the statement that two diplomats had disappeared without leave, but of course unable to reveal that they were suspected of espionage. Mrs Maclean and her three children disappeared while on a holiday in Switzerland in 1953, but the two men did not appear in person until February 1956 after the relevation of their spying activities following the defection of Vladimir Petrov in Australia in 1954 (see Australia: *Petrov Affair, 1954–55*). Petrov sold his story to the British newspaper the *People*, which began publishing details in September 1955. This prompted the government to issue a White Paper revealing some of the details of the case and admitting that Burgess and Maclean had been spies.

Burgess died in Moscow in 1963, while Maclean pursued a career with the rank of colonel in the KGB as a Foreign Ministry Adviser until his death in 1983.

The affair prompted serious questions about the reliability of the British security procedures and led to American protests at the infiltration of the British security services. An internal committee of inquiry was set up and recommended improving security checks. Despite calls for the discovery of the "third man" who had tipped off Burgess and Maclean the authorities failed to catch Kim Philby. The flight of both Burgess and Maclean had left Philby's position exposed, but although recalled and interrogated, he gave nothing away.

LP

Commander Crabb Affair (1956)

Lionel Crabb, naval officer and diver.

The Commander Crabb Affair caused acute, if temporary, embarrassment for the British Government during the official visit of Krushchev and Bulganin to Britain, and also raised further questions about the actions and accountability of the British security services.

Lionel "Buster" Crabb, born in 1920, had served with distinction as a naval officer during World War II. He became a proficient diver, specializing in underwater bomb disposal, and in 1944 was awarded the George Cross for defusing a torpedo head attached to a troopship. He continued as a member of the Royal Naval Volunteer Reserve after the War, and was seconded as a technical adviser to the Admiralty Research Establishment where he helped test new diving equipment. He also became involved in intelligence work, diving underneath the Soviet cruiser *Sverdlov* when it docked in Portsmouth in October 1955.

Commander Crabb was reported missing in Portsmouth on April 19, 1956. Police visited the Sallyport Hotel where Crabb and another unidentified man had spent the two nights before his disappearance and removed the page with their details from the register. Later, on April 29, after persistent newspaper reports on his disappearance, the Admiralty issued a statement saying that Crabb had disappeared while testing new diving equipment in Stokes Bay, three miles from Portsmouth Harbour, and that this had been done without the knowledge of the naval authorities in Portsmouth.

The day before Crabb's disappearance a Soviet cruiser, the *Ordjonikidze*, accompanied by other Soviet warships, had arrived in Portsmouth Harbour to bring the Soviet leader Nikita Krushchev and Foreign Minister Marshal Bulganin to Britain for an official visit. On May 4 an official at the Soviet embassy in London revealed that a frogman had been seen by sailors on board the *Ordjonikidze*. The figure had surfaced near the vessel before diving underwater again. The Soviet commander had contacted his British opposite number in Portsmouth at the time to make inquiries about the incident and was told that nothing could have happened as the diving establishment at Portsmouth was closed. An exchange of diplomatic correspondence between London and Moscow took place and was made public. The Soviets restated the claim of the sailors and protested at the possible spying implications of the case. In reply the British government denied that it had given permission or had any knowledge about Crabb's actions and regretted the incident. The Soviet government agreed to accept the British assurances.

The Prime Minister, Sir Anthony Eden, when questioned in the House of Commons about the circumstances of Crabb's death, refused to give details, citing the potential threat to national security. In a debate on the affair the Leader of the Opposition, Hugh Gaitskell, accused government ministers of lack of control over the security services and questioned how Crabb's dive could have occurred without the knowledge of senior officers. Eden, however, refused to elaborate and stood by his earlier statement that the government had neither known of, nor had given permission for, Crabb's dive.

In his memoirs Eden relates how he had specifically forbidden any covert operations during the Soviet visit, knowing that the intelligence services were interested in the Soviet naval vessels, and how he had been angered by the apparent disregard of this directive. Eden asked the Cabinet Secretary, Sir Norman Brook, to investigate and report on the circumstances of the operation. It seems likely that Crabb was authorised to undertake the dive by somebody in the Special Intelligence Service (SIS) in order to investigate whether the *Ordjonikidze* was equipped to lay nuclear mines through an underwater hatch. The calmness with which the Soviets reacted to the affair suggested that such an action had been expected and that Crabb had been caught and killed, or that he had got into difficulties on the dive. According to Eden, the report prompted not only disciplinary measures against those involved, but also discussion about ministerial responsibility and interdepartmental co-ordination of covert activities in the future.

Crabb's headless body was eventually retrieved near Chichester Harbour on June 8, 1957, still in his diving suit. An inquest held on June 26 returned an open verdict as the Coroner stated that the cause of death was impossible to determine.

LP

Suez Collusion Affair (1956)

David Ben-Gurion, Israeli Prime Minister.
Sir Anthony Eden, British Prime Minister.
Selwyn Lloyd, Foreign Secretary.
Guy Mollet, French Prime Minister.

The Suez crisis is often regarded as a turning point in the perception of British power and influence in the world. It also proved to be the downfall of Prime Minister Anthony Eden. The Suez intervention, although a qualified military success, was, from an economic and political point of view, a disaster. The allegation of "collusion" was one which haunted the participants in the affair, unable by their promises to reveal the truth.

The accession to power in Egypt of Col. Gamal Abdel Nasser in 1954, promoting a brand of fervent Arab nationalism, proved unwelcome to the Western powers and led to a deterioration in relations. On July 25, 1956, Nasser, piqued by US and British withdrawal from backing for the Aswan Dam project, announced the nationalization of the Suez Canal Company. Egyptian troops entered the Canal Zone and secured the installations. The seizure of the Canal represented a particular threat to Britain and France. Both countries had interests in the Canal Company and British troops had only recently been withdrawn from the Canal Zone. The Canal was also a vital lifeline for Western European oil supplies and other goods. Furthermore the French resented Nasser's support for the rebels in their colony of Algeria.

The British were not in a position to undertake immediate military action to intervene, so diplomatic initiatives were pursued in an attempt to seek a negotiated settlement, in concert with the other Western powers and the

United Nations. The use of force, however, was still reserved by the Cabinet as necessary in the "last resort". Mindful of the policy of appeasement in the 1930s, of which he had been a critic at the time, Prime Minister Eden was determined not to give way to "bullying" from Nasser, whom he equated with Hitler and Mussolini. He was further goaded into this position by some sections of the Conservative party and the press who wanted to see a firm response to the crisis.

Plans were formulated with the Chiefs of Staff for a possible attack on Egypt, but misgivings and delays led to indecision among the policy makers and restlessness among the forces mobilized in the Mediterranean. The French, meanwhile, dissatisfied with the British progress, opened secret negotiations with the Israelis over a possible attack on Egypt. Israel feared another Arab-Israeli war, and regarded a pre-emptive strike as the best way to deal with Egypt whose forces were rapidly being augmented by Soviet and East European supplies.

British attitudes to such a plan were thought to be influenced by fears of an Israeli attack on Jordan (heightened after a series of border incidents during the summer), in which eventuality Britain, by virtue of treaty obligations, would support Jordan. But British involvement was needed as only the Royal Air Force had the bombers that could immobilize the Egyptian Air Force and gain air cover.

The idea of a possible joint Anglo-French-Israeli plan of action was first outlined to Eden at a meeting with the French at Chequers on Oct. 14. Gen. Maurice Challe, the Deputy Chief of Staff of the French Air Force, proposed a plan whereby the Israelis would be encouraged to attack Egypt across the Sinai peninsula. Britain and France would allow the Israelis sufficient time to defeat the Egyptians before demanding that both sides withdraw from the Canal Zone. A joint Anglo-French force would then intervene to secure the canal installations.

Eden and Selwyn Lloyd, the Foreign Secretary, then flew to Paris on Oct. 16 to discuss the plan with the French Prime Minister, Guy Mollet and Foreign Minister, Christian Pineau. When Eden reported back to the full Cabinet on Oct. 18 about the meeting he did not reveal the possibility of collusion with the French and Israelis, but merely stated the general necessity of preventing damage to the canal in the event of an Israeli attack.

Some members of the Cabinet and Conservative party, however, already had serious doubts about the use of force. Walter Monckton, the Minister of War, resigned on Oct. 18, citing ill-health, but in fact worried by military involvement. He was replaced by Anthony Head whom Eden felt had more confidence in decisive action.

Selwyn Lloyd returned to France on Oct. 22, this time for a secret meeting at Sèvres also attended by the Israeli Prime Minister, David Ben-Gurion, and Chief of Staff, Gen. Moshe Dayan, at which the details of the plan were agreed. In accordance with Ben-Gurion's wishes, the details of the Sèvres meeting were kept secret. At the Cabinet meeting on Oct. 25 Eden did reveal that Israel was making plans for an attack and that Britain and France should prepare a plan for such a contingency, but he did not spell out the details of collusion. Except for the handful of ministers and officials in full knowledge of the facts, the official line on intervention was that it would be holding the two sides apart and was not co-operation with Israel.

The Israeli attack was launched on Oct. 29, and by determined fighting quickly overcame the Egyptian opposition. The following day Britain and France issued their ultimatum that both sides should withdraw 10 miles either side of the Canal. The Israelis were, of course, expecting the ultimatum, but the Egyptians rejected it as interference. Meanwhile at the United Nations Britain and France used their vetoes in the Security Council to block US and Soviet demands for Israeli withdrawal, something which would have removed the reasons for intervention. This duly took place when British and French aircraft bombed Egyptian military airfields and other targets.

The actions of the British and French and leaks of information were sufficient to allow Hugh Gaitskell, the Leader of the Opposition, to make allegations of collusion in a debate in the House of Commons on Oct. 31. Selwyn Lloyd, replying for the government, stated that "it is wrong to state that Israel was incited to this action by the government. There was not a prior agreement between us about it". The Suez crisis divided British public opinion and the press into those for and against the intervention. The Labour party vigorously opposed the military action, while most of the Conservative party supported Eden, apart from a handful of dissidents, including Anthony Nutting, the Minister of State for Foreign Affairs, who resigned in protest.

British and French paratroopers landed at Port Said on Nov. 5, but strong American disapproval and a run on the pound, caused by fears of an oil shortage and US pressure, persuaded Harold Macmillan, the Chancellor of the Exchequer, to urge Eden to halt the military action. This he eventually did, although the French were willing to continue, and a ceasefire was accepted on Nov. 7. A UN Emergency Force was mobilized and arrived in Egypt on Nov. 15.

In the aftermath of the crisis, Eden went to Jamaica to recuperate from illness, leaving Butler in charge as acting Minister. On his return on Dec. 14 it seemed inevitable that he would have to resign. He was questioned about collusion by Nigel Nicholson, an anti-Suez MP, at a meeting of the backbench 1922 Committee on Oct. 18, but gave no definite answer. He was eventually forced into giving a reply in the House of Commons on Dec. 20. Honouring the pledge he had given at Sèvres he said that there were no plans to attack Egypt and that he had no foreknowledge of the Israeli action. In doing so he lied, and several of those present knew he had lied. The truth about collusion did not emerge for several years. Selwyn Lloyd in his memoirs claimed that knowledge of collusion at the time would have damaged relations in the Middle East and he cited other precedents for withholding information from Parliament and Cabinet. But the charge remained that Eden had pursued his personal vendetta against Nasser as far as being prepared to use illegal means to unseat him.

LP

Bank Rate Leak Affair (1957–58)

Harold Macmillan, Prime Minister (1957–63).
Oliver Poole, Deputy Chairman of the Conservative Party (1957–59).
Enoch Powell, Financial Secretary to the Treasury (1957–58).
Peter Thorneycroft, Chancellor of the Exchequer (1957–58).
Harold Wilson, Shadow Chancellor of the Exchequer (1956–61).

One single and controversial public error of judgment by an ambitious and rising politician can easily ruin what otherwise might appear to be a career which is heading towards the commanding heights of British politics. One such controversial and public error involving a senior Labour politician and the City of London had in fact the opposite effect of what might normally have happened in such circumstances: The politician moved on up the political ladder to become the occupant of No. 10 Downing Street as Prime Minister, while a number of useful and interesting pieces of information came into the public domain for the first time in relation to the behavioural intricacies of the financial centre of the United Kingdom. The controversy was known as the Bank Rate Leak affair, while the politician involved was Harold Wilson.

Born in March 1916 in Huddersfield, West Yorkshire, James Harold Wilson attended Royds Hall Secondary School and Wirral Grammar School, winning a scholarship to Jesus College, Oxford, where he obtained a first-class honours degree in philosophy, politics and economics. He then appeared to embark upon a promising academic career, becoming a lecturer in economics at Oxford then research assistant to Wiliam Beveridge. However, with the outbreak of war in 1945, his academic career was unavoidably interrupted; he became a wartime civil servant, holding a variety of research and statistician posts within the Ministry of Supply, the War Cabinet Secretariat, the Ministry of Labour and the Ministry of Fuel and Power. Such experience gave him invaluable first-hand knowledge and training at the very centre of the civil service machine in Whitehall. His political career began in 1945 when he was elected to the House of Commons as the Labour member for Ormskirk, which became Huyton in 1948, where he remained until 1983. Upon his arrival in the Commons in 1945 he immediately became, at 29, the youngest member of the government of Clement Attlee as Parliamentary Secretary at the Ministry of Works; he further became, at 31, the youngest Cabinet Minister since Pitt in 1783, when Attlee appointed him President of the Board of Trade in 1947. With the move into Opposition of the Labour Party in 1951, it was therefore as Shadow Chancellor of the Exchequer, a post to which he had been appointed in 1956, that Wilson made what was apparently a disastrous error of political judgment, in the affair of the Bank Rate Leak.

On Sept. 19, 1957, the Bank of England announced that the Bank Rate was to rise from 5 to 7 per cent. Wilson wrote the next day to Enoch Powell, the Financial Secretary to the Treasury, to complain that the rise had been leaked 24 hours previously on the basis of which there had been an inspired selling of gilt-edged securities on the Stock Exchange. Wilson quoted a number of newspapers which had referred to strong evidence that an unauthorised leak of information had taken place, including the *News Chronicle* which had written of "heavy sales of Government securities . . . late on Wednesday and on Thursday by people who evidently knew that the Bank Rate was to be raised". The Shadow Chancellor was convinced that information on the bank rate rise had been leaked to at least one journalist in advance; in his letter to Powell, Wilson wrote ". . . I would ask you to draw this letter to the attention of your senior colleagues with a view to an inquiry being instituted". The government quickly rejected his call for an inquiry on the grounds that a careful and thorough investigation by officials of the Treasury had uncovered no evidence of the alleged disclosure. In a statement immediately following the government's decision Wilson said he was astonished at the reply, claimed that the failure to order an inquiry fell far short of the traditions which successive governments had maintained, and promised to press the matter when the new parliamentary session opened in October. He then wrote to the Prime Minister, Harold Macmillan, from the Labour Party annual conference at Brighton, saying that he had *prima facie* evidence indicating that the leak had come from a political source. The Prime Minister eventually agreed to refer the matter to his Lord Chancellor, who carried out an investigation and concluded that there were no grounds for inviting Parliament to establish an official inquiry. It was only at the start of the new parliamentary session, when Wilson continued to call for an inquiry and referred to Oliver Poole, the deputy chairman of the Conservative Party, as having "known City interests", that Macmillan finally agreed to an official inquiry, setting up the Bank Rate Tribunal under Lord Justice Parker.

Giving evidence to the Tribunal, Wilson stated that when he read an identical story in a number of newspapers, he had secured authorisation from his Labour colleagues to press for an inquiry. In response to questioning, Wilson suggested that Poole had "improperly, not corruptly, passed on a top secret document to a person not covered by the Official Secrets Act", referring to an official of Conservative Central Office. In fact Poole had been briefed about a number of financial measures other than the Bank Rate increase the day before the alteration was announced. The Tribunal eventually reported that the charges made by Wilson were groundless and that those supposedly involved were cleared. The House of Commons debated the report on Feb. 3–4, 1958, during which Wilson made a long, carefully prepared speech and was subjected to quite ferocious verbal attacks from Conservatives opposite. With insults and jeers being exchanged across the Chamber, the debate ended in disorder with the Government securing its majority in the division that followed.

Some years later Wilson admitted that the Bank Rate leak affair had been one of his more serious errors of judgment, particularly in relation to his "unprepared choice of words" when referring to Poole. Although it is clear that the Shadow Chancellor had found himself in a difficult situation largely of his own making, and the whole affair soured relations between him and the city for a long time, the future Party Leader and Prime Minister was always keen to point out that it was the Conservative Government which had set up the inquiry and their Attorney-General who had stated that such an inquiry was necessary.

WS

George Blake Affair (1961–90)

George Blake, Soviet spy.
Pat Pottle, Michael Randle, joint authors of *The Blake Escape*.

The post-war years in Britain have seen a British intelligence community characterized by the regular unmasking of a number of spies whose treason and betrayal were on an unprecedented scale. One such unmasking was that of George Blake, whose case in the 1960s involved one of the heaviest sentences ever imposed for espionage as well as a dramatic prison escape, and who continued to interest the British media into the 1990s as two of his alleged helpers in the escape came to trial.

During the late 1950s, Michael Goleniewski, a Polish intelligence officer of the UB (the polish equivalent of the KGB), was sending classified information to the Central Intelligence Agency (CIA) in the United States. Within his written reports was the claim that the Russians had been regularly receiving copies of British secret service documents. In 1960 Goleniewski was forced to defect because he had discovered that someone in the West had warned the KGB that there was a spy in the Polish UB acting on behalf of the CIA. With the realization that he himself must soon be suspected of espionage activity he decided it was time to escape, and he reached the United States via West Berlin towards the end of 1960.

Following his interrogation by American and British intelligence officers, a list of those who had had access to the documents the Polish officer had described was compiled and considered. Although George Blake appeared to be the principal suspect, it was decided that his successes precluded the possibility of his being a spy.

However, it then emerged that the movement of secrets to the Russians had stopped when Blake had in 1960 been posted to attend an Arabic course in the Middle East. It was the secret service station chief in Beirut, Nicholas Elliott, who was assigned the delicate task of persuading Blake to return to London without arousing the latter's suspicions. Elliott told Blake that he was to return to London for discussions about a new post involving promotion. When Blake returned to England in April 1961 he was arrested and interrogated, and confessed to being a spy.

Blake, who had joined the British secret service in 1948 after carrying out wartime intelligence work for the Navy, described how he had been present when Operation Gold was discussed and planned. This involved a 350-foot-long tunnel which was to be driven under the East–West demarcation boundary in Berlin for the purpose of intercepting Russian telephone lines. Blake stated that he had informed the Russians of this tunnel in 1954, before its construction had begun. He also confessed that while working in London at MI-6 headquarters he had betrayed everything he could about the secret service to the Russians, including the "battle order" — that is, details of secret service personnel, including how and where they were deployed. In West Berlin, to which he had been posted in April 1955, he had met KGB agents in the Eastern sector, and had handed over much classified information including copies of documents he had photographed.

Once Blake had been arrested and charged, Harold Macmillan, the Prime Minister, ordered the issue of a D-notice — a system which provides ministerial guidance to the media about material whose publication is regarded as detrimental to national security — restricting the reporting of the trial on the grounds that British agents allegedly placed in jeopardy by the spy were still being withdrawn from behind the "Iron Curtain". Blake pleaded guilty, and the trial was largely held *in camera* so that the public was given very little information to justify the sentence of 42 years' imprisonment. In October 1966 Blake made a sensational escape from prison and managed to reach the Soviet Union.

In March 1989 Michael Randle and Pat Pottle, a lecturer and antique dealer respectively, published *The Blake Escape*, which disclosed in great detail the way in which they, together with Sean Bourke, had planned and implemented the 1967 escape. All three had met Blake in prison in 1962, when Randle and Pottle were serving short sentences for anti-nuclear civil disobedience campaigns. Bourke, who was serving a seven-year sentence for sending an explosive device to a policeman and who died in 1982, had himself published in 1970 his own account of the escape entitled *The Springing of George Blake*.

Randle and Pottle had decided to write their book because work by researchers and journalists had virtually named them as having been involved in the Blake escape. They decided to publish their own full account of the escape in order to counter the widespread speculation and rumour that was then circulating throughout 1987–88 in a number of books and newspapers.

More specifically, the authors of *The Blake Escape* set out at length their reasons for helping George Blake to escape from prison. In their view, the 42-year sentence was vicious and indefensible, reflecting the obsessions of the Cold War and the hypocrisy and double standards over espionage activities by both East and West; there were serious anomalies about the Blake trial and the circumstances surrounding it, including the fact that both it and the subsequent appeal were held *in camera* so that the public were denied the means with which to judge whether or not justice had been done; and, further, that Blake's espionage activities were no more politically or morally reprehensible than much of the activity of the Western intelligence agencies.

The two men were eventually charged in 1989 by the Director of Public Prosecutions of aiding and abetting Blake's escape, an offence which carried a maximum sentence of five years' imprisonment. During the pre-trial hearings in March and April 1990, the men claimed that the decision to prosecute was an abuse of the legal process since, they argued, the police had sufficient evidence in 1970 that they had been involved but that a policy decision was made then to take no action. Meanwhile Blake, then aged 67, continues to live in Moscow, working at the Institute for World Economics and International Affairs.

WS

Vassall Affair (1962)

Thomas Galbraith, Conservative MP and Admiralty minister.
Sigmund Mikhailski, Soviet agent.
John Vassall, Admiralty clerk and Soviet spy.

The Vassall Affair served once again to expose the negligence of British security. British security procedures failed to detect Vassall's activities or his homosexuality for many years. Despite his seemingly lowly clerical position, Vassall's jobs brought him into contact with senior members of the Admiralty and the documents which passed through their hands, and which Vassall had been blackmailed into passing to the Soviets.

John Vassall was born on Sept. 20, 1924, the son of a Church of England clergyman. After leaving school he worked as a temporary clerk in the Admiralty before being called up and serving in the RAF between 1943 and 1946. In the RAF he was trained as a photographer. After being demobilized he returned to a permanent post in the Admiralty. In 1954 he volunteered to join the staff of the naval attaché at the British Embassy in Moscow. Here he met a Polish clerk named Sigmund Mikhailski who worked at the embassy. Mikhailski, a Soviet agent, invited Vassall to dinners and parties. It was at one of the parties that Vassall, a homosexual, was photographed in compromising positions by Soviet agents. He was then blackmailed into spying, which he began by passing over documents in the naval attaché's office.

In July 1956 he returned to London and was attached to the Naval Intelligence Division. In this post he had access to a wide range of secret documents concerning British and Allied naval operations, equipment, plans and intelligence. In 1957 he was appointed assistant private secretary to the Civil Lord of the Admiralty, Thomas Galbraith. He seems to have struck up a close working relationship with Galbraith and was once again entrusted with numerous important documents. In 1959 he moved to the secretariat of the Naval Staff. All this time Vassall was passing a regular flow of information from files he had removed to his contact, a councillor at the Soviet Embassy in London. The Soviets provided him with photographic equipment so that he could photograph files at home himself, rather than pass on the files for photography elsewhere.

Vassall received money for his spying activities, which he found useful for supporting an extravagant lifestyle. He estimated his "earnings" from spying at about £500–£700 per year, roughly equivalent to his net annual salary. In 1959 he rented a luxury apartment in Dolphin Square, London, and furnished it with fine antiques, yet his superiors seemed to raise no questions about a clerk so obviously living beyond his means. Neither did they question his extensive foreign holidays.

He was ordered by his Soviet contact to stop his activities in the aftermath of the Portland spy ring, but resumed in January 1962, after being transferred to the Military Division of the Admiralty. A review of security in the aftermath of the George Blake affair eventually raised questions about Vassall and when confronted he admitted everything. A Soviet defector to the USA also revealed the existence of a leak of information in the Admiralty. The authorities now discovered the facts about his homosexuality for the first time, something which should have prevented him from being sent to Moscow in the first place. Film containing pages from 17 documents was found in a hidden compartment behind a bookcase in his flat, along with the photographic equipment. He was arrested on Sept. 12, 1962 and convicted and sentenced to 18 years' imprisonment on Oct. 22. He was released in 1973 and, after a period in a monastery, retired to a quiet life under an assumed name.

The jailing of Vassall, however, did not prove the end of the affair. The Vassall case caused acute embarrassment to the British government and prompted Prime Minister Harold Macmillan to set up a Civil Service inquiry, chaired by Sir Charles Cunningham, as to how Vassall had escaped suspicion for so many years. Even so, opposition demands for an independent inquiry were insistent, as were the continuing press stories surrounding the case which grew increasingly lurid and which regularly ridiculed ministers. In particular Galbraith's relationship with Vassall was subjected to press speculation.

Eventually the Committee produced an interim report on Nov. 7 consisting of letters between Vassall and Galbraith. By doing this Macmillan hoped to halt some of the innuendo put forward by the press. Galbraith resigned from his post as Under-Secretary of State for Scotland the following day, saying that although the correspondence had cleared him of any wrongdoing he felt that his way of dealing with officials had become an embarrassment to the Government.

On Nov. 13 Macmillan announced the creation of a Tribunal of Inquiry, to be chaired by Lord Radcliffe, into all aspects of the case. The Tribunal had extensive powers to subpeona witnesses and demand answers — powers that were used to full effect during the hearings which lasted from Dec. 3,

1962 to Feb. 5, 1963. Journalists were summoned before the tribunal and questioned about the sources of their stories. Desmond Clough of the *Daily Sketch* was convicted and sentenced to six months' imprisonment for refusing to reveal his source for the allegation that Vassall had passed on information about secret NATO sea exercises. He based his defence on the journalist's traditional right to protect the anonymity of his source. He was only saved from prison by a press officer in the Admiralty revealing himself as the source. Two other journalists, Brendan Mulholland of the *Daily Mail* and Ronald Foster of the *Daily Sketch* were not so lucky. They too were sentenced to six months' imprisonment for contempt of court on Feb. 4 and were sent to prison after their request to appeal to the House of Lords was refused on March 6.

The Radcliffe Tribunal published its report on April 25. For the most part it exonerated the authorities by saying that no-one was to blame for the failure to detect Vassall's homosexuality, his unusual lifestyle or his spying activities. It confirmed that there had been nothing improper in the working relationship between Galbraith and Vassall. It criticized the Admiralty's selection, vetting and security procedures as inadequate and superficial. It also said that there had been insufficient control of contacts between staff and local employees at the Moscow Embassy and suspicions about Mikhailski had not been acted on.

The Vassall case proved to be the most damaging of the spy revelations surrounding the Macmillan government, even though the Radcliffe report cleared the Government of most of the blame. Although the Radcliffe report did not go out of its way to attack the press, the imprisonment of the two journalists contributed to the bad relations between press and government and probably played some part in the vehemence with which the press pursued the Profumo Affair a few months later (see below).

LP

Profumo Affair (1963)

Eugene Ivanov, Russian diplomat.
Christine Keeler, teenage girl.
John Profumo, Conservative MP and Minister of War (1960–63).
Stephen Ward, society osteopath and party organizer.
George Wigg, Labour MP and security enthusiast.
Harold Wilson, Labour MP (1945–76), Leader of the Labour Party (1963–76), Prime Minister (1964–70, 1974–76).

The Profumo affair begins with Christine Keeler who, at the age of 15, decided to escape to London, away from a drab existence in a converted railway carriage in a run-down part of the Buckinghamshire village of Wraysbury, a dull job in Slough and a stepfather she couldn't get on with. Within months her looks and self-confidence took her from being a waitress at a Greek restaurant to some modelling assignments and a job as a topless dancer earning £8.50 a week at Murray's Cabaret Club where she met Stephen Ward, 30 years her senior; a thin, elegant man and a talented artist who had qualified as an osteopath at Kirksville, Missouri. He combined his profession with his social charm and gregariousness to expand his Harley Street practice to cater for politicians, royalty and showbusiness figures: he was the "society osteopath" in the '50s. He liked company, he liked doing favours for people, he liked new experiences — including sex and drugs, and he frequently sought the friendship of attractive young women, often prostitutes.

He also rented for £1 a year a cottage from one of his patients, Lord Astor, in the grounds of Cliveden estate. The cottage was Ward's pride and joy, a rural retreat in upper-class surroundings to which he invited a cosmopolitan mix of weekend guests, one of whom was Eugene Ivanov, Assistant Naval Attaché with the rank of Lieutenant-Commander at the Russian Embassy in London since March 1960. In April 1961 Colonel Oleg Penkovsky, a senior officer of the Soviet GRU intelligence agency, was being debriefed by MI-6 and the CIA in London, which he was visiting as part of a Soviet Trade delegation, after offering to supply information to the West. Penkovsky named Ivanov as a GRU intelligence officer with a decided leaning toward Western decadence. By that time Ward was seeing Ivanov regularly after meeting him at the invitation of Sir Colin Coote, then editor of the *Daily Telegraph*, over lunch at the Garrick Club. (Coote was Ward's patient; Ward wanted to go to Russia to sketch the politicians and Coote knew Ivanov.) A recent suggestion is that Coote, a friend of Sir Roger Hollis, then head of MI-5, may have arranged the meeting to introduce Ivanov to Ward and thus to the delights of Ward's demi-monde with the hope of compromising him. Whatever the exact nature of their relationship, Ivanov was to meet Keeler at the Cliveden cottage; he was also there on one occasion when one of Lord Astor's guests was present — John Profumo.

Then 46, Profumo was a rising Tory politician. Son of a successful barrister, with a considerable family income invested in an insurance company and a country squire's lifestyle, Profumo moved from Harrow to Oxford to a world tour and the beginnings of a political career in East Fulham. In 1940, as a young army officer, he won Kettering with an 11,298 majority before ending up a Lieutenant-Colonel on F.M. Alexander's HQ staff. Losing his seat in 1945 he stayed with the army until 1947, joined the Conservative Central Office as the party's broadcasting adviser and won Stratford-upon-Avon in 1950. He got his first ministerial post in 1952, married the actress Valerie Hobson in 1954 and in 1960 was appointed Secretary of State for War. He had charm, enthusiasm and all the right connections.

The meeting with Keeler in July 1961 led to a brief affair which ended toward the end of that year. MI-5 were watching the Ivanov–Keeler friendship and had contacted Ward for information. Worried that Profumo's presence might affect any entrapment of Ivanov, MI-5 asked Sir Norman Brook, the Cabinet Secretary, to warn Profumo of their interest and then to ask for his help in the operation. Profumo refused but, in the mistaken belief that MI-5 knew of the affair with Keeler, hastily wrote her an affectionate note cancelling a meeting, a note she kept and which helped disprove his later protestations of innocence.

The unfolding of the scandal began in November 1962 when Profumo clashed with George Wigg, the security-minded Labour MP with a deeply-held passion for the army and the serving conditions of its men, over a June 1961 military training exercise. Wigg was left with a burning sense of resentment. In December one of Keeler's boyfriends, Johnny Edgecombe, fired a shot at the front door of Ward's house where she was staying. After his arrest, whether from panic or a wish to build up her own importance in the case, she began talking about her life to journalists, police and John Lewis, a former Labour MP who had a personal dislike of Ward and who repeated the story to George Wigg in January 1963. Lewis kept him informed of developments, including the security issue that was the spark of Wigg's sustained interest in Profumo — the claim by Keeler that Ward had asked her to find out from Profumo about the nuclear arming of West Germany. Meanwhile Fleet Street was also preparing to publish both this claim and other details of Keeler's life, including her relationship with Profumo and the note he had sent her. Both Ward and Profumo, independently and for different reasons, sought to stop publication. With increasing numbers of individuals, including lawyers and journalists, learning of the allegations it was only a matter of days before government ministers were being alerted. Sir John Hobson, the Attorney-General, and Peter Rawlinson, the Solicitor-General, questioned Profumo who denied the rumours; consequently they and other senior government officers met with Profumo on several occasions; the latter insisted that there had been no impropriety with Keeler and expressed his willingness to take legal action to defend his reputation.

The row did break publicly in March when Andrew Roth's weekly insider newsletter, *Westminster Confidential*, reported the outlines of the cancelled press story, the existence of the affectionate note and the security aspects. Since Keeler had at that time decided to go abroad on holiday shortly before she should have been a witness at her former boyfriend's trial, rumours began to multiply that she had been whisked away to avoid the scandal erupting. Two Labour MPs raised her absence in the Commons during a debate on the case of the journalists jailed during the Vassall affair (see above). The next day Profumo made a statement to the House denying any "impropriety whatsoever in my acquaintanceship with Miss Keeler".

Nevertheless Wigg, annoyed at what he saw as another evasion by Profumo, went on the TV programme *Panorama* and baldly stated that Ivanov and Ward were security risks. Ward contacted Wigg and wrote to other politicians with details of his life to deny the security allegations. The Labour Opposition used the existence of these letters to force Macmillan into proposing to set up an inquiry under Lord Dilhorne, the Lord Chancellor, to review the security issues. Profumo returned from holiday — he had learned both of Ward's allegations and the proposed inquiry — and resigned. Written on June 5, his letter to the Prime Minister said: "rumour had charged me with assisting in the disappearance of a witness and of being involved in some possible breach of security. So serious were these charges that I allowed myself to think that my personal associations with that witness which had also been the subject of rumour was, by comparison, of minor importance only. In my statement I said that there had been no impropriety in this association. To my very deep regret I have to admit that this is not true, and that I misled you and my colleagues, and the House."

The resignation released the restrictions on press comment — which immediately indulged in rumour and allegation that appeared to encompass most of the Establishment in decadence and cover-up — and gave the Opposition both the security issue and the hoodwinking of ministers as grounds for attacking the Government. In the parliamentary debate on June 21, Labour leader Harold Wilson offered a restrained recital of the events surrounding Profumo's resignation, referring to Macmillan's "unflappability and unconcern" as evidence of ignorance or collusion and taking a sideswipe at the effects of Tory leadership: "the sickness of an unrepresentative sector of our society should not detract from the robust ability of our people as a whole to face the challenge of the future. And in preparing to face that challenge, let us frankly recognize that the inspiration and the leadership must come first here in this House." The Prime Minister's response was poor, reflecting the deep personal hurt he had felt at the affair — the lies, the deception, the lack of information — but pinned his hopes on the argument that in acting as he did, "honourably and justly", then he should be believed to have acted "with proper diligence and prudence". He was, he argued, "entitled to the sympathetic understanding and confidence of the House and of the country". Unfortunately this did not convince his Party: the plaintiveness and lack of firm leadership only served to aggravate criticism within it. Facing poor health, Macmillan resigned in October. In the meantime, Ward had committed suicide, after being found guilty of living off the immoral earnings of Keeler and another of Ward's girlfriends. The affair was conveniently wrapped up with the publication of the official report into the security aspects of the affair — the Denning Report — which said there were no security leaks and that the press were responsible for creating the scandal, and concluded that no one politician was to blame for the Profumo affair other than the Prime Minister and his colleagues in their failure to act on a reasonable belief that Profumo was misbehaving.

Since the scandal, Profumo has dedicated his life to good works in the East End of London and never attempted a return to public life.

RAD

Commander Courtney Affair (1965–66)

Anthony Courtney, former intelligence officer, Conservative MP (1959–66). Zinaida Grigorievna Volkova, Intourist official and alleged Soviet agent.

The reaction of the Harrow East constituency to the embarrassment of Conservative Minister Ian Harvey's resignation in 1958 for a homosexual escapade that led to his arrest in Hyde Park was to choose as their candidate his intellectual and social opposite — an ebullient, middle-aged former naval officer with a bluff no-nonsense manner, Anthony Courtney. Before entering Naval Intelligence Courtney had become a fluent Russian speaker. He ended up in the British Naval Mission in Moscow during World War II. In 1946 he was put in charge of the Russian section of the Naval Intelligence Division which involved both co-operation with Russian officials in London over the disposal of German naval assets and an assessment of the Russian naval capabilities as the possible enemy of the future. His work also involved providing cover for Foreign Office staff attending a special Russian course at Cambridge University and discussions with the head of MI-6 over the use of submarines and other craft in its activities. On retirement, when he was almost recruited into the Secret Service, he took his first steps to find a Tory constituency and set up a company — Eastern Trading Group Consultancy Services — which involved numerous trips for industrial clients to Poland and Russia (and may have been used as an intelligence cover, a favoured MI-6 method at that time).

A few months after his election to Parliament as Conservative MP in 1959 he returned to Moscow, conducting his business from the Hotel Ukrania, where he met Zinaida Grigorievna Volkova, an Intourist official who ran the hotel car service for visitors. During his visit he became concerned that, on their own ground, the Russians were winning the Cold War, and in particular that they were gaining "moral ascendancy" over the embassy by harassing staff and making life uncomfortable for them. Harold Macmillan's lack of interest prompted a parliamentary campaign by Courtney and others to persuade the Government to stand up to the Russians. In 1961, two months after his first wife's death, Courtney went back to Russia for the British Industrial Exhibition and renewed his acquaintance with Volkova which led to a brief sexual liaison. On his return to England Courtney remarried — to Lady Elizabeth Trefgarne — and renewed his criticism of the Foreign Office, whom he thought "excessively gullible" over security matters and the Russians' Cold War strength in intelligence and espionage affairs: in July 1965 he asked Harold Wilson "when the Government were going to stop behaving like a lot of hypnotized rabbits in face of the efficient Soviet espionage organization".

A month later an anonymous broadsheet headed "I'm not a Profumo but . . ." and carrying pictures of Courtney in a compromising position with a woman reached the *News of the World*, Labour and Tory MPs and constituency officials. While the details in the broadsheet did not emerge in the press the immediate consequence was the break-up of his already shaky second marriage — a fact presumably known to the KGB after he and his second wife had discussed their deteriorating relationship over a Moscow telephone line. A second consequence was that the new Labour Government on the advice of George Wigg dissuaded Courtney from any further visit to Moscow, which effectively curtailed his business activities. The announcement of impending divorce proceedings on grounds of adultery — Volkova was named — was followed by a *Daily Telegraph* article in October 1965 written with Courtney's help that referred to the the Russians' attempt to smear him with the broadsheet. The emergence of this information into the public domain, together with the impending divorce, made the Party leadership nervous about the possibility of another sex scandal so soon after the Profumo affair (see above). Furthermore these events precipitated a split in his local constituency party, several of whose senior members found Courtney's manner and frequent absences on business irksome. In November 1965 he ws asked to stand down by the constituency party leadership, only to be reinstated the following February by a special general meeting of the constituency party. In 1966 he lost the seat to the Labour candidate in the general election of that year and subsequently left public life.

RAD

"D" Notice Affair (1967)

Col. L. G. Lohan, secretary of the Services, Press and Broadcasting Committee.
Chapman Pincher, investigative journalist.

The "D" Notice Affair surrounded the breaking of the "D" notice system which guarded against the disclosure in the media of information that could endanger national security. However, it was the government's response to this breach that raised questions.

On Feb. 21, 1967 the *Daily Express* newspaper published an article by Chapman Pincher, a journalist well-known for his interest in security matters, alleging that cables and telegrams were regularly being intercepted and scrutinized by the security services acting under a special ministerial warrant. The Prime Minister, Harold Wilson, claimed that the disclosure of this information was a breach of two "D" notices and on Feb. 28 an all-party committee of the House of Commons was set up under the chairmanship of Lord Radcliffe to investigate the "D" notice system.

The "D" notice system was a voluntary one, administered by a committee of representatives from the newspapers, television, radio, and the Services, known as the Services, Press and Broadcasting Committee. Under the system warning "D" notices would be issued to those media organizations planning to reveal something in connection with national security. In this case the *Spectator* magazine of March 3 published the texts of the two "D" notices concerned. These asked newspaper editors not to publish any information about secret intelligence work or the nature of ciphering or interception activities.

The Radcliffe Committee heard that Pincher had obtained his story from an ex-employee of Western Union, who had said that cables were routinely being transferred to the Foreign Office for reading before being passed on. Pincher made inquiries to verify his story and also telephoned the secretary of the "D" notice committee, Col. L. G. Lohan. Lohan told him that no "D" notice applied in this case. When Lohan subsequently reported to the Foreign Office he was told that the security services wanted the story suppressed and, although he was uncertain in his own mind whether a "D" notice applied, he promised to persuade Pincher to abandon the story. He failed, and a series of crossed communications and misunderstandings ensured that the message was not delivered properly and the story was duly published.

The Radcliffe Committee published its report on June 13. It said that little of substance could be done to improve the "D" notice system and that there had been no new changes in the methods or practice of interception. However, the government also published a White Paper on the same day, accepting the committee's recommendations on minor changes, but strongly disagreeing with the committee's findings on the original story. The White Paper accused the article of being "sensational and inaccurate" and said that the *Daily Express* should bear full responsibility for an affair which was of grave significance for national security. Lohan resigned his post as a result of the criticism of him made in the White Paper.

Lohan later complained about Harold Wilson's remarks made in the House of Commons debate on the subject about his relationship with Pincher and his security clearance. Wilson explained that anxieties about Lohan's contacts with journalists had arisen some time earlier and it had also been discovered that he had not been positively vetted. Other party leaders were invited to view the documents surrounding the case. A civil service inquiry later said that the government statements about Lohan were not unfair, but that no doubts had ever been raised about Lohan's character or patriotism.

LP

Cecil King Affair (1968)

Cecil King, newspaper proprietor and chairman of the International Publishing Group (1963–68).

The Cecil King Affair came about through the furore created by King's comments about Harold Wilson and his Labour government that led to his dismissal from the media conglomerate he was so closely identified with.

Cecil King had been brought up with newspapers, as his mother was sister to the two Harmsworth press barons, Lords Rothermere and Northcliffe. He joined the *Daily Mirror* in 1926 and became a director of the paper in 1929. He became chairman of the International Publishing Group (IPC), publisher of the *Daily Mirror*, in 1963.

On May 10, 1968 the *Daily Mirror* published an article written by King highly critical of the Labour government and of the Prime Minister, Harold Wilson, in particular. The paper had previously been a staunch supporter of the Labour party. In his article King accused Wilson of lack of leadership and said that the country was in the grip of "the greatest financial crisis in our history". He castigated the government for failing to arrest Britain's economic decline and suggested that Wilson should resign.

Although Wilson refrained from personal attacks against King, several Labour members did express their anger at his article. Further questions were raised about King's position as director of the Bank of England, a post he had resigned on May 9, when he had made references in his article about the state of Britain's foreign exchange reserves. On May 30 King was asked by the other members of the IPC board to resign. He refused to do so and was dismissed the same day and replaced by his deputy, Hugh Cudlipp. King alleged that influence from Labour members on the board had led to his sacking.

LP

Enoch Powell Affair (1968)

Enoch Powell, Conservative MP and former minister.

The Powell Affair centred around Enoch Powell's notorious "Rivers of blood" speech about immigration into Britain which effectively led to the end of his political career in the Conservative party.

Enoch Powell had first entered Parliament as Conservative MP for Wolverhampton South-West in 1950 and rose to be Minister of Health between 1960 and 1963. A controversial and somewhat maverick figure, he had also contested the party leadership in 1965. At the time of his speech he was the opposition front-bench spokesman on defence.

The speech was made on April 20, 1968 to a private meeting of the Conservative Political Centre's West Midlands area, although the text of the speech was made available afterwards. In it he strongly attacked the number of immigrants from the New Commonwealth and Pakistan coming into the country, called for a halt to further immigration, and suggested that a policy of repatriation should begin immediately. He said he was particularly concerned by the presence of large numbers of immigrants in inner-city areas, such as his Wolverhampton constituency. He claimed that British people were feeling like strangers in their own country and would be discriminated against in favour of the newcomers. He predicted that unless a policy of repatriation were adopted the numbers of British-born descendants of immigrants would rise and racial tensions would increase. In the most famous passage from the speech he said (quoting the Roman poet Virgil): "As I look ahead I am filled with foreboding. Like the Roman I seem to see 'the River Tiber foaming with much blood'."

The speech was widely condemned as stirring up racial prejudices, particularly in view of the forthright language used by Powell. It also provoked demonstrations of support for his views from some, such as London dock workers, who staged strikes in his support.

Powell's speech had not been cleared with the Conservative party leader, Edward Heath, or with the whips. It caused embarrassment among the Conservative leadership and Heath's reaction was to sack Powell from the shadow Cabinet on the following day. On May 2 it was decided not to prosecute Powell under the Race Relations Act for his remarks.

Powell did not repent of his views, claiming that they represented the views of the large majority of the British public. He pointed to the numerous messages of support he had received agreeing with his sentiments. Powell did not stand at the February 1974 election, but urged the public to vote Labour at the October 1974 election. He resigned from the Conservative party and joined the Official Unionists and served as MP for South Down from 1974 to 1987.

LP

Maudling Affair (1972–76)

John Cordle, businessman, right-wing Conservative MP, 1959–1976.
Jerry Hoffman, offshore property speculator.
Reginald Maudling, senior Conservative MP and Home Secretary (1970–72).
Eric Miller, property company chairman.
John Poulson, nationally prominent architect.
Albert Roberts, Labour MP since 1951.

Reginald Maudling was elected to the House of Commons in 1950. By 1955 he was a Cabinet Minister and Privy Councillor; by 1964, when the Conservatives lost office, he was Chancellor of the Exchequer. He was the epitome of the Party's middle-of-the-road, pragmatic image and a popular figure among colleagues and party members. In 1965 he lost the fight for leadership of the Party to Edward Heath and, embittered and suffering a drop of £5,000 in his annual income, turned to business to sustain his and his family's upwardly-mobile lifestyle. He knew what was expected: "after all, when a public figure becomes a director or chairman of a company it is presumably because his name and influence will be valuable". Within months he snapped up various directorships from which he was probably earning over £20,000 a year, about four times a ministerial salary. By the end of the 1960s he was a member of Lloyd's, a banker, a director of several companies, owner of a country house and a Regency home in Belgravia.

Taking on such commitments is not unexceptionable — or unacceptable — in British politics. The traditional view was that being an MP was not a full-time job and, because many MPs invariably had occupations before entering politics and were able to continue them while MPs, little attention was paid to their financial interests. There were few rules governing such interests other than a formal rule that they should be declared when voting in the House, a convention that they should be declared when speaking on related matters in the House and the commonsense awareness that they should avoid embarrassing or controversial interests. Additionally, ministers were expected not to have directorships or controlling shareholdings, not to accept gifts or services that would place the Minister "under an obligation to a commercial undertaking", and not to become involved in any business activity where insider knowledge could be suspected. The governing principle for ministers was that no conflict should arise, or appear to arise, between private interests and public duties.

Maudling, meantime, considered that his business interests should expand. He wanted capital, fringe benefits and something for his family and, in the next four years, he also accepted consultancies and directorships with three less reputable businessmen — John Poulson, Jerry Hoffman and Eric Miller, to whose schemes Maudling was not only prepared to lend his name but also actively to promote them. It was a fine distinction between who was exploiting whom.

In 1965 Eric Miller, who used the resources of his Peachey Property Corporation to win friends as Poulson used his to influence them, offered Maudling a directorship. Anxious to avoid paying more income tax and to protect his two houses from the proposed capital gains tax, he offered himself as a consultant and traded his fee for a deal in which Peachey bought the freehold of his country house from his wife — Maudling held a lease on the property from her — and paid to repair and improve it. The deal effectively gave Maudling years of salary in advance, without any tax loss, and was of no commercial advantage to Peachey.

In 1966 he signed up with Poulson. Born in 1910, John Poulson joined an architectural firm as a 17-year-old articled clerk; by the mid-1960s, his was the largest architectural practice in Europe, earning over £1,000,000 a year in fees. His success was largely accounted for in two ways; one in terms of business organization and the other in terms of a political market. On the advice of a Conservative MP and tax expert, Poulson set up an umbrella company that saved tax, allowed the accumulation of funds, and, as an all-in-one organization covering surveying, engineering, as well as architectural services, permitted Poulson to achieve savings when seeking work. He sought work by joining with a nationally-known local political leader, T. Dan Smith, to set up a series of public relations companies to employ key local politicians to push work from their councils towards Poulson. He used his political, social and freemason contacts in a similar manner to win contracts and bought key individuals by using the resources of his firm to provide them with fringe benefits — holidays, accommodation, mortgages and so on. By the mid-'60s Poulson was heavily engaged in corruption, an activity facilitated by one-party domination, the intricate world of local political networks, an enfeebled local press and inadequate means of official scrutiny. Then, by the device of placing nominal control of his firm in his wife's name, Poulson expanded his activities by establishing a building firm for the home market to erect ready-made houses and a design firm specifically for the overseas market.

He decided to hire MPs to front this company. He employed Labour MP Albert Roberts and right-wing Tory MP John Cordle. Poulson wanted a big name to front his overseas initiative and Roberts proposed Maudling who joined in 1966. Although any payment to Maudling was deferred until the company began to win orders Poulson employed Maudling's son, paid substantial amounts to a theatre charity that involved Maudling's wife and agreed that Maudling would be able to buy shares later in the company. In return Maudling began a series of Mediterranean and Middle East forays to charm the sheikhs and, in particular, persuade the Maltese Government to give Poulson a hospital contract on the island of Gozo. A charming talker and convivial host, he could open doors but could never raise private capital for Poulson's clients' projects. In Gozo, however, where British Government funds were involved, his influence helped win the contract and ensure Poulson was paid.

In the midst of these trips Maudling was proposed by Poulson's solicitor for the Board of the Real Estate Fund of America (REFA), the off-shore investment vehicle of Jerry Hoffman that promised massive tax-free profits on international property speculation. Maudling again rapidly agreed, waiving a fee in return for 250,000 shares in REFA's holding company. His function was to join a coterie of well-known public figures fronting REFA and intended to attract bank funds. He persuaded two foreign banks, solely on the basis of his involvement in REFA, to invest money in what was an international charade: Hoffman's operators were running an inter-locking network of companies intended to buy properties worldwide. Using investors' money they paid the deposit price while charging themselves commissions and fees on the basis of the full purchase price. This spread out investors' funds and inflated the apparent extent of the company's activities while making Hoffman and his colleagues rather rich.

By the end of the 1960s Maudling, too, was rather rich on paper but, in 1970, the Conservatives were returned to power and Maudling again took up ministerial office. Fortunately he had resigned from REFA in 1969 following adverse media criticism of Hoffman; he later denied any involvement in the activities of REFA and claimed he never attended any board meetings. In 1970 he resigned his Peachey consultancy and chairmanship of Poulson's overseas firm. Poulson, however, was in deep trouble, overextending his organization, frontloading his costs against large contracts that never materialised and forgetting to pay the taxman; in 1972 he filed for bankcruptcy and hearings were begun by his creditors to find out where the money had gone. The discovery that much of it went in salaries and rewards to politicians and public officials began both media and police inquiries into possible cases of fraud and corruption.

Reginald Maudling resigned as Home Secretary on the grounds that the Metropolitan Police Fraud Squad were beginning investigations into Poulson: The resignation was "solely because of my connection" with the police. He complained stridently at the mention of his name in the bankcruptcy hearings. The disingenuousness was blatant. The £8,000-a-year theatre charity convenant was only part of Maudling's indebtedness to business partners; his house was still owned by Peachey, he left Hoffman with a testimonial that REFA was an admirable concept that "can have a great future" and he kept his REFA shares for a further 12 months in the futile hope of realizing this "little pot of gold". More surprisingly he made it plain later that, if he had held any other post than that of Home Secretary, he would not have resigned from Poulson's company.

While the police inquiries were leading to a number of corruption trials, the Conservative Government was ousted in 1974. The new Labour administration tried to tighten up the parliamentary rules on Members' financial interests but were reluctant to act further, even trying to avoid the issue of those MPs who had had dealings with Poulson. In October 1976 the Attorney-General announced the end of further criminal inquiries but a damning article in the *Observer* newspaper forced Parliament to set up a Select Committee to look at Maudling, Cordle and Roberts. Despite its lack of investigative capabilities and the problem of determining what were the conventions on disclosure of interests prior to 1974, the Committee reported that all three had failed to declare their interests at appropriate times. Cordle was considered to have committed a "contempt" for advocacy for money; he had been signed up as a consultant and enthusiastically began promoting Poulson in West Africa. Unfortunately his airport hopping produced no contracts and Cordle wrote a lengthy defensive letter to Poulson spelling out his efforts, including taking part in a Commons debate "largely for the benefit of Construction Promotion (Poulson's firm)", and ending that the payment he had so far received "is uncomplimentary to myself". The other two were merely castigated for imprudence in not declaring an interest; Maudling was further rebuked for his lack of frankness in his letter of resignation in 1972. Cordle, already doomed by his self-justificatory letter to Poulson, chose to resign to avoid, as he put it, an "acrimonious and divisive" debate on the Committee's Report. In the subsequent debate Maudling resisted the findings of the Committee, was called an "honourable man" by former Tory Prime Minister Edward Heath and, surprisingly, was allowed to remain during the discussions. Albert Roberts objected to being considered with Maudling and Cordle because he had not known what standards he had been expected to obey and because he had only "transgressed in the shallow waters". Both MPs were given the benefit of the doubt and the Committee's conclusions relating to them were simply noted. Maudling retreated to backbench anonymity and died in 1979.

RAD

Lord Lambton Affair (1973)

Edward Heath, Conservative Prime Minister, 1970–74.
Anthony Lambton, former peer, wealthy landowner, Conservative MP and
   Parliamentary Under-Secretary of State, Ministry of Defence (1970–72).
Colin Levy, Norma's husband.
Norma Levy, a callgirl.

In 1973 the lifetime political career of Conservative Minister Lord Lambton
was to end abruptly. He had first been elected to Parliament in 1951
as Tory MP for Berwick-on-Tweed. He had served as a parliamentary
private secretary to Selwyn Lloyd from 1955–57, resigning over Suez,
and was a critic of Macmillan during the Profumo affair (see above).
His was the old-fashioned brand of Tory politics that was uncomfortable
with the "creeping socialism" of Macmillan's policies and with the later
managerial style of the Heath government. He was strong on patriotism,
defence and constituency matters but equally prepared to argue for the
rights of the individual or against the restrictions of censorship. Lambton
had married Belinda Blew-Jones in 1942 after one week's engagement.
They had six children but Lambton was not one to feel his individuality
constrained by the marriage. In any case he was, by 1972, living his life as
he wanted. Commander Bert Wickstead, head of the Metropolitan Police
Serious Crime Squad, who investigated Lambton, noted: "the remarkable
feature of his London home was that it had been divided precisely into
two halves. Lord Lambton's half was almost spartan in appearance, more
befitting a bachelor than a married man. Lady Lambton's half, by contrast,
was beautifully furnished and full of female fripperies."

   Lambton was very rich, adding £100,000 a year from the 25,000 acres of
farmland he owned in Durham and Northumberland to the personal family
fortune that had been first accumulated by his coal mine-owning ancestors.
In Durham he was a member of the county set, living in a 17th-century
mansion, Biddick Hall, where he owned racehorses and was reputed to be
one of the best shots in the country. In London he owned a house in St
Johns Wood and had a reputation of being a "man about town". He wrote
regularly for the press and could always be relied upon for independent, if
idiosyncratic, opinions, particularly about his love of politics.

   Certainly another Lord, Lord Carrington, thought enough of him to recommend him in 1970 for the position of Parliamentary Under-Secretary of
State at the Ministry of Defence, where Carrington presided, with specific
responsibility for the RAF. Able, intelligent, a good speaker, Lambton
performed his duties without any difficulty until Colin Levy, an unemployed
mini-cab driver, saw his name on a cheque given to his wife, Mary Levy,
an attractive 25-year old Irish woman who had graduated from nightclub
hostess and an escort agency employee to an exclusive high-class call-girl
ring. Sometime in 1972 Lambton obtained her telephone number and the
services of other sexual partners, one of whom was Mary Levy. Lambton
soon made no pretence of his identify to the point of signing his own cheques
for her fee. The Levys' relationship was tempestuous and, after Norma Levy

alleged to the police that her husband was abroad buying drugs for which he was searched on his return, Colin Levy mentioned Lambton to them both as a client of his wife and as a possible drugs user. The Levys then talked to Serious Crime Squad who were at that time investigating pornography, police corruption and rumours of a high-class vice ring in London. They passed on the Levys' story to MI-5 who were also investigating claims of a European vice-ring; the latter reported the information to the Home Office Minister Robert Carr. He told Prime Minister Edward Heath who, not wanting to be caught out without knowing the facts — the plaintive and damaging claim by Macmillan when the Profumo story broke — ordered MI-5 and the police to co-operate in securing the evidence.

Meanwhile Colin Levy was trying to sell his allegations to a mass-circulation Sunday newspaper which, not satisfied with the quality of Levy's covert photographs of Lambton with Levy's wife, took their own. Incredibly, when they decided not to publish the story, they returned their photographs to Levy who took them to another newspaper which turned the material over to the police.

Confronted by the police with the pictures of him together with Norma Levy and a black nightclub hostess he was casually indifferent: "she's a kind of prostitute . . . I liked her, but she played no important part in my life whatsoever." When the police raised his repeated reference to drugs on the tape Lambton knew that he was in trouble and immediately resigned for what he later told the press was a "casual acquaintance" with a call-girl and one or two of her friends, behaviour he termed "credulous stupidity". The same day, May 24, Earl Jellicoe, Lord Privy Seal and Leader of the House of Lords, was tendering his resignation (see *Lord Jellicoe Affair, 1973*, below). Heath was praised on all sides for his firmness, his openness and his immediate request to the Security Commission that it should look at the events leading to the resignations.

The Security Commission reported in July, emphasizing that there had been no security leaks, no European call-girl networks and no security implications — the issue that allegedly was the core to the concern over John Profumo's behaviour (see *Profumo Affair, 1963*, above). The Commission insisted that it would not express opinions on the moral aspects of the affair but only on the risk to security that the Lordships' behaviour may have involved. "Ordinary sexual intercourse" with a prostitute was not a real risk. If a criminal offence was involved the risk was greater. On the other hand, public figures were at risk if their behaviour was "punishable news" that could ruin their careers. Nevertheless, the Security Commission was condemnatory of the newspaper handing back to its informants "convincing evidence" which they previously lacked, calling the photographs "instruments of blackmail". What concerned the Commission was blackmailable behaviour that could endanger security. It did not see such liaisons in themselves as security risks and was almost congratulatory about Jellicoe's discretion and heterosexual orthodoxy but was less enthusiastic about Lambton. Although it considered that compromising photographs and sexual practices that "deviated from the normal" left him open to blackmail, the effectiveness of blackmail depended on a victim likely to betray his country. That, thought the Commission, was very unlikely with Lord Lambton. Its real concern was his use of cannabis which might lead him, "without any conscious intention of doing so," to reveal classified information "in a mood of irresponsibility". Heath accepted the conclusions of the Commission and announced that ministers would be reminded regularly of the standing instructions and guidance on security matters (the Commission did not think ministers should be subject to positive vetting). While Lord Jellicoe was allowed back into public life Antony Lambton left for his villa and his own way of life in Italy. He never took part in public life again.

RAD

Lord Jellicoe Affair (1973)

Edward Heath, Conservative Prime Minister (1970–74).
George Jellicoe, peer and Minister responsible for the Civil Service Department (1970–72).

The day after Lord Lambton resigned from the Conservative Government (see *Lord Lambton Affair*, 1973, above) another Conservative politician found himself caught up in the ensuing scandal; on May 24, 1973, Earl Jellico, Lord Privy Seal and Leader of the House of Lords, tendered his resignation. Like Lambton, George Patrick John Rushworth Jellicoe was an aristocrat with inherited wealth who enjoyed public service and politics. Born in 1918, son of Admiral of the Fleet Earl Jellicoe who commanded the Grand Fleet at the Battle of Jutland in World War I, godson of King George V, educated at Winchester and Cambridge and Hon. Page to King George VI, he served with the SAS and their Naval equivalent, the SBS, as well as the Coldstream Guards in World War II, earning the DSO, MC, Légion D'Honneur, Croix de Guerre and the Greek Military Cross. He entered the Foreign Service after the war, serving in Washington, Brussels and Baghdad. In the 1950s he switched to politics; by the early 1960s he was holding junior ministerial offices in the Home Office and Defence as well as being Deputy Leader of the Opposition in the House of Lords up to the election of a Conservative Government in 1970, at which time he became Minister in Charge of the Civil Service Department.

Unfortunately, as one of his associates put it, "if he had a fault; it is because he wears his weakness on his sleeve. He is not flamboyant but he was a hedonist". The hedonism took the form of hiring girls from two escort agencies advertised in the *Evening Standard* during 1972 and 1973. He dealt with the agencies under an assumed name and never consciously disclosed his name to his partners; he certainly never discussed his ministerial work where, as a member of the Cabinet, he had access to secret and some Top Secret material. The agencies were not connected with the Levy ring with whom Lord Lambton became involved but, apparently, his identity was guessed at and became the subject of gossip in the London vice underworld. This gossip soon reached the police through their informants — hardly surprising since the police were busily tapping all their sources of information on the "high-class call-girl" ring they were investigating at that time. The police watched his movements and then reported their information to Prime Minister Edward Heath. Asked about his knowledge of Lambton's activities and aware that other ministerial names were the subject of gossip Jellicoe admitted the relationships and offered to resign. He wrote: "when you told me yesterday that my name was being linked with allegations about a ring of call-girls, I thought it right to tell you that, unhappily, there was justification for this because I had had some casual affairs which, if publicized, would be the subject of criticism. I also said that, since this must be a grave embarrassment to you and to my colleagues, I felt I must resign . . .". Heath, unwilling to be put in a position where he could not deny the involvement of other ministers in the scandal, quickly accepted it. "Your decision accords with the best traditions of public life", he wrote in response.

The speed of the resignations and the unloading of the stockpiled stories in Fleet Street quickly took the edge off the scandal. The *News of the World* ran a three-page story on May 27, claiming a major role in bringing the story to light, before clashing with the *Daily Express* which expressed concern that "in this modern so-called permissive age a splendid member of parliament (Lord Lambton) and junior minister had been cast into the wilderness . . . can we really afford to discard men of talent, wit and partriotism because their personal lives fall short of blameless perfection?" Nevertheless, despite press talk of other names, Heath was able to state categorically on May 28 that no further ministers were involved and, despite some ministerial mutterings over his alacrity in accepting Jellicoe's resignation, was praised for his firmness and requested the Security Commission to investigate further.

The Security Commission reported in July and, while somewhat critical of the role of the press and Lambton's use of soft drugs, was almost con-gratulatory about Jellicoe's behaviour which it described as ". . . conducted with discretion. There was no abnormal sexual behaviour . . . no criminal offence nor any risk of compromising photographs . . .". The Commission concluded that the risk of indiscretions, blackmail or security leaks was negligible; the fact that the affairs came to light when they did was unfortunate and there was no reason why Jellicoe should not in future have access to confidential information. Heath accepted the conclusions of the Commission and announced that ministers would be reminded regularly of the standing instructions and guidance on security matters. Lord Jellicoe was to make a steady return to commercial and public life: he became Chairman of the Medical Research Council from 1982, Chancellor of Southampton University in 1984, Chair of the East European Trade Council in 1986, and member of various public committees as well as director of some major companies such as Sotheby's, Morgan Crucible, Smiths Industries, Davy Corporation, Booker Tate and Tate and Lyle.

RAD

Slag Heap Affair (1974)

Tony Field, Williams' brother and geology graduate.
Ronald Milhench, insurance broker and property developer.
Marcia Williams, Wilson's personal secretary from 1956.
Harold Wilson, Labour MP (1945–76), Prime Minister (1964–70, 1974–76).

The last years of Harold Wilson's premiership, and his return to the backbenches, was clouded by two controversies; the first concerned the financial affairs of some of his office staff and the second the award of honours at the time of his resignation. Harold Wilson was born in 1916 in Huddersfield, the son of a works chemist. His academic ability took him to Wirral Grammar School and then to Oxford where he graduated with a First Class degree in Politics, Philosophy and Economics and where he stayed as a Research Fellow in Economics. It was at Oxford he joined the Labour Party and although he was to spend some time during the War as a civil servant his interests increasingly lay in politics and, in 1945, he was elected Labour MP for Ormskirk in Lancashire (he later moved to the Huyton constituency which he was to represent throughout his political career). He was given immediate political office on election and in 1947, at the age of 31, he was appointed President of the Board of Trade and made a member of the Cabinet. In 1951, however, shortly before the Labour Government was to lose office to the Conservatives, Wilson resigned from the Cabinet over the imposition of health charges. He was to return to the front ranks of the Party during the 1950s as spokesman on economic and financial affairs as well as beginning a long, often bruising search for leadership of the Party. This he achieved in 1963 on the death of Hugh Gaitskell but success left Wilson unsure of his political power-base and keenly aware of the need to create coalitions and support out of individuals and groups of very different political persuasions and temperaments. He was to say later when in office that he was leading a contentious and often combative group of politicians: "I am running a Bolshevik Revolution with a Tsarist Shadow Cabinet" staffed by "bitterly hostile and suspicious, miserable creatures." As a result he became a politician who prized personal loyalty very highly.

In 1964 he led the Labour Party into government for the first time since 1945. Much of the campaign focused on the contrast of the weak leadership of the Conservative Government over the Profumo Affair (see above) and its apparent failure to respond positively to the rapid social and economic change the country was undergoing. Wilson, on the other hand, was, in the public's eyes, the undisputed leader of the Labour Party and self-proclaimed harbinger of the new technological era. Nevertheless, as Cabinet Minister and diarist Richard Crossman suggested, organizationally Wilson was ill-prepared for the demands of political office and often reluctant to devolve responsibility or control; "he is a general without any chief of staff and indeed without any structure of command . . . but above all he has no right-hand man to plan his political strategy and to put up suggestions to him".

Instead Wilson tended to rely on political cronies and a handpicked political office at whose head was Marcia Williams. The daughter of a Northampton builder, she graduated with a history degree and then took a secretarial qualification before becoming secretary to Morgan Phillips, the Labour Party General secretary, and then secretary to Wilson in 1956. Williams provided Wilson with the combination of organizational buffer and political loyalty throughout his political career. The various conflicts within the Party, the economic and foreign policy crises confronting Wilson during his first period as Prime Minister to 1970 tended to reinforce Wilson's reliance on his retinue and staff, much to the annoyance of several ministerial colleagues and party officials. Indeed Wilson sought private funding to run his office while he was leader of the Opposition between 1970 and 1974 (see *Wilson Resignation Honours Affair*, 1976, below) and thus free himself from reliance on the Party organization.

The core of the office revolved around Marcia Williams and also involved some of her relatives: Williams' father helped to find Wilson a house; her elder sister, Peggy Field, left her job at Hendon Technical College in 1969 to work as a secretary at 10 Downing Street; and her brother Tony Field moved from volunteer-driver and golf companion of Wilson to office manager for 18 months from 1971. Field was a graduate geologist who had spent a number of years in the Middle East working for the Iraqi Petroleum Company. On his return he worked as a quarry manager for the Bath and Portland Cement Company. He left in 1967 after the company did not act on his advice to buy a slag heap and quarry near Wigan. He set up his own company, J. Taylor's Slag Ltd., to buy the site. Slag, or aggregate, is a common base for roads and buildings and Field sold it for local motorways, road networks and power stations. Field also bought a gritstone quarry. He, his mother and Marcia were directors of one or other of the companies. The idea was to give them a return that would provide a steady income, and in the case of his sister, to establish a pension fund.

Although the slag business started well, the gritstone quarry was less successful. In 1973 Field, to keep his business interests going and to pay back a public sector loan that helped to purchase the original site, began to prepare a package of several pieces of land, including his own, as suitable industrial land to be offered to developers, one of whom was Ronald Milhench, a successful insurance broker who decided to get into the '70s property boom with backing from a London merchant bank. Milhench was interested in buying the land for resale; he was talking of spending nearly £1,000,000 on the purchase.

Milhench's enthusiasm to play the "Wilson connection" for his efforts to resell the land led, shortly before the 1974 February General Election, to an anonymous telephone call to *The Guardian* with some well-informed detail of the deals, the key to which was the incorrect but explosive claim that "Marcia Williams was investing money in speculative land deals on behalf of Harold Wilson". At the same time the *Daily Mail* obtained a forged letter which implied Wilson's involvement in the deals. Neither story was published before the election, which Labour won, but, following the media attention given to the death of Milhench's wife, the *Daily Mail* published the first details of the land deals story. In response another newspaper (the *Daily Express*) which was locked in a circulation war with the *Daily Mail*, published details of correspondence between one of Milhench's associates and Field relating to the sale of land about which the latter replied on official Downing Street notepaper.

The stories provoked a parliamentary furore, particularly when Wilson chose to defend the motives of those involved despite warnings from his political staff of the consequences. In April 1974 when provoked by a Tory MP (the Labour Party had regularly criticized the speculation and profits that were being made during the property boom) Wilson announced that "my honourable friends from Durham know the difference between property speculation and land reclamation .... This is not a laughing matter. My honourable friends know that if one buys land on which there is a slag heap 120 ft. high and it costs £100,000 to remove that slag, that is not land speculation in the sense that we condemn it. It is land reclamation". That stunned his party into silence and delighted both the media and Opposition MPs. The refusal to back away from the story only served to draw attention to it and give the Conservatives the opportunity to turn what was essentially a private matter into a political issue. Wilson and Williams rapidly issued writs (which they never followed up) while the press found that the other people were using the Wilson name in vain. The *Daily Mail* had picked up the *Daily Express* story about correspondence from No. 10 to a local council and found it was now incorporated into a developer's promotional material, while *The Sunday Times* found Wilson's name fraudulently mentioned on two more sets of documents.

In the meantime Wilson was convinced that the press, with whom he had long had an uneasy and often hostile relationship, was dedicated to his downfall as his statements later that year, when a second General Election was held, confirmed: "my colleagues and I throughout this summer have received many warnings ... about the assiduous and dedicated work going on to prepare stories held back, ready for issue as the election nears its climax. Cohorts of distinguished journalists have been combing obscure parts of the country with a mandate to find anything, true or fabricated, to use against the Labour Party". He said later that he believed that the aim was to spread allegations, "however vague, however hidden, of corruption at worst, dubious standards at best". Wilson believed that "his personal staff, any one connected with him, anyone even thought to be connected with him, ran — and runs — a constant risk of his or her private life being raked over".

Although Wilson had no connections with the deals, the fact that he did not disassociate himself from what had happened but used his public position to try and justify the private activities of private staff merely prolonged the affair, with Marcia Williams receiving the most press attention. Wilson then chose to crown the whole episode in July 1974 by putting his secretary into the Lords as Lady Falkender, a move that was to herald the second area of controversy — the 1976 Resignation Honours List (see below).

RAD

Crown Agents Affairs (1974)

John Cuckney, former Chief Executive, PSA, and Head of the Crown
    Agents (1974–78).
Judge E. S. Fay, author of an inquiry into the Crown Agents in 1977.
Judith Hart, Labour MP and Minister of Overseas Development (1969–70,
    1974–75, 1977–79).
Matthew Stevenson, author of an inquiry into the Crown Agents in 1974.

The Crown Agents affair held the record for the most number of official inquiries into how a small, little-known government body managed to run up hundreds of millions of pounds of losses in a few years. Set up in 1833 to act for the British Empire's colonial administrations in obtaining for them the means of government, from stamps to personnel, the Crown Agents symbolically changed its name in 1954 from the Crown Agents for the Colonies to the Crown Agents for Overseas Governments and Administrations. With its ready-made Empire clientèle dwindling the Crown Agents began to believe that UK governments had become indifferent to its future and so sought any overseas government seeking an experienced UK broker and agent. By the 1960s, the Crown Agents was being run by a Board of between one to four Agents (one of them the Chairman) with 12 heads of departments and some 1,500 executive and clerical staff. Its accounts were audited, without any formal liaison, by the Comptroller and Auditor-General (Parliament's auditor), the Director-General of Overseas Audit Service (wound up in 1970), and by commercial auditors for some of its subsidiaries. Its own sense of isolation discouraged contact with the Ministry of Overseas Development (ODM), which itself had no desire to interfere, and whose staff were not sufficiently conversant with CA activities had it wished to do so. "The usual apparatus of governance and accountability", warned the 1974 Stevenson Report, "which is found in the public — and to a lesser extent in the private — sector, is missing. The Crown Agents are unincorporated; they have no terms of reference such as are prescribed by statutes or other instruments of incorporation; and they have no prescribed limits for activities or borrowing; they have neither shareholders nor the usual kind of board of directors".

Worried that its general reserve (for pensions and so on) would be insufficient if its activities were wound down, the Crown Agents' Financial Directorate obtained the Board's assent in March 1966 to a proposal that funds directly under their control should be invested at their discretion to build up the reserves. A year later own-account transactions began and, by August 1968, the Crown Agents were borrowing from the City, putting clients' cash straight into the Finance Directorate's investment account (Finvest), and adopting an "adventurous" approach to its other own-account deals in currencies, share acquisitions, and property investments.

In October 1969 the Exchequer and Audit Departments (EAD) had already picked up the "size and unusual nature" of Finvest and reported it to the Treasury, with copies to the ODM. The EAD felt that their responsibility ended in pointing out the problems: it was the Treasury's job to investigate. A shiver of administrative paralysis pervaded Whitehall. In December 1970 the Bank of England stirred itself sufficiently to warn the Treasury of the Crown Agents' association with "some rather doubtful people and. . .some unsure investments". However suspicious it was of the Finvest account, the ODM was not willing to brief its minister, Judith Hart, to challenge the Crown Agents when there was no evidence of losses and no constitutional grounds for her intervention. Nevertheless the steady, accumulated concern by the various bodies with some responsibility for the Crown Agents' activities led to the setting-up in August 1971 of the Stevenson Committee to look at those activities and CA's constitutional status. Its report was critical of the lack of accountability and of some of the CA's partnerships, but was not unhappy with the conduct of own-account transactions. The report was suppressed to avoid upsetting clients, while the government issued a bland statement supporting the Crown Agents' "competent and economical" services. With an apparant acquittal, the CA joined the speculative fringes of the 1970s property boom, confirming the decision to do so by apparently successful wheeler-dealing and a self-confidence engendered by a feeling of being on equal terms with the City.

Following the Stevenson Report, the ODM was working towards control of the Crown Agents despite the latter's hostility and lack of co-operation and, in 1974 with the return of a Labour Government, Judith Hart returned to office as Minister for Overseas Development and announced restraints on Crown Agents' transactions and a new leadership structure. In October 1974 a new Crown Agent, John Cuckney, called in an outside accountant who revealed the extent of CA indebtedness. He then arranged for government funding (£85,000,000 with £50,000,000 standby credit), while Judith Hart established a Committee of Inquiry under Judge E.S. Fay, QC, in April 1975.

Fay's thorough Report published in December 1977 revealed that own-accounts transactions contributed little to Crown Agents' profits between

1967 and 1973, but considerably to the 1974 collapse. It demonstrated that, in the loss of its sense of direction in the "spiritual sense", the Crown Agents and its investment partners indulged in a secret underwriting commission, the support-buying of shares, balance-sheet window-dressing, and the avoidance of exchange control, and joined in triangular transfers of funds and tax avoidance. This shift, said the Report, lay in the "characteristics of the Finance Directorate" which, as a result of secrecy, insularity and absence of qualified staff, became involved in "unjustified risktaking, lack of regulation, aversion from taking advice, low standards of commercial ethics and haphazard choice of business associates". This in turn led to "a case of too many eggs in too few baskets"; £114,000,000 was lent and lost on two property companies — English and Continental and the Stern companies — and on property development in Australia. While most of the losses were incurred because the property market collapsed, the cause of the huge investments in a handful of speculative ventures and companies was blamed on favouritism, gifts, influence, ignorance of the market and a failure to understand the need to spread risk, trust in the overconfidence of the "associates" who saw the CA as a "soft touch" and whose lack of commercial morality so dominated the CA's behaviour that it, a government department, was prepared to set up deals that avoided paying UK tax — "in a class of its own", said the Report. Fay's conclusions angered Parliament sufficiently for it to override government wishes and demand a public Tribunal of Inquiry whose 1982 Report confirmed the findings of the earlier reports. Its detailed and lengthy exposition found few "guilty" names but thoroughly explained how the Crown Agents' own-account activities avoided organizational and institutional supervision. The Report noted that internal secrecy was extended towards ODM and that, in terms of external scrutiny within Whitehall, since the EAD's "clear warning" about own-account activities in 1969, government departments were more concerned with the Crown Agents' constitutional status than with finding out what the Crown Agents were up to. Thus the Ministry did not use the Stevenson Committee properly, the Treasury acquiesced in the Ministry's handling of the Crown Agents, while the Bank of England, often relying on informal and verbal contacts, helped neither. This Report again stressed how the absence of supervision and control led to imprudent transactions, conflict of interest and, ultimately in one case, corruption; one junior official with no previous experience was given £10,000,000 to invest in property "on a world wide basis", several senior officials took expensive gifts from one borrower and one went to a senior management position with another substantial borrower, while one official was charged with accepting bribes to ease his gambling debts.

The absence of Civil Service standards and procedures allowed the Crown Agents to indulge in organizational and personal activities which, if not forbidden, might have been much more circumspectly handled. However, it was the lack of clear lines of external accountability and responsibility that caused the secrecy and insularity which, together with the lack of willingness to break down the institutional secrecy or the "trench warfare" that the Crown Agents deployed to protect its activities, resulted in an initial debt of over £212,000,000. The CA was subsequently substantially reorganized and restructured; the affair was a salutary lesson in the financial consequences of inadequate or absent administrative control and political will.

RAD

Stonehouse Affair (1976)

Sheila Buckley, girlfriend and second wife of John Stonehouse.
Josef Frolik, Czech intelligence defector.
John Stonehouse, Labour MP (1957–76) and businessman.
Harold Wilson, Labour MP (1945–76), Prime Minister (1964–70, 1974–76).

At 4.05 pm on Nov. 20, 1974, John Stonehouse, a Labour MP and former government minister, walked out of the Fountainbleu Hotel in a pair of shorts and disappeared along the Miami, USA, seafront. On Christmas Eve, 1974, he was arrested by the Australian police on a passport offence. Stonehouse told the police he wanted to start a new life there, away from the pressures on him.

Stonehouse was an ambitious achiever born into a working-class socialist world. His mother was a president of the Southampton Co-operative Society and his father a union official. Stonehouse grew up in a political atmosphere of meetings, fundraising events and the espousal of left-wing causes. Leaving school at 16, he went to work as clerk in Southampton Council's Probation Department before joining the RAF during the war and subsequently went to the London School of Economics on an ex-serviceman's grant where he also met his future wife. There he began an involvement in politics that, in 1957, saw him elected to Parliament as a Labour MP. After the election of the Labour Government in the general election of 1964 he rapidly climbed the ministerial ladder to become Minister for Technology in 1967–68 and hence to become a Privy Counsellor and Postmaster General in 1968. He was energetic, hardworking, ambitious and increasingly mistrusted by his colleagues. Crossman described him as a "violent, fierce, implacable, unscrupulous young man. . .a kind of dangerous crook, overwhelmingly ambitious but above all untrustworthy. . .".

When Labour lost the 1970 General Election, Stonehouse chose to supplement his salary by establishing his business career. He took a consultancy with the UK computer firm ICL but most of his efforts were directed to setting up his own firms so that he had, as he put it, "enough to live reasonably comfortably, to afford to travel and to have the peace of mind to devote myself to political work"; he still had ambitions to become Prime Minister one day. Connoisseurs of Claret Ltd. was set up in March 1970 as sellers of wine by mail order. Its buying policy was erratic — "the work of either a madman or a person who just talks so big", said a colleague — and never made a profit. It folded in 1975 with a £48,000 deficit. Export Promotion and Consultancy Services Ltd. was set up in March 1970 as an export consultancy service and did a modest amount of trading before it collapsed in 1975 owing some £241,533. Global Imex Ltd. was set up in January 1972 to promote exports; its turnover never exceeded £90,000 and its projected deals collapsed because of political reversals, business competition and lack of available capital. Around the three main companies floated a host of subsidiaries which did little or nothing until the British Bangladesh Trust debacle unfolded.

This began in 1971, when the internecine conflict between West and East Pakistan exploded into bloody civil war. Stonehouse went out to report for the War on Want and Oxfam charities, returning committed to the Bangladeshi cause for which he raised funds and sought political support. When a Bangladeshi proposed a bank for migrants in the UK, Stonehouse was keen to seek Bank of England approval and other institutional assistance to set up the British Bangladeshi Trust. Stonehouse cobbled together a measure of financial assistance from a few institutions but the launch itself attracted little support from individual Bangladeshis and was only saved by Stonehouse borrowing from banks and using his other companies, nominee companies and employees to bolster the poor subscriptions for shares. Yet at the first meeting of BBT on Nov. 30, 1972, with Stonehouse in the chair, applications for loans and overdraft facilities to Stonehouse and Stonehouse companies of £215,000 were approved as fast as it took to read out the list. £140,000 of that money was drawn upon within two weeks to pay off the overdrafts of his companies which had been used to finance the shares applications for BBT. Most of the overdrafts were on Stonehouse's personal guarantee and the money-go-round was seen by Stonehouse as "a necessary and not very serious evil" until the shares were bought up. However, the advances remained unpaid and Stonehouse became enmeshed not only in trying to keep the company afloat but also the conceal the Stonehouse interest in supporting the shares — which involved using employees and relatives, windowdressing the accounts to make the company look profitable, inflating balance sheets, temporarily "settling" loans, and recycling loans through "middlemen" firms.

Unfortunately the Middle East Yom Kippur War of 1973 and the consequent rise in oil prices depressed the Stock Market just at the moment Stonehouse chose to try and use BBT money for dabbling in the stock market to raise funds. Faced with — for once — the caution of his colleagues ("a most imprudent transaction" said one), shares were bought through BBT subsidiaries but, with Stonehouse showing a marked reluctance to sell (he claimed he knew the chairmen of the companies in which he bought the shares), the gamble was "singularly unsuccessful". Stonehouse tried to conceal the losses from appearing in the 1974 accounts, but by this time the auditors steadily penetrated "what was, by then, a jungle dense with improprieties", with interconnected loans to Stonehouse companies and back again involving some £757,000 or 56% of BBT's total lending.

Now under investigation for possible fraud in the original launch of BBT and facing its imminent collapse, Stonehouse made one last effort to salvage the BBT disaster; he subsumed it into a new organization, the London Capital Group, in April 1974. As he felt he had cleared that hurdle Czech spy defector Josef Frolik published his autobiography which alleged that Stonehouse was one of his three contacts (another Labour MP, Will Owen, was charged in 1970 with receiving Czech money for information) and added a dramatic aspect to the impending collapse of his business career. As his last big deal — selling cement to Nigeria — failed, Stonehouse decided enough was enough. He chose the "psychiatric suicide" of himself and the emergence of another personality, which he planned by obtaining passports of two deceased constituents and siphoning money overseas from his firms. He staged a dress rehearsal escape to Miami where he secreted clothes and documents before returning to London. There his brokers asked him to pay for his loss-making share deals. Instead he chose to return to Miami and disappear. He re-emerged in Australia where his use of two false identities to open bank accounts attracted police attention because of possible fraud and he was arrested.

In January 1975 the House of Commons had set up a Select Committee to consider Stonehouse's position as an MP. It invited him to return to England and appear before them. Stonehouse wrote back that it "would be extremely dangerous to his psychiatric health" to do so. He himself sought another country in which to live but the advent of criminal charges, extradition proceedings and the threat of expulsion from the House prompted his return. He resigned as an MP in August 1976 on his being convicted of various offences at the end of his Old Bailey trial on charges relating to misuse of credit cards, forgery, false pretences, theft and fraud. Beside him in the dock was his secretary, 29-year-old Sheila Buckley, who was charged with stealing the proceeds of cheques and conspiracy to defraud. Buckley, the daughter of a South London butcher, became Stonehouse's secretary in 1968 when he was Minister of Technology. "It is not a crime when a pretty girl falls in love with a married man", said her defence, in describing the beginning of her affair with Stonehouse. She subsequently became a director of some of his companies. "I did not realize what was happening", she claimed.

The Crown's case was that Stonehouse, facing ruin, disgrace and bankruptcy over the failure of his various businesses — he owed banks and credit card companies some £250,000 — deliberately and systematically decided to fake his own suicide, illegally obtain passports, take money from sources still open to him, provide some £125,000 through short-term insurance policies for his wife and then begin a new life in a new country with his secretary. Stonehouse argued that the Crown had identified many aspects of the story but had failed to fit them together correctly because it had failed to take note of his mental state. Nevertheless, in his summing-up Mr Justice Eveleigh stressed that everyone is assumed sane and accountable for his actions unless the contrary was proved. The jury evidently agreed with the judge: the defendants were both found guilty of most of the charges against them. Stonehouse was sentenced to seven years' imprisonment (he received several concurrent sentences totalling over 23 years) while Buckley was given a two years' suspended sentence; a criminal bankruptcy order was also made against them.

From prison, Stonehouse lost his appeal to the Lords, resigned the Privy Council, suffered a heart attack and had his business and personal indebtedness spelt out — he had some £816,000 in liabilities and £137,185 in assets (including £115,000 in Zurich) — before the curtain was rung down in 1977 with the publication of the DTI report on the Stonehouse group of companies. This stated that the companies were "saturated with offences, irregularities and improprieties of one kind or another". Stonehouse, who died in 1989, never accepted their verdict, saying to the end that "I just wanted to get away and become a plain human being again. All right, so it wasn't a normal thing to do. I wasn't in a normal state of mind".

RAD

Wilson Resignation Honours Affair (1976)

Desmond Brayley, businessman awarded a life peerage by Wilson in 1973.
Joseph Kagan, businessman awarded a life peerage by Wilson in 1976.
Eric Miller, property developer awarded a knighthood by Wilson in 1976.
Marcia Williams, Wilson's personal secretary from 1956.
Harold Wilson, Labour MP (1945–76) and Prime Minister (1964–70, 1974–76).

Up to the middle of this century honours and titles were awarded as a form of public reward for a variety of activities, from dedicated public service to large donations to the party funds. Since 1925, however, the "rules" of who may get a honour for what have been governed by legislation to stop the growing practice of simply selling honours for donations to pay for the growing party machines, irrespective of the character or background of the donors.

After the legislative power of the House of Lords was broken at the start of this century there was an increase in the award of the more valued honours because such honours now represented social rather than political status, particularly hereditary peerages which were sought after by successful businessmen who were keen to secure a highly visible place for themselves and their heirs in society. Lloyd George, a Liberal who had been in coalition with the Conservatives during World War I, tried while in office to establish his own political party. A man with few scruples but with a large political following in the country, he decided to sell as many honours as possible to raise the necessary funds to do this. He used a number of political cronies and commercial touts to find suitable recipients who paid according to a sliding scale of charges for the whole range of honours, from the commonplace Order of the British Empire to a hereditary peerage. The scheme fell apart partly over the increasing number of minor honours being sold but primarily over King George V's and the Lords' annoyance over the poor quality of those seeking peerages, including some with criminal records and unsavoury business backgrounds. Lloyd George's organization was broken up and its chief tout spirited abroad by the Conservative Party and Lloyd George himself was forced to legislate his own practices out of existence.

Honours could still be granted for public service, but those for political purposes had to be vetted by a small committee of respectable public figures to ensure that those who received them were fit and proper persons. While this ensured that the excesses of Lloyd George steadily disappeared, parties still gave honours for political contributions and other party favours but now most of the recipients of such honours were also involved in other public or charitable works. Nevertheless there was a growing feeling, particularly among the Labour politicians, that honours were part and parcel of the class structure, a reward system for establishment figures and major party supporters which only perpetuated class bias and party favouritism.

In 1964 the new Labour Prime Minister, Harold Wilson, announced the end of hereditary titles and the exclusive use of life peerages and knighthoods, tenable only for the lifetime of the recipient and awarded solely for merit, with particular emphasis on the new type of peers having an important "job of work" to do in the House of Lords. In the next three years he underlined his reforms by deciding to discontinue honours for political service and reduce the numbers of automatic awards for senior civil servants. His final effort, to take away the legislative rights of hereditary peers, floundered in the press of government business at the end of the 1960s and, with it, Wilson's enthusiasm for future reforms. Thereafter the names began to reflect Wilsonian acquaintances and loyalists as well as "star dust" recipients from the world of sport and entertainment. Although there was some adverse comment at the enoblement of Wilson's personal secretary, Marcia Williams, after the Slag Heaps Affair in 1974 (see above) the 1976 Resignation Honours List focused public attention on Wilson's public stance and private inclinations.

On May 27, 1976, as is customary for retiring prime ministers, Wilson published a list of those he wished to reward; unlike the New Years Honours List which is issued by the Crown, this list is very much a Prime Minister's choice. Life peerages were announced for some eight people, including Wilson's publisher, doctor, raincoat manufacturer, former office manager and campaign assistant, but also for a property millionaire, an academic critic of Wilson policies and two entertainment moguls. There were also knighthoods for, among others, James Hanson, James Goldsmith, Sigmund Sternberg and Eric Miller — all successful and wealthy businessmen.

The list caused a predictable public row — "frankly distressing" said *The Guardian*, "such farce" said *The Times* — as over 100 Labour MPs signed a motion disassociating themselves from the List. The furore over the "lavender-coloured" list (so-called because it was allegedly written on notepaper belonging to Wilson's secretary, Marcia Williams) and the leakings of names before publication of the list only served to create a series of controversies as to why certain people had been picked. The row was further exacerbated by two members of the three-member Political Honours Scrutiny Committee, the committee that vets the suitability of awards, publicly expressing their astonishment that their reservations over "at least half the list" (although some names were withdrawn because of the reservations) were ignored: "we were, in fact, faced with a *fait accompli* which we had no power to upset", said Lady Summerskill. Wilson defended certain of the awards on the grounds that the recipients entertained "real" people: the others were rewarded because Britains's survival depended on "a really tough, almost piratical enterprise in foreign trade". Williams claimed that the critics were snobbish and anti-semitic, calling their complaints a "sanctimonious protest by the unimaginative half of the Establishment".

The list caused the media to begin to look not only at possible reasons for some of the names on the list but also at previous appointments. Some awards had been made to businessmen with whom Wilson had had dealings as a government minister from his days at the Board of Trade, from his support of export efforts or from their support of his political activities. Many of them were Jewish and/or had business connections with eastern Europe, both areas with which Wilson had close interests, while other businessmen-friends were supporters of his 1970 Office Fund, a story broken in 1977 by the *Daily Mail* and thus adding to the concern surrounding the list.

Explanations for various honours since 1964 were not always easy to determine; similarly it was not always evident that all of those elevated to a peerage had done "a job of work" in the Lords. Worse for Wilson, the controversy was to blight his retirement because of the involvement of three of those he honoured in criminal activities both before and after 1976. One was Desmond Brayley who, in 1970, became a knight in Wilson's resignation honours list (the first one) and a life peer in 1973. He had begun to make friends in Labour circles to the extent that Labour politicians used his yacht and Wilson his London flat after the 1970 election defeat. The takeover of the glassmaking firm he chaired at the same time as he was taking up a junior ministerial appointment ran into trouble as auditors for the purchasers began asking questions about payments to Brayley of £197,105, including commissions, expenses and travel. These concerned £30,000 commission paid to Brayley over eight years; £40,000 for expenses, including a £2,000 Jamaica trip for two; a payment by the company of £8,500 for his own Rolls Royce which was allegedly worth £3,000; £109,415 paid to Brayley by one of the firm's transport subsidiaries and payments of commission to haulage companies in which Brayley's friends and relatives had shares. He was swiftly persuaded to resign in 1974 and died shortly after, before the official inquiry into his firm could be carried out.

In 1977, on the Jewish Day of Atonement, Sir Eric Miller shot himself in the rear patio garden of his South Kensington home with a Walther automatic pistol. Miller, a working-class Londoner who had built up the Peachey Property Corporation into the largest owner of residential property in the country, was an avid seeker of social distinction who used his company and its funds to employ a number of politicians from both parties as well as providing receptions and offices for various Labour organizations. Boardroom discontent surfaced in 1976 over Miller's financial withdrawals from the company. By 1977 the company ousted Miller and slapped in claims for repayments of £282,000 as Edmund Dell, Labour's Trade Minister, ordered a DTI inquiry which later revealed that Miller used the funds of Peachey Property to pay for his extravagant lifestyle and to enhance his social standing. He moved money around to balance the books, took cash out of the company — £188,700 allocated for introductory commissions went directly to himself — or used its funds for personal entertainment, including Labour Party banquets and champagne for Harold's resignation party, as well as £1,280-worth of filing cabinets for Downing Street which Miller visited on several occasions between 1974–76. He used, said the DTI report, "the Company as his private bank".

As this report appeared so the Customs and Excise arrived on the premises of Kagan Textiles, looking for evidence of a major tax swindle by the Yorkshire-based manufacturer of Gannex raincoats and Peer of the Realm, Joe Kagan. Son of a Jewish Lithuanian mill-owner Kagan made a fortune when, in 1952, he invented a means to bond together nylon and wool which resulted in the warm and waterproof Gannex raincoat. He was assiduous in cultivating publicity for the raincoat by putting them on the backs of the rich and famous, including the Royal Family and Harold Wilson. Although he did not join the party until 1968 Kagan was already part of the Wilson entourage where he often helped with staff problems. Kagan Textiles was financially healthy — Kagan had a Lakeland home, a London flat, an 18th-century manor house near Halifax and a large detached house near Huddersfield — but was tightly controlled by its owner. In 1971 he took over a firm which made denim, just at the time that the material was coming back into fashion. Rather than pay the tax due on the increasing sales Kagan devised a scheme to export denim as substandard material for resale on the continent at full price and, later, to sell indigo dye for denim abroad without the authority of the manufacturer. All payments, over £700,000, were made to a secret Zürich bank account, but attracted the attention of the Swiss customs whose information to the British Customs and Excise resulted at the end of 1978 in warrants for the arrest of Kagan, his wife and business colleagues on charges of conspiracy to defraud the public revenue and to falsify records. Kagan was safely ensconced in Israel but in 1980 he was arrested in Paris and extradited on charges of theft and false accounting relating to the dye swindle. Accordingly, charges against the others were dropped and Kagan was only tried in relation to part of the charges first brought. Despite his argument that the Swiss money was intended to help Jewish refugees to reach Israel, the judge accused Kagan of disregarding all legal and moral restraints and weaving a tangled web of deceit. He then sentenced Kagan to 10 months' imprisonment and £135,000 in fines and costs (later reduced to £86,000); the total liability to him and his firms ran to £1,100,000. Stripped of his knighthood, Kagan is still a peer of the realm.

RAD

Thorpe/Scott Affair (1976)

Peter Bessell, Liberal MP (1964–70) and businessman.
David Holmes, best man at Thorpe's first wedding, Liberal Party Deputy Treasurer.
Norman Scott, male model.
Jeremy Thorpe, Liberal MP (1959–79) and Leader of the Party (1967–70).
Harold Wilson, Labour Prime Minister (1964–70, 1974–76), political friend of Thorpe.

In February 1974, after a four-year period of Tory rule that had been less than successful in dealing with the economy and militant trade unionism, the general election had left the Tory Government unable to command an overall majority in the House of Commons without the support of Liberal MPs. The Conservatives proposed a coalition with Jeremy Thorpe, the leader of the small Liberal Party, but this was rejected by his party, not the least because of his failure to consult before talking to the Conservatives. The Labour Party took office as Thorpe warned his party "not to shrink from the possibility of sharing power". For 15 years he had kept faith with a minority political party that had finally come close to seeing him promoted to the Cabinet and the key figure in a coalition government. He had not, despite his growing personal difficulties, been prepared to give up that opportunity willingly.

That singlemindedness was part of Thorpe's public make-up, dynamic, principled but with a well-developed sense of the art of the possible. Son of a barrister and former Tory MP, he was brought up in a comfortable upper middle-class environment and educated at Eton and Oxford. After work as a barrister and a television journalist he won the North Devon constituency as a Liberal in 1959 at the age of 30. Another Liberal parliamentary candidate in Devon, and later MP was Peter Bessell, a congregationalist lay preacher who campaigned in a Cadillac and pursued a variety of business schemes. Bessell introduced Thorpe to some of them, starting Thorpe on a series of directorships that led in 1971 to an appointment as a non-executive director of London and County Securities, a merchant bank. By this time Thorpe had been elected leader of the Party and had married. Despite rumblings of idealist discontent, particularly among Young Liberals, he had ruthlessly stamped his organizational mark and personal style of leadership on the Party and begun to develop strong links outside, particularly with figures like Labour Prime Minister Harold Wilson. By 1973, he was a Privy Councillor, confirmed leader of his Party, a national figure, with a comfortable lifestyle funded by several directorships. He had survived the shock of his first wife's death in a car crash and married Marion, Countess of Harewood. His political future was riding high on a general revival of the Party's fortunes, particularly at local level. Only one setback had occurred; London and County Securities, amidst the secondary bank boom of the early 1970s, had overextended its lending and collapsed. In January 1976 he had to take a public lecture from Department of Trade and Industry inspectors in their report on the bank's collapse about the inadvised practice of leading politicians taking paid directorships (in Thorpe's case £5,000 a year, a car and share options) in companies whose affairs they were ill-equipped to understand. He weathered the crisis, apologizing for not paying sufficient attention to the company's affairs. On the day the DTI Report appeared, however, Bob Carvel of the *Evening Standard* rang the Party's Chief Whip for his comments on another story. What, he asked, were Cyril Smith's comments on the Barnstaple courtroom outburst by a Norman Scott?

Norman Scott was a good-looking young man with underlying psychological problems stemming from his upbringing and his bisexuality, which were increasingly reflected in bouts of personal insecurity and highly-charged emotional intensity. A love of horses took him to a Chipping Norton riding stables where in 1960 he met the 31-year old Thorpe who offered a helping hand if ever he was in trouble. After treatment at an Oxfordshire clinic, a couple of drug overdoses and an increasingly complex private life, Scott decided to take up the offer. According to Scott — and repeatedly denied by Thorpe — he and Thorpe then began a homosexual relationship.

Certainly at that time Thorpe felt a personal responsibility for Scott, arranging accommodation and work for him, and told the police he was "more or less a guardian" to him when they were inquiring about a coat stolen from the clinic. Certainly he felt affectionate towards him; he was writing to "My dear Norman", nicknaming him "Bunnies" (because he looked like a startled rabbit) and professing that "I miss you". After a few months, however, Scott felt the relationship cooling. He reacted sharply; he was interviewed by the police in 1962 after being overheard threatening to kill Thorpe, he told his employers about the alleged relationship in 1965 and, in the same year, wrote to Thorpe's mother repeating allegations about the relationship and urging her to intercede with her son because he "was desperate". Thorpe turned for help to Peter Bessell who put Scott on a monthly retainer. Scott then underwent medical treatment, a shortlived marriage and a quest for documents (which he was to say later that Thorpe had retained) in a not particularly successful attempt to begin a new life. His complaints about Thorpe reached the Party through a concerned member and precipitated an internal Party inquiry, much to Thorpe's annoyance. He sought the support of the then Conservative Home Secretary and the Commissioner of the Metropolitan Police in convincing the inquiry that Scott's allegations were baseless fantasies. Equally upset by the inquiry's dismissal of his claims, Scott took them to the media, with one newspaper handing the story to a freelance reporter who was later to claim he was working for BOSS, the South African secret police.

In late 1975 one Andrew Newton was arrested (and subsequently convicted) on charges of possessing a firearm with intent to endanger life following the shooting of Scott's dog. Press speculation suggested a link to Thorpe. Then, in January 1976, Scott appeared in court in Barnstaple (Devon) on charges of defrauding the Department of Health and Social Security and claimed that he was being hounded because he had once had a sexual relationship with Thorpe.

After Scott's Barnstaple courtroom outburst the media began to investigate the activities of two of Thorpe's closest associates, Bessell and businessman David Holmes, who had been best man at Thorpe's first wedding and been appointed a deputy treasurer of the Party by Thorpe. Initially it was assumed that Bessell, known at least within the Party to have been paying Scott a retainer, was being blackmailed by Scott and that Holmes was helping him deal with the matter. Bessell, however, who had been willing to go along with the blackmail tale but was increasingly upset by the media's hostile attitude to him and his motives, denied in a *Daily Mail* interview in early May that he was at risk and claimed that he had been shielding Thorpe's reputation because he assumed that Scott posed a serious threat to it.

Intense media interest in Scott's allegations and growing concern within the Party forced Thorpe to resign on May 10, 1976. At the same time, Labour Prime Minister Harold Wilson claimed in Parliament that "I have no doubt that there is strong South African participation in recent activities relating to the Leader of the Liberal Party based on massive reserves of business money and private agents of various kinds and qualities". This claim triggered a series of media inquiries which invariably found no substance behind the allegations.

Investigations by journalists Roger Courtiour and Barrie Penrose traced a link from Andrew Newton to Holmes and two associates, George Deakin and John Le Mesurier. In October 1977 a newspaper paid Newton a substantial sum for his claim that "I was hired to kill Scott" and that he had accepted £5,000 from a top Liberal supporter — "it was a contract to murder". Meanwhile Bessell talked of a Mr X suggesting that David Holmes look for ways to kill Scott. In August 1978 Thorpe was charged, together with Holmes, Deakin and Le Mesurier, with conspiracy to murder. Thorpe was additionally charged with "incitement to murder".

The committal hearings were held in Somerset in November 1978 and, a few days after he was defeated in the general election of 1979, Thorpe was seated in the Old Bailey as the prosecution case began with Scott's long exposition of his alleged homosexual relationship with him. Bessell's tale concerned Thorpe's alleged decision to "get rid" of Scott — "it's no worse than shooting a sick dog" — as Scott staggered from one emotional outburst to another. Holmes' friend and contacts provided the conspiracy in action and the money was covertly diverted from party supporters' contributions. The defence strategy was to underline the unreliability and unprincipled nature of some of the prosecution witnesses — Bessell was Judas Iscariot, Scott was a liar and a scrounger, for example — and to argue that, while there was a strong suggestion of a conspiracy to frighten, there was none to kill. This line found favour with the judge who also pointed out that there had been no corroborated evidence about the threats to Scott, the source of the money or, more importantly, any conspiracy to kill. The defendants were acquitted.

Later Bessell published his autobiography in the USA in which he accused Thorpe of being as "ruthless as the rogue elephant, trampling all before him in the cause of self-preservation" and, two years later, Thorpe's closest friend David Holmes, in return for a "substantial fee" to charity, told the *News of the World* that Thorpe was the inspiration behind the attempts to silence Scott because of the threat Scott posed to his political career and the plan to frighten Scott (killing was a knee-jerk reaction that he believed Thorpe could not and would not sustain in reality) other actions were done "after discussion with Jeremy, and with his authorization". For many, the scandal was rooted in the allegations of homosexuality, for others it was exacerbated by party intrigue and conflict. Despite the acquittal, Thorpe never returned to public life.

RAD

Philby Affair (1963)

Harold Philby, British intelligence officer (1940–51).

Of all the British spy stories which have emerged in the post-war years, some have clearly been more sensational and dramatic than others, but perhaps none could be interpreted as singularly classic in the way that the Philby affair could.

On July 1, 1963, the British government revealed in the House of Commons that Harold "Kim" Philby, the former Foreign Office official who had been asked to resign from the security service in 1951 because of his past Communist associations, was now known to have been an agent of the Soviet Union before 1946, and further to have been the "third man" who in May 1951 had given fellow spies Guy Burgess and Donald Maclean a warning that enabled them to escape to the Soviet Union before the completion of investigations into Maclean's suspected spying activities (see *Burgess and Maclean Affair, 1951*, above).

Philby was born in January 1912 and educated at Westminster School and Trinity College, Cambridge. He entered the Foreign office as a temporary officer in 1941, served in Istanbul in 1947–49, and was a first secretary in the Washington Embassy from October 1949 to June 1951. He had been a friend of Burgess since they were undergraduates together at Cambridge and had shared a flat in Washington during the months before Burgess had been recalled to London in April 1951. After the defection of Burgess and Maclean to the Soviet Union, suspicion fell upon Philby and his background was subjected to further investigation. As a result of the discovery that he had had Communist associations before and after his university days he was asked to resign from the security service, in which he then held the position of Britain's principal intelligence liaison officer in Washington.

Although Philby was strongly suspected of having sent a warning to Maclean via Burgess, there was no precise proof at this stage. It was in those circumstances that on Nov. 7, 1955, Harold Macmillan, the Prime Minister, had stated in a Commons debate that, although Philby had been asked to resign, no evidence had been found of his alleged treason or of his identification as the so-called "third man". At the same time, MI-5 appeared totally convinced of his guilt and advised that he should never again have access to classified information.

In 1956, MI-6, the Secret Intelligence Service, decided to employ Philby as an agent to secure some information about Middle East affairs, based in Beirut and using as a cover the position of foreign correspondent for the *Observer* and the *Economist*. Two incidents then occurred which apparently strengthened the case of those who believed that Philby was a spy.

Firstly, at Christmas 1961 Anatoli Golitsyn, a KGB officer who had defected to the West, informed his CIA interrogators that Philby was a long-standing Soviet spy. Golitsyn could only identify the British agent through indirect means so that his evidence could not be admissible in a court of law.

Secondly, in July 1962 a Jewish woman was attending a party in Israel and passed comments on what she claimed were the anti-Israeli tone of newspaper articles then being written by Philby. She further remarked that before the war he had approached her and suggested that she should help him in "important work for peace". Another visitor from England reported the conversation on his return to London to Sir Dick White, the then head of MI-6, who subsequently talked to the woman and received an assurance from her that she would be prepared to sign a formal statement and appear as a witness against Philby in court. Thus 11 years after suspicion first fell upon him, there appeared at last to be some concrete first-hand evidence that Philby had been a Soviet spy for many years.

Following these two highly significant incidents, described in the Commons in July 1963 merely as "further information", both MI-5 and MI-6 needed to pursue a careful strategy with a view to extracting a confession from Philby.

Since he had been denied access to British secrets for a period of 11 years, it was agreed that Philby would be offered an immunity from prosecution. An MI-6 officer and an old friend of the suspected spy, Nicholas Elliott, was sent to Beirut to make contact with him. The interrogation took place early in January 1963. Various accounts of the meeting suggest that Philby appeared to be expecting the visit. He then confessed that he had been a Soviet agent since 1934, that he had indeed warned Maclean in 1951 of his imminent interrogation, and had also transmitted detailed secret information on a number of British intelligence operations to the Russians. However, the British security services were convinced that the KGB had been able, by some means, to monitor the Philby case from early in 1962 onwards and had further provided him with a plausible but incomplete account of his espionage activities with which perhaps to placate the British authorities.

On January 23, 1963, Philby disappeared from the Lebanese capital and went to Moscow, where he settled and eventually reached the rank of colonel in the KGB. He published a book in 1968 entitled *My Silent War*, which outlined his career as a Soviet spy, and died in Moscow on May 11, 1988.

The implications of the Philby affair were that, in the first place, he had somehow known of the intention of the British security service to confront him with their new evidence, and secondly, it appeared that there could possibly exist a "fifth man" — Professor Anthony Blunt having confessed to being the "fourth man" in 1964 and being publicly exposed as such in 1979 (see *Blunt Affair, 1979–80*, below) — who was or is operating within the highest reaches of Britain's intelligence services. It remains to be seen whether the Burgess-Maclean-Philby-Blunt quartet will yet become a quintet.

WS

Blunt Affair (1979–80)

Professor Anthony Blunt.

One of the more sensational statements by a British Prime Minister in recent years was that made in the House of Commons on Nov. 15, 1979, when Margaret Thatcher revealed that Sir Anthony Blunt, a prominent art historian, had from 1940 to 1945 regularly passed information to the Soviet Union while he was a member of the British security services.

Such a dramatic disclosure by the Prime Minister followed press speculation in the preceding few days and the publication earlier in the month of a book by Andrew Boyle, *The Climate of Treason*, in which indications were given that an (unnamed) person holding a high public position had been the "fourth man" in the Burgess-Maclean-Philby spy affair (see *Burgess and Maclean Affair, 1951*; *Philby Affair, 1963*; above).

In April 1964 Professor Blunt had admitted to the security authorities that he had been recruited by and had acted as a talent-spotter for Russian intelligence before the war, and passed information regularly to them while he was a member of the security service from 1940 to 1945. This admission had been made after he had been given an undertaking that he would not be prosecuted if he confessed. The security authorities had no reason either in 1940 or at any time during his service to doubt his loyalty to his country.

On leaving the security service in 1945 Professor Blunt had reverted to his profession as an art historian, holding a number of academic appointments. He was also appointed as Surveyor of the King's Pictures in 1945, and as Surveyor of the Queen's Pictures in 1952. He was awarded a knighthood in 1956 and on his retirement as Surveyor was appointed as an Adviser for the Queen's Pictures and Drawings in 1972, from which post he retired in 1978.

Professor Blunt had first come under suspicion in the course of the inquiries which followed the defection of Burgess and Maclean in 1951. Although Professor Blunt was interviewed 11 times between 1951 and 1964, no evidence was produced to support possible charges. However, early in 1964 new evidence was received by the security authorities which directly implicated him, without providing a basis upon which charges could be brought. Sir John Hobson, the then Attorney General, decided in April 1964, after consultation with the Director of Public Prosecutions, that the public interest lay in trying to secure a confession from Sir Anthony, not only to arrive at a definite conclusion on his own involvement but also to obtain information from him about any others who might still be in danger. It was apparently considered important to gain his co-operation in the continuing investigations by the security authorities, following the defections of Burgess and Maclean in 1951, and of Philby in 1963, into Soviet penetration of the security and intelligence services and other public services during and after World War II. Accordingly, the Attorney General authorised an offer of immunity from prosecution to Professor Blunt if he confessed.

Both at the time of his confession and subsequently, Margaret Thatcher revealed, Professor Blunt provided useful information about Russian intelligence activities and about his association with Burgess, Maclean and Philby.

Professor Blunt admitted to the security authorities that he had indeed become an agent of Russian intelligence and had talent-spotted for them at Cambridge University during the 1930s; that he had regularly passed information to the Russians while he was a member of the security service; and that, although after 1945 he was no longer in a position to supply the Russians with classified information, in 1951 he used his previous contact with the Russian intelligence service to assist in the arrangements for the defection of Burgess and Maclean. Professor Blunt was not required to resign his appointment in the Royal Household, since his position carried no access to classified information and no risk to security, while the security authorities believed it desirable not to put at risk his co-operation in their continuing investigations. It was agreed by successive Attorneys-General that, having regard to the immunity granted in order to obtain the confession, which had always been the only firm evidence against Professor Blunt, there were no grounds on which criminal proceedings could be instituted. On Nov. 16, 1979, his knighthood was withdrawn.

In his own statement issued on Nov. 20, Professor Blunt said that in the 1930s it seemed to him and to many of his contemporaries that the Communist Party and Russia constituted the only firm bulwark against fascism, since the Western democracies were taking an uncertain and compromising attitude towards Germany. He stated that he had been persuaded by Burgess that the cause of anti-fascism could best be served by working for the Russians. Professor Blunt stated that this was a case of political conscience against loyalty to country, and he had chosen conscience. He continued that when later he came to realize the true facts about Russia, he was prevented from taking any action by personal loyalty, since he was not prepared to denounce his friends. He said that in 1964, however, an event took place — believed to be the death in a car crash of a friend who had facilitated his recruitment into MI-5 in 1940 — which meant that he was no longer bound by this loyalty, and was relieved to give the authorities all the information in his possession.

The British government in 1979 and into the 1980s continued to resist demands for a full inquiry into the Blunt affair, while Professor Blunt died in London of a heart attack on March 26, 1983.

WS

Kincora Boys' Home Affair (1980–90)

Tam Dalyell, Labour MP for Linlithgow.
Colin Wallace, former information officer with Ministry of Defence in Northern Ireland.

Throughout 1989 and continuing into 1990 most serious allegations arose concerning incidents of child sexual abuse at the Kincora boys' home in Belfast, in Northern Ireland, occurring during the 1970s.

In 1980 an Irish newspaper had initially exposed the allegations, resulting in the imprisonment in 1981 of William MacGrath, a senior worker at Kincora, for sexual offences. Two inquiries were then held into the affair — one by Sir George Terry, the then Chief Constable of Sussex, the other by Judge Hughes — which were described by the British government as having been very thorough.

However, repeated allegations throughout the 1980s about the supposed real truth about the Kincora boys' home re-emerged in January and February 1990, as part of a package of wider allegations which had been circulated within the British media for a number of years by Colin Wallace — a former information officer with the Ministry of Defence (MOD) at British Army headquarters in Northern Ireland — that a "dirty tricks" campaign of smears and subversion against senior politicians which had existed in the province in the 1970s was extended to the mainland to include many leading British politicians. More specifically, Wallace alleged that boys at the home were in fact used by British army intelligence as "pawns" for blackmail purposes.

Wallace further alleged that the security forces in Northern Ireland deliberately covered up information relating to homosexual activities in Kincora, and that his superior officer, Peter Broderick, saw and initialled a report in 1973 by Wallace about Kincora; it was a further seven years before the matter was brought to the attention of the authorities. Despite further evidence which emerged in a television documentary programme in June 1990, that MI-5 repeatedly refused to allow the Royal Ulster Constabulary (RUC) to interview security service officers about Kincora, the British government continued to pursue the view that the affair was now complete. For instance, Peter Brooke, the UK Secretary of State for Northern Ireland, said in the House of Commons in February 1990 that the Kincora affair had been investigated "as fully and thoroughly as lies within the power of the government to investigate it, and that no purpose would now be served by a further inquiry".

Despite the consistency of the government's line on the Kincora boys' home affair, a number of questions appeared to remain unanswered, most notably pursued within the House of Commons by Tam Dalyell, the Labour MP for Linlithgow. The questions relate principally to the precise nature of government inquiries into the allegations made by Wallace about Kincora, the role of senior officials within the MOD who had been providing ministers with information and briefings in order to deal with parliamentary questions on the matter, and the way in which an increasing number of people involved in the political and security implications of the matter were now calling for a public inquiry into the alleged cover-up by the intelligence services of the Kincora affair.

WS

Geoffrey Prime Affair (1981–82)

Geoffrey Prime, government intelligence officer.

The detection of government employees who pass on secret information to other countries always raises a number of issues: how such a person was able to be engaged and retained on classified work and to escape notice as a spy for the relevant period in which the activity took place; how much and what information was passed to other countries and what damage was done; and whether such a person knew of any others in the public service who were or who might have been involved in espionage. The case of Geoffrey Prime, imprisoned in 1982 on espionage charges, was one in which such issues arose.

Prime, who had joined the Royal Air Force in 1946, had qualified in the Russian language in May 1964 and was engaged thereafter in work of a classified nature at RAF Gatow in West Berlin. In January 1968 he made contacts with secret service agents of the Soviet Union in Berlin, and in July of that year he left the RAF, obtaining a civil service post as a linguist in London. For the next four or five years he regularly conveyed information to the Russians, being for this purpose supplied with special equipment and trained in the use of miniature cameras, of short-wave radio transmitters and receivers, and of encoding and deciphering methods.

In the spring of 1975 Prime was given a briefing by his employers in London in order to receive and understand fresh material of a higher security classification, and he reported this immediately to his contact in Berlin. A number of meetings with this contact took place in Vienna in September 1975, when Prime handed over photographic copies of highly secret material and microfiche cards, receiving financial payments in return.

Prime was in March 1976 transferred to the Government Communications Headquarters (GCHQ) in Cheltenham, being promoted in November of that year to the position of a section head which gave him access to a wider and even more secret range of material. In May 1976 he had travelled again to Vienna and been paid for more photographic documents. Between that time and his resignation from GCHQ in September 1977 Prime took 15 rolls of film amounting to some 500 photographs of top secret documents. He had no further contact with Soviet agents until April 1980; in May of that year he handed over to a contact in Vienna the 15 rolls of film taken from Cheltenham, while in November 1981 he flew to Berlin and discussed top secret matters with a contact. After leaving GCHQ, Prime worked as a taxi driver and later as a travelling salesman for a wine company.

In a statement to police in June 1982 following his arrest, Prime had stated that he regretted the extent of his betrayal, and that he had embarked on such activities partly as a result of "a misplaced idealistic view of Soviet socialism which was compounded by basic psychological problems within myself".

On Nov. 10, 1982, he was found guilty of offences under the Official Secrets Act 1911 and sentenced to 35 years' imprisonment. He had faced seven charges under that part of the Act which prohibited the communication of information, for purposes prejudicial to the safety and interest of the state, which might be useful to an enemy.

Prime had initially come under suspicion in connection with an incident of indecent assault, but while he was in custody further investigations indicated that he had over a number of years been engaged in espionage activities. He received a further three years' imprisonment on the sexual offences charges.

In a statement to the House of Commons on Nov. 11, 1982, Margaret Thatcher, the Prime Minister, said that Prime had been positively vetted while in the RAF and again by GCHQ. Further positive vetting had followed in 1973, and nothing had arisen on these occasions to place in doubt his fitness for access to classified information. An application by Prime to appeal against his sentence was rejected by the Court of Appeal on April 23, 1983.

WS

Commander Trestrail Affair (1982)

Michael Rauch, male prostitute.
Cdr. Michael Trestrail, the Queen's Police Officer.

The Commander Trestrail Affair came as the result, not of any wrongdoing on the part of Trestrail, but by the unfortunate circumstances which forced him to admit to his homosexuality. As head of security for the royal family this could have compromised him, and he was forced to resign from the police force amid a wave of press publicity.

Trestrail had acted as the Queen's Police Officer (and therefore responsible for her personal security) since 1973. He was also head of the Scotland Yard squad in charge of protection of the royal family. The quality of this protection came under intense public scrutiny in July 1982 after a mentally disturbed man, Michael Fagan, succeeded in breaking into Buckingham Palace and entering the Queen's bedroom. Numerous questions were raised in Parliament and in the press about the case and other breaches of security surrounding the royal family.

It was in this atmosphere that Michael Rauch, a male prostitute with whom Trestrail had had a casual relationship three years earlier, attempted to sell his story to the *Sun* newspaper. Trestrail had broken off the relationship after an unsuccessful attempt by Rauch to blackmail him. The newspaper passed the allegations on to Scotland Yard, and when confronted Trestrail admitted the relationship publicly on July 17. He resigned from the Metropolitan Police on July 19. It was subsequently revealed that Trestrail had been positively vetted for the first time only three or four months before his resignation.

LP

General Belgrano Affair (1982–86)

Tam Dalyell, Labour MP (since 1962).
Margaret Thatcher, Prime Minister (from 1979).

There has been a long-standing debate amongst academics and practitioners about whether or not backbench members of the British House of Commons have enough power and indeed status to influence the public affairs of the United Kingdom. Whatever the truth of the matter, backbench MPs have demonstrated time and time again that persistent questioning of government ministers and a determined pursuit of answers to such questions can reveal details of cases in which the facts were quite evidently never intended to be revealed. One prominent illustration is the case of the *General Belgrano*, the Argentine battle cruiser sunk by the Royal Navy in May 1982 during the Falklands conflict, with the military and political circumstances of the incident being pursued relentlessly by Tam Dalyell, the Labour MP for Linlithgow.

Born in August 1932 Tam Dalyell was educated at Eton and at King's College, Cambridge. After qualifying as a teacher, he unsuccessfully contested Roxburgh, Selkirk and Peebles in the general election of 1959. He was elected to the House of Commons as Labour MP for West Lothian in 1962, which became Linlithgow in 1983. Dalyell was a member of the European Parliament in the period 1975–79, and has pursued his journalistic endeavours through the columns of the *New Statesman and Society* (previously *New Statesman*) since 1967.

The Argentine battle cruiser *General Belgrano*, carrying a crew of over 1,000 and equipped with Exocet missiles, was torpedoed and sunk on May 2, 1982, by the British nuclear-powered submarine *Conqueror*, about 30 miles south of the total exclusion zone established by the British government around the Falklands following the opening of hostilities in April 1982 between the two countries in a dispute over the sovereignty of the islands.

It was estimated that 368 Argentinians on board lost their lives, while the Ministry of Defence (MOD) stated that the cruiser had "posed a major threat to our ships".

The particular controversy over the sinking of the cruiser began in December 1982, when Dalyell published a book, *One Man's Falklands*, in which he argued that the decision to destroy the *Belgrano* had ended all chances of a peaceful settlement to the conflict and further that the Cabinet had taken the decision knowing that the Argentine army council had on the day prior to the sinking persuaded Gen. Galtieri, one of the joint leaders of the then Argentine military junta, to accept withdrawal from the Falklands Islands under the auspices of a United Nations proposal. He also claimed that the cruiser was on a 280 degree course in the direction of its home port of Ushuaia when it was sunk.

It was reported on March 20, 1983, that President Balaunde of Peru had confirmed to an Argentine journalist that his attempts to find a peaceful solution to the conflict had failed as a direct result of the sinking. The President had said that as the Argentine junta met to discuss a proposed Peruvian peace plan, they had received the news about the *Belgrano*. In May 1983 more than 150 Labour MPs called for a special inquiry into the British government's decision to order the sinking. Cranley Onslow, a Minister of State at the Foreign and Commonwealth Office, stated in the Commons that month that a thorough investigation of the records had confirmed that an outline of the Peruvian proposals was first communicated to London in a telegram from Washington over three hours after the attack on the *Belgrano*. Onslow accused Dalyell of pursuing a "wholly disgraceful vendetta" against Margaret Thatcher, the Prime Minister, which came close to an abuse of parliamentary procedure. The minister insisted that the Argentine cruiser was sunk for military reasons. Early in June 1983, Adml. Lord Lewin, the former Chief of the Defence Staff, who advised the Cabinet to order the sinking, said that the decision had been imperative to safeguard British lives.

The controversy over the sinking was revived in August 1984 when Dalyell revealed that he had in mid-July been sent some "leaked" confidential documents relating to the incident, which he had then passed to the Commons Foreign Affairs Committee. He said that the documents indicated that government officials had deliberately witheld from MPs details of changes made in the rules of engagement relating to the Falklands Islands conflict. He also claimed that Michael Heseltine, after becoming Secretary of State for Defence in January 1983, had ordered a secret inquiry into the sinking which showed that the Royal Navy had intercepted Argentine signals to the *Belgrano* and therefore knew that it had been ordered to return to port. In September 1984 the Prime Minister asserted that the "precise position and course of the *Belgrano* at that time were "irrelevant" and that for this reason the report of a change in the ship's course was not communicated to ministers in the hours preceding the sinking.

In February 1985, Clive Ponting, an MOD assistant secretary, was acquitted of charges brought under the Official Secrets Act 1911, following his disclosure that he had sent the documents to Dalyell in July 1984 (see *Clive Ponting Affair, 1984–85*, below).

A significant exchange of letters took place between various MPs and the Prime Minister during September–October 1984, with the main issue being raised of whether the government had in fact known that the *Belgrano* had changed course. In these Thatcher stated that there had been no intention by the government to misinform or mislead Parliament; that the British operational headquarters at Northwood did not tell the War Cabinet in London that the cruiser had changed course; and, that the cruiser could have altered course again and, acting in concert with other vessels, closed on elements of the Royal Navy task force.

On July 24, 1985, the Commons select committee on foreign affairs issued two conflicting reports on the sinking of the General Belgrano. In its majority report, the committee found that the decision to authorise the sinking was militarily justified, but that the failure of ministers to provide information in an effort to discourage further questioning about the incident was understandable but not wise. In a minority report, four Labour MPs accused the government of trying to conceal "a hasty and unjustifiable decision to risk many lives and possible disaster in order to ensure the life of an administration which was itself palpably negligent".

It is unlikely that the true facts of the communications to and knowledge of Thatcher's Falklands War Cabinet on the movements of the *General Belgrano* will ever be revealed. Equally certain is the continuing Commons documentation of Dalyell's pursuit of the affair since 1982 through a bewildering array of the procedures available to him, from oral and written questions to ministers to a multitude of persistent points of order and information.

WS

Parkinson Affair (1983)

Sarah Keays, House of Commons secretary.
Cecil Parkinson, successful businessman, Conservative MP since 1970 and Chairman of the Party (1981–83).
Margaret Thatcher, Conservative Prime Minister (from 1979).

During the first week in October 1983 the London-based satirical magazine *Private Eye* ran a speculative gossip column story: "why was Cecil Parkinson asked to step down as Tory Party chairman? I can assure readers that it had nothing to do with his marital difficulties which have recently caused raised eyebrows in Tory circles. Now comes the news that Parkinson's fun-loving secretary Ms Sarah Keays is expecting a baby in three months' time". The magazine was later to issue damages and apologies because of the errors and libellous comments about those it named, but the story drew wider media attention, a formal joint statement from Cecil Parkinson's and Sarah Keay's solicitors admitting the relationship, and the Prime Minister's announcement that she wished him to stay in office. Cecil Parkinson was then a rising Conservative politician with legitimate ambitions of one day leading the Party: while he then had no intention of resigning either from ministerial office or from Parliament he accepted that "if ever I ceased to be an asset and became a liability, and the Prime Minister felt so, then of course I would leave immediately".

Born in 1931 in Lancashire, the son of a railwayman, Parkinson had progressed from the Royal Lancaster Grammar School from where he won a scholarship to Emmanuel College, Cambridge. His first job was as a management trainee for the manufacturers Metal Box where, in 1955, he met Anne Jarvis, the privately educated daughter of a self-made building contractor. They married the next year; Parkinson's father-in-law encouraged him to take up accountancy and set him on a business career when he offered Parkinson a Stockport building firm. This he bought with the grandson of Woolworth's chairman. They then set up their own company, Hart Securities Ltd., and Parkinson was soon on his way to a modest fortune and homes in a former rectory in Hertfordshire, in Pimlico and in the Bahamas.

Parkinson became a Conservative through personal conviction, joining the Party in 1956; by 1966 he was chairman of the Hemel Hempstead association with Norman Tebbit (later a Cabinet colleague) as his deputy. Narrowly defeated for the Northampton constituency in the 1970 general election, he won the Enfield West seat five months later on the death of Iain Macleod. Good-looking, charming and self-made, he fitted many of the attributes that the new Tory Prime Minister, Margaret Thatcher, preferred. He began his ministerial career in 1972 but after the 1979 general election success he rose rapidly; Minister of State for Trade in 1979, Chairman of the Party in 1981 as well as Paymaster General and, in 1982, Chancellor of the Duchy of Lancaster, an appointment which saw him elevated to the Cabinet. In 1982, during the Falklands conflict, he was a member of the small "inner" Cabinet that met to plan the campaign and subsequent defeat of the Argentinian forces. In 1983 he was widely credited with a major role in securing the Conservative's sweeping success at the general election. He was at the Prime Minister's elbow at the celebrations and expected to climb even higher in the Cabinet.

Between the original *Private Eye* story and the Party Conference a week later the twin pursuit of the story — Thatcher's endorsement of her loyalty to Parkinson and the media' enthusiasm for a sex-and-politics thriller — ran heavily in Parkinson's favour. By the time Parkinson sat down after his anodyne Conference speech the response was sufficient to suggest that the Party could forgive, even if it could not condone, his behaviour. Parkinson certainly believed he had survived but then he clearly underestimated the consequences of the tactics adopted by his supporters in the Party and the media. To defend his political reputation the affair had to be marginalized as a temporary aberration in which he succumbed to the temptations of a high-pressure job in a particular environment from which his "fall from grace" was sufficiently punished by a full admission, financial restitution and an acceptance that higher office was no longer achievable. In that, he was buttressed by the loyalty of those who felt he had taken the right course of action — his wife and his leader — and by the joint statement issued at the same time that *Private Eye* published its allegations. This, agreed by both sides (with a further agreement that there would be no elaboration or discussion of the contents), stated the bare details of the relationship, Parkinson's retracted offer of marriage and the financial provisions for the child.

Unfortunately for Cecil Parkinson this exercise in damage-limitation reflected *his* views; it did not take into account those of Sarah Keays. Keays was born in 1947 into a comfortably-off, closely-knit family who lived in a country vicarage near Bath. Moving to London in 1967 with her sister she took various secretarial jobs before beginning work in the House of Commons and, within a year, becoming secretary to Cecil Parkinson with whom she began an affair shortly after their meeting — "a long-standing, genuine love affair", says Keays. It was marked by regular conflicts over what each wanted from the relationship. Clearly Keays valued her independence and her career and did not want to continue indefinitely as Parkinson's mistress. On the one hand she "loved him wholeheartedly and wanted nothing more than to spend the rest of my life with him", but there were also doubts about Parkinson's intentions. Despite his promises of marriage and undying affection he appeared content with the existing relationship. In 1979 Keays ended the relationship and took herself off to Brussels as secretary to Roy Jenkins, then President of the European Commission, where Parkinson arrived to resume the affair only to announce at the end of 1980 that marriage was out of the question because of family problems.

In 1981 he allegedly changed his mind again but the relationship again faltered firstly over Parkinson's annoyance at Keay's efforts to take up a career in politics and, more crucially, her discovery that she was pregnant. He allegedly told Keays to have an abortion, then told her he wanted to marry her. After telling the Prime Minister, supposedly on the day of the 1983 general election victory, he did not get promoted to the post of Foreign Secretary to which he aspired, but the Prime Minister did not want him to resign, believing the affair was "a private matter". In August, Sarah Keays was approached by journalists asking questions about her pregnancy. In September, Cecil Parkinson returned from holiday to announce he was staying with his wife. In that month the Prime Minister removed him from the Party chairmanship as Keays' father wrote to the Prime Minister warning her of the imminent public scandal which was precipitated by the *Private Eye* story and the joint statement.

Now in the public domain, the scandal intensified following Parkinson's appearance on *Panorama* and at the Party Conference. Sarah Keays chose that same evening to publish through *The Times* her own unexpurgated version of events because, she said, press comment, government pronouncements and continued speculation put her in an impossible situation and she felt it was both a public duty and a duty to her family to put the record straight. She said that the baby had been conceived in a "long-standing, loving relationship which I had allowed to continue because I believed in our eventual marriage". The statement also showed Parkinson to be a creature of vacillating emotions who had made the running in continuing the relationship with the intention of marriage but that he was unable or unwilling to keep his word. Parkinson's resignation from the Government was inevitable and immediate, taking place on Oct. 14 when it was announced at the Conference. His ministerial successor was Norman Tebbit.

Periodically his return to office was mooted in the media which also published Keays' comments on the affair and the behaviour of the Conservative Party; the 1985 Party Conference was enlivened by the serialization of Keays' autobiography in the *Daily Mirror*. The 1986 conference was presaged by a Keays interview in *Good Housekeeping* which talked of "the hypocrisy, the lying and the arrogance of the other people who interfered — Conservative politicians who were prepared to destroy me to protect themselves". Nevertheless, the Prime Minister kept faith and in close contact with one of her favourite colleagues and friends. Parkinson was again at her elbow after the success of the 1987 General Election, after which he was appointed Minister for Energy. He had paid his party dues, undertaking a large number of speaking engagements and travelling across the country during the campaign. Nevertheless his return to public life has not been smooth and both his private life and political activities have been subject to regular press scrutiny.

RAD

Bettaney Affair (1983–84)

Michael Bettaney, security service officer, 1973–83.

The well-documented history of British security service personnel spying for the Soviet Union demonstrates that no sooner does one spy scandal appear to be over than another one appears. This was typical of the case of Michael Bettaney, a middle-ranking official within MI-5, the British counter-espionage branch of the security services, who was on April 16, 1984, sentenced to 23 years' imprisonment on a total of 10 charges under the official secrets legislation. The Bettaney affair closely followed that of Professor Anthony Blunt, whose public exposure in Parliament in 1979 dominated security service news in the media then and in the early 1980s (see *Blunt Affair, 1979–80*, above).

Bettaney was born in Stoke-on-Trent, Staffordshire, and obtained a second-class degree in English from Pembroke College, Oxford. After passing the civil service examinations he was formally recruited into MI-5 in late 1973, and following a positive vetting became an officer there in 1975 having reached the minimum age of 25 to qualify for such a position. Between 1975 and 1980, he completed his basic training, studied the activities of the Communist Party of Great Britain, and worked in Northern Ireland on counter-terrorist operations. A second positive vetting which was due in 1980 was never completed due to an apparent disagreement over the references he had supplied. In 1982 he was transferred to counter-espionage work, based in London and dealing with the activities of the KGB. Bettaney was later to claim that he could not work against the Russians partly because of his disenchantment with the British security services. Rather than resigning, he began to carry out activities preparatory to communicating information to the Russians, by means of photocopying and photographing documents and taking notes about his work.

Bettaney then made four attempts to contact the Russians. On April 13, 1983, he delivered a letter to the home of Arkady Gouk, the first secretary of the Soviet Embassy in London and a KGB officer. The letter gave details of the reasons why MI-5 had expelled three Soviet intelligence officers in the previous month, and how such officers had been detected. Having had no response, Bettaney then delivered another letter to Gouk on June 12. This contained a classified document giving an estimate of the efforts of the Russian intelligence services in Britain. With still no response being forthcoming, Bettaney delivered a third letter on July 10.

The fourth attempted contact by Bettaney came after he had collected more than four dozen documents giving details of MI-5's activities and counter-espionage plans against the KGB. He then bought an air ticket to Vienna for a departure on Sept. 18, where he hoped to contact the Russians, but was arrested in London by British security service officers on the same day.

The trial of Bettaney in April 1984 was held almost entirely *in camera*, largely because classified information was to be discussed. The author of a number of books on espionage, Chapman Pincher, suggests in his *Too Secret Too Long* that the trial was also held in closed session because Bettaney's purpose in pleading not guilty despite making a confession was to use the trial as a vehicle for pro-Soviet propaganda.

Pincher also notes in his book that the Bettaney case demonstrated that positive vetting could sometimes be of scant value, that an officer of more than five years' service could become disillusioned and convert to pro-Soviet Communism without detection or suspicion, and that effective precautions about the security of classified documents were not being implemented within MI-5. It appeared, moreover, that lessons which could have been learned from previous spy cases had not been entirely taken on board.

On May 14, Gouk was expelled from the United Kingdom, while on Nov. 13 an appeal by Bettaney against his conviction was rejected by the Appeal Court.

WS

Sarah Tisdall Affair (1983–84)

Sarah Tisdall, clerical officer in Sir Geoffrey Howe's Foreign and Commonwealth Office.

Sarah Tisdall, a clerical officer employed in the private office of Sir Geoffrey Howe, the Foreign and Commonwealth Secretary, was on March 23, 1984, sentenced to six months' imprisonment after being found guilty of an offence under Section 2 of the Official Secrets Act 1911, for having sent to *The Guardian* newspaper documents carrying "secret" classification.

The main document in question, whose contents were carried in summary form by *The Guardian* on Oct. 22, 1983, and published in full on Oct. 31, comprised a photocopy of a briefing from Michael Heseltine, the then Secretary of State for Defence, to Margaret Thatcher, the Prime Minister, dated Oct. 20, 1983. The briefing assessed alternative courses to be adopted in the announcement and the parliamentary and public presentation of the delivery to the RAF base at Greenham Common, and the deployment, of launchers for cruise missiles and of the missiles themselves. An additional document, dealing with contingency security arrangements, was destroyed by *The Guardian* and not published.

The High Court in London on Dec. 15, 1983, ordered *The Guardian* to return its copy of the principal document to the Ministry of Defence, following the issue of a writ in the names of Heseltine and Sir Michael Havers, the then Attorney General, seeking such a return. The ruling was upheld in the Court of Appeal the following day, when the document was finally handed over by the newspaper's editor, Peter Preston. Tisdall was identified as the source of the leaked documents, which had been sent anonymously. She was charged on Jan. 9, 1984, and appeared in the magistrate's court the following day. At her trial on March 23 she pleaded guilty and sentenced, with leave to appeal being refused on April 9. Tisdall was released on July 23 upon completion of four months of her sentence.

On the same day the House of Lords began hearing an appeal by *The Guardian* against the original ruling of December 1983. In delivering a judgment on Oct. 25, 1984, the House of Lords rejected the newspaper's case that it had protection under Section 10 of the Contempt of Court Act 1981, which provided that courts could not order the disclosure of a source of information in a publication unless it was established that the disclosure was necessary in the interests of justice or national security, or for the prevention of disorder or crime.

It was by a three to two majority that the law lords ruled that evidence before the Appeal Court had been sufficient to establish that immediate delivery of the document was indeed necessary in the interests of national security.

WS

Oman Cementation Affair (1984)

Andrew Neil, editor of *Sunday Times*.
Brian Sedgemore, left-wing Labour MP.
Margaret Thatcher, Conservative MP (since 1959), Party leader (since 1975), Prime Minister (since 1979).
Mark Thatcher, son of Margaret Thatcher, racing driver and business-man.

"Some people think", said Mark Thatcher, son of Conservative Prime Minister Margaret Thatcher, in 1980, "that just because I'm Mrs Thatcher's son, it's plain sailing, but it isn't because at the end of the day I've got to earn my own living like everyone else. . ." Mark Thatcher was born one of twins in 1953: his twin Carole went on to make an independent career for herself in journalism. Mark went to Harrow public school, leaving at 18 in 1971 to work for Jardine Matheson, the Hong Kong trading company for a year. After a few months with a London stockbrokers he spent four years with accountants Touche Ross before leaving without a qualification. He joined a firm of jewellers in 1977 and the London office of an Australian freight company, IPEC, in 1978. In 1979 he left to devote himself to motor racing and to setting up an international consultancy firm, Monteagle Marketing (London) Ltd., with a racing colleague. His own scheme, Mark Thatcher Racing, soon ran into financial difficulties and Mark Thatcher himself became noteworthy for several expensive crashes, a period lost in the Sahara on a rally that had his mother in tears and controversial offers of sponsorship.

The row about how he earned his living broke in January 1984 when *The Observer* revealed that Mark Thatcher was acting as a consultant to a British civil engineering and building firm, Cementation International, a subsidiary of Trafalgar House. In 1980, the Sultan of Oman had announced his intention of building a university for his country of 1,500,000 people. In March 1981 an official plan emerged which stated that "a reputable establishment renowned for its experience in building universities will be selected". It also proposed that the competition for the contract would be by sealed tenders and that the successful firm would work under the supervision of an independent, government-appointed architect. In April 1981 Thatcher undertook a six-nation Middle East tour with her husband and daughter in the official party. She landed first in Abu Dhabi, then moved on to Oman with the official party, Mark arriving two days later to join her. There she pressed for the University contract to go to a British firm (the source of her repeated phrase that she was "batting for Britain"); several were interested in the contract but none, apart from Cementation, had got as far as conducting negotiations with the Sultan's officials. In September 1981 Cementation won the £230,000,000 building contract without tendering and by direct negotiations. No government-appointed architect was required; Cementation won the design contract as well.

The Observer revelations and the subsequent political row about how much his mother, as mother or as Prime Minister, knew of Mark Thatcher's activities, intensified during 1984 with further media allegations about Mark's Middle East connections, Cementation's university-building track-record and the Prime Minister's civil service briefing on the contract. In March 1984 the row widened during a *Sunday Times* inquiry into Monteagle Marketing whose activities, said an employee, involved catering: "by catering we mean that somebody who knows somebody can put somebody in touch with somebody else". What the newspaper had learnt during its inquiries was that Mark Thatcher was representing Monteagle in Oman and that the expected commission payment would go into Monteagle's bank account. To find out who was involved in Monteagle, two journalists paid in £25 to the account to check the names on the receiving account and discovered that not only was Mark's name in the company account but so was that of his father, Dennis Thatcher. The journalists' action was denounced by the Prime Minister as impersonation and deception. The bank itself complained that the confidentiality of client accounts was threatened. The bank claimed that the journalists used aliases, the newspaper retorted that the story was "based on hard fact confirmed by reputable journalistic methods". Said Andrew Neil, the editor: "allegations have been made that the Prime Minister's son benefited from the Prime Minister's work. Public figures have to live by different standards of disclosure than the rest of the country. They must not only be clean, but be seen to be clean. As the Prime Minister's son, Mark Thatcher is a public figure."

The Sunday Times' story pushed the Oman business into the public arena; the Monteagle aspect had raised the issue of whether members of her family had benefited financially from the Prime Minister's official endorsement of British interests in an Omani contract. Ministers are bound by the Members' Register which requires information on relevant pecuniary interests. In addition, ministers are required to be more circumspect and divest themselves of any interests in such a way that, as Thatcher said herself in 1980, "no conflict arises, or appears to arise, between their private interest and public duties". The requirements, however, do not, as in local government or the public sector, extend to disclosure of family or non-pecuniary interests. Nevertheless some Labour MPs began a campaign to have her position investigated by the parliamentary committee responsible for the Register and to ensure that MPs follow the rules on their financial interests, despite Mrs Thatcher's arguments that she was "batting for Britain" in general terms and that the activities of her son were a private matter. The matter was looked at by the relevant committee — the Select Committee on Members' Interests — but it decided that the Prime Minister had breached no existing rule or convention. Labour MPs pressed for a further meeting of the Committee to re-examine the case on the grounds that the Prime Minister had a financial interest, indirectly through her son and directly through her husband's involvement in Monteagle Marketing, on whose behalf the son was acting in a consultancy capacity. The Committee did not respond; it believed it was unnecessary "to investigate the validity of these allegations" and reaffirmed that there was no evidence of any financial benefit to the Member of Parliament concerned, Margaret Thatcher. There was no case to answer, said its Report, although it managed to place on record the full account of the allegations by Brian Sedgemore, the leading Labour critic.

It was a story now running out of steam. As one *Observer* executive put it: "there was a vein of truth, everyone knew, but several weeks of digging failed to lay it properly bare". In March 1984, Thatcher found a job in the USA as a £45,000-a-year director of Lotus Performance Cars and announced the end of his links with Cementation: "Only a fool", he said, "and I am not one — would claim there to have been no advantages in having the name Thatcher. I now know some of the disadvantages."

RAD

Clive Ponting Affair (1984–85)

Tam Dalyell, Labour MP (from 1962).
Rt Hon. Michael Heseltine, Secretary of State for the Environment (1979–83), Secretary of State for Defence (1983–86).
Clive Ponting, civil servant (1970–84).

The way in which the central administration of government in Britain is organized and operated raises the question of how much power and influence the civil service has and ought to have within that administration and, further, the precise nature of the roles, duties and indeed loyalties of particular civil servants. Is it the case that such loyalties should extend only to Ministers of the Crown, or could there be circumstances in which they might have a higher loyalty to Parliament or to the public interest? Such a dilemma was illustrated by the case of civil servant Clive Ponting, who passed confidential documents to a Labour MP and was prosecuted under the Official Secrets Act for such action.

Born in April 1946 in a middle-class suburb of Bristol, Clive Ponting attended Bristol Grammar School and the Universities of Reading and London. It was in the late 1960s when he was involved in research for a doctorate that Ponting became interested in public administration. He joined the Ministry of Technology in August 1970, moving through the Ministry of Aviation Supply and into the Ministry of Defence. He became a Principal in 1976 and an Assistant Secretary in 1981, becoming head of a Defence Secretariat division in March 1984. Ponting had been awarded the OBE in 1980; four years later he had resigned from the civil service and faced prosecution in the courts.

On Feb. 11, 1985, Ponting was acquitted on a charge under Section 2 of the Official Secrets Act 1911 of having on or around July 16, 1984, communicated to a person information to which he (Ponting) had access through his official position, although that person was not such a person to whom he was authorised to communicate it or to whom it was his duty to do so in the interests of the state.

The person involved was Tam Dalyell, the Labour MP for Linlithgow, who was conducting a protracted campaign against the Conservative Government over the sinking by the Royal Navy of the Argentine battle cruiser the *General Belgrano* in May 1982, during the Falklands conflict (see *General Belgrano Affair, 1981–86*, above). Dalyell was particularly concerned about an apparent change in the rules of engagement by the United Kingdom, given that the cruiser had been 30 miles south of the total exclusion zone then created around the islands.

Following two years of increasing political pressure upon the government to explain why the *Belgrano* had been sunk, Ponting was asked in March 1984 to produce a detailed study and chronology of the events surrounding the incident, including the significance and timing of a proposed Peruvian peace plan. The study had been requested by Michael Heseltine, the then Secretary of State for Defence, and was required in order to be able to respond to a letter from the Labour Shadow Cabinet on March 6,

1984, expressing concern about the apparent discrepancies in the various accounts of the sinking. The Prime Minister had also received a further letter from Dalyell on March 19, 1984, asking nine detailed questions about the detection of the *Belgrano*, its course on May 1–2, 1982, and about other aspects of the attack.

According to Mr Ponting's account of the affair, in his *The Right to Know: The Inside Story of the Belgrano Affair*, published in 1985, an internal departmental meeting had agreed that it was no longer possible to "keep up the pretence" that the *Belgrano* was detected on May 2, 1982, when a variety of other accounts suggested that such a detection had taken place many hours earlier. In the event, the reply to the Labour Shadow Cabinet was evasive, while the letter to Dalyell from Heseltine stated that there was nothing that it would be useful to add to replies already received by the Labour MP to earlier requests for information on the sinking. Later requests for information from Dalyell were, according to Ponting, to be treated with a refusal to answer with no reason given.

Ponting wrote in his book that the reply to Dalyell was "a deliberate attempt to conceal information which would reveal that Ministers had gravely misled Parliament for the previous two years". He then decided to send two documents to the MP in July 1984. The first outlined the way in which the Ministry of Defence should reply to questions from the House of Commons select committee on foreign affairs about changes in the rules of engagement, and the second was the draft of a letter, composed by Ponting for, but not sent by, Heseltine, on the course of the *Belgrano* on May 1–2, 1982. Dalyell immediately handed the documents over to the select committee whose chairman, Sir Anthony Kershaw, had in turn passed them to the Ministry of Defence. In the course of the subsequent investigation Ponting confessed to having passed the material over.

Ponting first appeared in the magistrates' court on Aug. 18, 1984, with the main proceedings before a jury opening on Jan. 28, 1985. He pleaded not guilty, while part of the proceedings were held in camera when certain classified documents were presented. Giving evidence, he said that he had sent the documents to Dalyell as "a duly elected MP and a man of considerable integrity who had been systematically misled" and that it was "in the wider interests of Parliament to be told how it was being misled and how the government was now proposing to mislead it".

Following Ponting's acquittal and the continued pursuit of the affair by Dalyell it remains uncertain whether or not further details of the sinking of the *Belgrano* have yet to emerge, but what is certain is that the trial was the strongest test to date of Britain's official secrets legislation.

WS

Stalker Affair (1984–88)

Sir John Hermon, Chief Constable of the Royal Ulster Constabulary (1980–1989).
Sir Patrick Mayhew, Attorney-General (1987–).
John Stalker, Deputy Chief Constable of Manchester (1984–87).
Kevin Taylor, Manchester businessman.

The peculiarities of an unwritten British constitution have often led to controversy and conflict between the variety of institutions that comprise the government and politics of the United Kingdom. The Stalker affair, which began in 1984 and remained prominent into the 1990s, was one such example of opposing political and security interests involving the Deputy Chief Constable of the Greater Manchester police force, the Chief Constable of the Royal Ulster Constabulary (RUC), the Secretary of State for Home Affairs, the Attorney-General, and, it is alleged, a variety of unseen and unknown senior Cabinet and Home Office civil servants. These, together with six dead terrorists, constituted the ingredients of an affair which had begun in an isolated farm building in County Armagh in November 1982.

Born in 1939 in north Manchester, John Stalker attended Chadderton Grammar School, and although his wish was to go on to university such a destination was precluded by the poor financial position of his parents. After an unsuccessful attempt to become a journalist, Stalker spent nine months with an insurance company before becoming a cadet with Manchester City police in May 1956. He joined the Criminal Investigations Department (CID) in 1961 and became the youngest Detective Sergeant in the history of the force in 1964. He then made a rapid rise through the ranks of the Manchester police force, becoming Detective Inspector in 1968, Detective Chief Inspector in 1974 and Detective Superintendent in 1976. In 1978 he moved to Warwickshire as Detective Chief Superintendent in charge of CID, returning to Manchester as Assistant Chief Constable in 1980. He became Deputy Chief Constable in March 1984, and it was in May of that year that he was appointed to investigate allegations of a cover-up surrounding accusations that the RUC had been operating a "shoot-to-kill" policy in Northern Ireland.

On Nov. 11, 1982, three IRA terrorists were killed by RUC officers after a car chase in Craigavon, Co. Armagh. The officers were in June 1984 acquitted of murder on the grounds that they believed shots to have been fired at them from the car. On Nov. 24, 1982, Michael Tighe was killed and Martin McCauley was injured by police near Lurgan, Co. Armagh, in an isolated farm building in which there were rifles but no ammunition. When McCauley was given a suspended two-year prison sentence in February 1985 for the possession of arms in suspicious circumstances, the judge said that he had had to exclude evidence given by three police officers after it had emerged that they had initially been instructed by senior officers to give a false account in order allegedly to conceal the involvement of special branch and an informant. In September 1982 Seamus Grew was shot dead by the

RUC, while allegations later arose that the officers involved had engaged in a cover-up to imply that Grew had been shot after driving through a police road block.

In September 1985 John Stalker submitted an interim report on his findings to Sir John Hermon, the Chief Constable of the RUC. That report was known to have uncovered new evidence on the shootings and recommended that seven senior RUC officers should be prosecuted on charges ranging from attempting to pervert the course of justice to conspiracy to murder. Stalker was at this time attempting to retrieve from the RUC an intelligence tape which apparently had recorded the November 1982 shootings, but was being frustrated in that attempt by Sir John Hermon. Just as Stalker was preparing to return to Ulster from Manchester intending to collect the tape, he was on May 30, 1986, dramatically sent on enforced leave of absence pending investigation of unspecified allegations against him of a possible disciplinary offence unrelated to Ulster, and was removed from the inquiry team. He was replaced on the team by Colin Sampson, the Chief Constable of West Yorkshire, who had also been appointed to lead the investigation into John Stalker.

These events drew criticism from many quarters. Seamus Mallon, MP for Newry and Armagh and deputy leader of the Social Democratic and Labour Party (in whose constituency the 1982 shootings had taken place), claimed that "sinister forces" were at work to prevent Stalker from completing his inquiry, while the Irish government expressed its disquiet at these events. The UK government stated that the absence of Stalker would not impair its progress, and that a report would be completed at the earliest possible opportunity.

In August 1986 the Greater Manchester Police Authority considered a report on Stalker, which had been prepared by Sampson, and which had recommended that a disciplinary tribunal should consider 10 accusations against him, including one of discreditable conduct over a long-standing friendship with a Manchester businessman, Kevin Taylor, an alleged associate of known criminals. The Police Authority rejected the report by 36 votes to eight and reinstated Stalker as Deputy Chief Constable. Stalker resigned from the police force in March 1987, claiming that the pressure arising from the RUC inquiry, and the inquiry into his own conduct and subsequent developments, had ended his career. On publication of his autobiography in February 1988 Stalker said that during his inquiry, while had not uncovered a formally articulated "shoot-to-kill" policy, he believed that he was removed from that inquiry because, had he continued, the consequences for the RUC would have been "disastrous". He claimed that he found it difficult to believe that the decision to replace him had been taken at anything lower than Cabinet level.

Two significant announcements were made in 1988 in relation to the RUC inquiry. In January 1988, Sir Patrick Mayhew, the Attorney-General, told the House of Commons that following the Stalker–Sampson report no further criminal prosecutions of RUC officers would take place, even though the Director of Public Prosecutions (DPP) for Northern Ireland had concluded that there was evidence of the commission of offences of perverting, or attempting or conspiring to pervert, the course of justice. The Attorney-General said that in reaching his decision, matters concerning the public interest and considerations of national security had been taken into account. In June 1988 the Police Authority for Northern Ireland announced that no disciplinary action would be taken against any senior RUC officers, in connection with allegations that they had obstructed the Stalker–Sampson inquiries into the alleged "shoot-to-kill" policy.

The matter was not, however, allowed to rest there. The affair re-emerged in January 1990 following the collapse of fraud charges against Kevin Taylor, after which a number of announcements that same month appeared to ensure that the Stalker controversy would continue throughout the new decade. The DPP urged the Greater Manchester police to investigate the Taylor trial in the light of allegations of police corruption; the Manchester police authority announced that it was itself to hold such an inquiry; David Waddington, the Home Secretary, rejected calls for a judicial inquiry into the original removal of Stalker in 1986; and John Stalker and Sir John Hermon engaged in a public argument over whether certain documents in the possession of the former showed that the 1986 decision had been taken by senior Cabinet and Home Office officials.

WS

Westland Helicopters Affair (1985–86)

Rt. Hon. Leon Brittan, Secretary of State for Trade and Industry (1983–86).
Rt. Hon. Michael Heseltine, Secretary of State for Defence (1983–86).
Sir Patrick Mayhew, Solicitor General (1983–87).
Margaret Thatcher, Prime Minister (from 1979).

The history of political resignations in the United Kingdom comprises a colourful multitude of personalities, issues, events and governments, where such resignations in the main did or did not lead to the professional demise of those leaving office. A classic example of the former was the temperamental George Brown, who resigned as Foreign Secretary in 1968, never to regain office; an example of the latter was Harold Wilson, who resigned as President of the Board of Trade in 1951, and went on to win four general elections as leader of the Labour Party. One particular resignation where the future of the politician involved remains undecided was that of Michael Heseltine, who resigned as Secretary of State for Defence in January 1986, over the Westland helicopters affair. Within two weeks of his departure, the Cabinet had also lost Leon Brittan, the Secretary of State for Trade and Industry, in the same controversy and who later became a commissioner within the European Community.

Born in March 1933 in Swansea, south Wales, Michael Heseltine attended Shrewsbury School and Pembroke College, Oxford, where he obtained a Bachelor of Arts and a further degree in philosophy, politics and economics. Having unsuccessfully contested Gower in 1959 and Coventry North in 1964, he moved into a successful publishing career, being chairman of Haymarket Press from 1966–70. Heseltine was elected to the House of Commons as MP for Tavistock in 1966, moving to the constituency of Henley in 1974. During the period 1969–79 he held various junior ministerial posts and occupied a number of senior frontbench positions in opposition. He entered the Cabinet as Secretary of State for the Environment in 1979, becoming Defence Secretary in 1983.

Westland, the only major helicopter manufacturer in the UK, had in the autumn of 1985 within the context of a developing financial crisis, held discussions (i) with United Technologies Corporation (UTC — the parent company of Sikorsky, the largest US helicopter manufacturer), with whose proposals for a 29.9 per cent shareholding in Westland the Italian Fiat company later became associated; and (ii) with a grouping comprising at that stage Messerschmitt-Bolkow-Blohm (MBB) of West Germany, the state-owned Aerospatiale of France and the Augusta company of Italy. In October 1985 the British government had confirmed that it was its intention to give encouragement to Westland to explore further what had become known as the European option, while Westland itself desired to see both options on its financial restructuring remaining as open as possible for the decision of its shareholders. Although in December 1985 firm proposals were sent to Westland by the European consortium these were rejected, and the company announced that it had reached an agreement in principle for UTC and Fiat between them to take a minority shareholding. The government stated then that it had ensured that Westland had access to an alternative European-based offer, but that as a private sector company it was for Westland itself to decide the best route to follow to secure its future.

A number of significant letters were then exchanged between the leading participants in the affair, some of which were published or leaked. On Jan. 1, 1986, Margaret Thatcher, the Prime Minister, indicated in a letter to Sir John Cuckney, the Westland chairman, that there were indications from European governments and companies that a number of projects in which Westland were expecting to participate might be lost if the UTC/Fiat proposals were accepted. Heseltine published on Jan. 3 a letter which he had sent to the financial advisers to the European consortium, repeating the central point of Margaret Thatcher's letter two days earlier. On Jan. 6 the Press Association news agency service carried the text of part of a letter sent that day to Heseltine by Sir Patrick Mayhew, the then Solicitor General, which maintained that Heseltine's own letter implied that all governments and all the companies involved in the collaborative battlefield helicopter and NH-90 projects had given this indication to the British government. Sir Patrick also said in his letter that since the British government was under a duty not to give incomplete or inaccurate information, he was advising Heseltine to rewrite his letter correcting the inaccuracies.

During the course of a Cabinet meeting on Jan. 9, Heseltine staged a dramatic walk-out having tendered his resignation as Defence Secretary, accusing the Prime Minister of having refused to allow discussion of Westland within a Cabinet committee, and of allowing the government in its official position to suggest the adoption of an even-handed approach between the viable offers, whereas in practice it had, he alleged, attempted to remove any obstacles to the US offer.

Margaret Thatcher confirmed on Jan. 14 that there would be an inquiry into the publication of correspondence between Sir Patrick Mayhew and Heseltine. The remaining days of the affair at its most prominent were taken up by the emerging role of Brittan and the outcome of that inquiry.

In a statement to the House of Commons on Jan. 23, Thatcher gave an account of the results of the inquiry. She stated that it was a matter of duty for the government to make it known publicly that there were thought to be "material inaccuracies" which needed correcting in Heseltine's letter. She also said that it was urgent that the letter became public knowledge before 4 pm on Jan. 6 when the Westland chairman was due to announce the recommendation of his board to its shareholders of a revised proposal from the UTC/Fiat consortium. These considerations were, the Prime Minister said, very much in the mind of Mr Brittan when he saw the letter early on the afternoon of Jan. 6.

The Prime Minister's office, and Brittan and his officials in the Department of Trade and Industry (DTI) eventually agreed, without directly approaching the Prime Minister (although she said in her statement that she agreed that the letter must be made public whilst wishing that a different way of doing it had been found), that the DTI should disclose such "material inaccuracies" and that in view of the urgency of the matter the disclosure should be made by means of a telephone communication to the Press Association. No proceedings were to be instituted under the official secrets act. Soon after Thatcher's statement a meeting was held of the Conservative backbench 1922 Committee at which it was understood that calls were made for Brittan to resign. He did so the following day, stating in his resignation letter to the Prime Minister that he had lost the confidence of his colleagues.

On Feb. 12, 1986, Westland shareholders voted by 67.8 per cent to 32.2 in favour of the Sikorsky–Fiat deal, whereby UTC and Fiat together acquired a substantial minority shareholding in the company. A further, but perhaps not the final, political commentary on the affair came with the publication on July 24, 1986, of two reports by the all-party Commons select committee on defence. The first report claimed that Britain's national interest would have been better served by the acceptance of the proposal from the European consortium, while the second described as "disreputable" the way in which Sir Patrick Mayhew's letter had been leaked to the press. The affair had cost the Prime Minister two Cabinet ministers and gave rise to what was generally regarded then and later as the most serious political crisis of her premiership to date.

WS

Zircon Affair (1987)

Duncan Campbell, journalist.
Rt. Hon. Douglas Hurd, Secretary of State for Home Affairs (1985–89).
Alasdair Milne, Director-General of the BBC.
Marmaduke Hussey, Chairman of the BBC.

The role of television broadcasting in an open society is an obviously crucial one as far as education, entertainment and culture are concerned. When politics enters the equation such a role must be diplomatic as well as delicate, given the uneasy relationship which has always existed between the broadcasting media and governments of whatever persuasion. That diplomacy becomes even more important when political documentaries and programmes involve information of a secret nature, as in the affair of the Zircon project.

Zircon was a Ministry of Defence project, the purpose of which was reportedly to develop a surveillance satellite to listen in to civilian and military radio communications. On Jan. 15, 1987, Alasdair Milne, the then Director-General of the British Broadcasting Corporation (BBC), decided to ban a programme on Zircon on grounds of national security, a decision from which arose a major controversy involving the BBC, the government and the security services.

On January 22, 1987, the government obtained an injunction in the High Court in London against Duncan Campbell, a journalist working for the *New Statesman* magazine (since renamed *New Statesman and Society*), who had researched and was to present the programme, preventing him from making any disclosures about the project, even though MPs and journalists had watched the film in a House of Commons committee room on Jan. 19 and 20, and Campbell had published an article on Zircon in the *New Statesman* on the day the injunction was served. Also on the same day, Bernard Weatherill, the Speaker of the House of Commons, banned any further showing of the film within the Palace of Westminster.

In a further development, Special Branch police officers searched both Campbell's home in north London and the offices of the *New Statesman* in central London, on Jan. 24–25, while on Jan. 31 officers also searched the Glasgow offices of the BBC and removed documents together with all six films in a series entitled "Secret Society", which included the Zircon documentary.

The chairman of the BBC, Marmaduke Hussey, protested to Douglas Hurd, the then Home Secretary, over the search in Glasgow, in a letter on Feb. 2. Hussey also complained about the wide-ranging nature of the search warrants and the timing and manner of the operation. On Feb. 25 the injunction against Campbell was withdrawn following his undertaking not to disclose further secret material about the project, and on the same day Weatherill removed the restriction on the banned film being shown at the Commons. Meanwhile copies of the film were shown during February 1987 at public meetings throughout the country. Four of the six programmes were subsequently broadcast by the BBC in late April and early May.

The Times reported on Aug. 6, 1987, that the Zircon project had "been abandoned at a cost of £70,000,000 after fears that its technology would be outdated by the time it was ready", but that "the Prime Minister and key Cabinet colleagues [had] decided to keep alive the idea of Britain having its own spy satellite by going ahead with a programme that [would] rely instead on American technology".

WS

Spycatcher Affair (1987–89)

Sir Robert Armstrong, UK Secretary to the Cabinet (1977–89).
Margaret Thatcher, Prime Minister (from 1979).
Peter Wright, retired member of the security services.

The publication of books on the British security and intelligence services, particularly by its former members, has always proved to be a difficult and delicate problem for governments to resolve. This has been especially true in recent years as authors and publishers become more dependent on recourse to the legal system to secure the fact of publication. Perhaps the most spectacular example of this occurred when a lengthy series of court cases in Australia, the United Kingdom and elsewhere, during the period 1987–89, arose from the attempts of the British government to ban *Spycatcher*, the memoirs of Peter Wright, whose anonymity as an agent was in stark contrast to his very public profile as an author.

Wright served in the British (counter-intelligence) security service MI-5, from September 1955 until his retirement in January 1976. Following his retirement, Wright went to live in Tasmania, Australia. On July 16, 1984, he appeared on a British television programme and claimed that Sir Roger Hollis, the director-general of MI-5 during 1956–65, had been a double agent working for the Soviet Union. Wright subsequently wrote his memoirs, entitled *Spycatcher*, to be published in Australia by Heinemann Publishers Australia, containing detailed allegations about Sir Roger, about what the author himself perceived as shortcomings, irregular activities and treachery within MI-5, and about a supposed plot by MI-5 officers and others to remove from office Harold Wilson during his 1974–76 term as Prime Minister.

The initiation of legal action began when a temporary injunction was granted to the UK government in the New South Wales Supreme Court in Sydney in September 1985, preventing publication of the book, with the government submitting that it contained material covered by the Official Secrets Acts of 1911 and 1920 and that Wright was still bound by duty to the British Crown. When the case opened on Nov. 17, 1985, Sir Robert Armstrong, the UK Secretary to the Cabinet, presented four affidavits to the court. These maintained that publication of the book would be in breach of the duty of confidentiality owed by Wright to the Crown and was likely to cause "unquantifiable damage" by reason of the disclosures involved; that the allegations would endanger intelligence officers and their families; that the disclosures would impair MI-5's liaison with other friendly security services because an unauthorised publication would diminish confidence in its ability to keep confidential information; and that the disclosures would assist hostile intelligence services.

On March 13, 1987, the court rejected the UK government's application for a permanent injunction against Wright and Heinemann. In its judgment, the court ruled that although Wright was not bound by a contractual relationship with the government there was an obligation of confidence and duty to the Crown which would continue during such time as any information which he discovered during his service with MI-5 retained its confidential quality; however, the information contained in the book was no longer bound by that confidentiality, since most of it had already been published elsewhere, and the remaining information which might be regarded as confidential did not cause any detriment to the UK or MI-5. Further, it was in the public interest of Australia, insofar as the liaison between the security services of the two countries were concerned, that the book should be published. The UK government in September 1987 lost an appeal against the judgment, with the book going on sale in Australia on Oct. 13, 1987, being already on sale in the United States and elsewhere. In June 1988 the High Court in Australia rejected the government's appeal against the September 1987 ruling.

In addition to its efforts to have the book itself banned from publication, the UK government had at the same time tried to prevent the dissemination of its allegations and information in newspapers throughout the world, but most notably within the UK itself. Thus throughout the period 1986–88 the government had secured a series of injunctions against national newspapers prohibiting them from publishing extracts from *Spycatcher* or, in some instances, publishing certain comments on the issue. The newspapers included *The Guardian*, *The Independent*, *The Sunday Times* and the London evening paper, the *Standard*. Each of these newspapers was from June 1986 and at one time or another afterwards prevented from publishing information from the book or information by Wright while he served with MI-5. In most cases the newspapers had already done the deed by publishing extracts of varying length and content.

The High Court in London on Dec. 21, 1987, and the Court of Appeal on Feb. 10, 1988, rejected the government's request for the permanent ban on publication by the British media of material from the book. The December 1987 decision was based partly upon the fact of publication and worldwide dissemination of the book since July 1987 which had abrogated any duty of confidence lying on newspapers or other third parties in relation to information contained in the book. The judgment also included the comment that the government had, in contrast to its strenuous efforts in this case, shown a lack of action in relation to many of the previously published books or television programmes which had already carried all of the more obviously important information. The February 1988 decision, similarly, emphasized that the worldwide dissemination of the information in question meant that the right of confidence formerly enjoyed by the Crown no longer bound third parties.

The House of Lords on Oct. 13, 1988, sitting as the final court of appeal, rejected the final appeal of Sir Patrick Mayhew, the Attorney General, on a number of matters arising from the government's attempts to prevent the dissemination of allegations and information contained in *Spycatcher*. The decision meant that the government could no longer prevent British newspapers from publishing such material, and was taken on the grounds that, given the book's publication abroad and its easy availability in the UK, any damage which it was likely to do to national security had already been done. At the same time the Court upheld the principle that members of the security services had a lifelong obligation not to disclose information about their work, a principle enshrined in the new Official Secrets Act 1989.

WS

Gibraltar Shootings Affair (1988)

Sir Geoffrey Howe, Foreign and Commonwealth Secretary (1983–89).

Shrouded as it is in myth and mystery, the role and activities of the British security service attracts both fascination and friction within the minds of the public and the politician. This is especially true when the media pay detailed attention to the events and interpretations of a particular case, even when the truth of what really happened can never be revealed. One such case began in March 1988, when three members of the Irish Republican Army (IRA) were shot dead by British security services in Gibraltar, with both incident and subsequent inquest causing much controversy.

The three IRA terrorists had been killed on March 6, 1988, following the reported discovery by the Spanish authorities of what was believed to be the final preparations for a bomb attack against a changing of the guard ceremony outside the Governor's residence in the colony. The IRA confirmed that the three — who were named as Daniel McCann, Mairead Farrell and Sean Savage — had been part of an "active service unit" in Gibraltar.

Early reports of the killing of the three — who had, it emerged, been under surveillance by the Spanish authorities since November 1987 — had indicated that a 500-lb bomb had been found on March 6 in a car parked near the home of the Governor. However, in a statement to the House of Commons on March 7, Sir Geoffrey Howe, the then British Foreign and Commonwealth Secretary, said that although a controlled explosion had been carried out on the car by the British army, the initial reports about the discovery of a bomb had been wrong. Sir Geoffrey further disclosed that one of the three had been seen to park a rented car close to where the military band was due to assemble for the ceremony, and was then seen making some adjustments to the vehicle before leaving it on foot to join the other two members of the team. According to Sir Geoffrey, the three had been challenged by members of the British security services while making their way back on foot towards the Spanish border, and responded with "movements which led the military personnel operating in support of the Spanish police to conclude that their own lives and the lives of others were under threat. In the light of that threat, they were shot. Those killed were subsequently found not to have been carrying arms".

On March 6 and 8 two other cars rented by the three were found. The first, discovered on the Spanish side of the border, contained false passports and items of bomb-making equipment, while the second, found in the Spanish resort town of Marbella, contained a 140-lb bomb together with a timing device and ammunition. The circumstances surrounding the shootings prompted expressions of concern from various quarters. The government of the Republic of Ireland stated on March 8 that it was "gravely perturbed" that three unarmed Irish citizens had been shot dead when reports suggested that they could have been arrested by the security forces. Members of the European Parliament of the European Community, notably from the United Kingdom, Ireland, Spain, Denmark and the Netherlands, expressed alarm at the killings, while on March 22 the international human rights organization Amnesty International, demanded a full public explanation of the shootings, in view of the possibility that they might have been "extrajudicial executions".

Following a number of delays and amidst intensive international media coverage, an inquest held in Gibraltar into the deaths reached a verdict on Sept. 30, 1988, that the three had been lawfully killed. During the hearing lawyers for the families of the deceased sought to establish that the security forces had had a predetermined plan to kill the IRA members. This was strenuously denied by six members of the team carrying out the operation, as well as by a senior member of the British security service (MI-5), each of whom appeared at the inquest screened by a curtain from the press and the public so as to exclude the possibility of their being personally identified; they were each referred to during the hearing only by a letter.

The inquest was told that the British security service had identified the changing of the guard ceremony as a target for IRA terrorist activity, and had believed that a car parked by the three near the ceremony had contained explosives which could be detonated by remote control, although the car in fact contained no explosives. The security forces insisted that their plan had been to arrest the three, and that it had been the necessity to prevent the detonation of what they had believed to be a car bomb which had led to the shootings.

The hearing also heard a number of discrepancies in evidence related to the timing of the shots fired and whether or not the victims had attempted to surrender. One witness had claimed that shots had been fired while McCann and Farrell lay on the ground, while another said that Farrell had put her open hands in the air towards a British soldier just before she was shot dead. A further witness claimed that she had seen McCann and Farrell raise their hands immediately before they were killed. Following the inquest verdict, two independent reports into the shootings were published in April 1989. The National Council for Civil Liberties and Amnesty International in their reports called for judicial inquiries into the shootings, claiming that the inquest had been an inadequate forum in which to ascertain the true reasons for the killings.

The Gibraltar shootings had cast an unwanted spotlight upon the operational activities of the British security services, but it was likely that despite the inquest and the intensity of the press and television coverage before, during and after the hearing, the precise truth of the main point of contention — the timing of the shots and the movements of soldiers and victims — would never be known.

WS

Cathy Massiter Affair (1985)

Cathy Massiter, former MI-5 officer.

The Massiter Affair raised allegations that MI-5, responsible for domestic intelligence work, was exceeding the controls on its operations by monitoring a number of left-wing individuals and organizations. It also cast further doubt on the Official Secrets Act as a piece of legislation suitable for protecting national security.

Cathy Massiter had been recruited into MI-5 after leaving university. As a relatively junior officer she had been employed in monitoring the activities of a number of people and organizations. Disillusioned with this type of work she had left the service.

On Feb. 28, 1985, the Independent Broadcasting Authority banned the screening of a documentary film by Channel 4 called *MI-5's Official Secrets* on the grounds that its showing would violate the Official Secrets Act. In the film Massiter and another former MI-5 employee (who chose to remain anonymous) stated that MI-5 had monitored individuals and organizations filed as "subversive". These had included the National Council for Civil Liberties (NCCL), the Campaign for Nuclear Disarmament (CND), Mgr Bruce Kent of CND, Arthur Scargill, President of the National Union of Mineworkers, and Ken Gill, a prominent trade unionist. They alleged that the organizations had been infiltrated by MI-5, that telephone and mail interceptions had taken place without the issuing of ministerial warrants and that the information gleaned had been used for political purposes.

On Feb. 28 the Home Secretary, Leon Brittan, ordered an inquiry into the allegations contained in the programme to be headed by Lord Bridge, chairman of the Security Commission. The Commission's report came to the conclusion that no illegal intercepts had been made, but this failed to contain anger among opposition politicians at what they saw as a cover-up and an attempt to avoid the real question of the accountability of the security services. On March 12 Brittan said that the Director of Public Prosecutions, Sir Thomas Hetherington, had asked the Metropolitan Police to investigate whether any charges should be brought against MI-5 officers.

Meanwhile, on March 5 the Attorney-General, Sir Michael Havers, announced that those involved in the film, including Cathy Massiter, would not be prosecuted under the Official Secrets Act, and transmission of the programme could go ahead. This duly happened on March 8.

LP

Maurice Oldfield Affair (1987)

Sir Maurice Oldfield, former director-general of MI-6.
Chapman Pincher, investigative journalist.

Maurice Oldfield was born on Nov. 6, 1915 and educated at Manchester University. During World War II he became involved in intelligence work and remained working for the security services in the post-war period, serving in South-East Asia and in Washington, DC. In 1973 he was made Director-General of the Special Intelligence Service (MI-6), a post he held until his retirement in 1978.

The following year he was called out of retirement by the Prime Minister, Margaret Thatcher, to undertake a special job as security co-ordinator in

Northern Ireland. This job involved liaising between the Army and the Royal Ulster Constabulary over security issues at a particularly difficult time, not long after the murder of Lord Mountbatten by the IRA. Already in poor health, Oldfield found the job strenuous and was replaced in June 1980. He died a year later on March 11.

In 1987 the journalist Chapman Pincher, well-known for his interest in espionage matters and the author of a series of books on the subject, published *Traitors: The Labyrinths of Treason* in which he claimed that Oldfield had been a practising homosexual. He alleged that Oldfield had regularly associated with male prostitutes — something that could have compromised his security position — and that he had failed to reveal his homosexuality in the positive vetting procedures.

On April 23, 1987 the Prime Minister, Margaret Thatcher, revealed in a written parliamentary answer that Oldfield had indeed admitted his homosexuality during the course of a review of security in March 1980. As a result of this his positive vetting clearance had been removed and he had been replaced as Northern Ireland security co-ordinator.

Thatcher also revealed that an extensive investigation had been conducted into the aspects of the case, but no evidence had been found to suggest that Oldfield had compromised security, although his homosexuality had provided a potential risk. The results of the case were made known to the Security Commission which had begun a review of security procedures in March 1981. As a result the Commission recommended the strengthening of the vetting process.

LP

UNITED STATES OF AMERICA

The pattern of US scandal 1945–90

Three themes have dominated the pattern of American political scandal since World War II: those of corruption, loyalty, and the limits of executive power.

Corruption has been a running sore in American public life throughout these years. No administration has been spared, and the petty and not-so-petty self-seeking of many White House officials during the Reagan years (see especially the *Sleaze Factor Affair, 1984*) was perhaps no greater than the now largely forgotten and historically inconsequential plundering and cronyism of the Truman administration at the start of the period. Equally, none of the three branches of government has been spared. High White House officials who have left office in the face of allegations of impropriety have included Eisenhower's top adviser Sherman Adams (1959), Nixon's Vice-President Spiro Agnew (1973), Carter's Budget Director Bert Lance (1977), and Reagan's Attorney General Edwin Meese (1988). Congressmen who have been deprived of their seats or forced to resign have included Adam Clayton Powell (1967) and Speaker Jim Wright (1989), while in the Abscam Affair (1980–82) seven members of Congress were sentenced to prison terms. Even the Supreme Court has been affected, as in the case of Abe Fortas (1969).

Two factors aggravate the problem of corruption in American public life. The first is the relentless turnover of personnel. The career life of most in the highest reaches of the executive branch is short, with a fast-moving revolving door which propels individuals from business life to high office and back again to business life (sometimes lobbying the very government agencies they have recently left). It was well seen that Ronald Reagan, at the end of eight years in the White House, had trouble recalling the names of some who had served in key posts under him. There is in consequence a lack of a culture of public service; all presidents have tended to pack their staffs with cronies to whom they owe favours as much as with the "best and the brightest".

The second, and more creditable, factor is the competitive nature of American institutions, in which each of the three branches of government and, today, the media) jostle for dominance. Congress and the courts have proved especially ready in recent years to launch and sanction investigations of the White House, probing matters which in most countries remain cloaked in confidentiality. Through the 1980s a series of independent counsels (formerly known as special prosecutors) were appointed to investigate wrongdoing by current or former White House officials. This practice is governed by the 1978 Ethics in Government Act. While the appointment of an independent counsel is formally requested by the Attorney General, and the counsel is responsible to the courts, in practice the real initiative for such appointments has come from stampedes set up by Congress and the press. Once appointed, independent counsels have tended to initiate wide-ranging investigations in which they have wandered where they please. This process, moreover, has been a one-sided one, for independent counsels cannot investigate the legislative branch. The media, for its part, enjoying the protection of the First Amendment to the Constitution upholding the right of a free press, freely investigates all branches of government alike. And, unlike in Britain, where the effect of the libel laws (and punitive awards in libel cases) has been to weaken significantly the investigative energies of the serious press, the American media are effectively unrestricted in their power to make allegations on the thinnest of evidence. Likewise, all boundaries of restraint have now seemingly been overstepped. In the 1988 presidential election each candidate for nomination was pestered by questions as to whether he had ever used drugs, or committed adultery, and each felt obliged to answer. Two decades earlier, in contrast, President John Kennedy had indulged in an orgy of promiscuity, involving even a girl-friend linked to the Mafia, without a word being breathed in the media at the time.

The theme of *loyalty* — to the country and the Constitution — dominated the great affairs of the 1940s and 1950s. Most dramatic were the series of congressional investigations and trials in which executive branch officials were accused of being Communists or agents of the Soviet Union (see especially *Harry Dexter White Affair, 1947–53, William Remington Affair, 1948–53 and Joseph McCarthy Affair, 1950–54)*. These affairs represented not just personal tragedies, but marked the painful process by which the isolationist self-contained America of the 1930s adjusted to its new role of global power and in the course of a few years moved from ally of the Soviet Union to its worldwide adversary. The stresses of this adjustment, and the delimitation of what America could and could not attempt, surfaced in other ways too, as in the *Gen. MacArthur Affair (1951)*, the *Bay of Pigs Affair (1961)*, and the *Gulf of Tonkin Affair (1964-71)*. The failure in Vietnam led to unrest at home — see *Chicago Seven Affair (1968–70)*, and *Kent State Massacre Affair (1970)*. In the *My Lai Massacre Affair (1969–71)* American troops stood trial for war crimes and the case united in an ugly alliance those who thought that no individuals could be held accountable for crimes in Vietnam because it was the "system" and the war itself that was to blame, and those who seemingly believed that it was wrong to tie the hands of their boys abroad. By this time it was clear the war was unwinnable and that America was entering another bout of isolationist indifference to the world beyond its shores. The CIA, the agency which for three decades had projected US interests throughout the world, had its closest secrets disclosed and its apparatus all but wrecked by congressional and media exposure in the mid-1970s (see *CIA "Family Jewels" Affair, 1974–76)*. Then, in the 1980s, in the face of Soviet expansion into the vacuum left by the USA, the Reagan administration revitalized US global commitments. Loyalty was still a theme, with a virtual spy-hunting mania gripping the country in the mid-1980s. This time round, however, the spies were not top officials but relatively low-ranking government officials or servicemen (see especially *Walker Family Espionage Affair, 1985*). The process seemed complete when George Bush, a former Director of the CIA, became President in 1989.

At times entangled with these issues of US global commitment has been that of the *limits of executive power*. The connection has been explicit in cases involving the power of presidents to make foreign policy without any real congressional oversight. A consequence of the Vietnam War, where successive presidents had committed US forces without a clear congressional mandate (Nixon ultimately relying on his powers as Commander-in-Chief), was that Congress sought a broad oversight of White House foreign policy activities, especially where these had military implications. This process reached its climax in the *Iran–Contra Affair (1986–90)* where, in the face of congressional investigation, Reagan abandoned to their fate those White House officials who had been running the operation in a limbo where their actions were neither explicitly approved nor disapproved.

The Iran–Contra issue had many echoes of the *Watergate Affair (1972–74)*, which brought down President Nixon; where it differed is that Nixon had tried to shield his aides and become entangled in a cover-up. If Reagan had learned from Nixon's experience, it was also true that Congress had become a more formidable adversary precisely because of Watergate.

In the two decades following World War II an imperial presidency had grown up in which practical authority over the great issues of foreign policy and defence had become concentrated in the White House, with minimal and often retrospective reference to Congress. By 1972–73 the fast emerging prospect of the failure of US policy in Vietnam was already undermining the presidency, and the Watergate scandal — perhaps survivable in other times — brought the house crashing down, with Congress, the courts and the media concerting their efforts against the President. Congress's triumph soon turned sour, however, as US policy vacillated and stagnated in the 1970s without a strong executive. Presidential powers recovered in the 1980s, but remained clearly less than those enjoyed by Presidents from Eisenhower to Nixon. Congress has proved able to administer rebutts and humiliations even to a President so strongly entrenched in public favour as Ronald Reagan.

FJH

"Hollywood Ten" Affair (1947)

The so-called "Hollywood Ten" were a group of writers and directors of varied standing in the motion picture industry who refused to answer questions about Communist associations put to them before the House Committee on Un-American Activities in October 1947. All were subsequently convicted of contempt of Congress; meanwhile, their case pushed the film studios into implementing a blacklist of reputed Communists and their sympathizers which lasted a decade.

The 1947 hearings of the House Un-American Activities Committee were conducted amid a blaze of publicity as movie stars trooped to Washington to tell what they knew about Communist subversion of their industry. In truth, little enough was revealed. Ronald Reagan testified that Communist efforts to control the Screen Actors' Guild (of which he was president) had come to nothing, and, while there was more evidence that members of the Screen Writers' Guild had espoused or flirted with Communism, it was far from clear that they had achieved any propagandist impact with their screenplays such as would have been detectable to the average film-goer. Had it not been for the inflated posturing of the "Hollywood Ten", whose egos in several cases seemed out of proportion to the reputation of their work, and who took turns to harangue and defy the Committee rather than merely quietly pleading the Fifth Amendment (which gives the right to remain silent when the alternative might be self-incrimination), the issue might have subsided. Instead, in the face of pressure from sections of the press and the money men who stood behind them, the movie moguls met at the end of 1947 to agree the indefinite suspension of the rebel ten and, in effect, to initiate the blacklist.

In subsequent trials the ten were convicted of contempt of Congress and sentenced to fines and prison terms of up to one year. They were the writers Albert Maltz, Lester Cole, Alvah Bessie, Ring Lardner Jr, Samuel Ornitz, Adrian Scott, John Howard Lawson, and Dalton Trumbo; and the directors Herbert Biberman and Edward Dmytryk. None of them had any connection with espionage, and none of them, except perhaps Lawson, was of much significance in Communist activity; their fanaticisms were primarily of the literary kind, and their exaggerated defiance before Congress (in contrast to the calculated evasions of those more deeply implicated in subversive activities) perhaps expressed the frustrations of these would-be propagandists whose writings were inescapably shaped to the needs of the Hollywood dream machine. All were blacklisted on their release from prison, but the more talented such as Trumbo carried on screen writing under assumed names at a fraction of their former fees. Trumbo finally re-emerged under his own name as screenwriter on epics such as *Ben Hur* and *Spartacus*.

The blacklist deprived Hollywood of many of its most talented artists in the years that followed. In addition, bitter resentments were born of the decision of some one-time Communists to name (some said betray) former friends and colleagues who had shared their faith. Among these was one of the Hollywood Ten, Edward Dmytryk, who in 1951 co-operated with the Un-American Activities Committee and resumed his career, and Elia

Kazan. Others, such as Edward G. Robinson, who had never been Communist but had shared some Communist associations and enthusiasms, were forced to stand penitent and humiliated before the Committee before being reinstated in their profession. In 1953, the Screen Actors' Guild instituted a loyalty oath and banned Communists from membership, a step followed by the Screen Writers' Guild the next year. A preoccupation with the potential of the arts to corrupt the foundations of Americanism remained apparent in Washington for many years, and a series of encounters between congressional committees (especially the Un-American Activities Committee) and such figures as singer Paul Robeson and dramatist Arthur Miller both made headlines and contributed to the increasing disrepute of the Un-American Activities Committee and its emulators.

FJH

Harry Dexter White Affair (1947–53)

Elizabeth Bentley, self-confessed Soviet espionage courier and White's accuser.
Whittaker Chambers, self-described Soviet spy, who also accused White.
Harry S. Truman, President of the United States, (1945–1953).
Harry Dexter White, Treasury official and first US executive director of the IMF.

Harry Dexter White, a top official of the Treasury Department who had played the leading role on the US side in the creation of the International Monetary Fund (IMF), serving as its first American executive director in 1946–47, was publicly named as a Soviet espionage agent before the House Committee on Un-American Activities by self-confessed former Soviet courier Elizabeth Bentley on July 31, 1948, and by Whittaker Chambers three days later (the same day that Chambers first publicly named Alger Hiss—(see *Hiss/Chambers Affair (1948–50)* below). Appearing before the Committee on Aug. 13, 1948, White vigorously rejected the charges made against him, but three days later he died of a heart attack at his summer home in New Hampshire. Five years later the White case became the focus of a bitter controversy when Republican Attorney General Herbert Brownell accused former Democratic President Harry S. Truman of having nominated White to the IMF despite having received an FBI report casting doubt on White's loyalty.

Harry Dexter White, who was born of Lithuanian Jewish immigrant parents in Boston in 1892, entered the Treasury from academic life in 1934, the second year of Franklin D. Roosevelt's New Deal, and soon became established as a close adviser to Treasury Secretary Henry J. Morgenthau Jr. Throughout World War II White had responsibility for supervising the Treasury's considerable foreign policy involvements, and was the leading influence behind the creation in 1944 of the Morgenthau Plan for post-war Germany. This visualized the de-industrialization and dismemberment of Germany and, despite the opposition of the State Department and Whitehall, had some short-term influence over Allied planning, until being finally buried for good with the inception of the Marshall Plan in 1947. White was also, with Lord Keynes of Britain, the chief architect of the Bretton Woods agreement of July 1944 which led to the establishment of the International Monetary Fund. In recognition of his work he was appointed first US executive director of the Fund when it came into being in 1946, resigning in March 1947.

Meanwhile, in August 1945, Elizabeth Bentley had gone to the FBI with the story of her secret life as a Soviet espionage courier in the late 1930s and through much of World War II. Bentley (who died in 1963) was a Vassar graduate who on her own account had joined the Communist Party in 1935, detaching herself from the open party to undertake underground espionage work in 1938. To the FBI she named some 30 current or former government officials as having supplied her directly or indirectly with material which was passed on to her Soviet contact, Jacob Golos, until his death in November 1943. Her principal contact in government had been Russian-born Nathan Gregory Silvermaster, and it was through him, she said, that she had received material from Harry Dexter White, whom she had never met. Others named to the FBI by Bentley included several individuals connected with the Treasury's Division of Monetary Research (which White had headed as director until January 1945), including Frank Coe (who had succeeded White as head of the Division), Victor Perlo (who had been recruited by Coe to the Division in December 1945, after formerly leading, according to Bentley, a group of spies in the War Production Board), Harold Glasser (who had succeeded Coe as head of the Division when Coe went to join White at the IMF in 1946), and William Ludwig Ullmann.

An FBI memorandum referring to White as being of suspect loyalty was passed to Gen. Harry Vaughan, a Truman aide who acted as liaison with the FBI, on Dec. 4, 1945, but despite this President Truman on Jan 23, 1946, nominated White to become executive director of the IMF. A further detailed report, this time focusing solely on White, was sent to the White House by the FBI on Feb. 4, 1946. Truman, Secretary of State James F. Byrnes and Treasury Secretary Fred Vinson (who had succeeded Morgenthau in 1945) met to discuss the report on Feb. 6, but the same day the Senate confirmed White's appointment and White took up his new post without a breath of public controversy. FBI reports on the charges laid by Bentley circulated within the government during 1946, and Silvermaster resigned from government service at the end of 1946 and Ullmann in March 1947. White himself remained at the IMF, under FBI surveillance, until the spring of 1947, when he resigned, citing a wish to return to private business. In a letter of April 7, made public the following day, Truman accepted White's resignation with "sincere regret and considerable reluctance", declaring that "your unfaltering efforts have been a source of great pride to me". Press speculation noted that White had been in ill health, and that old New Dealers like White were generally being moved out of senior posts. There was not the slightest hint of any taint to White's career.

A federal grand jury was empanelled in New York City in March 1947 to hear Bentley's charges and interviewed White in March 1948, but eventually failed to return indictments against any of the people named by Bentley. (The same jury did return indictments against the leaders of the Communist Party in July 1948 and against Alger Hiss in December 1948, for which see respectively *Communist Party "Top Eleven" Affair (1948–56)* and *Hiss/Chambers Affair (1948–50)* below). This left the way clear for the sensational hearings before the House Committee on Un-American Activities in the summer of 1948, whose highpoint proved to be the interrogations of Whittaker Chambers and Alger Hiss. On July 31, 1948, Bentley told her full story for the first time in public (having named William Remington in a preliminary session the previous day, see *William Remington Affair (1948–53)* below). White was recognizably the most important person named by her. Then, on Aug. 3 Whittaker Chambers told the Committee that he had known White from the mid-1930s to 1938 as the member of an "elite group" whose aim was to achieve "power and influence". (Chambers had earlier, independently of Bentley, named White to State Department security officer Ray Murphy in 1945.) Although Chambers did not at this time testify to any espionage activity by White, unlike Bentley he did say that he had known him personally (though the relationship had not been a close one) and claimed that after his own defection from the Communist Party in 1938 he had tried to persuade White to follow his example.

On Aug. 13, 1948, before the House Committee, White had what fate would decree to be his only public opportunity to counter the charges laid against him. Easily fending off somewhat disorganized and random questions from the Committee, and enjoying the sympathy of most of the spectators, White resolutely denied ever having been a Communist (neither Bentley nor Chambers had actually charged him with being a party member), or anything close to one, ever having handed over government documents to unauthorized persons, or ever having known Chambers. White said that he could not be absolutely sure of never having met Chambers—"I must have met anywhere from 5,000 to 10,000 people in the last 15 years"—but could be sure that he had never met anyone who had tried to persuade him to sever his links with the Communist Party, as Chambers said he had sought to do in 1938.

White's death of a heart attack three days later meant not only that controversy about him subsided but also that he never had the opportunity to defend himself against later evidence. It was clear from the line of questioning adopted by Congressman Richard Nixon, at the Aug. 13 hearing, that Nixon had intended to focus on White's denial of ever having known Chambers (the same tactics as in the Hiss case). Indeed, among the documents retrieved by Whittaker Chambers from a Brooklyn dumbwaiter shaft in November 1948 which proved pivotal in the Alger Hiss perjury case was one long memo, covering Treasury foreign affairs interests in a period in early 1938, handwritten in what government experts concluded was White's own hand. During the second Hiss perjury trial, Chambers claimed that, with Hiss himself and Julian Wadleigh (both at the State Department), White had been one of his main sources of material during his espionage years in the 1930s. This claim, advanced almost parenthetically in the context of Hiss's struggle to avoid conviction, seemed to seal the verdict on White, whose posthumous reputation found few defenders.

In 1953 the White case revived in sensational circumstances when Attorney General Brownell told a Chicago audience on Nov. 6 that "incredible though it may seem" Truman had nominated White to the IMF even after receiving a report labelling him as a security risk. Truman initially claimed not to remember receiving such a report and insisted that "as soon as we found out that White was wrong we fired him", but his former Secretary of State, James F. Byrnes (who had defected to the Republican banner in the 1952 elections), revealed that he had a perfectly clear recollection of discussing the matter with Truman and advising him not to proceed with White's appointment. In a nationwide broadcast on Nov. 16, Truman modified his story, now admitting he had seen the second FBI report on White (but could not remember the first) but claiming that he had let through White's appointment so as not to hamper FBI investigations by alerting other suspected Communists, and that White had been "separated from the government service promptly" when the necessity for secrecy had passed. Somewhat extraordinarily, Truman also advanced the argument that he had abandoned plans to put forward White to become the IMF's managing director (its top post) in view of the doubts about his loyalty, and that his board position at the IMF was "less important and much less sensitive, if it were sensitive at all, than the position then held by him as Assistant Secretary of the Treasury". To Truman's critics this seemed to amount practically to a statement that under Truman—at least back in 1946, before espousal in 1947 of the Truman Doctrine and the onset of the Cold War—spies in government service could expect to be punished by nothing more painful than diminished promotion prospects.

Truman's broadcast exercise in self-justification—he refused to appear before a congressional investigation on grounds of executive privilege—and his claims that Brownell had "degraded his office" and that the Eisenhower administration had "embraced McCarthyism"—hardly dispelled the doubts about the circumstances of White's appointment in the minds of any but the most partisan Democrats. Truman's position was not helped when the FBI director, J. Edgar Hoover, told Congress that the FBI had not been a party to the decision to let White's appointment go ahead, and that Vinson (now dead) had not wanted White's appointment to proceed or for him to remain at Treasury. Here was substantial grist to the mill of those who considered the Truman administration had been guilty of the most egregious laxity in its handling of the problem of Communist subversion in Washington. It was one thing, however, for Joe McCarthy as a maverick Senator to accuse relatively inconsequential government officials and private citizens of having protected Communists, and quite another for an Attorney General to seem to point the finger of suspicion directly at a former President. Eisenhower showed little appetite for the discomfiture of Truman (reports were leaked from the White House suggesting Eisenhower had never authorized Brownell's Chicago speech) and Brownell backed off from the thrust of his earlier exposure, insisting that he had never meant to impute disloyalty to Truman but rather had wished to suggest "a certain unwillingness of Mr Truman and others around him to face the facts". Having briefly threatened to precipitate a major crisis, the Brownell exposé was quietly suffocated by the Republican leadership.

What did not escape unscathed was Harry Dexter White's posthumous reputation. His death in 1948 had left his case in a sort of limbo; he had been named by Chambers and Bentley, but he had never been convicted of anything by a court, or brought to trial, and he had not been indicted in 1947 by the New York grand jury. In 1953, however, it seemed to be taken for granted by all concerned, including Truman ("as soon as we found out that White was wrong we fired him"), that White had been guilty of espionage. Brownell not only told Congress unequivocally that White had passed secrets to the Soviets, but also explained that he had engineered the appointment to the IMF of two other espionage agents, Harold Glasser (who resigned from government at the end of 1947) and Frank Coe (who was ousted from the IMF in 1952, going in 1958 to China, where he died in 1980), and referred to the possession by the FBI of wiretap evidence which had not been admissible before a federal court. No one, not even Morgenthau, for whom he had worked throughout most of the New Deal and the war, rallied to the cause of the dead man.

Left altogether unclear was what, if he had been an agent of the Soviet Union, White's primary role had been. Was it merely passing information, or had his aim been to influence US policy-making in the interest of Moscow? According to Bentley, White "on our instructions" had "pushed hard" the Morgenthau Plan (of which he was undoubtedly the leading protagonist) for the post-war de-industrialization and dismemberment of Germany; and he had also acted on instructions in 1944 in arranging the handing over to the Russians of duplicate printing plates for the manufacture of US-redeemable banknotes—Allied Military (AM) marks—for use in occupied Germany. (The three Western occupying powers subsequently released some 10,500 million AM marks in their zones of occupation, while the Soviets released at least 78,000 million.) Both the Morgenthau Plan and the decision to hand over the printing plates, while actively promoted by White, had been widely debated in both civilian and military circles, and the Morgenthau Plan, though given some play in Allied planning in 1944–45, had not come to set the predominant course of Anglo-American policy. Nonetheless, to critics of the foreign policies of the Roosevelt and Truman administrations, such allegations raised the spectre that behind the Yalta accords, the deference to Soviet interests in Eastern Europe, and the somewhat utopian aspirations behind the formation of new international agencies such as the UN and the IMF, lay not the dictates of wartime expediency, or naivety about Soviet intentions, or plain muddled thinking, but rather the influence of highly-placed Soviet agents such as White and Alger Hiss.

This was not a line of reasoning which appealed to the mainstream of

US political thinking by the 1950s, however. The internationalist aspirations for global economic stability embodied in the IMF had dwindled as the Soviet Union refused to join it, and the Marshall Plan, aimed at the rebuilding of Western Europe, to counter the Soviet menace, had come to dwarf anything the IMF achieved. At the core of Democratic and Eisenhower Republican thinking alike by the early 1950s were shared assumptions about the direction of US international policy, with its focus on the Western alliance as a counter to Soviet ambitions. In that context, McCarthyite red-baiting and neo-isolationism were an irritating irrelevance, and Eisenhower Republicans had no great wish to upset the bipartisan consensus by raising questions about the influence of men like White in the period of the wartime alliance with the Soviets.

Despite his arguably greater importance in terms of access to US policy-making (Morgenthau enjoyed a particular intimacy with Roosevelt, as did White with Morgenthau), especially in the critical wartime years, White never achieved the status of Alger Hiss as martyr or villain of the post-war purge of Communists and fellow-travellers from the government. And yet, if the case for Hiss (who has found many adherents) is crucially undermined by documentary evidence, White's guilt was more tenuously established primarily by the word of Bentley and Chambers alone. Unlike Hiss, he had a more recognizable political profile before being accused of espionage; he was known as being on the progressive wing of the Democratic Party and was tipped by some as the choice of Henry Wallace for Treasury Secretary in 1948, when Wallace led the most left-wing elements of the party, in alliance with Communists, in a notably unsuccessful third-party insurgency. If there is a case to be made that leftists and liberals in government were framed by Bentley and Chambers, it could perhaps be more seriously made of White than of Hiss. His case was never properly heard, however, and little is known about the motivations that may have governed White's life, so that much went with him to the grave.

FJH

William Remington Affair (1948–53)

Elizabeth Bentley, Soviet espionage courier.
William Walter Remington, Commerce Department official.

William Walter Remington, a high-ranking Commerce Department official, was publicly named before a Senate Committee in 1948 as a former espionage contact by Elizabeth Bentley, a self-confessed courier between US government officials and a Soviet agent (see also *Harry Dexter White Affair, 1947–53*, above). He stood trial for perjury in 1951, was convicted, and then had the judgment set aside before being convicted a second time for perjury committed at his first trial.

Remington was born into an upper-middle class family in 1917 and was recruited to the Young Communist League while a student at Ivy League Dartmouth College in the mid-1930s. While there he met his future wife, Ann Moos, a banker's daughter and Radcliffe student who also became a Communist. Remington joined the Commerce Department under New Deal economist Thomas C. Blaisdell and later followed Blaisdell to the War Production Board, where in late 1942 he first made contact with Elizabeth Bentley (code-named "Helen"). According to Bentley he went on to pass information on such matters as airplane production schedules and synthetic rubber research, for onward transmission to Soviet agent Jacob Golos (though Remington claimed he had known Bentley only as a reporter).

Bentley first told the FBI of her contact with Remington in 1945, but despite FBI warnings to his superiors—including Blaisdell, who was satisfied with Remington's personal assurance that he was not a spy—Remington was able to advance by 1948 to a key post under Blaisdell in the Commerce Department's Office of International Trade. After being publicly named by Bentley before the Senate subcommittee on investigations in the summer of 1948, Remington was in September 1948 relieved of his post by a Civil Service Commission regional loyalty board, but then reinstated on Feb. 10, 1949, after an appeal to the President's loyalty review board, which had the final say on such matters. Remington was hailed by liberal commentators for his courage in having stood up to the anti-Communist "witch-hunters" and won. When Elizabeth Bentley repeated her charges without immunity on the National Broadcasting Company's radio programme "Meet the Press", Remington filed suit and won a $10,000 out-of-court settlement from NBC and the programme's sponsor, the General Foods Corporation.

Remington remained under suspicion, however, facing further public hearings (this time before the House Committee on Un-American Activities) and a grand jury investigation. At last he was brought to trial in 1951 and convicted on charges of having committed perjury before the grand jury in denying that he had ever been a member of the Communist Party. Among those who gave damning evidence at his trial was his recently divorced wife Ann. A US Appeals Court subsequently reversed his conviction on the ground that the trial judge had been "too vague and indefinite" in defining Communist Party membership to the jury. In January 1953, however,

Remington was convicted after a second trial of having committed perjury at his first in having denied knowledge of the Young Communist League at Dartmouth and passing secret information to Bentley.

In February 1953 Remington was sentenced to a three-year prison term and entered Lewisburg penitentiary. To this point his story had mirrored that of Alger Hiss (see *Hiss/Chambers Affair, 1948–50*, below): the youthful fascination with Communist ideology which led to the seedy fringes of the world of espionage; the early warnings to the FBI which were passed on but went ignored by other federal agencies; the public accusation before a congressional committee by a sole accuser; the defence of having known the accuser but as a different sort of person; the adoption by liberals as a martyr to oppression; the indictment for perjury; the double trial; even the incarceration in Lewisburg. Its end, however, was tragically banal. On Nov. 24, 1954, Remington was beaten to death in prison with a brick by fellow inmates; there was no political motive.

FJH

Hiss/Chambers Affair (1948–50)

Whittaker Chambers, Hiss's accuser and self-proclaimed Soviet spy.
Alger Hiss, former State Department high official.
Priscilla Hiss, Alger Hiss's wife.
Richard Nixon, member of House Committee on Un-American Activities.

On Aug. 3, 1948, Whittaker Chambers, a *Time* magazine senior editor, told the House Committee on Un-American Activities in public session that he had been a member of the Communist Party in the 1920s and 1930s, and that he had been in touch in the 1930s with members of the "Communist underground apparatus" in Washington, among them Alger Hiss, then an official at the State Department. In the months to come he would elaborate a tale which implicated Hiss in a web of past espionage and cast doubt on his current allegiances. Hiss was but one of the many who faced such charges in the Cold War period, and Chambers just one of many such accusers, but their duel, in its intensity and many ambiguities, became the pre-eminent *cause célèbre* of the era.

With Elizabeth Bentley—who claimed to have acted as courier for a Washington spy ring and among others named William Remington (see

William Remington Affair, 1948–53, above) and Harry Dexter White (who would also be implicated by Chambers—see *Harry Dexter White Affair 1947–53* above)—Chambers was the star turn of the Un-American Activities Committee's hearings in its vintage summer of 1948. In addition to Alger Hiss, Chambers named as his former Communist associates Hiss's brother Donald, John Abt, Henry Collins, Charles Kramer, Victor Perlo, Lee Pressmen and Nathan Witt, all former government officials, and Harold Ware, who had died in 1935. From August 3–25, all the surviving alleged Communist associates of Chambers except the Hisses appeared before the Committee and pleaded the Fifth Amendment against self-incrimination; Donald Hiss did give evidence, saying he had never met Chambers. The whole group, Chambers said, had been headed by one J. (Joszef) Peters (who refused to answer questions about Chambers and Hiss and was deported by the Justice Department to his native land of Hungary in April 1949 although potentially still an important witness).

Alger Hiss was the epitome of what the anti-Communist zealot most feared and despised: the privileged liberal. Born in 1904, he graduated from Harvard Law School and clerked briefly for Supreme Court Justice Oliver Wendell Holmes. After private practice, in 1933—with Pressman, Abt and Witt—he joined the New Deal Agency, the Agricultural Adjustment Administration, which became a stronghold for radicalism. In 1936 Hiss joined the State Department. He was a member of the US delegation at the Yalta conference, where Joseph Stalin, Roosevelt and Winston Churchill decided the shape of post-war Europe; executive secretary at the Dumbarton Oaks conference; and temporary secretary-general at the April 1945 San Francisco conference, where the UN Charter was adopted. Behind the scenes, however, there were already doubts about his loyalty. Alerted by secret evidence from Chambers and Bentley and by information from Soviet defector Igor Gouzenko (see Canada: *Gouzenko Affair, 1945–46*) that the Russians had a high-ranking State Department agent, the FBI placed Hiss under surveillance at the end of 1945, maintaining this through Hiss's last year at State. In March 1946 Secretary of State James F. Byrnes told Hiss that two congressional committees were investigating him for Communist links, and Hiss went to the FBI at Byrnes' suggestion in an attempt to clear his name. At the end of the year, his State Department career effectively frozen, Hiss resigned and went on to become president of the Carnegie Endowment for International Peace in New York. In June 1947 he was again interviewed by the FBI and first confronted with the name of Whittaker Chambers. In March 1948 he secretly told a New York grand jury investigating Communist activities that he did not know Chambers.

David Whittaker Chambers, a pudgy, ill-kempt and unprepossessing individual, made an unfortunate contrast to the elegant, patrician Hiss. Born Jay Vivian Chambers in 1905, he became involved with the Communist movement in the 1920s, working on the *New Masses* newspaper before going underground in 1932 and living under various aliases. According to his own statements, he broke with communism in 1938, spending some months in hiding in fear for his life. (In his earliest statements Chambers said he had left the Communist Party in 1937, a discrepancy made much of by Hiss's defenders; it seems clear, however, that Chambers went through a transitional state and that in late 1937 and early 1938 was undergoing a painful period of disengagement from his long-held allegiance.) In 1939 he took a job with *Time* magazine, and in September of that year, following the Nazi-Soviet Pact, discussed his past Communist associations with Assistant Secretary of State Adolf A. Berle (the President's adviser on internal security affairs), including his links with Hiss. In 1945 he told the State Department's security officer, Raymond Murphy, and the FBI that he had known Hiss as a Communist. He had also by this time discovered the consolations of religion, becoming a Quaker in 1942.

On Aug. 5, 1948, two days after Chambers aired his charges, Hiss appeared before the Un-American Activities Committee in public session and, exuding self-confidence and integrity, insisted that he had never even heard of Chambers until questioned about him by the FBI in June 1947. Such was Hiss's self-assurance that only Congressman Richard Nixon and the Committee's Chief of Staff, Robert Stripling, wanted to continue the investigation. Recalled by the Committee on Aug. 7, however, Chambers (this time in executive session) offered many details of the one-time friendship between him, his wife Esther, and Alger and his wife Priscilla, recalling how Hiss ("a man of great simplicity and a great gentleness and sweetness of character") had known him as Carl. At a second private appearance before the committee on Aug. 16, Hiss reluctantly conceded that photographs shown to him of Chambers brought to mind one George Crosley, "a sort of deadbeat", a would-be freelance writer he had once known slightly and helped (even sub-letting him his apartment in 1935) but had finally dropped after concluding he was a freeloader.

Also on Aug. 16, Harry Dexter White died of a heart attack a few days after being grilled by the Committee, an event which brought hostile press comment on the Committee's methods (see *Harry Dexter White Affair, 1947–53*, above). The next day, however, Nixon brought together Hiss and Chambers in a dramatic confrontation at the Hotel Commodore in New York; after prevaricating and bizarrely insisting on examining Chambers' teeth, Hiss reluctantly conceded that Chambers was the man he had known as Crosley and challenged him to make his charges outside the Committee hearings (where they were privileged). On Aug. 25 Hiss, no longer exuding self-confidence, told the Committee that he had met this "George Crosley" about a dozen times during 1934–36. On Aug. 27 Chambers repeated his charges in a radio broadcast, declaring that "Alger Hiss was a Communist and may be now". A month later, on Sept. 27 (after the *Chicago Tribune* had run a story saying he was planning to flee the country), Hiss brought his threatened legal action for slander.

Chambers faced a double threat: the Hiss suit, and the danger that he might be prosecuted himself. The FBI, directed by President Truman's Justice Department, seemed less concerned with investigating Hiss (that role had fallen by default to Nixon and Stripling) than with building a case against Chambers. Deeply in trouble, Chambers now raised the stakes to include espionage, even though on Oct. 15, 1948, he had told the New York grand jury that he had not known of any espionage activities. On Nov. 14, on his own account, Chambers retrieved from their hiding place in the dumbwaiter shaft of a Brooklyn apartment house the following material: 65 typewritten documents, summarizing or copying 70 State Department reports and one from the War Department; several memoranda in the hand-writing of Hiss and Harry Dexter White; two strips of developed microfilm; and three containers of rolls of undeveloped microfilm. (Chambers' story about the dumbwaiter was confirmed by Esther Chambers' nephew, Nathan Levine, who lived in the apartment house.) At a pre-trial deposition in Baltimore on Nov. 17, Chambers handed over the documents, which came from a period from January to April 1938 (when he was planning his defection from the Communist Party, and so was taking out "insurance"), as documentary evidence of his association with Hiss. In his 1952 memoir *Witness*, Chambers would later record that he contemplated suicide in the time between recovering the documents and handing them over. On Dec. 1 Chambers told Nixon and Stripling that he had kept back some of the material from the dumbwaiter shaft (the microfilms) as an insurance policy in case the Justice Department tried to suppress evidence. Nixon responded by ordering Chambers to hand over the microfilms direct to the Un-American Activities Committee. The next day Chambers travelled with Committee investigators to his Westminster (Maryland) farm and at dead of night in his garden patch produced the microfilms from where he had secreted them in a hollowed-out pumpkin.

The sensational publicity given to the "pumpkin papers" helped to shore up the position of the Un-American Activities Committee, which had seemed precarious after Truman's unexpected re-election and the election of Democratic majorities to both Houses of Congress in the Nov. 2 elections. Chambers then went on to tell the New York grand jury on Dec. 6 that he had acted as courier for a Communist spy ring in Washington from 1934–38, delivering microfilms to Col. Boris Bykov (who headed Red Army intelligence in the USA). On Dec. 14 the grand jury heard from an FBI documents examiner, Ramos Feehan, that the Brooklyn documents produced by Chambers had been typed with the same typewriter used to type the "Hiss standards"—letters and other material known to have been typed by Priscilla Hiss in the 1930s. The next day the grand jury heard testimony from Alger Hiss, who reportedly provoked outright laughter from jurors when he declared: "Until the day I die, I shall wonder how Whittaker Chambers got into my house to use my typewriter." That same day the grand jury indicted Hiss on charges of having committed perjury in saying that he had not known Chambers after Jan. 1, 1937, and that he had not passed to him documents in the early months of 1938. (Espionage charges could not be brought because the statute of limitations then precluded prosecution for peacetime espionage or treason after a mere three years.) Exactly who should be indicted had remained bitterly contentious right through to Dec. 15. The Democratic-controlled Justice Department wished to indict Chambers rather than Hiss for perjury; the FBI favoured indicting them both; and Nixon and the House Committee pressed for Hiss alone to be indicted. It was essentially a political battle which Nixon won thanks largely to the dramatic impact on public opinion of the pumpkin papers incident.

The first trial of Alger Hiss for perjury took place from May 31 to July 8, 1949. In trial testimony Chambers said that he had been introduced to Hiss by J. Peters in 1934 and had then met him regularly until April 1938. Chambers claimed to have been present at a meeting in 1937 between

Hiss and Colonel Bykov at which Hiss had agreed to pass on State Department documents; that Alger or Priscilla had copied documents on her typewriter and had given him (Chambers) the copies to pass to Bykov; and that the Hisses had been sent an oriental rug as "a present from the Russian people in gratitude for the work of American Communists". Chambers said he had last met Hiss about the Christmas of 1938, when he had unsuccessfully appealed to him to abandon communism. Chambers' account of his friendship with the Hisses was supported by his wife, Esther, though her testimony was on occasion vague as to time and date and spectators at the trial seemed bemused by her statement that "we (the Chambers) never had a last name to them (the Hisses)" and were only known as "Carl" and "Liza". The Chamberses in particular recalled details from their acquaintance with the Hisses after the Hisses changed address in December 1937, by which time Hiss claimed that he had long severed his connection with "Crosley".

Alger Hiss, who showed great poise on the witness stand, denied ever handing over any documents to Chambers, claimed that he had never met Col. Bykov, and insisted that he had known Chambers only as George Crosley, meeting him first in December 1934 or January 1935 and breaking off relations with him not later than May or June of 1936 because "Crosley" owed him money. While Chambers was able to illustrate his knowledge of the Hisses' private life in the 1930s with innumerable picturesque details, in this respect it was essentially his word (and that of his wife) against that of Hiss (who was equally supported by the testimony of Priscilla). What lent most substantial weight to Chambers' case was the evidence by Ramos Feehan that the 1930s Hiss "standards" known to have been typed by Priscilla and all the Brooklyn documents produced by Chambers (save the one War Department report) had been typed with the same typewriter. Even though the defence itself had produced the typewriter, (a Woodstock model), there was no plausible explanation offered by the defence as to how Chambers had managed to copy State Department documents with the Hisses' own typewriter. (Priscilla Hiss claimed that she had given away the typewriter to a servant, Claudia Catlett, in 1937, but the evidence from the Catlett family on this point was entirely confused and contradictory, for all their evident desire to help the Hisses.) The defence's only explanation was that Chambers had somehow gained access to the typewriter and himself used it to copy documents he had also somehow gained access to by rummaging in wastepaper baskets and stealing from desks at the State Department. (The defence's production of the typewriter was a less candid act than it seemed; Hiss had tracked its whereabouts down by early December 1948, before he was even indicted, but then left the FBI to comb Washington in a massive operation for five months, with the complicity of his brother Donald and the Catlett family, until it became clear that the FBI would inevitably locate it.) At the same time the government was able to bring forward as a witness Henry Julian Wadleigh, who said he had handed documents over to Chambers (whom he had known as Carl Carlson) while employed at the State Department in 1936–38 but that none of the Brooklyn material had originated with him; while Wadleigh had no direct knowledge of espionage by Hiss, this was corroboration for Chambers' claim that he had been an espionage courier.

The defence based its case on a comparison of the respective characters of the two principals. Hiss was, according to his principal attorney, Lloyd Paul Stryker, without "blot or blemish", and the defence brought forward a dazzling array of character witnesses including two Supreme Court justices (Felix Frankfurter and Stanley Reed, whose appearances before the Court were quite unprecedented), former (1924) Democratic presidential candidate John W. Davis, and future Democratic presidential candidate Governor Adlai Stevenson of Illinois. Meanwhile the defence excoriated Chambers' own reputation, calling him a "thief", "liar", "blasphemer", "moral leper", "Communist conspirator", "thug", and "psychopathic sadist". Among the facts brought out by the defence were that Chambers' grandmother had died insane; that his brother had committed suicide; and that Chambers himself had had to leave Columbia University after writing a "blasphemous" play, had been dismissed from a job at the New York Public Library for stealing books, had frequently used false names, had led an immoral private life (he was said to have shared a house with a prostitute), and had committed perjury in 1937 when applying for a government post. That Chambers had perjured himself at some point was of course self-evident, for he had first told the grand jury that he had known of no espionage by Hiss and then changed his story.

The first Hiss trial ended in July 1949 in a hung jury, apparently split eight to four for conviction. What divided the jurors was whether or not it was inevitably the case that if the Hisses' typewriter had been used one of the Hisses (and this was presumed to be Priscilla) must have done the typing. Meanwhile, leading congressional Republicans charged that trial judge Samuel H. Kaufman had showed systematic bias in favour of Hiss in his handling of the case.

A second trial began—in front of a new judge, Henry W. Goddard—on Nov. 17, 1949. Little substantive new evidence was heard, although Hede Massing, the former wife of Gerhard Eisler (see *Gerhard Eisler Affair, 1949*, below) testified that she had known Hiss as a member of the Communist underground in the 1930s. The defence tried to shift the blame for stealing the State Department documents onto Julian Wadleigh, but without being able to explain how the copies of them had come to be typed on the Hisses' typewriter. A further difficulty was that Wadleigh, unlike Hiss, had had no obvious access to some of the State Department documents, leading the defence to some highly speculative theorizing that Wadleigh may had a confederate. Again, the weight of the defence's case rested on an assault on Chambers' personality. One Dr Carl Binger psychoanalyzed Chambers from the witness box and found him to be a "psychopathic personality" (this was the first time psychiatric evidence had ever been allowed in the federal courts). Brushing this aside, the government prosecutor, Thomas F. Murphy, shifted the basis of his case in the second trial from the credibility of Chambers to the objective evidence relating to the typewritten documents. On Jan. 21, 1950, the jury voted for conviction and four days later Judge Goddard sentenced Hiss to the maximum sentence of five years' imprisonment. He began his sentence in March 1951 after the Supreme Court had refused to review his case by four votes to two. (Justices Frankfurter and Reed, who had appeared as his character witnesses, and former Attorney General Tom Clark, disqualified themselves from sitting on the case.)

Throughout the two trials the defence attorneys had sought to explain away the typewriter evidence by arguing that the Woodstock must have somehow fallen into Chambers' hands to enable him to copy the State Department documents. It was a difficult argument to sustain, and required an imaginative leap to suppose that Chambers would have sought to frame Hiss in this way and then would wait ten years to produce his evidence. In fact, it is now known, two experts hired by the defence in 1948–49 had concluded not only that it was the Hiss Woodstock which had been used to type the Brooklyn State Department documents but that it was Priscilla Hiss who had typed them. Not surprisingly, these experts were not called at either of the trials, the defence merely letting rest unchallenged the evidence of the FBI's expert which traced the Brooklyn documents and the 1930s Priscilla Hiss documents to the same typewriter, without giving a judgment as to the typist of the Brooklyn material. After his conviction, however, Hiss hired a new team of attorneys and a typewriter expert dedicated to proving a new proposition, that Chambers, perhaps with associates, had constructed a fake typewriter which would mimic exactly the characteristics of the old Hiss Woodstock.

Fantastic though this theory must seem (and Hiss's expert laboured for a year and could not exactly reproduce the Hiss Woodstock), it formed the basis for an appeal by Hiss in 1952, which was rejected. It was also enthusiastically taken up with variations by a string of pro-Hiss writers, including Fred J. Cook (in *The Unfinished Story of Alger Hiss*, 1958), William Reuben (*The Honorable Mr Nixon and the Alger Hiss Case*, 1956) and Meyer Zeligs (*Friendship and Fratricide*, 1967). All manner of co-conspirators have been alleged to have helped Chambers including the FBI, Richard Nixon, the CIA, Trotskyists, proprietor of *Time* magazine Henry Luce, and the "China lobby", and Hiss himself has flirted with most of these theories at one time or another. According to one version (Ronald Seth, *The Sleeping Truth*, 1968) it was the KGB which had manufactured a fake Woodstock so that Chambers could create confusion in the US government by accusing Hiss. Not one shred of serious evidence has ever been advanced for any of these theories.

Despite his conviction, Hiss still had friends in high places: on the day of his sentencing, the Secretary of State, Dean Acheson, declared: "I do not intend to turn my back on Alger Hiss." Such Democratic partisanship on his behalf only confirmed the view of many Republicans that the whole line of policy taken in foreign affairs under Roosevelt and Truman had been deeply compromised by the influence of Communists and "fellow travellers" in the government. At the least, it seemed, there had been complacency to excess. Told about Hiss by Chambers in 1939, Adolf Berle had not checked Chambers' charges until 1941, and had then been satisfied with glowing character references from Frankfurter and Acheson; and although the FBI had first interviewed Chambers as early as 1942, it failed to follow up the interview for three more years, reflecting the general weaknesses of its response (under political direction) to Soviet espionage during the wartime period. Within weeks of Hiss's conviction, Senator Joe McCarthy launched his spectacular career with a speech claiming he had a list of known Communists in the State Department (see *Joseph McCarthy Affair, 1950–54*, below). Moreover, Republican orators around the country lost no opportunity to recall that Hiss had been at Yalta, at the creation of the UN, at every turning-point decision where the wartime victory had supposedly been sold out to the forces of international communism. In retrospect, Hiss's influence loomed larger than it had ever done in reality at the time. The biggest winner of all from the affair was Richard Nixon, who had stuck by Chambers when other members of the Un-American Activities Committee had weakened in the face of Hiss's self-assurance: for him the case was a make or break point in his career. In 1952 he went on to win the Republican vice-presidential nomination on Eisenhower's victorious ticket.

Hiss was released from prison in November 1954 and three years later published *In the Court of Public Opinion* as his counterblast to Chambers' own 1952 bestseller *Witness*. In 1960 he left Priscilla (they never divorced) and began a modestly successful if unglamorous career as a stationery sales-man. For some years interest in his continued insistence in his innocence was at a low ebb, but his cause was helped dramatically in the early 1970s when Nixon became implicated in dirty tricks and cover-ups and was finally dragged down by Watergate. As Hiss now explained it, to enthusiastic college audiences around the country, he had been the original victim of Nixon's dirty tricks, framed by a conspiracy between the Congressman and the FBI. (Chambers, and the typewriter, were practically dropped from the record.) In a 1973 article "My Six Parallels" (a reference to Nixon's book *My Six Crises*) Hiss drew parallels between his own case and what had become known about the activities of the White House plumbers (see *Pentagon Papers Affair, 1971–74* and *Watergate Affair, 1972–74*, below), including supposed use of illegal wiretaps and "forgery by typewriter" (a reference to Howard Hunt's efforts to forge State Department cables to implicate President John Kennedy in the 1963 assassination of South Korean leader Ngo Dinh Diem). Such were the times that in March 1972 a federal court even restored his government pension.

As Watergate receded into historical perspective and the political mood shifted in the late 1970s, enthusiasm for Hiss's cause again ebbed. Particu-larly damaging was the publication in 1978 of Allen Weinstein's *Perjury: The Hiss-Chambers Case*, a massively researched account which made use of FBI records obtained by Weinstein under the Freedom of Information Act and concluded that Chambers had essentially told the truth about Hiss. Weinstein demonstrated that Hiss had lied systematically to Congress, the courts, and his own attorneys, and had worked to cover up evidence. Hiss has nonetheless persisted in his claims of innocence, endlessly reworking variations on the theme that he was framed; he still finds sympathetic liberal audiences prepared to believe that he was a victim of anti-Communist hysteria and "McCarthyism". For the right, too, the affair has retained its vitality. In his 1965 memoir *Where's the Rest of Me*, Ronald Reagan wrote of the influence that Chambers' writings had had on him. In 1984, as President, Reagan posthumously awarded Chambers a Medal of Freedom, and in May 1988 Reagan's Interior Secretary, Donald P. Hodel, granted national historical landmark status to Chambers' Pipe Creek Farm at Westminster, Maryland, where the pumpkin papers were hidden. Chambers was, Hodel declared, "a figure of transcendent importance in the nation's history".

Those persuaded of Hiss's guilt have differed as to his motivation in denying Chambers' charges against him. Some have believed that Hiss remained a Soviet agent of influence throughout the 1940s and that he lied to cover this fact and protect what he knew about other Soviet agents. More general, perhaps, has been the view that Hiss had engaged in mild espionage in the 1930s, in the Popular Front period, a time of naive faith in the Soviet experiment in some New Deal circles; that he had since quietly abandoned this flirtation; and that he lied to try to save himself from losing all that he had achieved in his professional life, for indiscretions which belonged to what must have seemed a different life in a different age. On this view, Hiss's greatest crime, perhaps, was not his 1930s espionage, but his refusal to tell the truth about his past, and his effort to destroy the lives and reputations of others—most especially Chambers—in an attempt to save himself. Another theory has been that Hiss was led into espionage by his wife, who had been the more zealous Communist, and was protecting her as much as himself. Priscilla Hiss died in 1984, without ever modifying the version of events presented by her and her husband at the 1949–50 trials.

Chambers' own motivations have prompted endless speculation. Why did he wait for months, until he faced a defamation suit and the threat of imminent indictment, to produce the Brooklyn documents? Chambers' life had been racked by the conflicts caused by his bisexuality, and some have concluded that he was in part infatuated with Hiss, wishing to hurt him and claim his affection at one and the same time. Chambers had confessed to many past homosexual encounters to the FBI (he said he had broken free of his homosexual tendencies after coming under religious influences), leading to anxiety at the agency that this would surface at the Hiss trials. The FBI in particular was concerned that the defence might try to suggest that Chambers had had a liaison with Hiss's stepson, Timothy Hobson (who lived with the Hisses in the late 1930s and had been discharged from the Navy in 1945 on grounds related to homosexuality), and that Hobson might have given him access to the typewriter. Why this issue did not surface is not fully clear, though it was not for any excess of moral delicacy on the part of the defence which had placed its whole emphasis on trying to destroy Chambers' character. Some close to the case speculated that Hiss feared the revelation of a more intimate relationship with Chambers than he dared to admit, though Chambers had told the FBI he had never had sexual contact with Hiss. At the root of this theory lay the notion of Chambers as a spurned lover, or would-be lover, who was now taking his revenge. It was a theory which seemed to be lent credence by the emotional volatility shown by Chambers, who spoke of Hiss by turns with resentment and affection.

Beyond this, Chambers saw himself as an actor in a historical as much as a human drama, forced by historical necessity to betray a man he claimed had been his friend, as an act of principle, an act which in its significance for the salvation of the West had meaning beyond the petty fate of him and Hiss. As he told the Un-American Activities Committee on Aug. 25, 1948: "We were close friends, but we are caught in a tragedy of history. Mr Hiss represents the concealed enemy we are all fighting . . . . I am testifying against him with remorse and pity. But at this moment of historic jeopardy at which this nation now stands, so help me God, I could not do otherwise." The conspiratorial, apocalyptic mentality which had drawn Chambers to the Communists in the 1920s—a time when their cause was far from fashionable in the circles from which Hiss came—in the 1940s drew him into the world of traitor-hunting as defender of Civilization against the concealed forces of communist Evil. In this he saw himself as pitched against not just Hiss but the whole closed ranks of a duplicitous establishment, an unwelcome bringer of ugly truth. Chambers' life after the conviction of Hiss was seemingly one of little contentment. He had lost his $30,000-a-year job with *Time* magazine, and while hailed as a hero of the right drew little satisfaction from his celebrity. In 1957 he took a job as a writer on William Buckley's *National Review*, with his main theme being the decline of the West, but resigned in 1959 and retreated to spend his last years on his farm self-consciously pursuing a life of simple labour. He died in July 1961 at the age of 60, apparently of a heart attack (although some Hiss partisans speculated that he had actually killed himself). Neither he nor Esther Chambers ever changed the account of the affair that they had given in the Hiss trials.

Alger Hiss remains to this day a determined advocate of his innocence. To some this seems a proof of the righteousness of his cause, the unending quest for justice of an honourable man; others, however, consider that falsehood does not become truth merely by repetition, and suggest that this may be Hiss's ultimate vanity or crime, a refusal to come to terms with his own past. In 1949 Hiss was tried in one age—the Cold War—for what he did in another age, the time of the New Deal and the Popular Front against fascism. But time has moved on since then: the seduction of the intellectuals by communism in the 1930s is now more pitied than condemned; Hiss might by now have thrown himself at the mercy of historical perspective, and found the rest that others of his time have done. That he has not done so would suggest that he truly believes himself innocent of those offences for which he went to jail, or else has never repented of them to himself.

FJH

Communist Party "Top Eleven" Affair (1948–56)

The so-called "Top Eleven" leaders of the US Communist Party were in October 1949 convicted of conspiracy to overthrow the US government and sentenced to prison terms. Four of them jumped bail after conviction.

During the New Deal era of the 1930s, the Communist Party, though a minor force in electoral terms, did succeed in gaining significant footholds in a number of labour unions, and in influencing the agenda of liberal and socialist groups through the Communist technique of creating "front" organizations. It was also, as would be shown in the Alger Hiss, Harry Dexter White, William Remington and other cases (see above), active in recruiting converts in the Washington bureaucracy. During World War II, with the USA and the Soviet Union fighting on the same side, the party emphasized its full-blooded Americanism. In 1944 it formally dissolved itself and reformed as the "Communist Political Association" to "promote Soviet-American friendship and co-operation in stemming Nazi aggression". Immediately after the war, however, the party was reorganized, its leader Earl Browder deposed for "revisionism" and the party firmly brought into line as an instrument of the foreign policy interests of the Soviet Union. As the Cold War gathered force, this brought upon the party a level of persecution that it had never before experienced in the USA.

The 12 leading members of the party were on July 21, 1948, indicted on charges of conspiring to advocate the overthrow of the US government "by force and violence" under the 1940 Smith Act. They were party chairman William Z. Foster (who was subsequently held to be too ill to stand trial, leaving the so-called "Top Eleven"), Benjamin J. Davis (a member of the New York City Council), Eugene Dennis (general secretary), John Williamson (labour secretary), Henry Winston (organizing secretary), Jacob Stachel (director of propaganda and education), John Gates (editor of the *Daily Worker*, the party organ), Irving Potash (vice-president of the Fur and Leather Workers' Union), Robert Thompson (New York state party chairman), Gilbert Green (Illinois state party chairman), Carl Winter (Michigan state party chairman), and Gus Hall (Ohio state party chairman).

The trial of the Top Eleven began before federal judge Harold Medina in New York in January 1949. Although all the defendants pleaded not guilty, on Oct. 14 all eleven were found guilty and were sentenced to five years' imprisonment except Thompson, whose sentence was reduced to three years in recognition of his war record (he had won the Distinguished Service Cross). All the defendants were also fined $10,000 each.

The government's case was essentially that, in reconstituting itself in 1945 and abandoning the revisionist theory of class collaboration, the party had become an agent of a foreign power committed to the overthrow of the democratic government of the United States. The government's evidence, much of which came from FBI agents infiltrated into the party's ranks, ranged from such revelations as that in 1945 the party form of greeting had been changed from "Dear Brother" and "Dear Sister" to "Dear Comrade", through to reports that party leaders had said that in the event of a revolution Soviet troops would enter the country through Alaska and Canada. In their defence, the Communist leaders claimed that theirs was an open political party and not a conspiracy, that if violence came about it would be the counter-revolutionary violence of the capitalists in opposition to peaceful transformation, and—irony of ironies—that the trial was a denial of the constitutional protection of the rights to freedom of speech and the press. In the use of conspiratorial techniques, the Communists compared themselves to the early Christians in Rome and the Jews in Nazi Germany, and warned that if the party was declared illegal it would simply re-form underground.

The convictions were upheld by the Supreme Court on a six to two vote on June 4, 1951. In the majority decision Chief Justice Fred M. Vinson declared that the defendants had been "properly and constitutionally convicted for violation of the Smith Act". Vinson continued: "We reject any principle of government helplessness in face of preparation for revolution. . . . The mere fact that from 1945 to 1948 the activities of the petitioners did not result in any attempt to overthrow the government by force and violence is not an answer to the fact that there was a group ready to make the attempt. . . . Their conspiracy to organize the Communist Party and teach and advocate the overthrow of the government of the United States creates clear and present danger."

Seven of the eleven began their sentences the month after the Supreme Court decision, but Hall, Winston, Green and Thompson failed to surrender themselves to the authorities. As a result of the flight of the four, Frederick Vanderbilt Field (of the plutocratic Vanderbilt family), Dashiell Hammett (the detective-story writer) and two other trustees of the bail fund of the Civil Rights Congress (a Communist front organization which had stood bail for the defendants) received prison terms for failing to disclose the names of persons who had contributed to the fund. All four escapees ultimately went to jail: Hall was deported to the USA from Mexico later the same year; Thompson was captured at a mountain hideout in California in August 1953 (and sentenced to an additional four years for contempt of Congress); Green and Winston surrendered on Feb. 27 and March 5, 1956, respectively, each receiving additional three year sentences. Thompson died as a result of injuries inflicted on him by a prison inmate. The seven imprisoned in 1951 were released from late 1954 to early 1955. Potash (who was born in Kiev) and Williamson (a British subject), with official permission, emigrated after their release to Poland and Britain respectively. A government motion to bring William Z. Foster to trial was rejected by a federal judge in April 1956 on the ground of his ill health.

On April 3, 1950, FBI director J. Edgar Hoover told the Senate that, although the official membership of the Communist Party was only 54,174, there was a potential "fifth column" of ten times that number willing to do its work. He said that following the conviction of the 11 Communist leaders the party had been driven into "concentrated underground activity", membership records were no longer kept, and the party had a "loyalty programme" to try to counteract FBI infiltration.

The apparatus of government control was further tightened during 1950 with the enactment, over President Truman's veto, of the Internal Security Act. This required that all Communist and Communist "front" organizations must register with the Department of Justice, and provided for the creation of a new Subversive Activities Control Board to determine which organizations were Communist or Communist "fronts". The Act also denied passports to any member of a Communist organization, barred Communists from work in any defence plant, provided for sweeping powers of arrest in time of war, barred immigration to all persons who had ever been a member of a Communist Party and naturalization to any person who had joined a Communist or "front" organization within ten years of arrival in the USA, and extended the statute of limitations for espionage cases from three years to ten. By April 1954 105 of the party's principal leaders had been indicted since 1948, of whom 67 had been convicted. In August 1954 President Eisenhower signed into law the Communist Control Act which (against the wishes of the administration) explicitly outlawed the Communist Party as "a conspiracy to overthrow the government of the United States". (The banning amendment to what had originally been a more modest administration bill had actually been sponsored by liberal Democrats, anxious not to be seen as weak on communism in the run-up to the November 1954 mid-term elections.)

This was the high-watermark of government repression of the Communist Party, ironically at a time when the real domestic influence of communism as a mass movement was lower than at any point since the Bolshevik Revolution. What lay behind the persecution was less any apprehension of the internal menace posed by the Communists than a working out of the frustrations caused by the advance of communism on the global stage: the Russian and Chinese Communists were unreachable, but their American followers were not.

In 1957 the Warren Court (in a case involving California Communists) applied a new demanding standard for Smith Act prosecutions, causing the Justice Department to abandon pending cases. Thereafter, more liberal judicial rulings in combination with dwindling political interest in the supposed domestic Communist menace, led to a gradual easing of pressure on the party. Following a 1965 Supreme Court decision striking down the registration requirements of the 1950 Internal Security Act, the party again became an open organization, publishing programmes and holding conventions.

FJH

Gerhard Eisler Affair (1949)

Gerhard Eisler, German Communist.

Eisler (alias Hans Berger), a former prominent member of the German Communist Party, fled the USA on board a Polish ship while on bail pending his appeal against convictions for contempt of Congress and making false statements in applying for an exit visa, but was arrested by the British police at the request of the US authorities on May 14, 1949, as the ship lay at anchor in British waters. In the face of US demands for his extradition, however, he was released by the British courts, and travelled to the Soviet zone of Germany, where he had been offered the post of professor of Social Science at Leipzig University.

Eisler had entered the United States in 1941, and seems to have been active in enforcing Comintern discipline on the US Communist Party. He was, according to his sister, Ruth Fischer, "the perfect terrorist type" and had been involved in purges in China in 1930 and the deaths of many dissident comrades elsewhere including Nikolai Bukharin. He was named to the House Committee on Un-American Activities in October 1946 by Louis F. Budenz, former managing editor of the Communist *Daily Worker*, shortly before he was about to leave the country (his exit visa was cancelled) but refused to answer questions or even to take the stand when brought before the Committee in February 1947. In 1948 he was sentenced to prison for making false statements in applying for an exit visa from the USA and for contempt of Congress. His fate became a matter of international leftist concern. When he was held in Britain, members of the ruling Labour Party claimed that his extradition was being demanded for purely political reasons.

Gerhard's brother, Hans Eisler, was permitted to leave the USA voluntarily in 1948 (travelling to Czechoslovakia) after it became known he had disguised his past Communist associations when entering the USA. Gerhard's former wife, Hede Massing, gave evidence against Alger Hiss in 1949 (see *Hiss/Chambers Affair, 1948–50*, above). Legislation passed by Congress in 1954, designed to prevent a repetition of the Eisler affair, made it a criminal offence to jump bail.

FJH

James Forrestal Affair (1949)

James V. Forrestal, Secretary of Defence (1947–1949).

James V. Forrestal, the first US Secretary of Defence, fell to his death from a 16th-floor window at Bethesda US Naval Hospital at about 1.50 am on May 22, 1949. His death was almost universally termed a suicide, but some on the American right have suspected that Forrestal was murdered.

Forrestal, formerly the Navy Secretary, was appointed to the new post of Secretary of Defence in September 1947 but was ousted from the job by President Truman in March 1949. He had become a particular target for liberal commentators such as Drew Pearson as the supposed voice of Wall Street and for his opposition to the formation of the State of Israel. On April 2 he was hospitalized at Bethesda for "operational fatigue" and remained there until his death. Immediately after his fatal fall, a hospital statement announced flatly that Forrestal "took his own life", a view confirmed by a coroner. Press reports noted Forrestal had shown symptoms of acute paranoia and had appeared convinced there was a conspiracy against him by Jews, Communists and enemies within the White House. He had apparently made more than one suicide attempt in the weeks before his death. A bathrobe cord had been found wound tightly round his neck and had seemingly snapped as he hung from the window with the cord tied to a radiator. Scratch marks on the windowsill led to speculation he may have attempted to climb back into the room. Although a special naval board investigated the death, its inquiries resulted only in an anodyne public statement which said little more than that Forrestal had died as the result of a fall (there was no police investigation).

Speculation that Forrestal might have been killed, by person or persons unknown, was subsequently confined primarily to the McCarthyite wing of American politics. Suggestions were made that the White House had effectively incarcerated Forrestal to gain control of his diaries (subsequently published in an edited form in 1951 after screening by the White House) and to prevent him from developing plans for freelance anti-Communist activity on a worldwide scale, and that Forrestal had been isolated at Bethesda from trusted confidants. Russian agents were seen as the most likely assassins, and parallels were drawn with a number of other notable violent deaths usually dismissed as suicides or accidents, including those of Soviet defector Gen. Walter Krivitsky (found dying of gunshot wounds in a Washington hotel room on Feb. 10, 1941), former State Department official Laurence Duggan (who fell from a window of a Manhattan office building on Dec. 20, 1948, after his name had surfaced as a former Communist fellow traveller in connection with the Alger Hiss affair—see *Hiss/Chambers Affair, 1948–50*, above); wartime ambassador to Britain John G. Winant (found shot to death on Nov. 3, 1947); J. Robert Oppenheimer's Communist mistress Jean Tatlock (found dead in her bathtub on Jan. 6, 1944); and Senator Robert M. La Follette Jr (found shot in his Washington apartment in 1953).

To some it seemed possible that these deaths had been murders carried out by Soviet agents to silence former supposed ultra-liberals who were changing allegiance and might influence opinion (Winant, La Follette), or to prevent the risk of current or former Communists from revealing what they knew about others (Duggan, Tatlock), or as a warning to would-be defectors (Krivitsky). Parallels were also drawn with the death of Czech statesman Jan Masaryk, who fell—or was pushed—from a window in Prague in 1948 (see Czechoslovakia: *Masaryk Affair, 1948*). Why, however, the Soviets would have taken the immense risk of killing a former US Cabinet officer after he had already been removed by President Truman from a position of power was far from clear. Forrestal remains the most high-ranking US official ever to have taken his own life.

FJH

Atom Spies Affair (1950–53)

Harry Gold, US espionage contact of Klaus Fuchs, who gave indirect evidence against the Rosenbergs.
David Greenglass, Ethel's brother, who gave evidence against the Rosenbergs.
Irving Kaufman, trial judge in the Rosenberg case.
Ethel Rosenberg, Julius' wife, executed for espionage.
Julius Rosenberg, executed in 1953 for spying for the Soviet Union.
Morton Sobell, friend of Julius Rosenberg, also convicted of espionage.

The most sensational and bitterly disputed espionage case of the Cold War period arose from the apparent uncovering of a Soviet spy ring which had targeted the US atomic weapons programme (Manhattan Project) during World War II. In the USA alleged members of the ring were rounded up following the confession of Klaus Fuchs in Britain in early 1950 (see United Kingdom: *Klaus Fuchs Affair, 1949–50*), and the affair reached its climax with the execution in 1953 of Julius and Ethel Rosenberg.

In the years before Fuchs' confession there had been mounting concern that the relative laxity of wartime security procedures had allowed the Soviet Union to learn US atomic secrets. In 1946 revelations by Soviet defector Igor Gouzenko in Canada and the conviction of Gouzenko's informant Allan Nunn May in Britain, had exposed the efforts made by the Soviets in this area (see Canada: *Gouzenko Affair, 1945–46*). In September 1948 the House Committee on Un-American Activities had actually named five individuals as having carried out wartime spying on the Manhattan Project for the Soviet Union, charging that the Truman administration had failed to take action despite having a "complete record" of their activities. Nevertheless, the Justice Department refused to take action against the five, calling the charges against them "hearsay". When the Soviet Union exploded its own first atomic bomb in 1949 (an event made public in the USA in the September of that year) there was a widespread conviction that this shocking development could only have come about because of betrayal of US secrets.

Following Fuchs' confession in Britain, the FBI between May 23 and Aug. 18, 1950, rounded up eight individuals openly labelled in the press as members of a Red atom spies network. Midway through this period war broke out in Korea, further heightening excitement and panic over the arrests. The first to be arrested was Harry Gold, a 39-year old Philadelphia chemist. According to contemporary press reports, Gold had been named by Fuchs as his wartime espionage contact in the USA, where Fuchs had served on the British mission to the Manhattan Project; however Gold had in fact been detained (and according to the FBI confessed) before Fuchs was said to have identified him from a photograph. (Gold was already known to the FBI, having appeared briefly in 1947 before a grand jury investigating charges made by Elizabeth Bentley, the self-confessed Soviet espionage courier—see *Harry Dexter White Affair, 1947–53*, above). Arrested in the following weeks were David Greenglass, a former machinist and briefly foreman in a machine-shop at the Los Alamos facility of the Manhattan Project in the last stages of World War II; Julius Rosenberg, 32, and his wife Ethel, 34, who was Greenglass's sister; and Morton Sobell, a radar and electronics technician who was a friend of Julius. Julius Rosenberg, a New Yorker born in Europe of Russian parents, had been a civilian inspector in the Army Signal Corps in World War II, but was removed from his post in early 1945 because of allegations of Communist Party membership; he had then gone on to open a small machine-shop in which Greenglass had also invested after his return to civilian life in 1946. Also arrested were bit players in the drama, Abraham Brothman, Alfred Dean Slack and Miriam Moskowitz.

Slack, who had served on the Manhattan Project at the Oak Ridge facility, went on to plead guilty to passing information on explosives unrelated to atomic weapons to Gold and was sentenced to 15 years; Brothman and Moskowitz were finally never linked to atomic espionage, but were convicted of obstruction of justice for having pressured Gold into lying to the grand jury investigating the Bentley charges.

The Rosenbergs and Morton Sobell went on trial before Judge Irving Kaufman in the Foley Square Federal Court House—in the same Number 110 courtroom which had witnessed the trials of William Remington and the Communist Party "Top Eleven" (see above)—in New York on March 6, 1951, charged with conspiring to deliver atomic secrets to the Soviet Union from June 6, 1944, to June 16, 1950. Named as a fourth co-conspirator was one Anatoli Yakovlev, the former Soviet vice-consul in New York, who had returned to the Soviet Union in 1946 and was said to have co-ordinated wartime Soviet espionage in the USA. Meanwhile, Gold had already pleaded guilty separately to espionage charges (and been sentenced on Dec. 7 to 30 years, a sentence which he seemed to accept with curious equanimity), while Greenglass had entered a guilty plea but had had sentence deferred. These two were to be the prosecution's star witnesses against the Rosenbergs.

During the trial, David Greenglass (who with his wife Ruth had been a youthful convert to Communism) described how he had memorized secret data at Los Alamos which he had passed to the Rosenbergs in 1945. Much was heard of sketches that Greenglass said he had given to Julius at the beginning of 1945 of a special lens mould designed for use in detonating an atomic weapon. Harry Gold also corroborated Greenglass's espionage activities, testifying that he had travelled to New Mexico in June 1945 to meet Greenglass, and provided the link to Yakovlev, saying that he had passed to the Russian material supplied by Greenglass and Fuchs. The

Rosenbergs for their part maintained that they had not even heard of Los Alamos before its existence was made public after Hiroshima and Nagasaki and had never known Yakovlev or Gold. Julius testified that Greenglass's wife Ruth had told him that she was worried because David had plans to steal from the Army, but he (Julius) assumed this meant "taking parts and gasoline". The defence's theme was that Greenglass, facing capital charges, had fabricated a story in which he had been merely a tool of the Rosenbergs, realizing that Julius was a "clay pigeon" because he had once lost his job as an alleged Communist. The defence also emphasized that Julius and Greenglass had had business differences which could have coloured Greenglass's testimony, and that at the time of his arrest Greenglass had been planning to prosecute a financial claim against Rosenberg arising from the severing of his (Greenglass's) connection with the machine-shop business. The defence, perhaps unwisely, chose not to attack Gold's testimony, concentrating instead on the point that Gold had never had any communication with the Rosenbergs, only with Greenglass.

As for Sobell, the prosecutors never actually implicated him in atomic espionage. Much of the evidence relating to Sobell (who did not give evidence) related to the reasons why he had fled (his defence said he had merely gone on extended vacation) with his family to Mexico after the arrests began. Sobell's principal accuser was Max Elitcher, his long-time closest friend, who said he had first learned of the Rosenbergs' and Sobell's espionage activities in 1944. Elitcher himself was under threat of perjury charges for having denied Communist Party membership in 1947 in a federal loyalty oath form.

Weak in documentary evidence (the only sketches of bomb components were crude replicas drawn by Greenglass while in custody), the prosecution's case against the Rosenbergs was lent spice by substantially irrelevant testimony designed to prove the extent of the Rosenbergs' Communist and leftist involvements. There was even an appearance by Elizabeth Bentley, who thought that she might once, in her days as a self-confessed Soviet agent, have spoken to Julius Rosenberg over the telephone—she certainly could recall speaking to someone by the name of Julius. The Rosenbergs repeatedly pleaded the Fifth Amendment to questions about their Communist associations, a lack of candour which cannot have failed to influence jurors at a time when all Communists were being portrayed as ready tools of Soviet power.

The jury found the defendants guilty on March 29, 1951, and Judge Kaufman passed sentence a week later. Notwithstanding his conclusion that Sobell had had no involvement with atomic espionage, Judge Kaufman sentenced him to 30 years' imprisonment. The Rosenbergs received sentence of death, Judge Kaufman declaring: "I consider your crime worse than murder. . . . I believe your conduct in putting into the hands of Russia secrets of the atomic bomb has already caused Communist aggression in Korea, with resultant casualties exceeding 50,000 Americans. . . . I believe that by your betrayal you have altered the course of history." Julius he described as the "prime mover in this conspiracy" and Ethel as "a fully-fledged partner in this crime". The next day Kaufman sentenced Greenglass to 15 years for his part in the conspiracy, a punishment which shocked Greenglass, who had thought to be more lightly treated.

While the sentences were generally greeted as appropriate to the gravity of the offences, there were even at the time some who felt that the death sentences had more to do with the Cold War atmosphere of 1951 than with the nature of offences committed at a time when the USA and Soviet Union were allies. Whatever Judge Kaufman might have said on the subject, it was apparent to sober-minded technical observers that the quality of the information that could have been passed by Greenglass, whose scientific knowledge was unimpressive (he had only a high school education), was rudimentary. The sketches that he drew for the trial were of such crudity that they would have been of no assistance to any country with the technical apparatus needed to contemplate the construction of an atomic weapon. Even had Greenglass, a corporal with limited security clearance, understood all that went on in his machine-shop, that shop was but a tiny part in a vast industrial operation involving the deployment of scientific expertise on a scale unequalled in history. There was no atomic "secret" that could be passed; rather, the ability to make a bomb depended on a nation possessing a wide and developed range of technologies. The public perception of what the Rosenbergs had done, however, was shaped not by the reading of technical journals but by press comment, at times bordering on hysteria, fed by the anxieties of the age. (Symptomatically, the launch of the first Soviet sputnik in 1957 triggered a fresh flurry of press speculation that this had been helped by "secrets" collected by the Rosenberg "ring".)

Others saw in the case a human drama. There was some evidence that the Rosenbergs had helped Greenglass in life, but that relations had cooled, and that at the last he had turned on them. There was distaste that a sister—the mother of two young children—should be condemned on a capital charge by the testimony of her brother, especially one whose own wife, Ruth, who had admitted to her own involvement in espionage, had escaped prosecution in return for his testimony. Conversely, Ethel prompted dislike for being seen as the dominant personality in her relationship with Julius, a consideration which seems to have influenced Eisenhower's decision not to extend clemency to her. There was, too, an oddly incestuous character to the drama, for Judge Kaufman, the lead prosecutor Irving H. Saypol, and all the defendants and star prosecution witnesses were Jews. Old questions of Jewish loyalty and identity were never far below the surface.

The Rosenberg affair dragged on for two more years, during which the case was considered five times by the Supreme Court, two appeals were made to the White House for clemency, and three postponements of the date of execution were announced. Finally, the pair were executed at Sing Sing prison (New York) on June 19, 1953, having protested their innocence throughout. They were the first—and to date the only—persons sentenced to death in peacetime for espionage in the USA. Most unsatisfactorily, the Supreme Court seemed to wish to have it both ways on the case, finding no grounds to quash the conviction (which it could review) but implying that it did not favour the sentence (which it said that it could not review). Likewise, President Truman failed to act on the Rosenbergs' first clemency petition, leaving office on Jan. 20, 1953, and handing the decision to his successor, Dwight D. Eisenhower.

The defence through the appeals process variously argued that the death penalty was a "cruel and unusual punishment"; that the 1917 Espionage Law was unconstitutional; that the defendants should have instead been tried under the 1946 Atomic Energy Act, which did not provide for a death penalty; that Judge Kaufman had conducted the trial unfairly; that the sentence was influenced by political hysteria; that pre-trial publicity had prevented a fair trial; and that there had been perjured testimony by government witnesses. The affair stirred great passions which affected even the nine just and sober men of the Supreme Court itself: liberal Justice William Douglas unilaterally granted a stay of execution based on a newly-advanced technical argument just 36 hours before sentence was finally carried out, before being overruled (by six to three) by his colleagues.

The Rosenbergs themselves, through the two long years between conviction and execution, seemed almost set on their own deaths. It was common knowledge that the government was prepared to see their lives spared if they confessed and co-operated. However, pleading their absolute innocence to the end, they would not seek forgiveness for crimes which they denied having committed. At the same time, they assumed such a manner of outraged martyrdom that they compelled little sympathy among those who thought them rightly convicted but wrongly sentenced. There is in their published prison correspondence, as in their various public appeals, an oddly impersonal, rhetorical style, an unswerving conviction that history would sanctify them and condemn their accusers. The very language has an affected loftiness which suggests that they wrote for posterity rather than out of immediate fear or hope. Nor were the Rosenbergs much helped by the outpouring of rhetoric from defence committees which flourished in Europe. From France, especially, came a stream of denunciations of American paranoia and barbarism from what the French called their intellectuals (Americans recognized no such class). Yet many Americans remembered how supinely the French themselves had surrendered to Nazi barbarism, how indifferent they had been to the demands of patriotism, and questioned how great their commitment was even now to resisting the totalitarian threat from the East. Most Americans resented European suggestions that this was another Dreyfus case; even liberals, after the embarrassment of the Alger Hiss case and with McCarthy in full spate, thought this poor ground on which to make a stand.

That the grounds on which the Rosenbergs were executed were unsound can hardly be doubted today. Echoing the words of Judge Kaufman, President Eisenhower, on the day of the executions, declared: "By immeasurably increasing the chances of atomic war, the Rosenbergs may have condemned to death tens of millions of innocent people all over the world." The Rosenbergs were in effect executed for what their actions might have led to, rather than what they had actually done. It cannot be maintained however that what the Rosenbergs are said to have done advanced Soviet progress to becoming an atomic power by as much as a day. What is more, within little more than a decade of their executions, American military strategists had embraced the doctrine that security was best achieved by the doctrine of "mutually assured destruction", where neither side had an unbalancing advantage in atomic weapons which could tempt a devastating first strike.

It was precisely this argument—that the world would be a safer place if no one country had a monopolistic power to lay waste its rivals—which the Rosenbergs had, according to David Greenglass, used to persuade him to hand over atomic secrets.

In a statement issued on their behalf on June 3, 1953, the Rosenbergs declared: "History will record—whether we live or not—that we are the victims of the most monstrous frame-up in the history of our country." The frame-up, they believed, was the FBI's work, and Gold and Greenglass the FBI's mendacious instruments. History has, however, recorded no such unambiguous verdict, although there are many crucial questions which beg answers. What reliance should have been placed on the testimony of Gold, a lonely fantasist who found in the trial a celebrity in which he revelled? (Gold in another case in 1955 admitted he had lied to a grand jury when he said that he had known Elizabeth Bentley's controller, Jacob Golos, and confessed that he had made up phone conversations with Golos.) Should not have greater scepticism been shown towards Greenglass, who, facing a capital charge for which he had yet to be sentenced, had a clear interest in minimizing his own importance in the affair? (A secret Justice Department report later concluded that Greenglass was a man without conscience and untrustworthy.) Did the FBI not shape and mould the testimony of their star witnesses through hours of pre-trial coaching, ironing out many troubling inconsistencies to be found in their initial statements? Was it not unethical that Judge Kaufman discussed the sentence with prosecutors even before the jury had reached its verdict? Some have even claimed, less plausibly (and with shades of the "forgery by typewriter" claimed in the Alger Hiss case—see *Hiss/Chambers Affair, 1948–50*, above), that the FBI fabricated material evidence, including a hotel reservation card which authenticated Gold's visit to New Mexico in 1945, though why the FBI should have shown such determination to frame such obscure individuals as the Rosenbergs had been is far from apparent. And yet, coloured though the trial was by hysteria about Communist subversion, the case was argued on evidence as well as on prejudice. In one sense, the strongest argument for the Rosenbergs' innocence has always been that they were prepared to insist on it to the death, even knowing that confession and penitence could save their lives. It is not a finally conclusive argument, however, for many a guilty man has died proclaiming his innocence, and to those persuaded of their guilt the Rosenbergs had merely gone to their deaths blinded to the end by fanatical devotion to their cause.

With the Rosenbergs dead, the cause of Morton Sobell—a peripheral figure in many ways—assumed a symbolic significance for those who had sought to save the Rosenbergs' lives. They had died, but his innocence could be proved, his release secured. No such vindication through the legal system ever came, however, and Sobell was finally released early for good behaviour only in January 1969. David Greenglass was released in late 1960, and Harry Gold in 1966 (he died in 1972).

FJH

Joseph McCarthy Affair (1950–54)

Roy M. Cohn, McCarthy aide.
Dwight Eisenhower, US President (1953–61).
Joseph McCarthy, Republican senator from Wisconsin (1947–57).
David Schine, McCarthy aide.
Robert T. Stevens, Secretary of the Army.

Joe McCarthy, hitherto an obscure junior Republican senator from Wisconsin, came suddenly to fame with one speech in Wheeling, West Virginia, on Feb. 9, 1950, in which he claimed to have a list of 205 employees of the State Department who were known Communists. In the following years he waged a bitter campaign against what he saw as treason in the State Department and other areas of the government, employing a battery of techniques—the reliance on unnamed informers, charges made under cover of congressional immunity, exaggeration of policy differences into evidence of treachery, and systematic fomenting of suspicion against whole categories of public officials—which came to be known as McCarthyism. Finally he overreached himself, challenging the integrity of the Army and the presidency, and was formally condemned by the Senate. In retrospect, he seems at once the most strident of the Cold War enemies of Communism, a zealot whose philosophy had at its root a know-nothing isolationism which came to threaten the Western alliance, but also a fiery advocate of the right of Congress to question the privileges of the ascendant imperial presidency of the post-war era.

Joseph Raymond McCarthy was born to Catholic Irish–American parents in 1908 in a remote rural area of Wisconsin known as the "Irish settlement". He first stood for public office in 1936 as a Democrat; became a state judge in 1939; served in the Pacific in World War II (when he met John F. Kennedy and became a friend of the Kennedy family); and was elected to the US Senate as a Republican in 1946, defeating Senator Robert "Young Bob" La Follette in a campaign which capitalized on La Follette's isolationist record. In his early years in the Senate McCarthy made little impact and said little about the increasingly potent issue of Communist subversion in government.

The timing of McCarthy's Wheeling speech was opportune. The Cold War in Europe had set in with a vengeance in 1948, and in 1949 after years of civil war the Communists had secured total power in China. Facing a dangerous world, many Americans were inclined to look for evidence of treachery in the State Department and other areas of the Truman administration to explain how it was that the victory of 1945 had so quickly led to such setbacks. In January 1950 Alger Hiss was convicted of perjury after denying he had committed espionage for the Soviet Union while a high-ranking State Department official in the late 1930s, and to some the most disturbing aspect of the case was the manner in which so much of the Washington policy-making establishment had been prepared to cover-up and provide glowing testimonials for Hiss (see *Hiss/Chambers Affair, 1948–50*, above). Secretary of State Dean Acheson himself, after Hiss's conviction, had declared that he would not abandon Hiss. The Hiss case seemed compelling evidence to Republicans and many in the country that the Truman administration's loyalty programme for screening out security risks (in effect since 1947 and under which some 4,353 federal employees had either been dismissed or resigned in the face of investigation by January 1950) was ineffective and perhaps compromised at the highest levels.

A Democratic-controlled special subcommittee of the Senate Foreign Relations Committee, under Senator Millard E. Tydings, a conservative Maryland Democrat, opened hearings on McCarthy's charges on March 8, 1950, and proved unsympathetic to McCarthy. The senator was forced to concede that he did not in fact have a list of 205 Communists in the State Department—he first revised the figure to 57 and then to 81—and only nine individuals, not all of them affiliated to the State Department, were ever publicly named during the Tydings subcommittee hearings.

McCarthy's principal targets turned out to be two individuals linked to US policy-making on China, ambassador-at-large Dr Philip Jessup and Prof. Owen Lattimore of Johns Hopkins University, the latter being described by McCarthy as "the architect of our Far Eastern policy". According to McCarthy, Jessup was merely a "front" for Lattimore, his case against whom seemed to be based on his loose links to a number of Communist "front" organizations; after Jessup produced glowing testimonials to his patriotism from Dwight D. Eisenhower and Gen. George C. Marshall, McCarthy rather quickly backed off. Jessup survived the attack, remaining ambassador-at-large for the rest of the Truman presidency, and later being appointed US representative on the International Court of Justice under President Kennedy. Lattimore, however, escaped less easily. He had served as personal adviser to Chinese Nationalist leader Chiang Kai-shek at President Roosevelt's instigation in 1941–42, and since that time had been a significant voice on China policy questions primarily in his capacity as a leading member of the Institute of Pacific Relations, an international research-oriented body which in the USA had close links to the State Department. On March 27, 1950, the press reported that McCarthy had named Lattimore to the Tydings subcommittee as the "top Russian espionage agent" in the USA. McCarthy subsequently retreated from his charges of espionage but maintained his claim, based primarily on evidence given by Louis Budenz, the former managing editor of the Communist *Daily Worker*, that Lattimore had been part of a Communist cell which effectively controlled the Institute of Pacific Relations and had exerted a powerful influence over State Department policy-making. Lattimore, in contrast, denied that he had ever been a Communist, insisted he had had little influence over policy-making, and that McCarthy was making the US government "an object of suspicion in the eyes of the anti-Communist world and undoubtedly the laughing-stock of the Communist governments".

Ultimately, the Tydings subcommittee agreed with Lattimore, calling the charges against him a "fraud and a hoax". This was not the end, however, of what Lattimore, in the title of a 1950 book, had called his *Ordeal By Slander*. In July 1952 the Senate Judiciary Committee's internal security subcommittee (the McCarran Committee) concluded that Lattimore had been a "conscious, articulate member of the Soviet conspiracy" and with others associated with the Institute of Pacific Relations had influenced US policy. In December of that year a grand jury brought somewhat nebulous perjury charges against Lattimore, and it was not until June 28, 1955, after a judge had twice dismissed key counts, that the government abandoned its case against Lattimore. By that time the public careers of other prominent State Department "China hands" linked to the Institute of Pacific Relations, such as John Carter Vincent and John Stewart Service, had been terminated because of concerns about their reliability.

To his defenders, Lattimore had been condemned primarily because he had been right in foreseeing that the Chinese Nationalist government would not survive and that the Communists would take power. To McCarthy, however, it was evident that Lattimore, like others linked to the Institute of Pacific Relations, had used his influence to bring about the very results that he had forecast. In this McCarthy was the howling voice of American frustration that the world would not be just as America wished it to be. On its surface, it was a policy for global confrontation with Communism, but in its bowels it was the old Midwestern isolationism, a know-nothing attitude to the complexities of the world shot through with suspicion of the cynical ways of the East Coast liberal establishment. Given its head, it was an attitude which led straight on to "America First-ism", a repudiation of the Old World, and retreat from the American guarantee to Western Europe.

Throughout 1951 and 1952 McCarthy kept up his attacks on subversion in government, and on the Truman administration's supposedly complacent attitude to the issue, building a private network of informants in the bureaucracy to counteract the administration's policy of withholding security information from Congress. By 1952 the term "McCarthyism"—reputedly coined by Owen Lattimore—was established as a pejorative description of a type of smear attack and guilt by association, with McCarthy engaged in a bitter running feud with liberal media commentators and such organs as the *New York Post*, the *Washington Post* and *Time* magazine. McCarthy's assault on the administration was politically partisan but it was also a hidden attack on some of the basic assumptions of the post-war settlement. Most striking, perhaps, was his notorious June 1951 condemnation in a 60,000-word speech read into the congressional record of the whole career of former Secretary of State and Army Chief of Staff George C. Marshall as "steeped in falsehood", a product of "a great conspiracy, a conspiracy on a scale so immense as to dwarf any previous such venture in the history of man".

What Marshall most clearly symbolized by the turn of the 1950s was an historic decision by the USA that its vital interests lay in the reconstruction of Western Europe—through the Marshall Plan—rather than in endless conflict with Communism in Asia. Although this was a philosophy with which many mainstream Republicans were in sympathy, while out of office the Republican Party leadership was seemingly prepared to abide by the blanket attacks made by McCarthy on the State Department and wartime heroes, swallowing their scruples in the hope of gaining political advantage. In partial admission of the truth of some of McCarthy's charges, the State Department was in any case by 1951–52 weeding out more or less discreetly some of the individuals named by McCarthy. Such was McCarthy's strength that when a partisan Democratic-controlled Senate subcommittee sought to investigate claims that he had accepted "influence money" from the Lustron

Corporation, manufacturers of prefabricated homes, he simply refused to appear before it.

In November 1952, however, the Democratic presidential candidate, Adlai Stevenson, was defeated by the Republican Dwight Eisenhower, and the Republicans also took control of Congress. In January 1953 McCarthy became chairman of his own committee, the Senate Committee on Government Operations, and of a subcommittee of this, the permanent subcommittee on investigations. He now at last had a budget to hire investigators, powers to subpoena witnesses, to conduct their interrogation and to seek documents from the executive branch. With the Republicans now in control of the executive branch, McCarthy found himself increasingly on a collision course with the Republican leadership. He was quickly in conflict with the White House over such issues as diplomatic appointments (he called Eisenhower's choice of ambassador to Moscow, Charles E. Bohlen, a "bad security risk" and unsuccessfully demanded that he should take a lie-detector test before being confirmed by the Senate) and the continued trading of America's European allies with Communist China. McCarthy also showed ambitions to run his own unilateral foreign policy, announcing on March 28, 1953, that he had secured an agreement with Greek shipping owners that they would not trade with Iron Curtain countries. On May 30, 1953, he amended his catchphrase "20 years of treason", used to describe the Roosevelt and Truman presidencies, to "21 years of treason".

Meanwhile, in April 1953, following on from a destructive investigation of the Voice of America radio station (which was run by a branch of the State Department), McCarthy despatched his permanent investigating subcommittee's chief counsel, Roy M. Cohn, and its "chief consultant", G. David Schine, both of them 26 years old, on a highly-publicized tour of US information centres and libraries operated by the State Department in Europe. This led to the resignations (in May) of Theodore Kaghan, the deputy director of the US High Commission's Public Affairs Division, after he had been charged with past Communist connections, and of Raymond Swing, the principal political commentator on the Voice of America, who claimed that the Information Service had been "crippled" by the McCarthy attacks and the State Department had been guilty of "spineless failure" to support Voice of America. Press reports in May–June 1953 showed that the State Department had ordered the withdrawal of books by more than 40 authors from libraries overseas, including books by Dashiell Hammett, Owen Lattimore, Lillian Hellman, Joseph E. Davies (former ambassador to Moscow) and (ironically) Whittaker Chambers' *Witness*. On June 14, however, Eisenhower counter-attacked against the "book burners", and on June 24 criticized those who "would try to defend freedom by denying freedom's friends the opportunity of studying communism in its entirety—its plausibilities, its falsities, its weaknesses".

Secretary of State John Foster Dulles had largely stood aside as McCarthy renewed his attack on the State Department, an action which led to widespread demoralization in the agency. The stage was now set, however, for the conflict which proved to be McCarthy's undoing, namely his attempt to investigate the Army. In August 1953 hearings opened in an investigation of the US Army Signal Corps laboratories at Fort Monmouth (New Jersey), and, contrary to McCarthy's broad hints that this would expose a major espionage ring, little was conclusively shown beyond lax security procedures. McCarthy then opened up the case of Dr Irving Peress, a captain in the Army Dental Corps, showing that Peress had been called to active service in January 1953 despite having pleaded the Fifth Amendment in declining to answer questions about membership in subversive organizations at the time of his call-up, and had been promoted subsequently despite a series of recommendations that he should be dismissed on security grounds. Finally, Brig.–Gen. Ralph W. Zwicker, Peress' commanding officer at Camp Kilmer (New Jersey) allowed Peress an honourable discharge on Feb. 2, 1954, three days after Peress had appeared before McCarthy's subcommittee and again pleaded the Fifth Amendment. At best, this seemed a case of Army incompetence, and at worst a cover-up. To his face, McCarthy on Feb. 18 described Gen. Zwicker, who had evaded questions about his conduct in the affair by pleading a 1948 Truman directive requiring the "absolute confidence" of information relating to the loyalty of federal employees, as "not fit to wear" his uniform.

By this time plans were well afoot within the White House and the Pentagon to head off McCarthy, who had rejected informal soothing overtures from Eisenhower. Following a secret Jan. 21, 1954, conference between Army Counsel John Adams, Presidential Assistant Sherman Adams, Attorney General Herbert Brownell, and Eisenhower's 1952 campaign manager Henry Cabot Lodge, John Adams warned McCarthy to abandon his Army probe or face accusations that improper pressure had been placed on the Army by him and Cohn to give preferential treatment to Schine (who had been called up as a private in late 1953). When McCarthy proved unaccommodating, the Army on March 12, 1954, publicized its charges concerning Schine.

Hearings on the Army's charges were held before the investigating subcommittee from April 22 to June 18, 1954, with Senator McCarthy stepping down to let Senator Karl Mundt take the chair. Preceding this the Army filed a series of charges with the committee which hinged on allegations that McCarthy and Cohn, and other members of McCarthy's staff, had threatened to subject the Army to harrassing investigation if Schine were not given a commission and posted on special assignment to New York and given other preferential treatment. According to these allegations Cohn had threatened to "wreck the Army" if Schine were posted overseas. Following the hearings, the investigating subcommittee split on a strictly partisan basis. The four Republicans rebuked Cohn but only mildly criticized McCarthy for failing to exercise "more vigorous discipline" over his staff. The three Democrats thought McCarthy had "fully acquiesced in and condoned" the "improper actions" of Cohn.

Both sides found fault in the conduct of the Army. Particularly damaging was evidence that Army Secretary Robert T. Stevens had at first sought to conciliate McCarthy and Cohn, promising to give Schine a soft berth if they abandoned their investigation. It was heard how Schine's parents had entertained Stevens, McCarthy and Cohn to dinner at New York's Waldorf-Astoria hotel the previous October, and a famous photograph produced in evidence showed Private Schine and Secretary Stevens posed together at Fort Dix military base. Cohn in turn told the hearings that

Army Counsel John Adams had offered to feed him damaging evidence about other branches of the services—including the name of an Air Force base with a high proportion of "sex deviates"—if he would drop the Army investigation. John Adams also admitted that the plan to draw up a report on the pressure brought to bear in favour of Schine had originated in the White House. When Eisenhower on May 17, 1954, ordered all executive branch employees not to give testimony on this in order to preserve "a proper separation of powers between the executive and the legislative branches of the government", McCarthy accused the administration of itself pleading the Fifth Amendment.

Two decades later President Nixon's assertion of executive privilege in the Watergate affair would be fought tooth and nail by Congress (see *Watergate Affair, 1972–74*, below). In 1954, however, many in Congress were prepared to look the other way while the administration moved against McCarthy. Ultimately what mattered was less the facts of the case—what after all did it matter if McCarthy himself had tried to help Schine, for such patronage was the daily round in Washington?—than image and appearances. The Army–McCarthy hearings reached millions of homes through television, and what the public saw destroyed McCarthy. The Senator's worst characteristics, his humourless, hectoring, monotonous style of speech, his endless points of order, his occasional flashes of violent temper, were exposed for all to see, as was the studied insolence of the youthful Cohn. Nor, in truth, did McCarthy's appearance, with his lowering heavy-set features and perpetual "five o'clock shadow", suggest anything but an unpleasant bully. Against them stood the highest officials of the Army, bedecked in medals and standing firmly on their dignity, their cause most skilfully argued by Boston attorney Joseph Welch. Welch's legendary emotion-laden rebuke to McCarthy when he alluded to a past Communist association of a young member of Welch's law firm, one Frederick G. Fisher—"Little did I dream you could be so reckless and so cruel. . . . I fear he shall always bear a scar needlessly inflicted by you. . . . Have you no sense of decency, sir, at long last? Have you no sense of decency"—moved millions who witnessed the scene to question McCarthy's basic humanity, and Welch reinforced the lesson by breaking down in tears afterwards before a dozen press photographers. No matter that the story that Welch had dropped plans to employ Fisher in the hearings because of his past Communist affiliations had already been reported in the *New York Times*, almost unobserved, and that Welch's breakdown may not have been unrehearsed. The image of the kindly-looking Welch in distress, the faltering tone of his voice, and the harsh uncaring manner of McCarthy were what caught the popular imagination.

The hearings also had a subplot, perhaps unfamiliar to many in the country but well-known around Washington, namely a whispering campaign of innuendo that in the mutual affection of Schine and Cohn (bachelors both) and the cosseting of them by McCarthy (who had married only the previous year, in middle age) there was something of the unwholesome. It became a fashion among the knowledgeable to speculate that in their obsessive campaign against suspected Communists in the Establishment McCarthy and his young men were pursuing the abnormal fanaticisms of those who felt outsiders from mainstream society. This sentiment came to help to shape the growth of opinion in the Senate, in most circumstances an institution most protective of the privileges of its members, that McCarthy was not fully a member of the club.

Cohn resigned as chief counsel to the McCarthy investigating subcommittee on July 20, 1954. On Aug. 2 the Senate agreed the formation of a special committee of three Republicans and three Democrats to investigate charges against McCarthy, under the chairmanship of Senator Arthur V. Watkins of Utah, an Eisenhower Republican. On Aug. 24 this committee announced that it would hear evidence relating to five charges: (i) that McCarthy had shown contempt for the Senate by refusing, among other things, to answer questions before the Senate subcommittee on privileges and elections when it investigated his finances in 1951–52; (ii) that he had encouraged federal employees to break the law and violate their oaths of office or executive orders to give him information; (iii) that he had received classified or confidential documents from executive branch files; (iv) that he had "ridiculed his colleagues in the Senate, defaming them publicly in vulgar and base language"; and (v) that he had "attacked, defamed and besmirched military heroes of the United States", in particular Gen. Zwicker. The proceedings of the Watkins committee were essentially political in character, and McCarthy by this time seemed subdued and for all the odd flash of temper, a man resigned to the inevitable; on the advice of his counsel, Edward Bennett Williams, he had also agreed to the exclusion of cameras and microphones from the hearings.

The committee's report published on Sept. 27 unanimously recommended that McCarthy should be censured for contempt of the Senate subcommittee on privileges and elections and defamation of Gen. Zwicker, but not on the other counts. On Nov. 8, the Senate reconvened in special session to consider the Watkins committee recommendations and, after a delay while McCarthy entered hospital, voted on Dec. 2 by 67 to 22 to condemn McCarthy for contempt of the subcommittee on privileges and elections, and for insults to the Senate itself during the censure proceedings (including charges that the Watkins committee was a "lynch party" and the "unwitting handmaiden" of the Communist Party). The proposal to censure him for his abuse of Gen. Zwicker was not voted on. All 44 Democrats present and the one independent (Senator Wayne Morse) voted for the censure, the Republicans present dividing equally for and against McCarthy. It was only the third time that the Senate had so condemned one of its own members, and it was the first time that the root issue was one of political conduct. (Previous cases had involved two senators who engaged in a fist fight on the Senate floor in 1902, and a case of corruption in 1929.) On Dec. 4, 1954, President Eisenhower called Senator Watkins to the White House and privately congratulated him on having done a "very splendid job".

To counteract McCarthy, Eisenhower had in April 1953 issued a directive broadening the grounds on which federal employees could be dismissed. Three weeks before the November 1954 elections the Civil Service Commission had announced that 6,926 individuals had been dismissed under the new programme. (Only more than a year later was it revealed that 40 per cent of these had been hired since Eisenhower took office.) The issue was fading, however. No more Elizabeth Bentleys or Whittaker Chamberses were coming forward to tell their stories and feed the fires, and there were no figures of the stature of Hiss or Remington or Jessup coming under suspicion. East–West relations remained strained, but the general shape of the post-war settlement, after the cataclysmic disruptions of the late 1940s, had become clear. Most Americans felt that the nation's security was in safe hands with Eisenhower at the helm. Even had McCarthy not overreached himself by attacking the Army, his sun would doubtless have burnt itself out. He was no Nixon, who had launched his career as an anti-Communist zealot on the House Committee on un-American Activities, but had moved easily with the subtle changing of the tide, and would, two decades later, as President, visit Communist China and cement détente with the Soviet Union.

McCarthy had automatically lost his committee chairmanships as a result of the Democrats gaining control of the Senate in the November 1954 elections. After this he took little part in political life (although he was re-elected in November 1956), spending increasing amounts of time away from the Senate watching soap-operas, gazing into the fire in his living room, and drinking more heavily than ever. He was the only member of Congress systematically excluded from White House functions. Meanwhile, his health was deteriorating and he died on May 2, 1957, of liver disease, aged only 48. His Wisconsin seat was captured by a liberal Democrat, Edward W. Proxmire. His most celebrated assistant, Roy Cohn, went on to live a life of notoriety. A closet homosexual to the end, he died of AIDS in August 1986 shortly after being disbarred in New York state for unethical conduct.

McCarthy's downfall was rich in irony. In bringing it about, the Senate not only broke McCarthy as an individual and repudiated McCarthyism, it also conceded important limitations on the powers of Senate committees to interrogate the executive and of individual senators to conduct themselves as they pleased in pursuance of their legislative responsibilities. McCarthy's Democratic critics on the investigating subcommittee even urged the Justice Department to consider whether McCarthy had violated the espionage laws in receiving confidential FBI documents and then producing them in evidence before his committee. For the next two decades foreign and intelligence policy would remain clearly defined as the prerogatives of the executive branch. The Army–Eisenhower victory over McCarthy was shrewdly fought. McCarthy had gone too far for most in Congress to stomach, but in the reaction broad executive powers were asserted. The consequences of this would be seen in the Vietnam War, when successive Presidents and the military establishment put themselves beyond reach of Congress.

FJH

Gen. MacArthur Affair (1951)

Gen. Douglas MacArthur, Commander of UN forces in Korea (1950–51).
Harry S. Truman, President (1945–53).

President Harry S. Truman's decision in April 1951 to relieve Gen. Douglas
MacArthur of all his Far Eastern commands precipitated a violent controversy about the limits of the powers of military men to set military policy,
and about the purpose of US involvement in the Korean War, which was
then at its height. To Truman's detractors, MacArthur's dismissal set the
seal on a policy of largely passive containment of the Communist forces,
which culminated in the partition of Korea. To Truman's supporters, the
dismissal of the general was a rightful humbling of a man who had exceeded
his powers and posed a threat to the supremacy of civilian command.

Following the defeat of its Japanese rulers in World War II, Korea was
effectively divided into zones of Soviet and US influence along the line of
the 38°N parallel. In 1949 the Soviet Union withdrew its forces from the
North, and the USA from the South, but in June 1950 military forces of
the Communist North invaded the South. In the absence of the Soviet
Union (which was at the time boycotting its proceedings), the UN Security
Council urged UN member states to come to the aid of the South, and
Gen. MacArthur became Supreme Commander of all UN forces in Korea
(the majority of which were American). His choice was a natural one, for
MacArthur was a dominating figure in the region, having led US forces to
victory over Japan in the Pacific in World War II and then demonstrated
considerable diplomatic skills in overseeing the reconstruction of Japanese
society, without inflicting humiliation, in his capacity as Supreme Allied
Commander in Japan.

The early months of the Korean War witnessed a see-saw campaign. The
North's initial highly successful onslaught, which included the capture of the
Southern capital, Seoul, was fairly quickly repelled, and by October 1950
allied forces had retaken Seoul and advanced north of the 38th parallel. The
commitment of large numbers of Chinese forces on the side of the North
then led to a further reversal, Seoul falling for the second time in December,
before allied forces regained the ascendancy, reconquering Seoul on March
14, 1951.

MacArthur was from the start tightly constrained in his conduct of the
war. Although most of the men and money on the allied side were
contributed by the USA, the campaign was conducted in the name of
the UN, giving the European allies, most of whom had limited enthusiasm
for the fight, a restraining influence over military tactics. MacArthur was
not permitted, in particular, to bomb targets inside China or to make free
use of the air power at his disposal against Chinese troop concentrations.
To a man who had acted under no such restraints in the total war of
1941–45, these inhibitions seemed inimical both to the chances of bringing
the North to terms and the safety of the men under his command. From the
earliest weeks of the war, there was public comment on policy differences
between MacArthur and the administration. Meanwhile, Truman followed

a policy of soothing MacArthur, even travelling to meet him for private conversations at Wake Island in the Pacific in October 1950.

On March 20, 1951, with the war at a stalemate but with the North Koreans and the Chinese driven back across the 38th parallel, Truman told the allied nations and MacArthur that the time had come to look for an armistice and a negotiated peace. On March 24, however, MacArthur, on his own authority, announced that he had directed US forces to cross the 38th parallel if and when this became tactically advisable; that he believed that the extension of the war to China's interior bases and coastal areas would "doom Red China to the risk of imminent military collapse"; and that he was willing to confer with the commander of the Chinese forces at any time to bring about a settlement. It was an ultimatum which seemed to be directed as much at Washington as at China, and Truman's supporters began to wonder how long he would tolerate MacArthur's assumption of policy-making powers. On April 5 Joseph W. Martin (the Republican leader in the House of Representatives), a strong opponent of administration Far Eastern policy, read to the House a letter from MacArthur in which the General expressed support for the idea of using Chinese Nationalist forces in Formosa (Taiwan) to open a second front to relieve pressure on UN troops in Korea. MacArthur added that in Asia "we fight Europe's war with arms, while the diplomats there still fight it with words. . . . if we lose the war to Communism in Asia the fall of Europe is inevitable".

Truman would later assert that he decided to dismiss MacArthur in direct response to his March 24 statement. His approach was cautious, however, and he did not act before he had secured the assent of all his top advisers, including Defence Secretary George C. Marshall and Secretary of State Dean Acheson, and all the Joint Chiefs of Staff. At 1.00 am on April 11, 1951, at a press conference hastily arranged to beat a scoop in that day's *Chicago Tribune*, a White House spokesman announced that Truman had "with deep regret" relieved MacArthur of all his Far Eastern commands, adding that he had proved "unable to give his wholehearted support to the policies of the US government and of the United Nations in matters pertaining to his official duties". In defensive anticipation of the storm to come, Truman released the texts of communications with MacArthur showing that efforts had been made to restrain the General's public statements, and warning him of "strong UN feeling" in favour of further diplomatic efforts before any advance beyond the 38th parallel. In a broadcast later the same day, Truman explained that the purpose of US involvement in Korea was to contain Communist expansionism without a general war, and that to take steps such as bombing Manchuria or assisting Chinese Nationalist troops to land on the mainland would be to run "a very grave risk of starting a general war".

MacArthur's dismissal polarized opinion. To some, Truman had acted to ensure the supremacy of civilian control over the military, and to prevent a catastrophic military escalation. To others, Truman had acted to appease the faint-hearted European allies and his faint-hearted Secretaries of State and Defence by humiliating a great American hero. Senator William Jenner of Indiana demanded that Truman should be impeached, warning that "the country today is in the hands of a secret inner coterie which is directed by agents of the Soviet Union". Many leading Republicans made no secret of their view that they believed that in terms of military strategy MacArthur was in the right. The Republican minority leaders in both Houses of Congress introduced a resolution which declared that Truman's action had "precipitated a situation fraught with danger for the national defence" and invited MacArthur to address Congress to "present views and recommendations for the policies and courses in Korea and Asia generally". Truman and the Democrats tactfully bowed before the storm, and MacArthur was duly invited by unanimous vote of both Houses to address a joint session.

When MacArthur left Japan on April 16, 1951, 1,000,000 people lined his route to Tokyo airport, and on April 17 he was greeted by 500,000 people on his arrival in San Francisco. It was the first time he had set foot in the USA since 1937. However, to the relief of the White House, his address to Congress on April 19 proved to be valedictory rather than a further challenge. "Like the old soldier" of a barracks song of his youth, he declared, "I now close my military career and just fade away, an old soldier who tried to do his duty as God gave him the light to see that duty". The next day New York gave the General the greatest ticker-tape procession the city had ever seen.

Hearings on MacArthur's dismissal were held by a Senate committee from May 3 to June 25, 1951, in secret but with extensive edited transcripts appearing in the press. As the hearings went on, it became clear just how unanimous was the view among the nation's leading military officers that MacArthur had outlived his usefulness, so that the White House position strengthened. At the last, the committee never produced a majority report, merely transmitting a transcript of the hearings to the Senate "for its information".

To many at the time, MacArthur embodied all the dangers of the "man on a white horse", a military man made ambitious by victories in war, a threat to the principle of civilian control of the military as exercised by the President in his capacity as Supreme Commander. And, indeed, in his swagger, his tendency to see himself as the final authority in the Pacific region, MacArthur did have something of the temperament of the soldier-who-would-be-king. The case was always overstated, however. Ambitious though he may have been, MacArthur's dispute with Truman was about the conduct of a specific military operation; if Truman had to consider broader political issues in his policy-making, those issues included matters of expediency and diplomacy which an active military commander might reasonably have deemed unworthy. To MacArthur, as a military man, war was about victory, not compromise. With his removal, the US military for two decades settled into the ways of compromise without victory. As Vietnam would show, it was a way of thinking which had its price. In that long and useless war no policy was ever followed beyond an ever-shifting strategy of containment, while the military men and the White House lied to each other, and both lied to the American people, about what they were achieving.

It was Truman's Defence Secretary Gen. George C. Marshall, who told Congress after MacArthur's dismissal that MacArthur's policies not only risked a breach with the allies, but also threatened all-out war with both China and Russia and a possible Soviet invasion of Europe. Administration officials and the Chiefs of Staff queued up to tell Congress that MacArthur, with the limitations of a field commander, had got Korea out of proportion, and had missed the big picture in which it was but one of a series of limited and sometimes inconclusive engagements with communism. Whether or not history has vindicated that interpretation, or whether perhaps history was consciously shaped to favour that interpretation, must be a matter of opinion. Fewer now than then, no doubt, would dispute MacArthur's arguments that the Soviet Union's Far Eastern interests were primarily defensive; that the Soviet Union and China were not indissoluble allies but potential adversaries; that the Pacific would emerge as a strategic cockpit; that the Soviet Union would not risk war for Korea; or that Soviet policy in Europe would unfold essentially independently of what was happening on the far side of Asia. In their fear that the preoccupation of the right with resisting Communism in Asia would weaken the more important and sustainable commitment to Europe, the policy-makers in Washington arguably took too negative a view of the potential for the USA to influence events in Asia on a large scale, settling instead for that policy of limited engagement which culminated in Vietnam. Yet that view prevailed decisively after the fall of MacArthur. The war in Korea dragged on for three more years, petering out into an uneasy armistice under which the 38th parallel remained the border between North and South.

What the Truman administration established, and Eisenhower and successive Presidents followed, was a broad strategic policy which assumed that the engagement with Communism would be of indefinite duration. US security would be secured by its strategic forces; the alliance with Western Europe would be the pivotal element in resisting Soviet ambitions; and limited skirmished would be fought out around the world and would have to be contained. Many of those who urged MacArthur's case had no such vision which could describe the future: they wanted rather to abolish Communism, abolish the present, rediscover a past when America was not burdened with global entanglements. (A Republican minority on the Senate committee which held hearings on MacArthur's dismissal produced a report which both praised MacArthur's military strategems and yet condemned Truman for involving the USA in Korea in the first place, demanding that the USA should "never again become involved in war without the consent of Congress".) MacArthur's most bellicose supporters were—it now seems paradoxical—precisely those on the isolationist wing of the Republican Party who were arguing against the stationing of troops in Europe and in favour of a "look homeward", "Fortress America" policy. Resenting the present, they could not plan for the future, and their strategy lacked coherence for the realities of the post-war world. It was the Truman-Acheson-Marshall vision of the global situation which would prevail for want of a consistent alternative.

FJH

Oppenheimer Affair (1954)

J. Robert Oppenheimer, US atomic scientist.

Dr J. Robert Oppenheimer, who headed the US atomic bomb project at Los Alamos in the later stages of World War II, was in 1954 stripped of his security clearance primarily on the grounds that he had shown defects of character in his past Communist associations and had failed to sever these even while leading a top-secret project.

Oppenheimer had been appointed director in January 1943 of the atomic bomb facility then about to be built at Los Alamos (New Mexico) as part of the overall Manhattan Project; he had overseen the development of the bomb through to completion and use at Hiroshima and Nagasaki. In October 1945 he had returned to academic life, and since 1947 had been director of the Institute for Advanced Study at Princeton, but had retained a considerable influence in US atomic policy-making.

Oppenheimer's suspension as consultant to the general advisory committee of the Atomic Energy Commission (AEC) and as a member of the science advisory committee under the Office of Defence Mobilization was announced by the AEC on April 13, 1954. The decision was made by President Eisenhower in consultation with defence and atomic energy officials. The ground announced by the AEC was the "substantial derogatory information" in Oppenheimer's security file. The announcement followed publication in US newspapers the previous day of correspondence (supplied by Oppenheimer himself) between Oppenheimer and Maj.-Gen. K.D. Nichols (the general manager of the AEC), including a letter sent by Nichols to Oppenheimer in December 1953 listing allegations that had been made against him. These included association with members of the Communist Party and its front organizations in the late 1930s and early 1940s, and that he had opposed research on the hydrogen bomb and had "definitely slowed down its development". Nichols had noted that Oppenheimer himself had admitted in 1953 that although not a Communist he had "probably belonged to every Communist-front organization on the West Coast"; that his wife and brother (Frank Oppenheimer, who had also worked on the Manhattan Project) had been Communist Party members; and that there were reports that he had been a party member himself in the early 1940s. (In addition, Oppenheimer's mistress, Jean Tatlock, found dead in her bath in questionable circumstances in 1944, was a prominent Communist—see also *James Forrestal Affair (1949)* above.) Nichols also charged that in the winter of 1942–43 Oppenheimer had been approached by the Soviets for information on the work being done at the Berkeley Radiation Laboratory, using Oppenheimer's friend Haakon Chevalier as a go-between; according to Nichols, Oppenheimer had not only failed to report the approach until August 1943 but even then had not given Chevalier's name for several more months.

In a letter of self-defence of March 4, 1954, Oppenheimer had conceded his association with left-wing groups, portraying himself as an apolitical scientist whose enthusiasms had been engaged by the "united front" policies after 1936 on issues such as the Spanish Civil War and the plight of Jews in Germany. In 1939–40, however, he had suffered a disillusionment with Communist politics (he said that he had never been a party member), and his leftist associations had been ended by the time he went to Los Alamos. He denied having sought to impede the hydrogen bomb programme, saying that all members of the AEC general advisory committee had been opposed to a "crash" programme for this in 1949 (when the issue became one of intense concern after the Soviets exploded their first atomic bomb in the August); however once Truman announced his decision in January 1950 to proceed with the programme, the committee had not questioned the decision.

On June 1, 1954, the AEC personnel security review board, after holding hearings on the case from April 12 to May 6, voted by two votes to one that Oppenheimer's security clearance should not be reinstated. It cited both past conduct and a lack of candour before the board, arguing that Oppenheimer's known lack of enthusiasm for the hydrogen bomb "undoubtedly had an adverse effect on recruitment".

Many leading scientists had rallied to Oppenheimer's support before the review board; he also enjoyed the support of Lt.-Gen. Leslie R. Groves (the wartime head of the Manhattan Project), who had engaged him to run Los Alamos. To those who sided with Oppenheimer, the real security interests of the United States seemed to lie in freedom of thought, in allowing the first-rate to flourish without the dreary censorship and pious condemnation of watch-committees of the mediocre, who had never erred because they had never thought or imagined. When the transcripts of the review board hearings were published on June 16, however, it was seen that a principal witness against Oppenheimer had been Dr. Edward Teller, a Hungarian-born physicist widely credited with the post-war development of the hydrogen bomb. Teller had testified that if "at the end of the war some people like Dr Oppenheimer would have lent moral support . . . we could have kept at least as many people in Los Alamos as we then recruited in 1949 under very difficult conditions . . . . if we had gone to work in 1945 we could have achieved the thermo-nuclear bomb just about four years earlier". To some familiar with the case, Teller's charge appeared motivated in part by professional jealousy. Yet it was a critical factor in building a picture of Oppenheimer as somehow cut from the same compromised cloth as those State Department and other officials who had supposedly lost the peace for the USA and allowed the Communists to achieve ascendancy over vast areas of the globe.

When on June 29, 1954, the AEC Commissioners announced that they had rejected by four votes to one Oppenheimer's appeal against the findings of the security review board, the ground appeared to have shifted somewhat. On the hydrogen bomb question, the AEC said nothing, merely observing that "enthusiasm" for a project could not be a security requirement. What weighed against Oppenheimer was instead "proof of fundamental defects in his character" in that his association with Communists (since 1942, when he was picked to head Los Alamos) had "extended far beyond the tolerable limits of prudence and self-restraint". Particularly obnoxious was his association with Haakon Chevalier, with whom he had associated as late as December 1953, and his repeated "falsehoods, evasions and misrepresentations".

That Oppenheimer was a victim of the McCarthyite political mood of the times can scarcely be doubted; indeed, the Eisenhower administration acted in the face of warnings from McCarthy that he intended to investigate the hydrogen bomb programme. Characteristically, the hearings which led to Oppenheimer's condemnation featured innuendo, hearsay, guilt by association, outdated evidence presented out of its historical context, and a constantly shifting focus as to what the charges actually were. Disturbing as Oppenheimer's Communist associations may have seemed (and it was clear that he had remained a fellow-traveller of sorts long after the Nazi-Soviet Pact had fatally alienated from the party many former enthusiasts among the intellectuals), little evidence was produced that had not been known to security officials a decade earlier, when Oppenheimer's influence over atomic developments had been far greater. Groves himself had taken on Oppenheimer to head Los Alamos although he knew that he had "you might say, a very extreme liberal background" and had subsequently taken a distinctly relaxed view of FBI and military intelligence reports of Oppenheimer's continuing Communist associations and of his unwillingness to name Chevalier (which Groves thought merely the "typical American schoolboy attitude that there is something wicked about telling on a friend").

The resurgence of the Chevalier incident was an ironic case of nemesis, however, for Oppenheimer had revealed to security officials that there had been an approach for secrets only in an attempt to prove his reliability. Initially he had spun an elaborate yarn suggesting that the approach had not been made to Oppenheimer himself, only reported to him; not until September 1946 did he admit to his own direct involvement, and had in time also given Chevalier's name for the same reason. Wishing to prove he was not a security risk, but at the same time not wishing to incriminate a friend, Oppenheimer had enmeshed himself in deceits which would in time be seen as showing a defect of character and personality. A less favourable interpretation is that nothing of the story would have come out anyway, had Oppenheimer not given the initial report, and that he must have believed that the trail would be traced back to Chevalier in time. Curiously, Chevalier himself was not even interviewed by the FBI until 1946, and after the Oppenheimer affair broke Chevalier (resident in France since 1950) maintained his complete innocence. Claiming that he had only told Oppenheimer that he (Chevalier) had been approached in order to warn him (Oppenheimer) of Soviet attempts to infiltrate the project, he also suggested that Oppenheimer had given his name in an attempt to ingratiate himself with the authorities, and that the intelligence agencies had suspected this and so had not taken the story seriously.

Oppenheimer, who did not appeal against the AEC's ruling in the courts, remained excluded from public service for the rest of his life. Within a short time of the 1954 controversy, however, increasing sentiment developed that he had been unfairly judged. In 1963 President Lyndon Johnson personally presented him with the AEC's Enrico Fermi Award (and Teller and Oppenheimer shook hands), but Oppenheimer declined to respond to suggestions he should apply to have his case reopened. He died in February 1967.

FJH

Sherman Adams Affair (1958)

Sherman Adams, assistant to President Eisenhower (1953–58).

Sherman Adams, from 1953 President Eisenhower's Assistant (the equivalent of the modern White House Chief of Staff), resigned on Sept. 22, 1958, in the wake of revelations that he had accepted gifts and favours from a New England textile manufacturer, Bernard Goldfine. He had effectively run the White House since President Eisenhower suffered a stroke in November 1957.

The revelations resulted from the investigations of the Senate subcommittee on legislative oversight, which produced records showing that between December 1953 and May 1958 Goldfine had paid hotel bills for Adams totalling $3,096 and given him material for a vicuna fur coat worth $700. It was charged that Adams had on three occasions intervened with the Federal Trade Commission (FTC) and the Securities and Exchange Commission (SEC) to assist Goldfine's business interests.

Adams himself admitted to the subcommittee that he had received gifts, but said that Goldfine was an "old personal friend" and that there had been "no strings attached"; he had made enquiries at the FTC and the SEC for Goldfine, and might have acted "a little more prudently", but had never exerted influence on his behalf. Goldfine in turn testified that he had never asked Adams to do "anything out of line", and that Adams had also given him gifts, including a wristwatch which he showed the senators. Goldfine conceded, however, that he had given gifts to a number of officials and paid hotel bills for three senators, writing these costs off as "business expenses". He refused to produce some records required by the subcommittee.

Richard Nixon, Eisenhower's Vice-President, later recorded his view that Adams had made a mistake of judgment rather than morality, and "left his job a relatively poor man". In later years Adams operated a New Hampshire ski resort. He died on Oct. 27, 1986.

FJH

Martin/Mitchell Espionage Affair (1960)

William H. Martin; Bernon F. Mitchell, NSA employees.

The defection of two employees of the top-secret National Security Agency (NSA) to the Soviet Union in 1960 was the most serious publicly-known security lapse to have affected the intelligence-gathering agency to that point. The NSA was exposed to unprecedented and unwelcome publicity as a consequence.

The two who defected, both mathematicians, were William H. Martin (29) and Bernon F. Mitchell (31). They disappeared in late June 1960, re-appearing at a press conference in Moscow on Sept. 6 where they advanced a somewhat confused mix of personal and political motivations for their action. These included concern at the penetration of Soviet airspace by US planes for intelligence-gathering, and the interception and deciphering by the NSA of the secret communications of the USA's own allies.

Defence Department statements focused on minimizing the significance of the secrets in the possession of the pair, who were described as junior mathematicians employed in "limited areas of communications statistical work", and on undermining their credibility. Mitchell, it was revealed, had been undergoing psychiatric treatment immediately before their disappearance, and both were "obviously confused". Most embarrassing were the allegations that the USA had spied on its own allies.

According to James Bamford's book on the NSA, *The Puzzle Palace*, Mitchell had admitted to NSA investigators after a lie-detector test at the time of his recruitment in 1957 that he had carried out "sexual experimentations" involving animals as a teenager, yet had still been given a security clearance; in the weeks before his defection, moreover, he had told his psychiatrist of his bisexuality. A report by the House Committee on Un-American Activities in 1961 implied that the principal reason for the defections was homosexuality, but Bamford suggests that the reasons were more likely naively ideological.

Following the defection of Martin and Mitchell, some 26 NSA employees were dismissed for "indications of sexual deviation". Also dismissed was NSA personnel director Maurice H. Klein, who was found to have falsified his own personnel file.

FJH

Bay of Pigs Affair (1961)

Fidel Castro, Cuban President.
John F. Kennedy, US President (1961–63).

On April 17, 1961, a force of about 1,000 Cuban exiles opposed to the Communist regime of Fidel Castro, with the backing of the US Central Intelligence Agency (CIA), landed in Cuba at the Bahia de Cochinas (Bay of Pigs) in an attempt to secure a bridgehead to stir a national uprising. After three days of fighting, during which there were heavy losses on both sides, the invaders were completely routed. US involvement in the fiasco would leave a malign legacy which has been detected in many later affairs, including the assassination of President Kennedy in 1963 and the Watergate break-in in 1972 (see *John F. Kennedy Assassination Affair, 1963–79*, and *Watergate Affair, 1972–74*, below).

The Cuban revolution had followed an increasingly anti-American and bloodthirsty course since the overthrow of the Batista regime in January 1959. US property had been nationalized; Castro had despatched teams elsewhere in Latin America and the Caribbean to foster insurgency; the hundreds of "counter-revolutionaries" executed had included some of Castro's early supporters. The USA had broken diplomatic relations with Cuba in January 1961, by which time there were some 100,000 Cuban refugees in the USA. As early as the end of 1959, the CIA was laying plans to dispose of Castro, and in 1960 contacts were made with Mafia figures to scheme Castro's assassination. Plans were also underway to stage a direct military operation, and Kennedy gave his endorsement to these after he succeeded Eisenhower as President in January 1961. On April 12, 1961, however, less than a week before the landings at the Bay of Pigs, Kennedy publicly pledged that the USA would in no way assist in any military action against the Cuban government. Moreover, in the immediate aftermath of the event US officials flagrantly misrepresented the level of US involvement, which was actually described more accurately by the Cuban government. On April 18, in a letter to Soviet leader Khrushchev, Kennedy denied any US involvement, while endorsing the action of "Cuban patriots". In a speech on April 20, with disaster becoming apparent, Kennedy declared that "while we could not be expected to hide our sympathies, we made it repeatedly clear that the armed forces of this country would not intervene in any way".

Many different views have been taken of what went wrong at the Bay of Pigs. Fundamentally, perhaps, it was never clearly resolved what its purpose was to be. On the one hand, the Bay of Pigs was a classic World War II-type beachhead landing, complete with a command "war room" set up in the White House with the Kennedy brothers (John, and his Attorney General, Robert) in personal command. On the other hand, the administration's anxiety to avoid political complications, and to make what happened seem like a "spontaneous" uprising triggered by the arrival of freelance Cuban exiles, meant that effective support to the bridgehead was lacking. Most critically, Kennedy refused to sanction air strikes against

Cuban communications and forces or to provide adequate air cover for the bridgehead, leaving the Cuban air force as masters of the skies. Many Cuban exiles concluded that Kennedy had wantonly sacrificed the lives of those who took part in the operation (some 150 died, the rest were captured).

It was widely charged at the time that the failure of the operation had been due to a misreading by the CIA of the probability of a supporting spontaneous anti-Castro revolt within Cuba. This, certainly, was the view put about by White House insiders. According to the later accounts of CIA officials, however, CIA thinking on this question was all along ambiguous and divided, notably in that some CIA analysts believed that Castro was too firmly entrenched to be dislodged by any conceivable US intervention. It was in any case never supposed that any significant level of internal unrest could develop until the bridgehead had been firmly established, something which only adequate US military backing could have guaranteed.

Following the fiasco, an investigation of the CIA was put in the hands of former Army Chief of Staff Gen. Maxwell Taylor, a protagonist of non-conventional guerrilla warfare. Several months later, Allen Dulles, who had headed the CIA since 1953, quietly resigned, while in 1962 Richard Bissell, who as Deputy Director of Operations had prime operational responsibility at the CIA for the Bay of Pigs, was moved out and replaced by Richard Helms. The CIA was not fundamentally restructured, however. No one in the Kennedy administration resigned, although—perhaps because—ultimate responsibility for the bungling of the operation had lain with the White House.

Kennedy's failure at the Bay of Pigs undoubtedly encouraged the Soviet government to press home its advantage in Cuba, a process which culminated in the Cuban missiles crisis the following year. The CIA diverted its anti-Castro planning into equally ineffectual assassination plots against the Cuban leader, activities which some have believed led indirectly to the assassination of President Kennedy in November 1963 (see *John F. Kennedy Assassination Affair 1963–79*, below).

FJH

Soblen Affair (1962)

Robert Soblen, New York psychiatrist and convicted spy.
Jack Soble, Soblen's brother and fellow spy.

The flight from the USA in 1962 of Dr Robert Soblen after conviction on espionage charges precipitated a three-cornered international incident, involving the USA, Israel and Britain, which was resolved only by Soblen's suicide.

Soblen, a Lithuanian-born Jew who had become a psychiatrist at New York hospital, was arrested on Nov. 29, 1960, on charges of having conspired to steal US defence secrets for the Soviet Union during and after World War II. Three years earlier his younger brother Jack (known as Soble), Jack's wife Myra Soble, and an associate called Jacob Albam, had pleaded guilty and been sentenced to prison terms on similar charges, but sufficient evidence to bring charges against Soblen had not been found at that time.

Soblen was said to have spied for the Soviet Union with his brother in Europe before the war. He came to the USA (with Jack and other family members) in 1941 under the name Ruvelis Sobelevicius, and took citizenship in 1947. Soble and Soblen apparently concentrated their wartime espionage activity on gathering information on the Office of Strategic Services (OSS), the predecessor of the CIA. At his trial, the principal witness was his brother Jack, who was serving a seven-year term arising from his 1957 conviction. On Aug. 7, 1961, Soblen was sentenced to life imprisonment, although he was suffering from leukemia and was considered unlikely to live more than a year. On June 25, 1962, the day on which the US Supreme Court refused to review his conviction, Soblen jumped bail and fled to Israel on the passport of a dead brother, Beras Sobolevicius. In a letter to the *New York Times* on June 29, he claimed he had been convicted on the evidence of a psychotic (Jack Soble) and an informer, Mrs Johanna Koenen Beker.

A remarkable aspect of the case was that Soblen had based his unsuccessful appeal against conviction on the argument that the US government had kept from the defence knowledge of the true identity and whereabouts of Dr. Hans Hirschfeld, a German refugee employed by the OSS in 1943–45 who was said to have passed information to Soblen. The prosecution had said it did not know where Hirschfeld was, but since the trial he had been identified as a close associate of Willy Brandt, then Chief Burgomaster of West Berlin (and later West German Chancellor). Hirschfeld denied the allegations.

Soblen was expelled from Israel on July 1, 1962 (the Israeli government surviving motions of no confidence on the issue in the *Knesset*), but stabbed himself on board the aircraft taking him to the USA and was disembarked in London. The British government turned down his application for political asylum, and there followed a complex international legal wrangle. Britain demanded that Israel should return Soblen to the USA on board a flight of its national airline El Al, on which he had arrived, a demand which the Israeli government—facing domestic pressures from the left-wing parties and those who advocated an unrestricted right of return to Israel for all Jews—would not concede. Britain, conversely, would not allow Soblen to be carried by El Al to any country other than the USA. Faced with Israel's unrelenting non-co-operation, the British government ordered the deportation of Soblen on board a US airliner, but on his way to London airport on Sept. 6, Soblen was found to be suffering from barbiturate poisoning. He died five days later.

FJH

John F. Kennedy Assassination Affair (1963–79)

Fidel Castro, Cuban President.
John Connally, Governor of Texas.
Jesse Curry, Dallas Chief of Police.
Sam Giancana, Mafia boss.
J. Edgar Hoover, Director of the FBI.
Lyndon B. Johnson, Kennedy's Vice-President, US President (1963–69).
John F. Kennedy, US President (1961–63).
Yuri Nosenko, Soviet defector.
Lee Harvey Oswald, Kennedy's presumed assassin.
Marina Oswald, Lee Harvey Oswald's wife.
Jack Ruby, Lee Oswald's killer.
J. D. Tippit, Dallas police officer presumed killed by Oswald.
Earl Warren, Chief Justice of the United States.
Abraham Zapruder, bystander who filmed the Kennedy assassination.

Little is certain about the assassination of President John F. Kennedy other than the place and time of the event itself: Dealey Plaza, Dallas, Texas, Nov. 22, 1963. Lee Harvey Oswald, the man charged with Kennedy's murder, was himself shot and killed on Nov. 24 by Jack Leon Ruby while being transferred from Dallas police headquarters. No one has ever been convicted of involvement in Kennedy's murder (or, other than Ruby, in that of Oswald). The new President, Lyndon B. Johnson, appointed a special seven-member commission under Chief Justice Earl Warren of the US Supreme Court to investigate the assassination, but the Warren

Commission's report, presented in September 1964, has widely come to be seen as being deficient to a greater or lesser degree.

What the Warren Commission said

The principal findings of the Warren Commission were that President Kennedy was shot and killed (and Governor John Connally of Texas, also travelling in the presidential limousine, wounded) by Lee Harvey Oswald, a 24-year-old ex-Marine; that there was no evidence that Oswald was involved with anyone else in a plot to kill the President; and that Jack Ruby had shot Oswald without accomplices on a momentary impulse, and had had no previous connection with Oswald. The report was agreed unanimously in whole by the Commission, whose other members were Senator Richard Russell of Georgia, Senator John Sherman Cooper of Kentucky, Representative Hale Boggs of Louisiana, Representative Gerald R. Ford of Michigan, Allen W. Dulles (a former head of the CIA) and John J. McCloy (a former disarmament adviser to President Kennedy and former President of the World Bank).

The Commission concluded that Oswald had fired on the presidential motorcade, using a rifle which he had purchased under the name of A. Hidell from a mail order company in March 1963, from a position at the south-east corner window on the sixth floor of the Texas School Book Depository. This provided a perfect vantage point to overlook the route of the presidential motorcade as it moved away from the Depository along Elm Street across Dealey Plaza at just after 12.30 pm. (The President rode in an open car without the protection of running boards carrying secret servicemen.) The Commission found that the "weight of the evidence" indicated that Oswald had fired three shots (three spent cartridges identified as having been fired from his rifle being found at the "sniper's nest" on the sixth floor) and concluded that two shots had hit the President. The first had hit him in the base of the neck, exited through his throat and then inflicted injuries on Governor Connally (who recovered after surgery), sitting immediately in front of him. This bullet would not have proved fatal to the President, but the second hit entered his skull at the rear causing catastrophic damage. Kennedy was rushed to Parkland Hospital, where a faint heartbeat was detected, but he had lost much of the brain matter on the right-hand side of his head and there was no possibility of recovery. He was pronounced dead at 1.00 pm and Vice-President Lyndon Johnson, also present in the motorcade but in a different car, was sworn in as President at 2.38 pm on board the presidential jet Air Force One as it stood waiting to fly back to Washington. Also on that flight back to Washington were the President's body, en route to autopsy at the National Naval Medical Centre at Bethesda (the Secret Service had insisted on the body being taken back to Washington immediately), and Kennedy's wife, Jacqueline, who had been sitting beside her husband at the time he was shot.

The situation at Dealey Plaza was inevitably one of extreme confusion after the shots were fired, a confusion which would be reflected in the differing eyewitness accounts of what had happened. A police motorcycle patrolman, Marrion L. Baker, believing the shots had come from the Book Depository, entered the building and within less than two minutes of the shots being fired challenged a man on the second floor. Patrolman Baker let this man go, however, when building superintendent Roy Truly identified him as an employee at the Depository, Lee Harvey Oswald. According to the Warren Commission's account, Oswald then left the Depository by the front door, and proceeded by foot, bus and taxi to his lodgings in a rooming house at 1026 N. Beckley Avenue in the Oak Cliff section of the city, where he arrived at 1.00 pm. He went out again within a few minutes and at 1.15 pm, at a point nearly one mile from his lodgings, was approached by a police officer, J. D. Tippit, as a man fitting the general description of a suspect being sought in the Kennedy shooting. Oswald drew a revolver, however, and shot Officer Tippit dead. Half an hour later, after his retreat from the scene had been watched by several witnesses, he was arrested after a struggle inside the Texas Theatre motion picture house, still carrying the revolver used to kill Officer Tippit. At 7.10 pm he was charged with the murder of Officer Tippit and later the same night with that of President Kennedy.

Shortly after 2.00 pm on the day of the assassination it was discovered at police headquarters that the only one of the 15 Book Depository warehouse employees who had not been located (the building having been sealed by 12.40 pm) was one and the same as the man arrested for the Tippit shooting. At 3.00 pm on Nov. 22 the police visited the house in a Dallas suburb where Oswald's wife Marina was living apart from him, and discovered that a rifle which she knew he kept in the garage there was missing. By this time a rifle, a 1940 Italian-made 6.5 mm Mannlicher-Carcano, had been found hidden on the sixth floor at the Depository, and by the next day the FBI had clear evidence that this was a rifle bought by Oswald under a false name from a mail order company. Under interrogation Oswald denied any involvement in the murders of President Kennedy or Officer Tippit, said he had been eating lunch at the time of the Kennedy assassination, and denied that he owned a rifle, claiming that a photograph of him holding one had been faked. He also refused to answer questions about a selective service card found on him in the fictitious name of Alek J. Hidell, the name that he had used as president of a "Fair Play for Cuba" committee branch in New Orleans and to purchase his rifle by mail order. Within hours of his arrest the media were carrying reports detailing Oswald's past activities supporting Cuba's Communist regime and disclosing that he had once defected to the Soviet Union.

During the nearly 48 hours that Oswald was held at Dallas police headquarters, a state bordering on chaos prevailed in the building, which swarmed with pressmen and the curious. No contemporaneous tapes, transcript or even notes were made of the 12 hours of interrogation of Oswald carried out by local detectives, the FBI and the Secret Service. Amid the melée, Oswald in fact spent most of his time undisturbed by interrogators; information was disclosed to reporters, some of it wrong, in the course of impromptu press conferences in the corridors; and Dallas Police Chief Jesse Curry brought Oswald himself before a midnight press conference, those present including Jack Ruby, a 52-year-old Dallas night club operator. Apparently concerned at the lack of security in the building, Curry decided to remove Oswald to the county jail, and a large crowd of newsmen and others gathered to see the suspect escorted from the basement of police headquarters at 11.20 am on Sunday Nov. 24. From the crowd emerged Jack Ruby, who killed Oswald with one revolver shot to the abdomen in front of a live television audience of millions.

The Warren Commission provided an account of Oswald's life story. His father had died two months before his birth and his childhood had been unsettled, including a stay as a small child in an orphanage. Oswald's mother, Marguerite, remarried twice after his father's death, and a jury found that she had physically abused her third husband; she too was a drifter, having been dismissed from one job after another. As he entered his teenage years, Oswald became a chronic truant from school and needed psychiatric counselling, a social worker describing him as "seriously detached", "withdrawn", and "emotionally starved" and believing that his mother did not care for him. At the age of 17 in 1956 he joined the Marines, where he was court-martialled twice, for possessing an unregistered pistol and profanity towards an officer. He frequently expressed Marxist sympathies to his fellow Marines and was regarded as a "loner". In September 1959 he left the Marines at his own request and on Oct. 16 he arrived in Russia on a six-day visa, immediately applying for Soviet citizenship. On Oct. 21 he was ordered to leave the country but slashed his wrist in an apparent attempt at suicide. On Oct. 31, after his release from hospital, he told officials at the US Embassy in Moscow that he was a Marxist and wished to become a Soviet citizen. He was subsequently permitted by the Soviet authorities to stay on a year-by-year basis, and on April 30, 1961, he married a Russian girl, Marina Nikolaevna Prusakova, whom he had met working as a labourer in Minsk. Oswald then began to lobby to return to the USA, and in January 1962 wrote to Senator John Tower of Texas "beseeching" him to "raise the question of the holding by the Soviet Union of a citizen of the United States against his will and expressed desires". It was established that Oswald had never formally renounced US citizenship, and in June 1962 he, Marina and their baby daughter came to America with financial assistance from the State Department.

Back in the USA, Oswald drifted from place to place and job to job, spending periods apart from his wife and baby. He was interviewed twice by the FBI concerning the reasons for his stay in the Soviet Union, but revealed little. The Oswalds meanwhile made contacts in the Russian exile community in Dallas-Fort Worth, which provided them with material assistance out of sympathy for Marina, who spoke no English; they were also befriended by Ruth Paine, a Communist sympathizer who was chairman of an "East–West Contacts Committee". On April 6, 1963, Oswald lost his job with a photography firm in Dallas, and a few days later took an unsuccessful potshot with his newly-acquired rifle at Maj.-Gen. Edwin Walker (Resigned, US Army), a prominent local member of the right-wing John Birch Society. On April 24 he left for New Orleans where he then lived for five months, being joined by Marina in May. While in the city he formed a pro-Castro "Fair Play for Cuba" committee, was interviewed twice on radio, and was arrested once after a scuffle when he was distributing pamphlets. At the same time, the Warren Commission reported, he sought unsuccessfully to join an anti-Castro group. On Sept. 23 Marina and the baby travelled back with Ruth Paine from New Orleans to the Paine home in Irving (a Dallas suburb), where Marina remained until Nov. 22. Oswald himself, meanwhile, travelled to Mexico where on

Sept. 27 he visited the Soviet and Cuban embassies, but was denied visas to travel to either country. He then took lodgings in Dallas (under a false name), visiting Marina (who gave birth to a second daughter on Oct. 20) at the Paine home at weekends and starting work at the Book Depository on Oct. 16. On Nov. 21 he spent the night at the Paine home, travelling into work with a fellow Book Depository employee, Buell Wesley Frazier. Oswald was carrying a package which he told Frazier contained curtain rods but the Warren Commission said held his rifle, which he had kept hidden in a blanket in a garage at the Paine home.

In its detailed account of his life, the Commission portrayed a confused drifter, unhappy in both the USA and the USSR. No "definitive determination" of his motives could be made, but the Commission thought the factors which may have been involved were: (i) "his deep-seated resentment of all authority"; (ii) "his inability to enter into meaningful relationships with people"; (iii) "his urge to try to find a place in history"; (iv) his "capacity for violence, as evidenced by his attempt to kill Gen. Walker"; (v) "his avowed commitment to Marxism and Communism, as he understood the terms and developed his own interpretation of them."

The Commission made no assessment of the motives of Jack Ruby on the grounds that his appeal against conviction for the murder of Oswald was pending, but did see fit to note that Ruby had told the Commission that he had done what he did to spare Jacqueline Kennedy the ordeal of returning to Dallas for Oswald's trial. The Commission found no evidence of any previous connection between Ruby and Oswald which would supply another motive.

Criticism of the Warren Commission

The initial reaction to the release of the Warren Commission report in September 1964 was overwhelmingly favourable. Apart from a fringe of conspiracy theorists—who variously took the view that Oswald was a tool of the Cubans and Russians, of anti-Castro Cuban exiles, of extreme right-wing Dallas businessmen, or even an innocent look-alike for a "second Oswald", perhaps a KGB agent who did the killing and then vanished—the prevailing view was one of relief that the killing of the President, however tragic, had been an isolated event. 1966, however, brought the publication of two apparently well-documented books (Mark Lane's *Rush to Judgment* and Edward J. Epstein's *Inquest: The Warren Commission and the Establishment of Truth*) which questioned practically every aspect of the Warren Commission's work and became massive bestsellers. In the following year New Orleans District Attorney Jim Garrison began a sensational and irresponsible probe into the assassination, this culminating in the indictment but subsequent acquittal of a local businessman, Clay Shaw, for involvement in a supposed conspiracy to kill Kennedy.

As the critical literature piled up, two things became apparent. The first was that no theory was too far-fetched, devious or downright scurrilous not to be able to find a publisher. The second was that the Warren Commission, in presenting the case as cut-and-dried, had chosen to take some evidence as fact while emphatically—indeed arbitrarily—rejecting contradictory evidence. Some witnesses' testimony had been accepted at face value, while that of others (including evidence from police officers) was disregarded; and in some cases parts of an individual witness's testimony had been accepted and other parts which did not fit the Warren Commission's interpretation brushed aside as mistaken. In particular, the Commission ignored any evidence which might have suggested that Oswald did not act alone, including statements that he had been seen being picked up by a station wagon behind the Depository 15 minutes after the Kennedy shooting. By the late 1960s practically every detail of the Warren Commission's account of the affair had been attacked from one quarter or another, even including the belief that Oswald had killed Tippit, the offence for which he was separately arrested in the first place.

There was in particular unrelenting criticism of the Commission's reconstruction of the few seconds of the Kennedy assassination itself. The Commission accepted that the "preponderance of the evidence, in particular the three spent cartridges", was that three shots had been fired, and on the basis of a home movie 8 mm film taken by a bystander, Abraham Zapruder, determined that the elapsed time from the first to the last shot could have been no more than 5.6 seconds. This was the interval between the moment Kennedy emerged into Oswald's line of fire from behind the cover provided by an oak tree (frame 210) to the point on the film (frame 313) where the horrific effects of the bullet to Kennedy's head were seen, the film running at 18.3 frames per second. Test firings by FBI marksmen with Oswald's bolt-action rifle, however, showed that it could not have been fired with any degree of accuracy three times in the elapsed time, leading the Commission to the conclusion that one bullet was fired off wildly, missing completely.

Even more difficult for the Commission was the problem that the Zapruder film clearly showed the President reacting in pain on frame 225 (when he emerged from behind a traffic sign shielding him from Zapruder's view since frame 210) but Connally showing no reaction until frame 236 at earliest. Knowing that it was physically impossible for Oswald to have scored two hits in the elapsed time between frame 210 and frame 236 (which was about 1.5 seconds, whereas the FBI had found that Oswald's rifle could be fired no more quickly than with an interval of 2.25 seconds between shots), the Commission concluded that Governor Connally had suffered a delayed reaction on being hit by the same bullet which hit the President's neck and exited through his throat. It was a theory with a number of obvious weaknesses: Governor Connally's emphatic insistence that he was hit by a separate bullet; the lack of major damage to a bullet found on Connally's stretcher at Parkland which the Commission believed was the one which had passed through two bodies; and the somewhat devious trajectory (itself much-debated) that a single bullet would have had to follow to cause the wounds that it supposedly did. It was also, however, a theory which seemed absolutely central to the Commission's contention that there was only one gunman. (A possible alternative advanced in subsequent literature, is that Oswald had shot first through branches of the oak tree, which by late November was substantially bare of foliage. In this case, he could have fired as early as the Zapruder 186th frame, creating a total elapsed time of seven seconds, which FBI marksmen had shown was sufficient for Oswald to have taken aim and fired three good shots, and for him to have hit Kennedy in the neck, then Connally, and then Kennedy in the head, in sequence. It is also possible that one of the three cartridges found at the "sniper's nest" had not contained a bullet and that Oswald fired only two shots.)

The apparent weakness of the Commission's "single bullet" theory, as it became known, strengthened speculation that one bullet had actually hit the President from in front and to his right. This was encouraged by eyewitness accounts, of varying degrees of coherence, suggesting that there had been shooting from the area of the so-called Grassy Knoll, a gentle elevation which abutted Elm Street ahead and to the right of the President at the moment of the shots and was topped by a picket fence well camouflaged by bushes and trees. Of 75 witnesses who reported hearing shots, 39 thought at least one had come from the Grassy Knoll area. It was also encouraged by the fact that the initial statements of the doctors at Parkland Hospital spoke of an entry wound in the President's throat, this being redefined as an exit would only after the autopsy at Bethesda Naval Hospital (no autopsy was carried out at Parkland). Furthermore, there were rumours that the original Bethesda autopsy findings had been rewritten. Speculation on this score was not lessened by the seeming indifference with which the Commission accepted both the admission of the presiding doctor at the Bethesda autopsy that he had burned his original notes and the non-availability of autopsy X-rays and photographs (which were held back from the Commission by the Kennedy family and not released until 1966, although Connally's X-rays and medical photographs were published by the Commission). Against this background, suggestions were made that there may have been a conspiracy to disguise from the American people evidence that there was more than one gunman, or even that the shots had not been fired by Oswald at all.

Much of the debate was highly technical, a mix of the scientific and the pseudo-scientific, and of shrewd investigation and crackpot theorizing. What the critics lacked, however, was any strong plausible alternative scenario to the one provided by the Warren Commission. If Oswald had not acted alone, or was not to blame at all, then who were the guilty men? There were many rumours that Ruby, Oswald and Tippit, far from being total strangers, were well acquainted with each other, but what did these rumours mean? The Commission had, after all, received every assistance from the FBI and the CIA in determining that there had been no conspiracy. Those who argued otherwise were in effect arguing against the massed ranks of the US government.

During the 1970s the picture began to change. In 1975 the Church Committee investigation of the CIA by the US Senate (see *CIA "Family Jewels" Affair, 1974–76*, below) revealed that from 1960 the CIA had contacts with Mafia chieftains Sam Giancana, Santos Trafficante and John Rosselli aimed at plotting the assassination of Castro, with Robert Maheu of the Hughes Corporation (a figure who would reappear in the Watergate affair—see below) acting as a go-between. So close were the ties between elements of the government and organized crime during the Kennedy administration that John Kennedy shared a girlfriend (Judith Campbell Exner, apparently introduced to him in 1960 by Frank Sinatra) with Mafia boss Sam Giancana, despite the fact that his brother Robert (Bobby) Kennedy (the Attorney General) had made his political name as chief counsel to the McClellan

Committee's organized crime investigation in the 1950s. In 1975 Exner denied that Kennedy had known of her Mafia ties, but in a February 1988 article in *People* magazine she said that she had arranged face-to-face meetings between Kennedy and Giancana in 1960–61 and had acted as a courier. In mid-1962, however, John Kennedy under pressure from Bobby and FBI Director J. Edgar Hoover, ended his relationship with Exner and then, after the Cuban missiles crisis of October 1962, contacts with the Mafia were terminated and US backing for anti-Castro groups was scaled down. CIA plans to eliminate Castro continued, however, right until the time of Kennedy's assassination, and there is evidence that Castro was well aware of this.

What this all meant was far from clear. On the one hand, it clearly established an incentive for Castro to have set Kennedy's assassination in motion. On the other hand, a motive seemed to be established for the Mafia, for after being courted by the government all contacts were dropped, and Bobby Kennedy kept up his campaign against organized crime. That Bobby was a hated figure among Mafia figures, and that he was seen as deriving all his power from the fact that his brother was President, was well known. Furthermore, links had developed between the Mafia—desperate to get back its lucrative Havana casino business abolished by Castro—and anti-Castro exiles in the USA. Many of these exiles believed they had been betrayed by Kennedy in April 1961 when he refused to provide air cover for the CIA-planned invasion of Cuba by exiles at the Bay of Pigs, thus sentencing those involved to a slaughter. After the Cuban missile crisis, moreover, the Kennedy administration had put increasing pressure on the exile community in the USA, breaking up its military training camps and making it clear that thenceforth its hot war with Cuba would become a cold one.

Had Kennedy then been assassinated by an alliance of anti-Castro exiles and the Mafia? That the CIA would not have wanted this possibility to be looked at by the Warren Commission was clear enough, for not only would its own operations have been severely compromised, but its plots might have been seen as a primary cause of the President's death. In such circumstances, the fact that ex-CIA director Allen Dulles had been a Commission member appeared of obvious significance. Jack Ruby's role in shooting Oswald also seemed to fall into place on such a theory, for Ruby was a relatively small-time underworld figure with connections to more powerful Mafia bosses. As a local man, sufficiently friendly with local police to have easy access to police headquarters, and as a man who knew that he was in any case dying of cancer, Ruby seemed an appropriate candidate to act as the Mafia's executioner. At least a dozen individuals have claimed that they saw Ruby and Oswald together, at Ruby's Carousel Club or elsewhere, in the months before the assassination.

At the same time, some of the new evidence could also be seen as pointing back to the Soviet Union. Through congressional probes and the release of evidence under the Freedom of Information Act, it became known that at the beginning of February 1964 Yuri Ivanovich Nosenko, a KGB official under cover as a member of the Soviet team at the Geneva disarmament talks and who had had contacts with the CIA since 1962, had defected to the USA with the amazing information that he had personally supervised the

KGB file on Oswald, and that he knew that Oswald had never been a Soviet agent. This confirmed the documentation on Oswald's period in Russia provided by the Soviet Union a week after Kennedy's death. Nosenko's claims pitched different elements of the intelligence community against each other. Hoover, desperate that the FBI should not be proved to have been negligent in its monitoring of Oswald, eagerly accepted Nosenko's claim that Oswald had been seen as too unreliable to be of use, a theory which tied in exactly with the Hoover line that Oswald was a lone crackpot whose action could not have been foreseen. To others, however, including the CIA's Soviet Russia and counterintelligence divisions, Nosenko seemed unreliable and possibly to have been sent by the Russians precisely to establish their innocence in the assassination. The conflict within the intelligence community was never finally resolved, although Nosenko, after being kept for three years under hostile interrogation in a windowless room, was finally allowed to take up a new identity in the USA.

In September 1976, after disclosure by the Church Committee of the CIA–Mafia plots, the House Select Committee on Assassinations was set up to look at the killings of John Kennedy and also those of Bobby Kennedy and Martin Luther King in 1968. The report of the Assassinations Committee, issued on March 29, 1979, in many respects followed the conclusions of the Warren Commission 15 years earlier. Like the Warren Commission, and against the views of many writers on the subject in the intervening years, the Committee, on the basis of exhaustive scientific studies using computer enhancement and other techniques not available in the 1960s, concluded that Kennedy had been hit by two bullets fired by Oswald from the sixth floor of the School Book Depository; that the first bullet had also hit Connally; and that the second had fatally wounded Kennedy in the head. The Committee also presented research to explain as a neuromuscular reaction the apparent initial powerful backward movement (i.e. in the approximate direction of the Book Depository) of Kennedy's head after the second bullet hit. Ever since the Zapruder film (hitherto known to the public only from stills) had graphically revealed this movement when shown on television in 1975, there had been much speculation that the second bullet had been fired from behind the picket fence on the Grassy Knoll, and not by Oswald. However, whether the initial movement of Kennedy's head was actually backward, as the film appeared to show, has itself been a matter of controversy. Computerized analyses of the critical frames 312 and 313 have indicated that there was in fact an initial violent forward movement which is not apparent to the viewer of the film because it was faster than the speed of the film and camera.

The Assassinations Committee believed that there was convincing evidence that Oswald had killed both Kennedy and Officer Tippit. Where it fundamentally differed from the Warren Commission was in its view that there had been a conspiracy. On the basis of highly sophisticated acoustical analysis of a dictabelt recording of sounds picked up by a police radio microphone, the Committee came to the view that four shots had been fired that day, three by Oswald and one from the Grassy Knoll area. This bullet, however, had missed the Kennedy limousine entirely.

Whether the recording of the sounds heard in Dealey Plaza does in fact show four shots is of critical significance, because the elapsed time between the supposed Grassy Knoll shot and the closest to it of Oswald's shots was such that all four shots could not have been fired from Oswald's rifle. For their part, the Dallas police maintained that the sounds on the dictabelt recording were not even from Dealey Plaza but had been picked up by a motorcycle in the Dallas Trade Mart area, more than two miles away. As for the authenticity of the analysis made of that recording (if the recording was indeed from the time and place of the assassination), it is impossible for anyone untrained in such techniques, and who has not seen the evidence, to come to any judgment, other than to note that the report of the scientific analysts spoke in terms of probabilities rather than certainties. But this, of course, has always been the nub of many of the dilemmas associated with the assassination. Amid the masses of evidence there are bits and pieces to give a degree of support to innumerable interpretations. Even the most disinterested and judicious observer faces the problem that many of the controversies revolve around very technical questions—autopsy evidence, ballistics evidence, photographic and acoustics analysis—on which it is difficult for the uninitiated observer to express an opinion.

This was a problem which also confronted the Warren Commission, however upright the motives of its members. Most of the Commission's work was done by junior staff members, few of whom had significant knowledge in the complex evidentiary questions involved. The illustrious members of the Commission, and the most senior members of the staff, in many cases involved themselves with the inquiry with a deplorable superficiality, with little sacrifice of private pursuits to the public service. In the circumstances, the Commission relied heavily on the work presented to it by the FBI. Whatever the motives of the FBI—and there have been strong suggestions that it did not wish to see exploration of its own ties to Oswald and that it naturally preferred to have the case regarded as "solved" rather than expose its own inadequacies in protecting the President—it reached its own verdict in remarkably short order, giving the Commission its report within a fortnight of the assassination. Indeed, as early as the day after the assassination, Hoover told Lyndon Johnson that Oswald had been a sole assassin. In relying on investigations by the secret service, the FBI and the Dallas police, the Commission put its trust in the very people who had failed to protect the President's life and to discover a conspiracy if there had been one. Thus the FBI was itself asked to investigate reports from Texas law enforcement officials that Oswald had been a paid FBI informer.

Furthermore, the Commission showed a remarkable indifference in its own work to the unavailability, inadequacy or disappearance of much evidence, including the failure of the Dallas police to provide any contemporaneous record of more than 12 hours of interrogation of Oswald, the disappearance of autopsy, X-ray and photographic evidence, and the admission that the original Bethesda autopsy notes had been burned. This was compounded by the failure of the Commission to scrutinize witnesses under the adversarial procedure used in a court of law, the absence of public hearings, and the interviewing of many witnesses by staffers without a single Commission member in attendance. Furthermore, internal discussions among the Warren Commission staff are now known to have demonstrated considerably less certainty on many points than appeared from the final report. It is clear that there was great pressure to wrap up matters in a conclusive manner before the 1964 election, and no conclusion other than that Oswald had been the lone assassin would have made this possible.

It is, moreover, fairly clear that this was very much the preferred conclusion at the highest levels of the government. Those who knew of the Castro assassination plots—and one of the Commission members, Allen Dulles, most certainly did, because he had participated in planning them—had no wish for Kennedy's death to seem a consequence of their bungled plotting. Nor was it desirable for anything to be seen of the ties between Kennedy, the CIA and the Mafia. And, of course, there was little desire to make much of Oswald's Soviet connections, for any public belief that Kennedy had been killed by a Soviet agent could have led to calamitous consequences. When Johnson appointed the Warren Commission, he wanted the public to be calmed, not aroused to indignation or panic. Earl Warren later confirmed that Johnson had prevailed on him to take on the job of chairing the inquiry by saying that it needed to be headed by someone of his stature who could lay to rest wild rumours which threatened international stability, and that if the public became aroused against Castro and the Soviet Union there might be war.

In the 1970s, in contrast, Watergate and the Church Committee hearings established a widespread perception that there was a conspiracy around every corner; the theorizings of fringe "assassination buffs" came into the mainstream, to the extent that there became almost a presupposition in favour of there having been a conspiracy to kill Kennedy. All manner of theories were given currency. David Lifton, in *Best Evidence: Disguise and Deception in the Assassination of John F. Kennedy* (1980), a massive tome packed with pseudo-scientific data and published by a major house (Macmillan), claimed that Kennedy's head was operated on after his death to conceal the fact that he was shot from in front, and that this had been done by a murky conspiracy at the highest levels of the government. Perhaps the most distasteful in its consequences was the claim of Michael Eddowes, in *The Oswald Files*, that Oswald's identity had been taken while he was in the Soviet Union by a Soviet agent. This led to the exhumation in October 1981 of Oswald's body at the request of Marina Oswald Porter (by this time remarried), and the conclusive establishment through dental and other records that the body in Oswald's coffin was that of none other than Lee Harvey Oswald.

That the Warren Commission understated the real uncertainties of the assassination is beyond doubt. It is equally clear that things are now known about the FBI, the CIA and the Mafia which were not taken account of by the Warren Commission and which may put the affair in a different context. But does this mean that the Commission was wrong in its basic conclusions? The Commission strung together a series of probabilities and drew from them conclusions which it presented as certainties. In 1964 the pressure was to produce a final verdict leaving nothing to doubt, to close the affair, but with the passage of time that approach can easily seem to have involved misrepresentation to fit a preconceived judgment. Any more ambiguous judgment in 1964 could have had grave implications for the conduct of the US intelligence agencies and for US relations with Cuba's sponsor,

the Soviet Union; there was in that sense a sort of political inevitability
about the verdict. The unfortunate consequence of this, however, is that
the bending of facts, the smoothing out of rough edges, to remove all shade
of doubt, came to be seen as outright fraud.

When the House Select Committee on Assassinations came to review
the evidence, it agreed with the Warren Commission on many key points.
It differed principally in its conclusion that Kennedy's death had been the
result of a conspiracy. The evidence for this was thin, however, based on
an analysis of a recording of questionable authenticity which in any case
left unexplained why the supposed marksman on the Grassy Knoll had fired
off only one shot when Oswald had managed three, had missed from much
closer range than the Book Depository when Oswald had scored two hits,
and why no evidence of such a bullet was ever found. In the late 1970s,
against the background of the Church Committee revelations, there was
a natural disposition to find signs of a conspiracy—just as in 1964 the
Warren Commission had been disposed not to find one—yet the evidence
produced was thin indeed. The Committee absolved the governments of
the Soviet Union and Cuba primarily on the basis that the assassination
of Kennedy would have involved too great a risk, yet ignored the logic
of this conclusion in favouring the view that the President was killed by
anti-Castro zealots in combination with the Mafia, whose position would
presumably have become desperate had their plot been uncovered.

In this respect the Warren Commission's approach was arguably the
more consistent. After his return from the Soviet Union, Oswald lived
a life which has invited suspicion at every turn. He corresponded with
Trotskyist groups, but also had contacts with the Soviet embassies in
Washington and Mexico. He set up a "Fair Play for Cuba" committee
branch, but also had contacts with known opponents of the Castro regime.
He lied incessantly to those around him, disappeared for periods, changed
address constantly, used forged documentation. According to the Warren
Commission, all this activity ultimately added up to very little. Oswald was
an inadequate personality in whose thought processes and actions there
may not have been the logic which investigators have constantly sought
to find. It may be too that this was what those KGB and FBI officials who
spoke to Oswald also concluded: that he was a figure of little consequence,
reliability or value. By an irony of history, however, one action of his
in Dallas meant that his whole life story in its every detail and random
action would take on a significance seemingly demanding the explanation
of a deeper pattern. If this is true, then the FBI—and the KGB—had
every reason to distance themselves entirely from Oswald, so that their
own connection with him, however incidental, should not seem to assume
dreadful proportions. Whether sent by the KGB or not, what Nosenko said
on his defection was exactly what the KGB would have wanted to be heard,
just as it was exactly what J. Edgar Hoover wanted to hear.

Whether the truth would be any clearer had Oswald lived might be
doubted. In his time at Dallas police station Oswald lied continuously, and
told lies— such as that he did not own a rifle—that were easily disproved.
This was not much like a man acting out a well-laid part in a cover story who
might have been broken with time, but much more like a man for whom
the boundaries between truth and fiction and logic and illogic were not well

marked. The case of Jack Ruby might also be borne in mind. Ruby was tried and convicted in 1964 for Oswald's murder. At his trial he maintained that he had killed Oswald in a moment of blind rage (and there was substantial evidence that he was a man of violent impulses) and he never changed his story in numerous interviews with lawyers and investigators until his death—in Parkland Hospital—of cancer on Jan. 3, 1967, while awaiting a re-trial. This has done nothing whatsoever, however, to dampen down speculation that Ruby killed Oswald to silence him. Why, it has been asked, was it that Oswald shot Tippit only two blocks from Ruby's house? Why did so many people who had or may have had knowledge of a possible Ruby connection with both Tippit and Oswald meet strange deaths within a few years of the assassination? Could it be mere coincidence that the one citizen of Dallas who felt such outrage that he chose to kill the President's assassin was also someone with Mafia connections? As with so many aspects of the affair, the questions outnumber the answers and any individual's assessment will come down to a broad judgment based on a balance of probabilities.

In a press conference at Dallas police headquarters, Lee Harvey Oswald told newsmen that he was "just a patsy" (a "patsy" for whom he did not say). If this was the truth, then the most dramatic single event in American history has never yet been explained and guilty men went free. Probability, for all the murky and unresolved questions that have been raised over the years, still favours the Warren Commission conclusion that Oswald killed Kennedy acting alone. Between probability and certainty, however, stands a gulf which may never be bridged.

FJH

Gulf of Tonkin Affair (1964–71)

Lyndon B. Johnson, President (1963–69).

In response to what the administration said had been attacks on two US destroyers (the *Maddox* and the *C. Turner Joy*) in the Gulf of Tonkin by North Vietnamese torpedo boats at the beginning of August 1964, US President Lyndon Johnson ordered the bombing of North Vietnamese torpedo boat bases and an oil storage depot. The action marked a key event in the escalation of US involvement in Vietnam, which had developed progressively since the French abandoned the country in the mid-1950s. It also came to be regarded as symbolic of the way in which the USA had become mired in Vietnam by military and White House decisions made without close scrutiny or control by Congress. A major consequence, in the atmosphere of disillusionment and defeatism regarding the war which prevailed in later years, was the passage of the 1973 War Powers Act, which sought to place limits on the President's powers to wage war without the approval of Congress.

President Johnson announced his retaliatory action on Aug. 4, 1964, and the next day sent to Congress a resolution calling for Congress to give him broad powers to "take all necessary measures" to prevent further aggression and to use armed force "as the President determines" to assist US allies in South-East Asia. The resolution was to have effect until "the President shall determine that the peace and security of the area is reasonably assured by international conditions", unless terminated by concurrent resolution of Congress. The resolution passed the House on Aug. 7 by 414 votes to nil and the Senate the same day by 88 votes to two. The two opposed senators were Wayne Morse (Oregon) and Ernest Gruening (Alaska), Morse criticizing its "blanket authority to wage war" and Gruening declaring that Vietnam was "not worth the life of a single American boy".

US officials stressed at the time that they had acted only in a limited way in response to unprovoked aggression. In the following years, however, Johnson frequently cited the Gulf of Tonkin resolution to justify the escalation of what was an undeclared war (the power to declare war being reserved to Congress under the Constitution). On Nov. 6, 1967, the majority of the Supreme Court refused to hear a case directly involving the constitutionality of the war, stating that it raised "political and military" issues beyond the Court's jurisdiction. In February 1968 the administration's version of the Tonkin incident itself came under question in the Senate Foreign Relations Committee (which included among its members several of the most prominent opponents of the administration's Vietnam policy, including its chairman, J. W. Fulbright). On that occasion, questions were raised as to whether the North Vietnamese attacks might have been provoked by coastal forays by South Vietnamese naval vessels provided by the USA, or by the US vessels having intruded into North Vietnamese territorial waters, and even whether they took place at all (neither destroyer having been hit).

On June 24, and again on July 10, 1970, the Senate voted to repeal the Gulf of Tonkin resolution, though the move had limited significance as President Richard Nixon, since taking office in January 1969, had asserted that he was continuing military operations under his authority as Commander-in-Chief, rather than under the authority of the Gulf of Tonkin resolution. Then, in 1971, the publication in the *New York Times* and other newspapers of the Defence Department's secret history of the war, generally known as the Pentagon Papers (see also *Pentagon Papers Affair, 1971–74*, below), clearly indicated that the attacks by North Vietnamese patrol boats which had led to the passage of the resolution had been the direct result of previous attacks on North Vietnam by South Vietnamese ships and US aircraft. The Papers raised the possibility that the Aug. 2 attack on the US destroyer *Maddox* had been a mistake by North Vietnamese torpedo boats looking for South Vietnamese vessels which had staged amphibious commando raids against two North Vietnamese islands on July 30; and that the Aug. 4 torpedo attacks on the *Maddox* and on the *C. Turner Joy* may never have happened at all. The Papers also seemed to show clearly that former Defence Secretary Robert McNamara had lied to the Senate at the time in saying the US Navy had been unaware of any South Vietnamese naval actions.

These revelations, set in the context of the broader disillusionment with the course of the Vietnam War, led to the passage of the War Powers Act in 1973 over Nixon's veto. Every President since Nixon has challenged the constitutionality of the Act (which requires the President to inform Congress on all occasions on which troops are introduced into combat zones, and to withdraw troops within 60 days unless otherwise authorised by Congress). Congress has only once attempted to enforce the legislation, in 1983, when US Marines were landed in Lebanon. On that occasion, Congress agreed to extend the deadline for compliance by 18 months and the Marines were then withdrawn by President Reagan before there was a showdown.

FJH

Adam Clayton Powell Affair (1967)

Rev. Adam Clayton Powell, Democratic representative for Harlem, New York (1944–67).

The decision of the House of Representatives in 1967 to refuse to seat the Rev. Adam Clayton Powell, the black Democratic representative for the Harlem district of New York, precipitated a bitter controversy in which the details of his financial improprieties became blurred in accusations of racial bias.

Powell, the pastor of the Abyssinian Baptist Church in Harlem, had entered Congress in 1944, becoming known for his opposition to racial discrimination and retaining great popularity with his electorate notwithstanding a luxurious lifestyle and allegations of tax evasion. Until the emergence of Martin Luther King, he was the best-known black American political leader. Since 1963, when he failed to pay damages of $156,000 awarded against him in a defamation suit, he had visited New York only while Congress was in session (when as a Congressman he could not be arrested in connection with a civil suit) and during recess on Sundays (when civil writs could not be served). Following conviction in New York of criminal contempt for failing to produce his financial records, he was declared a fugitive from justice on Nov. 23, 1966, liable to arrest whenever he returned to the state.

A report by the House Administration Committee on Jan. 3, 1967, found that Powell as chairman of the Education and Labour Committee had abused his position to provide pleasure trips for himself and others at the public expense and had kept his wife on the committee payroll at $20,578 a year without her doing any work. On Jan. 10 the House voted not to permit Powell to take his seat until he had been investigated by a special committee.

On Feb. 23, 1967, this committee recommended that Powell should be permitted to take his seat, but should be censured, lose his seniority, and be fined $40,000. On March 1, however, the full House rejected the report and by 307 votes (134 Democrats, 173 Republicans) to 116 (105 Democrats, 11 Republicans) decided to exclude Powell. The decision was bitterly resented by many black leaders, who argued that many white congressmen had behaved similarly without suffering such consequences. No one elected to Congress had been excluded since Victor Berger, a Socialist convicted under the Espionage Act at the time of World War I, who was finally seated in 1923 after a Supreme Court ruling. On April 11, 1967, Powell ran again for his Harlem seat and was re-elected with nearly seven times as many votes as the Republican candidate, but the House refused to seat him. Thereafter, Powell was a marginal figure in national black politics, having failed entirely to adapt his idiosyncratic style to the different mood and temper of the civil rights movement (or to accept his displacement as a national figure by a new generation of black leaders). He lived mostly on the resort island of Bimini, and died on April 4, 1972, aged 63.

FJH

Martin Luther King Assassination Affair (1968–79)

Martin Luther King, Black Civil Rights Leader.
James Earl Ray, his assassin.

The Rev. Dr Martin Luther King (39), the leading figure in the black civil rights movement in the 1960s and Nobel Peace Prize winner in 1964, was shot and killed by a single bullet while standing on a balcony of the Lorraine Hotel in Memphis, Tennessee, on April 4, 1968. James Earl Ray, a 40-year-old white drifter, was later convicted of the murder.

Ray had a criminal record dating back to 1949, and in April 1967 had escaped from the Missouri state penitentiary, where he had served seven years of a 20-year sentence for armed robbery. He was first identified as a suspect by the FBI on April 17 under the alias Eric Starvo Galt and then from fingerprint records on April 19 under his real name. He had registered at the rooming house from which he shot Dr King under one of his several aliases, John Willard. Ray (travelling on a Canadian passport in the name of Ramon George Sneyd) was arrested at Heathrow Airport (England) on June 8, 1968, while in transit between Lisbon and Brussels, and he was returned to the USA on July 18.

Ray pleaded guilty at his trial in Memphis in March 1969, and was sentenced to a 99-year prison term. At his trial both the prosecution and Ray's lawyer, Percy Foreman, agreed there was no evidence that Ray had been part of a conspiracy. This was the view also officially announced by Attorney General Ramsey Clark and the Memphis police chief the day after the assassination, when there was still no suspect. Ray, however, appeared to indicate that there had been a conspiracy. A week after his conviction Ray dismissed Foreman and retained as his counsel J. B. Stoner, a Georgia lawyer who was once the head of the Ku Klux Klan in Tennessee. He then demanded a new trial on the ground that he had been "pressurized" into pleading guilty, but this was rejected.

Such doubts as there were about Ray's guilt arose from contradictions between the original FBI warrant for the arrest of "Galt" and later details about Ray. Galt in particular had been described as a conspirator with a man he said was his brother, and various details of Galt's life had been given for the period when Ray was in the Missouri state penitentiary. In addition, Ray had apparently spent money freely in the weeks before the assassination, despite having no known source of income.

The King assassination became a focus of congressional investigation again in 1976 with the creation of the House Select Committee on Assassinations (see also *John F. Kennedy Assassination Affair, 1963–79*, above). Ray himself told the Committee that he had not shot King and speculated that the assassination could have resulted from a conspiracy between the FBI and the Memphis police. In the face of conclusive evidence placing him at the rooming house and linking him to the murder weapon, Ray claimed that the day before the shooting he had given the gun to a man named "Raoul", whom he had met in Canada some months before and with whom he had since engaged in smuggling activities. Ray claimed that he never saw the rifle again and at the time of the murder was at a petrol station repairing a car tyre; on returning to the rooming house he had seen police activity and fled. He claimed that his attorney, Percy Foreman, had pressurized him into pleading guilty, convincing him that it would "somehow be in my financial interests to plead guilty" and that his brother and elderly father would be imprisoned if he failed to do so. Foreman, however, told the Committee that Ray had told him in prison interviews that he had killed King in the hope of becoming a "hero to the white race" and that he had left the rifle near the lodging house in a hope of achieving fame. Foreman also said that Ray himself had wanted to plead guilty to avoid the death sentence.

In its final report (released in July 1979) the Committee concluded that Ray had indeed shot King, but that the assassination had "probably" originated in a conspiracy of right-wing St Louis businessmen; that Ray may have been motivated by reports of a $50,000 "bounty" on King's head; and that his brothers John and Jerry might have been involved. (The bounty had allegedly been offered by businessmen John Sutherland and John Kauffman, both of whom had since died). The Committee also strongly criticized the FBI for its "Cointelpro" intelligence and black propaganda campaign against King (which had included FBI assistant director William Sullivan sending an anonymous letter to King in 1964 advising him to commit suicide before "your filthy, abnormal, fraudulent self is bared to the nation"): The Committee found, however, no evidence of any complicity by the FBI or other government agency in King's death.

One Republican member of the Committee (Harold S. Sawyer) described the conspiracy theory as based merely on "totally fabricated" testimony about the bounty. The Justice Department declined to follow the Committee's request that it should reopen the case, reflecting a widespread view that the evidence for a conspiracy was tenuous. Ray has not to date won a retrial.

Many of King's former associates remain convinced that his death was the result of a conspiracy. The Rev. Ralph Abernathy, King's successor as leader of the Southern Christian Leadership Conference, said in 1988 that King was "gotten rid of" by a conspiracy among the "evil forces of this nation", which included the FBI. As in the case of the 1963 assassination of President John F. Kennedy, much of the conspiracy-theorizing that followed King's death reflected little more than a widespread reluctance to accept the banality of his death. "Assassination" seemed too grand a word to associate with the likes of Ray and Lee Harvey Oswald, inconsequential drifters without clear motivations beyond a vague desire for fame and notoriety. Many Americans longed for the deaths of King and Kennedy to stand in proportion to the scale of their lives, and so it became necessary to believe that they had been the victims of vast political conspiracies rather than just two more of the countless victims of the easy availability of firearms to those clearly unsuited to possess them.

FJH

Abe Fortas Affair (1968–69)

Abe Fortas, Supreme Court Justice (1965–69).
Louis Wolfson, Florida financier.

In October 1968 Supreme Court Associate Justice Abe Fortas became the first nominee to the position of Chief Justice of the United States to be rejected by the Senate since 1795. Subsequently, in May 1969, he was forced to stand down from the Court altogether in the face of charges of an improper financial relationship.

President Lyndon Johnson announced in June 1968 his nomination of Fortas as Chief Justice in succession to the 77-year old Earl Warren, who wished to retire, and his choice of Homer Thornberry, a Texas judge, to take Fortas's place as one of the Supreme Court's eight Associate Justices. Following a Senate filibuster against his appointment, however, Fortas on Oct. 2 asked Johnson to withdraw his nomination, and Warren agreed to stay on as Chief Justice (he was succeeded in June 1969 by Warren Burger, appointed directly as Chief Justice without serving as an Associate Justice). Thornberry's nomination lapsed automatically because there was no longer a vacancy to be filled.

On the surface, the opposition to Fortas centred on the fact that he was a long-time close friend of Johnson (who had appointed him to the Supreme Court in 1965), and had seen fit to give the President private advice on policy matters since joining the Court. Neither of these objections had proved fatal to several illustrious past appointees, however, and the root issue appeared to be a feeling that Fortas was too liberal, the coalition that formed in Congress against his appointment consisting of conservative Republicans and southern Democrats. Under Earl Warren (since 1954) the Court had shown increasingly liberal inclinations and had asserted itself powerfully as a force for change on civil rights issues in particular, a tendency which conservatives were reluctant to see consolidated.

On May 14, 1969, Fortas was forced under pressure from his fellow Justices to resign from the Supreme Court following the publication of an article in *Life* magazine on May 4 charging that after he joined the Court he had accepted, but had later returned, a fee of $20,000 from the Family Foundation of Louis E. Wolfson, a Florida financier. According to Bob Woodward and Scott Armstrong in their book *The Brethren: Inside the Supreme Court* (1979), the information was fed to a *Life* magazine reporter by President Nixon's Justice Department. In a statement in response to the *Life* study, Fortas conceded he had accepted the money (in January 1966), but said this was in return for "research functions, studies and writings" connected with the Family Foundation's work for racial and religious harmony; he added that he had never given Wolfson or the Foundation any legal advice or made any representations on their behalf since joining the Court. Fortas's law firm had, however, represented Wolfson in litigation connected with his financial affairs since 1965; Fortas had returned the $20,000 only in December 1966, after Wolfson was indicted on stock manipulation charges; and Wolfson had in September 1967 been convicted and sentenced to a year in prison. In the view of most in Congress, Fortas had failed to avoid "the appearance of impropriety" and his resignation was generally welcomed. No prosecution was ever brought against him. He died on April 5, 1982.

Fortas's resignation seemingly delivered President Nixon an unexpected opportunity to place another conservative on the Court. However his first two nominees to take Fortas's seat, Judges Clement F. Haynsworth and G. Harrold Carswell, both southern conservatives, were rejected by the Democratic-controlled Senate. Nixon's third and successful choice, Harry A. Blackmun, from Minnesota, proved in time to be a stalwart of the Court's liberal wing.

FJH

Chicago Seven Affair (1968–70)

The Chicago Seven: Rennie Davis, David Dellinger, John Froines, Tom Hayden, Abbie Hoffman, Jerry Rubin, Lee Weiner.
Mayor Richard Daley, Mayor of Chicago.
Julius Hoffman, Trial Judge.
William Kunstler, attorney.
Leonard Weinglass, attorney.

The 1968 Democratic National Convention, held in Chicago from Aug. 26–29, was the scene of chaotic disturbances in both the convention hall and on the streets outside. The disturbances vividly demonstrated to the nation the scale of opposition that had developed among the younger generation to the Vietnam War, and the internal divisions of the Democratic Party on this issue. The immediate consequence was the defeat of the Democratic candidate, Hubert H. Humphrey, in the November 1968 presidential election, as the "silent majority" rallied to Republican Richard Nixon. However, the events in Chicago also marked a watershed following which the general drift of US policy would be towards disengagement from Vietnam, a policy brought to a conclusion by the Republican Presidents Nixon and Ford.

By 1968, after several years of escalation following the Gulf of Tonkin incident (see *Gulf of Tonkin Affair 1964–71*, above), US troops had become bogged down in a seemingly unwinnable war in Vietnam. It was, moreover, a war whose purpose and justice was being increasingly questioned at home. On March 31, 1968, unable to reconcile the conflicting needs of the war effort with the growing anti-war sentiment in his own party, Lyndon Johnson announced he would not run for another term as President. Senator Robert Kennedy, the brother of the late President, made a strong race for the nomination but was assassinated in early June 1968 immediately after winning the California primary. By convention time Vice-President Hubert Humphrey (who declared his candidacy only on April 28) had emerged as the favoured candidate for the party establishment, with Senator Eugene McCarthy of Minnesota, running on an anti-administration platform that promised a quick withdrawal from Vietnam, as the choice of the party's left wing, and Senator George McGovern as a late-entrant anti-war alternative to McCarthy.

As the Democratic Convention prepared to convene, thousands of loosely-organized hippies, yippies, draft evaders, anti-war militants and other young people converged on Chicago to express their contempt for the political system and their opposition to the continuance of the war. Chicago was not San Francisco, however, and the Chicago police under the direction of Mayor Richard Daley—an old-time Democratic "hard-knuckle" politician of the rawest type—backed up by the Illinois National Guard, staged a series of brutal and one-sided engagements with the demonstrators in front of national television. Within the Convention McCarthy and McGovern supporters denounced Daley's "police state" methods, Daley responding by bringing in police to remove some delegates. According to Senator McGovern, the conduct of the police was "like Nazi Germany". In scale and ferocity, the demonstrations were scarcely akin to the black riots that had devastated many cities in the past few years (there was not one fatality), but most of those who protested at Chicago were white, middle-class, and well-educated. The evidence of their uncomprehending and incomprehensible dissatisfaction proved profoundly unsettling to many of the nation's mainstream opinion-formers, with great consequences for the political mood of the 1970s.

The convention chose Humphrey as its candidate, giving him more than twice as many delegate votes on the first ballot as McCarthy and McGovern combined, on a platform broadly endorsing Johnson's Vietnam policies. In the election, however, Humphrey lost narrowly to the Republican candidate, Richard Nixon, who played on an appeal to the "silent majority" of law-abiding citizens afraid of the chaos they had seen at Chicago. In 1972 the radical wing of the party and the centre combined to secure the selection of the ultra-liberal George McGovern as the party's candidate, ensuring a second term for Nixon. By this time, however, the anti-war mood in the nation was so pervasive, and the commitment of the nation's policy-makers and intellectual establishment to continuing the war so uncertain, that Nixon pulled out of Vietnam (leaving the South to its ultimate capitulation in 1975) on terms and in circumstances that would have been seen as a national humiliation in 1968.

The trial of eight leaders of the disturbances began in Chicago on Sept. 24, 1969, before federal district judge Julius Hoffman. They were Black Panther Party chairman Bobby Seale (34); David Dellinger (53), John Froines (30) and Lee Weiner (30) of the National Mobilization Committee to End the War in Vietnam; Rennie Davis (29) and Tom Hayden (29) of Students for a Democratic Society; and Abbie Hoffman (32) and Jerry

Rubin (31), the founders of the Youth International Party (the yippies). All were charged with charges involving incitement to riot.

In the early stages of the trial a series of violent diatribes by Seale directed at what he styled the "racist, fascist pig" judge, culminated in Seale being bound and gagged and ordered to stand trial separately. In addition, he was sentenced to four years in prison on 16 counts of contempt, described by some lawyers as the longest sentence for contempt in Anglo-American jurisprudence. The trial then proceeded with just the "Chicago Seven", as they became known, present. Presentation of evidence lasted four months, again with outbreaks of abuse and obscenity and courtroom scuffles. There were repeated heated exchanges between Judge Hoffman and defence counsel William Kunstler, who had one point accused Judge Hoffman of carrying out a "legal lynching". The Judge refused to allow Ramsey Clark, who had been Attorney General at the time of the 1968 disturbances, to give evidence for the defence.

After the jury had retired on Feb. 14, 1970, Judge Hoffman sentenced all the defendants and defence attorneys Leonard Weinglass and Kunstler to prison terms for contempt of court, Kunstler's sentence of four years 13 days being the longest ever given to a lawyer for contempt in American history. Liberal sections of the press excoriated Judge Hoffman for his supposedly biased conduct of the trial. The jury gave a mixed verdict on Feb. 18, 1970, acquitting all the defendants on one conspiracy charge, but finding all but Froines and Weiner (both of whom were academics) guilty of inciting and organizing riot. All five convicted were given the maximum possible sentence, namely five years imprisonment and a $5,000 fine.

The mood of the trial, and the severity of the sentences, reflected the worsening domestic political situation. Anti-war protest had turned increasingly violent and disruptive, with bombings of military and corporate targets by Weathermen and other militant underground groups; in 1969 there were 93 explosions in New York city and 62 in San Francisco. In June 1970 the situation would be further exacerbated by the killings of student protestors at Kent State University by National Guardsmen (see *Kent State Massacre Affair, 1970*, below).

Jerry Rubin, with Abbie Hoffman perhaps the leading figure among the Chicago Seven, has in recent years run a business promoting parties which people pay to take part in to meet others who can advance their careers; he has been called a "yippie-turned-yuppie". Abbie Hoffman's death following a drugs overdose in April 1989 provoked a wave of 1960s nostalgia among a generation now facing middle age.

FJH

Chappaquiddick Affair (1969)

Edward Kennedy, Senator from Massachusetts.
Mary Jo Kopechne, former campaign worker, who died in his car.

On the night of Friday July 18, 1969, Senator Edward Moore Kennedy, then aged 37, the younger brother of John (assassinated while President in 1963) and Robert (assassinated in 1968 while campaigning for the Democratic presidential nomination), drove his car off a narrow bridge on Chappaquiddick Island (off the Massachusetts coast at Martha's Vineyard) into the waters of a salt water inlet known as Poucha Pond. He escaped, but his 28-year-old passenger, Mary Jo Kopechne, a former secretary on the campaign staff of Robert Kennedy, did not. Throughout the rest of that night Kennedy failed to contact the authorities to raise the alarm. By the time he notified the police the next morning that an accident had occurred, the car had already been discovered by two anglers and Kopechne's body retrieved from inside it. No autopsy was ever performed, but the diver who found the body believed that Kopechne had died of suffocation after three or four hours trapped in an air lock. The accident, and Kennedy's behaviour in the hours that followed, excites controversy to this day, and the unanswered questions arising from Chappaquiddick have hung over his presidential ambitions like a pall.

During the evening of July 18 Kennedy had been one of six men (none of them under 30, and all but one, including Kennedy, being married) at a reunion party at a cottage on the island with six female Kennedy campaign workers, all of whom were under 30 and single. In a statement to the local police on the morning of July 19, Kennedy explained that he had left the party at 11.15 pm to catch the ferry back to his hotel at Edgartown on Martha's Vineyard, and that Kopechne had been accompanying him to return to her own hotel. He said that the accident occurred after he took a wrong turning along a dirt road; that he had repeatedly dived into the water to try to rescue Kopechne; and that when this failed he had walked back to the party cottage in a state of shock and exhaustion, after which "someone" had driven him back to Edgartown where he returned to his hotel. The statement added: "when I fully realized what had happened this morning, I immediately contacted the police."

In the following days press speculation focused on the possibility of a relationship between Kopechne and Kennedy (whose wife Joan was three months pregnant), and on whether he had been drunk. Meanwhile, back at the Kennedy compound at Hyannis Port, many of the most famous names in Democratic politics gathered to discuss the problem and devise a solution which would not destroy Kennedy's career. On July 25, after a plea bargain had been worked out with friendly local prosecutors, Kennedy appeared in court before Judge James Boyle on Martha's Vineyard and pleaded guilty to the minor charge of leaving the scene of an acccident, and failing to report it, for which he received a suspended two-month jail sentence and was banned from driving for one year. That same evening he appeared on national television to give a full account of his version of events. In broad outline his story remained the same as first given on July 19 but some details were added. In particular, he recalled that on returning to the beach party he had alerted two of the men there (his cousin Joseph Gargan and legal adviser Paul Markham), and that the three had then returned to the scene of the accident, diving repeatedly into the waters to try to locate Kopechne's body. After this had proved unavailing, Kennedy's account went, they had driven to the ferry crossing point, where, finding that the last ferry had gone, he "suddenly jumped in to the water and impulsively swam across [a distance of some 160 yards], nearly drowning once again in the effort". He had got back to his hotel in Edgartown about 2.00 am, and had collapsed in a state of exhaustion. There had been, Kennedy asserted, no "immoral conduct" between him and Kopechne (a "gentle, kind and idealistic person"), and neither had he been driving "under the influence of liquor". As for his failure to raise the alarm, this had been the result of confusion, grief, fear and panic—he had suffered, his doctors had told him, "a cerebral concussion as well as shock", though he did not seek to "escape responsibility" on this count. So scrambled were his thoughts, Kennedy declared, that he had wondered that night whether "some awful curse did actually hang over all the Kennedys".

Many were unpersuaded by Kennedy's account then and have remained so since. The simplest explanation for the failure to raise the alarm, many thought, was not exhaustion but a desire to construct an alibi and allow the effects of alcohol to wear off. How, it was wondered, could a sober man have driven off the side of a bridge, albeit a narrow one without guard rails? How could he, sober or drunk, have driven off the only paved road on the island and set off down a dirt road which led in exactly the wrong direction, to the ocean shore? Why had his two friends not tried to raise the alarm themselves? What was to be made of a report by a local police officer that he had seen a car similar to Kennedy's being driven in the vicinity of the bridge much later in the evening, after the last ferry had already gone? Was it not significant that Kennedy had reportedly made some 17 phone calls from his hotel room in the small hours of July 19, without contacting the police? Why, if he was distraught and confused and not intent on a cover-up, had Kennedy emerged from his hotel at 7.30 am dressed for boating and in apparently casual mood? In the hustling away of those who had been at the party by Kennedy aides, the failure to perform an autopsy on Kopechne, and the low-key investigation by local police (in what was the Kennedys' political backyard), opponents of the Kennedy "dynasty" saw the clan exercising its power to protect its own. Some have seen a peculiar horror in the possibility that Kopechne remained alive for hours, slowly consuming the oxygen in an air lock, while Kennedy failed to organize a rescue but concerned himself with saving his own career.

Following the July 25 plea bargain, no further charges were ever brought against Kennedy. In December 1969 a local court turned down a request by a Massachusetts district attorney for the exhumation of Kopechne's body. An inquest was held the following month before Judge Boyle, who concluded that Kennedy had not taken a wrong turning but was heading to a secluded beach and had driven "negligently", but did not recommend prosecution. On the instructions of the Massachusetts Supreme Court, press and public were excluded from the inquest proceedings. A grand jury investigation of the case was frustrated by intense pressure on the jurors by the Massachusetts judiciary. Despite this—or because of it—what happened at Chappaquiddick was never laid to rest in the way the Kennedy family hoped. Theories advanced in the extensive speculative literature on the subject have varied from a claim that Kopechne was pregnant and that Kennedy had murdered her before diving clear of his car as it went over the Dyke bridge in a fake drowning incident (Zad Rust, *Teddy Bare* (1971)) to the suggestion that Kennedy was not even in the car and that Kopechne drove it off the bridge herself (Jack Olsen, *The Bridge at Chappaquiddick* (1970)). Most persistent have been doubts about whether Kennedy actually tried to rescue Kopechne and the reasons for the hours of delay in reporting the accident. In September 1969 columnist Jack Anderson claimed that Gargan and Markham actually rowed Kennedy back to Edgartown in an attempt to create an alibi for him at the Shiretown Inn. Variations on this theme have persisted, and in a 1988 book by Leo Damore (*Senatorial Privilege: The Chappaquiddick Cover-up*) Gargan was reported as saying that Kennedy had planned to say that Kopechne was driving the car by herself and was only dissuaded the following morning by him and Markham.

Given the doubts surrounding the Chappaquiddick incident, its impact on Kennedy's career might be considered surprisingly slight. What saved him was the fact that he was a Kennedy, America's own royal family. That reflected lustre has continued to bathe him, however much the exposure of the tawdry undersurface of the Kennedy presidency has become plainer through the years. He has remained a US senator, a leading force in his party (even a stern moralist in condemning the lapses from grace of political rivals), and a perennial possibility for its presidential nomination notwithstanding his possession of arguably more modest talents that those of his brothers. In his only sustained run for the nomination, however, in 1980 (when he pursued his campaign all the way to the convention), questions were raised about his electability as the press turned over old stones and opinion polls showed that nearly one-third of the American people did not believe his account of what happened on that 1969 night.

FJH

My Lai Massacre Affair (1969–71)

Lt. William Calley, convicted of leading the My Lai massacre.
Capt. Ernest Medina, Calley's commanding officer.
Ronald Ridenhour, Vietnam veteran who exposed details of the massacre.

It became public knowledge in November 1969 that a platoon of troops under the command of Lt. William Calley had massacred a large number of unarmed civilians, including many women and children, in a South Vietnamese hamlet called My Lai on March 16, 1968. The subsequent trial and conviction of Calley for murder aroused intense and contradictory reactions, focusing public attention on the individual responsibility and guilt of soldiers in war, the morale and morality of US forces in Vietnam, and the responsibility of the government and senior commanders for waging the type of warfare in which such incidents could occur.

"My Lai 4" was the name of one of six hamlets in Quang Ngai province which together made up the village of Song My, nicknamed "Pinkville" by US forces. The Song My area had been effectively controlled by the Viet Cong since 1964, and was a designated "free fire zone" in which any Vietnamese was assumed to be hostile and could be fired upon. In the March 16 operation a company of US troops under Capt. Ernest Medina was ordered to occupy and destroy the My Lai hamlet. Calley's platoon led the advance, met no resistance, and then at Calley's order indiscriminately massacred civilians. At his trial Calley was charged with the murder of at least 102 people, and was convicted of the murder of at least 22. There was one American casualty in the operation, a soldier who accidentally (or deliberately to avoid participation in the massacre) shot himself in the foot, while a few soldiers refused to obey Calley's orders. Recent accounts by participants show that victims were in many cases not just shot, but mutilated, scalped, raped and disembowelled and that hundreds were killed. It has also been disclosed that up to 100 civilians were similarly massacred in a simultaneous action in the neighbouring hamlet of My Khe.

Capt. Medina ordered his company to say nothing of the incident, and two investigations by Col. Oran Henderson (commander of the 11th Infantry Brigade, who had himself monitored the operation from a helicopter), made in response to eyewitness and survivor claims, rejected any suggestion of a massacre. In March 1969, however, Ronald Ridenhour, a former soldier who had served in Vietnam and heard details of the massacre from members of Calley's platoon, sent full accounts of it to government officials and 23 congressmen. Following this, on April 23, Chief of Staff General William Westmoreland ordered a full investigation, which led to charges being preferred against Calley on Sept. 5, the day before he was due to be released from the Army. News of the investigation first appeared in the US press on Nov. 12, 1969. Medina was also charged with murder in March 1970. A number of senior Army officers were charged with offences relating to concealment of the massacre, but those against all except Henderson were ultimately dropped. Eleven members of Calley's platoon were charged with murder and assault, but two were acquitted and nine had the charges against them withdrawn on the grounds of insufficient evidence.

Calley's trial before a military court at Fort Benning, Georgia, ended with his conviction on March 29, 1971, on charges of premeditated murder, and his being sentenced by the military jury to life imprisonment on March 31. By April 2, 90,000 telegrams had reached the White House, these being said to be 100 to one in favour of clemency. All the jurors were forced to change their phone numbers because of the flood of condemnatory calls. The right-wing Governor of Alabama, George Wallace, announced that he would try to prevent the conscription of young men from his state and paid Calley a personal visit; Governor Edgar Whitcomb of Indiana ordered all State flags to be flown at half-mast in protest; and the legislatures of several states (particularly in the south) passed resolutions calling for clemency. Jimmy Carter, the Governor of Calley's home state of Georgia, asked those who supported Calley to drive with their car headlights left on. In Congress many right-wing southern congressmen publicly announced their support for clemency and belief that Calley was being burdened with the responsibility for the war. There were many resignations of members of local draft boards.

The pro-Calley sentiment showed a confusion of motivations. Some politicians who had for years supported every escalation of the war now discovered that they were opposed to its continuation, apparently because it could not legally be fought with the tactics employed by Calley. Isolationism, which had in the past few years become the property of student radicals, rediscovered its authentic populist and conservative roots. Others who had opposed the war appeared prepared, with an indulgence that bordered on hypocritical cant, to accept Calley as in some way the war's victim, a luckless "scapegoat" for more senior commanders. Calley himself encouraged this interpretation at his trial, maintaining that he had been "indoctrinated" by the Army to regard all Vietnamese, including children, as potential enemies, and that he even considered children more dangerous than adults because they threw grenades and planted landmines. At the same time, he sought to attribute direct responsibility to his superior, Capt. Medina; according to Calley, Medina had ordered "everything" to be destroyed, and had told him to "waste" his prisoners when they were slowing down the advance.

In the face of a barrage of criticism of Calley's conviction, President Nixon on April 1, 1971, ordered him to be released from the stockade at Fort Benning and returned to his quarters while his conviction was being reviewed. On Aug. 20, 1971, the Army reduced Calley's life sentence to 20 years. After serving three years under house arrest at Fort Benning, he was released when his conviction was overturned by a federal district judge. He was not returned to house arrest when an appeals court reinstated his conviction. He now runs a jewellery business in Columbus, Georgia, an apparently respected local businessman.

On Sept. 22, 1971, Capt. Medina was acquitted by a military court on charges of murder and involuntary manslaughter. Most of the witnesses at his trial said that he had not ordered or been present at any killing of non-combatants, although two said that they had seen him personally kill a wounded woman. On Oct. 15 he received an honourable discharge from the Army. The series of trials ended on Dec. 17, 1971, when Col. Oran Henderson was acquitted by a court martial of charges of failing to investigate war crimes, dereliction of duty and false swearing.

The My Lai massacre was a sordid insight for the American public into the real nature of the war being fought in Vietnam. It demonstrated that the conduct of troops had degenerated under the stress of fighting, without conventional military objectives, a largely unseen enemy which melted into the civilian population. And it reinforced a growing sense of national self-doubt and debasement whose full consequences would be seen in the following few years.

FJH

Kent State Massacre Affair (1970)

Richard M. Nixon, President (1969–74).
James Rhodes, Governor of Ohio.

Four students were killed in a clash with National Guardsmen at Kent State University, Ohio, on May 4, 1970. The incident proved a landmark event in the escalation of domestic opinion against US military involvement in Vietnam.

On April 30, 1970, President Nixon announced in a broadcast his decision to commit US ground forces to a major incursion into Cambodia directed at Viet Cong and North Vietnamese bases in that country. The decision triggered a wave of violent protests in US colleges, leading President Nixon on May 1 to denounce "these bums blowing up the campuses". Clashes at Kent State University between students and police began on the night of May 1–2, when a curfew was imposed. On May 2 the campus ROTC (military officers' training corps) building was burned down and that evening martial law was declared and National Guardsmen were deployed to drive the students back to their dormitories with tear gas. On May 3 James Rhodes, the state Governor, visited the campus and assured the National Guard there that he would back any action they took to the hilt, asserting that the demonstrations were part of a "national revolutionary conspiracy". At noon on May 4 some 1,500 to 3,000 student demonstrators gathered in the college grounds; the National Guard at first fired tear gas to disperse them, but when they were pelted with gas canisters and stones the Guardsmen opened fire without orders and without warning. Other students going to and from classes were drawn into the conflict as bystanders. Ironically, none of the students killed were apparently participating in the demonstration, and one was a member of the ROTC; none of them had been less than 85 yards from the Guardsmen at the time they were shot. National Guard spokesmen at first claimed that the men had opened fire because they had been attacked by a sniper positioned on a roof; however it became clear that the Guards had in fact not come under such attack but had panicked.

The incident intensified the wave of college strikes and protests, many supported by faculty members, and there were clashes between National Guards and students at several colleges over the next few days. On May 6, 1970, President Nixon received a delegation of six students from Kent State University and promised them that the Justice Department would produce a full report on the shootings. The following day he received a delegation of heads of leading universities, and promised that top administration officials would stop making antagonistic comments about students. On May 9 Nixon also made an extraordinary pre-drawn excursion from the White House to talk informally to students gathering at the Lincoln memorial in Washington prior to an anti-war demonstration. On June 13 Nixon appointed a Commission on Campus Unrest, headed by former Republican Governor of Pennsylvania William Scranton. In June 30 the Senate passed a resolution banning expenditure to maintain US troops in Cambodia, but no action was taken on this by the House.

The Scranton Commission, reporting on Oct. 4, 1970, specifically on the Kent State affair, while noting the "violent and criminal" actions of some of the students, found that the "indiscriminate" firing of rifles into the crowd (28 guardsmen fired 61 shots between them) was "unnecessary, unwarranted and inexcusable". On Oct. 16, however, an Ohio grand jury exonerated the National Guard, blamed the students and the university administration, and indicted 25 students and faculty. The grand jury report emphasized that National Guardsmen fired in an "honest and sincere belief" that they were at risk of "serious bodily injury", that 58 had been injured by objects thrown at them, and that they had been confronted by a much larger force of demonstrators hurling missiles and a stream of obscenities and shouts of "kill, kill, kill". The report found that the administration of the university had "fostered an attitude of laxity, over-indulgence and permissiveness with its students and faculty", which had allowed matters to get out of hand. On Oct. 30, the Justice Department produced another version of events which noted that the Guardsmen had not been in serious danger when they fired and that only one had been injured seriously enough by a missile to require hospital treatment. The Justice Department unequivocally concluded there had been no sniper fire at the Guards.

In January 1979, in an out-of-court settlement of a civil liability suit, the state of Ohio approved the payment of $600,000 to parents of students who had been killed or injured. A statement by Governor Rhodes and 27 Guardsmen who were defendants in the case expressed "regret" for the "tragedy of May 4, 1970".

FJH

Pentagon Papers Affair (1971–74)

Matthew Byrne, trial judge.
Charles Colson, Special Counsel to President Nixon.
John Ehrlichman, President's Assistant for Domestic Affairs.
Daniel J. Ellsberg, leaker of the Pentagon Papers.
Lewis Fielding, Ellsberg's psychiatrist.
E. Howard Hunt, White House "plumber".
Henry Kissinger, Nixon's National Security Adviser.
G. Gordon Liddy, White House "plumber".
Richard M. Nixon, President (1969–74).
Anthony Russo, Ellsberg's collaborator.

The *New York Times* on June 13, 1971, began publication of excerpts from a secret 2,500,000-word Defence Department history of the war in Vietnam (officially known as *History of US Decision-Making Process on Vietnam Policy*), which became known as the "Pentagon Papers". The response of the Nixon administration to the leak was to create the "plumbers' unit" in the White House and set in motion intensified surveillance of its "enemies", a road which culminated in Watergate and Nixon's resignation.

At one level the leaking of the Pentagon Papers was scarcely a damaging blow to the Nixon administration, for their subject was how America had become embroiled in the war under Democratic presidents Kennedy and Johnson (although the papers did include some sensitive current intelligence secrets). However, both Nixon and his National Security Adviser, Henry Kissinger, were convinced that their policies were being undermined by a growing disloyalty in government, and that such leaks were reducing the confidence of US allies and emboldening America's enemies.

The Justice Department first tried to block publication of the Papers on national security grounds. On June 30, 1971, however, the Supreme Court ruled by six votes to three, in a case involving the *New York Times* and the *Washington Post*, that publication was protected by the First Amendment to the Constitution, guaranteeing a free press, notwithstanding the subject-matter and the fact that the Papers had been stolen.

Every one of the nine members of the Court gave a separate opinion on the case, and those offered by the majority showed the extent to which the Court now felt qualified to speak on foreign policy and national security issues formerly regarded as well outside the province of the judicial branch, and how out of temper it was with the Nixon administration. The government had told the Court that publication could damage national security, the process of negotiating an end to the Vietnam war, and relations with America's allies. Justice William Douglas, however, took the opportunity to question the validity of "presidential wars" not declared by Congress and to justify publication as a contribution to the national "debate" on Vietnam. Justice Potter Stewart theorized that the contending needs of an "enlightened citizenry" and confidentiality in relations between governments were best served by "the maximum possible disclosure, recognizing that secrecy can best be preserved only when credibility is truly maintained". At root the justices were defining their position on policy issues. Thus Stewart could see no "direct immediate and irreparable damage to our people" to justify an overriding of the First Amendment. Justice William Brennan seemed to regard it as a defining mark that the government had not shown that publication entailed a risk equivalent to the unleashing of a "nuclear holocaust". Justice Hugo Black thought the two newspapers should be "commended" because "paramount among the responsibilities of a free press is the duty to prevent any part of the government from deceiving the people and sending them off to distant lands to die of foreign fevers and foreign shot and shell".

Meanwhile, Dr Daniel J. Ellsberg, a former Pentagon analyst (and one time assistant to Kissinger), who had been a co-author of the study while attached to the Rand Corporation, revealed that he had leaked the Papers. To the disgust of the White House, he immediately became a hugely fashionable figure in circles opposed to continuance of the war, which by this time included much of the media and intellectual establishment. An outraged Nixon set his aides the task of destroying the reputation of Ellsberg, one ploy seriously considered being to issue a statement that he had had nothing to do with leaking the Papers, in an effort to deflate his ballooning celebrity. In the event, Ellsberg was initially (on June 28) indicted in Los Angeles for possession of stolen documents, this being followed on Dec. 30 by a grand jury indictment on more sweeping charges of espionage, theft and conspiracy. Also indicted at that time was a former Rand Corporation colleague of Ellsberg's, Anthony Russo, who had helped Ellsberg to photocopy the Papers in October 1969.

After months of preliminary manoeuvrings, the trial opened before Judge Matthew Byrne in Los Angeles in January 1973, at just the time that the Watergate cover-up was beginning to unravel, so that the trial proceedings became entwined with developments in that larger story. As events unfolded it seemed increasingly that it was not Ellsberg and Russo, but the government, that was on trial. The government contention that publication of the Papers could have harmed national security was from the start put under intense scrutiny, and found to be precariously based, if mere embarrassment were to be excluded as a consideration. Meanwhile, behind the scenes, developments in the Watergate affair were spelling catastrophe for the government in the Ellsberg case. On April 14, 1973, White House turncoat John Dean, trading information in an attempt to win immunity from prosecution, told Watergate prosecutors that two of the key figures in the Watergate break-in, G. Gordon Liddy and E. Howard Hunt, had earlier (on Sept. 3, 1971), on orders from within the White House, supervised a break-in at the Los Angeles office of Ellsberg's psychiatrist, Dr Lewis Fielding, in an attempt to get hold of Ellsberg's file. On April 26 it became known publicly that acting FBI Director L. Patrick Gray (whose confirmation in the post was stalled in the Senate) had burned documents from Hunt's White House safe given him by Dean. Attorney General Richard Kleindienst and top Watergate prosecutor Earl Silbert warned Nixon that he must allow them to tell Judge Byrne of the Hunt and Liddy operation against Ellsberg's psychiatrist to avoid them all becoming involved in obstruction of justice when the information leaked out otherwise.

Judge Byrne's public disclosure of the Hunt and Liddy operation on April 27 (the day Gray announced his resignation) was a sensation. An FBI report of an April 27 interview with top White House aide John Ehrlichman, disclosed at the trial on May 1 (the day after Ehrlichman's resignation from the White House), further revealed that Liddy and Hunt had been working as part of a unit set up by Ehrlichman on President Nixon's orders to investigate unauthorized leaks after the Pentagon Papers became public. The task of organizing the "plumbers", as the leak-pluggers were called, had fallen on Ehrlichman's aide, Egil "Bud" Krogh, and a National Security Council official, David Young. Scarcely less damaging was Judge Byrne's disclosure that at meetings with Ehrlichman earlier in April he had been offered the post of Director of the FBI, Nixon having already decided that Gray should be dropped.

Further evidence showed that Hunt had, prior to the Fielding break-in, received from the CIA false identity papers, a speech alteration device, a wig, and other accessories for a "very sensitive operation" authorized by the White House, although the CIA had subsequently backed out of giving further help to Hunt. Testimony was also heard that the Fielding break-in was carried out by a three-man team of Cubans recruited by Liddy which included two of the Watergate burglars, Eugenio R. Martinez and Bernard L. Barker. Ehrlichman's right-hand man in organizing the plumbers, Egil Krogh, resigned as Under-Secretary of Transportation on May 9, saying that Hunt and Liddy had acted in excess of his instructions, and that no more senior officials had known of the Fielding break-in. On May 10 Judge Byrne announced that he had been told by the new acting FBI Director, William D. Ruckelshaus, that the FBI had in 1969–70 made wiretaps of conversations at the home of Morton Halperin, a former Deputy Assistant Secretary of Defence who had supervised compilation of the Pentagon Papers, and these included conversations with Ellsberg. All records and transcripts of these conversations had "disappeared", however (although they reappeared from Ehrlichman's safe immediately after the case was closed). The following day Judge Byrne dismissed all charges against Ellsberg and Russo, stating that the conduct of the government had precluded a fair trial.

With Ellsberg and Russo freed, those implicated in the Fielding break-in now found themselves brought to trial. Ehrlichman, Krogh, Liddy and Nixon's former counsel and "hit man", Charles Colson (who had found the money to finance the burglary), were all given prison sentences, while Barker and Martinez received suspended sentences. Ehrlichman, the principal target of the prosecutors, was on July 31, 1974, given a term of from 20 months to five years in prison for conspiracy and perjury. He maintained that he had never approved the Fielding break-in, but was convicted of authorizing it and later lying about it primarily on the word of Young.

To Ehrlichman and others who had served in the White House in 1971–2 it seemed that the world had turned upside down, when Ellsberg was feted as a defender of civil liberties and government officials acting in what they believed to be the interests of national security found themselves imprisoned. In retrospect, it is arguable that the indictment and conviction of Ehrlichman had about it more than a little of the political show trial. Its ultimate target was the increasingly isolated figure of Richard Nixon, who refused to come to court to testify for Ehrlichman. As for Nixon's own role in the affair, this became a matter of bitter retrospective debate and accusations. In his 1982 memoir *Witness to Power*, Ehrlichman claimed that Nixon had now admitted to confidants that he himself had prior knowledge of, and had encouraged, the break-in at Ellsberg's psychiatrist's; Ehrlichman argued the idea for the break-in (which he says he knew of "a few hours after it occurred") had probably come from Hunt and Liddy and been passed on to Nixon through Colson. ("In those days Charles Colson and Richard Nixon had few secrets from each other".) Dean claimed that Krogh had told him that "that one came right out of the Oval Office". Nixon, in his own memoirs, was curiously ambiguous as to how much he knew about the break-in and when. In Ehrlichman's view, the break-in was the "seminal Watergate episode" because it was panic that investigations into Watergate might expose the link back from Hunt to Colson and then to Nixon himself in the Ellsberg case which led Nixon to involve himself in the Watergate cover-up.

The prosecution of Ellsberg and Russo was the last attempt to use the espionage laws to stop leaks to the press until the case of Samuel Loring Morison in 1985, when the defendant was convicted in a very different political atmosphere to 1973 (see *Samuel Morison Affair, 1985*, below). Because of the wiretapping, the Fielding break-in and the murky presence of Hunt and Liddy, the government's claim to be defending national security came to appear like the grubby special pleading of an administration obsessed with spying on its own citizens and punishing all deemed to be enemies. Ironically, nothing in the Pentagon Papers—other than the fact of the leak itself—was damaging to Nixon. Indeed, some of their material, such as evidence that the Kennedy government had connived at the coup which led to the murder of President Diem in 1963, and that Johnson had misled the public by underestimating the real strength of the enemy in Vietnam, could be seen as confirming the view that Nixon was facing the task of extricating the country from a mess the Democrats had made for him. In its hounding of Ellsberg the administration veered from the course suggested by political expediency, and paid the penalty in convicting only itself. Coinciding with the endless revelations and accusations in the Watergate affair, the collapse of the Ellsberg trial and the disclosures about the plumbers built up a popular perception of an administration engaged in wholesale illegal monitoring and subversion. The plumbers came to be looked on as a sort of secret police.

In retrospect, however, what is perhaps most striking about the affair is the fact that the Nixon White House was so insecure that it felt unable to call on the normal resources of the state—the FBI and the other intelligence agencies—to plug the leaks; Nixon himself later wrote that in the Ellsberg case J. Edgar Hoover was "dragging his feet" and not co-operating with the White House. It was the breakdown of the national consensus on security issues of the 1950s and early 1960s—when secrets had been safe in the hands of executive branch employees, congressional committees, and even newspapers like the *New York Times*— that led the White House to have recourse to an amateurish little band of freelance operatives, the plumbers, to whose bunglings the administration itself became hostage.

FJH

Thomas Eagleton Affair (1972)

Thomas F. Eagleton, Democratic Senator.

Senator Thomas F. Eagleton of Missouri was named by Democratic presidential candidate George McGovern as his vice-presidential running mate on July 13, 1972, at the Democratic national convention. On July 31, however, Eagleton stepped aside after controversy over his mental health, being succeeded as vice-presidential nominee by Kennedy clan intimate Sargent Shriver.

Eagleton admitted at a press conference on July 25 that he had been hospitalized three times between 1960 and 1966 for "nervous exhaustion and fatigue", adding that he had on two of these occasions received electric shock therapy. Eagleton conceded that "I still am an intense person, I still push very hard" but insisted that "I pace myself a great deal better than I did in earlier years. The past six years . . . I've experienced good, solid, sound health". McGovern's initial reaction was to insist that he would not drop Eagleton from the ticket, although he had not known of his previous problems; however, under pressure from key aides and leading pro-Democratic newspapers he reluctantly agreed to Eagleton's replacement in the interests of party unity.

The incident, and McGovern's vacillating handling of it, confirmed the opinion of many voters that McGovern's judgment was uncertain. McGovern's first choice as his running-mate had actually been Senator Edward Kennedy—only three years after Chappaquiddick (see *Chappaquiddick Affair*, 1969, above)—but Kennedy had declined the invitation. In the November election the McGovern–Shriver ticket was routed by the incumbent Republican Nixon–Agnew combination.

FJH

Watergate Affair (1972–74)

Carl Bernstein, *Washington Post* reporter.

Fred J. Buzhardt, special Watergate counsel to Nixon.

Charles Colson, Nixon's special counsel.

Archibald Cox, Watergate Special Prosecutor (May 18–Oct. 20, 1973).

John W. Dean III, White House counsel to April 30, 1973; later Nixon's chief accuser.

John D. Ehrlichman, President's Assistant for Domestic Affairs (resigned April 30, 1973).

Sam J. Ervin, Chairman of the Senate Watergate Committee.

L. Patrick Gray III, Acting FBI Director from May 1972 (resigned April 27, 1973).

Gen. Alexander M. Haig, Haldeman's successor as White House Chief of Staff.

H. R. (Bob) Haldeman, White House Chief of Staff (resigned April 30, 1973).

Richard Helms, Director of the CIA.

J. Edgar Hoover, Director of the FBI until his death in May 1972.

Howard Hughes, reclusive billionaire industrialist.

E. Howard Hunt, White House "plumber" and Watergate burglar.

Leon Jaworski, successor to Archibald Cox as Watergate Special Prosecutor.

Herbert Kalmbach, Nixon's personal attorney, CRP official and Watergate "bagman".

Richard Kleindienst, Attorney General (resigned April 30, 1973).

Egil Krogh, Ehrlichman's aide.

Frederick C. LaRue, Mitchell aide at Committee to Re-elect the President, Kalmbach's successor as "bagman".

G. Gordon Liddy, White House "plumber", official at Committee to Re-elect the President, and Watergate burglar.

Jeb Stuart Magruder, Deputy Director, Committee to Re-elect the President.

James W. McCord, Security co-ordinator, Committee to Re-elect the President, Watergate burglar.

John N. Mitchell, Attorney General (resigned Feb. 15, 1972), then head of Committee to Re-elect the President (resigned July 1,1972).

Richard M. Nixon, President 1969–Aug. 9, 1974.

Lawrence F. O'Brien, Democratic Party national chairman at time of Watergate break-in.

Henry Petersen, Assistant Attorney General.

Charles "Bebe" Rebozo, Nixon intimate.

Elliot Richardson, Kleindienst's successor as Attorney General (resigned Oct. 20, 1973).

Earl J. Silbert, first Watergate chief prosecutor.

John J. Sirica, Watergate trial judge.

Maurice H. Stans, Finance Chairman, Committee to Re-elect the President.

Gordon Strachan, Haldeman aide.

Bob Woodward, *Washington Post* reporter.

Ronald L. Ziegler, White House press secretary.

The Watergate affair began with a break-in at the national headquarters of the Democratic Party in the Watergate hotel and apartment complex in Washington DC in the early hours of June 17, 1972. It ended on Aug. 9, 1974, when Richard Nixon became the first President of the United States to resign his office. Between those dates the US political system went through the most sustained and debilitating crisis of this century, and the imperial presidency which Nixon had inherited from Eisenhower, Kennedy and Johnson was brought to earth.

The origins of Watergate

The roots of Watergate lay partly in the character of Richard Nixon, and partly in the consequences of the war in Vietnam. Nixon trusted few men; he feared and detested the "eastern establishment"; and he saw himself as the victim of a perpetual vendetta by the liberal press. The son of a small-town small California businessman of populist views, Nixon travelled east to make his career, joining the ranks of the rich and powerful, but never, even as President, overcame a sense that he was an outsider. In the late 1940s he gained prominence as a member of the House Committee on Un-American Activities, where he was influential in the downfall of Alger Hiss (see *Hiss/Chambers Affair* 1948–50 above). In 1952 Nixon's career faced a crisis when, selected as Eisenhower's running mate, he faced accusations that he controlled a secret slush fund set up by wealthy Californian businessmen. In his notorious "Checkers" speech, Nixon won public sympathy by claiming that the only gift he had ever accepted from these backers was a little puppy dog which his children had called "Checkers", but among his opponents Nixon was henceforth known as "Tricky Dicky". In 1960, after two terms as Vice-President, Nixon was the Republican nominee to succeed Eisenhower, but lost narrowly to John F. Kennedy (possibly as a result of Democratic ballot-stuffing in some critical districts.) In 1962 he was again defeated, this time in an attempt to become Governor of California, and the day following the election bitterly told reporters: "For 16 years . . . you've had a lot of fun [attacking] me . . . . You won't have Nixon to kick around any more because, gentlemen, this is my last press conference."

Notwithstanding these words, and the further humiliation of being convicted and fined along with his campaign manager H. R. (Bob) Haldeman for unfair campaign practices, Nixon's appetite for power proved unsated. Following the rout of Barry Goldwater as the Republican candidate against Lyndon Johnson in 1964, Nixon re-established himself as the leading figure in the party. In 1968, a year of domestic strife highlighted by the assassinations of Robert Kennedy and Martin Luther King (see *John F. Kennedy Assassination Affair, 1963–79; Martin Luther King Assassination Affair, 1968–79*, above), race riots, and the chaos in the streets of Chicago at the time of the Democratic convention, he won election on a platform pitched at what Nixon styled the "silent majority" and stressing issues of law and order.

The new President's closest advisers were men without experience of public office, men essentially without political ideas and policies beyond the acquisition and exercise of power for its own sake. Haldeman became White House Chief of Staff, controlling access to the President; John Ehrlichman, an old friend of Haldeman and like him a former public relations man, became the President's Assistant for Domestic Affairs; John Mitchell, Nixon's former law partner and 1968 campaign manager, was rewarded with the post of Attorney General. In power Nixon retained many of the instincts of an outsider; he distrusted everything to do with the establishment, everyone not under his personal control. Preoccupied with the threat of domestic sedition arising from opposition to the Vietnam War, Nixon mistrusted the FBI as too much the tool of its powerful Director, J. Edgar Hoover, and he despised the CIA for what he saw as its Ivy League pedigree and history of accommodation with America's enemies; furthermore Nixon appeared to see no distinction between the national interest and his own. Against this background he and the little clique which surrounded him grew ever more deeply involved in schemes to create their own private intelligence capability, responsible only to the White House.

By 1970–71 a variety of projects for bugging opponents and harrassing Democrats and the press were underway. Some of the schemes were sophomoric to a degree: suggestively, perhaps, several of those who would achieve notoriety through the Watergate exposures—Haldeman's aide Gordon Strachan, Nixon's appointments secretary Dwight Chapin, White House press secretary Ronald Ziegler, and lawyer Don Segretti—had all begun their careers as members of the Trojan Knights, a student club at the University of South California which had specialized in stuffing ballot boxes and other dirty tricks.

At the same time other men with harder operational experience were taken on board. In June 1971 the *New York Times* began publication of the "Pentagon Papers", a secret Defence Department history of the war in Vietnam leaked by Daniel Ellsberg (see *Pentagon Papers Affair, 1971–74*, above). In response Nixon ordered the creation by his aides of the "special investigations unit", the so-called "plumbers", designed to collect information on Ellsberg and his links to the Democrats. Those particularly involved were Ehrlichman, his aide Egil Krogh, National Security Council staff lawyer David Young, and Nixon's own special counsel and action man Charles Colson. Colson recruited E. Howard Hunt, known as an ex-CIA man who had been involved at the Bay of Pigs, to try to discredit Ellsberg and link him to the Kennedys, Nixon most fearing the prospect of facing Edward Kennedy, draped in the mantle of his dead brothers, as the Democratic presidential candidate in 1972. Also recruited to the plumbers unit, which was set up in the basement of the old Executive Office Building, was an ex-FBI agent and assistant district attorney, the unstable G. Gordon Liddy. On Sept. 3, 1971, Hunt and Liddy stood guard while three Cubans burgled the office of Ellsberg's psychiatrist.

In December 1971 John Dean, the White House counsel, despatched Liddy to work at the Committee to Re-elect the President (CRP, or "Creep"), nominally as its general counsel and later as counsel to its finance committee, under Jeb Stuart Magruder. John Mitchell was in effect in charge of the CRP from its formation in Spring 1971, though he formally only took charge after resigning as Attorney General in February 1972. Liddy's job was to be political intelligence-gathering, though he was called CRP general counsel. In a meeting with Mitchell, Magruder and Dean on Jan. 27, 1972, Liddy outlined plans, which he called "Operation Gemstone" and said would require a budget of $1,000,000, to fight the election with a broad programme of sabotage, blackmail, kidnappings, break-ins and electronic surveillance. The plan was rejected by Mitchell as too expensive and too far-fetched, but Liddy was not discouraged from drawing up modified proposals concentrating on wiretapping and electronic surveillance. On March 30 Mitchell probably gave Liddy approval to put these plans into effect, with a budget of $250,000. Mitchell himself, though not denying that the meetings with Liddy had occurred, insisted later that he had never given Liddy authorization.

According to the later account of Jeb Stuart Magruder *(An American Life: One Man's Road to Watergate)*, Mitchell agreed to this watered-down Gemstone only with reluctance: he let it happen because he was preoccupied with other things—difficulties created by the eccentricities of his wife Martha and in countering allegations of misconduct in connection with an anti-trust case involving ITT—and because he was under pressure from the White House to deliver results. Mitchell's star was fading, and Haldeman, Ehrlichman and Colson were pushing at him constantly. At the same time, having let Liddy loose, Mitchell was too distracted to keep him under control. On the nights of May 26–27, 1972, Liddy and Hunt supervised attempted break-ins by teams of Cubans directed against the campaign headquarters of George McGovern—who had emerged as the probable Democratic candidate instead of Kennedy—and the Democratic National Committee (DNC) in the Watergate. The attempts to enter the McGovern headquarters were entirely unsuccessful, but at the Watergate James W. McCord, the CRP "security co-ordinator" and a former chief of physical security for the CIA, placed two wiretaps. Only one of the taps worked and the other produced little more than secretarial gossip.

The Watergate break-in and start of the cover-up

On the night of June 16–17, 1972, another break-in was staged at the DNC headquarters but ended in disaster when an alert night watchman called the local District of Columbia police. Five men carrying bugging devices, walkie-talkies and substantial sums of money were arrested that night, all of whom at first gave false names but quickly admitted their true identities: one was McCord; the other four would become generally known as the "Cubans", three of them being Cuban-born (Bernard L. Barker, Eugenio Martinez, Virgilio R. Gonzales) and one, Frank Sturgis, alias Frank Fiorini, a US-born mercenary who had fought both for and against Castro. Supervising the break-in from a distance, and not arrested, were Hunt, Liddy and Alfred C. Baldwin, a former FBI agent.

When the arrested men appeared in local court later the same day, they identified themselves as "anti-Communists" and McCord whispered "CIA" to the judge. Press reports, however, immediately identified McCord as security co-ordinator of the CRP, while Mitchell issued a statement describing McCord as merely a temporarily hired security consultant who had been let go a month earlier. On June 20 the *Washington*

Post—which had assigned two youthful reporters, Bob Woodward (29) and Carl Bernstein (28), to the case—reported from police sources that address books found on two of the burglars had contained the name of E. Howard Hunt, whom the *Post* said had been identified as an ex-CIA man who until March 29 had worked as a consultant to Charles Colson. At the White House all telephone books were recalled and amended in an attempt to disguise the fact that Hunt still had an office there, while Colson claimed to Ehrlichman and Dean that he had not seen Hunt for months. Meanwhile, Baldwin, who was possibly an FBI informant all along, had named both Hunt and Liddy to the FBI. Behind the scenes, Dean had on Ehrlichman's orders (Dean's story) or on his own initiative (Ehrlichman's version) told Liddy to get Hunt out of the country (Hunt disappeared briefly until July 7), while Liddy had melodramatically offered to Dean to stand on a street corner where he could be gunned down.

It is fairly clear in general terms who did know or should have known that Liddy had set in motion a programme of bugging and that the DNC headquarters was a target. Magruder, Dean and Mitchell had participated in the initial discussions of Gemstone; Dean later said that he thought the plan had been dropped, but Mitchell approved its implementation and the results of the first Watergate taps were communicated to Magruder, Mitchell and Haldeman's aide Gordon Strachan. But who approved the second break-in and why is far from clear, partly because the immediate response of those most closely involved to the arrest of McCord and the Cubans was to start lying to each other. Magruder says in his account that he knew of the second break-in only when Liddy phoned him to say that McCord had been arrested; Mitchell never said anything significant in public, but according to Dean personally confessed to him at the end of March 1973 that he had authorized the operation. In one sense, this question scarcely mattered to those concerned, because they knew that the Watergate break-in did not stand alone; it was the "other things" that would emerge if the stone was upturned that they feared.

The President's closest advisers were potentially at risk: Haldeman, because his aide Strachan had received reports from the first Watergate tap (Haldeman later claimed Strachan had not told him this, but Strachan said that he had kept Haldeman informed on all CRP espionage activities); Ehrlichman, because of his involvement with Hunt and Liddy in the plumbers' activities. And, it was instinctively realized by those around him, even the President himself was not in the clear, because whatever cover he had in terms of deniability, no one would believe that all these things, involving all his most senior aides, could have happened without his knowledge. This was especially so as Hunt had been brought in by Colson, who was the President's man of action and fixer. Thus it was that at both the CRP and the White House a cover-up began by consensus, without deliberation. Documents relating to the Ellsberg case and other "dirty tricks" were destroyed—by Liddy, by Strachan, by Magruder—and Mitchell, Magruder and Dean planned a cover story which would allow the operation to be traced back no further than Liddy, who would be portrayed as having been hired only for legitimate intelligence-gathering and as having acted on his own in the Watergate operation. The silence of the burglars would be bought by paying them hush money. Damage limitation was to be the policy. Meanwhile Hunt's White House safe had been broken open on Dean's orders and sensitive materials removed, including bugging equipment, information on Ellsberg, and cables forged by Hunt to link former President Kennedy with the overthrow and murder of South Vietnamese President Ngo Dinh Diem in 1963. According to Dean, Ehrlichman told him to shred the documents and "deep six" (i.e. put at the bottom of the Potomac) the bugging equipment, while Dean in Ehrlichman's presence handed over some of Hunt's documents to Acting FBI Director L. Patrick Gray, with the admonition that they "should never see the light of day". As with many Watergate episodes, this incident can be interpreted more than one way: as an injunction to Gray to destroy the documents, as Gray took it to be, or as a step to avoid leaks by lower level FBI officials, as Ehrlichman later claimed had been intended.

The curious fact about the cover-up story is that—narrowly considered in terms of the second break-in—it may even have been the truth. No one has yet come forward to say that they sanctioned Liddy and Hunt to go ahead with that second break-in. Given the gung-ho attitude of the two men involved, and the fact that the first break-in had produced no objections from the CRP or the White House, it may be that events had simply proceeded under their own momentum. The problem for those involved in the cover-up was that their story, while it would prove hard to dislodge, of its very nature excited suspicion, for why should these men have undertaken the break-in for reasons of their own? Their motives were incomprehensible.

A further weakness of the cover-up was that those implementing it had very different views of whom and what they were trying to protect. Furthermore, they were never all on the same team; to Haldeman and Ehrlichman, Mitchell and Magruder were the ones who had got them into difficulties; to Mitchell and Magruder, it was White House pressure which had led them to sanction Liddy's schemes. They were bound together by the "other things", but mutual resentment and suspicion meant that they were never really playing on the same team.

Nixon's involvement in the cover-up

Of all the remaining mysteries of Watergate, the greatest is what Nixon himself did or did not know. Nixon was never called as a witness in the Watergate perjury trials which convicted his closest aides, and has never testified on these matters under oath. In his 1978 memoirs, however, he maintains that the break-in (which he learned of while on vacation at his summer home at Key Biscayne, Florida) came as a complete surprise to him and that his reaction had been that the choice of the DNC headquarters as a place to bug had seemed incomprehensible ("anyone who knew anything about politics would know that a national committee headquarters was a useless place to go for inside information on a presidential campaign"). Nixon concedes that when the *Washington Post* on June 20, 1972, speculatively linked his special counsel Colson indirectly to the break-in, this "gave me a start" and "I wondered if he might have gone too far", but says that Colson told him he was uninvolved. Nixon also says that he believed John

Mitchell had not been involved, arguing that Mitchell was preoccupied with the increasingly erratic behaviour of his emotionally unstable wife Martha, and that because of this things had got out of hand at the CRP: "Without Martha", Nixon says, "I am sure that the Watergate thing would have never happened." If anyone actually explicitly authorized the break-in, on Nixon's account, it was probably Magruder, but, he emphasizes, he was far from clear in his own mind just who might have been involved and was receiving conflicting assessments from his aides.

That Nixon became involved in the cover-up almost immediately is incontrovertible. It is proved by the "smoking gun" tape recording of June 23 (whose later revelation had a shattering effect on his attempt to cling to office), in which he discussed with Haldeman trying to use the CIA to block the FBI's inquiries. As Nixon later explained it, the June 23 conversation arose from his anxiety lest there should be exposure of the activities Hunt had undertaken for Colson as part of the plumbers' operation, which was "the only White House vulnerability about Watergate that I was worried about exposing". He also quickly knew that pay-offs were being made to the Watergate burglars. This in no way proves, however, that Nixon knew in advance of either of the Watergate break-ins. The question matters: if he did, then Nixon let other men go to jail for covering up a crime he himself had committed. This question will inescapably shape the judgment of history on his presidency, however much the perspective of time may seem to lessen the seriousness of the crimes involved.

Little consideration was given back in 1972–74 to the thought that Nixon himself might have ordered the break-in. Nobody seriously imagined the President personally instructing Hunt and Liddy. The trail instead was seen rather as leading back from these low-level operatives through a string of increasingly more important intermediaries, whose personal direct responsibility decreased at each step away from the crime itself. And it was, of course, for the cover-up, and not for the break-in, that Nixon lost the presidency.

As time has gone by, however, another theory has gained ground which hinges on the view that the break-in was not so much a symptom of a general malaise—the view back in 1972–74—but a very specific operation related to Nixon's own personal concerns. The prime target of the Watergate bugging was Democratic Party national chairman Lawrence (Larry) O'Brien, about whom Nixon had his own anxieties. In 1969 O'Brien had been retained as the Washington representative of the reclusive billionaire industrialist Howard Hughes—who had not been seen in public since the 1950s—but in 1971 had been pushed out of his reputedly highly lucrative position when the faction within the Hughes empire with which he was identified was overthrown. Nixon himself, however, had also been effectively on the Hughes payroll in 1969–70 (i.e. when he was President), $100,000 of Hughes money in supposed campaign contributions having been channelled to Charles "Bebe" Rebozo, the President's closest friend and the man who reputedly kept his private "cash box". (Nixon later claimed that Rebozo, fearing that Nixon could be embarrassed by exposure of a Hughes connection, had kept the money without telling him about it, returning it to a Hughes representative in June 1973.) Nixon must have assumed, the argument goes, that O'Brien may have found out about the money and could turn it against Nixon in the campaign. Nixon had been hurt by the Hughes connection before, his painfully narrow defeat in the 1960 presidential election at the hands of John Kennedy often being attributed to press reports of a $250,000 loan, never repaid, made by Hughes to Nixon's brother Donald in 1957.

That Nixon had told several members of his staff of his desire to "nail" O'Brien is incontrovertible. This was a general obligation but, according to Haldeman in his 1978 account *The Ends of Power*, the greatest pressure was on Charles Colson, the President's "hatchet man". Haldeman explicitly states his view that the President was involved from the beginning and that Hunt was working for Colson specifically on this project. Haldeman indeed dismisses the idea that Mitchell, whom he pictures as a shrewd and instinctively cautious man, would have become involved in the Watergate operation, if only because he would have known, like all "Washington insiders", that the DNC headquarters was but a "ceremonial shell" unlikely to reveal much of value. The burglary, in sum, was the peculiar consequence of Nixon's obsession with the danger posed to him by his Hughes connection. (Ironically, according to Watergate historian J. Anthony Lukas, as reported in the *New York Times*, O'Brien told him in 1987 that he had not even known about the Hughes' payments to Rebozo.) At the same time, according to Haldeman, the operation was compromised from the beginning because both Hunt and Martinez were reporting to the CIA.

All this is, of course, circumstantial. Colson himself in his 1976 memoir *Born Again* reiterated his earlier claim that he had not seen Hunt for months before the break-in and knew nothing about it. (By this time Colson had undergone a much publicized religious conversion, but his memoirs demonstrated a wish to turn the page on past misdeeds, to turn the cheek and not blame others, rather than the spirit of purgative confession.) If the theory of direct Nixon involvement is true it also goes against the grain of what prime movers in the cover-up such as Dean and Magruder—and Haldeman himself—believed to be the case at the time: that the break-in was the result of a general pressure on the CRP for "results", something that had perhaps got out of hand, rather than a specific deliberate operation prescribed by the President. (At a 1987 conference, however, Magruder said that "as far as I know" the "primary" purpose of the break-in had been to find out what O'Brien knew about the Hughes loan to Rebozo, and that he had discussed this problem with both Mitchell and Haldeman in the weeks prior to the break-in.) That Nixon participated to some extent in the evolution of the cover-up is undeniable: it is in the evidence of the transcripts of the White House tapes. But interpreting the evidence of those tapes is not easy; and it often seems, indeed, that Nixon's critics have been prepared to take at their face value any remarks of his which appeared to show knowledge of the cover-up, while discounting as for effect or insincere those which showed ignorance. Even John Dean himself, who became the President's prime accuser, conveys in his account of the affair, *Blind Ambition* (1976), the impression of a President "mostly . . . rambling and forgetful" who seemed aware of some things but in the dark about others, constantly and irrelevantly reminiscing about the supposed lessons of how he had trapped Alger Hiss; a participant in a cover-up, but not its mastermind. Nixon may only have suspected the links of Mitchell and other aides to Watergate, but four months from an election, with the Democrats desperate for any issue to rescue their flagging campaign, elementary political expediency quite apart from any personal guilt led in only one direction.

Moreover, once it is assumed that the Hughes-Rebozo-O'Brien triangle may be the key to the affair, other aspects of the break-in, also largely overlooked in 1972–74, take on a different aspect. It may indeed be that even if the target was O'Brien, other fish were being fried on that night in June 1972. When O'Brien was pushed out as Hughes's man in Washington he was replaced by Robert Bennett, the president of the Robert R. Mullen public relations film company, and Bennett was Howard Hunt's employer and the man who had introduced Hunt to Colson in the first place. Bennett, for sure, and the Hughes faction he represented, had an interest in knowing what the powerful and disgruntled O'Brien might know which was dangerous to Hughes. What is more, the Mullen company was a front for the CIA and—as would be learned in the congressional investigations of the CIA later in the 1970s (see *CIA "Family Jewels" Affair*, 1974–76, below)—the CIA had many ultra-secret connections with Hughes. Hunt was known even in 1972 as an ex-CIA man, but it seems fairly probable that—if only because of the tie-up with the Mullen company—he was still a CIA asset. Could it be, then, that on that fateful night Hunt was in reality working not for Richard Nixon, or for Mitchell, but for Howard Hughes or the CIA?

What the people knew, June–November 1972

In the first days after the break-in considerable attention was given in the press—especially the *New York Times*—to the possibility that the burglars, given their past records, were looking for evidence to link the Democrats to Castro. Indeed, Nixon records in his memoirs that he even briefly hoped to gain political mileage from the break-in if the supposed Cuban connection "caught on" by sending his friend Bebe Rebozo to whip up sympathy among the Cuban exile community in Miami for the arrested men and so turn the heat of ethnic politics on George McGovern. Quite quickly, however, this aspect of the situation slipped from view, the "foot soldiers" who had carried out the break-in were dismissed as inconsequential bit-part players, and the search was on to link the break-in instead with high-ups in the CRP and at the White House. Through a mix of dogged detective work and leaks from more or less well-placed sources—and especially from Woodward's "Deep Throat" (whose identity is still not clearly established and who according to Woodward chose to vouchsafe his secrets in an underground car park), the *Washington Post* reporters learned enough to keep a steady flow of stories coming, but not enough to complete the jigsaw. How far up in the CRP had the burglary been authorized, if indeed it had been authorized there?

John Mitchell resigned on July 1, after several days of bizarre attempts by his wife to claim media attention—including telephone calls to a reporter that she was being held as a "political prisoner"; however, this was before any significant evidence had emerged to link him directly to the break-in, and White House leaks indicated only that Mitchell had wished to stand down so he could look after his emotionally disturbed wife. On July 22 a Long Island afternoon newspaper broke the story that G. Gordon Liddy had been dismissed from his job with the CRP more than three weeks earlier after refusing to answer the FBI's questions, and on July 25 the *New York Times* linked Liddy directly to the burglars; but was this dismissal evidence of CRP's determination that the FBI should get to the truth, or a put-up job? (It was, in fact, the latter: the idea was that Liddy, who was expected not to break his silence, and never did, was expendable).

On Aug. 1, 1972, the *Washington Post* reported that money in the bank account of one of the burglars (Barker) had been traced back to undisclosed campaign contributions to the CRP which had been laundered through Mexico. Over the following weeks the *Post* published a sequence of stories stating or implying the existence of a CRP "secret fund" used for espionage and other illicit purposes, and identifying those with authority to authorize payments from the fund as Mitchell, Magruder, CRP finance chairman Maurice Stans and (finally, on Oct. 16) Herbert W. Kalmbach, the President's personal attorney, who had also been the CRP deputy finance chairman until April 7. The *Post*, in trying to illustrate what uses had been made of this money, declared on Oct. 10 that FBI agents had "established that the Watergate bugging incident stemmed from a massive campaign of political spying and sabotage" and over the next week or so named a young California lawyer, Donald Segretti, as having recruited operatives throughout the country, with Dwight Chapin (Nixon's appointments secretary) and Howard Hunt as his link to the White House and Kalmbach as the paymaster.

In fact, Segretti's activities were, for the most part, little more than what he himself called "political hijinks", stunts and escapades to fluster the Democrats, most of which were probably not illegal. Woodward and Bernstein were chipping away at the story, aware that there was a story, but that they had not found real paydirt. What had not been reported was that from straight after the break-in pay-offs had been made to the burglars using cash campaign contributions distributed through Kalmbach. Kalmbach was Mitchell's choice and a shrewd one, for it clearly tied the White House tightly to the success of the cover-up and limited the risk that Mitchell himself could be sacrificed; Mitchell's aide at the CRP, Frederick C. LaRue, took over the job in September 1972, when Kalmbach could no longer take the pressure. Nor had any information come to light that Nixon's involvement went any further than being embarrassed by the excesses of a few relatively minor officials. Few at this point even suspected the personal involvement of Nixon in a cover-up. The President's announcement on Aug. 29, 1972—his first public comment on the break-in—that the White House counsel John Dean had conducted a thorough investigation and that no one "presently employed" in the administration had been involved in this "very bizarre incident" met with a generally favourable reaction other than among Democratic partisans.

Meanwhile, FBI investigations had continued, these being pushed with more enthusiasm by field agents than their superiors or the Justice Department (where Assistant Attorney General Henry Petersen was in charge of the investigation). On Sept. 15 a federal grand jury handed up indictments against the five burglars, Hunt and Liddy; no mention was made of any sponsorship by higher officials, or of the money controlled by Stans. The policy of containment appeared to be working. In the run-up to the election, Watergate was just a side issue to most of the press, and the big three television networks had assigned just one reporter between them to the story. The public seemed to believe the White House line that the *Washington Post's* stories were simply McGovern campaign propaganda, and on Nov. 7, election day, buoyed up by the "New Majority" and McGovern's image as an ultra-liberal, Nixon swept to victory.

November 1972–April 1973: the cover-up begins to unravel

In the weeks following the election major Watergate stories all but dried up in the press: Aware that the story appeared to have died on them, Woodward and Bernstein, and the *Washington Post's* editor, Ben Bradlee, prepared for the expected counter-attack from the White House. But all was not well at the White House: Hunt was back for more money, on behalf of all the burglars, and Dean was worrying whether he had involved himself in a cover-up which would go on for ever; too many people had become involved one way or another, increasing the risk of exposure. On Dec. 8, 1972, Hunt's wife—carrying $10,000 in $100 bills used in the pay-offs—was killed in a plane crash, and Hunt's state of mind thereafter began to give increasing concern to Colson. As the trial of the "Watergate Seven" indicted in September approached, Nixon's aides were beginning to turn against each other, Haldeman and Ehrlichman telling Nixon that they feared Colson knew more than he had admitted, and he saying the same of them. And yet, even at this point, few of those involved had realized, in their preoccupation with distancing themselves from any connection with the Watergate break-in itself, that the real danger to them all had become their involvement in the cover-up.

The first Watergate trial, which took place from Jan. 8–30, 1973, before Judge John J. Sirica in Washington, passed off without any major disclosures, notwithstanding the prosecutorial manner adopted by Sirica, who considered that the government team headed by Earl J. Silbert was handling the defendants with kid gloves. Silbert pictured Liddy as the ringleader of the group who had been given funds by Magruder to carry out legitimate intelligence gathering but had exceeded his brief. Magruder testified that he had been too preoccupied with other CRP affairs to monitor Liddy. All seven defendants were found guilty but none had implicated anyone other than those standing trial. The press was full of rumours that the men had been paid off, but nothing had come out in court.

Other inquiries were under way, however. On Feb. 7, 1973, the Senate voted by 77 to nil to establish a special investigatory committee (the Senate Select Committee on Presidential Campaign Activities) under the chairmanship of Senator Sam J. Ervin, a 76-year old North Carolina Democrat and self-styled homespun country lawyer described by his admirers as a constitutional expert. Endless and uncontrolled leaks from this Senate "Watergate Committee", some based on fact and others on speculation, were to build up pressure on the White House as the finger of suspicion was pointed at one White House official and then another. Meanwhile, on Feb. 28, the Senate Judiciary Committee opened hearings on Nixon's nomination of L. Patrick Gray, Acting Director of the FBI since the death of J. Edgar Hoover in May 1972, to become FBI Director on a permanent basis. Exactly why Nixon insisted on pushing forward the nomination at this sensitive time, to the bewilderment of much of the press and against the opposition of many of his advisers, is unclear, though it may be that Nixon was afraid that Gray could not be relied on unless he was firmly on board. Whatever the reason, Gray's testimony proved to be a series of blunders and shocks. In the first few days of testimony, in which he persistently volunteered more than he was asked, Gray confessed that FBI agents had not interviewed Martha Mitchell, at her husband's request, because of an "innate sense of courtesy"; that he had allowed John Dean to sit in on FBI interviews of White House staff and had handed him evidence relating to the case; and that Dean had removed files and other items from Hunt's White House safe. Gray was on a slippery slope which would end with his resignation as Acting Director of the FBI on April 27 following press reports the previous day that he had burned documents from Hunt's safe handed to him by Ehrlichman and Dean at a White House meeting on June 28, 1972. Gray later told the Ervin Committee that he thought Ehrlichman and Dean had clearly implied he should destroy the documents because they were "political dynamite".

"I think we ought to let him hang there. Let him twist slowly, slowly in the wind" was how Ehrlichman on March 31 advised Dean to look upon Gray's discomfiture. Dean, however, had other worries, for Gray's statements had suddenly cast the spotlight on him for the first time. Until Gray spoke, Dean had been barely mentioned in reporting of the affair; thereafter, however, he was to be the key to its unravelling. Dean had taken on the job of chief co-ordinator of the cover-up because no one else had wanted the job; he was young (35) and ambitious and took the chance to make his mark at the White House. But Dean's very availability testified to his weakness: he was inexperienced, cunning but naively so, and he lacked the mental resources to stay the course. On March 14, backed by a ruling from Nixon that his staff would not give testimony to Congress on the ground of executive privilege, Dean refused to appear before the Ervin Committee; he had, however, begun to lose his nerve, and to worry that he was in some way being set up to be the scapegoat. Moreover, it was clear that Congress would not fail to contest Nixon's attempt to block his staff from giving testimony, Ervin warning on April 2 that members of the White House staff were not "nobility or royalty" and that if they failed to obey subpoenas to come before the Senate he would recommend that the Senate should issue warrants for their arrest.

On March 23, 1973, Judge Sirica showed his displeasure with the way the government had conducted the trial of the burglars, imposing swingeing sentences on six of the defendants—up to 20 years for Liddy, and up to 35 years for Hunt and 40 years for Barker, Gonzalez, Martinez and

Sturgis (more than they might have expected for murder in the District of Columbia) while announcing that (except in Liddy's case) the sentences were provisional and would be reviewed depending on how the defendants co-operated with the Senate Watergate Committee and the continuing work of the Federal Grand Jury. At the same time Sirica read out a letter from McCord claiming that "political pressure" had been applied on the defendants to plead guilty and remain silent, that perjury had been committed, that others involved in the Watergate operation were not identified in the trial, that "I know for a fact" that it was not a CIA operation, and that "several members of my family have expressed fear for my life if I disclose knowledge of the facts in this matter". McCord himself had his sentencing postponed and was released from jail (Sirica subsequently granting him immunity from further prosecution).

Two days earlier (March 21), in a taped conversation that would become famous, Dean warned Nixon that there was a "cancer within—close to the presidency—that's growing". Dean did not disguise his agitation over his own vulnerability. He had, he told Nixon, recommended Liddy's appointment to the CRP to serve as the White House's eyes and ears on the committee; he knew that Magruder had specifically ordered Liddy to make a second attempt to place wiretaps at the Watergate; and he had made arrangements in Mitchell's presence for Kalmbach to carry out the pay-offs to the defendants with money made available by Haldeman. Dean also warned Nixon that Hunt was demanding more money, and had threatened to bring down Ehrlichman over his link to the break-in at Ellsberg's psychiatrist's. It was not Hunt, however, but Dean himself who was now the real danger. On March 26 the *Los Angeles Times* reported that McCord—who was almost certainly saying more than he knew—had told prosecutors that not only Magruder but also Dean had known of the Watergate break-in in advance: the investigation was reaching ever closer to him. On April 8, after preliminary negotiations through a lawyer, Dean began to talk to the prosecutors, while remaining in the White House. Concurrently, Haldeman and Ehrlichman were still trying to get Dean to persuade Mitchell to take the blame for the break-in, believing that this would end the problem. Magruder, too, was also talking to the prosecutors by this time, describing the Gemstone plan, how he had been coached by Mitchell and Dean to commit perjury as the cover-up began, and the payments of hush money to the burglars.

On April 15, 1973, Nixon learned from Attorney General Richard Kleindienst and Assistant Attorney General Henry E. Petersen that Dean was co-operating fully with the prosecutors, implicating Haldeman in the pay-offs to defendants and Ehrlichman in the destruction of evidence from Hunt's safe. Nixon then made a series of tactical blunders that allowed Dean to slip beyond his control. On April 15 and 16 Nixon interviewed Dean in the White House, phrasing his questions in such a deliberate way and framing his own participation in such an "innocuous perspective" that Dean, as he later testified, first began to suspect that the conversation was being taped. Nixon also tried to persuade Dean to sign a resignation letter citing "my involvement in the Watergate affair". On April 17 Nixon announced that no White House staff would be granted immunity from prosecution, a move which he evidently believed would reinforce Dean's dependence on him as the only source of a pardon. But quite the opposite occurred, for Dean, being skilfully hauled in by the prosecutors, proved willing to say more and more in an effort to win the reward of immunity from the prosecutors. On April 19 Dean said in a press statement: "Some hope or think that I will become a scapegoat in the Watergate case. Anyone who believes this does not know me, know the true facts, or understand our system of justice." On April 26, however, columnist Jack Anderson ran a story fed to him from White House sources to the effect that Mitchell and Dean had known in advance about the break-in and had orchestrated the cover-up and payments to the burglars; that Nixon had been misled by Dean; and that Ehrlichman and Colson had laboured to bring out the truth. Meanwhile, as Nixon dithered, Dean had remained at the White House collecting damaging documentary evidence about administration dirty tricks.

With his aides now openly at war with one another, the danger signs were beginning to appear for Nixon personally, so he resolved to make a sacrificial offering to the growing circle of his enemies. In a television broadcast on April 30 he told the nation that he had received "continuing assurances" from those investigating the break-in ("this senseless, illegal action") that no administration officials were involved, and had "remained convinced . . . that the charges of involvement by members of the White House staff" were false until he received "new information" which caused him to initiate a new investigation on March 21. This, it would later emerge, was a reference to the "cancer on the presidency" meeting with Dean. Nixon went on to announce the resignations of Haldeman and Ehrlichman ("two of the finest public servants it has been my privilege to know" and with "no implication whatsoever of personal wrongdoing on their part"); the resignation of Attorney General Richard Kleindienst (for ethical reasons because of his personal ties to individuals involved in the Watergate case, with which he was otherwise entirely unconnected); and the resignation of Dean (which Nixon announced without comment). The President solemnly pledged that "I will do everything in my power to ensure that the guilty are brought to justice . . . there can be no whitewash at the White House" and praised the work of "a determined Grand Jury, honest prosecutors, a courageous judge, John Sirica, and a vigorous free press". As if to demonstrate the White House view that the truth must be told, and that Nixon had been in the dark all along, his press spokesman, Ronald Ziegler, the next day issued an awkward apology to Woodward and Bernstein for the vilification he had previously heaped upon them.

The breaking of the President (May 1973–August 1974)

Far from appeasing Nixon's critics, the April 30, 1973, purge merely encouraged them. By linking the departure of Haldeman and Ehrlichman to his discovery that there had after all been a cover-up, Nixon seemingly confirmed that all the press speculation about their role in Watergate (much of which had been ill-founded) had been right on target: Not only did he thereby prejudice their case in later legal battles, he also sent an unmistakeable signal to those around him that Richard Nixon was now preoccupied with his own survival and that even his closest associates were expendable. (Haldeman remained a frequent visitor to the White House; Ehrlichman did not speak to Nixon again.) From this point on it would be every man for himself. Nor were his critics convinced by Nixon's claims that everything was now being fully investigated. On May 1 the Senate, showing a lack of faith in the integrity of the Justice Department, by unanimous voice vote called on Nixon to appoint a special prosecutor independent of the executive branch, and on May 18 Elliot Richardson (the new Attorney General) named Archibald Cox (professor of law at Harvard, and a former Solicitor General under Kennedy and Johnson) to this position. It was a damaging choice from Nixon's point of view: Cox was a Kennedy clan intimate and packed his staff with Nixon opponents. Meanwhile, on May 11 in the Pentagon Papers case, which was now seen as closely meshed with the origins of Watergate, Judge Byrne dismissed all charges against Ellsberg and Anthony Russo on the ground of "government misconduct", after being told that the FBI could not locate wiretap records he had demanded. (Byrne had already on April 27 revealed that the Watergate prosecutors had told him that Hunt and Liddy had supervised the burglary of Ellsberg's psychiatrist's office.) In a lengthy statement on May 22, Nixon, while maintaining an absolute denial that he had known in advance about the Watergate burglary or had participated in any way in a cover-up, provided a fairly full account of the background to the creation of the "plumbers" under Ehrlichman's direction; though denying that he had approved illegal activity, he accepted that "because of the emphasis I put on the crucial importance of protecting the national security, I can understand how highly motivated individuals could have felt justified in engaging in specific activities that I would have disapproved had they been brought to my attention".

On May 17, 1973, the Senate Watergate Committee under Sam Ervin began its public televised hearings on the affair, the hearings lasting through the summer. By this time attention was shifting from what the men around the President had individually known: the "central question" had become, as Senator Howard Baker put it: "What did the President know, and when did he know it?" McCord gave inconclusive testimony that a Treasury Department official, John J. Caulfield, had in January 1973 brought him an offer of clemency "from the very highest levels of the White House" in exchange for his silence at the Watergate burglars' trial. Caulfield, however, testified that the offer of clemency had come to him only from Dean, who had never explicitly said that the President had authorised it, only that it came "from way up at the top". Magruder, while thoroughly implicating his former boss Mitchell in both the Liddy espionage operations and the cover-up, said that to the best of his knowledge Nixon had no advance knowledge of the break-in and had not been involved in the cover-up. Mitchell himself, who denied any advance knowledge of the Watergate burglary or having authorised Gemstone, also insisted that as far as he was aware the President had not known about the cover-up, while freely implicating Haldeman and Ehrlichman. Kalmbach testified how he had raised $220,000 for the Watergate burglars on orders from Dean and Ehrlichman, but had no evidence to link the President to the pay-offs. Ehrlichman argued that neither Nixon nor his other top advisers had given more than a passing thought to Watergate during the summer months of 1972, amid the pressing distractions of vital matters of state and had relied on John Dean to give them accurate information but Dean had not done this, a theme echoed by Haldeman.

In the most dramatic testimony of the hearings, from June 25–29, however, John Dean (who had for his pains won only a limited immunity from prosecution, which would save him from prosecution based on testimony to the Committee, but not based on evidence collected by the Grand Jury) disclosed that Nixon had kept an "enemies list" of targets for harrassment by the FBI and Internal Revenue Service; that he (Dean) had never carried out an investigation of the sort claimed by Nixon but had rather worked with the FBI and the Justice Department to discover what they had learned to enable "plausible scenarios" to be constructed; and that his impression of a Sept. 15 meeting with Nixon was that the President had been well aware of his (Dean's) cover-up activities. Most damagingly of all, Dean also declared that at his March 21 meeting with Nixon, with Haldeman also present, the President had assured him (Dean) that there was "no problem" in raising $1,000,000 to buy the continuing silence of the Watergate burglars.

Asked whether he was "fully aware of the charges you have made under oath against the highest official of our land", Dean replied: "I realize it's an almost impossible task, it's one man against another. And it's not a very pleasant situation." As a self-confessed perjurer, Dean's testimony could hardly command universal credibility, for all the tide of opinion beginning to flow against Nixon. Then came perhaps the most dramatic development of the whole Watergate affair when on July 16 Haldeman's former assistant, Alexander Butterfield, revealed publicly before the Committee what he had testified to in executive session on July 13: that Nixon had a system for taping conversations in his private offices. On July 23 both the Senate Watergate Committee and Special Prosecutor Archibald Cox issued subpoenas to obtain access to the White House tapes, setting in motion a legal battle that would culminate a year later in Nixon's fall from office.

Since it was the tapes that in the end brought down Nixon—for without them it would only ever have been his word, and the word of some of his advisers, against some others of his advisers—the question has often been asked: why did he not destroy them, either before the Butterfield disclosure, or immediately thereafter, and assert that he was defending executive confidentiality and national security (Leon Jaworski, Cox's successor as Special Prosecutor, and other key figures in the affair later concluded that Nixon could probably have survived had he taken this course.) In his memoirs Nixon admits that he thought about destroying the tapes the moment their existence became known but that the balance of opinion among his advisers was that this would be politically and legally unwise. Nixon apparently concluded that to destroy the tapes would look like an admission of guilt, and he also somehow regarded them as an insurance policy: "I was prepared to believe that others, even people close to me, would turn against me just as Dean had done, and in that case the tapes would give me at least some protection". Perhaps fundamentally, Nixon did not at this point seriously imagine he could ever be forced to surrender the tapes, and so believed that he could still control any use to which they might be put on a selective basis.

On Aug. 29, 1973, Judge Sirica ordered that Nixon should deliver the tapes of eight specified conversations to him personally for evaluation to determine whether they should be handed over to the Grand Jury, an order upheld by the Appellate Court in Washington on Oct. 12, while on Oct. 17 Sirica dismissed a suit by the Senate Watergate Committee asking for the tapes to be handed over to it. On Oct. 19 Nixon announced that he was prepared to make available a "summary" of the tapes to Sirica and the Senate Committee, the authenticity of which would be verified by one Senator, John C. Stennis of Mississippi, who would have full access to the tapes, and that he had ordered Cox to make no further attempts to seek tapes. (The ageing Stennis was a curious choice: he was partially deaf, and the tapes were often hard or impossible to follow accurately even to those with the most acute hearing.) Cox, however, was emphatically opposed to this solution. In the face of his resistance, Nixon abolished the office of Watergate Special Prosecutor and ordered Attorney General Richardson to dismiss Cox, a demand which led both Richardson and his deputy William Ruckelshaus to resign, the order finally being carried out by the third-ranking Justice Department official, Solicitor General Robert Bork.

This, the so-called "Saturday Night Massacre" of Oct. 20, led to Cox's famous observation that "whether ours shall continue to be a government of laws and not of men is now for the Congress and ultimately the American people to decide". A million telegrams and letters of protest poured into Washington, and in the face of a massive and near universal hostile response, and the initiation of steps in the House to move his impeachment, Nixon on Oct. 23 suddenly backed down and agreed to surrender the subpoenaed tapes to a surprised Sirica. Having conceded this principle, he had effectively lost the war, though he seemed not to know it. On Oct. 26 Nixon also announced that he had asked Acting Attorney General Bork to appoint a new Special Prosecutor, to which post Leon Jaworski, a veteran Texas trial lawyer, was named on Nov. 1. Meanwhile, against the backdrop of the larger drama, Vice-President Spiro Agnew had resigned on Oct. 10 over his own involvement in an entirely separate business scandal (—*Spiro Agnew Affair, 1973*, see below). On Oct. 12 Nixon named Gerald Ford to succeed Agnew. Agnew's departure increased the willingness to consider impeachment of Nixon among those who had feared Nixon's replacement by the demagogic Agnew: with the lacklustre but sober Ford as vice-president, the presidential succession seemed in safe hands.

Over the next few months the Nixon White House slipped progressively into impotence, Nixon himself becoming increasingly isolated from his own top advisers, brooding and introspective. In the face of further allegations about his tax affairs, Nixon emotionally told a press conference on Nov. 17: "I am not a crook", an expression that would be endlessly thrown back at him by jeering demonstrators in the months to come. Nixon had lost all the close advisers who had steered him through his first term, and Haldeman's successor as White House Chief of Staff, Gen. Alexander Haig—widely regarded as Henry Kissinger's rather than Nixon's man—was determined to keep himself clear of participation in any further cover-up. Even the economy had entered a crisis after the Yom Kippur War, with inflation soaring and fuel shortages caused by the Arab oil embargo. On Nov. 21 Nixon's counsel, J. Fred Buzhardt, was obliged to give the embarrassing news to Sirica that 18½ minutes of the chronologically first of the subpoenaed tapes—from June 20, 1972 (the day Nixon returned to the White House after the arrest of the Watergate burglars) had mysteriously been erased, a circumstance explained—to almost universal derision—by the President's long-time secretary Rose Mary Woods as the result of a bizarre error on her part. (A special independent panel of technical experts appointed by Sirica later concluded that the erasure was the result of at least five separate operations, and it is possible that Nixon had begun an attempt to clean the tapes—naturally beginning with the first one relating to Watergate—which he came to realize was futile.) Meanwhile, Nixon continued to resist demands to hand over further documents and tapes to Jaworski and the Senate Watergate Committee, pleading the principle of executive confidentiality which he had already surrendered.

On Feb. 6, 1974, the House of Representatives voted by 410 to 4 to give the House Judiciary Committee broad powers to conduct an inquiry into grounds for impeachment of the President (impeachment being the method to bring to trial before the Senate officials of the executive branch). With Haldeman, his former aide Strachan, Ehrlichman, Mitchell, Colson, and two peripheral CRP figures, Robert Mardian and Kenneth Parkinson, indicted by the grand jury on March 1 on charges of conspiracy, perjury and obstruction of justice, Nixon began a process of partial backtracking. On March 6 he promised to provide the Judiciary Committee with all the tapes surrendered to the special prosecutor and admitted for the first time that Dean had told him in the "cancer on the presidency" conversation of March 21, 1973, that payments had been made to buy the silence of the Watergate burglars. On April 29, after fighting a rearguard action against sweeping demands from the House Judiciary Committee for more tapes, Nixon suddenly announced his intention to release transcripts, edited for relevance and national security considerations, of all the conversations the Judiciary Committee was seeking the tapes for, and others it had not sought, and to allow the senior members of the Committee to hear the original tapes in full to verify the editing. The tapes would, Nixon assured the nation in a televised broadcast, prove that he had had no prior knowledge of the break-in, and knew nothing of the cover-up until told of it by Dean in the "cancer on the presidency" meeting of March 21, 1973, as a result of which he had ordered Dean to deliver to him a written report and then, when Dean failed to do this, had ordered a fresh investigation by Ehrlichman.

The public release of the 200,000-word edited transcripts the following day (April 30) did Nixon no good at all. The sensibilities of his dwindling band of supporters in the country were shocked by the 146 gaps marked "expletive deleted" and the clear evidence that, far from seeking to determine the truth, Nixon had been actively involved in discussions of misleading "scenarios" to explain away the steady stream of damaging disclosures. Nixon himself admitted in his April 29 broadcast that the tape of March 21, 1973, in which he, Dean and Haldeman discussed how to respond to Hunt's demands for money had "potential for misinterpretation"; the correct interpretation, said Nixon, was that while he had admittedly ("thinking out loud") discussed the implications of buying Hunt's silence, he had contemplated the idea only to prevent disclosure of national security secrets unrelated to Watergate and had in any case gone on to reject the idea. (Those national security secrets, Nixon would later explain, after many other things had become known, related to Hunt's activities against Daniel Ellsberg.) Most who read the transcripts, however, found clear evidence of Nixon engaging deeply in the cover-up, unconcerned about legal or moral issues but only what the risks were of the cover-up coming unstuck. Whether or not the conversation concluded with an understanding that Hunt could and should be paid off was essentially a matter of interpretation, interpretation which depended on an assessment of what was likely to have been unstated, implicit, taken for granted. The many ambiguities of the transcripts, likewise, seemed to reflect Nixon's apparent inability to sustain a logical and orderly sequence of thought as he moved, at times gruntingly incoherent, from one tangential meditation to another: it seemed an alarming insight into the processes of the presidential mind.

At the same time, the transcripts of the tapes were challenged by the House Judiciary Committee, which on July 9 published its alternative version of what some of the fuzzy and often indistinct tapes actually said. (The chairman of the judiciary committee, Pete Rodino, delicately noted that the Committee had enjoyed the use of superior audio equipment.) There were some striking contrasts with the White House version, such that a remark of March 22, 1973, by Nixon to Dean, recorded in the White House transcript as "in order to get off the cover-up line" became, in the Judiciary Committee alternative, "in order to get on with the cover-up plan". Particularly damaging was the inclusion in the Judiciary Committee version of a passage, not found in the White House edition and also from March 22, 1973, where Nixon discussed with Mitchell the relative merits of a total cover-up or adopting the tactic of "just letting it out there" and trying to see things through. Like much else in the transcripts, the passage was profoundly ambiguous as to the real intent in Nixon's words, but a tide of opinion was now flowing strongly that Nixon himself had either orchestrated or sanctioned the cover-up and interpretations sympathetic to the President were accorded an ever-diminishing credibility. And all the suspicions seemed to many to be only confirmed by Nixon's dogged insistence—which seemed to have nothing more to do with the notion of executive confidentiality, which Nixon had breached when he first agreed to give eight tapes to Sirica—that he alone would determine what tapes would be handed over and to whom.

On June 7, 1974, Sirica confirmed what had been widely reported since mid-May, that the grand jury, in handing up indictments on March 1, had secretly named Nixon himself as an unindicted co-conspirator: only the status of his office, it meant, had saved Nixon from criminal indictment (it being far from clear that a sitting President could in fact be indicted). Nixon's position was nonetheless still not hopeless. In a parliamentary system he would have been long gone, or else the scandal would have been long buried, but there was no precedent for the resignation of a President while in office. To remove him required not a congressional vote of no confidence, but his impeachment by the House and his trial by the Senate, something for which there was no precedent. Even some of Nixon's enemies wondered whether the credibility of the whole system of the balance of powers between President and Congress might be put under fatal strain by such a contest, and whether Congress might not be overreaching itself. Nixon still commanded enough votes in the Senate to make a trial there by no means a foregone conclusion: two-thirds of the senators would need to vote for conviction, and the consequences of a vote less than near-unanimous were potentially disastrous for the Congress itself. When the House Judiciary Committee voted on the articles of impeachment on July 27–30 the three articles were passed by votes of 27 to 11, 28 to 10, and 21 to 17: substantial margins for most purposes, for sure, but arguably not substantial enough to justify the impeachment of a President, especially given that the Committee had a partisan majority, with 21 Democrats to 17 Republicans. (Two articles of impeachment, citing Nixon's alleged evasion of taxes and secret bombing of Cambodia, were voted down.) While the Democratic leadership, frantic that it might have overreached itself in pressing for impeachment, was mobilizing all its resources for one last great push against Nixon, a faint but perceptible counter-current of opinion was beginning to flow that the Judiciary Committee, with its relentless bias, its endless prejudicial leaking, and its adoption of nakedly political rather than judicial criteria, had neither conducted itself with appropriate objectivity or gravity nor finally proved a sufficient case.

At this point, however, Congress was joined by the third party to the constitutional system, the independent judiciary. On July 24, 1974, the Supreme Court unanimously by eight to nil (one justice, William Rehnquist, did not sit on the case) ruled that Nixon must hand over the tapes of 64 more conversations subpoenaed by Sirica at Jaworski's request for use in the pending trial of the seven Watergate "cover-up" case defendants. The gist of the Court's argument was that, executive confidentiality notwithstanding (and Nixon himself had surrendered that principle), the defendants were entitled to have all the evidence brought forward to ensure a fair trial. (It was a curious argument in that the tapes were being sought by the prosecution not the defence.) We know now—from the accounts of Haldeman and others—that Nixon's impulse was to fight the Court had any of the justices taken his side. As it was, faced with a unanimous bench, and the unanimous advice to accede of his advisers, Nixon bent the knee and submitted.

What finally sealed Nixon's fate was the evidence of one of the tapes that the Supreme Court had ordered him to hand over to Sirica. Nixon had kept his own attorneys in the dark as to the content of the tapes but on July 24, 1974, the day of the Supreme Court decision, he told J. Fred Buzhardt, his counsel in charge of the tapes, to listen to the conversation of June 23, 1972, in which he ordered Haldeman to try to get the CIA to block the FBI's investigation of the source of the money found on the Watergate burglars. Buzhardt realized at once that this was the "smoking gun" which once made known would make Nixon's position untenable. In the following days Buzhardt, Nixon's counsel James St Clair, White House Chief of Staff Haig, and the most powerful Cabinet member Henry Kissinger, privately worked to persuade Nixon to end the misery of his administration by resigning; St Clair and Haig also privately briefed congressional Republican leaders. On Aug. 5 Nixon himself made public the transcript of his June 23, 1972, discussion with Haldeman, conceding that "portions . . . are at variance with certain of my previous statements" but insisting that "the record, in its entirety, does not justify the extreme step of impeachment and removal of a President". By the next day, however, all the members of the House Judiciary Committee who had voted against impeachment had changed their minds and on Aug. 7 Republican congressional leaders told Nixon that 425 of the 435 members of the House would now vote to impeach him, and that he could no longer count on even a dozen senators to vote against conviction.

To much of America these final days were a classic case of nemesis, a vindication of the American system of a balance of powers and a free press, even a reassertion of good over evil. To Nixon, however, it seemed that he was the victim of political misjudgments only—by his aides, more than his own—and perhaps of the iconoclastic, mood of the times. The attitude of his fellow Republicans in Congress seemed a violation of his own creed of political ethics: "I campaigned for a lot of people", he complained, "some were turkeys, but I campaigned for all of them." Announcing his resignation to the nation on Aug. 8 in a speech which trumpeted his foreign policy achievements and barely mentioned Watergate, Nixon portrayed his problem as essentially one arising from political difficulties, declaring that "it has become evident to me that I no longer have a strong enough political base in the Congress". The next day he formally resigned, and Gerald Ford became the 38th President of the United States without ever having sought the office. Echoing the words of Archibald Cox at the time of the Saturday Night Massacre, in an inaugural statement Ford declared: "Our long national nightmare is over. Our Constitution works. Our great Republic is a government of laws and not of men. Here, the people rule."

The aftermath

Nixon disgraced was not Nixon forgiven. On Sept. 8, President Ford announced that, because Nixon was in poor health and because it would be years before he could get a fair trial, he had decided to grant him a "full, free and absolute" pardon for "all offences against the United States". Ironically, this essentially humane gesture would cost Ford dear, for the bitter reaction it caused—even his own press secretary resigned in protest—is widely considered to have tipped the result of the presidential election of 1976 against him to Jimmy Carter. What irked America was that Nixon never apologized. In 1976 he appeared in a series of television interviews with David Frost in an apparent attempt to begin his rehabilitation, but what the viewers saw was no remorse for the damage he had inflicted on the country, but only bad words for the deeds of his staff, and self-pity that he had become embroiled in their blunders. Since that time Nixon has never, in the simplest, most straightforward sense, really apologized for Watergate, and despite his occasional pronouncements on the affairs of the day he has never been readmitted to the inner councils of his party or accorded a role by the White House. He remains, a decade and a half later, an exile in his own land.

Nixon's attitude was also a cause of bitter resentment for some who had been his closest allies. Nixon failed to act on Haldeman's suggestion to him that as his last presidential act he should pardon all those involved in Watergate, and nearly all the principals in the Watergate cover-up—Haldeman, Mitchell, Dean, Ehrlichman, Magruder, Kalmbach, LaRue, Colson—went to jail either directly on Watergate-related charges or alternatively or additionally for illegal fund-raising (Kalmbach) or connection with the plumbers' activities against Ellsberg in the Pentagon Papers affair (Colson, Ehrlichman and Krogh). Segretti and Chapin went to jail for the exposure of their pre-Watergate "dirty tricks". (No one other than the original "Watergate Seven" was ever charged in connection with the Watergate break-in itself.) Of the more significant figures in the cover-up, only Strachan escaped altogether, charges against him being dropped because of a limited immunity agreement under which the Senate Watergate Committee had obtained his testimony, while Stans escaped with a fine. Nixon himself, however, not only escaped indictment but also refused, despite the protection of a presidential pardon, to come to the assistance of his former aides. Subpoenaed by Ehrlichman as a defence witness in the main Watergate cover-up trial (which also involved Mitchell, Haldeman, Mardian and Parkinson), Nixon entered hospital for treatment for phlebitis on Sept. 23, 1974, his attorneys insisting that he was too unwell to give evidence either orally or in writing. And, despite the finding of three court-appointed doctors that the former President would be able to provide at least written answers in the New Year, Sirica, to the dismay of the defendants, ruled on Dec. 5 that the trial must proceed without Nixon's testimony. All the defendants save Parkinson were convicted of perjury, conspiracy and obstruction of justice (Mardian's conviction being reversed in 1977).

Gordon Liddy served the longest sentence of anyone convicted in connection with Watergate or the activities of the White House "plumbers": 52 months. Haldeman and Ehrlichman served 18 months, Mitchell 19, Colson seven and Dean four. When John Mitchell was released on parole in January 1979, he was the last of the 25 persons jailed in connection with Watergate to be freed.

The subsequent lives of the Watergate principals took different courses but none has re-emerged as a political figure: all are in effect known primarily for only one thing, their role in Watergate (though Ehrlichman has become a successful author). Their personal accounts of Watergate earned them large sums of money. Haldeman (now a businessman in California) earned a reputed $100,000 for one 1975 CBS TV interview and even today Gordon Liddy is said to earn $1,500,000 per year as a celebrity speaker on the lecture circuit. Magruder and Colson for their part discovered the consolations of religion, Magruder becoming a Presbyterian minister and Colson a lay preacher; in March 1988 Magruder became head of the city commission of values and ethics in Columbus, Ohio. John Mitchell died on Nov. 10, 1988, the only one of the key figures who never published his version of Watergate, possibly taking with him to the grave the solution to several of the key mysteries of the affair.

Many views can be taken about the real heinousness or otherwise of what happened at the Watergate and the cover-up that followed. One thing that can be said with some assurance, however, is that at any time other than the mid-1970s the affair would never have assumed such proportions. As

Nixon complains on seemingly every other page of his memoirs, he did not invent dirty tricks and wiretapping of opponents: Lyndon Johnson, his predecessor, had bugged his own Vice-President, Hubert Humphrey, and those working for the CRP accepted it as fact that the Democrats had bugged and tried to sabotage Nixon's 1968 campaign and would be trying to do it again in 1972. Even Woodward and Bernstein were not above basing their reports on illegally-acquired phone records or making illegal approaches to the grand jury. Nor was Nixon the first President to have a taping system: Franklin Roosevelt was the first to do this—with a microphone hidden on the lamp on his desk—and the tradition was certainly continued by Kennedy and Johnson: indeed, Nixon had Johnson's system removed when he came to power in 1969 but later had second thoughts and installed his own. Covering-up for political aides was also as old as politics itself and had reached a high point under Johnson. Bigger secrets than Watergate were still being tightly held at that time, as the later investigations of the CIA's "family jewels" affair would show.

What in retrospect is striking about the Watergate cover-up is not how massive and sinister it was, but how chaotic, ad hoc, and liable to implosion. Part of Nixon's problem indeed, was not that he was playing too hard but that he was not playing hard enough. He—or his aides—leaned on the FBI and the Justice Department to ease back their investigations, but they never tried hard enough to succeed. Anaemic though these investigations were, they led to the original trial of the Watergate burglars, and it was the trial—more than the reporting of the *Washington Post*—which began the opening of the can of worms. At many points Nixon seems to have had a chance to "hang tough", but to have backed away from it: in allowing his staff to go before congressional committees; in accepting the appointment of a special prosecutor; in bending before the legal process which led to the surrender of his tapes rather than simply destroying them and defying anyone to do something about it. Every insider's account of the Watergate cover-up shifts the blame to someone else, but one thing is a constant theme: Nixon was there, enough to incriminate him, but never enough to be in charge. He never adopted a tough-it-out hands-on approach to the problem, and his own remoteness and indecisiveness discouraged those around him, weakened their resolve, and at the last led to a breaking of ranks. To read the transcripts of the tapes is to see Nixon casting about for ways out of his difficulties, elliptic in his thought processes, at times rambling, incoherent, only vaguely in control of the facts of the situation.

It may be, as Haldeman maintains, that the Watergate break-in was the result of Nixon's pressure on Colson to get something on Larry O'Brien. It may also be that it was instead, as Dean presumed, the consequence of pressure on the CRP people—Mitchell, and especially Magruder—from White House aides like Haldeman and Ehrlichman. There is perhaps no fully plausible theory of the break-in which has Nixon directly ordering it; equally, there is none which does not trace its inception back, however indirectly, to pressure from Nixon himself. It was not, however, for the break-in but for the cover-up that Nixon finally fell, and there we have some mysteries too. We know—it was there on the famous "smoking gun" tape—that Nixon told Haldeman on June 23, 1972, to blackmail the CIA into ordering the FBI not to "follow the money" found on the burglars;

his argument, he told Haldeman, should be that there was a danger of
opening the "whole Bay of Pigs thing" again. Was Nixon just fishing,
encouraged by the fact that the burglars were Cubans and that Hunt
had been involved in the Bay of Pigs? Was this a hidden reference,
which Haldeman would not have understood but CIA Director Richard
Helms most certainly would, to the dangerous inter-connections between
the CIA's early 1960s plots (in which Helms was closely involved) to kill
Castro and the assassination of President John F. Kennedy (see *John
F. Kennedy Assassination Affair, 1963–79; CIA "Family Jewels" Affair,
1974–76*, above)? Certainly he touched a sore enough nerve for the CIA
to react by putting some mild pressure on Gray at first, but by July 6,
1972, Gray was reporting back to Nixon that the CIA's view was that it
had nothing to hide and was happy for the investigation to proceed.

Helms's personal fate was to be discussed by Nixon after the election,
but the CIA as an institution was barely touched by Watergate. Curiously,
perhaps, the whole CIA-Bay of Pigs-Cuba aspect of the break-in very
rapidly disappeared from investigation of the affair. The minority (Republican) staff of the Senate Watergate Committee explored a variety of
links back to the CIA: that one of the burglars (Martinez) was an
acknowledged current CIA "asset" and that all of them had past CIA
links; the relationship between Hunt and the Mullen enterprise, which
was a CIA front; reports that a CIA operative had visited McCord's
home immediately after the break-in and burned documents; evidence
that the CIA through Robert Bennett had fed Woodward and Bernstein
with information designed to lead them away from the CIA connection
and to the CRP and the White House. Fred Thompson, who headed
the minority Committee's staff, became convinced that the CIA had at
the last monitored the operations of the Hunt-Liddy group, and possibly
even sabotaged it to weaken the White House, a view later endorsed by
Haldeman. Both Thompson and Haldeman also formed the view that
knowledge of the activities of the group had become fairly widespread
among a murky underworld of intelligence operatives and tipsters, and
that key figures in the Democratic Party may have known about the plans
for the break-in advance; this view implies that the arrests on the night of
June 17 were perhaps not simply an accident but the result of a laid trap.
Neither the Democratic majority on the Watergate Committee, however,
nor the press, which had set their sights on Nixon and his aides as their
target, showed much interest in the CIA aspect of the affair, and the
CIA most effectively stonewalled the investigation, with the complicity
of the congressional oversight committees which nominally monitored the
agency. It would only be after Nixon had been deposed that the CIA itself
would become a target of investigative journalism, with the exposure of the
"family jewels" in the winter of 1974–75.

As Haldeman notes, Nixon and the CIA were old enemies. Nixon
had demanded access to the CIA files on the Bay of Pigs, and effectively been refused. He resented, perhaps feared, its Ivy League aura
and its ability to set its own course regardless of which administration was in power, and had made no secret of his wish to tame the
agency. There was little affection for Nixon at the FBI either—despite
the muddled obsequiousness of Gray—or indeed in many other areas

of the executive branch. Here was a President who had made no secret of his intention to bring the executive under his control, to bypass normal channels and work through his own men—men for the most part, like Haldeman and Ehrlichman, who had no other loyalties in public life than to Nixon himself. He had failed, for all the power of his office, to gain this ascendancy in his first term, but openly boasted of his plans to do so on the back of a massive election victory in 1972. Many people in Washington had little love for Richard Nixon, and no sooner had the break-in occurred than the consequences of this friendlessness began to appear. Nixon, at the end, was a President who sought to wield a power which the bureaucracy, the Congress and the press, did not wish him to possess, and he was not strong enough, decisive enough, or wily enough, to avoid encirclement by his enemies.

Victim of his own ambitions and weaknesses, Nixon was no less a victim of the times. His Democratic predecessors, Kennedy and Johnson, had led America into a massive military involvement in Vietnam which had led to the bitterest national turmoil since the Civil War. Nixon had set himself to extricate America from the war—had begun secret, frustrating negotiations with North Vietnam right in the early days of his presidency in 1969—but the war still dragged on, and he was the target of the hatreds aroused by it. Many of the normal decencies of politics were in abeyance. The President's men bugged the Watergate, but the Republican campaign was under attack too: Republican offices were sacked or burned in several cities; locally, Democratic workers mobilized the disaffected young in mob actions. The Democratic Party convention of 1972 was a chaos, as every ultra-liberal faction and minority sought to make policy, and the presidential nominee McGovern was far outside what had been the Democratic mainstream since Roosevelt created the modern party. No excess of rhetoric seemed beyond McGovern, who three times likened the President of the United States to Hitler, and the Grand Old Party to the Ku Klux Klan.

Nixon may have carried the "silent majority" in 1972, but the intellectuals, the opinion-formers, had seemingly turned against Nixon's America. The office of the presidency had once carried an innate authority which had put its holder on a different plane from lesser mortals; all-powerful in his own sphere, the physical embodiment of the national identity. Now those who made opinion were seeking a casting down of idols; it was time, it seemed, for even the President of the United States to stand naked. In Nixon—a man whose evident unease among his "betters" was still evident 30 years after he first came to Washington, who surrounded himself with Californian advertising men rather than the east coast Ivy League intelligentsia of Kennedy's Camelot, whose political sobriquet was "Tricky Dicky" and who sweated too much under television cameras—they found an idol who lacked real authority, who could be toppled. After Nixon would come only Ford, an apologetic uncertain figure who could not even claim the authority that came from election, and Jimmy Carter, a man whose own embarrassment in the face of the opportunities of power ultimately embarrassed America itself.

In the election in 1980—and re-election in 1984—of Reagan, America at one level appeared to put behind the years of national self-doubt: this, indeed, was the very theme on which Reagan campaigned. There is, nonetheless, an insecurity about the office of the President which was not there before Watergate. If one President may resign—and for crimes rather less than the vilest recorded in this world this century—then others may be made to follow. The cry of impeachment went up in some quarters at the time of the Iran–contra affair in 1986–87 (see below) over little more than an exaggerated clash of decision-making authority in foreign policy, and Reagan ditched his White House intimates at the first sign of problems. He, it was clear, would be no Nixon, defiantly defending the men around him simply because they were the men around him. Reagan would benefit from a new mood of national self-satisfaction, just as Nixon suffered from a mood of national self-doubt, and the benefits of being seen as an amiable custodian of traditional virtues; yet Reagan's presidency proved an oddly personal one, a personal as much as presidential rule. The imperial presidency that Nixon inherited and had wrested from his grip has yet to be restored. It may be that Watergate conclusively established the ultimate supremacy of the other branches of government over the executive.

FJH

Spiro Agnew Affair (1973)

Spiro Agnew, Vice-President (1969–Oct. 10, 1973).
Gerald Ford, Agnew's successor as Vice-President.
Gen. Alexander Haig, White House Chief of Staff in 1973.
Richard M. Nixon, President (1969–74).

Spiro Agnew resigned as Vice-President of the United States on Oct. 10, 1973, in the face of allegations that he had taken tens of thousands of dollars in bribes from engineering contractors in a period from the early 1960s to December 1972. In normal times his fall would have been a major political event, but against the background of Watergate (see *Watergate Affair, 1972–74*, above) it passed with relatively little sensation. President Nixon then nominated Gerald Ford, the Republican minority leader in the House of Representatives, to become Vice-President. Ford, considered a dull but respected figure, faced little congressional opposition, and was sworn in on Dec. 6, 1973.

Spiro Agnew was chief executive of Baltimore County in 1962–66, and then served as Governor of Maryland before taking office as Richard Nixon's Vice-President in 1969. His reputation as Vice-President was based on little more than his demagogic attacks on radical students and "effete" liberal intellectuals. He had few allies in the Nixon administration, and Nixon himself had wished to drop him from the ticket for his second-term race in 1972 in favour of former Democratic Texas Governor John Connally, before reluctantly concluding that this would be politically inadvisable.

It was in February 1973 that Agnew first learned that he had become a target of federal prosecutors investigating the payment of kickbacks in the awarding of construction contracts in Baltimore. In other times, perhaps, the investigation could have been quietly put to sleep without further ado, but Agnew's misfortune was that his troubles began just as the Watergate cover-up (in which he personally was totally uninvolved) was beginning to break apart. Neither Nixon nor the Justice Department were able, even had they wished, to extend to Agnew the level of protection and sympathetic consideration which a Vice-President might normally have expected; indeed, Agnew was to suffer a display of particular zeal from the Justice Department, which had come under heavy fire for its half-hearted investigation of the Watergate break-in. Once news that Agnew was under investigation became public (with a story in the *Wall Street Journal* of Aug. 7), he was effectively set adrift by the White House. His efforts to stabilize his position were undermined by a systematic campaign of leaking of allegations against him by those involved in prosecuting the case, to a degree that even some liberals bitterly opposed politically to Agnew considered that his rights to a fair trial had been compromised. While Agnew at first assured his loyal supporters that he was innocent and would fight the charges against him, and also flirted with the idea of throwing his case before the House of Representatives, behind the scenes his lawyers sought to negotiate a plea bargain with the Justice Department which would allow him to accept a relatively minor misdemeanour charge, avoid jail, and resign without forcing the spectacle of a trial in the courts of impeachment by the House. (There were conflicting views as to whether a Vice-President could be forced to stand trial before the courts or would instead have to be impeached by the House and convicted by the Senate.)

On Oct. 10, the day of his resignation, Agnew pleaded *nolo contendere* in federal court in Baltimore to a single misdemeanour charge of income-tax evasion arising from payments made to him by engineering contractors while Governor of Maryland in 1967. He was fined $10,000 and placed on probation for three years. (A *nolo contendere* plea, while technically not a guilty plea but only a statement of unwillingess to contest charges, in law has the same effect.) Judge Walter E. Hoffman accepted the plea bargain "in the light of the overwhelming national interest". The prosecutors submitted a 40-page summary of evidence which detailed all the charges they would otherwise have brought against the Vice-President.

In his 1980 account of the events leading to his resignation, *Go Quietly . . . Or Else*, Agnew asserted his innocence of the charges made against him in 1973. He claimed that he had been hounded from office by ambitious glory-seeking Baltimore prosecutors who had browbeaten witnesses into giving perjured testimony, by the personal hostility of Attorney General Elliot Richardson (pictured by Agnew as a sanctimonious anti-ethnic WASP prig with presidential ambitions which Agnew stood in the way of), by the machinations of White House Chief of Staff Gen. Alexander Haig and President Richard Nixon (who thought to serve up Agnew as a sacrificial offering to ease his own Watergate difficulties), and by a hostile media assisted by prejudicial leaks from the Justice Department. While admitting that he had accepted gifts from contractors, Agnew claimed that he had regarded these as campaign contributions rather than personal presents or bribes; such campaign payments by individuals hoping to do business with the state had long been the normal practice in Maryland, whichever party was in power; and he had never awarded a contract just because a contribution had been paid, though of course it had been normal practice to favour "friends" rather than "enemies" where other factors were equal.

Agnew claimed that he agreed finally to a single count *nolo contendere* plea because of exhaustion, because he realized that the prosecutors and the Justice Department were out to destroy him at whatever cost, because he believed that he would not get a fair trial in predominantly black Baltimore, and because he realized that Nixon had determined to throw him to the wolves in an effort to save himself. Most bizarrely, Agnew claimed that a conversation between his military aide, Gen. Mike Dunn, and Gen. Haig on Oct. 4, had led him (Agnew) to conclude that his own life might be in danger if he did not resign, possibly from an order by Haig (who according to Agnew was by that point the de facto President) to the CIA to eliminate him. Agnew wrote that he had "perhaps" overreacted because of his mental state, but that the congressional CIA investigations of the later 1970s, which had disclosed CIA involvement in plots to assassinate foreign leaders, meant that he now realized "even more than before that I might have been in great danger".

While Nixon, who had never been close to Agnew, was temporarily relieved to see him resign, the Vice-President's departure from office in fact backfired on Nixon. As long as Agnew stood next in line for the presidency, even Nixon's most determined enemies hesitated at the thought of Agnew succeeding him. With the accommodating middle-of-the-road Gerald Ford installed as Vice-President, Nixon's own position became significantly weakened, and momentum gathered for his impeachment.

After his resignation Agnew (disbarred as a lawyer in Maryland in 1974) began a business career. His fines, legal costs and back tax liabilities of $160,000 (which Agnew has claimed were charged on income he never received, but agreed to pay to avoid further litigation and harrassment) were paid by his friend Frank Sinatra. In April 1981, at the end of a civil damages suit brought by three Maryland taxpayers, Agnew was ordered by a Maryland court to repay to the state of Maryland some $248,735 in alleged kickbacks, plus accumulated interest, that he had taken while Governor and Vice-President.

FJH

Mitchell/Stans/Vesco Affair (1973–74)

John Mitchell, Attorney General under Richard Nixon.
Maurice Stans, Nixon's Secretary of Commerce.
Robert Vesco, financier.

John Mitchell, formerly Richard Nixon's Attorney General, and Maurice Stans, formerly Nixon's Secretary of Commerce, were on April 28, 1974, acquitted by a New York jury on all counts relating to payments made by New Jersey financier Robert Vesco to President Nixon's Committee to Re-elect the President (CRP) in April 1972. Mitchell had at the time headed CRP while Stans was its finance director.

Mitchell, Stans, Vesco, and a New Jersey politician named Harry L. Sears had been indicted on May 10, 1973, on charges of conspiracy and obstruction of justice, while Stans and Mitchell were also accused of perjury. It was charged that Mitchell and Stans had negotiated a $200,000 payment from Vesco to be made to the CRP in return for a pledge that they would influence a Securities and Exchange Commission (SEC) investigation into Vesco's management of his Swiss-based company Investors Overseas Services Ltd. In January 1973—with its finances under intense scrutiny because of the Watergate affair (see above)—the CRP had returned the $200,000 to Vesco. By the time of the indictment Vesco had fled the United States, and during 1973 unsuccessful attempts were made to extradite him from Costa Rica and the Bahamas (see Bahamas: *Pindling Affair, 1983–88*).

A key prosecution witness was John Dean, who had also become President Nixon's chief accuser in the Watergate affair. The White House thus drew some brief comfort from the indication that one jury at least had not found Dean a credible witness, or had been reluctant to see Mitchell and Stans punished for offences which had not profited them personally but could be be seen as part of the political game. While these parallels with Watergate were obvious, it was also true by 1974 that many Americans had begun to feel that crimes committed by CRP officials or at the White House should more properly be laid at the door of the President himself.

In a separate case, Stans was fined $5,000 on May 14, 1975, after pleading guilty to accepting illegal campaign contributions from corporate contributors on behalf of the CRP in 1972. Mitchell was sentenced to jail to his involvement in the Watergate cover-up. Since leaving the United States, Robert Vesco has remained an elusive figure, shuttling from one Caribbean destination to another. In August 1986 Fidel Castro disclosed that Vesco had been living in Cuba, where he was receiving medical treatment.

FJH

John Connally Affair (1973–75)

John B. Connally, Secretary of the Treasury (1971–72).

John B. Connally, a former Democratic Governor of Texas who had gone on to serve as Secretary of the Treasury in the Nixon administration in 1971–72 (formally joining the Republican Party in 1973), was on April 17, 1975, acquitted on charges of accepting bribes.

Connally (who had come to national fame when wounded in the assassination of President Kennedy for which see *John F. Kennedy Assassination Affair, 1963–79*, above) had been accused of accepting a bribe, while Secretary of the Treasury, offered by Jacob Jacobsen, a lawyer retained by a group of milk producers, in exchange for recommending an increase in federal milk price supports. Jacobsen, the principal prosecution witness, claimed that he had handed over $10,000 to Connally, but the jury believed Connally's version that he had twice rejected offers of money from Jacobsen.

Speculation about the supposed milk money scandal was rife in 1973–74 and contributed to a popular sense that the Nixon administration was contaminated by corruption. In retrospect it is a remarkable commentary on the mood of the times that the Justice Department elected to bring charges against such a prominent public figure on the basis of evidence which a jury would find flimsy to a degree. Connally went on to become a candidate for the 1980 Republican presidential nomination, but lost out to Ronald Reagan.

FJH

CIA "Family Jewels" Affair (1974–76)

James J. Angleton, CIA counter-intelligence chief.
Frank Church, chairman of Senate select committee which investigated
   the CIA.
William E. Colby, Director of CIA (Sept. 4, 1973–June 30, 1976).
Gerald Ford, President (1974–77).
Richard Helms, Director of CIA (1966–Feb. 2, 1973).
Nelson Rockefeller, Ford's Vice-President.

The *New York Times* on Dec. 22, 1974, charged that the CIA had under
the Nixon administration engaged in a massive programme of domestic
surveillance of anti-war activists and other dissidents (in violation of
its charter, confining the CIA to foreign operations). The next month
President Ford—anxious not to become entangled in such a cover-up as had
engulfed Nixon, whom he had succeeded but five months earlier(see *Watergate Affair, 1972–74*, above)—appointed a special blue-ribbon commission
headed by Vice-President Nelson Rockefeller to investigate the charges.
Congress in turn quickly took up the issue, and a Senate Committee headed
by Frank Church developed a series of exposures which did severe damage
to the CIA's reputation and morale.
   The CIA was already in deep trouble by late 1974. It was widely
accused of engineering the bloody overthrow of Salvador Allende in Chile
in September 1973; it was vaguely linked in the popular mind to Watergate;
it had proved unable to foresee and prepare for the energy crisis triggered
in the winter of 1973–74 by the OPEC oil cartel. The CIA, often suspected
by conservatives and isolationists in the 1950s as a tool of the east coast
liberal establishment, had by the 1970s become a worldwide symbol of US
imperialism, resented both at home and abroad. At the same time, those
who wielded power looked on its autonomy with resentment, and under
Nixon relations between the agency and the White House had become ever
more frosty, especially after CIA Director Richard Helms refused to assist
Nixon to block the FBI's investigation of the Watergate break-in (a refusal
for which Helms was dismissed after the 1972 election).
   Internal CIA politics played a part in the agency's misfortunes. On Dec.
20, 1974, William Colby, the CIA's Director since September 1973, met
New York Times reporter Seymour Hersh and confirmed the essentials of
Hersh's forthcoming story (while assuring him that illegal practices had
now been ended). He then used his knowledge that the story was to be
published to demand and obtain the resignation of James Jesus Angleton
who, as the agency's long-time counter-intelligence chief, was personally
implicated in many of the domestic intelligence activities. Angleton's chief
assistants were also purged. The Dec. 22 *New York Times* story meanwhile
attributed domestic surveillance operations specifically to Angleton.
   Some of his colleagues thought that Colby, who had personally supervised
one of the cruellest operations in the CIA's history in the 1960s—"Operation Phoenix" in Vietnam—had "got religion"; others that he was motivated
by animosity to Angleton; a few Angleton loyalists wondered whether

Colby might not be the top-level Soviet mole whom the counterintelligence staff had sought for years. Others saw Colby as seeking to save the agency by making a full confession of past misdeeds, and some (including Colby) believed that Angleton's obsessive fear that the agency had been penetrated by Soviet moles or misled by KGB "disinformation agents" (spurious defectors) bordered on the paranoid and had actually weakened the agency by fostering mutual suspicion and operational hesitancy. The issue had arisen most acutely in the case of the 1964 KGB defector Yuri Tvanovich Nosenko, who had "cleared" the Soviet Union of involvement in the assassination of President Kennedy (see *John F. Kennedy Assassination Affair, 1963–79*, above), but whose story was disbelieved by Angleton and some others in the CIA, who interrogated Nosenko in solitary confinement for three years. The forces unleashed by Colby proved unstoppable, however, crippling the covert side of agency operations and demoralizing many who worked for it.

Over Christmas 1974 Colby sent to President Ford a several-hundred-page account of the agency's so-called "skeletons" of "family jewels", these being the agency's deepest and most embarrassing secrets including its involvement during the Eisenhower and Kennedy administrations in plots to assassinate Cuban leader Fidel Castro. From this point Ford and his administration began to distance themselves from the bad odour in which the agency found itself, leaving it increasingly vulnerable. As Ford later explained: "In the aftermath of Watergate, it was important that we be totally above board about these past abuses and avoid giving any substance to charges that we were engaging in a 'cover-up'." Ford himself had been one of a small group of congressmen responsible for oversight of the CIA in the 1950s and 1960s, yet seemingly knew nothing of the assassination plots until told about them by Colby. To balance the needs of avoiding the appearance of a cover-up while not disclosing too much, Ford set up the Rockefeller Commission to investigate judiciously and not too intrusively (the Commission's investigations being conducted in private).

The Rockefeller Commission report, published on June 10, 1975, was a rather anodyne document, concentrating on the charges made by the *New York Times* story concerning the CIA's role in domestic surveillance. The CIA's activities were said by the Commission to have included some "plainly unlawful" methods, including opening of mail, wiretapping, room bugging, burglaries, monitoring of overseas phone calls, administering drugs to unsuspecting persons, and infiltration of political groups. Some of the most controversial activity had occurred as part of "Operation Chaos" in the late 1960s and 1970s, which was designed to provide intelligence on disorders associated with the anti-war movement and campus radicalism. Unacceptable as all this seemed to many, this was a pattern of activity difficult to see as of the most heinous character (other than for those with a fundamental hostility to the principle of governmental intelligence-gathering per se), for while the CIA had monitored dissidents, this had been primarily to investigate any connections with foreign governments (of which it found little evidence), and it had not engaged in active attempts at sabotage and disruption of their efforts. Furthermore, the Commission found that "the agency's own recent actions, undertaken for the most part in 1973 and 1974, have gone far to terminate the activities upon which this investigation has focused". The Commission, acknowledging that "allegations that the CIA had been involved in plans to assassinate certain leaders of foreign countries" had come to its attention, blandly asserted that "time did not permit a full investigation" of the charges, while President Ford announced that material bearing on this topic would not be published because it was "incomplete and extremely sensitive".

By this time, however, the Senate and House both had select committees investigating the CIA and other intelligence agencies, and the press was on the scent of more revelations. The first media rumours of the assassination plots were aired at the end of February 1975, and on June 5 the *New York Times* published details of the "family jewels".

Before Congress Colby (whose efforts to tell the Rockefeller Commission more than it wanted to hear had been politely rebuffed) admitted to all the "family jewels" activities in turn, many of which had been known to only a very few even within the agency. With the hearings held in the open without recourse to executive sessions, Americans were treated to accounts of CIA drug tests on unsuspecting American citizens, and to the sight of the CIA Director brandishing before the Church Committee a special gun designed to fire poison pellets.

The main focus of the congressional hearings was on alleged CIA involvement in attempts to assassinate foreign leaders. Most of these involved plans to remove obscure Third World leaders whose names were far from familiar to most Americans, but a series of revelations concerning CIA plots against Castro proved both sensational and profoundly disturbing. Americans learned for the first time that the CIA, working through an ex-FBI agent called Robert Maheu (an operative for the Howard Hughes interests), had in August 1960 asked Mafia mobster John Rosselli to locate Cubans willing to attempt to assassinate Castro, and that Rosselli had then brought two other top organized crime figures, Sam Giancana and Santos Trafficante, into the scheme. Nothing ultimately came of the plotting (which revolved around ideas to poison Castro), but those who had long felt that there must have been some significance to the fact that President John F. Kennedy's presumed assassin, Lee Harvey Oswald, had connections with both pro- and anti-Castro Cubans, now felt they had the evidence they needed. The CIA, it seemed possible, in plotting with the underworld and anti-Castro exiles (whose operations were sure to have been penetrated by Cuban intelligence), had encouraged Castro to strike down Kennedy first. Whether or not the President himself had been informed (the Church Committee came to no conclusion on this question) scarcely matterd on this scenario, for the CIA would inevitably have been seen as the President's tool. On the very day that Kennedy was assassinated, a CIA contact within the Cuban government was offered a pen with a poison needle with which to assassinate Castro, rejecting it as "too amateurish" (see also *John F. Kennedy Assassination Affair, 1963–79*, above).

Sam Giancana was killed on June 19, 1975, a few days before he was due to give testimony to the Church Committee; Rosselli, who did testify, was found the following year, with his legs sawn off, in an oil drum in Biscayne Bay (Florida). Another key witness, Judith Campbell Exner, admitted only in 1988 that she lied when she told the Church Committee that she had not told John Kennedy (whose mistress she had been) of her simultaneous dealings with Giancana and Rosselli.

In its key report, issued on Nov. 20, 1975, under the title "Alleged Assassination Plots Against Foreign Leaders", the Church Committee concluded that the CIA had instigated plots to kill Fidel Castro and the late Patrice Lumumba (former Prime Minister of the ex-Belgian Congo, later Zaîre), and that CIA and other government officials had "encouraged or were privy to" the coup which had led to the death in 1963 of President Ngo Dinh Diem of South Vietnam, the 1961 assassination of the dictator of the Dominican Republic, Generalissimo Rafael Leonidas Trujillo, and the 1970 murder of Gen. René Schneider, the commander-in-chief of the Chilean armed forces, who was seen as an obstacle to attempts to prevent Salvador Allende taking office as President of Chile. However, as Castro was still alive and Lumumba had actually been killed independently by Congolese rivals in 1961, it did not appear that the CIA had ever directly killed any foreign leader itself, and the Church Committee also found itself unable to conclude that any President had definitely known of any plan to kill a foreign leader. Other reports followed, but it was the assassinations question that got the publicity.

The CIA also faced problems, in the strange atmosphere of the times, arising from some of its own former employees. One such, Philip Agee, who had left the agency in 1969, in 1975 published *Inside the Company: CIA Diary*, which included the names of hundreds of CIA operatives and front organizations. Agee also became involved with a publication called *Counterspy*, compiled by CIA renegades, and on Dec. 23, 1975, Richard Welch, the CIA station chief in Athens, was murdered after his name and address appeared in the magazine. This incident, and strong warnings from the Ford administration about the damaging results of excessive revelations, contributed to the decision by the House on Jan. 29, 1976, not to publish the (much-leaked) report of its own CIA investigating committee headed by Representative Otis Pike until it had been vetted by the White House. On Feb. 17, 1976, President Ford warned that it was "essential that the irresponsible and dangerous exposure of our nation's intelligence secrets be stopped".

Colby himself had been dismissed in January 1976, as Ford sought to reinforce the sense that all had changed and was now in order at the CIA; his new man for the newlook CIA was George Bush, who headed the agency until Jimmy Carter became President. To some, Colby had all but betrayed the agency in his appeasement of the post-Vietnam, post-Watergate witch-hunters on Capitol Hill. Particularly resented was the way in which he had exposed ex-CIA Director (from 1966–73) Richard Helms, for information provided to the Justice Department by Colby showed that Helms had lied when he told Congress in February-March 1973 that the CIA had not sought to overthrow Allende. As a result of this, Helms in October 1977 had little choice but to enter a *nolo contendere* plea to charges of having committed perjury before Congress and was sentenced to a $2,000 fine and a suspended jail term. (The fine was collected by passing the hat at a rally of ex-CIA officers later the same day.)

Others, however, believed that Colby had made the sacrifices necessary to secure the long-term survival of the agency. The Church Committee, for all the ballyhoo of its hearings, ultimately took a pragmatic view of the agency's failures, reprimanding it for past errors but not demanding its dissolution, and its mollification was at least partly the work of Colby. Furthermore, it was at least arguable that many of the "family jewels" had become tarnished by age, and that their exposure was overdue.

New formal checks on the CIA followed the "family jewels" affair. 1974 legislation had already imposed on the Director of the CIA an obligation to give notice of covert operations in advance to eight separate congressional committees, and in 1976–77 both Houses set up new intelligence oversight committees to monitor the agency. The politics of oversight had come full circle since the 1950s, when congressional isolationists and right-wingers had led the call for oversight of suspect internationalist-minded agencies like the CIA. In a message to Congress on Feb. 18, 1976, President Ford announced that he had issued an executive order stating: "No employee of the United States Government shall engage in, or conspire to engage in, political assassination". He also announced strict limitations on the surveillance of US citizens by whatever means, and barred burglaries and drug tests on unsuspecting persons, with a range of exemptions.

The neutralization of the CIA seemed to have reached its apotheosis when incoming President Jimmy Carter nominated former conscientious objector Theodore Sorenson to head the agency; the choice proved too much for Congress to accept, however, and Admiral Stansfield Turner instead headed the CIA through the Carter administration (1977–81). At least in respect of covert operations, these appear to have been years of little activity, as the agency feared a revival of opposition to its work. With the election of Ronald Reagan (who took office in 1981) and the replacement of Turner by the freewheeling William Casey, a one-time operative in the CIA's World War II predecessor, the OSS, a less restrictive era opened up for the CIA. The shadow of the agency in covert operations has been seen particularly in Central America, especially in providing support for the anti-government contra guerrillas in Nicaragua. Some of the formal restrictions on the agency have also been eased, and in December 1982 President Reagan signed an executive order which for the first time authorized the CIA to conduct covert operations within the USA, in cases where "significant foreign intelligence" was sought.

There are nonetheless residual and profoundly felt limitations to such activity, and it appeared in the Iran–contra affair (see below) that Casey had worked through Col. Oliver North, a National Security Council official, and his team of freelance operatives precisely to circumvent the restrictions imposed on the CIA and the hesitancy of its bureaucracy. Particularly difficult for the CIA is the modern pattern of oversight by Congress under which dozens of congressmen and their aides come to learn the agency's secrets, and in some cases do not hesitate to leak what they discover. Matters are a far cry from the 1950s and the early 1960s when leaks were practically unknown and all-powerful committee chairmen who were well-disposed to the agency kept a tight lid on its affairs. After Casey's resignation as CIA Director because of ill-health in January 1987 (he died four months later), and the damage caused by exposure of even the indirect and marginal CIA involvement in the Iran-Contra fiasco, the agency appeared again to assume a more defensive posture.

Keeping its own employees under restraint has also proved a problem for the agency. Philip Agee, regarded as an adviser to the Cuban intelligence service, was stripped of his passport by the State Department in 1979 and has not been able to re-enter the USA since. The order was upheld by the Supreme Court in 1981, and in 1982 it became a crime to disclose the names of US intelligence agents operating abroad. In 1978 the government sued ex-CIA employee Frank Snepp for violating security in a book, *Decent Interval*, which gave a critical account of the US withdrawal from Vietnam, and Snepp was ordered by the courts to relinquish his profits from the book.

The wrath that overtook the CIA in the mid-1970s arose, paradoxically, from the agency's failures rather than its successes. The fall of South Vietnam in April 1975 came as the humiliating culmination of years in which the American people had been misled about the course of the war and in which the CIA had failed to make an accurate and powerful contribution to policy-making. In the McCarthyite years of the early 1950s, setbacks in China and Korea were blamed on a domestic scapegoat, the traitors in the State Department; in the early 1970s, those who adhered to the conspiracy theory of history found in the CIA the source of all the woes of America. No major power has ever exposed its intelligence services to such public contempt and dissection as were experienced by the CIA in the "family jewels" affair, and the episode gives ample testimony to what many Europeans have regarded as the American inability to differentiate between matters of state and matters of morality. In the congressional exposures of the CIA, the righteous belief in American perfectibility achieved one of its periodic moments of triumph.

FJH

Bert Lance Affair (1977)

Jimmy Carter, President (1977–81).
Bert Lance, Carter's first Budget Director (resigned Sept. 21, 1977).

President Carter's Director of the Office of Management and Budget (OMB), Bert Lance, resigned on Sept. 21, 1977, amid controversy over his past business and banking practices.

Lance had been head of the State Transportation Department while Jimmy Carter was Governor of Georgia from 1970 to 1974, and had then been president of the National Bank of Georgia in 1974–76, acting as Carter's liaison with business in the 1976 presidential campaign. Rewarded with the position of OMB Director, Lance found the post an uncomfortable one from the beginning. At his confirmation hearings before the Senate Governmental Affairs Committee in January 1977, he promised to rid himself of his 200,000 shares in the National Bank of Georgia by the end of 1977 to avoid the appearance of a conflict of interest. However the value of his stock dropped sharply and in July 1977 Carter asked the Committee to release Lance from his pledge because of the "undue financial burden" it had placed on him and other stockholders. By this time there was also controversy concerning a $3,400,000 loan Lance had received in January 1977 from the First National Bank of Chicago, and on Sept. 7 it was disclosed that he and his wife had over a 13-year period received some $3,500,000 in loans from the Fulton National Bank (Georgia) in which the Calhoun National Bank, of which he had been an executive, maintained a substantial account under a so-called correspondent relationship.

Lance insisted that he had been guilty of no wrongdoing, and he was not charged with criminal offences, but his resignation became politically inevitable. In a characteristically sincere but inapposite letter of reply to his resignation message, Carter referred to knowing Lance "as if he was my own brother" and as a "good and an honourable man" who had "told the truth" in the face of "unproven allegations". Carter to some extent was hoist on his own petard, for he had campaigned on a platform of bringing a new homespun morality to Washington but had then appointed a Georgia crony to a top economic post. In 1979 the Justice Department announced that it had no evidence of wrongdoing in the dealings between the Carter family peanut business and the National Bank of Georgia, which had loaned the Carter family business $10,000,000 in 1975–77.

In April 1980 Lance was acquitted by a federal jury in Atlanta, Georgia, on nine of 12 counts of bank fraud; the remaining counts were also subsequently dropped by the Justice Department. In 1984 Lance was apparently restored to favour in the Democratic Party, taking a key role—in an evident attempt to attract southern voters—in Walter Mondale's unsuccessful presidential campaign. In February 1986 he was permanently barred from any association with any banking institution as part of a settlement in a suit brought by the Comptroller of Currency alleging illegal use of bank funds by Lance in 1983–84.

FJH

Tongsun Park Affair (1977–79)

Tongsun Park, South Korean lobbyist.

The activities in the USA of South Korean businessman Tongsun Park resulted in 1978 in a prison term for one former US congressmen and reprimands from the House of Representatives for three Democratic congressmen. The affair became known in some quarters as "Koreagate".

Tongsun Park—otherwise known as Park Tong Sun—was indicted in August 1977 on charges of conspiring to bribe public officials. According to the indictment, he had with the help of the Korean Central Intelligence Agency given campaign contributions and cash gifts to congressmen, as well as laying on all-expenses paid trips to Korea and lavish parties, to create a favourable climate of opinion towards South Korea in Congress. The money for this largesse had come from his position as sole agent for US rice sales to South Korea. In December 1977 the Justice Department reached an agreement with the South Korean authorities whereby Tongsun Park (who had returned to South Korea) would testify in court cases in the USA but the indictment against him would be dropped. Tongsun Park went on to tell a congressional committee in April 1978 that he had made gifts and campaign contributions to 30 present or former congressmen.

Former Congressmen Richard Hanna, a California Democrat, was charged with being a co-conspirator with Tongsun Park, receiving at least $75,000 in return between 1967 and 1974, and was sentenced to a prison term after pleading guilty in March 1978 to one count of conspiracy to defraud the US government. He spent just over one year in jail. In October 1978 the House formally reprimanded three current members—John McFall, Edward Roybal and Charles Wilson, all Democrats from California—for failing to report the receipt of cash gifts from Tongsun Park. Despite this, Roybal and Wilson were re-elected to Congress the following month, perhaps reflecting a public perception that such influence-peddling in Congress was common if rarely brought to the surface. On April 1, 1979, ex-Congressman Otto Passman, a Louisiana Democrat, was acquitted on charges of accepting bribes from Tongsun Park.

FJH

Agent Orange Affair (1978–88)

Following years of litigation, originating in a class action suit filed in 1978, a programme for the disbursement of $240,000,000 in compensation for victims of Agent Orange was announced by a federal judge on July 5, 1988.

Agent Orange was a herbicide used by US forces in the Vietnam War to defoliate jungle cover shielding enemy troops. It contained traces of dioxin, a chemical which has been linked to cancer in animals, and according to the Vietnam veterans who sued the chemical companies which had made Agent Orange, it had produced cancers and other illnesses in them. The companies consistently denied such allegations, and the medical evidence was ambiguous, but in May 1984 the companies agreed a $180,000,000 settlement. Some claimants refused to accept this settlement, however, and litigation continued into 1988, when the Supreme Court refused to hear an appeal by the dissenters. Meanwhile suits brought against the government itself had been rejected by the courts on the basis of the doctrine of sovereign immunity (which had also applied in cases brought by victims of radiation from atomic tests).

Under the settlement plan announced in July 1988 disbursement of some $240,000,000 (representing the $180,000,000 agreed in 1984 and accumulated interest) was to begin in 1989. Some 250,000 veterans and their families were reported to have filed claims, and $5,000,000 was reserved for veterans from Australia and New Zealand. The real number of veterans actually exposed to Agent Orange, and the herbicide's effect on their health, remained controversial, however. In 1987 officials of the federal Centers for Disease Control abandoned a study of the effects of Agent Orange on the ground it had proved unable to find enough veterans who had clearly suffered exposure.

FJH

Hamilton Jordan Affair (1979)

Hamilton Jordan, White House Chief of Staff

President Carter's White House Chief of Staff, Hamilton Jordan, in 1979 became the first person to be investigated by a special prosecutor under the provisions of the 1978 Ethics in Government Act after allegations that he had used cocaine.

Jordan (who became Chief of Staff on July 17, 1979) came under investigation after Steven Rubell and Ian Schrager, the owners of the fashionable Studio 54 discotheque in New York, claimed in August 1979 that Jordan had used cocaine while on a visit to the discotheque in 1978. The charges came two months after Rubell and Schrager had been indicted on tax evasion charges, on which they were convicted in November 1979. Other accounts spoke of Jordan using cocaine at parties in Los Angeles in 1977.

In deference to the rigorous requirements of the 1978 Ethics Act, Attorney General Benjamin Civiletti asked for a court-appointed special prosecutor to investigate the charges, even while the White House put out statements seeking to clear Jordan in advance. New York lawyer Arthur H. Christy was appointed special prosecutor on Nov. 29, 1979, and on May 28, 1980, announced that a special grand jury had concluded there was insufficient evidence to support the charges against Jordan.

President Carter's national campaign manager, Tim Kraft, was also investigated on charges of cocaine use in 1980, and in his case also there was no indictment. He had accompanied Jordan on his 1978 visit to Studio 54 and had denied that Jordan had used cocaine at that time.

FJH

Billy Carter Affair (1980)

Billy Carter, brother of Jimmy Carter.
Jimmy Carter, President (1977–81).

The already beleaguered presidency of Jimmy Carter was further weakened in 1980 by revelations concerning the handling of his brother's registration as an agent of the Libyan government of Col. Moamer Gaddafi.

Billy Carter, a small-town Georgia businessman without political background or sense, tried to capitalize commercially on his brother's elevation to the presidency by acting as a representative for Libya. Although then still having normal trading relations with the USA, Col. Gaddafi's regime was already widely seen in the USA as a sponsor of terrorism and a fanatical enemy of America's ally, Israel. In September 1978 Billy went on a much publicized trip to Libya with other Georgia businessmen and politicians which horrified Jewish Democrats who smelled the odour of unreconstructed southern redneck anti-semitism. He failed to register with the Justice Department as an agent of a foreign government, as required by law, until July 14, 1980, and then only in response to a court order made at the request of the Justice Department. On July 22 it became known that President Carter had in November 1979 used his brother to arrange a meeting between National Security Adviser Zbigniew Brzezinski and Libyan officials aimed at gaining the assistance of Libya to persuade Iran to free the US embassy hostages being held in Tehran.

On July 25, 1980, Benjamin Civiletti, the Attorney General, admitted (after repeated earlier statements to the contrary) that he had spoken to President Carter about the problem of his brother on June 17, after the Justice Department had learned of Libyan payments to him of $220,000 (Billy claimed the money was a loan). Following this disclosure, President Carter on Aug. 4 sent to the Senate a report denying any impropriety in his conversation with Civiletti, or that he had realized from the conversation that Billy was being paid by the Libyans, or that he had told his brother of it. The President insisted that Billy had never had any influence on US policy and disclosed that he (Jimmy) had tried repeatedly to get his brother to reduce his Libyan contacts.

While a special (Democrat-controlled) subcommittee went on to report on Oct. 2, 1980, that there had been no illegality in the handling of Billy Carter's registration (a conclusion which would be endorsed by a Justice Department report in April 1981), several aspects of the affair contributed to a sense of disquiet about the Carter presidency. Jimmy Carter's defence against complaints that he had failed to restrain his brother—"I don't have authority to order Billy to do something . . . . Anyone who knows Billy knows that no one can push him around"—inevitably caused some to wonder how a President who could not control his own brother could stand up to America's foreign enemies. Furthermore, his insistence that Billy had never influenced US policy caused critics to wonder why in that case he had been prepared to use Billy to contact the Libyans on the hostages issue, and sat uneasily with the fact that other members of the Carter family—notably his wife Rosalynn and mother "Miss Lillian"—had been used for important diplomatic initiatives and were known to wield significant influence around the White House (even the meeting with the Libyans by Brzezinski had apparently been suggested by Rosalynn). Clearly the Libyans had believed that there could be a direct conduit to the Oval Office through Billy, and Jimmy Carter's insistence that he had never known (though "it occurred to me") about the Libyan payments to Billy (known for his love of get-rich-quick schemes) until after his registration as a foreign agent struck most Americans as absurdly naive.

Ultimately, the damage done to Jimmy Carter by the Billy Carter affair lay not in any sense that he had abused his power to protect his brother, but that he had been too powerless to restrain him. Weakness and hesitancy, regarded by his critics as the hallmarks of the Carter presidency, were the root of the problem. In the November 1980 presidential election Jimmy Carter became the first incumbent President since Herbert Hoover not to be re-elected, losing all but six states and the District of Columbia to his Republican challenger, Ronald Reagan.

In 1981, with his brother no longer in office, Billy Carter sold his service station, house and other property in Plains, Georgia, to pay off his debts. He died in 1988.

FJH

Abscam Affair (1980–82)

Six US Representatives and one Senator were convicted in 1980–81 on charges arising from an FBI operation, initiated in 1978 and made public on Feb. 2, 1980, designed to trap public officials suspected of corruption. The operation was condemned by some as involving "entrapment" in crimes which would not have existed had the FBI not invented them in the first place.

The Abscam operation involved FBI agents, posing as an Arab sheikh "Kambir Abdul Rahman" and his agents, offering officials bribes in return for promises of help with supposed immigration and business problems. (The term Abscam was initially reported as being a contraction of "Arab Scam", but after a complaint from Jimmy Carter's Justice Department that this was "offensive" to Arab countries and Arab-Americans, it was redefined as derived from the name of the sheikh's imaginary business "Abdul Enterprises Ltd".) Videotapes shown in courtrooms and on television featured congressmen receiving bags containing tens of thousands of dollars in return for their offer of services.

The seven members of Congress convicted in the affair were Senator Harrison A. Williams and Representative Frank Thompson of New Jersey, Representatives Michael J. Myers and Raymond F. Lederer of Pennsylvania, Representative John M. Murphy of New York, Representative John W. Jenrette of South Carolina and Representative Richard Kelly of Florida. None of the seven (all of whom except Kelly were Democrats) were among the more prominent members of Congress. Also mentioned in the indictment but never charged was Representative John Murtha, a Pennsylvania Democrat, who gave evidence against Murphy and Thompson. Others convicted in the affair included state and city officials from Pennsylvania and New Jersey.

Much as some in Congress resented this mass targeting of their colleagues by the Justice Department, the videotapes showing greed at its most uncomplicated and cynical so disgusted public opinion that most on Capitol Hill prudently avoided any appearance of siding with the wrongdoers. By

March 11, 1982, when Senator Williams resigned from the Senate in the face of a pending vote to expel him (by resigning he saved his pension entitlements), all seven guilty men had either failed to win re-election or been expelled or resigned from Congress. Myers on Oct. 2, 1980, achieved the distinction (by 376 votes to 30) of becoming the first member of the House of Representatives to be expelled since 1861. All those convicted received prison terms.

The affair spawned considerable litigation, the accused, primarily resting their case on the issue of entrapment. In May 1982 a federal district judge overturned Kelly's conviction on precisely that ground, but the conviction was restored by an apellate court and upheld by the US Supreme Court in October 1983. Appeals by the other former congressmen also came to nothing.

FJH

Westmoreland Libel Affair (1982–85)

Gen. William C. Westmoreland, US Commander in Vietnam War.

In 1982 retired Army General William C. Westmoreland, who had headed US forces in Vietnam at the height of the Vietnam War from 1965, filed a $120,000,000 libel suit in response to a CBS News television documentary which suggested that he and others had conspired to deceive policy-makers about the enemy's strength. He dropped the suit in early 1985, however, midway through a trial which had exposed sharp conflicts in the evidence.

Named in the libel suit were CBS officials and programme makers and Samuel Adams, an ex-CIA officer who had been consultant for the programme. The trial began on Oct. 11, 1984, in New York. According to past Supreme Court rulings, Westmoreland was required to meet the demanding test of having to prove that CBS had shown "actual malice" and "reckless disregard" for the truth to win his case. As the trial progressed, however, it became clear that, notwithstanding some signs of personal animus and bias against Westmoreland on the part of the programme-makers, the programme's general theme was one which was at least an arguable interpretation of the evidence. Substantial testimony by former intelligence officers and government officials created an overall impression that intelligence reports of enemy strength had been put in as favourable light as possible, largely so as not to alarm public opinion. Westmoreland had himself told the Joint Chiefs of Staff in August 1967 that the press could reach "erroneous and gloomy conclusions" if estimates of enemy strength included the so-called Vietcong "self-defence forces" (irregular, occasionally-employed guerrilla saboteurs, indistinguishable from ordinary civilians, which Westmoreland had removed from the Order of Battle count of enemy strength), although the activities of these forces ultimately proved highly significant in undermining the morale of US troops by creating a sense that the whole population of the countryside was secretly against them (see also *My Lai Massacre Affair, 1969–71*, above). What was far from clear was whether Westmoreland had been solely or principally to blame for this. It was, rather, the case that military leaders were under political pressure to present an optimistic view of how the war was going, and they responded to that pressure by abandoning the demands of objective assessment. It was a course which led in time only to domestic disillusion with what proved to be an unwinnable war, and the humiliating surrender of South Vietnam to the North in 1975 when the USA abandoned thousands of its Vietnamese intelligence operatives and others closely identified with the US military in the scramble to evacuate Saigon.

On Feb. 18, 1985, it was unexpectedly announced that an out-of-court settlement had been reached. CBS insisted that it stood by its original broadcast, while stating that CBS "never intended to assert, and does not believe, that General Westmoreland was unpatriotic or disloyal in performing his duties as he saw them". Westmoreland in turn claimed that he had received an apology from CBS and that he had "won", but he received no financial compensation. In the view of some critics, CBS had woefully neglected its responsibilities to the public interest and to the right of the media to free comment in failing to see the suit through to the end.

FJH

Sleaze Factor Affair (1984)

In the face of the personal popularity of President Ronald Reagan, running for a second term in office, and an upturn in the economy, the Democrats in the 1984 election campaign sought to capitalize on what their strategists called the "sleaze factor": i.e. the high incidence of allegations of corruption directed at Reagan appointees. As a strategy it failed, however, partly because the Democrats had developed their own "sleaze factor" as a result of the vice-presidential candidature of Geraldine Ferraro, (see *Geraldine Ferraro Affair, 1984*, below); for this and other reasons the Democratic presidential candidate, Walter Mondale, was trounced in the November 1984 elections.

Among those Reagan officials who had been touched by charges of corruption were both his Attorney Generals: William French Smith, who announced his decision to step down in January 1984 after being dogged by allegations of tax dodging; and Edwin Meese, formerly Reagan's counsellor, who faced and survived an investigation by a special prosecutor during 1984 but was not finally confirmed by the Senate until February 1985 (see *Edwin Meese Affair, 1984–88*, below). On Oct. 1, 1984 the indictment of Raymond Donovan was announced, the first of a serving Cabinet member on criminal charges, after he had been accused of fraud and forgery. He resigned office in May 1985 after being on leave since October 1984 (see *Raymond Donovan Affair, 1984–87*, below). Paul Thayer, Deputy Secretary of Defence, resigned in January 1984 to contest charges of insider trading brought against him by the Securities and Exchange Commission. He pleaded guilty to obstruction of justice charges in March 1985. In March 1984, White House Chief of Staff James Baker, his deputy Michael K. Deaver, National Security Adviser Robert C. McFarlane, and four other White House staff members turned in to the government sets of gold cufflinks given them in 1983 as gifts by the South Korean government.

Numerous minor officials, unknown before and forgotten since, also had their day of notoriety, resigning in the face of, or surviving, allegations of improprieties of a financial nature. They included Victor Schroeder (resigned August 1983 as president of the federal Synthetic Fuels Corporation); Arthur Hall Hayes (resigned September 1983 as Commissioner of the Food and Drug Administration); J. Lynn Helms (resigned January 1984 as head of the Federal Aviation Administration); Max Hugel (resigned as Deputy Director for Operations of the CIA in July 1981); Guy Fiske (resigned as Deputy Secretary of Commerce in May 1983); and Thomas C. Reed (a special assistant to the President for national security affairs, dismissed March 1983). Reagan's first National Security Adviser, Richard Allen, had also resigned in January 1982 after taking leave of absence on Nov. 29, 1981, in the face of charges of having accepted gifts including $1,000 from Japanese journalists who had interviewed Nancy Reagan at the White House. Meanwhile, the Environmental Protection Administration had attracted intense adverse criticism, and high officials had been forced to resign, in the face of charges of favouritism towards certain large corporations in the administration of a multi-billion dollar toxic waste clean-up programme.

The high incidence of charges of financial irregularities reflected the simple fact that this was an administration of businessmen-politicians; not sexual misconduct, or treason, but tax-dodging and favouring cronies were the substance of the charges. The more ideological Carter administration had had only one major corruption case, that of budget director Bert Lance (see *Bert Lance Affair, 1977*, above). In addition, the 1978 Ethics in Government Act, establishing a system for the investigation of charges against high officials by special prosecutors operating independently of the executive branch, was beginning to have an effect—an effect which would be most acutely felt in Reagan's second term. Many of those tainted, however, were riders on the coat-tails of the administration, and not its key policy makers. The major players in setting the image of the administration—the President himself, Secretary of State George Shultz, Defence Secretary Caspar Weinberger—seemed to their admirers to rise like Olympians above such petty malfeasance.

FJH

Geraldine Ferraro Affair (1984)

Geraldine Ferraro, Democratic vice-presidential nominee (1984).
John Zaccaro, Ferraro's husband.

Geraldine Anne Ferraro, a member of Congress for New York, was Democratic candidate Walter Mondale's running-mate in the 1984 presidential election. Her candidature was surrounded by controversy concerning the business affairs of herself and her husband, John Zaccaro. In the election on Nov. 6 President Reagan won every state except Mondale's home state of Minnesota and the District of Columbia. Ferraro retired from Congress in January 1985 and effectively disappeared from public life.

Mondale named the 48-year-old Ferraro as his vice-presidential choice on July 12, 1984, after a highly public search for a running-mate which came increasingly to seem like the quest for a qualified woman. She was the first woman candidate of either major party for President or Vice-President. She had been first elected to the House of Representatives in 1978 and had become known as a liberal and a party loyalist, although with a slight legislative record. On Aug. 20, 1984, she and husband Zaccaro sent a $53,459 cheque to the Internal Revenue Service to cover back taxes said to have been overlooked because of an accountant's error. Ferraro also admitted that she was a co-owner of a real estate firm owned by Zaccaro from which she had received a salary and dividends. This latter revelation was of significance because while in Congress Ferraro had declined to provide details of her husband's finances on the ground that their affairs were entirely separate and that she derived no benefit from his interests. No less damaging were reports and rumours implying that Zaccaro's real estate activities were questionable and even that he was linked to organized crime. On Sept. 12, under pressure from Republicans taking revenge for the Democrats' use of the so-called "sleaze factor" in their campaign (see *Sleaze Factor Affair, 1984*, above) the House Ethics Committee agreed to investigate charges that Ferraro had violated congressional standards in not disclosing fully her sources of finance. Following the election, the Committee reported on Dec. 4 that Ferraro had violated congressional rules but also concluded that this had been unintentional and that no action should be taken.

The controversy probably had little effect on the magnitude of the defeat of the Mondale–Ferraro ticket in the election, but it led to Ferraro's disappearance from the political scene. In January 1985 her husband was convicted on a misdemeanour charge of fraud in connection with a real estate deal, and was subsequently ordered to serve a sentence of community service. (He was acquitted in October 1987 on charges of trying to extort $1,000,000 from a cable television company.) In addition, her son, John A. Zaccaro Jr, was sentenced by a Vermont court on June 16, 1988, to four months in prison for selling cocaine to an undercover police officer in 1986.

In December 1985 Ferraro ruled herself out as a candidate for the Senate because of continuing Justice Department investigations into her 1978 campaign finances and financial reports filed while in Congress. In February 1985, capitalizing on her transient fame, she filmed a commercial for Diet Pepsi for which she received a fee from PepsiCo. Inc. variously reported as between $75,000 and $500,000

The Justice Department announced on Feb. 20, 1987, that it had ended a 30-month investigation of Ferraro's financial affairs and did not seek to bring charges.

FJH

Raymond Donovan Affair (1984–87)

Raymond Donovan, Secretary of Labour (1981–85)

Raymond Donovan, then Secretary of Labour, in September 1984 became the first serving Cabinet member ever indicted on criminal charges. (The indictment was made public on Oct. 1.) He immediately took leave of absence and then resigned in March 1985, and after an eight-month trial for fraud was acquitted with his seven co-defendants on May 25, 1987. His political career, however, was at an end.

Donovan came to the Cabinet direct from business at the start of President Reagan's first term in 1981, having been an executive of the Schiavone Construction Company in New Jersey. In 1981–82 he faced a series of investigations by the FBI, a Senate committee and a special prosecutor into allegations that he had links with organized crime and labour union racketeering (both powerful factors in the Jersey construction industry). None of these investigations led anywhere, but a Democratic district attorney in New York (Mario Merola) remained at Donovan's heels. In September 1984 he and seven others (five of them Schiavone executives) were indicted by a state grand jury in New York on charges of having defrauded the New York City Transit Authority of $7,400,000 on a subway construction project in 1979–80. Legal manoeuvres delayed the start of the trial until September 1986.

According to jurors who spoke after the trial ended in acquittals, the jury believed that the indictment had been politically motivated and that Merola and the chief prosecutor (Stephen R. Bookin) had been looking for publicity and to advance their own careers.

FJH

Edwin Meese Affair (1984–88)

James McKay, Independent counsel who investigated Meese.
Edwin Meese, US Attorney General (1985–88).
E. Robert Wallach, Meese's personal lawyer.

President Reagan's second Attorney General, Edwin Meese, survived several years of allegations of official misconduct before leaving office more or less voluntarily in the closing months of Reagan's second term. According to his critics, his tenure as Attorney General had tarnished the reputation of both the Justice Department and the administration as a whole, but to his admirers Meese stood out as an uncompromising reformer who had sought to remodel the justice system in accordance with the mandates of the "Reagan revolution".

Meese was a long-time California associate of Ronald Reagan, and when Reagan became President in January 1981 Meese moved into the White House (with the title of counsellor) as one of the triumvirate of closest Reagan intimates (along with Michael Deaver and James Baker). Reagan's first Attorney General, William French Smith, announced his intention to step down in January 1984, following press and congressional criticism of his tax affairs, and Reagan nominated Meese as his successor on Jan. 23. The nominee quickly ran into a storm of allegations of corruption, however, these focusing on the appointment to high federal posts of a number of people with whom he had had business dealings, including several officials of a Californian bank, the Great American Federal Savings Bank, which had extended him a mortgage loan which reached $423,000 in 1982. Meese survived unscathed an investigation by a special prosecutor (Jacob Stein), who reported in September 1984 that there was "no basis for bringing a prosecution" against him. A strong sense remained, however, that mere absence of conclusive evidence of criminality was not the strongest recommendation for the appointment of the nation's highest law officer, and Meese was confirmed by the Senate only in February 1985, and with 31 votes against.

In May 1987 James McKay, the independent counsel (special prosecutor) investigating former White House aide Lyn Nofziger in connection with the Wedtech scandal (see *Wedtech Affair, 1987–90*, below), extended his investigations to include Meese. After several months of press speculation that Meese could be indicted because of his links to Wedtech through his friend and personal lawyer E. Robert Wallach and financial adviser W. Franklyn Chinn, McKay announced in December 1987 that he would prosecute Wallach and Chinn but not Meese. McKay had by this time, however, moved on to examine Meese's role in 1985 in supporting the proposed construction by the Bechtel engineering group of a $1,000 million oil pipeline running from Iraq to the Jordanian port of Aqaba. This inquiry came to focus on a memo, whose existence first became public on Jan. 29, 1988, sent by Wallach (who appeared to have been retained by Bruce Rappaport, a financier working in collaboration with Bechtel, because of his White House access) to Meese in September 1985 which referred to payments to be made to Israel in return for a pledge not to bomb the pipeline. These payments were, according to the memo, to include secret funding direct to the Israel Labour Party. Under the Foreign Corrupt Practices Act of 1977, Meese as Attorney General would have been obliged to prosecute any individual or corporation offering corrupt inducements to a foreign official; Meese, however, maintained that he could not recall seeing this part of the memo, and no evidence could in any case be produced that any such payments had ever been made or actually offered to the Israel Labour Party.

The pipeline affair generated considerable excitement in sections of the media which scented another Iran–Contra debacle (see *Iran–Contra Affair, 1986–90*, below). Despite some of the same elements of Middle Eastern intrigue, however, the resemblance was only superficial. The pipeline idea was a legitimate commercial project which foundered because its political and strategic complications could not be resolved. The abandonment of the project before it ever really started in early 1986 reflected Iraqi doubts about the reliability of Israeli guarantees and a lack of enthusiasm in the US administration about its practicability. Meese, it seemed, had provided Wallach with access to persuade National Security Adviser Robert McFarlane to take up the plan, but when McFarlane was replaced by Admiral John Poindexter at the end of 1985 tentative US support for the project had been dropped. Meese's influence clearly had either not been sufficient to shape this aspect of foreign policy (which was, the Democrats loudly insisted, nothing to do with the job of Attorney General, though they perhaps forgot the example of their own Robert Kennedy) or had only been weakly applied. On April 1, 1988, McKay announced he did not intend to bring an indictment against Meese "based on the evidence developed to date".

This did not close the affair. On March 29, 1988, six senior Justice Department officials—including Deputy Attorney General Arnold I. Burns and Assistant Attorney General William F. Weld—had resigned their posts, reflecting a growing sense in the Department that its work was being hampered by the continuing problems of its chief official. Other close aides left in the following weeks, including Meese's press spokesman, Terry Eastland. Being seen as too close to Meese had clearly become a deleterious career move even for those, like Eastland, Burns and Weld, whom Meese had brought to the Justice Department in the first place. On July 5, hours after McKay filed his sealed report on the Meese investigation with a special panel of federal judges, Meese announced that he had been "completely vindicated" by the McKay report, and now felt able to step down later in the summer. By this time the Meese "sleaze factor" had increasingly the appearance of a millstone around the neck of Republican candidates in the coming elections in November 1988, and there was barely-disguised relief in many Republican quarters that Meese was withdrawing from the limelight.

When the 830-page McKay report was made public on July 18, 1988, it proved something less than a "complete vindication" of the Attorney General, who was accused of having "probably violated the criminal law" in four instances while in office, although not to an extent warranting prosecution. With some feeling, Meese retorted that McKay had violated "every principle of fairness and decency" in reaching such a conclusion. "They had nothing to show for all of their work in almost 14 months of effort and $1,700,000 of the taxpayer's money", Meese complained, adding: "Then they belatedly had to find something that they could show to justify their efforts." That something was four rather minor instances involving an inaccurate tax return, failure to pay capital gains taxes when due, and two possible violations of conflict-of-interest laws by participating in telephone industry regulation when he had an (actually rather slight) financial interest. Even the *New York Times*, no friend of Meese, could find in these charges only "literal violation of two very tough statutes".

In the opinion of his political enemies, Meese had once again slid out of a hard place, leaving behind him a pervasive odour of corruption. At the very least, on this view, Meese was unfit to have held office as Attorney General for as long as he did, and the President's indifference to the "appearance of impropriety" was an index of the more general ethical complacency of his government. Some others, however, felt that Meese had been harried by politicized investigations, and that the type of probe carried out by McKay—moving from Wedtech, to the pipeline, then finally coming to rest on some small-scale financial irregularities which only emerged in the general sweep—was a measure of the extent to which the role of independent counsels, as licensed inquisitors seemingly accountable to no one, had run out of control and beyond reason. As only Republicans were being affected by this—because special prosecutors could investigate only the executive branch and not the Congress– there was arguably a case that ethical double standards were being applied.

On Aug. 12, 1988, Richard Thornburgh was sworn in as the new Attorney General, having been confirmed by the Senate the previous day without a vote against. He came to office as a man with a reputation for iron integrity. Immediately before stepping down, Meese announced that he had signed an order providing for the appointment of independent special prosecutors directly by the Attorney General in the case of allegations of misconduct by members of Congress, a move generally interpreted as his parting revenge.

FJH

Samuel Morison Affair (1985)

Samuel Morison, intelligence analyst.

Samuel Loring Morison, the grandson of the noted naval historian Samuel Eliot Morison, was convicted on espionage charges in 1985 arising from his "leaking" of secret photographs to a British magazine.

Morison was arrested on Oct. 1, 1984, while working as a civilian analyst of the Naval Intelligence Support Centre at Suitland, Maryland, and charged with having leaked photographs to *Jane's Defence Weekly*, a British publication well-known for its informed analysis of defence issues. Morison had, at the time, a part-time job as US editor for a companion publication, *Jane's Fighting Ships*. The photographs showed the first Soviet nuclear-powered aircraft carrier under construction and had been taken by a US spy satellite.

At his trial Morison maintained that he had sought only to warn the public of the dangers of the Soviet arms build-up, and that the Soviet Union already had full knowledge of the capabilities of the KH-11 spy satellite involved (thanks to a low-level CIA official William Kampiles, who had sold the Soviets a copy of the KH-11 technical manual for a mere $3000, for which he had been sentenced to 40 years in jail). Morison was nonetheless convicted on Oct. 17, 1985, on charges of espionage and theft of government property and subsequently sentenced to two years' imprisonment. He was the first person convicted under the 1917 espionage law for leaking information to the media (the only parallel prosecution, of Daniel Ellsberg and Anthony Russo, having foundered in 1973–see *Pentagon Papers Affair, 1971–74*, above), and civil libertarians suggested that his case represented an attempt to muzzle the freedom of the press guaranteed by the First Amendment to the Constitution. The press itself, however, perhaps reflecting the mood of anxiety about espionage stirred by the Walker Family Espionage Affair (see below), proved hesitant and divided about taking up the issue with any vigour, although news organizations supported Morison's appeal against conviction.

A three-man federal appeals court in Richmond on April 4, 1988, upheld Morison's conviction, but two of the judges also conceded that the First amendment issues involved had been "real and substantial".

FJH

Walker Family Espionage Affair (1985)

Arthur J. Walker, former naval officer, John Walker's brother.
John A. Walker, former naval officer, presumed dead.
Michael L. Walker, naval clerk, John's son.
Jerry A. Whitworth, former naval radio operator.

The uncovering of the Walker family naval spy ring in 1985 shocked US opinion not just for the importance of the secrets betrayed to the Soviet Union, but because three members of an apparently normal mainstream family, US citizens of native stock, had been drawn into treason for no higher motive than greed. It led directly to the passage of legislation by Congress, given force by a presidential directive in February 1986, providing for the restoration of the death penalty for espionage by members of the armed forces in peace time.

Within a fortnight from May 20, 1985, the FBI arrested John A. Walker (47), usually described as the leader of the ring, who had retired from the Navy with the rank of chief warrant officer in 1976; his son, Michael L. Walker (22), a clerk in the operations room of the aircraft carrier *Nimitz*; his brother, Arthur J. Walker (50), who had left the Navy in 1973 with the rank of lieutenant commander; and his friend, Jerry A. Whitworth (45), who had left the Navy in 1983 when he was a senior chief radioman.

According to prosecutors, John Walker had begun his spying as early as 1968, when he needed money to rescue a failing business venture;

his arrest, which supposedly followed information provided to the FBI from his former wife and daughter, was made as he attempted to pass documents to a Soviet agent (who had subsequently left the USA). There were conflicting assessments of the role of Arthur, who told the FBI that he had been recruited only in 1980 when he had taken work with a naval contractor, but according to some estimates may have been involved at a far earlier stage.

In each case the motivations appeared to be financial—hundreds of thousands of dollars had reached the conspirators—with no ideological conviction involved. John Walker himself had boasted, in a note apparently intended for his Soviet contact, that all the members of his group were "psychologically well-adjusted and mature", with "no drug users, alcoholics, homosexuals".

John and Arthur both received life sentences, and Michael 25 years, for their part in the ring, their sentences being worked out as part of a plea bargain under which John gave evidence against Whitworth, against whom the case was largely circumstantial. Whitworth himself was sentenced to 365 years in prison, the severity of his sentence reflecting the apparent importance of the coding and other information he had passed. Estimates of the significance of their activities varied widely. According to some intelligence experts and government officials, the secrets handed over had potentially compromised the security of the entire US nuclear submarine fleet; others suggested that the information given the Soviets—such as code keys—had been of only transient value. On April 16, 1987, Caspar Weinberger (the Defence Secretary) claimed that the KGB regarded the Walker operation as "the most important in their history" and that it had been one of the greatest espionage setbacks ever suffered by the USA. Whatever the truth of this, the case served to underline the apparently still potent significance of old-fashioned cloak-and-dagger espionage in an age of technical surveillance.

According to Justice Department records, more people were arrested for espionage in 1985 than in any year on record (see also *Samuel Morison Affair, 1985*, above, *Jonathan Pollard Affair, 1985–87*, below). The resultant political storm led to the reinstatement of the death penalty for peacetime espionage. This had been inoperative since a Supreme Court decision and no one had been executed for espionage since the Rosenbergs in 1953 (see *Atom Spies Affair, 1950–53*, above). It also resulted in a tightening-up on the numbers of people employed by the Pentagon or military contractors with access to classified information. According to the Defence Department in February 1987, the number of individuals with security clearances had been cut from 4,100,000 in June 1985 to 2,500,000.

FJH

Jonathan Pollard Affair (1985–87)

Jonathan Jay Pollard, naval intelligence analyst.

The arrest on Nov. 21, 1985, and subsequent trial and conviction of Jonathan Jay Pollard, a civilian intelligence analyst for the Naval Investigative Service, on charges of spying for Israel led to friction in that country's relations with the USA, and served to underscore the fundamental scepticism of the Jewish state about the reliability of even friendly nations.

Pollard, an American Jew, was arrested in Washington after attempting to take refuge in the Israeli embassy, where he was denied entry; his wife, Anne Henderson Pollard, was also arrested the next day on charges of unauthorised possession of stolen documents. Initial accounts suggested that the Pollards may also have passed or sought to pass information to Pakistan and China, but it soon became clear that Pollard had been interested only in aiding Israel, which he knew was being denied various types of intelligence about its Arab neighbours gathered by the USA. Within a few days of his arrest, US press reports had identified Pollard as having been controlled by a special unit within the Israeli Ministry of Defence known as LEKEM (Science Liaison Bureau) which was headed by Rafi Eitan, who had served as counter-terrorism adviser to Israeli Prime Ministers Menahem Begin and Shimon Peres from 1978 to 1984; two Israeli diplomats attached to LEKEM, Ilan Ravid and Yosef Yagur, had abruptly left the USA on Nov. 22, and on Nov. 28 Prime Minister Peres indicated that Israel would deny the USA access to the two.

Following some sharp diplomatic exchanges—and complaints in the Israeli press that US espionage activities in Israel had been unmasked without any public disclosure—Israel abandoned its initial posture of non-co-operation with the USA, while continuing to insist that any espionage carried out by LEKEM in the USA had been entirely unauthorised at government level. A team of US investigators was admitted to Israel and on Dec. 20, 1985, the State Department announced that Israel had disbanded LEKEM and returned to the USA documents which had been improperly acquired. Pollard himself was sentenced on March 4, 1987, to life imprisonment for espionage, and his wife to a term of five years for acting as an accessory.

While it evidently suited the foreign policy interests of both governments to play down the implications of the affair, its reverberations were slow to die down. At his trial Pollard insisted that he had acted as part of a highly-co-ordinated Israeli espionage operation, and on March 3, 1987, Col. Aviem Sella, a senior Israeli Air Force officer, was indicted in absentia by a US federal grand jury on charges of conspiring with Pollard. (Under the terms of the US extradition treaty with Israel, Sella could not be extradited for espionage and could be arrested only if he came to the USA voluntarily.) According to a report in the *Jerusalem Post* of March 20, 1987, the Israeli view was that former CIA Director William Casey had changed the rules of the game by recruiting an Israeli military officer as a spy, and the

CIA had not wanted the FBI to set in motion the prosecution of Pollard because of this. Two official investigative reports issued in Israel on May 26, 1987, concluded that Pollard had been recruited by LEKEM without the knowledge of top government officials, but the validity of the conclusions was not universally accepted. Neither report recommended that anyone should be punished (LEKEM's chief, Eitan, having already resigned). On May 27 the Israeli Cabinet, in an effort to appease US opinion, announced that it accepted collective responsibility for the affair—a gesture with no obvious practical consequence.

According to press reports in April 1989, Israel was paying $5,000 per month into an Israeli bank account for Pollard while he served his sentence.

FJH

Michael Deaver Affair (1986–87)

Michael Deaver, Lobbyist and former White House official.
Whitney North Seymour Jr, Independent Counsel who investigated Deaver.

Michael Deaver, a former deputy White House Chief of Staff who had become known as President Reagan's "image-maker", was convicted on Dec. 16, 1987, on three of five charges of lying to Congress and a grand jury about his contacts as a lobbyist after he left the Reagan administration in May 1985. His conviction was the first ever won by an independent counsel (special prosecutor) appointed under the 1978 Ethics in Government Act.

Deaver had known Ronald Reagan since the 1960s, and as deputy White House Chief of Staff from 1981 to May 1985 he had been an intimate adviser of the President. He then left the White House to set up a lobbying business, Michael K. Deaver and Associates, quickly attracting lucrative clients and assuming an unusually high-profile image. He remained a regular visitor to the White House, even appearing on the front cover of *Time* magazine on March 3, 1986, for a story on "influence peddling in Washington" in which he boasted of having "as good access as anybody in town". Such ostentation attracted mounting congressional and press attention, and on April 28, 1986, Deaver himself called for the appointment of an independent counsel to investigate him under provisions of the 1978 Act which barred certain categories of lobbying by former high government officials. Whitney North

Seymour Jr was appointed as independent counsel by a federal court at the request of the Department of Justice on May 29.

Seymour ultimately did not charge Deaver with violations of the Ethics Act, but instead on March 18, 1987, Deaver was indicted on charges of having committed perjury before a congressional committee and a grand jury assembled by Seymour. Thus Deaver was obliged to stand trial not on the legality of his activities as a lobbyist, but rather on the truthfulness of what he had said about those activities while under investigation. After the indictment Seymour ruffled diplomatic feathers in both Washington and Ottawa by a sustained (if ultimately unsuccessful) campaign to compel testimony from the Canadian ambassador to the USA, Allan Gotlieb, and his wife Sondra (with whom Deaver was said to have discussed lobbying the US administration in favour of the Canadian position on acid rain). At his trial Deaver was acquitted of charges relating to his lobbying for Canada, but was convicted on charges of perjury in respect of his work in contacting White House officials on behalf of South Korea, Puerto Rico and Trans World Airlines (TWA).

Because Deaver's conviction was for perjury it was not put to the test whether or not he had violated the complex and largely untested provisions of the 1978 Ethics Act. Thus the first person convicted under the 1978 Act was former Reagan aide Lyn Nofziger, in February 1988 (see *Wedtech Affair, 1987–90*, below). Deaver, apparently, had initially assumed he had not violated the Act, though once his trial for perjury approached, his defence came to rest on the argument that his memory and judgment in giving testimony had been clouded by alcohol abuse. This defence, rejected by the trial judge as inadmissible, in itself raised intriguing questions, for it emerged that Deaver had been hospitalized twice for alcohol abuse in his last months in the White House when still playing an active role in the Reagan administration. Within weeks of Deaver's conviction, on Jan. 22, 1988, an appellate court in a separate case ruled the independent counsel provisions of the Ethics Act unconstitutional, raising the possibility that Deaver's conviction might not stand. (Deaver himself had tried to avoid standing trial by arguing that the role of the independent counsel was unconstitutional, although he had himself called to be investigated by one in the first place.) On June 29, however, the Supreme Court reversed the appellate court, and on Sept. 23 Deaver was fined $100,000 and ordered to do 1,500 hours' community service; a three-year prison sentence was suspended.

FJH

Iran–Contra Affair (1986–90)

William Casey, Director of the CIA (died May 6, 1987).

Albert Hakim, North's partner in Iran–Contra operation.

Robert McFarlane, President Reagan's National Security Adviser (resigned December 1985).

Edwin Meese, Attorney General.

Oliver North, Marine Colonel, member of National Security Council staff.

John M. Poindexter, McFarlane's successor as National Security Adviser (resigned Nov. 25, 1986).

Ronald Reagan, President (1981–89).

Donald Regan, White House Chief of Staff (resigned Feb. 27, 1987).

Richard V. Secord, North's partner in Iran–Contra operation.

George Shultz, Secretary of State.

John Tower, Former US Senator; investigated Iran-Contra affair for Reagan.

Lawrence Walsh, Independent Counsel who investigated Iran–Contra affair.

Caspar Weinberger, Secretary of Defence.

During the winter months of 1986–87 the Reagan administration was shaken to its foundations by a series of sensational revelations that it had sold weapons to Iran (which had been publicly denounced by the President as a "terrorist state") in an effort to secure the release of Americans held by pro-Iranian groups in Lebanon, and that top national security officials had then diverted money from the sales to help anti-government contra rebels in Nicaragua. However, while excited comparisons were made by the press and Democratic politicians to the Watergate affair (see above) which brought down President Nixon, President Reagan himself came through battered but unbroken. Ultimately, it seemed, whereas few Americans could believe that the consummate political manipulator Nixon had not known of everything that his servants were doing, most were quite ready to accept that in President Reagan they had a leader who had opted for a style of lazy delegation, or who could not be judged fully accountable even for decisions arrived at in his presence.

The crisis of winter 1986–87

The Iran-contra affair—the term "Irangate", with its overtly pejorative implications, never quite came to stick—began with the revelation by a Lebanese magazine, *Al Shiraa*, on Nov. 3, 1986, that Robert McFarlane, the President's National Security Adviser to December 1985, had in 1986 carried out a secret mission to Tehran (Iran) involving the transfer of military parts. This story was confirmed, the next day by the Speaker of the Iranian parliament, Hojatolislam Hashemi Ali Akbar Rafsanjani, who, however, claimed that the Americans had been arrested, confined to their hotel for five days, and then expelled. Over the following days increasingly detailed reports began to appear in the US press (its investigative fervour heightened by pique that it had been scooped by an obscure Lebanese publication) linking an arms trade to the release in Beirut (Lebanon) of US hostage David P. Jacobsen by an Islamic faction on Nov. 2, and naming the National Security Adviser, Vice-Adml. John M. Poindexter, and Col. Oliver North, a National Security Council (NSC) official, as intimately involved.

On Nov. 13 President Reagan publicly admitted for the first time that the administration had secretly sold "defensive weapons and spare parts" to Iran, though claiming that the aim had been to forge links with moderate elements in that country and not to deal for hostages. "Since US government contact began with Iran", Reagan declared, "there's been no evidence of Iranian government complicity in acts of terrorism against the US". (Secretary of State George Shultz, however, publicly rejected this claim on Nov. 16.) By this time, as would later emerge, administration officials were in a state of panic, giving misleading information not just to the press and public but to each other. On Nov. 19 a statement by Reagan that no third country had been involved in the arms trading was almost immediately contradicted by a White House statement, it quickly becoming obvious that Israel had been a party.

On Nov. 20 Edwin Meese, the Attorney General, began an internal White House inquiry on the President's orders, and on Nov. 25 an apparently overwhelmed and disorientated Reagan and a rather more self-possessed Meese appeared together at a White House press conference to announce that Poindexter had resigned and that North had been dismissed as a result of the discovery that North had diverted between $10,000,000 and $30,000,000 in profits from the sales of arms to Iran to assist the contra rebels in Nicaragua with the knowledge of both Poindexter and his predecessor McFarlane, who, however, had learned of it only after leaving office. While the apparent decisiveness of Meese's inquiry won praise at the time—the press had not latched on to the "contra diversion" before Meese's disclosure of it—it would only later be learned that he had conducted the investigation with such laxity that he had informed Col. North on Nov. 23 that his role in the diversion of profits had come to light, but then failed to seal North's office for another two days, during which time North and his secretary, Fawn Hall, worked long hours shredding documents at whose significance later investigators could only guess. On Nov. 26 President Reagan appointed a special three-man review board, headed by former Senator John Tower of Texas, to investigate the role of the NSC in the affair; and under intense congressional pressure the President on Dec. 2 agreed to the appointment of an independent counsel (special prosecutor), a federal court appointing Lawrence Walsh to the job on Dec. 19. Congress in turn set its own inquiries in motion, these leading to joint public hearings before special committees of the House and Senate (headed, respectively, by Democrats Lee H. Hamilton and Daniel K. Inouye) from May to August 1987.

Unlike in the Watergate affair, however, where the process of investigation led to a steady accumulation of damaging evidence and a gradual erosion of President Nixon's position, most of the salient details in the Iran–contra affair came to light in the very first weeks. Part of the reason for this lay in the fact that the administration was divided against itself. The plans of North, Poindexter and CIA Director William Casey to cover up as much as possible were thwarted by other top officials, especially Secretary of State George Shultz. After Poindexter and North were removed there was only one other top-level administration casualty of the affair, the White House Chief of Staff, Donald Regan, who resigned on Feb. 27, 1987, after the report of the Tower review board (issued the previous day) had declared that "he must bear primary responsibility for the chaos that descended upon the White House" after the initial disclosures. Ironically, Regan had apparently tried to warn President Reagan against the Iranian sales and had not even known of the contra diversion, but his many enemies—and especially, it seems, the President's wife Nancy—used the opportunity to persuade the President that Regan had failed to manage the crisis properly. In his 1988 book *For the Record: From Wall Street to Washington*, Regan claimed that in the early stages of the affair he had warned Nancy Reagan that her husband must act decisively, but she had refused, based on the warnings of an astrologer, to let the President face the media.

The transfers of arms to Iran

The origins of the whole Iran–contra affair appear to have lain in the President's overriding concern to secure the release of seven US citizens abducted in the Lebanon since March 1984 who were believed to be in all or most cases held by Shia Moslem fundamentalist groups controlled or strongly influenced by Iran. President Jimmy Carter's failure to win the release of 52 hostages held in the US embassy in Tehran by Islamic Revolutionary Guards for 444 days from Nov. 4, 1979, cast a pall over his presidency and eased the way for Reagan's victory over him in the November 1980 presidential election. (The Tehran hostages were finally released on Jan. 20, 1981, the day of Reagan's inauguration). By the summer of 1985 President Reagan was himself under pressure from US opinion to assert US power to win the release of US citizens in Lebanon. The President had publicly vowed, however, that he would not deal with terrorists, and the use of force was considered a hopeless proposition given the poor state of US intelligence about the location and identity of the murky groups which held the Americans.

Exactly who originated the idea that the USA might win back its hostages by the indirect route of selling weapons to Iran—itself hard-pressed in its protracted war with Iraq, which enjoyed the support of most of the Arab world—is still not entirely clear. Those involved from an early stage, however, included a number of international arms dealers and middlemen, including Manucher Ghorbanifar (an expatriate Iranian who was used despite failing a CIA lie detector test), Adnan Khashoggi (a Saudi Arabian financier and arms dealer), Yaacov Nimrodi (an Israeli who had been the head of the Tehran station of Mossad, the Israeli secret service, from 1956 to 1970) and Al Schwimmer (an Israeli arms manufacturer with close ties to Shimon Peres, the then Israeli Prime Minister). Also clearly involved at a high level was the Israeli government, which already had its own plans to sell weapons to the Iranians, US involvement beginning in the summer of 1985 following a meeting between David Kimche, the director of the Israeli Foreign Ministry, and McFarlane. The identities of all those involved on the Iranian side were more than a little obscure, but they were known to include Hojatolislam Rafsanjani (said to be the most powerful man in the country after the Ayatollah Khomeini) and the Prime Minister, Hossein Moussavi, and it is hard to imagine that such a relationship with the "Great Satan" of the USA could have been undertaken without the backing of the Khomeini himself. Certainly Rafsanjani survived the exposures unscathed (and was later to attain supreme power following Khomeini's death in June 1989). According to press reports, the *Al Shiraa* account of Nov. 3 which broke the story had been planted by Mehdi Hashemi, a clerical ally of Rafsanjani's arch-rival, Ayatollah Hossein Ali Montazeri, but in 1987 Hashemi was brought before an Islamic court and convicted of a variety of charges including murder, kidnap and sabotaging foreign relations.

While the interests of the arms dealers, the Iranians and the Israelis in embroiling the USA in the intrigues of the Gulf War were clear enough, the interests of the US side were never well-defined. In retrospective self-justification, much was made by US officials of the supposed objective of cultivating Iranian "moderates" in preparation for the succession to Ayatollah Khomeini, but the evidence was overwhelming that the real impetus to the operation came from the hostages issue. The Secretaries of Defence (Caspar Weinberger) and State (George Shultz), after raising objections in the early stages of the operation (objections described by themselves as strenuous, but by others as only token), were then quickly "frozen out" of—or on some accounts excused themselves from—its further development. Both Shultz and Weinberger later testified that they believed the operation had been discontinued at the end of 1985 following their objections; in fact, several shipments of weapons and spares, direct from US stocks or via Israel, took place in 1986. With the State and Defence departments out of the picture, and the CIA apparently proving frustratingly inert and suspicious of the middlemen brokering the sales, the burden of implementing the policy fell upon the staff of the NSC, a small agency within the executive office of the President largely closed to congressional scrutiny and headed by the National Security Adviser.

In particular, it fell on the ever-willing shoulders of Col. North of the US Marines, a self-styled man of action who had been appointed to the NSC staff in 1981 despite a record of some emotional volatility. In 1974 North had entered Bethesda Naval Hospital for treatment for "emotional distress" after threatening suicide. He was also a fantasist, who boasted to colleagues of regular meetings with the President which never actually occurred. North in turn recruited to the operation Maj.-Gen. Richard V. Secord, a retired US Air Force officer whom he had first met when they served in Vietnam, and Secord's Iranian-born business partner, Albert Hakim. Secord had met Hakim while stationed in Tehran during 1975–78, when the Shah still ruled, and had later taken a senior Defence Department job in the Reagan administration. In 1983, he had resigned under a cloud after an FBI investigation of his business relationship with a renegade CIA operative, Edwin Wilson, who had been sentenced to 52 years' imprisonment in 1982 for selling arms to Libya and plotting to kill federal prosecutors.

In the words of the Tower Commission, North conducted the Iran sales in an "amateurish" way, to the extent that from the first transfer of arms to Iran in August 1985 (100 TOW anti-tank missiles from Israeli stocks) to the exposure of the operation in November 1986 the USA won the release of only three of its hostages (Rev. Benjamin Weir, Fr Lawrence Jenco, and David Jacobsen), while with other seizures six remained in captivity. Meanwhile, US officials had engaged in a series of bizarre initiatives, including a trip to Tehran in May 1986 with a planeload of spare parts for anti-aircraft missiles by Col. North and Robert McFarlane (in the company of Shimon Peres' anti-terrorism adviser, Amiram Nir), when both the Americans carried suicide pills for use in the event of their detention. According to some accounts, supporters of Ayatollah Montazeri attempted to seize the hotel occupied by McFarlane and North, but were repelled by Revolutionary Guards loyal to Prime Minister Moussavi. North was also involved in separate direct attempts to ransom hostages with money put up by wealthy Americans. And, while the total of missiles shipped was relatively small—anti-tank and anti-aircraft missiles for which the Iranians paid $30,000,000—and certainly too small to influence the balance in the Gulf War, the arms sales made a mockery of President Reagan's denunciations of Iran as an outlaw state and boasts that he would never deal with terrorists. At the very time that arms were being sold to Iran, the USA was publicly trying to sustain a worldwide embargo on arms sales to Iran known as "Operation Staunch", while in August 1986 the President had signed the Omnibus Diplomatic Security and Anti-Terrorism Act. This prohibited the export of arms to countries identified by the Secretary of State as supporting terrorism, a category which had included Iran since 1984.

Exactly what President Reagan's active role had been in the policy-making on the Iran sales was unclear. On some accounts he had actively pushed the initiative, but on others he had been largely disengaged, leaving matters to advisers. Reagan himself told the Tower Commission that he could not recall exactly whether or not he had orally approved the first shipments of arms from Israeli stocks in 1985, as McFarlane had said was the case, or had only done so restrospectively, as Donald Regan had told Congress on the President's behalf. In a confusing broadcast explanation after the Tower Commission had reported that in its view he probably had given approval from the start, and had done so because of his concern for the hostages, Reagan observed on March 4, 1987: "A few months ago I told the American people I did not trade arms for hostages. My heart and my best intentions still tell me that is true, but the facts and the evidence tell me it is not. What began as a strategic opening to Iran deteriorated in its implementation into trading for hostages." That it had begun as any such strategic initiative was in any case fairly generally discounted. In July 1987 Adml. Poindexter told the congressional hearings that the first official directive on the affair signed by the President ("on or about" Dec. 5, 1985) had been concerned solely with the hostage question, and that only later, in a further directive signed on Jan. 17, 1986 (whose existence was already public knowledge), had any reference to a strategic opening been put in such a document. This Dec. 5 finding, like many other documents, had been destroyed, in this case by Poindexter himself, on his own evidence in an attempt to save the President from possible embarrassment after the operation became public.

Diversion of funds to the contras

After the early weeks of the affair, however, the attention of President Reagan's opponents came to focus less on the Iran arms sales, which for all the enormity of the contradictions exposed in administration policy had involved only relatively marginal and highly debatable violations of US laws, than on the diversion of proceeds to help the contras. Over several years Congress and President had feuded over the degree of support to be given the contras. After revelations that the CIA had mined Nicaraguan harbours, Congress had in October 1984 imposed restrictions (known as the Boland Amendment, as earlier and later different congressional restrictions on US aid to the contras were also somewhat confusingly referred to) which were intended to preclude the involvement of US intelligence agencies directly or indirectly in military or paramilitary operations in Nicaragua. (The restrictions imposed in October 1984 were, however, somewhat ambiguously weakened by 1985 legislation which allowed the intelligence agencies to provide the contras with "advice" and also set up a programme to supply the rebels with $27,000,000 in "non-lethal" aid, this including military support equipment such as trucks: the formula was a fudged compromise, the Senate having wanted to give the contras military aid while the House had refused.)

The discovery that Col. North and Adml. Poindexter had used the Iranian profits to help the contras buy weapons seemed to many of the administration's opponents to mean only one thing: that President Reagan, frustrated by Congress in the pursuit of his goal (albeit never explicitly acknowledged) of unseating the left-wing Sandinista government in Nicaragua, had gone behind Congress's back and broken the Boland amendment by stealth. The old Watergate questions were revived: "What did the President know, and when did he know it?" And would a "smoking gun" be discovered? President Reagan himself, beyond telling *Time* magazine at the end of November 1986 that he regarded Col. North as a "national hero", remained practically incommunicado and closely supervised by his aides in the critical months following the fall of North and Poindexter. It fell to his spokesmen to repeat denials that he had known anything about the diversion, which administration spokesmen freely conceded had been both illegal and unauthorised.

There were rumours, excitedly latched onto by Democratic politicians who thought they sniffed another Watergate, that Adml. Poindexter was preparing to defend himself by saying that he had twice told President Reagan of the diversion. Poindexter, the argument went, was a grey, anonymous functionary, who would not have set out on such a hazardous escapade without approval in triplicate, and had suffered deep disillusionment when set adrift by his master in the White House. When, however, Poindexter finally broke his post-resignation silence at the congressional Iran–contra hearings on July 15, 1987, he said instead that he had never explicitly told the President (or anyone else in the administration) that money from the Iran arms sales was being used to help the contras, but had merely inferred support because the President already knew of efforts by his staff to encourage private fund-raising and donations by third countries to assist the contras. And so, as Poindexter put it: "Although I was convinced that we could properly do it and that the President would approve if asked, I made a very deliberate decision not to ask the President so that I could insulate him from the decision and provide some future deniability for the President if it ever leaked out." "On this whole issue", Poindexter asserted, "the buck stops with me." As Col. North also conceded to Congress that he had never communicated directly with the President on the subject (but had only sent some unacknowledged memos via Poindexter, which the latter said he could not recall and copies of which North said he had shredded), the "smoking gun" was never found.

One vital witness was taken from the scene before his story could be told: William Casey, the Director of the CIA, who fell seriously ill with a brain seizure on Dec. 5, 1986—just a fortnight after the removal of North and Poindexter—and remained in hospital until his death on May 6, 1987. Before Casey fell ill he told Congress that he had learned of the contra diversion only when told of it by Meese, subsequently shifting the date back a month when other facts came to light. Whether or not Casey, as he lay in hospital, confirmed his earlier knowledge of the diversion to *Washington Post* reporter Bob Woodward (as claimed by Woodward in his book *Veil: The Secret Wars of the CIA, 1981–87* (1988), a claim which was vigorously denied by Casey's wife, who said Woodward had never once been at her husband's bedside), the view became fairly general that Casey had been a key player in the whole operation. Col. North himself told the congressional committees in July 1987 that he had worked with Casey to support the contras since 1984, when CIA involvement was curbed by the Boland Amendment, and that Casey ("a man of immense proportions") had known of the diversion since it was first conceived in early 1986. (That North's job was to help the contras one way or another was hardly a total secret: he had already faced inconclusive congressional investigation in 1985 after press exposés.) According to Clair George, the Deputy Director of the CIA responsible for operations, who admitted to extensive knowledge of the contra re-supply network managed by North, Casey had found the style of the CIA too cautious and bureaucratic and had responded to North's buccanneering spirit.

Indeed, Casey seemed to wish to break free altogether of the shackles which still restricted the CIA in the aftermath of the Church and Pike Committee's investigations of the mid-1970s (see *CIA "Family Jewels" Affair, 1974–76*, above). Col. North testified that Casey had envisaged the use of proceeds from the Iran sales to create an "off-the-shelf, self-sustaining, stand-alone entity that could perform functions for the United States" beyond assisting the contras. To some it seemed that Casey had been the mastermind of the whole Iran–contra operation, using North to bypass obstacles in the Washington bureaucracy, with both men understanding that North was to be—as North told the congressional committees—the "fall guy" if anything went wrong. (Curiously, however, Poindexter said he had never talked to Casey about the diversion, not wishing to involve the CIA because of the Boland Amendment.) At the same time, Casey had been a link to a group of current and former CIA operatives whom North had recruited to assist in the contra re-supply operation.

Behind this lay one conception of idealistic patriotism, and in his appearances at the congressional hearings from July 7–14, 1987, Col. North—deploying to full effect what the *New York Times* called his "smirks and winks and teary eyes. . .the 'Peck's Bad Boy' grins and the earnest altar-boy gazes"—lost no chance to drape himself in the flag. Congressmen were put consistently on the defensive as North portrayed himself as a decent soldier who was just doing what he believed his superiors intended and what he believed was right. He resented, he declared, George Shultz's description of him as "a loose cannon on the gundeck of state at the NSC". "That wasn't what I heard while I worked there," North insisted: "people used to walk up to me and tell me what a great job I was doing". For a few heady days of high summer North seemed to hold the nation in thrall and telegrams deluged Washington calling on Congress to cease and desist its harrassment of the man: "Olliemania" was compared to the (equally ephemeral) wave of popular sympathy for Gen. Douglas MacArthur after his recall from Korea in 1951 (see *Gen. MacArthur Affair, 1951*, above).

Not all the proceeds of the Iran sales ended up helping what North called the contra "freedom fighters", however. Albert Hakim, an Iranian-born US citizen who was the self-confessed director of finances of what those involved called the "enterprise", told the congressional hearings that for him the operation had never been more than a business proposition. In all, he said, the enterprise had taken in some $30,000,000 from the Iran arms sales and $17,700,000 from other sources; $8,000,000 remained in bank accounts, which he was not willing to surrender. North's closest associate, Gen. Secord, claimed that his motives were entirely patriotic, but his patriotism had according to Hakim not precluded the purchase of a Porsche and a light aircraft for his private use, and Secord furiously resisted US requests to the Swiss authorities for details of his bank accounts. Col. North himself, while clearly a man of genuine zeal for the contras' cause, had still accepted a $16,000 security fence for his house paid for by Secord and then, after the affair broke open, accepted backdated invoices for the work. Only Adml. Poindexter among the major figures in the diversion seemed entirely free of the taint of private advantage.

Before the investigatory committees North and Poindexter both pictured their acknowledged attempts to mislead Congress as justified by the need to conduct a foreign policy not compromised by endless leaks from bloated and partisan congressional staffs. Both declared that they had not seen the Boland Amendment as applying to the NSC staff (an interpretation which Reagan himself had flirted with briefly in a statement on May 16 before dropping the argument, perhaps for tactical rather than constitutional reasons). Both also emphasized that they had worked to keep faith with the contras (which the USA itself had largely created as a fighting force) in the face of what North termed the "fickle, vacillating, unpredictable" policy adopted by Congress. The point was not without merit: although North and Poindexter were hauled before Congress for violating the far from simple terms of the Boland Amendment—of which there were actually a series of five quite different versions in the period 1982–86, the October 1984 version being the most restrictive of the five—Congress had itself in August 1986, before the Iran-contra affair broke open, again reversed itself to allow the resumption of US military aid and direct CIA activity on behalf of the contras, with effect in the October. Here, arguably, were real issues about the credibility of the USA as a world power, and about the balance of authority between the legislative and executive branches over foreign relations, a matter which divided both constitutional theorists and practical politicians. The Reagan administration, however, conspicuously refused to broaden the issues in this way, clearly signalling that North and Poindexter were to be isolated as rogue miscreants. The calculation, presumably, was that if Congress's privileges were fully and fulsomely acknowledged, the less would be the political heat on the President himself.

And so the spokesmen of the administration, Secretary of State Shultz in particular, waxed moralistic at the congressional Iran–contra hearings about the undesirability of covert actions beyond the oversight of Congress, a theme which brought both satisfaction and relief to legislators who could not have relished a bruising dispute about what the administration could in practice have done to make a consistent policy out of Congress's constant shifts and shiftily-worded compromises on the contra issue. Other scores as well were perhaps being settled, for the exposure of the Iran–contra operation had helped to restore an authority to the State Department which had clearly been seriously compromised at a time when North and Poindexter, with direct access to the President, had conducted an independent mini-foreign policy in collusion with a miscellaneous assortment of international arms dealers and security agents of foreign governments. In a remarkable indication of the extent to which the nominally responsible Cabinet officers had been bypassed, Shultz and Weinberger both told Congress that they thought the Iran initiative had been discontinued after the initial transfers of arms from Israeli stocks. Shultz testified that he learned of the McFarlane–North trip to Tehran in May 1986 only when the affair broke open in November 1986, and Weinberger said he had found out about it only through the intelligence service of another government.

Congressional report on the affair

Despite the often prosecutorial tone of the questioning, the congressional hearings effectively laid the affair to rest as a politically critical issue, the administration and congressional leaders reaching a form of accommodation. The majority report of the joint investigating committees, published on Nov. 18, 1987, while attributing "ultimate responsibility" to President Reagan for the contra diversion for having allowed a "cabal of the zealots" to make policy, nonetheless drew short of charging that he had known of the diversion himself or had committed any impeachable offences. Col. North, it was concluded, had been the "central figure" in the diversion, with approval or tacit support from McFarlane, Poindexter and, probably, Casey, but no one still in government was linked to this side of the affair. A minority report, signed by eight of the Republicans on the 26-member committees, concluded that while there had been errors of judgment, "there was no constitutional crisis, no systematic disrespect for the 'rule of law', no grand conspiracy and no administration-wide dishonesty or cover-up", and that Congress itself had been seeking unjustifiably to aggrandize its foreign policy-making role.

At the same time, the President announced that he would in future notify the congressional intelligence committees of covert action within 48 hours (rather than just give "timely notice" as required by current law), and would inform Congress of any involvement by third governments or private parties. Congress was also assured in February 1988 that NSC officials had been forbidden to provide any assistance for fund-raising for the contras. And, in a gesture to those concerned that the CIA under Casey had come to resemble the old CIA of the days before the exposures of the mid-70s, the new CIA Director, William Webster, in December 1987 dismissed or reprimanded four operatives who had been involved in supporting the contras, and replaced Clair George as Deputy Director for operations. Gen. Secord had testified that some CIA and other US officials in Central America had helped the enterprise but others had refused, one of the latter group apparently being John Ferch, ambassador to Honduras, who was relieved of his post in 1986.

On a longer perspective, however, the conflict between Congress and the executive over the control of sensitive areas of foreign policy was ultimately not capable of any final resolution. Through successive presidencies this conflict had led to periodic crises and was inherent in the global, and necessarily covert, nature of US operations, in conjunction with the tension between the different branches of government which the Founding Fathers—in simpler days—had seen fit to build into the nation's constitution.

Criminal prosecutions of North, Poindexter and others

If the political accommodation was one which might have been achieved in many states, the affair still retained its peculiarly American dimension in the determination to put someone on trial. The real issues were political, about the morality and credibility of dealing in arms for hostages, and about the degree to which administrations could or should keep faith (as in the case of the contras) with allies about whom the Congress was alternately blowing hot and cold. Special prosecutor Walsh, however, backed by a small army of dogged investigators, was on the trail of criminality. On March 11, 1988, Robert McFarlane (a broken man, who had attempted suicide in February 1987) pleaded guilty to misdemeanour charges of misleading Congress (principally in 1985, when he had said that North was not fund-raising to assist the contras) as part of a plea-bargain to win his evidence against the men targeted by Walsh as the criminal principals: North, Poindexter, Secord and Hakim. These four were indicted five days later on sweeping charges of conspiracy, fraud, embezzlement, and obstruction in the use of arms sales funds to support the contras and for their private benefit (no claim was made that the transfer of arms to Iran had been illegal per se). A further indictment, against the former CIA station chief in Costa Rica,

Joseph F. Fernandez, was returned on June 20, 1988 (all criminal charges against him were dismissed in November 1989).

This narrowing-down of the affair to the criminal culpability of just a few men, none of them now in government, was inevitably very much in the interests of the administration. While President Reagan continued to make occasional blandly favourable observations about what he thought must have been the decent motives of North and Poindexter, the White House absolutely refused to extend any meaningful co-operation to the defence or to surrender important documents demanded by it. Prosecutor Walsh sought at first to put all the defendants in court at once in a set-piece show trial, but trial Judge Gerhard Gesell ordered that they should be tried separately in sequence. The defendants' right to a fair trial, Gesell ruled, had not been compromised by the testimony they had given to Congress under immunity (in the case of North, Poindexter and Hakim—Secord had testified without immunity), but each defendant had to be allowed to use the immunized testimony of the others in his own defence. (Congress had compelled testimony by a grant of immunity, which meant that nothing self-incriminating said by those testifying could be used against them in legal proceedings.) North, chosen by Walsh to lead the procession, fully demonstrated in months of pre-trial manoeuvres that he no longer felt bound to be the "fall guy", demanding the handover of government documents relating to other intelligence operations and that George Bush and Reagan should be put on the witness stand. North's counter-attack provoked alarm in the government and intelligence communities at the prospects of further disclosures unrelated to the case, and Walsh was forced to back off some of the most sweeping conspiracy charges before the trial even got underway.

Ultimately, little evidence was advanced at North's trial that was not amply familiar from the earlier congressional hearings, though this would not have led to any sense of tedium on the part of the 12 jurors (nine men and three women, all of them black); their primary qualification, established at jury-vetting, was that they were so indifferent to public affairs that they had neither read nor heard a word of anything to do with the case which might have led them to form even the slightest prejudicial assumption. And yet, while this process of jury selection might have struck a rational observer as like something from the pages of *Alice in Wonderland*, the final verdict of the jury seemingly approximated to what most Americans thought about the affair, as shown by opinion polls. On May 4 the jury, after 13 days of sequestered deliberation, announced that it had found North guilty on three counts of shredding government documents, accepting an illegal gratuity in the form of a security fence for his home, and falsifying records after investigations started; as North had effectively admitted all three points, the jury's conclusion was hardly unexpected. On nine counts, however, including the key charges of conspiracy to conceal the contra supply network from Congress, the jury found North innocent. It was clear from post-trial statements that most of the jurors had accepted North's defence that he had only been obeying orders, or had thought he was obeying orders—from McFarlane, Poindexter and Casey directly, and indirectly from the President himself—in what he had done to assist the contras. Accurately reflecting the balance of the jury's verdict, Gesell on July 5, 1989, sentenced North (who now professed penitence for his deeds) to only a suspended three-year prison sentence, 1,200 hours of community service, and a $150,000 fine. Perhaps the hardest part of the sentence for North was Gesell's ruling that he could never run for public office, for North's admirers had started a bandwagon for him to become a Republican candidate for Congress.

Gesell's decision not to jail North saved President Bush from a potentially embarrassing decision as to whether to accede to right-wing pressure to give North a pardon. Before the November 1988 elections much had been made by the Democrats of Bush's supposed ties to the contra re-supply operation through his former national security adviser, Donald Gregg, but the mud had not stuck. Bush had won a comfortable electoral victory, and as President had confidently gone on to nominate Gregg to become his ambassador to South Korea. By 1989 there was too a mood of boredom with the Nicaragua issue, perhaps even an uneasy sense that while Congress and the White House had been squabbling over the fate of a few thousand rebels of doubtful fervour in a tiny Central American country, America had been failing to respond properly to developments crucial to the national interest, whether Gorbachev's global peace initiatives, or the challenge of Europe and Japan to US economic pre-eminence. Bush himself had relegated the Nicaragua issue to a low place on his order of priorities and espoused a bi-partisan policy of marching in step with Congress on the subject. If Nicaragua had ultimately been a foolish, empty sideshow for the Reagan years, there seemed little point to letting its legacy poison the Washington atmosphere for another administration.

Meanwhile, however, the legal process trundled on. McFarlane had been fined and sentenced to two years on probation on March 3, 1989. On Jan. 24, 1990, Secord, and on Feb. 1, Hakim, were also both sentenced to two years' probation and fines after entering plea bargain deals in which they pleaded guilty to relatively minor charges (involving the diversion of money from the arms sales to North's personal use) in return for their co-operation with the investigation. Hakim also agreed to hand over to the US government $7,300,000 in proceeds from arms sales frozen in Swiss bank accounts.

Poindexter's trial in 1990 was in many ways a re-run of the Watergate trials of the mid-1970s. Having sought to protect his president at the height of the political crisis, Poindexter now maintained that much of what he had done had been with Reagan's broad knowledge. Abandoned was his 1987 claim that: "On this whole issue, the buck stops with me." At the same time, the charges brought against Poindexter related not to what he had done *before* the affair broke open in November 1986, but what he had done in the *aftermath*, all counts relating to his support of the contras having been dropped in June 1989 in the face of the government's refusal to release classified documents.

Poindexter's attempts to force the introduction into evidence of Reagan's diaries and private papers ended in a compromise whereby Reagan on Feb. 16–17, 1990, gave videotaped replies in private to questions put to him by Poindexter's lawyers. The former President's answers showed him confused and vague even in dealing with apparently innocuous questions, and cast no further light on the genesis of the affair. At his trial, which began on

March 5, 1990, Poindexter himself did not give evidence and the most damaging testimony came from North, who stated that Poindexter had supervised a November 1985 arms shipment to Iran: four of the five counts on which Poindexter was convicted on April 7 related to his statements to Congress that he had not learned of the arms trades until January 1986. Like Haldeman and Ehrlichman a decade-and-a-half earlier, Poindexter was convicted of involvement in a cover-up rather than for his role in any criminal activity which had precipitated the cover-up in the first place.

On June 11, 1990, Poindexter was sentenced to six months in prison. In passing sentence Judge Harold Greene declared that any lesser punishment would be "tantamount to a statement that a scheme to lie and to obstruct Congress is of no great moment". Poindexter remained at liberty pending an appeal, however, and on July 20 an appellate court reversed North's conviction for destroying documents and ordered Judge Gesell to conduct an inquiry into whether North's conviction on two other counts had been prejudiced by his prior congressional testimony.

Meanwhile, in Nicaragua, elections held in February 1990 had resulted in the defeat of the Sandinistas and the election of the National Opposition Union of Violeta Chamorro, to the evident relief of the Bush administration. By the summer of 1990 most of the remaining contra rebels had surrendered their weapons, marking an apparent end to the country's civil war.

FJH

Gary Hart Affair (1987)

Gary Hart, candidate for 1988 Democratic presidential nomination.
Donna Rice, model and actress.

Then a relatively obscure Senator from Colorado, Gary Hart succeeded in coming second to Walter Mondale in the race for the Democratic presidential nomination in 1984 by staging a "new ideas" campaign which survived revelations that he had changed his name from Hartpence to Hart in the early 1960s and was misrepresenting his age as 46 when it was 47. In the race for the 1988 nomination, Hart emerged as the early front-runner, but withdrew on May 8, 1987, following press reports of a liaison with Donna Rice, a 29-year-old model and actress, whom he had accompanied on a cruise to Bimini (55 miles off the Florida coast) on a yacht called *Monkey Business*.

In the view of many, Hart's basic political judgment was at issue more than his private morality, for although publicly reconciled with his wife (from whom he had separated briefly in 1979 and 1981) there had been widespread rumours in Washington circles of various extra-marital liaisons. Indeed the *New York Times* on May 3—the day the *Miami Herald* carried the first reports of the Donna Rice liaison—carried an interview with Hart in which he challenged the press: "Follow me around. I don't care . . . If anybody wants to put a tail on me, go ahead. They'd be very bored." The *Miami Herald* had done precisely that, staking out Hart's Washington town house on the night of May 1–2 and then revealing that he had spent the night there with a woman other than his wife.

Hart's withdrawal followed several days in which he entangled himself in increasingly unsustainable evasions and falsehoods about his relationship with Rice, culminating in reports that the *Washington Post* was about to give details of other relationships. It was greeted with undisguised relief by many Democratic insiders, who regarded him as a loner and a risk-taker. His own former poll taker referred to him as having a "death wish", and the affair triggered an avalanche of journalistic psychoanalyzing of Hart's career, from his severely puritanical and religious small-town midwestern background to jet-set party-goer and intimate of film star Warren Beatty (his so-called "Gatsby problem"). His announcement on Dec. 15, 1987, that he had decided to re-enter the contest produced consternation, and claims that this was further evidence of his arrogance, vanity and belief that he was above the normal rules of the game. Apparently this was also the view of the voters. After a series of disastrous primary results, Hart withdrew for good on March 11, 1988, claiming that his problem had been the difficulty of turning his complex ideas on policy issues into simple slogans.

FJH

Joseph Biden Affair (1987)

Joseph Biden, candidate for 1988 Democratic presidential nomination.

Senator Joseph Biden (44), of Delaware, withdrew as a candidate for the 1988 Democratic presidential nomination on Sept. 23, 1987, after allegations of plagiarism in his speech-making and falsification of his college record. Up to that point he had seemed among the strongest of the so-called "seven dwarfs" left in the Democratic field after the withdrawal of Gary Hart (see *Gary Hart Affair, 1987*, above).

The charges raised against Biden might in other times have proved survivable. His unattributed lifting of rhetorical flourishes from the speeches of past Democratic leaders, including John Kennedy, and even of the current British Labour Party leader, Neil Kinnock, arguably said more about the calibre of his speech-writers than his personal rectitude, though the news he had been reprimanded for plagiarism while in law school in the 1960s perhaps testified to a chronic addiction to this particular vice. In 1987, however, the US media had the scent of blood in their harrying of public figures. Having started with the driving out of Donald Regan as White House Chief of Staff thanks to a tenuous connection with the Iran arms fiasco (see *Iran–Contra Affair, 1986–90*, above), the year continued with the withdrawal of Gary Hart from the race for the Democratic nomination after being caught in a compromising situation by investigators of the *Miami Herald* (see *Gary Hart Affair, 1987*, above) and would culminate with the rejection of two successive Supreme Court nominees (see *Bork/Ginsburg Affair, 1987*, below). A week after Biden's withdrawal rival Democratic presidential candidate Michael Dukakis dropped two of his top campaign aides (John Sasso, his campaign manager and Paul Tully, his political director) after Sasso admitted having given reporters a videotape juxtaposing practically identical sections of speeches by Kinnock and Biden, and Tully that he had tried to mislead *Time* magazine by saying the Dukakis campaign was not responsible for anti-Biden leaks. With the removal of Biden, however, following that of Hart, the way in effect became clear for the relatively little-known Dukakis to make his way to the nomination.

FJH

Bork/Ginsburg Affair (1987)

Robert Bork; Douglas H. Ginsburg, Reagan nominees to Supreme Court.

In the autumn of 1987 President Reagan failed to seat two nominees to the Supreme Court in succession, in one case because the Senate did not care for the nominee's judicial philosophy, and in the other because of controversy over the nominee's private life.

President Reagan announced his choice of Judge Robert H. Bork

(60), a federal appeals court judge for the District of Columbia circuit, to replace the 79-year-old Justice Lewis F. Powell, who was retiring because of ill-health, on July 1, 1987. Bork, as a member of perhaps the most important of the appellate courts and a prolific writer on legal issues, was not challenged for his learning and competence but for his activist conservative beliefs, and faced an unprecedently intense lobbying campaign against him led by liberal, civil liberties and women's groups. In the view of these groups the nomination had a key significance, because Powell had been the "swing" vote on the Court, holding the balance between its liberal and conservative wings on a range of issues. Nor did it help Bork that many in the Senate still held against him his role in the 1973 "Saturday Night Massacre" in the Watergate affair, when he had carried out President Nixon's order to dismiss special prosecutor Archibald Cox after the Attorney General and the Deputy Attorney General had resigned rather than do so (see *Watergate Affair, 1972–74*, above).

Bork's misfortune was to be nominated at a time when the Reagan presidency was in decline, and after the Democrats had recaptured the Senate (i.e. the body responsible for confirming Supreme Court appointees) in the November 1986 elections. Had his nomination come any time from 1981 to late 1986 (when the Iran–contra affair—see above—further weakened the President), he would doubtless have been confirmed. As it was, Bork was rejected by the Senate by 58 votes to 42 on Oct. 23, 1987, after stubbornly keeping his name before the Senate long after defeat became inevitable (amid conflicting reports as to whether or not this was with the President's encouragement). He was probably the first Supreme Court nominee rejected on ideological grounds alone for half a century. Three months later, apparently embittered by his experience, he announced his decision to quit the federal bench altogether.

Reagan's nomination on Oct. 29, 1987, of Judge Douglas H. Ginsburg, a libertarian conservative, as his alternative to Bork was, in contrast, a case of a poorly-thought-out choice which quickly became embarrassingly indefensible. Ginsburg's candidature came under attack on a variety of counts, including his operation while a student of a computerized dating service which had been investigated by consumer groups. It also emerged that while at the Justice Department he had argued before the Supreme Court in favour of easing government regulation of cable television when he had made an investment of $140,000 in a cable television company. His cause was fatally damaged by his admission on Nov. 5 of the truth of reports circulated by former colleagues that he had smoked marijuana while teaching at Harvard Law School in the 1970s, and he withdrew on Nov. 7, a day after President Reagan had embarrassedly assured the public that his nominee was "not an addict. . .nothing of that kind". There had hardly been time for critics to latch onto Ginsburg's lack of experience: 41 years old, he had been a judge for only a year, and his lack of significant published work was apparently regarded as a benefit in the White House, because it meant that, unlike Bork, he had left no "paper trail" to betray his ideological predilections.

Following the Ginsburg debacle, President Reagan nominated California federal appeals court judge Anthony M. Kennedy to the Supreme Court vacancy. In the opinion of many, Kennedy—who was seen as close in judicial philosophy to Justice Powell—would have been the best choice in the very beginning, and on Feb. 3, 1988 the Senate confirmed his selection without a vote against. Overall, the Bork/Ginsburg affair showed that the Senate was no longer willing to acquiesce meekly in President Reagan's much-boasted strategy of preserving his political legacy by packing the federal courts with conservative judges. It also proved a further push in the downward slide of Attorney General Edwin Meese (see also *Edwin Meese Affair, 1984–88*, above), who was blamed by many in the administration for the fiasco caused by the nomination of his protegé Ginsburg.

FJH

Wedtech Affair (1987–90)

Mario Biaggi, Congressman convicted in Wedtech affair.
Robert Garcia, Congressman convicted in Wedtech affair.
James C. McKay, Independent Counsel who investigated Nofziger and Meese.
Lyn Nofziger, lobbyist and former Reagan aide.
Edwin Meese, Attorney General.

Connection with the tangled affairs of the Wedtech Corporation, a relatively modest defence contractor located in New York's South Bronx district, resulted in the late 1980s in a string of indictments and convictions of local and national officials, including two US Congressmen from New York, Mario Biaggi and Robert Garcia, and a former top Reagan aide, Lyn Nofziger. The Wedtech affair had also triggered an investigation of the Attorney General Edwin Meese, although no prosecution had been mounted in his case (see also *Edwin Meese Affair, 1984–88*, above).

Wedtech was founded in 1965 as the Welbilt Electronic Die Corporation, by John Mariotta, whose parents had come from Puerto Rico. Until the early 1980s it remained a modest enterprise, but after 1982 it grew rapidly as a defence contractor, benefiting from a federal Small Business Administration programme discriminating in favour of businesses owned by members of minority groups under which it received $250,000,000 in contracts in the four years to the end of 1986. The company was hailed as a minority business success story in an area of acute urban blight, and corruption and political objectives went hand in hand in the favouritism shown it. During 1986, however, Wedtech's affairs came under scrutiny as part of a broader ethics probe in New York, and in December of that year it went into bankruptcy. In early 1987, four former Wedtech executives agreed with prosecutors to name public officials who had taken bribes in connection with the awarding of contracts.

In February 1987 a federal independent counsel (James C. McKay) was appointed to investigate the lobbying activities of Lyn Nofziger (President Reagan's former assistant for political affairs) on behalf of Wedtech and a California rice company since he left the White House in January 1982, and McKay's investigations were subsequently broadened to include the Attorney General Edwin Meese at Meese's request after much speculation as to his own links with Wedtech. Meese was known to have intervened in 1982 (when he was special counsellor to President Reagan) to assist Wedtech to secure a $32,000,000 Army contract, and in 1985 he had invested $60,000 with W. Franklyn Chinn, a Wedtech consultant who subsequently joined the Wedtech board. Meese's personal lawyer, E. Robert Wallach, had also been paid more than $1,000,000 in fees and stock by Wedtech for his services for the company, which appeared to have included introducing Meese to it.

Nofziger was indicted in July 1987 and convicted on Feb. 11, 1988, of illegally lobbying former White House colleagues on behalf of Wedtech and two other clients within a year of leaving the White House (such immediate lobbying being barred by the 1978 Ethics in Government Act). The key to the case was evidence that he had intervened on behalf of Wedtech with Meese (whom he had known since they first worked for the then Governor Reagan in the 1960s) in April 1982 to assist it in winning a $32,000,000 Army contract (Nofziger's consultancy had received $886,000 from Wedtech in 1983). His was the first conviction ever under the 1978 Ethics Act, although Michael Deaver had been convicted two months earlier on perjury charges arising from a similar special prosecutor investigation (see *Michael Deaver Affair, 1986–87*, above). Nofziger was sentenced on April 8 to a 90-day prison term and a fine of $30,000, complaining that McKay had made "mountains out of molehills". On June 26, 1989, a federal appeals court reversed Nofziger's conviction, finding that the law was ambiguous and that Nofziger might not have known he was acting illegally.

In December 1987 Wallach and Chinn were indicted on charges of having taken bribes from Wedtech partly in exchange for influencing Meese. McKay announced that he had insufficient evidence to bring charges against Meese, although he continued to investigate other areas of the Attorney General's affairs. Wallach was sentenced to six years in prison and a fine of $250,000 on Oct. 16, 1989, while Chinn was sentenced to three years and a fine of $100,000.

After a five-month trial Mario Biaggi and five others (including former Bronx borough president Stanley Simon, Biaggi's son Richard, and

John Mariotta) were convicted by a federal grand jury in Manhattan on Aug. 4, 1988, on racketeering and other charges. Biaggi himself—who resigned from Congress with immediate effect two days later, and had already been convicted in November 1987 in a separate case involving acceptance of illegal gratuities—was found to have extorted about 5 per cent of Wedtech's stock, worth $1,800,000, for lobbying on behalf of the company. The prosecution case was based largely on the evidence of the four former Wedtech executives obtained under the plea-bargain deal set in January 1987, while Biaggi's main defence theme was that with Reagan administration insiders apparently in its pocket, Wedtech hardly needed to bribe a mere congressman. Such an argument conflicted, however, with extensive evidence that Wedtech had bought the services of numerous politicians and other public officials at every level of government.

Biaggi and his five co-defendants were sentenced to prison terms on Nov. 18, 1988 (Biaggi and Mariotta each got eight years). In a further case, New York congressman Robert Garcia was sentenced to three years in prison on Jan. 19, 1990, after being convicted of extorting cash and gifts from Wedtech. He had resigned his congressional seat on Jan. 7.

FJH

Dan Quayle Affair (1988)

George Bush, Republican presidential candidate (1988).
J. Danforth Quayle, Republican candidate for Vice-President (1988).

George Bush's choice of J. Danforth Quayle, a little-known senator from Indiana, as his running-mate on the 1988 Republican presidential ticket, threatened briefly to lead either to the dropping of Quayle or serious electoral difficulties for Bush. By election day, however, controversy over Quayle had largely subsided and the Bush/Quayle ticket secured a substantial victory.

Bush announced his decision to run with Quayle on Aug. 16, 1988, during the Republican National Convention, and there were immediate media reports that Quayle, who came from a wealthy and prominent family, had used family connections in 1969, after he graduated from DePauw University, to gain entry to the National Guard rather than be conscripted for service in Vietnam. (Only a very few Guard units had been despatched to Vietnam, and only 97 of the 58,000 Americans killed in Vietnam were Guardsmen.) While in the Guard, it emerged, Quayle had spent most of his six part-time years preparing press releases and articles for the *Indiana National Guardsman* and had scored below average on tests of military knowledge.

The disclosures stirred very mixed reactions. While many of military age had joined the Guard to avoid Vietnam, and others had fled the country altogether, Quayle had as a senator become known as a hawk, joining the ranks of what the *Village Voice* magazine called the "chicken-hawks"—those who were now military hardliners but had skipped service when faced with their own chance to take part in a war. To his bitterest detractors, Quayle seemed to represent cowardice and hypocrisy in equal measure. Other views were less hostile, however. National Guardsmen resented the implication that they had not also served their country, and many even of those who had supported the Vietnam War at the time had come to look upon it as an ignoble episode which had involved a worthless sacrifice of life. Certainly, there had been no post-Vietnam equivalent of the post-World War II generation of politicians, like Richard Nixon and John Kennedy, who had been helped to win seats in Congress by their wartime service. Hypocrisy was indeed present in abundance on every side, as liberal Democrats who had been mealymouthed about, or opposed, the Vietnam War suddenly shuddered at this evidence of unpatriotic behaviour by a vice-presidential candidate, while many of those who had been altogether in favour of the Vietnam War at the time now decided that dodging service in it was nothing to be ashamed of. For example, conservative columnist William Buckley claimed that Quayle's ingenuity in dodging Vietnam had been the "American way" of doing things.

Quayle himself, while conceding that "phone calls were made,. . .I don't know the specifics of that" to get him into the Guard (there were widely conflicting accounts as to how easy or difficult it had been to join the Guard at the time, but most emphasized the difficulty), denied that he had been guilty of anything more than wanting to stay at home so he could go straight to law school (which he duly did, despite a mediocre college record, again apparently helped by the family name). As he plaintively remarked at a news conference on Aug. 17: "I did not know in 1969 that I would be in this room today." George Bush for his part seemed satisfied that if his running-mate had not exactly been a war hero (was there a Vietnam war hero?), he had not been an out-and-out draft-evader: he "didn't go to Canada, and he didn't burn his draft card, and he damned sure didn't burn the American flag". Quayle indeed had quiet appeal for a whole generation of middle-class Americans, now settled into firmly patriotic middle age, who had never particularly supported and never particularly opposed the Vietnam War. Vietnam had after all—unlike World War II, when the college and high school educated had figured disproportionately among the casualties—been a war fought disproportionately by those without family connections or college attendance, 25 per cent of the 2,150,000 who served coming from below the poverty line.

Embarrassed by the Vietnam issue, and by a rehashing of lurid old stories—first aired in 1981—by model and former lobbyist Paula Parkinson of how she had spent a "golfing vacation" in 1980 with Quayle and two other congressmen, Quayle found himself cocooned by Republican campaign aides to the extent that he scarcely appeared for public questioning in the latter stages of the campaign. This finally seemed not to matter, however, in a campaign dominated by "sound-bites"—one-liner remarks packaged for the evening television news—in which Quayle's qualifications to stand a "heartbeat away" from the presidency were never seriously scrutinized. Even George Bush, many commentators surmised, had seen in Quayle little more than a boyishly attractive young man with a record of appealing to women voters (some saw a passing resemblance to Robert Redford) and who had solid conservative credentials but was unlikely to complicate a Bush presidency by emerging as a significant political force in his own right.

FJH

Jim Wright Affair (1989)

Tony Coelho, majority (Democratic) Whip in House of Representatives.
Jim Wright, Speaker of House of Representatives.

Speaker of the House of Representatives Jim Wright (Democrat, Texas) announced his resignation on May 31, 1989, in the face of continued erosion of his influence and reputation caused by corruption allegations. His decision to stand down from the most powerful job on Capitol Hill followed the resignation days earlier of fellow Democrat Tony Coelho, who as Majority Whip was the third most powerful Democrat in Congress, rather than face a long drawn-out probe into charges of corruption. While the accusations made against Wright and Coelho could doubtless have been made against many similarly influential congressmen over the years, Wright and Coelho came under scrutiny at a time when the old bipartisan consensus on Capitol Hill about turning a blind eye to all but the most flagrant culpability seemed to have broken down. In his resignation speech Wright urged his fellow Congressmen to "resolve to bring this period of mindless cannibalism to an end".

Wright, 66, had served in Congress for 34 years, succeeding "Tip" O'Neill as Speaker in 1987. Since then, however, he had faced sustained media examination of his relationship with Texas businessman George Mallick. Republican Congressmen, in little mood to compromise after years of Democratic attempts to tarnish the reputation of the Reagan adminis- tration with the so-called "sleaze factor" (see *Sleaze Factor Affair, 1984*, above) pressed for an investigation of Wright and on April 17, 1989, the House Ethics Committee (on which Democrats held the majority) issued a 270-page report, compiled by a committee-appointed special prosecutor (Richard Phelan), accusing Wright on 69 counts of financial impropriety. These included the acceptance of $145,000-worth of gifts and benefits from Mallick in the period 1979–88, $54,600 in unreported gifts in royalties from his book *Reflections of a Public Man*, and acceptance of gifts from Texas businessmen with interests in legislation pending in Congress.

Wright immediately declared his intention to "fight with the last ounce of conviction and energy that I possess" to prove his innocence. It quickly became apparent, however, that Republicans intended to press for Wright's expulsion from the House, threatening a long period of rancorous dispute, and that Wright, regarded as a political loner, did not have the breadth and depth of personal support among his fellow Democrats to enable him to survive. Nor was he helped by revelations in early May that he had used his influence in the mid-1970s to ensure that John Mack, the brother of his daughter's husband, served only 30 months in a soft suburban jail after being convicted of an horrifically brutal hammer and knife attack on a woman shop assistant who had barely survived, and that this same Mack had gone on to become Wright's top aide in Congress.

Tony Coelho's resignation was precipitated by newspaper stories linking him to insider dealing on a bond issue by Michael Milken, the so-called "junk-bond king" of brokers Drexel Burnham Lambert, who was under indictment, and the threat of twin investigations by the House Ethics Committee and the Justice Department.

The twin resignations brought to a climax a period of acute partisan conflict on Capitol Hill as Republicans sought to undermine the Democratic majorities in both Houses by focusing on charges of wrongdoing.

FJH

ZIMBABWE

Willowgate Affair (1988–89)

Jacob Mudenda, Governor, Matabeleland North.
Dzingai Mutumbuka, Minister of Higher Education (1988–1989).
Callistus Ndlovu, Minister of Industry and Technology (1985–1989).
Enos Nkala, Minister of Home Affairs (1985–1988); Minister of Defence (1988–1989).
Maurice Nyagumbo, Minister in the Office of the President responsible for Political Affairs, (1988–1989).
Frederick Shava, Minister of State for Public Affairs (resigned March 1989); elected secretary, Midlands branch of ZANU-PF (October 1989).

At the end of December 1988 President Robert Mugabe ordered a judicial inquiry headed by Justice Wilson Sandura, a high court judge, into a car sales racket thought to involve as many as 20 Cabinet ministers. The scandal had come to light as a result of investigative reporting by *The Chronicle* (Bulawayo), which claimed that government ministers had used their position to obtain cars from the state-owned Willowvale car assembly plant, which were then resold at huge profit on the black market, in breach of regulations forbidding the resale of vehicles above a certain price. The affair became known as "Willowgate".

Two ministers resigned in March 1989, just before the submission of the Sandura Commission's report, namely Frederick Shava (Minister of State for Public Affairs), who admitted lying to the inquiry and encouraging others to do likewise, and Enos Nkala, the Defence Minister, who also admitted giving incorrect evidence to the Commission.

The Commission presented its report in April 1989. It found that a number of government members had acted improperly in obtaining cars and in profiting from their resale. It also found that five ministers (among them Shava and Nkala) had perjured themselves in giving evidence to the Commission. Three more ministers resigned on the day the Commission's report was made public: Maurice Nyagumbo (one of the three senior Ministers in the Office of the President, responsible for Political Affairs); Dzingai Mutumbuka (Higher Education); and Callistus Ndlovu (whose portfolio of Industry and Technology covered the car assembly business). The Governor of Matabeleland North, Jacob Mudenda, also resigned.

Nyagumbo died on April 20. Three days later Mugabe confirmed that his death had been suicide, apparently caused by taking poison. The Sandura Commission had described his conduct as "improper and dishonest", and found that he had used his position to help friends obtain imported cars. He denied profiting from this, but accepted in his resignation letter to Mugabe that "my image in the leadership of both the party and the government has completely tarnished your name, party and government". He had been a prominent figure in the independence struggle.

Shava was sentenced to a nine months' gaol sentence and fined £50,000 for lying to the judicial inquiry. On July 6, 1989, however, he was pardoned by Mugabe.

The government showed reluctance to prosecute others implicated in the affair and Shava's involvement did not prevent him from standing in party provincial leadership elections in October 1989, when he was elected secretary for the Midlands province branch of Mugabe's ZANU-PF party.

Nonetheless, in November 1989 Nkala, a veteran member of the ZANU-PF political bureau and close confidant of Mugabe, was found guilty of violating price control laws and fined nearly £26,000.

A low electoral turnout and widespread apathy towards the general election of March 1990 was partly attributed to popular disillusionment exacerbated by corruption in government circles.

KD

INDEX

Abdul Razak 39
Abe, Shintaro 162
Abernathy, Ralph 368
Abitbol, Felix Messoud 170
Abt, John 311
Abu-Hatzeira 141
Acheson, Dean 316, 331, 340
Adams, John 335–336
Adams, Samuel 335, 427
Adams, Sherman 299, 346
Adenauer, Konrad 98–100
Agee, Philip 418, 420
Agnew, Spiro 299, 384, 401, 410–412
Ahlers, Conrad 98–100
Ahmansson, Nels-Erik 208
Albam, Jacob 350
Alexander, Field Marshall 233
Allen, Jani 194
Allen, Richard 429
Allende, Salvador 415, 418
Ambatiellou, Tonis 107
Amin, Idi 134
Amry, Herbert 27–28
Anagnostopoulos, Col. P. 111
Anderson, Jack 375, 398
Andreatta, Beniamino 148
Andropov, Yuri 118–119, 198–199
Androsch, Hannes 21–22
Angleton, James J. 415
Anselmi, Tina 151
Aoki, Ikei 161–162
Apostolopoulos, Sotiris 114
Aquino, Benigno 178
Aquino, Corazon 178
Arafat, Yasser 136
Aragu, Kazunobu 157
Ardbo, Martin 124, 126
Arens, Moshe 137–138
Aridor, Yoram 142
Armstrong, Sir Robert 292–293
Armstrong, Scott 369
Arnold, Henry 216
Astor, Lord 233
Athanassopoulos, Nikos 114
Atherton, Ray 44
Attlee, Clement 38, 42, 44, 213, 215, 216–217, 226
Augstein, Rudolf 99–100
Aung San 37–40, 42
Averoff, Evangelos 116
Azerad, Nelly 81, 83

B.J. 56
Ba Maw 37

Ba Nyun 41
Ba Sein 38
Ba Win 39
Babangida, Maj.-Gen. Ibrahim 170
Bacilek, Karol 59–60
Baker, James 429, 432
Baker, Howard 399
Baker, Marrion L. 352
Balaunde, President 274
Baldwin, Alfred C. 388–389
Bamford, James 347
Bannister, Everette 29–30
Bar-Kochba, Maj.-Gen. Moshe 137–138
Barak, Aharon 132–133, 136
Barak, Alexander 169–170
Baranès, André 69–70
Barba, Jean-François 95–96
Barker, Bernard L. 382, 388, 396
Barre, Raymond 84–85, 91
Barwick, Sir Garfield 13
Barzel, Rainer 103
Beatty, Warren 453
Beck, Bernard 90–91
Becker, Hans-Detlev 99
Begin, Menachem 132, 136, 438
Beijsky, Moshe 141-142
Beker, Johanna Koenen 350
Belcher, John 213, 215
Belcher, Louise 214
di Bella, Franco 150
Ben Barka, Mehdi 73–75
Ben-Gurion, David 129–131, 223–224
Beneš, Dr Edvard 54–55
Bennett, Max 130
Bennett, Robert 393, 408
Bentley, Elizabeth 303–304, 308–311, 327, 330
Benya, Anton 20, 22
Bérégovoy, Pierre 97
Berger, Hans see Eisler, Gerhard
Berger, Victor 366
Beria, Lavrenti 54, 56, 58–59, 180, 183
Berle, Adolf A. 312, 316
Berman, Yitzchak 136
Bernhard, Prince 167
Bernier, Philippe 73–75
Bernstein, Carl 385, 389, 394–395, 398, 407–408
Bessell, Peter 262–264
Bessie, Alvah 302
Bettaney, Michael 278–280
Beveridge, William 226
Biaggi, Mario 457–459
Biaggi, Richard 458
Biberman, Herbert 302

Biden, Joseph 454
Binger, Carl 315
Bingley, John S. 40
Bissell, Richard 349
Black, Hugo 381
Blackman, Harry A. 370
Blais-Grenier, Suzanne 51–52
Blaisdell, Thomas 309
Blake, George 228–230, 231
Blaney, Neil 127
Blattman, Yonah 138
Blecha, Karl 26–28
Blew-Jones, Belinda 245
Blunt, Anthony 210, 220, 267–269, 278–279
Boggs, Hale 352
Bohlen, Charles E. 334
Bokassa, Jean Bedel 86–88
Boland, Kevin 127
Bonassoli, Aldo 90
Bonnet, Christian 82–83
Bookin, Stephen R. 432
Bork, Robert H. 401, 455–456
Botha, Pieter Willem 188–191, 193
Boublil, Alain 97
Boucheseiche, Georges 73
Boulin, Mme 85
Boulin, Robert 84–85, 97
Bourassa, Robert 50
Bourke, Sean 229
Boyer, Miguel 204
Boyle, Andrew 267
Boyle, James 373–374
Bradlee, Ben 395
Brandt, Willy 104–106, 350
von Brauchitsch, Eberhard 102
Brayley, Desmond 258–259
Brennan, William 381
Brezhnev, Leonid 198–199
Brezhneva, Galina 198
Bridge, Lord 297
Briggs, Gen. 40
Brittan, Leon 288, 290, 297
Broda, Christian 18–19
Broderick, Peter 270
de Broglie, Jean 80–83, 97
Brook, Sir Norman 222, 234
Brooke, Peter 270
Brothman, Abraham 326
Browder, Earl 320
Brown, Bettina 9
Brown, George 288
Brownell, Herbert 303, 306–307, 335
Brzezinski, Zbigniew 425
Buckley, Sheila 257–258
Buckley, William 319, 450
Budenz, Louis F. 323, 332
Buhari, Maj.-Gen. Mohammed 169
Bukharin, Nikolai 323
Bulganin, Marshal 222

Burger, Warren 369
Burgess, Guy 210, 219–221, 265–266, 267–269
Burke, Edmund 11
Burns, Arnold I. 434
Buryatia, Boris 198–199
Bush, George 176, 301, 418, 451–453, 459–461
Butler, R.A. 225
Butterfield, Alexander 400
Buzhardt, Fred J. 385, 401, 404
Bykov, Col. Boris 313–314
Byrne, Matthew 380–383, 399
Byrnes, James F. 304, 306, 311

Caille, Jean 74
Cairns, James 12
Calley, Lt. William 376–377
Calvi, Roberto 145–147, 151
Campbell, Duncan 291
Carboni, Flavio 145, 147
Çarçani, Adil 2
Cardin, Lucien 48–49
Carino, Oscar 179
Carlson, Carl (alias David Whittaker Chambers) 314
Carlsoon, Ebbe 208
Caron, Michel 46
Carr, Robert 245
Carr, Sam 45
Carrington, Lord 219, 245
Carswell, G. Harrold 370
Carter, Billy 424–426
Carter, Jimmy 377, 405, 409, 418–421, 424–426, 429, 443
Carter, "Miss Lillian" 425
Carter, Rosalynn 425
Carvel, Bob 263
Casey, William 419, 438, 441, 443, 447–451
Castro, Fidel 348–349, 351, 357–358, 361, 388, 414, 416–418
Catlett, Claudia 314
Caulfield, John J. 399
Chad, Margaret see Papandreu, Margaret
Chaddha, Win 124–126
Challandon, Albin 90
Chalier, Yves 94–95
Challe, Gen. Maurice 224
Chambers, David Whittaker 303, 305–308, 310–319, 323, 330, 386
Chambers, Esther 312, 317
Chambers, Jay Vivian (later David Whittaker) 311
Chamorro, Violeta 453
Chapin, Dwight 387, 394, 406
Charles, Prince 7
Chevalier, Haakon 343–345
Chiang Kai-shek 332
Chinn, W. Franklyn 433, 458

Chirac, Jacques 85
Chmielewski, Lt. Waldemar 183–184
Chondrokoukis, Col. D. 111
Christy, Arthur H. 424
Chrostowski, Waldemar 184
Churbanov, Col.-Gen. Yury 198–199
Churbanova (née Brezhneva), Galina 199
Church, Frank 415
Churchill, Winston 213, 219, 311
Cindy 140
Civiletti, Gen. Benjamin 424–425
Claes, Willy 31–32
Clark, Sir Andrew 218
Clark, Ramsey 367, 372
Clark, Tom 316
Clementis, Vladimir 58–59
Clough, Desmond 232
Clutter, John W. 153, 158–159
Coates, Robert 51–52
Coe, Frank 304, 307
Coelho, Tony 461–462
Cohen, Chaim 129, 131
Cohn, Roy M. 331, 334–336, 338
Colby, William E. 415–419
Cole, Lester 302
Collins, Henry 311
Colombo, Franco 150
Colson, Charles 380, 382–383, 385, 387–392, 395, 398, 402, 406–407
Connally, John B. 351–352, 356–357, 359, 411, 414
Connor, Reginald 12
Constantine, King 109–112
Cook, Fred J. 316
Cools, André 31
Coote, Sir Colin 233
Cordle, John 241, 243–244
Coste-Floret, Paul 66–67
Costigan, Francis 14–15
Cotler, Irwin 207
Courtney, Anthony 236
Couve de Murville, Maurice 77
Cox, Archibald 385, 399–400, 405, 456
Crabb, Lionel "Buster" 221–223
Cripps, Sir Stafford 214
Crociani, Camillo 144
Crosley, George (alias David Whittaker Chambers) 312, 314
Cross, James 50
Crossman, Richard 250
Cuckney, Sir John 252–253, 289
Cudlipp, Hugh 240
Cunningham, Sir Charles 231
Curry, Jesse 351, 353
Curtis-Bennett, Derek 41

Daher 65
Dai, Hadji 27
Daimler, Hans Peter 26

Daley, Richard 370–371
Dalton, Hugh 215
Dalyell, Tam 269–270, 273–274, 284–285
Damore, Leo 375
Daoust, Raymond 46
Davies, Joseph E. 334
Davis, Benjamin, J. 320
Davis, John W. 314
Davis, Rennie 370
Daw Aung San Suu Kyi 42
Dayan, Gen. Moshe 129–132, 224
Deakin, George 264
Dean III, John W. 381, 383, 385, 388–390, 395–400, 406–407, 413
Deaver, Michael K. 429, 432, 439–440, 458
Debizet, Paul 88
Debré, Michel 71–72
Deferre, Gaston 65, 89
Dell, Edmund 261
Dellinger, David 370–371
Delon, Alain 76
Delpey, Roger 86–87
Delvalle, Eric 175
Denis, Raymond 46–47
Dennis, Eugene 320
Der'i, Aryeh 135
Diaz Herrera, Roberto 174–175
Dides, Jean 69–70
Diederichs, Nicholas J. 189
Diefenbaker, John 48–49
Diem, President 383
Dikko, Umaru 169–171
Dilhorne, Lord 235
Dlimi, Ahmed 73, 75
Dmytryk, Edward 302
Donner, Andreas 168
Donovan, Raymond 429–431
Dori, Ya'akov 129–130
Dorion, Frédéric 47
Dorman-Smith, Sir Reginald 37–38
Douglas, William 329, 380
Dovey, Margaret 11
Dreyfus, Captain 62, 329
Driberg, Tom 40
Ducret, Jean 81–83
Dugdale, Sir Thomas 217–219
Duggan, Laurence 324
Dukakis, Michael 455
Duke, Brig. 41
Dulczin, Ari 142
Dulles, Allen W. 349, 352, 358, 361
Dulles, John Foster 58
Dunn, Gen. Mike 412

Eagleton, Thomas F. 384
Eastland, Terry 434
Eastwood, Christopher 217–219
Eddowes, Michael 361
Eden, Sir Anthony 40, 222, 223–224

Edet, Okon 169–170
Edgecombe, Johnny 234
Ehrlichman, John D. 380, 382–383, 385, 387–390, 395–399, 402, 406–407, 409, 453
Eichmann, Adolf 206
Eisenhower, Dwight D. 58, 306–308, 317, 322, 328–329, 386, 416
Eisler, Gerhard (alias Hans Berger) 315, 322–323
Eisler, Hans 323
Eitan, Rafi 438–439
Eitan, Raphael 135–136
Elgey, Georgette 63
Elitcher, Max 327
Elizabeth II, Queen 7, 11, 13
Ellicott, Robert 13
Elliott, Nicholas 228, 266
Ellsberg, Daniel J. 380–383, 387, 389–390, 397, 399, 403, 406, 436
Elly 45
Emmanuelidis, Emmanuel 107–108
Endara, Guillermo 176
Enomoto, Toshio 155–156, 158
Ephraim, Brig.-Gen. Yonah 136
Epstein, Edward J. 352
Erasmus, Rudolph P.B. 190, 192
Erhard, Ludwig 99
Erlander, Tage 208
Ervin, Sam J. 385, 395–396, 399
Erwin, Dudley 10
Escaro, André 78
Eshkol, Levi 131–132
Evans, Gareth 8
Evatt, Dr Herbert 3–5
Eveleigh, Mr Justice 257
Exner, Judith Campbell 357–358, 417
Ezoe, Hiromasa 161–163, 165

Fabius, Laurent 92, 95
Fadden, Sir Arthur 4
Fagan, Michael 272
Falkender, Lady see Williams, Marcia
Fanali, Gen. Duilio 144–145
Farge, Yves 64–66
Farquhar, Murray 15
Farrell, Mairead 294, 296
Favreau, Guy 46–48
Fay, Judge E.S. 252–253
Feehan, Ramos 313–314
Fell, Zara 6
Ferch, John 450
Fernandez, Joseph F. 451
Ferraro, Geraldine 429, 430
Field, see Vanderbilt Field, Frederick
Field, Peggy 250
Field, Tony 249–250
Fielding, Lewis 380–381
Figon, Georges 73–75

Finochetti, Jean-Bruno 88
Fiorini, Frank 388
Fischer, Ruth 323
Fischi, Otto 58–59
Fisher, Frederick G. 336
Fiske, Guy 429
Flatto-Sharon, Samuel 133–135
Flick, Friedrich 102
Foccart, Jacques 73
Ford, Gerald R. 352, 370, 401, 405, 409–410, 412, 415–419
Foregger, Egmont 26
Forlani, Arnaldo 150
Forrestal, James V. 323
Fortas, Abe 299, 369–370
Foster, Ronald 232
Foster, William Z. 320–321
Foucar, E.V. 41
Fourcaud, Col. 66–67
Fraissinet, Jean 65
Francis, Antoine 34
Franco, Gen. Francisco 201–203
Franju, Georges 73
Frank, Jozef 58
Frankfurter, Felix 315–316
Fraser, John 51–52
Fraser, Malcolm 8, 10–14
Frazier, Buell Wesley 355
Frèche, Gerard 80, 83
Frederiki, Queen 107
Freijka, Ludvik 58
Frey, Roger 76
Friderichs, Hans 102
Frischenschlager, Friedhelm 23
Froines, John 370–372
Frolik, Josef 255, 257
Frost, David 405
Fuchs, Klaus 215, 325–326
Fujinami, Takeo 161, 164
Fulbright, J. W. 364
Fulton, Davie 48–49

Gaddafi, Col. Moamer 27, 424
Gaitskell, Hugh 222, 225
Galbraith, Thomas 230–231
Gallucci, Achille 151
Galtieri, Gen. 274
Gandhi, Indira 122–124
Gandhi, Rajiv 124–125
Gandhi, Sanjay 122–124
Garcia, Robert 457, 459
Gargan, Joseph 373, 375
Garouphalias, Konstantinos 110–111
Garrison, Jim 355
Gates, John 320
de Gaulle, Gen. Charles 61, 71, 75–77, 86–89
Gdlyan, Telman 198–200
Gehrling, Serge 83

Gelli, Licio 145–146, 149–152
Gemayel, Bashir 135–136
Geminder, Bedrich 58
Generalov, Ambassador 3
Gennimatas, Gen. 110
George, Clair 447, 450
Gerö, Ernö 119
Gesell, Gerhard 451–453
Ghorbanifar, Manucher 443
Giancana, Sam 351, 357–358, 417–418
Gibson, George 215
Gignac, Robert 46–47
Gil Robles, Jose María 202
Gill, Ken 297
Gimes, Miklós 120
Ginossar, Yossi 139
Ginsburg, Douglas H. 455–457
Girardot, Captain 66–67
Giraud, André 90, 95
Giscard d'Estaing, Valéry 80, 82, 84–87,
    90–91
Giudice, Gen. Raffaele 151
Glasser, Harold 304, 307
Goddard, Henry W. 315
Goddard, Lord Chief Justice 216
Gold, Harry 216, 325–326, 330
Goldfine, Bernard 346
Goldsmith, James 259
Goldwater, Barry 386
Goleniewski, Michael 228
Golitsyn, Anatoli 266
Golos, Jacob 304, 330
Gomez, Drexel 29–30
Gonzales, Virgilio R. 388, 396
Gorbachev, Mikhail 182–183, 195, 198, 452
Gore-Booth, Sir Paul 42
Gorton, John Grey 8–12
Gotlieb, Allen 440
Gotlieb, Sondra 440
Gotto, Ainsley 9–10
Gottwald, Klement 54, 57–58, 60
Guoin, Félix 64–66
Gouk, Arkady 279–280
Gouzenko, Andrei 43–44
Gouzenko, Anna 43–44
Gouzenko, Igor 43–45, 311, 325
Gratz, Leopold 23, 26–28
Gray III, L. Patrick 381–382, 385, 390,
    396, 408
Green, Gilbert 320–321
Greene, Harold 453
Greenglass, David 325–328, 330
Greenglass, Ruth 327
Gregg, Donald 452
Grew, Seamus 286–287
Grey, Anthony 6
Grivas, Gen. 110–111
Groenwald, Jan 194
Gromyko. Andrei 207
Groves, Lt.-Gen. Leslie R. 344–345

Gruening, Ernest 364
Guerrero, Oscar 140
Gui, Luigi 144–145
Guillaumat, Pierre 90
Guillaume, Christel 104
Guillaume, Günter 104–106
Gupta, Alak Chandra 123

Haavik, Gunvor Galtung 172
Habsburg, Otto 17–18, 91
Haig, Gen. Alexander M. 385, 401,
    410–412
Hajdu, Vavro 58–59
Hakim, Albert 441, 444, 448, 450–452
Haldeman, H.R. (Bob) 385–389, 391–392,
    395, 397, 399–401, 404–409, 453
Halfon, Ya'akov 133–134
Hall, Fawn 442
Hall, Gus 320–321
Halperin, Morton 382
Hamdan, Awad 139
Hamilton, Lee H. 442
Hammett, Dashiell 321, 334
Hamre, Gen. Sverre 173
Hananiya, Maj.-Gen. Haldu 169–170
Hanna, Arthur 29
Hanna, Richard 422
Hanson, James 259
Harada, Ken 163
Harel, Col. Yosef 130
Harewood, Marion Countess of 263
Harish, Yosef 137–139
Hart, Gary 453–454, 455
Hart, Judith 252–253
Harvey, Ian 236
Hasegawa, Takashi 163
Hashimoto, Tomisaburo 157–158
Hasluck, Paul 9
Hassan, King 73, 75
Hattori, Tsuneo 162
Haughey, Charles 127–128
Havel, Vaclav 60
Havers, Sir Michael 280, 297
Hawke, Bob 16
Hayden, Tom 370–371
Hayes, Arthur Hall 429
Haynsworth, Clemkent F. 370
Hazak, Reuven 138
Hazbiu, Kadri 1
Head, Anthony 224
Heath, Edward 240, 244–248
Hees, George 48–49
Hellman, Lillian 334
Helms, J. Lynn 429
Helms, Richard 349, 385, 408, 415,
    418
Henderson, Col. Oran 376–377
Hermalig, Yosef 139
Hermon, Sir John 286–288

Hernu, Charles 92–93, 95–96
Hersh, Seymour 415
Herzog, President 139
Heseler, Gerda see Gerda Munsinger
Heseltine, Michael 274, 280, 284–285, 288–290
Hetherington, Sir Thomas 297
Himmler, Heinrich 102
Hinduja, G.P. 126
Hirschfeld, Hans 350
Hiss, Alger 303, 305–308, 310–320, 323, 329–331, 386, 392
Hiss, Donald 311, 314
Hiss, Priscilla 310, 312, 314
Hitler, Adolf 215, 224, 409
Hiyama, Hiro 153, 155–156
Hobson, Sir John 234, 268
Hobson, Timothy 318
Hobson, Valerie 234
Hodel, Donald P. 317
Hodza, Fadilj 2
Hoffman, Abbie 370–372
Hoffman, Jerry 241, 243
Hoffman, Julius 370–372
Hoffman, Walter E. 411
Hollis, Sir Roger 44–45, 233, 292
Holmes, David 262, 264–265
Holmes, Oliver Wendell 311
Holt, Harold Edward 6–9
Hoover, Herbert 425
Hoover, J. Edgar 306, 321, 351, 358–360, 362, 383, 385, 387, 396
Hopf, Volkmar 99
Horwood (South African Finance Minister) 191–192
Horwood, Owen 188
Howe, Sir Geoffrey 170, 280, 294–295
Hoxha, Enver 1–2
Hugel, Max 429
Hughes, Howard 385, 391–393, 417
Hughes, Judge 269
Humphrey, Hubert H. 370–371, 407
Humphreys, Kevin 15
Hunt, E. Howard 317, 380–383, 385, 387, 397, 399, 402–403, 408
Hurd, Douglas 291
Hurwitz, Eli 141
Hurwitz, Yigael 142
Hussein, Saddam 25
Hussey, Marmaduke 291

Ikeda, Katsuya 164
Inouye, Daniel K. 442
Itakura, Hiroshi 162
Itoh, Hiroshi 155–156, 158
Ivanov, Eugene 233–235
Ivanov, Nikolai 198–200
Izat, Nafsu 139

Jacobsen, David P. 442, 445
Jacobsen, Jacob 414
Japhet, Ernest 141–143
Jaruzelski, Gen. Wojciech 182–183, 185
Jarvis, Anne 276
Jaworski, Leon 385, 400, 402, 404
Jellicoe, Lord 210, 246–247
Jenco, Fr Lawrence 445
Jenkins, Roy 277
Jenner, William 340
Jenrette, John W. 426
Jessup, Philip 332
Jibli, Benjamin 129–131
John Paul II, Pope 145, 148
Johnson, Lyndon B. 7, 345, 351–352, 360–361, 363–364, 369, 371, 380, 383, 386, 399, 409
Juan Carlos, King 202
Jordan, Hamilton 423–424
Joseph II, 21
Joxe, Pierre 97
Juliana, Queen of Netherlands 167

Kádár, János 118–121
Kadotani, Masahiko 162
Kagan, Joseph 258, 261–262
Kaghan, Theodore 334
Kahan, Yitzchak 135–136
Kaifu, Toshiki 161, 165
Kalkani, Sokratis 114, 117
Kalmbach, Herbert W. 385, 394, 397, 399, 406
Kampiles, William 435
Kanellopoulos, Konstantinos 111
Kapelonis, Emmanuel 108
Karamanlis, Konstantinos 107, 109, 112
Karl, Emperor 17
Karp, Yehudit 137–138
Kashev, Gen. Ilya 35–36
Kato, Mutsuki 157
Kato, Takashi 163
Kauffman, John 368
Kaufman, Irving 325–330
Kaufman, Samuel H. 315
Kawasaki, Kanji 164
Kazan, Elia 303
Keays, Sarah 275, 277
Keeler, Christine 233–234
Kellock, R.L. 44
Kelly, James 128
Kelly, John 128
Kelly, Richard 426–427
Kennedy, Anthony M. 457
Kennedy, Edward Moore 373–375, 384, 388
Kennedy, Jacqueline 352, 355
Kennedy, Joan 373
Kennedy, John F. 300, 317, 331–332, 348–349, 351–359, 361–363, 368, 373,

380, 386, 390, 392, 399, 407–409, 414,
   416, 418, 455, 460
Kennedy, Robert (Bobby) 348, 357, 359,
   371, 386, 434
Kent, Mgr Bruce 297
Kerr, Sir John 11, 13–14
Kershaw, Sir Anthony 285
Key, Charles 215
Keynes, Lord 304
Khashoggi, Adnan 177–179, 443
Khomeini, Ayatollah Ruhollah 444
Khruschev, Nikita 348
Kikunaga, Kazunori 157
Kimche, David 444
King, Cecil 239–240
King, Martin Luther 359, 365–368, 386
King, William Lyon Mackenzie 44
Kinnock, Neil 455
Kissinger, Henry 380–381, 401, 404
Kiszczak, Gen. Czeslaw 184
Klein, Maurice H. 347
Kleindienst, Richard 381, 385, 397–398
Kodama, Yoshio 153, 155, 158–159
Koldunov, Marshal Aleksandr 195–196
Kollias, Konstantinos 111
Komuro, Naoki 160
Konstantinov, Marshal Anatoly 197
Kopacsi, Sandor 120
Kopechne, Mary Jo 373–375
Koskotas, Yiorgos 113–117
Kostov, Vladimir 35–36
Kotchian, A.C. 153, 155, 158–159
Kotchian, Carl 167
Kotzamanis, Spyros 107–108
Koutsogiorgas, Agamemnon 112, 115, 117
Koutsogiorgas, Athanasios 116
Kraft, Tim 424
Kramer, Charles 311
Kravets, Gen. V.I. 200
Kreisky, Bruno 17–18, 20–22, 27
Krivitsky, Gen. Walter 324
Krogh, Egil "Bud" 382–383, 385, 387, 406
Krushchev, Nikita 59, 119, 221
Kunstler, William 370, 372
Kyaw Myint 41

La Follette, Robert "Young Bob" 324, 331
Lacina, Ferdinand 27
Lambert, Drexel Burnham 462
Lambrakis, Grigoris 107–108
Lambsdorff, Graf 102, 104
Lambton, (Lord) Anthony 210, 245–248
Lamontagne, Pierre 46
Lampert, Jerry 52
Lance, Bert 299, 420–421, 429
Landau, Moshe 137, 139
Lane, Mark 352
Langfelder, Vilmos 206
Laporte, Pierre 50

Lardner, Ring 302
LaRue, Frederick C. 385, 394, 406
Lattimore, Owen 332–334
de Lattre de Tassigny, Gen. 68
Lauer, Koloman 205
Lavon, Pinchas 129–131
Lawson, John Howard 302
Leburton, Edmond 31–32
Lechausser, Eddy 46–47
Lederer, Raymond F. 426
Leijon, Anna-Greta 208
Lemarchand, Maître Pierre 74
Le Mesurier, John 264
Le Ny, Julien 73
Leone, Giovanni 144–145
Le Pen, Jean-Marie 72
Le Roy, Marcel
Le Roy-Finville 74–75
Letendre, André 46
Levi, David 135–136
Levine, Nathan 313
Levy, Colin 245–246
Levy, Moshe 137–138
Levy, Norma 245–246
Lewis, John 234
Lewin, Adml. Lord 274
Liani, Dimitra 112–113
Liddy, G. Gordon 380–383, 385, 387–391,
   394–397, 399, 408
Lifton, David 361
Ligachev, Yegor 200
Lilov, Aleksandur 36
Listowel, Lord 41
Lloyd, Selwyn 223–225, 245
Lloyd George, David 258–259
Lo Prieto, Gen. Donato 151
Löbl, Evzen 58–59
Lodge, Henry Cabot 335
Lohan, Col. L.G. 238–239
London, Artur 58–59
Longo, Pietro 151
Lopez, Antoine 73–76
Lord, Guy 46
Losonczy, Geza 120
Louvaris, Yiorgos 113, 115
Luce, Henry 316
Lukas, Anthony 392
Lumumba, Patrice 418
Lütgendorf, Karl 20–21, 26
Luykx, Albert 128
Luyt, Louis 189–90
Lynch, Jack 127

MacArthur, Gen. Douglas 300, 339–342,
   448
McCann, Daniel 294, 296
McCarthy, Eugene 371
McCarthy, Joseph (Joe) Raymond 300,
   306, 316–317, 329, 331–338, 345

McCauley, Martin 286
McClellan, George 48
McCloy, John J. 352
McCord, James W. 385, 388–389, 397,
    399, 408
MacDonald, Malcolm 44
McEwan, John 8–10
MacGrath, William 269
Mack, John 462
Maclean, Donald 210, 219–221, 265–266,
    267–268
Macleod, Iain 276
Macmillan, Harold 224, 226–227, 229,
    231–232, 235, 236, 245, 266
Mafart, Alain 92
Magruder, Jeb Stuart 385, 387, 390,
    394–395, 397, 399, 406–407
Maheu, Robert 357, 417
Mahn Ba Knaing 39
Malafosse, Pierre 64–66
Maleter, Gen. Pal 118, 120
Malka, Rafi 138
Mallick, George 462
Mallon, Seamus 287
Mandelbaum, Moshe 141–142
Marcellin 78
Marcinkus, Archbishop Paul 145–147
Marcos, Ferdinand Edralin 177–179
Marcos, Imelda 177–179
Mardian, Robert 402, 406
Margolius, Rudolf 58
Marie, Jean-Joseph 88–89
Marin, Manuel 204
Mariotta, John 457, 459
Markham, Paul 373, 375
Markov, Annabel 36
Markov, Georgi 35–36
Markovic, Stefan 76
Marshall, Gen. George C. 332–333,
    340–341
Marten, Lt-Cdr George 217–218
Martin, Paul 47
Maung Sein 47
Martin, William H. 347
Martinez, Eugenio R. 382, 388, 392, 396,
    408
Masaryk, Jan 54–58, 324
Masaryk, Thomas 54
Masse, Marcel 51–52
Massie, Jacques 88–89
Massie, Pierre 88
Massing, Hede 315, 323
Massiter, Cathy 210, 296–297
Masson, Guy 46
Mast, Gen. 66–68
Mathur, D.S. 122–123
Matz, Albert 302
Matsuno, Raizo 155
Maudling, Reginald 241–244
Maung Ohn 39

Maung Sein 39, 41
Maung Soe 39, 41
Mauroy, Pierre 91
May, Allan Nunn 44–45
Mayhew, Sir Patrick 286–289, 294
McFall, John 422
McFarlane, Robert C. 429, 433, 441–442,
    444–445, 449–452
McGoff, John 190, 192–193
McGovern, George 371, 384, 388, 393,
    395, 409
McKay, James, C. 430, 433–434, 457–458
McMahon, William 8–11
McNamara, Robert 365
McNeil, Hector 220
Meagher, Douglas 15
Medina, Capt. Ernest 376–377
Medina, Harold 320
Medvedev, Roy 200
Meese, Edwin 299, 429, 432–435, 441–442,
    447, 457–458
Meir, Golda 132
Mendès-France, Pierre 69, 71
Mennini, Luigi 146
Menzies, Robert 3, 5–7, 9
Merola, Mario 432
Messmer, Pierre 78
Mijal, Kazimierz 186
Mikhailski, Sigmund 230–231
Mikoyan, Anastas 57, 60
Milewski, Lt.-Gen. Miroslaw 185
Millhench, Ronald 249–251
Milken, Michael 462
Miller, Arthur 303
Miller, Eric 241–242, 258–261
Milne, Alasdair 291
Milson, Menachem 136
Mitchell, Bernon F. 347
Mitchell, John N. 385, 387–394, 397–398,
    399, 402–403, 406–407, 413–414
Mitchell, Martha 396
Mitsiou, Gen. 108
Mitsotakis, Konstantinos 116
Mitterand, François 69–72, 91–94, 96–97
Mitzna, Gen. Amram 136
Miyazawa, Kiichi 162
Mizrachi, Bezalel 133
Moch, Jules 65–68
Moda'i, Yitzchak 141, 143
Mollet, Guy 223
Monckton, Walter 224
Mondale, Walter 421, 429, 430, 453
Mons, Jean 69–70
Montazeri, Ayatollah Hossein Ali 444–445
Moore, Major 40
Moos, Ann 309
Morberg, Per Ove 125
Mordechai, Brig.-Gen. Yitzchak 138
Morgenthau, Henry J. 304, 307–308
Morison, Samuel Eliot 435–436

Morison, Samuel Loring 383
Morita, Ko 162
Moro, Aldo 144
Morrison, Herbert 58
Morse, Wayne 337, 364
Moskowitz, Miriam 326
Mostert, Anton 189–190
Mountbatten, Lord Louis 37, 298
Moussavi, Hossein 444–445
Mudenda, Jacob 463
Mugabe, Robert 463–464
Mulder, Dr Cornelius Petrus "Connie" 188–193
Mulholland, Brendan 232
Mullen, Robert R. 393, 408
Mulroney, Brian 51–53
Mundt, Karl 335
Munsinger, Gerda 48–49
Munsinger, Michael 48
Murphy, John M. 426
Murphy, Lionel 14, 16
Murphy, Raymond 305, 312
Murphy, Thomas F. 315
Murtha, John 426
Musameci, Gen. 152
Mussolini, Benito 224
Mutumbuka, Dzingai 463
Myers, Michael J. 426

Nagy, Imre 118–121
Nakasone, Yasuhiro 153, 160–165
Nase, Nesti 2
Nasser, Col, Gamal Abdel 130, 223
Navon, Yitzchak 135–136
Ndlovu, Callistus 463
Ne Win 42
Negoro, Yasuchika 164
Neil, Andrew 281–282
Nemeth, Miklós 120
Newton, Andrew 264
Ngo Dinh Diem 317, 390, 418
Nicholas, Maj.-Gen. K.D. 343
Nicholson, Nigel 225
Niedzielak, Fr Stefan 186
Nielsen, Erik 47
Nikaido, Susumu 157
Nimrodi, Yaacov 443
Nir, Amiram 445
Nixon, Donald 392
Nixon, Richard M. 157, 301, 305, 310, 312–313, 316–317, 336, 346, 364–365, 369–371, 377–383, 384–387, 390–393, 395–415, 441, 443, 456, 460
Nkala, Enos 463–464
Nofziger, Lyn 433, 440, 457–458
Nottage, Kendal 29
Noriega, Gen. Manuel Antonio 174–175
North, Oliver 419, 441–453
Northcliffe, Lord 239

Nosaka, Akiyuki 160–161
Nosek, Václav 55
Nosenko, Yuri Ivanovich 351, 358–359, 362, 416
Nucci, Christian 94–95
Nugent, Ian 218–219
Nunn May, Alan 325
Nutting, Anthony 224
Nyagumbo, Maurice 463

O'Brien, Lawrence (Larry) 385, 391–393, 407
O'Neill, Thomas "Tip" 461
Ofer, Avraham 132
Ofner, Harald 22, 26
Okada, Mitsunori 156
Okubo, Toshiharu 155–156
Olah, Franz 18–20
Oldfield, Sir Maurice 210, 297
Olsen, Jack 375
Olshan, Yitzchak 129–130
Onslow, Cranley 274
Oppenheimer, Frank 343
Oppenheimer, J. Robert 324, 343–345
Ornitz, Samuel 302
Ortalini, Umberto 149, 152
Osano, Kenji 155, 158–159
Ostrovsky 141
Oswald, Lee Harvey 351–363, 368, 417
Oswald, Marguerite 354
Oswald, Marina 351, 353–355, 361
Oufkir, Gen. Mohamed 73–75
Owen, Will 257

Packer, Sir Frank 10
Paine, Ruth 354
Palme, Lisbet 208–209
Palme, Olof 207–209
Papadopoulos, Yiorgos 111
Papandreou, Andreas 109–117
Papandreou Jr, Andreas 112
Papandreou, Margaret 113
Papandreou, Nikos 112
Papandreou, Sophia 112
Papandreou, Yiorgos 112, 115
Papandreou, Yiorgos (George) 109–112
Papaterpos, Col. A. 111
Paraskevopoulos, John 111
Park, Tongsun (a.s.a. Park Tong Sun) 422
Parker, Lord Justice 227
Parkinson, Kenneth 402, 406
Parkinson, Paula 461
Parkinson, Cecil 210, 275–278
Pasqua, Charles 94–95
Passman, Otto 422
Pearson, Drew 324
Pearson, Lester 46–49
Peiers, Prof. 216

Pekala, Lt. Leszek 183–184
Pelat, Roger-Patrice 97
Penkovsky, Col. Oleg 233
Penne, Guy 94
Penrose, Barrie 264
Peres, Shimon 129–133, 138, 140–141, 444–445
Peress, Dr Irving 335, 438
Perlo, Victor 304, 311
Perón, Juan 149
Pesquet, Robert 71–72
Peters, Jozsef 311, 313
Petersen, Henry 385, 395, 397
Petrov, Evokiya 3
Petrov, Vladimir M. 3–4, 221
Petsos, Yiorgos 117
Petterson, Christer 207, 209
Peyré, Roger 66–68
Peyrefitte, Alain 84–85
Peyrefitte, Roger 87
Philby, Harold "Kim" 219–220, 265–267
Phillips, Morgan 250
Pietruszka, Col. Adam 183–185
Pika, Gen. 59
Pike, Otis 418
Pinay, Antoine 90
Pincher, Chapman 45, 238, 279, 297–298
Pindling, Sir Lynden 29–30
Pineau, Christian 224
Piotrowski, Capt. Grzegorz 183–185
Piterrmann, Bruno 18–19
Platek, Maj.-Gen. Zenon 183–184
Plummer, Leslie 211
Poindexer, John M. 433, 441–443, 445–453
Polak, Henry 41
Pollard, Anne Henderson 438
Pollard, Jonathan Jay 437–439
Pompidou, Claude 76–77
Pompidou, Georges 76–77, 88–89
Poniatoski, Jean 80–83, 86
Poniatowski, Michel 80
Ponting, Clive 210, 274, 284–285
Poole, Oliver 226–227
Popieluszko, Fr Jerzy 183–186
Porter, Marina Oswald see Oswald, Marina
Potash, Irving 320–321
Pottle, Pat 228–229
Poulson, John 241–242
Powell, Adam Clayton 299, 365–366
Powell, Enoch 226, 240
Powell, Lewis F. 456–457
Pózsgay, Imre 120
Pressman, Lee 311
Preston, Paul 280
Prieur Dominique 92
Prime, Geoffrey, 271
Pritt, D.N. 41
Profumo, John 210, 232–236, 245–246, 250
Proksch, Udo 26

Proxmire, Edward W. 338
Prusakova, Marina Nikolaevna see Oswald, Marina

Quayle, J. Danforth 459–460
Queuille, Henri 66–67
Quilès, Paul 95

Rabin, Yitzchak 132–133
Rabin, Leah 132–133, 138
Rabinovich, Yehoshua 132–133
Radai, Peleg 138
Radcliffe, Lord 231–232, 238
Rafsanjani, Hojatolislam Hahemi Ali Akbar 441, 444
Rákosi, Mátyás 119
Ramadier, Paul 66–68
Rance, Sir Hubert 37, 38–42
Randle, Michael 228–229
Rappaport, Bruce 433
Rashidov, Sharaf 198–199
Rauch, Michael 272
Ravid, Ilan 438
Rawlinson, Peter 234
Ray, James Earl 366–368
Reagan, Nancy 429, 443
Reagan, Ronald 299, 301–302, 317, 365, 410, 419, 425, 428–430, 432–433, 439–446, 448, 450, 452, 455–459
Rebozo, Charles "Bebe" 385, 391–393
Reder, Walter 23
Reed, Stanley 314
Reed, Thomas C. 429
Regan, Donald 441, 443, 445, 455
Rehnquist, William 404
Reicin, Gen. Bedrich 58
Reid, Alan 9
Remington, William Walter 300, 305, 309–310, 320, 326
Reuber, William 316
Revers, Gen. 66–68
Reynders, Loot 191, 193
Rhodes, James 378–379
Rhoodie, Eschel 188, 190–193
Rhoodie, Nic 193
de Ribemont, Patrick 80, 83
Rice, Donna 453–454
Richardson, Elliot 385, 399, 401, 412
Ridenhour, Ronald 376
Rizzoli, Angelo 148, 150
Rivard, Lucien 46–47
Roas, John 212
Roberts, Albert 241, 243–244
Robertson, Norman 44
Robeson, Paul 303
Robinson, Edward G. 303
Rocard, Michel 97
Rockefeller, Nelson 415–416

Rodino, Pete 403
Roosevelt, Franklin 304, 307–308, 311, 316, 332, 407, 409
Rose, Fred 45
Rose, Paul 50
Rosen, Pinhas 131
Rosenberg, Ethel 325–330, 437
Rosenberg, Julius 325–330, 437
Rosone, Roberto 148
Rosselli, John 357, 417–418
Roth, Andrew 234
Rothermore, Lord 239
Rouleau, Guy 46–47
Roux, Inspector 82
Roybal, Edward 422
Rubell, Steven 424
Rubin, Jerry 370–372
Ruby, Jack Leon 351–355, 357–358, 363
Ruckelshaus, William D. 382, 401
Ruiz Mateos, Jose Maria 202–204
Rumor, Mariano 144
Russell, Bertrand 107
Russell, Richard 352
Russo, Anthony 380–383, 399, 436
Rust, Mathias 195, 197
Rust, Zad 375
Ryan Sydney 16

Saguy, Yehoshua 135–136
St. Clair, James
St. Laurent, Louis 43
Sakharov, Andrei 207
Salcher, Herbert 22
Salengro, Roger 84
Sampson, Colin 287–288
Sandura, Wilson 463
Santovito, Gen. Guiseppe 150
Sasakawa, Ryoichi 159
Sasaki, Hideyo 157
Sasso, John 455
Sato, Eisaku 154
Sato, Takayaki 157
Savage, Sean 294
Sawyer, Harold S. 368
Saypol, Irving H. 328
Scargill, Arthur 297
Schine, G. David 331, 334–336
Schmelz, Hans 99
Schmidt, Helmut 106
Schneider, Gen. Rene 418
Schrager, Ian 424
Schramm, Maj. Augustin 54–56
Schroeder, Victor 429
Schwimmer, Al 444
Scott, Adrian 302
Scott, Norman 262–264
Scranton, William 379
Seale, Bobby 371–372
Sears, Harry L. 413

Secord, Maj.-Gen. Richard V. 441, 444, 448, 450–452
Sedgemore, Brian 281, 283
Segretti, Don 387, 394, 406
Sella, Col. Aviem 438
Selva, Gustavo 150
Service, John Stewart 333
Seth, Ronald 316
Sévigny, Pierre 48–49
Seymour Jr., Whitney North 439–440
Shagari, Shehu 169
Shalom, Avraham 137–139
Shamir, Yitzchak 133, 135–136, 138–139, 141–142
Shapiro, Lev-Arie 170
Sharett, Moshe 129–130
Sharon, Ariel 135–137
Shava, Frederick 463–464
Shaw, Clay 352
Shcholokov, Gen. Nikolai 198–199
Shehu, Feçor 1–2
Shehu, Mehmet 1–2
Sherman, Harry 214
Sherman, John 352
Shopov, Grigor 35–36
Shoshan, Daniel 139
Shriver, Sargent 384
Shultz, George 173, 430, 441–444, 448–449
Sica, Dominico 141
Silbert, Earl J. 381, 385, 395
Silvermaster, Nathan Gregory 304
Simard, Francis 50
Simon, Stanley 458
Simone, André 58
Simone, Guy 80–81, 83
Simou, Lieut.-Gen. 111
Sinatra, Frank 357, 412
Sindona, Michele 146, 150, 152
Singh, V.P. 124–125
Sinowatz, Fred 25, 27–28
Sirica, John J. 385, 395–398, 401–404, 406
Skardon, William 216
Slack, Alfred Dean 326
Slánský, Rudolf 57–60
Slánský Jr., Rudolf 60
Sling, Otto 58
Smith, Cyril 263
Smith, George 29
Smith, Howard 29
Smith, Sir James 29
Smith, T. Dan 242
Smith, William French 429, 432
Snepp, Frank 420
Sobelevicius, Beras 350
Sobelevicious, Ruvelis see Sovlen, Robert
Sobell, Morton 325–327, 330
Soble, Jack 350
Soble, Myra 350
Soblen, Robert 350–351
Soderblom, Staffan 206

Sokolov, Marshal Sergei 195, 197
Sorenson, Theodore 419
Souchon, Louis 73–75
Spadafora, Hugo 174
Spadolini, Giovanni 149–150
Spassov, Mircho 35–36
Spence, Gerry 179
Spence, W.F. 49
Spencer, George Victor 48
Springer, Axel 190
St Clair, James 404
St Laurent, Louis 43
Stachel, Jacob 320
Stalin, Marshal Joseph 57, 60, 119, 311
Stalker, John 210, 286–288
Stammberger, Wolfgang 100
Stanley, Sidney 213
Stans, Maurice H. 385, 394–395, 406,
    413–414
Stein, Jacob 433
Steinhardt, Laurence 59
Stennis, John C. 401
Stephanopoulos, Stephanos 110
Stephenson, William 44
Stergious, Dimitris 116
Sternberg, Sigmund 259
Stevens, Noreen 53
Stevens, Robert T. 335
Stevens, Sinclair 51, 53
Stevenson, Adlai 315, 334
Stevenson, Matthew 252
Stewart, Donald 14–15
Stewart, Potter 380–381
Steyrer, Kurt 24
Stonehouse, John 255–258
Stoner, J.B. 367
Stoyanov, Lt.-Gen. Dimitur 35–36
Strachan, Gordon 385, 387–388, 402, 406
Strachey, John 211
Straka, Pavel 56
Strauss, Franz Josef 98–100
Street, Sir Laurence 14–15
Stripling, Robert 312–313
Stryker, Lloyd Paul 315
Sturgis, Frank 388, 397
Suchowolec, Fr Stanislaw 186
Sullivan, William 368
Summerskill, Lady 260
Suslov, Mikhail 198–199
Sutherland, John 368
Svab, Karel 58–59
Sverma, Jan 59
Svitak, Ivan 55
Swing, Raymond 334
Szilagyi, Jozsef 120
Szürös, Mátyás 120

Tachibana, Takashi 159
Tachikawa, 158

Takeshita, Noburo 161–164
Tanaka, Kakuei 153–161, 165
Tanaka, Naoki 153
Tanassi, Mario 144–145
Tanikawa, Kazuo 164
Taschereau, Robert 44
Tassin Din, Bruno 148, 150
Tatlock, Jean 324, 343
Taylor, Kevin 286–288
Taylor, Gen. Maxwell 349
Tebbit, Norman 276, 278
Teller, Dr Edward 344–345
Terre'Blanche, Eugune 194
Terry, Sir George 269
Tessèdre, Serge 80, 83
Thakin Kyaw Nyein 41
Thakin Mya 39
Thakin Nu (U Nu) 37, 39–42
Thatcher, Carole 281
Thatcher, Dennis 282
Thatcher, Margaret 140, 276–268, 272–276,
    280–283, 288–290, 292, 297–298
Thatcher, Mark 281–283
Thayer, Paul 429
Theodorakis, Mikis 108
Théret, Max 97
Thet Hnin 39, 41
Thompson, Frank 426
Thompson, Fred 408
Thompson, Robert 320–321
Thornberry, Homer 369
Thornborough, Richard 435
Thorneycroft, Peter 226
Thorpe, Jeremy 210, 262–265
Tighe, Michael 286
Tindemans, Leo 33
Tippit, J.D. 351–352, 356–357, 359, 363
Tisdall, Sarah 210, 280
Titcombe, Ronald 7–8
Titov, Gennady 173
Tixier-Vignancour, Jean-Louis 69–70, 72
Tlass, Mustafa 20
Tombras, Theophanis 114
Torrijos, Brig. Gen. Omar 174
Torrisi, Adm. Giovanni 150
Toupin, Robert 53
Tournet, Henri 84–85
Tower, John 354, 441–442
Tozer, Christopher 218
Trafficante, Santos 357, 417
Trefgarne, Lady Elizabeth 237
Trehoit, Arne 172–173
Treholt, Thorstein 172
Tremblay, René 46
Trestrail, Cdr Michael 272–273
Treurnicht, Andries 193
Tricot, Bernard 92
Trudeau, Pierre Elliot 50–51
Trujillo, Rafael Leonidas 418
Truly, Roy 352

Truman, Harry S. 44, 217, 299, 303–307, 312–313, 316, 321, 324, 325, 328, 339–341, 344
Trumbo, Dalton 302
Tsimas, Kostas 114
Tsovolas, Dimitris 114, 117
Tsukamoto, Saburo 164
Tsvigun, Gen. Semyon 198
Tully, Paul 455
Tunik, Yitzchak 141–142
Turenge, Alain *see* Alain mafart
Turenge, Sophie *see* Dominique Prieur
Turner, Admiral Stansfield 419
Tydings, Millard E. 332
Tzannetakis, Tzannis 114, 117
Tzoumakas, Stephanos 116

U Saw 37–41
U Tun Byu 41
Ullman, William Ludwig 304
Uno, Sosuke 164–165
Urvalek, Jiri 59–60
Usmankhodzhayev, Inamszhan 200

van den Bergh, Gen. Hendrik 187, 189, 191–192
Vanden Boeynants, Paul 33
Vanderbilt Field, Frederick 321
Vanunu, Mordechai 140
de Varga, Pierre 80–81, 83
Vassall, John 230–231
Vaughan, Gen. Harry 304
Vertanes, Captain Benjamin Raphael 41
Vesco, Robert 413–414
Vila Reyes, Fernando 201
Vila Reyes, Juan 201–202
de Villegas de Saint-Pierre-Jette, Alain 90
Vincent, John Carter 333
Vinson, Fred M. 304, 321
Violet, Maître Jean 90
Vivian, Captain David 40, 42
Vlachou, Eleni 117
Voitot, Roger 73, 75
Volkova, Zinaida Grigorievna 236
Vorster, Balthazar Johannes 188–189, 191–193
Vranitzky, Franz 22, 25, 28

Waddington, David 288
Wadleigh, Henry Julian 306, 314–315
Wakasa, Tokuji 157–158
Wakefield, J.A. 211
Waldheim, Kurt 24–25
Walker, Arthur J. 436–437
Walker, Maj.-Gen. Edwin 354–355
Walker, John A. 436–437
Walker, Michael L. 436–437

Wallace, Colin 269–270
Wallace, George 377
Wallace, Henry 308
Wallach, E. Robert 432–433, 458
Wallenberg, Raoul 205–207
Walsh, Lawrence 441–442, 450–451
Ward, Stephen 233–235
Ware, Harold 311
Warren, Earl 351, 361, 369
Watanabe, Kozo 160
Watanabe, Naoji 158
Watkins, Arthur V. 337
Weatherhill, Bernard 291
Webster, William 450
Weech, George 29
Wehner, Herbert 105
Weichselbaum, Alois 20–21
Weinberger, Caspar 430, 437, 441, 444, 449
Weiner, Lee 370, 372
Weinglass, Leonard 370, 372
Weinstein, Allen 317
Weir, Rev. Benjamin 445
Weizmann, Ezer 136
Welch, Joseph 336
Welch, Richard 418
Weld, William F. 434
Westmoreland, Gen. William C. 376, 427–428
Whitcomb, Edgar 377
White, Sir Dick 266
White, Harry Dexter 300, 303–308, 311, 313, 320, 326
Whitlam, Edward Gough 7, 11–14
Whitworth, Jerry A. 436–437
Wicht, Col. 99
Wickstead, Commander Bert 245
Wigg, George 233–235, 237
Wilcox, Claude 217, 219
Willes, Edwin 29
Williams, Harrison A. 426–427
Williams, Edward Bennett 337
Williams, Marcia (Lady Falkender) 249–251, 258
Williamson, John 320–321
Willsher, Kay 44
Wilson, Charles 422
Wilson, Edwin 445
Wilson, Herald 7
Wilson, James Harold 214, 226–227, 233, 235, 237–239, 249–252, 255, 258–264, 288, 292
Wilson, Michael 51, 53
Winant, John G. 324
Winston, Henry 320–321
Winter, Carl 320
Witt, Nathan 311
Wolfson, Louis E. 369
Woods, Sir John 219
Woods, Rose Mary 402

Woodward, Bob 369, 385, 389, 393, 395,
    398, 407–408, 447
Wran, Neville 14–16
Wright, Jim 299, 461–462
Wright, Peter 292

Yadlin, Asher 132
Yagur, Yosef 438
Yakovlev, Anatoli 326–327
Yamamoto, Admiral Isoruko 160
Yan Gyi Aung 39, 41
Yazov, Dmitry 197
Yeltsin, Boris 197
Yiotas, Evstathios 114
Yoshida, Shigeru 154
Yosmas, Xenophon 108

Young, David 382, 387
Yusufu, Mohammed 170

Zabotin, Col. 45
Zaccaro Jr, John A. 431
Zaccaro, John 430
Zamir, Yitzchak 137–138
Zapruder, Abraham 351, 356
Zeligs, Meyer 316
Zhivkov, Tudor 35–36
Ziçishti, Llambi 2
Ziegler, Ronald L. 385, 387, 398
Zilliacus, Konni 57–59
Zorea, Maj.-Gen. Meir 137–138
Zwicker, Brig. Gen. Ralph W. 335–336
Zych, Fr Sylwester 186